INSIDERS' GUIDE® TO
SAN DIEGO

Help Us Keep This Guide Up to Date

Every effort has been made by the authors and editors to make this guide as accurate and useful as possible. However, many things can change after a guide is published—establishments close, phone numbers change, hiking trails are rerouted, facilities come under new management, etc.

We would love to hear from you concerning your experiences with this guide and how you feel it could be improved and be kept up to date. While we may not be able to respond to all comments and suggestions, we'll take them to heart, and we'll also make certain to share them with the authors. Please send your comments and suggestions to the following address:

The Globe Pequot Press
Reader Response/Editorial Department
P.O. Box 480
Guilford, CT 06437

Or you may e-mail us at:

editorial@globe-pequot.com

Thanks for your input, and happy travels!

Insiders' Guide®
to San Diego

THIRD EDITION

Jacquelyn Landis and Eva Shaw

Revised and updated by
Maribeth Mellin and Jane Onstott

Guilford, Connecticut

An imprint of The Globe Pequot Press

Copyright © 2000, 2002 by The Globe Pequot Press
A previous edition of this book was published by Falcon Publishing, Inc. in 1999.

ISSN 1533-5224
ISBN 0-7627-2258-4

Maps by Brandon Ray; ©The Globe Pequot Press
Front cover photo by Mark Gibson, Index Stock

Manufactured in the United States of America
Third Edition/First Printing

Contents

Directory of Maps

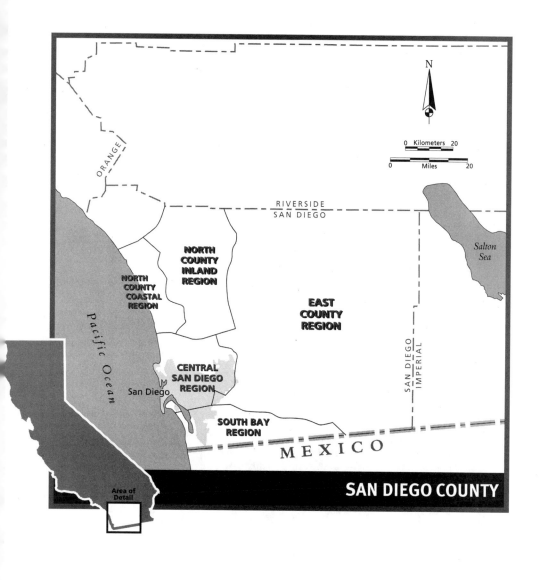

N

0 Kilometers 20
0 Miles 20

ORANGE

RIVERSIDE
SAN DIEGO

NORTH
COUNTY
INLAND
REGION

NORTH
COUNTY
COASTAL
REGION

EAST
COUNTY
REGION

Pacific Ocean

Salton
Sea

CENTRAL
SAN DIEGO
REGION

San Diego

SAN DIEGO
IMPERIAL

SOUTH BAY
REGION

M E X I C O

Area of
Detail

SAN DIEGO COUNTY

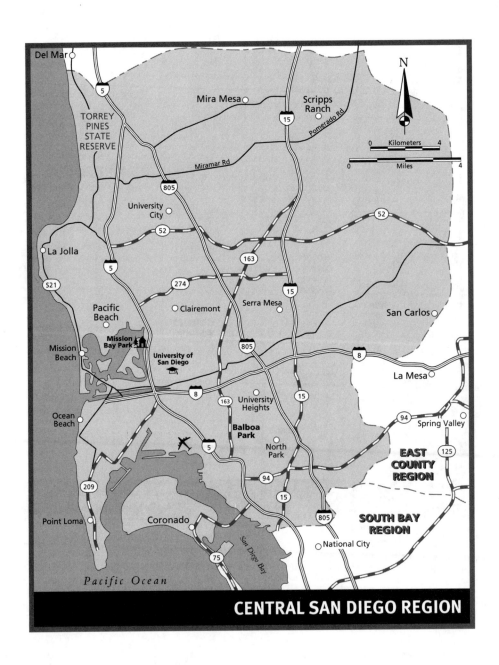

CENTRAL SAN DIEGO REGION

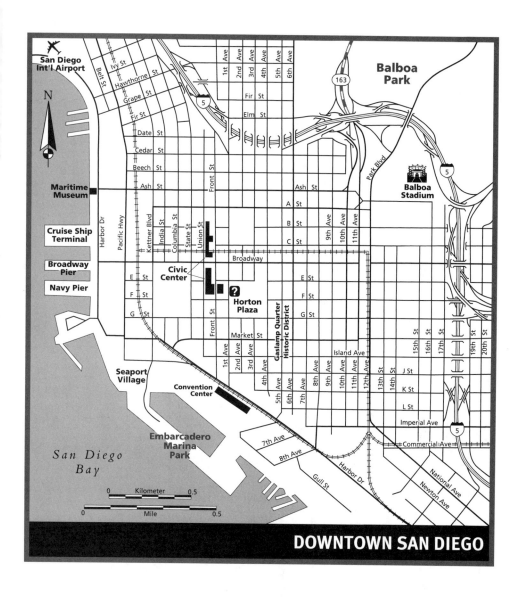

DOWNTOWN SAN DIEGO

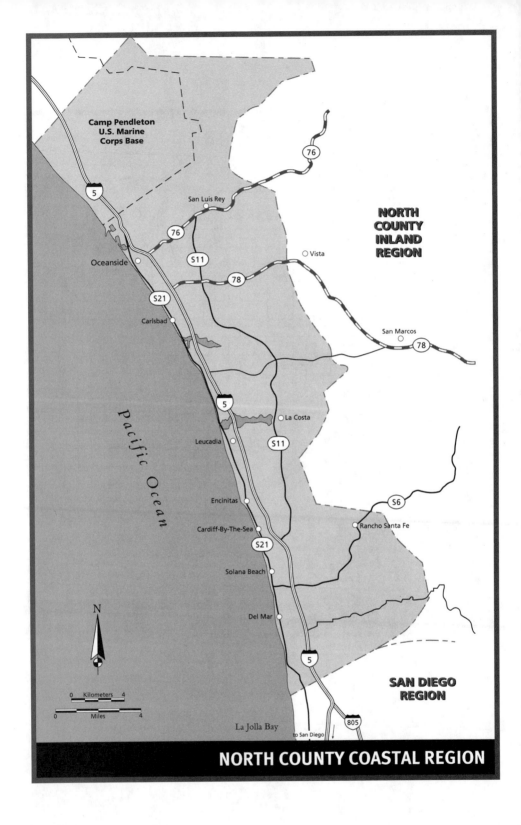

NORTH COUNTY COASTAL REGION

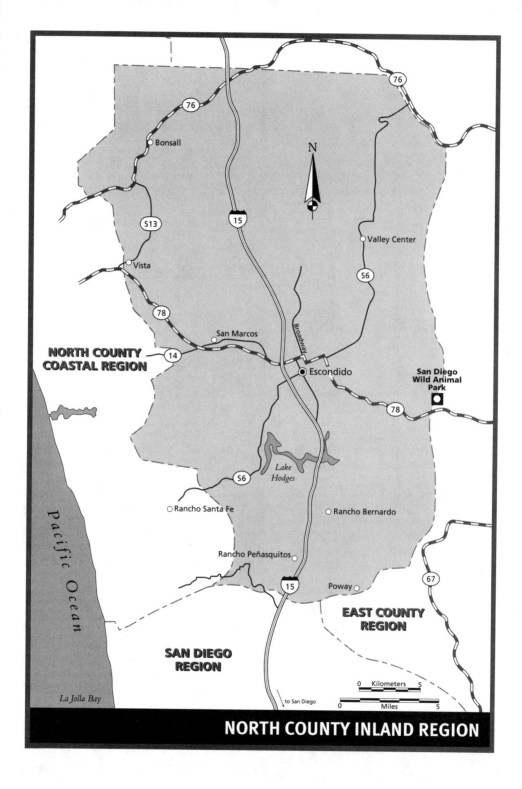

N

NORTH COUNTY COASTAL REGION

Bonsall

Vista

San Marcos

Valley Center

Escondido

Broadway

San Diego Wild Animal Park

Lake Hodges

Rancho Santa Fe

Rancho Bernardo

Rancho Peñasquitos

Poway

Pacific Ocean

EAST COUNTY REGION

SAN DIEGO REGION

La Jolla Bay

to San Diego

0 Kilometers 5

0 Miles 5

NORTH COUNTY INLAND REGION

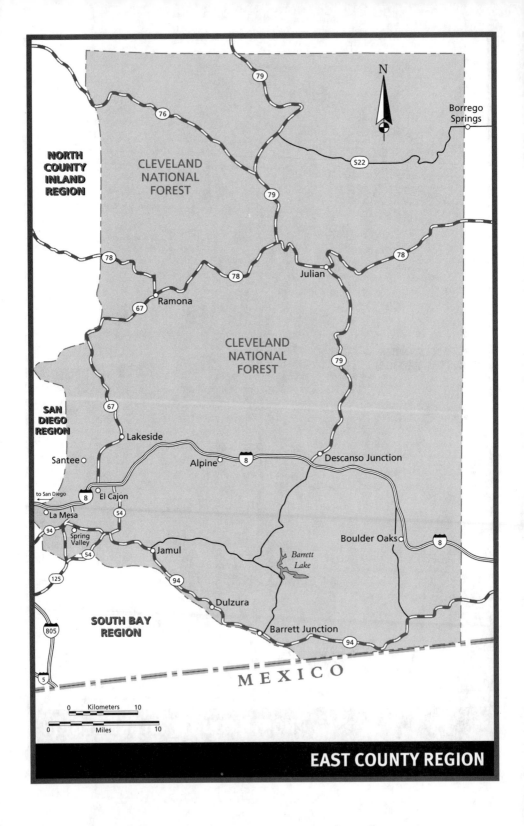

EAST COUNTY REGION

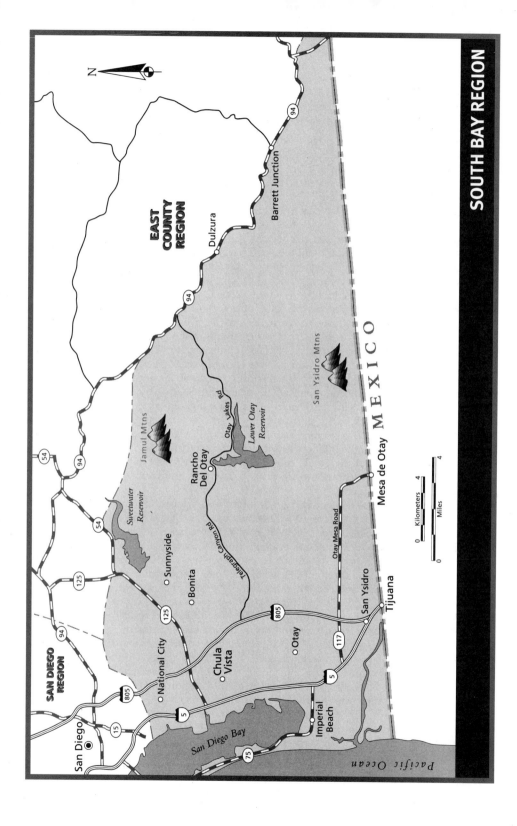

SOUTH BAY REGION

Preface

Welcome to San Diego, a.k.a. America's finest cities.

Haven't seen the word "cities" showing up in the glossy advertisements? That's because they're only talking about the city of San Diego. As Insiders know, San Diego is much more than one location or destination.

We're inviting you to explore all of the enticing locales that form San Diego County. Stretching south from Orange County to our international border with Mexico, this is one of the best places in America to visit or to live. On the west, you'll find the Pacific Ocean, and lining its shores, dozens of interesting communities, with their own flavor and style. To the east rise several beautiful mountain ranges, and beyond, the Anza-Borrego Desert—stark and eerie and flat—with a beauty all its own.

Like many first-time visitors, you might be a bit surprised by the diversity. Even those of us who live here have to remind ourselves to stray beyond our favorite, most familiar haunts to explore the myriad landscapes that make up our county. You can rough it on a weekend camping trip to unmarked tracts of desert or treat yourself like a queen at a high-end spa. Hang glide above the beach, stalk native or migratory birds in the estuaries, or just lie back amid the tall grasses in a riparian forest. Gallop through the mountains on a well-fed horse, or just dine at a classic country eatery. There's just nothing like San Diego for diversity of scenery and choices of outdoor activities.

Here in San Diego we take recreation seriously. However it's not all about sweat and sinew, blading and surfing. San Diego County also has boatloads of cultural activities. Our reputation is for being laid-back rather than high-energy like Los Angeles or cutting-edge like New York. But our easygoing spirit doesn't keep us from being ambitious. In San Diego you'll find biotech and telecommunications firms sharing economic indicator statistics with the military, tourism, and agriculture. Together with a substantial artistic community, these San Diego players contribute to one of the country's most eclectic lifestyles and cultures. And we work, play, study, and create under a cerulean-blue sky in a perfect climate.

On any given day, San Diego offers a smorgasbord of possibilities. You might start your day with a sunrise walk along a wide, sandy beach, with a stop at a surfer hangout for a kicked-back breakfast. Your biggest problem? Whether to order a spicy breakfast burrito or yogurt with fresh fruit and granola—not to mention which beautiful beach to walk on and at which patio restaurant to cool your heels. You might spend the day inspired by sunshine and the scent of sage in the lonely desert. And, not to put too fine a point on our diversity, you could end the evening with dinner in the mountains under a firmament of stars. If there's one thing San Diego does not lack, it's variety.

We can offer a choice of weather, too. For those folks who actually like to shovel snow (or at least play in it), San Diego County encompasses towns that experience the four seasons. That's right. Every winter our mountain communities get at least a dusting—if not more—of winter white. If you prefer wearing cool cotton clothing and sandals year-round, that's just the uniform some folks have adopted. You might have to dress up a bit for your boss or clients, but then it's back to the shorts and sandals. In general, clothing here is casual, except for the few occasions when grown-up clothes are required. Weddings, funerals, and the opera spring to mind, but even at the opera you'll see the range of tastes and fashion statements that mark San Diego as unique.

With so much to offer, it's no surprise that tourism is a mainstay of our economy. Visitors from the north and east flock here in winter to escape harsher climes. "Zonies" head for the sea during summer, when temperatures in their home state of Arizona soar to unbearable highs. But no matter where you're from, you'll not feel like an outsider. Although most don't like to admit it, relatively few San Diegans are natives themselves. Most of us weren't born here, truth be told, but selected the county as the place to live, go to school, or raise a family because we like it here.

So you're coming to San Diego, or you live here, and you want to explore. The Daytrips chapter offers great getaways, including sunny Palm Springs and Temecula's wine country. If you want to just relax, the Spas and Resorts chapter can direct you to a place where you can tune up your body and unburden your mind. And if you're bringing along your sweetie, the Bed-and-Breakfast Inns chapter can help you find the perfect romantic getaway.

Welcome to San Diego. It's a great place to visit and the best place to call home. But maybe we should just keep that to ourselves.

Acknowledgments

When we began the first edition of this book in early January 1998 we were colleagues. We quickly became friends and are now the closest of friends. An added pleasure and dimension to our friendship happened when we discovered that our funny bones were in the same spots.

Without each other's support, warmth, and mutual admiration, this collaborative project would never have gone so smoothly, perhaps never have been possible.

"Thank you, Jackie. You're the best."

"Thank you, Eva. You're the best."

"No, you're the best."

"No, you're the best."

"You're the best."

"You're the best."

Ad infinitum . . .

—Eva Shaw and Jacquelyn Landis

We would like to thank Susan Humphry, Joe Timko, Robert Arends, Tanisha Carden, Will K. Shilling, and Robin Klerin. We also express our thanks to everyone at the San Diego Convention and Visitors Bureau and Leslie Gaul and the San Diego North Convention and Visitors Bureau.

—Maribeth Mellin and Jane Onstott

How to Use This Book

Most visitors and residents think of San Diego in regions. San Diego County is so large (4,255 square miles) that it has to be broken down into more manageable areas. We refer to them as Central San Diego, North County Coastal, North County Inland, East County, and South Bay.

The actual city of San Diego includes the spectacular buildings and gorgeous harbor you may have seen if you arrived at the San Diego International Airport, locally known as Lindbergh Field. For our purposes the Central San Diego area includes Downtown, the Gaslamp Quarter, Mission Hills, Hillcrest, several beach communities, Coronado, La Jolla, the Golden Triangle, and some inland communities. Some Insiders will bristle at the divisions. It's tough to slice a perfect pie. Our goal with the format was to make it easy for newcomers and tourists to get around.

To make it easier to locate what you want and need in San Diego County, we've broken the outer regions into the four, smaller areas noted above. These are the labels Insiders use, so you'll see and hear these areas referred to in the newspaper, on television, and in conversations.

Think of the regions as making a circle around the core of our county. Out of the city proper we move north, up the coast using Interstate 5, to North County Coastal. This area includes the beach communities that touch or are close to the Pacific Ocean. Included are the communities of Rancho Santa Fe, Del Mar, Solana Beach, Cardiff, Encinitas (with its neighborhood region called Leucadia), La Costa, Carlsbad, and Oceanside.

East of the ocean is the region we called North County Inland. It includes the communities of Vista, San Marcos, Escondido, Fallbrook, Valley Center, Bonsall, Rancho Bernardo, Rancho Peñasquitos, and Poway.

The next region is East County. For our purposes it includes the cities of La Mesa, Lemon Grove, Spring Valley, El Cajon, Santee, Bonita, Lakeside, and Alpine. East County also embraces the mountain towns of Pine Valley, Ramona, and Julian and spreads farther to the desert area of Borrego Springs.

Completing the circle is the South Bay area. It includes Chula Vista, National City, Imperial Beach, and San Ysidro, the communities close to the border between the United States and Mexico. Because much of our region is bicultural, you'll find information and recommendations on activities, shopping, accommodations, and dining for Mexico in our chapter titled South of the Border.

When organizing the book we followed the outline of these natural regions. It made sense. There were exceptions, of course. Sometimes, such as in the chapter on Higher Education, we've listed colleges and universities by category. Beaches and Watersports and our Media chapters are also organized by categories.

Even if your family has been in California since the Gold Rush days, you'll enjoy reading the History chapter to get the full scope of San Diego. It will give you a feel for San Diego's terrain, our traditions, and our colorful and somewhat checkered past. In the Area Overview we bring you up to date on our industries, cultural activities, distinct population, role in the international marketplace, and close bonds with Mexico.

Annual events are listed with month-by-month notations. If you're visiting San Diego County in the summer, you may want to find out about the Roar and Snore Camp at the Wild Animal Park near Escondido. If you're here during the December holidays, you won't want to miss Christmas on the Prado in Balboa Park. These events are just examples of the many possibilities we've listed.

You'll notice by looking at the table of contents that we've devoted separate chapters to Golf, Spas and Resorts, Retirement, and Balboa Park. These are "big ticket items" in our county and make us unique. In Balboa Park alone, you can find museums, plays, and concerts along with the world-famous San Diego Zoo and its treasure trove of botanical exhibits. As long-time residents of San Diego, we know that you can't devote just one afternoon to our Balboa Park. It deserves repeat visits.

To make this book really useful, we've cross-referenced places and events. We've tried to keep repetition to a minimum but have allowed some duplication of entries to save you the trouble of flipping back and forth. For example, a great picnic area might be mentioned in the Parks chapter and in the Kidstuff chapter. Each entry will probably be slightly different depending on its placement. For example, the entry in Kidstuff might include the fact that this is the site of Easter egg and candy hunts for youngsters. Check the index if you want to read everything on a particular site.

The book's regional divisions and cross-referenced entries should make it easy for you to find the closest bed and breakfast inn, Asian grocery store, Cinco de Mayo fiesta, or beach. Keep in mind that Insiders never blink at traveling across the county for dinner, to visit a theater, or to attend a festival or event. For instance, when snowflakes sprinkle Mount Laguna, San Diegans often take off to let the kids (of all ages) play in the snow. For those of us living on the coast, it's a fun drive that's well worth the time. Since we feel that all of San Diego is our backyard, distance isn't an obstacle. Don't make it one for you.

Our roads and highways are clearly marked and referred to locally by number. As an example you'll hear people say, "Take 5 to 78 and then 15." Translated that means to go north on Interstate 5 to U.S. Highway 78, which begins in Carlsbad and takes travelers to the North County Inland area. After about 20 miles, U.S. Highway 78 easily merges with Interstate 15, and the signs are large and noticeable.

When navigating the county by car, we recommend buying a map. Most bookstores have them. Maps are also available at the Transit Store, 102 Broadway. The Transit Store is on the northeast corner of First Avenue and Broadway, and the phone numbers are (619) 234-1060 and (619) 233-3004 (for bus routes). They're open Monday through Friday 8:30 A.M. to 5:30 P.M., Saturday and Sunday noon to 4:00 P.M.

Parking isn't a big problem in the county, except at the beaches. However, if you're attending a well-publicized event, parade, or a Chargers football game, you could be in for a short hike. Remember, sneakers are acceptable here; comfortable clothes are the fashion choice for most San Diegans.

Throughout the book distances and times are given from the downtown area of San Diego, traveling on multilane freeways and highways, unless noted otherwise. Allow about 20 minutes to get from the downtown hotels to Del Mar. Rush hours and the occasional rainstorm always play a role in the time it takes to get anywhere. So if you're meeting friends after work in Solana Beach (North County Coastal) and it's stormy, give yourself extra time. Yes, there are traffic jams even in Paradise.

A few words on our area codes. It's doesn't take a rocket scientist to notice that the region is booming. (Although we have plenty of rocket scientists in the area who will discuss this at length.) With a recent influx of high-tech firms and high-tech folks, we finally stretched the limits of our area codes. As we go to press, we have three area codes for the county, so next to each telephone listing you'll find the area code along with the phone number. A fourth, and possibly a fifth, may be added soon.

Now for addresses. We provide street addresses, where available, to help you find your way around. Reading the Getting There/Getting Around chapter will help you further, by identifying some of San Diego's major districts. Once you know those, you can take a shuttle from the airport to the Gaslamp Quarter, for example, by asking for it by name. No numbered address is needed, unless you want to go to a specific building in the area.

Throughout the chapters, we've included Insiders' Tips. These are recommendations you won't find in tour books and are guaranteed to make your visit or move here more enjoyable or memorable. The Close-ups will let you meet the people and places that make the area exceptional. For instance, we've even included a once-secret guacamole recipe that recently received a first-place ribbon at a local avocado festival. Folks in San Diego County eat a lot of avocados. Check out the festival and recipe in the Annual Events chapter.

We hope you'll make this book your own. We wrote it for you. You might want to keep it in your desk for daydreaming or trip-planning purposes. You could put it in your briefcase to study during your morning commute or your flight into Lindbergh Field. Or add it to the glove box of your car when you're maneuvering around San Diego.

Use highlighting pens, sticky notes, and corner folds on the pages to plan an itinerary, a weekend, a holiday adventure, or your future. You've already started to feel comfortable here because, at this very moment, all of San Diego is at your fingertips.

Area Overview

When the Census of 2000 was completed, San Diego lost its ranking as the sixth-largest city in the United States. Phoenix took over that position, and San Diego became the nation's seventh-largest city. Guess what? That doesn't bother San Diegans a bit. It's not a sign that things have taken a turn for the worse. In fact, just the opposite is true. The economy is strong, jobs are plentiful, crime is down, and the weather is still balmy. All it means is that Phoenix is growing faster than San Diego. Good for them.

San Diegans have always appreciated quality over quantity, and while all reports indicate continued population growth, city leaders prefer to be ready for it. Predictions are that the next 20 years will bring more than a million newcomers to San Diego, and those already here are taking steps to ensure that the same quality of life they now enjoy will be preserved for generations to come.

Slipping to the seventh-largest spot is hardly a tragedy. In spite of the city's burgeoning reputation as a major player in international business, in spite of the fact that it continues to grow on a dozen different levels, it still relentlessly preserves its low-key and slow-paced image right alongside its more polished one.

Regions

Describing San Diego geographically can sometimes be a challenge. It's a city, but within that city are over 100 separate, identifiable neighborhoods. It's also a county. And within San Diego County are 18 incorporated cities (including the city of San Diego) and many more unincorporated towns and communities. The county stretches south from the Orange County line all the way to the U.S.–Mexico border. Its western boundary is the Pacific Ocean, and its eastern reaches include the Laguna Mountains and the Anza-Borrego Desert.

When locals try to describe where they live, they usually tack a few qualifiers onto the end of their description. Someone living in the tiny northern town of Jesmond Dene, for example, would say "I live in Jesmond Dene, a little town in San Diego, in the North County." Or even if their hometown is within the city limits, it occasionally needs a bit more information to pinpoint its location. "I come from Nestor. It's in San Diego, in the South Bay." Even though residents of every locale within the boundaries of the county feel enormous pride for their neighborhood, sometimes it's just simpler to say we all live in San Diego. And that's what most Insiders do.

To make things easier for you to understand, we've separated the county into five regions: Central San Diego, North County Coastal, North County Inland, East County, and the South Bay. The lines separating the regions are indistinct, and some locals may disagree about which region, in fact, contains their neighborhood. But each region has different characteristics that give it a definable flavor all its own. As you travel around the county, you'll soon discover that San Diego is indeed a complex place. And we have little doubt that you'll like what you find.

Central San Diego

It would be easy to say that the city of San Diego is the center of all the action. That may have been true at one time, but not anymore. Everything that makes San Diego a great place to visit and an even

Sailboat masts and skyscrapers—the San Diego skyline. PHOTO: JAMES BLANK, COURTESY OF SAN DIEGO CONVENTION AND VISITORS BUREAU

greater place to live can be found in other regions. But Central San Diego is still the heart of the county, the metropolitan center where the largest concentration of people live. From the lazy, sun-soaked beaches to the no-nonsense high-tech companies in Sorrento Valley; from the nightlife of the Gaslamp Quarter to the bedroom communities nestled inland, Central San Diego has it all.

The rhythm of life is a little faster around downtown than in other regions of the county. A good number of the major businesses are located within the city limits. If you fly into Lindbergh Field, San Diego's International Airport, you'll notice that you're almost downtown already. Of course, you probably figured that out while your plane was making its hair-raising descent through the maze of high-rises.

Within San Diego are three separate business areas: Downtown, Mission Valley, and the Golden Triangle. Although downtown has the highest concentration of banks and law firms, and Mission Valley has more than its share of shopping malls, the Golden Triangle is where the upstarts congregate. Located east and north of La Jolla, the area is home to many of San Diego's high-tech, biotech, and telecommunications firms.

The neighborhoods within the city limits are defined by several factors. Downtown and the surrounding neighborhoods of Uptown, Golden Hill, Bankers Hill, and Hillcrest are all urbane and trendy. Ocean, Pacific, and Mission Beaches are just what you'd expect: casual beach communities where businesses must post signs asking customers to wear shoes and shirts. Mission Valley, the Golden Triangle, and the College area, which are close to universities, tend to have lots of twenty-something inhabitants. La Jolla is inhabited by an upscale population who can afford multimillion-dollar, ocean-view homes. For purposes of this book, we have included all the neighborhoods south of Del Mar, north of Chula Vista, and west of La Mesa in the Central San Diego region. For detailed descriptions of the neighborhoods and cities within the entire San Diego County, check out our Neighborhoods and Real Estate chapter.

SAN DIEGO VITAL STATISTICS

Mayor/governor: Mayor Dick Murphy/Governor Gray Davis

Capital/major cities/outlying counties:
Sacramento/Los Angeles, San Francisco/Los Angeles County to the north, Riverside-San Bernardino County to the northeast, Imperial County to the east

Population: City: 1.2 million, County: 2.813 million

Area (sq. miles): City of San Diego: 320 sq. miles,
County of San Diego: 4,255 sq. miles

Nickname/motto: America's Finest City

Average temperatures (high/low): July: 76/65

Average temperatures (high/low): January: 65/48

Average rain/days of sunshine: Rain: 9 inches annually, sunny days: 72%

Founded: 1850

Major universities:
University of California, San Diego; San Diego State University; University of San Diego; California State University, San Marcos

Important dates in history: September 28, 1542 (Cabrillo landed in San Diego Bay)

Major area private employers: SharpHealth Care, Scripps Health, Pacific Bell

Famous sons and daughters:
Baseball legend Ted Williams, actors Gregory Peck and Cliff Robertson, actress Annette Bening, Ted (Dr. Seuss) Geisel

State/city holidays:
All national holidays; schools close for California Admission Day—Sept. 9

Toll roads/major airports/major interstates:
San Diego-Coronado Bay Bridge (toll-free as of July 2002)
San Diego International Airport (Lindbergh Field)
Interstates 5, 8, 15, & 805

Public transportation: Amtrak, Coaster, Trolley, Bus, Taxi

Military bases: Marine Corps Recruit Depot, Marine Corps Air Station, Naval Base Coronado, Naval Base Point Loma, Naval Base San Diego

Driving laws: Seatbelts–yes, car seats–yes, speed limit–65 mph, wipers/headlights–no, HOV lanes–2+ per vehicle

Alcohol laws:
21, DUI Limit: .08, alcohol available in liquor stores, convenience stores, supermarkets, drug stores 7 days a week; bars open until 2:00 A.M.

Daily newspapers: *San Diego Union-Tribune, North County Times*

Sales tax: 7.75% on everything but most foods

Room tax/meal tax: Room tax is 10.5%, meal tax is same as sales tax, 7.75%

Chamber of commerce:
San Diego Regional Chamber of Commerce
402 W. Broadway, San Diego
(619) 544–1300; www.sdchamber.org

Time/weather: (619) 853–1212/(858) 675–8706

North County Coastal

Stretching north from Del Mar to Oceanside, San Diego's North County Coastal region has some of the area's prettiest beaches, offbeat clubs and cafes, clusters of interior design businesses, and its own collection of emerging high-tech and manufacturing headquarters. In short, North County Coastal has just about everything Central San Diego has—even its own airport. You can catch regular commuter flights to Los Angeles from Palomar Airport in Carlsbad.

Also in Carlsbad, behind the rainbow of flower fields visible from Interstate 5, is an explosion of new office complexes. Numerous businesses moving into San Diego have chosen Carlsbad as their base. This ever-growing business community has provided an economic shot in the arm to North County Coastal as well as the rest of the county.

Houses in beach communities such as Del Mar, Solana Beach, and Encinitas command some of the most spectacular views in California. A few miles inland, interspersed among thousands of eucalyptus trees, is the village of Rancho Santa Fe. Here you find sprawling estates, a gentrified country atmosphere, and some of the most expensive real estate in the United States.

Drive around North County Coastal for a few hours and you'll see why this region has grown so quickly in recent years. In the first place, there was land to develop. Housing developments have sprouted up all over canyons and fields, and a dozen or more instant neighborhoods have sprung up. Access to the coast makes it desirable, as does the abundance of new businesses. It's just like Central San Diego—only newer, farther away from downtown, with more of a vacation attitude. Those differences give it its own special charm.

North County Inland

Continuing the circle of San Diego County, we come to North County Inland. Home to the cities of Vista, San Marcos, Escondido,

and Poway, North County Inland also has smaller communities with such charming names as Harmony Grove and the Elfin Forest. These are not misnomers, either. Trees, chaparral, horses, and hiking trails are abundant, and life has a decidedly more rural flavor.

As more and more people gravitate to San Diego, many have found their way to North County Inland, where housing tends to be more affordable and traditional family neighborhoods are more common than in Central San Diego. Many residents commute to Central San Diego for work, but they don't seem to mind. They prefer the more relaxed atmosphere of the northern region over the hustle and bustle of San Diego.

An emerging trend in North County Inland is to live, work, and play within the confines of the region. Many residents have moved or started their businesses close to home, avoiding the commute altogether and taking advantage of the quality of life in the northern reaches of the county.

The communities are a good mix of folks who have been around for a couple of generations and young families just starting out. Families are drawn to North County Inland for another reason too: top-notch schools. Poway High School, for instance, has one of the highest percentages of graduates in the county who go on to college.

Million-dollar villas surround the luxurious Four Seasons Resort Aviara near Carlsbad.

East County

Largest in terms of physical area, East County includes the suburban communities just east of the San Diego city limits, the Laguna Mountains, the Cuyamaca Mountains, Palomar Mountain, and the desert city of Borrego Springs. East County is where you'll find the hottest temperatures during the summer months and the coldest in wintertime.

East County is even more rural than North County Inland. East County residents share their neighborhoods with farm animals and country western bars. And if you're looking for the ultimate cowboy hat or the perfect pair of boots, you're in the right place.

But don't let the casually rugged appearance of some of the inhabitants fool you. Hidden treasures of a most sophisticated nature abound in the region. The East County Performing Arts organization in El Cajon stages a variety of wonderfully entertaining productions every year. The annual Oktoberfest in La Mesa draws folks from all over the county. And the Palomar Observatory, in the mountains, is a magnet for international professional and amateur astronomers. Borrego Springs, located in the desert east of San Diego's mountains, is home to one of the most venerated resorts in the county, La Casa del Zorro (see our Spas and Resorts chapter for a detailed description).

East County has more than its share of pleasures. Give the residents credit for having figured out how to enjoy the best of both worlds. They have the serenity of the quiet life, but the lights of the big city are only a short drive away.

South Bay

At the southernmost end of the county, the South Bay has beautiful beaches and great neighborhoods. By now you've noticed that's not unique within the county. But South Bay does have something that no other region can claim: an international border. Only 20 minutes from downtown San Diego, the U.S–Mexico border is the gateway to Baja California and a whole different set of experiences, which you'll find described in our South of the Border chapter.

Palm trees and sailboats on calm water are San Diego specialties. PHOTO: JAMES BLANK, COURTESY OF SAN DIEGO CONVENTION AND VISITORS BUREAU

Horton Plaza's exciting stores and restaurants draw crowds to the revitalized downtown district.

PHOTO: JOHN BAHU, COURTESY OF THE SAN DIEGO CONVENTION & VISITORS BUREAU

Even locals are surprised to learn that within the entire county, South Bay's Chula Vista has the second fastest growing population in the country. Chula Vista is also home to BF Goodrich Aerospace (formerly called Rohr Industries), an aircraft manufacturer and one of the county's largest employers.

As the county's population slowly spreads to outlying regions, the South Bay has not been ignored. As in North County Inland, many young neighborhoods, such as EastLake and Otay Ranch, are springing up to complement the older ones, like National City, Imperial Beach, and San Ysidro, and home prices are among the most affordable in the county.

Several attractions draw visitors and residents to South Bay. The Olympic Training Center is a hub for international athletes. The Coors Amphitheater, a 20,000-seat outdoor amphitheater, has become the most popular venue for the biggest concert stars. As with San Diego's other regions, the South Bay is constantly looking to the future and finding ways to make its little corner of paradise even better.

Government

Describing the structure of government is almost as confusing as describing the geography of San Diego, but if you remember the cities and the regions within the county, then you'll have a pretty good idea of the various governments, which tend to follow those same separations. The city of San Diego has a mayor and an eight-member city council, which represents eight different areas within the city limits. The 17 other incorporated cities within the county also have mayors and city councils.

Representing the entire county is a board of supervisors, composed of five elected members who represent areas that generally correspond to the regional divisions we use here. Even those hardy souls who live in the most remote speck on the county map still have an elected official representing their interests.

Demographics

To give you an idea of the geographic reach of San Diego, it lies in the southwest corner of California, 120 miles south of the city of Los Angeles. The city of San Diego encompasses an area of 320 square miles; add in the other four regions, and the area of the entire county jumps to 4,255 square miles. The population of the city is about 1.2 million, while the county's numbers remain around 2.813 million.

Like most other major cities in the United States, San Diego's minority population has increased significantly in recent years, especially because of its proximity to the U.S.–Mexico border. Estimates are that the Hispanic population will increase to 30 percent by 2020, and the Asian population will jump to 11.8 percent.

In addition to being the seventh-largest city in the country, San Diego is the second-largest city in California, behind Los Angeles. Living in the shadow of that megalopolis to the north has been both a blessing and a curse. National newspapers and magazines tend to overlook San Diego in favor of Los Angeles. When something newsworthy happens in La Jolla or Rancho Santa Fe, it will often be referred to by the national press as "a community south of Los Angeles."

Insiders' Tip

To learn more about San Diego's politics and government, visit the city's Web site at www.sannet.gov, or check out the county's at www.co.san-diego.ca.us. Both sites have great inside information about current issues affecting the city and county.

SANDAG Helps Make Sense of It All

Think about it: 18 incorporated cities exist within the county of San Diego. That's 18 mayors, city councils, and cities full of citizens fiercely protective of their quality of life within their geographic limits. Add another layer of government, the county board of supervisors, which is responsible for the five geographic regions that encompass all 18 cities. How in the world do they all get along?

The answer is SANDAG. Although the name conjures up pictures of some critter burrowing in the sand, SANDAG is actually a serious organization dedicated to facilitating the smooth flow of cooperation and understanding among the cities and regions of San Diego. Formally known as the San Diego Association of Governments, SANDAG is a forum for regional decision-making. Its goal is to build consensus among the various governments of San Diego County when it comes time to making decisions about strategic planning and allocation of resources.

Who runs SANDAG? That's where the brilliance of the association is most evident. The very people who oversee the cities and the county regions are the same people who make up SANDAG. Mayors, council members, and county supervisors from all 18 cities are the voting members of SANDAG's board of directors. Representatives from other agencies, including the U.S. Department of Defense (the military has long been influential in San Diego because of its strong physical presence), the San Diego Unified Port District, Caltrans (California Department of Transportation), and Tijuana/Baja California/Mexico serve as advisors.

Each month, SANDAG meets to consider crucial issues including growth, transportation, environmental management, housing, open space, air quality, energy, fiscal management, economic development, and criminal justice. Sounds like a monumental task, but San Diego County's leaders understand that planning cannot be effective if done in a piecemeal manner. With everyone working together through SANDAG the odds of making plans that enhance life for all San Diegans are greatly improved.

One of the appealing features of SANDAG is that the average citizen has access to the organization. Public forums are encouraged whenever an issue is about to be decided, whether that issue is recycling or traffic management. Citizens and special interest groups are actively involved in SANDAG's planning process. They serve on committees, attend workshops, and participate in public hearings.

Legally, SANDAG is a "joint powers agency," created in 1966 as the Comprehen-

The County Administration Building, with its Art Deco construction, is a designated historical building. It is home to the San Diego County Board of Supervisors, one of the arms of SANDAG. PHOTO: JACQUELYN LANDIS

sive Planning Organization. It was renamed SANDAG in 1980. Each May SANDAG pools local, state, and federal funds and develops a budget to tackle its goals for the upcoming year.

The organization has accomplished plenty.

In 1975, SANDAG developed a comprehensive Regional Transportation Plan. In 1992, the association helped form a five-county rail coalition. Four years later, SANDAG convinced Congress and the California state legislature to allocate funds for massive amounts of sand to replenish local beaches.

In keeping with its history, current plans are far-reaching. SANDAG is working on growth management in anticipation of the million newcomers expected by the year 2020. It also is focusing on habitat conservation, criminal justice research, hazardous waste management, and traffic management.

It sounds like a lot. It is. But this is a coalition of leaders with the same goal: to improve the quality of life in San Diego. Keeping things running smoothly among 18 cities in the same county is a big job. SANDAG is up to the challenge.

Even though locals bristle at that kind of liberal manipulation of county lines, there's a certain quiet satisfaction in believing that their city still has an aura of secrecy about it. It's not that we mind sharing it with visitors, we just prefer to keep it as quiet as possible. No one wants to spoil a good thing.

Industry and Jobs

Ask an Insider what the top industry is in San Diego and the likely response will be, with hardly a pause, "Tourism." Sometimes even Insiders can be wrong. Although tourism is a driving force in San Diego's economy, it's not number one. It's not even number two. San Diego's industries rank as follows: manufacturing, military defense, then tourism.

From the early days, manufacturing has been a leader in supporting the local economy. The types of goods produced have shifted in the past decade, however. The aerospace industry used to be the giant in town, and it still is strong. The local defense industry creates several billion dollars in contract work for local companies. And San Diego has shipyards large enough to build and repair the Navy's huge ships. But other industries are

coming to the forefront. For example, San Diego has become a golf equipment manufacturing center. Callaway Golf, makers of the famed Big Bertha driver, employs 5,000 San Diegans. Gateway, that computer upstart with the big cow spots on its boxes, has its headquarters in Poway with 500 employees. The big mover and shaker, Qualcomm, is San Diego's leading technology industry, employing 6,500 San Diegans. The homegrown telecommunications company has become a visible force in the local community. The football stadium even carries its name.

Research and development companies, biotechnology upstarts, and other high-tech industries have flocked to San Diego, thanks to the intellectual resources at our many institutes of higher education and our long-standing research facilities. The San Diego Super Computer Center at UCSD has some of the fastest computers in the world—a valuable resource for research teams. San Diego is home to 499 biomedical companies employing 29,000 workers. The leader in the employment race for the foreseeable future is the electronics business, which employs about 20,000 San Diegans. The demand for workers in these areas is extremely strong. Many companies have launched international searches and are stuffing

San Diego Bay offers a combination of harbor, urban, and coastal lifestyles. PHOTO: COURTESY OF SAN DIEGO CONVENTION AND VISITORS BUREAU

employment packages with perks to try to lure engineers, researchers, and technicians to San Diego.

The ties between San Diego and its good neighbor to the south continue to strengthen. A joint international marketing program with Baja California helps attract investment in research and in manufacturing, and a vigorous trade between the two countries helps bolster the ever-growing maquiladora industry. Maquiladoras are companies with offices and manufacturing facilities on both sides of the border, a venture that has been quite successful for the two countries.

The military remains a strong contributor to the economy, pumping nearly $9.8 billion annually into the local coffers. Tourism, even though it ranks third, will never be under-appreciated, as 15.2 million visitors yearly add another $5.2 billion to the pot. More than 177,000 San Diegans work in fields directly related to the tourist industry, including lodging, food service, attractions, and transportation. A large proportion of the new jobs created in San Diego are in the service-producing industries and in wholesale and retail trade.

The construction industry continues to be strong. Its growth seems to be limited only by the amount of available land for new homes. With an annual growth rate of 40,000–50,000 new residents, the demand for homes continues to keep construction firms busy, and the construction industry employs some 74,000 workers.

The median income for San Diegans is $48,900, yet the average salary is $37,500. Many San Diegans work more than one job just to keep up with the high cost of living in this place many see as their personal paradise. Fortunately, unemployment is at its lowest rate in four decades, down to 3.0 in the year 2000. There are plenty of jobs to be had, and many exciting opportunities for training in cutting-edge fields.

Cost of Living

There's a price to be paid for living in a paradise where the weather's great, jobs are plentiful, and attitudes are casual. A true dollars-and-cents price. The cost of living in San Diego is undeniably higher than in many other cities, and the main reason is real estate. Real estate has traditionally been the barometer of the local economy, rising and falling with the fortune of the rest of the city. However, even at its lowest, real estate is rarely a bargain in California's southernmost cul-de-sac. Housing prices fluctuate, of course, but the median price of a single-family house in 2002 was $274,000 and climbing.

Gasoline prices seem to be higher than in other places, too. And since San Diegans tenaciously cling to their autos as the preferred mode of transportation, they pay for it.

But the good news is that bargains are always to be found. Inexpensive dining, off-price shopping, and discount entertainment opportunities are common. With judicious planning, a visit or even a permanent move to San Diego doesn't have to break the bank.

Weather

San Diego is famous for many things: the zoo, Sea World, Balboa Park, Dr. Seuss, and Scripps Institution of Oceanography, to name a few. But ask anyone what comes to mind when they think of San Diego, and more likely than not they'll say the weather. Let's face it. The average daytime temperature is 70 degrees, and most days are sunny. Humidity is usually low, even during the summer, and winter temperatures rarely dip below 40 degrees at night. It doesn't get much more pleasant than that.

Of course, if you travel to the far ends of the county you can find some extremes. Desert temperatures in Borrego Springs soar over 100 degrees for most of the summer, and the mountains get cold enough to keep snow on the ground for at least a few days during the winter. But aside from a few heat waves during the summer and cold snaps during the winter, it's generally comfortable around town most of the time.

Visitors from the Midwest are astonished to find that a winter wardrobe is

Insiders' Tip

To report a crime in progress, or for any life-threatening situation, dial 911 immediately. If you are the victim of a crime that happened while you were away, or to give information concerning a crime or any suspicious activity, call the police at (619) 531-2000.

nonexistent in San Diego. Most locals' idea of a winter wardrobe is their summer wardrobe—with a sweater. And no matter how cold it gets during the winter months, some stalwart souls refuse to give up their shorts.

Rainfall averages less than 10 inches per year, except in the El Niño years, when anything can happen. The only other weather oddity is the occasional condition known as a Santa Ana. During a Santa Ana, hot and dry winds blow in from the desert, the temperature climbs into the high eighties or low nineties and the humidity plunges to 10 percent or less. Most common during the late fall or early winter months, these winds usually last only a few days, and are more a subject for water-cooler conversation than a cause of major discomfort.

Earthquakes

Anyone who has endured an earthquake of any magnitude will confirm that they are nothing to be scoffed at. They are every bit as frightening as a tornado or a hurricane and can cause devastating damage. The good news is that the big ones are few and far between. Even though earthquakes are almost a daily occurrence in

Lush foliage surrounds this coastal beacon. PHOTO: BOB YARBROUGH, COURTESY OF SAN DIEGO CONVENTION AND VISITORS BUREAU

A downtown San Diego skyline is the backdrop to a group of sailing enthusiasts. PHOTO: DALE FROST, PORT OF SAN DIEGO

and around Southern California, most are too small to be noticed. The wise traveler or resident is prepared for any eventuality, though, and will have evacuation routes planned in advance, just as you would in case of fire.

The White Pages of the local telephone book have comprehensive instructions and suggestions for earthquake safety. Knowing what to do ahead of time will lessen the scare factor of the occasional shaker.

Crime and Personal Safety

We want your time in San Diego to be safe. Although crime is down according to police and sheriff's department statistics, this still is a big city, and it still has crime and safety issues like every other large city. It's always wise to keep in mind the same basic safety precautions you would take in

your hometown or in any other major metropolitan city.

Whether sightseeing, dining, or shopping, it's a good idea to travel in groups. There's safety in numbers, and you will lessen the opportunity to be singled out as a target. Also, try to have a good idea of your current surroundings and where

> ### Insiders' Tip
> The 16½-block historic Gaslamp Quarter is home to almost 400 businesses, and most of its 93 historical buildings have been renovated within the past 10 years.

you're headed. The more confident you appear, the less vulnerable you are to unscrupulous strangers.

Finally, like every other major city in the world, San Diego has a homeless population concentrated in its urban areas. Most homeless people are harmless, but some are chronic criminals and drug or alcohol abusers who are eager to take advantage of the unsuspecting. We suggest you treat transients with respectful caution, and avoid contributing to panhandlers.

Now, you have an idea of what San Diego is all about, hop in your car, head for the trolley, and explore. You'll like what you find. And don't forget to bring your *Insiders' Guide*.

Insiders' Tip

Weather in San Diego can be changeable. Those Pacific breezes aren't always balmy. Insiders layer clothing and keep a sweatshirt in the car, just in case it turns cool.

Getting Here, Getting Around

San Diego is a destination city. In fact, it is often referred to as the cul-de-sac of the Southwest, a distinction that rankles most locals, but ultimately they grudgingly agree. Few people come through San Diego on their way to someplace else, as they do with major hubs like Los Angeles, Chicago, or Dallas. Of course, Lindbergh Field is called San Diego International Airport, but unless you're headed to Mexico, leaving the country usually involves a stop in Los Angeles first. Once you're here, well, there's really no reason to go anyplace else aside from an occasional daytrip. As you'll soon discover, that's not such a bad thing. The city has more than enough attractions and entertainment to amuse even the most hard to please. And if you're really determined to go someplace else when you leave San Diego, we'll get you there . . . eventually.

Another distinction San Diego has is the location of its primary airport, Lindbergh Field. It sits right smack in the middle of the city, not on the outskirts of town like most major airports. That means when you land, you're already here. You don't have to spend an hour or more finding your way into the city. Oh, and just a word about the landing. Because the airport is right next to downtown, your pilot will have to navigate some high-rises during final approach. But don't let that worry you—they've been doing it for years and they're used to it. Just wave to the office workers on the top floors as you fly by.

We've designed this chapter to help you find your way to San Diego and how to get around once you're here. We've included all the traditional modes of transportation as well as a few that may surprise and delight you, such as water taxis and ferries. Just be sure to always have a map with you, and you'll find your way around with ease. If you do get lost, half the fun of traveling is finding your way home.

San Diego is an excellent home base, and there's so much to do here that there's really little reason to venture farther afield. But should you choose to venture north—to visit Disneyland and Knott's Berry Farm—or to Temecula's wine country or the old mission at San Juan Capistrano—we won't hold it against you. We'll be here to welcome you back at the end of the day.

Getting Here

By Air

San Diego International Airport/Lindbergh Field
3707 N. Harbor Dr., San Diego
(619) 231–2100, (619) 686–8065

Named for aviation pioneer Charles A. Lindbergh, whose famed *Spirit of St. Louis* was built in San Diego, San Diego International Airport carries his name as tribute to his epic solo flight across the Atlantic Ocean. Lindbergh Field opened in 1928, and although the airport has changed substantially over the years, it remains at its original location—sandwiched between Pacific Highway and Harbor Drive.

More than 15 million passengers travel through the airport annually on more than 600 daily flights. Terminal 1

19

has been in existence since 1967, with quite a bit of remodeling in the ensuing years, and Terminal 2 opened in 1979. The Commuter Terminal was added in 1996 and handles 25,000 passengers daily. A major expansion and renovation of Terminal 2 was completed in 1998.

For the past 30 years, even while in the midst of remodeling, talk about the airport has mostly been, where should we move it? The drawbacks to having an airport in the middle of the city are many: The land the airport occupies is precious. Nearby residents constantly complain about airplane noise, and many consider the steep descent to pose a hazard with every landing. But 30 years of talk have produced nothing—not even a consensus of opinion on whether it should be moved, much less where it should go. Chances are it'll stay right where it is. For convenience and proximity to downtown, it can't be beat.

Arrivals

Terminal 1 and Terminal 2

Once you have deplaned, signs will direct you to the baggage-claim area as well as to ground transportation. If you've arrived at one of the far gates, it can be a bit of a hike, especially in Terminal 2, so muster up your extra energy and concentrate on the delights that await you. You'll have to take the escalator or elevator down to the baggage area, but once you're there, lighted signs will indicate which carousel will deliver your bags. Should your bags not arrive (this almost never happens in San Diego, but then, we believe hardly anything bad ever happens here), lost-baggage offices are conveniently located in the claim area, and friendly agents will do their best to reunite you with your luggage.

Located within the baggage-claim area are rental car and hotel information boards with telephones that will connect you directly to your preferred agency or hotel for pick-up, information and reservations. As you leave the baggage area, you can proceed directly to the outside curb if you are taking the Metropolitan Transit Service bus called the Airport Flyer. The bus stop is curbside as you exit either ter-

Insiders' Tip

If you're picking up or dropping off passengers at San Diego International Airport, keep in mind that both arrivals and departures share curb space in front of the terminals. Traffic is always heavy, and airport security is vigilant. Don't leave your car unattended or linger longer than necessary.

minal, and the 10-minute Airport Flyer service will transport you to or from downtown, Amtrak, the Coaster, the Trolley and other bus routes for a $2 fare.

If you've arrived at Terminal 1 or 2, you can cross the street at the light (or via the skybridge in inclement weather) and proceed to the transportation plaza or the parking lot. There you will find taxis, shuttles, and rental car transport.

Commuter Terminal

From destinations such as Los Angeles and Fresno, a half dozen commuter airlines arrive at one of the ten gateways of the Commuter Terminal. (These are Alaska Commuter, American Eagle, Northwest Airlines, Skywest, Delta Connection, and United Express.) Smaller but just as efficient, the Commuter Terminal has much the same system as Terminals 1 and 2. The only difference is that ground transportation is available curbside as soon as you leave the baggage area. In addition to taxis, shuttles, and The Airport Flyer, a complimentary red airport shuttle bus transports passengers between the Commuter Terminal and Terminals 1 and 2. Pedestrians may not walk between the Commuter Terminal and Terminals 1 and 2, so make sure you know from which your flight departs before leaving for the airport, be it by taxi, shuttle, or in your own car.

Rental Car Agencies
Alamo (619) 297–0311, (800) 327–9633
Avis (619) 688–5000, (800) 230–4898
Budget (619) 498–1144, (800) 527–0700
Dollar (619) 234–3388, (800) 800–3665
Enterprise Rent-a-Car (619) 294–3313,
    (800) 736–8222
Hertz (619) 220–5222, (800) 654–3131
National (619) 497–6667, (800) 227–7368

Departures

The most convenient way to reach the airport is to have a friend drive you, or take a cab, bus, or shuttle. Access to Lindbergh Field is from Interstate 5, either south or north. If you're traveling south, take the Sassafras Street exit, and follow the airport signs to Laurel Street, where you will turn right. Laurel Street feeds into North Harbor Drive, which takes you directly to the airport. From I–5 north, take the Hawthorn Street exit to North Harbor Drive and turn right. Signs will direct drivers to specific airlines at the three terminals.

Ticketing is downstairs at both the Commuter Terminal and Terminal 1, and upstairs and downstairs in Terminal 2, depending on your airline. A variety of shuttle services are available to transport you to the airport, as well as taxis and park-and-ride facilities. Be aware that onsite airport parking is limited; competition for the lot's 3,000 spaces can be fierce. Leave extra time for finding a spot, use off-site airport parking, or arrange another form of transportation. Airport parking rates are as follows:

0–$\frac{1}{2}$ hour $ .50
$\frac{1}{2}$–1 hour $1
1–2 hours $3
2–3 hours $5
3–4 hours $7
4–5 hours $10
5–6 hours $13
6–7 hours $16
7–24 hours $12
Per day (or partial day) after 1st day $24

Private Airport Shuttles

Rates vary widely from company to company. Some charge a per-person rate, others

Well-placed art makes airport travel a little more relaxing. PHOTO: PORT OF SAN DIEGO, COURTESY OF SAN DIEGO CONVENTION & VISITORS BUREAU

a per-carload rate. Still others charge by the mile. Van or sedan service is available, depending on the company.

5 Star Shuttle (619) 294–3300
Airport Shuttle (619) 234–4403
Cloud 9 Shuttle (619) 505–4950,
   (800) 974–8853, www.cloud9shuttle.com
Coronado Livery (619) 435–6310
Prime Ride Shuttle (619) 297–7463
Xpress Shuttle (619) 295–1900,
   www.xpressshuttle.com
Torrey Pines Transfer (858) 587–1184,
   www.torreypinestrans.com

Many travelers take advantage of the numerous park-and-ride facilities located near the airport. You can park your car in their secured lot, and they will shuttle you to and from the airport for a fee that is substantially less than the airport's parking fee. Fees range from $6 to $13 per day, depending whether you choose open-air or covered parking. Here are a few park-and-ride companies:

ACE Parking (800) 440–7275
Aladdin Parking Garage (619) 696–7275
Laurel Travel Center (619) 233–0412
Park and Ride Co. (619) 295–2832

Regional Airports

The following airports located around the county are mostly private or small airports serving small planes and corporate aircraft. The exception is Palomar Airport in Carlsbad, which, in addition to its private aircraft facilities, has daily commercial flights to Los Angeles.

Landing information and fees should be obtained in advance from each airport. As the fees and availability change frequently, we recommend you contact the desired airport well in advance of your arrival to make arrangements for landing.

Brown Field Municipal Airport
1424 Continental St., San Ysidro
(619) 424–0455

Owned and operated by the city of San Diego, Brown Field is located just north of the U.S.–Mexico border and has two runways, 8,000 and 3,000 feet long. The airport has two fuelers and three FBOs

(Fixed Base Operators) for full-service maintenance. Amenities include a restaurant and bar, and rental car arrangements can be made at the airport.

Gillespie Field
1960 Joe Crosson Rd., El Cajon
(619) 956–4800

Located in East County, Gillespie Field has three runways, 5,300, 5,000, and 2,800 feet long. Fuel services and maintenance facilities are available. Inside the small terminal is a comfortable lounge with soft drink and coffee vending machines, and there are two small restaurants. Rental cars are not located on site, but Enterprise Rent-a-Car has an arrangement with Gillespie Field to pick up travelers and transport them to the agency, usually within 30 minutes.

Montgomery Field
3750 John J. Montgomery Dr., San Diego
(858) 573–1440

City-owned Montgomery Field has two parallel runways, 4,600 feet (with displaced threshold) and 3,400 feet long, and a cross runway of 3,400 feet. Located in the Kearney Mesa business district of San Diego, the airport has full fueling services as well as three FBOs for aircraft maintenance. Car rentals are available, and the Casa Machado restaurant and bar is situated overlooking the runway.

Oceanside Municipal Airport
480 Airport Rd., Oceanside
(760) 966–2940

Oceanside Airport has one runway, 3,061 feet in length. Full-service fueling is available, as well as an FBO that services both planes and helicopters. Inside the terminal is a small lounge complete with snack and coffee machines. Enterprise and Avis will deliver rental cars to this airport.

McClellan-Palomar Airport
2198 Palomar Airport Rd., Carlsbad
(760) 431–1328

Daily flights to and from Los Angeles International Airport and Phoenix Sky Harbor Airport are available from McClellan-Palomar on America West Express and

Despite years of debate, San Diego's airport, Lindbergh Field, occupies prime real estate overlooking San Diego Bay. PHOTO: PORT OF SAN DIEGO, COURTESY OF SAN DIEGO CONVENTION & VISITORS BUREAU

United Express Airlines. Most of the traffic at Palomar, however, is private aircraft. The single runway is 4,600 feet for landing and 5,000 feet for take-off. Three FBOs provide full-service maintenance and fueling. A restaurant is located on site, and rental cars are available too.

By Train

Amtrak
(800) USA–RAIL (872–7245;
www.amtrak.com), reservations
Oceanside Station, 235 S. Tremont St.
(760) 722–4622
Solana Beach Station, 105 Cedros Ave.
(858) 259–2697
San Diego's Santa Fe Depot, 1050 Kettner Blvd.
(619) 239–9021

Traveling by train is probably one of the more pleasant ways to reach San Diego, and train routes feed from every part of the country. Scenic rides down the coast of California are popular. For overland routes through the deserts to points east of San Diego, one must connect with trains in Los Angeles. Amtrak makes three stops in San Diego County: Oceanside,

Solana Beach, and the Santa Fe Depot in downtown San Diego.

Taxi stands are prominent at all three stops, and bus service is available from all three too. The San Diego Trolley, which serves much of San Diego, also has a station at the Santa Fe Depot.

Checked baggage service is available at all stations. A five-year, $1.3 billion investment proposed by Amtrak in early 2002 will enhance Southern California trains with improved windows and seats (the latter with laptop dataports), classier menus, new business-class coaches, and expanded storage facilities, including storage racks for surfboards and bicycles.

Reservations may be made in advance through any travel agent, at Amtrak stations or by calling the 24-hour toll-free number listed above. Tickets can also be purchased the day of travel at Amtrak stations. Amtrak accepts cash and all major credit cards. Seniors 62 and older receive a 15 percent discount. Animals are not permitted on trains unless they are certified guide or service animals accompanying passengers with disabilities, and Amtrak requires that you carry necessary documentation.

By Bus

Greyhound Bus
Fare and Schedule Information
(800) 231-2222
www.greyhound.com

If you're on a tight budget, Greyhound Bus may be the perfect solution. In an effort to attract more customers, it seems that Greyhound always has some kind of special, such as two-for-one fares. Greyhound offers half-price fares for kids 11 years of age and younger. Babies younger than 2 (one per paying adult) travel for free.

Greyhound has several stations throughout San Diego County, which we've listed below.

San Diego: 120 W. Broadway
(619) 239-3266
El Cajon: 250 S. Marshall
(619) 444-2591
San Ysidro: 799 E. San Ysidro Blvd.
(619) 428-1194
Oceanside: 205 S. Tremont St.
(760) 722-1587
Escondido: 700 W. Valley Pkwy
(760) 745-6522
Vista: 505 S. Santa Fe Ave.
(760) 631-7715

By Car

To reach San Diego from Washington, Oregon, or Northern California, take I-5 and keep your car pointed south; it'll lead you all the way into the city. If you're not in a hurry and would like a more scenic drive, Calif. Highway 101, which begins in Eureka, California, is a nice alternative. It'll keep you close to the coast as you drive through such picturesque towns as Big Sur, Monterey, and San Luis Obispo. From points east, hook up with Interstate 15 in Nevada or Utah, or Interstate 8 in Arizona. Both freeways end up in San Diego. I-15 takes you through Las Vegas and the high desert in eastern California and I-8 winds through the desert and the Laguna Mountains before entering San Diego.

Getting Around

Now that you're here, let us show you how easy it is to move around the county. You have many options: auto, bus, taxi, trolley, train, and a few unusual modes, too. Take a map and your *Insiders' Guide* and go exploring.

By Car

Roadways

California is known for its excellent freeway system, and San Diego has one of the best systems in the state. With a combination of interstate, state, and county highways, navigating the county should be a snap, except during morning and afternoon commutes, when traffic throughout the county ranges from slow-and-go to stop-and-go. Avoid traveling from 7:00 to 9:00 A.M. and 4:00 to 6:00 P.M. when possible. If you're in the exploring mood and happen to see one of San Diego's trademark blue and yellow signs with a big white seagull on it, follow it. That's the sign for a scenic drive, and there are many throughout the county, especially along the coast.

All interstate and state highways have emergency call boxes spaced every quarter mile or so. These provide direct connections to emergency services, such as police, ambulance, fire, and towing.

> **Insiders' Tip**
> Sometimes a special event deserves a special touch. Ask your hotel concierge or receptionist to help you arrange for private limousine service to drive you in style to the wine country or a restaurant or even for a day of sightseeing. Enjoy a bit of luxury.

The Greyhound Bus Line takes visitors on day excursions to nearby Tijuana, Mexico.

PHOTO: THORN VOLLENWEIDER

U.S. Interstate Highways

Interstate 8

I–8 begins at the western edge of San Diego, at Sunset Cliffs Boulevard, and travels east through Mission Valley, East County, across the mountains and desert and into Arizona. It's the main east/west artery in the city. Every north/south interstate, state and county route intersects with I–8.

It has a tendency to bunch up between the East County and downtown during rush hours, the westbound lanes in the morning and the eastbound lanes in the afternoon. With more and more people commuting, and most using their own cars, traffic on Highway 8 at peak times is frustrating. Avoid I–8 during these times, or practice the Zen of driving.

Interstate 5

I–5 begins at the U.S.–Mexico border and ends at the U.S.–Canada border. It meanders north along the coastal region of San Diego, offering some spectacular ocean views before veering inland once it passes the county line.

Its rush-hour bottlenecks are in North County Coastal: during morning hours they happen in southbound lanes; the ones leading north back up in the afternoon. As North County continues to grow, even weekend traffic on I–5 can be slow, although a HOV (high-occupancy vehicle) lane speeds things up for families and carpoolers.

Interstate 15

The second major north/south freeway is I–15. Its southern leg emerges from I–5 in National City, and it travels north through inland San Diego and North County, eventually leaving the county in Riverside.

Rush-hour slowdowns are in North County Inland, southbound in the morning and northbound in the afternoon. An auxiliary lane on I–15 from north of Friars Road to I–8 should help ease some major slowdowns at the merge between I–15 and I–8. Its completion date is fall 2004. An 8-mile HOV eases congestion somewhat. The direction of the lanes is switched from south to north to accommodate morning and afternoon heavy traffic.

Interstate 805

I–805 provides a much-needed north/south inland sweep between I–5 and I–15. It emerges from I–5 in San Ysidro, just north of the U.S.–Mexico border, and makes its way north through central San Diego, reconnecting with I–5 in Sorrento Valley at the infamous "merge." Traffic at the merge is always heavy, especially when North County residents make their way home during the afternoon commute.

California State Highways

All state highways have the familiar green sign with white numbers that designate them as California highways, but in truth, some are little more than surface streets or roadway extensions of highways that may or may not be completed one day. Here we will mention only those that qualify as true highways. If you're looking at a map and see the California State Highway designation, and it hasn't been described here, keep in mind that it may well be a winding, two-lane road through the mountains or a busy commercial street that you'd just as soon avoid.

California Highway 54

We'll start in the South Bay with Calif. 54. This is a fairly new freeway that travels east/west and connects I–5 and I–805 and has been helpful in relieving a lot of traffic on South Bay surface streets. Its eastern end is in Bonita. It will connect to SR–125 by 2005 and eventually with Calif. 94, where another segment of Calif. 54 currently links to I–8.

California Highway 94

Moving north, you come to Calif. 94, another east/west freeway that connects I–5 and Calif. 125 before continuing east through Jamul and Dulzura in the East County. Also called the Martin Luther King Jr. Freeway, it is heavily traveled during commute hours, west in the morning and east in the afternoon. If you bypass Calif. 125 and stay on Calif. 94, it turns into a surface road that becomes a scenic back route through the foothills of East County, near the Mexican border.

California Highway 163

Calif. 163 (the downtown section is also known as the Cabrillo Freeway) has historic status in San Diego. It is a north/south freeway whose southern end is downtown. As it travels north, it winds through Balboa Park, and is about as scenic a freeway as you'll ever see, surrounded by lush greenery and soaring old trees. If you drive it during rush hour, south in the morning and north in the afternoon, you'll have ample opportunity to enjoy its beauty. It continues north through Mission Valley and ultimately connects with I–15 near the Miramar Marine Corps Air Station.

California Highway 125

Now we're moving into the East County, where you'll find Calif. 125. It is a north/south connector between I–8 and Calif. 94. It's a short freeway, but provides a much-appreciated link between the two freeways.

California Highway 67

Calif. 67, another north/south freeway eases congestion for commuters traveling to and from Lakeside and Santee in the East County. If you're looking for an adventure, keep driving north on Calif. 67 to Ramona, a slowed-down, laid-back community on the way to the mountain town of Julian. It's a journey back in time.

California Highway 52

Calif. 52 has been called San Diego's godsend. It is an east/west freeway that intersects four other major north/south freeways: I–5, I–805, Calif. 163, and I–15. Currently petering out in Santee, in the

East County, it is scheduled to intersect with Highway 67 in the next few years. It doesn't seem to suffer the same rush-hour traffic as San Diego's other freeways, and it has provided a much-loved link between the coast and East County.

California Highway 56

Located just south of Del Mar, four-lane Calif. 56 will one day be a sorely needed east/west link between North County Coastal and North County Inland. Right now it's about one-quarter finished, with an expected completion date of fall 2004.

California Highway 78

This is the existing major east/west artery connecting North County Coastal with North County Inland. Calif. 78 begins in Oceanside and travels east through Vista and San Marcos, before turning into a surface street in Escondido and continuing to Ramona. It too is heavily congested during rush hour—in both directions, both morning and afternoon.

San Diego County Routes

Identified by a white hexagonal sign with a black "S" followed by a number, county routes are exclusively surface streets and roads. Some are major business streets, others are scenic drives that meander through the back country. If you're looking to get somewhere fast, don't mistake a county route for a shortcut. The county route designation is mostly an indication of who is responsible for maintenance—in this case, the county rather than the city in which they are located.

Taxi Service

San Diego has about as many taxi companies as it has animals in the zoo. Fees vary by company, but all are clearly posted on the outside of the cab. If you're catching a taxi from the airport, they will be queued up in the transportation plaza outside the terminals.

Taxis usually gather around major hotels and are available on demand. If none are immediately available, your hotel doorman or receptionist will be happy to call one for you. Unfortunately, taxis aren't hailed from the street; they don't cruise for fares. If you're leaving a club or restaurant, ask the host or hostess to call a taxi for you.

Be wary if a taxi driver doesn't engage the meter as soon as you depart. This is strictly against the law, and you should bring it to the driver's attention.

Here are a few taxi companies:

American Cab (619) 234–1111
Crown City Cab (619) 437–8885
North County Cab:
  San Diego (619) 260–1003
  North County Coastal (858) 485–5544
  North County Inland (760) 480–0110
Orange Cab (619) 291–4444
San Diego Cab (619) 226–8294
Silver Cab (619) 280–5555
Yellow Cab (619) 234–6161

Public Transporation

Metropolitan Transit System
(619) 233–3004
www.sdcommute.com

The Metropolitan Transit System (MTS) includes the bus system and the San Diego Trolley. Dating back to 1886, the MTS began when the first streetcar made its way up Fifth Avenue from the downtown

Insiders' Tip

Traffic reports will often refer to a back-up at the "merge" or the "S-curve." The merge refers to the area just north of La Jolla where I-5 and I-805 join to become one freeway going north; the S-curve is the portion of I-5 that runs through downtown, snaking back and forth like an S.

waterfront. San Diego was the second city in the nation to replace the horse with electric streetcars, but by 1945 all the streetcars had been replaced by buses.

The bus system covers 570 square miles on 87 routes and serves the cities of San Diego, Chula Vista, National City, Coronado, El Cajon, Imperial Beach, La Mesa, Lemon Grove, National City, Poway, San Diego, and Santee, as well as adjacent unincorporated sections of San Diego County. The system also connects with other regional systems, including the North County Transit District (which serves inland and coastal cities in the North County) and Direct Access to Regional Transit (DART). Residents of Paradise Hills, Mira Mesa, Rancho Bernardo, Scripps Ranch, and the mid-city areas can call ahead to DART at (877) 841–DART for transport to the nearest bus stop.

All buses accommodate wheelchairs and are equipped to carry bicycles on racks mounted on the back. Most bus route fares are $2.00 one-way, and exact change is required. Deposit your fare into the box by the driver when you board an MTS bus. Children five years and younger ride free with any paying passenger, and discounts are available for seniors and disabled riders. Day Tripper passes provide unlimited access to all MTS buses and the Trolley. They are available for one day ($5), two days ($8), three days ($10), or four days ($12). Passes can be purchased at the Transit Store at 102 Broadway, San Diego.

Transfers are free; they are good for two hours. Printed bus routes and schedules are available in many hotels and at the Transit Store.

North County Transit District
Route Information
(800) 266–6883

The North County Transit District (NCTD) serves all of North County, both coastal and inland. Connections to San Diego MTS buses are plentiful and easy, and many routes connect to Greyhound, the Coaster, and Amtrak at the Oceanside and Solana Beach Transit Centers.

Basic fares are $1.50 for adults and free for children ages 5 and younger traveling with any fare-paying passenger. Seniors and the disabled (with NCTD photo ID card) pay 75 cents. Transfers are free.

Coaster
(800) 262–7837

The Coaster operates regional rail service between Oceanside and San Diego. The blue, green, and white express train mainly serves commuters, but it's a good way to travel between San Diego and North County Coastal. Moving north from the Santa Fe Depot in downtown San Diego, it stops in Old Town, Sorrento Valley, Solana Beach, Encinitas, Carlsbad Poinsettia, Carlsbad Village, and Oceanside.

Numerous round-trips are scheduled during weekdays, and a modified schedule is offered on Saturdays. Extra trains are added during special events such as the Street Scene in downtown San Diego or the annual Holiday Bowl at Qualcomm Stadium.

Tickets are purchased from vending machines on the station platform before boarding the train, and the machines accept cash (dispensing a maximum of $10 in change), VISA, and MasterCard. Fares range from $3.50 one way to $4.75, depending on the distance you travel. All tickets must be validated before boarding the train by validating machines that are also located on the station platform.

Passengers must present a validated ticket to the conductor, ticket inspector, or police upon request. Coaster tickets provide a free transfer to all connecting

Insiders' Tip

Plan to drive a rental car to Mexico? Make sure the rental agency allows its cars to travel across the border. Some do and some do not.

The Coaster runs through a downtown San Diego intersection. PHOTO: COURTESY OF THE SAN DIEGO CONVENTION AND VISITORS BUREAU

San Diego MTS buses, Trolleys, and NCTD buses within two hours from the time validated. Your Coaster ticket also provides a free transfer to the Airport Flyer, which departs for Lindbergh Field from the Santa Fe Depot in San Diego.

San Diego Trolley
(619) 233–3004
www.sdcommute.com

Part of the MTS, this light rail system with bright red cars serves San Diego, East County, and the South Bay. Connections to the Trolley from Amtrak and the Coaster are available at the San Diego Santa Fe Depot, and an additional connection from the Coaster is available at Old Town.

The Trolley has two lines, the Blue Line and the Orange Line. The Blue Line is an S-shaped line that serves San Diego from the Rancho Mission stop (east of Qualcomm Stadium and near San Diego Mission de Alcalá), west through Mission Valley and Old Town, and south through downtown to the U.S.–Mexico border. The Orange Line makes a loop through downtown San Diego serving Centre City as well as Seaport Village, the Convention Center, and the Gaslamp Quarter, then continues to the East County, to El Cajon and Santee.

Trolley tickets are purchased at vending machines located on the station platform and are priced according to the distance to be traveled. One-way fares range from $1.25 to $2.50, with senior and disabled-rider discounts available. Passengers with bicycles are charged 50 cents extra. Day Tripper passes give visitors one- to four-day unlimited access to the Trolley and MTS buses for the same prices as listed under the MTS section. Passes can be purchased at Trolley stations or at the Transit Store at 102 Broadway, San Diego. If you're using a prepaid pass, you must validate it before boarding the Trolley. Validating machines are located on every Trolley platform near the ticket-vending machines.

Trolley tickets serve as transfers to MTS buses, with connections at most stations. Keep your tickets with you while on the Trolley. They won't be collected as you board, but Trolley officers periodically check to make sure all passengers have tickets.

San Diego-Coronado Bay Bridge

This graceful blue bridge soars across San Diego Bay and links downtown San

Diego with the peaceful island enclave of Coronado. The views of both the San Diego skyline and Coronado are breathtaking from the top of the bridge. The bridge is quite high and narrow, and the trip across can be a little hair-raising. So if you're the driver, let your passengers describe the view to you.

The $1.00, one-way (San Diego to Coronado) toll was suspended in July 2002.

San Diego-Coronado Ferry
(619) 234–4111

If you prefer a waterborne approach to Coronado, try taking the ferry across San Diego Bay. Ferrying passengers and bicycles only (no autos), it departs from the San Diego Harbor Excursion Dock at 1050 North Harbor Drive, San Diego, and docks at the Ferry Landing Marketplace on Coronado. It leaves San Diego every hour on the hour from 9:00 A.M. to 9:00 P.M. Sunday through Thursday, and until

10:00 P.M. Friday and Saturday. It leaves Coronado every hour on the half hour from 9:30 A.M. to 9:30 P.M. Sunday through Thursday, and until 10:30 P.M. Friday and Saturday. The fare is $2.00 per person, one way. If you're bringing your bike, the fare is $2.50.

San Diego Water Taxi
(619) 235–8294

San Diego Water Taxi offers on-call boat transportation service along San Diego Bay for a $5.00 per person fare; it operates between 10:00 A.M. and 10:00 P.M. (often until midnight on weekends in summer). You can take in skyline scenery on your way to waterfront hotels, restaurants, and shopping centers. San Diego Water Taxi offers service to all points in San Diego Bay, including Shelter and Harbor Islands, Coronado, and Downtown; there's a $20 minimum for service to Chula Vista and the South Bay.

The Coronado ferry makes a quick trip across the bay. PHOTO: COURTESY OF SAN DIEGO CONVENTION & VISITORS BUREAU

Crossing the Border

Some folks feel that no visit to San Diego would be complete without a trip across the border to Mexico. All the details of a visit to Tijuana and beyond are covered in our South of the Border chapter, but we'll give you a general idea of how best to approach it here.

If all you're planning is a shopping and dining expedition to Tijuana, the best way to get there is via the San Diego Trolley. The Trolley ends right at the border, and you can walk across. Should you be driving, you can park in one of several lots on the U.S. side of the border and, again, walk across. Once you've passed through the border checkpoints, you can hail a Tijuana taxi to take you to the main shopping area or the restaurant of your choice. If you're just headed to the main tourist areas, walking is another option.

For more adventurous drivers, it's perfectly safe to venture south of the border. Just remember that the streets are not laid out quite as efficiently as they are north of the border, and it's easy to get lost. Also, be sure to purchase Mexican insurance from one of the many storefront insurance shops before you drive into Tijuana. If you were to have an accident, your Mexican insurance policy will make life much easier while dealing with the local authorities.

History

Although most San Diego schoolchildren above fourth grade know the name Juan Rodríguez Cabrillo, historians in general pay him scant attention. After all, he was just one of many who set out in the wake of Christopher Columbus, Hernán Cortés, and other explorers to chart new territory for Spain. When Cabrillo sailed with his two ships into San Diego Bay on September 28, 1542, he wasn't eager to spend much time exploring. Profit and glory lured him northward; Cabrillo's quest was to discover a Northwest Passage linking the Pacific and Atlantic Oceans. Still, he couldn't help admiring the natural attributes of the bay he had happened upon. Its south-facing opening, between the Point Loma peninsula and Coronado, made a U-turn and traveled southward between the mainland and a narrow stretch of land to the west. Cabrillo noted that the bay was well situated to withstand both violent storms and seafaring intruders.

The First San Diegans

Cabrillo's arrival on the eve of the feast day of St. Michael the Archangel inspired him to name his discovery San Miguel. He and his crew continued exploring to the north, but Cabrillo returned to San Miguel only to be buried. He died at sea that winter as a result of an infected wound.

As might be expected, native people had inhabited the area long before Cabrillo and his men arrived to admire the perfection of its port. As far back as 9000 B.C., Indians now known as the San Dieguito were settling in San Diego. They were descendants of Asians who had traversed the bridge of land that connected Asia and North America in prehistoric times, and of others who had traveled westward across North America, crossing the Sierra Nevada Mountains and moving down the coastal plains.

The Kumeyaay Indians joined the San Dieguito around 1000 B.C., and they lived in relative harmony until Cabrillo's arrival more than two millennia later. Although they greeted Cabrillo guardedly, they had little to fear—at least for the moment.

Lacking gold and other resources that drove the Spanish exploration at the time, the area was abandoned for future generations to explore and conquer.

In 1602 Spanish explorer Sebastián Vizcaíno sailed into San Miguel during a voyage to inspect the west coast of New Spain. Fortunately for the resident Indians, Vizcaíno had no more interest in settling the territory than had Cabrillo. His only contribution was to rename the area San Diego, in honor of his flagship's patron saint, San Diego de Alcalá. Like Cabrillo, Vizcaíno quickly left to sail northward, and the Indians once again were left in peace.

Reluctant Colonization

By the mid-1700s, Spain's reluctance to colonize the Baja California peninsula and Alta (or Upper) California was overcome by the encroachment of Russian fur traders. Moving down the Pacific Northwest and into California, they threatened to claim Spain's territories for themselves. Spain's previous lack of interest evaporated with the threat of losing the region to its competitors. Forts and adjacent missions from San Diego to the San Francisco Bay would provide defensive settlements to repel foreign invaders and to populate the area with settlers loyal to Spain. Also, Spain sincerely wished to convert the "heathen" Indians, although this desire sprang from convenience as much as from true religious fervor.

Along with the Catalonian military governor Don Gaspar de Portolá, King Charles sent Father Junipero Serra, a Franciscan priest who would establish a string of missions throughout California. De Portolá and Serra began their quest in Loreto, Baja California, and finally arrived in San Diego in 1769. Although de Portolá quickly pressed on, Father Serra remained behind, dedicating the first of 21 missions in California on July 16, 1769. Located atop Presidio Hill, Misión San Diego de Alcalá overlooked the bay and the Pacific Ocean beyond.

As in mission settlements in northern Mexico and Baja California, the local Indians were conscripted for construction, agriculture, and other tasks. After several initial rebellions, they accepted the inevitability of their new life under the dominion of the mission fathers and the presidio's soldiers. However, they had no natural defenses against introduced European diseases such as smallpox and measles. By the year 1800, mission records show that more than half of the 16,000 converts during the previous 10 years had succumbed to disease. Many were buried in mass graves.

San Diego de Alcalá mission remained on Presidio Hill for only five years before it was moved to its current location in Mission Valley, on the banks of the San Diego River. A lack of arable land, fresh water, and a good-sized population of potential indigenous converts prompted the move.

Despite its rocky start and scant resources, the mission was a success, with irrigated fields of wheat, vineyards, orchards of dates and fruit trees, and herds of cattle and sheep grazing in the arid countryside. Spain's claim to California was strengthened, and peace reigned until 1821, when Mexico achieved its independence from Spain. San Diego and its two missions were now under the authority of Mexico and would remain so until the end of the Mexican-American War.

Seeing the strategic value of San Diego's natural harbor, the United States was quick to wrest control of it from Mexico and met little physical resistance. By the time the war ended in 1847 and San Diego, along with the rest of California, officially became part of the United States three years later, the population was fewer than 1,000 people, most of them settled at the foot of Presidio Hill in the area now known as Old Town.

The Beginnings of a City

Although blessed with a mild climate and a beautiful port, San Diego didn't grow as quickly as you might think. By the end of the Civil War, the population had dwindled considerably, because San Diego residents flocked to Northern California to join the gold rush. What finally started San Diego on the path to becoming a city

Misión San Diego de Alcalá: one of the city's very first structures. PHOTO: CECE CANTON

was the same commodity that fuels its economy today: real estate.

First-time visitors to San Diego will note the popularity of the name Horton, seen at the popular downtown shopping mall Horton Plaza, the stately Horton Grand Hotel, and tiny Horton Avenue.

Alonzo Erastus Horton was the city's official founding father, and he was among the first to recognize the value of real estate in San Diego. Unlike others before him, he wasted little time in capitalizing on it.

Horton was living in San Francisco when he attended a lecture on the ports of California. The discussion about the prospects of San Diego caught his interest, and within three days he was on a steamer to San Diego with dreams of building a great city. He pulled into San Diego Harbor on April 15, 1867, disembarking at what is now the foot of Market Street. Horton's first stop was Old Town, the original settlement nestled beneath the burned-out ruins of the old Presidio. Scarcely disguising his contempt for what he saw, he declared his intention to relocate the heart of the city to the area near

the wharf. "I have been nearly all over the United States," Horton said, "and that is the prettiest place for a city I ever saw."

Horton's first land purchase was enviable even by 19th-century standards: 960 acres for $265, or about 27½ cents per acre. Horton swiftly began to develop the parcel, and within three years New Town had far outpaced Old Town with a population that had swelled to 2,301. The economy of the young city was precarious, however, because it was tied so closely to land speculation. From 1867 forward San Diego's economy would fluctuate between boom and bust as the price of real estate rose and fell.

In Search of a Railroad

Adding to the uncertain land market was speculation about the arrival of a railroad. Three barriers kept stalling the prospects: the two natural barriers of the mountains to the east and the ocean to the west, and the political barrier of the Mexican border to the south. Commerce-hungry San Diegans would not give up their dream, though, and whenever rumors spread that the railroad was finally coming, land prices would soar. Then when the bubble burst with the news that there would be no railroad, the real estate market would plummet, followed by the population, and the city's economy would be left in shambles. In 1872 the news that San Diego would become the western terminus for the Texas & Pacific Railroad produced wild speculation. Residents and outsiders alike scraped together whatever money they could to buy property and build, build, build. The population soared to 4,000. But when railroad plans fell through, the economy collapsed and the population dropped to less than half that number.

Alonzo Horton took a financial bath during the bust of the 1870s and was never again the same driving force in San Diego. His contribution to the city is well remembered, however, as is evidenced by the many visible tributes to him.

The railroad did finally make its way to San Diego in the mid-1880s. The Santa Fe-Atlantic & Pacific Railroad built its West Coast terminus in National City, just south of San Diego. The line went north and then east, through Barstow in central California. Once again the economy boomed, and the population grew to more than 35,000. New Town boasted 71 saloons, playing host to such notable visitors as Wyatt Earp, who lived in San Diego for a time and operated a handful of gambling casinos. Prostitutes were abundant, occupying 120 bawdy houses, and nearly outnumbering the more traditional business people. Hotels, restaurants, rooming houses, opium dens, and dance halls were bursting at the seams.

But true to the shape of San Diego's short history, bust was right around the corner. The Santa Fe-Atlantic & Pacific Railroad never became much more than a spur line. Most of the real rail traffic went north to Los Angeles, already a commercial rival. By 1889 San Diego had crashed again. The wharves and warehouses were empty, and half the city's population had disappeared—along with a good number of jobs. Those who had their fortunes tied up in real estate suffered greatly as the bottom dropped out of the land market. Once again, San Diego would have to reinvent itself.

Spreckels to the Rescue

Whenever San Diego's fortunes looked especially bleak, a savior was inevitably waiting in the wings. As was Alonzo Horton, John D. Spreckels was captivated by the temperate climate of this city by the bay. Heir to the Spreckels sugar fortune, he liberally poured his family money into his adopted city and for the next 20 years laid claim to much of its assets. He owned the streetcar system, most of Coronado and North Island, the historic Hotel del Coronado (a million-dollar property even then), two of the three newspapers, the water company, the ferry system, and numerous businesses.

Spreckels's most prized holding was undoubtedly the Hotel del Coronado. A favorite getaway for the rich, famous, and notorious, it was also home to Tent City. In the summer of 1900 Spreckels erected a sea of tents on the beach just southeast of the hotel. There families could spend the summer in a casual but elegant fashion, literally living in a luxurious tent on the sand. Along with the square tents, Tent City featured a dance pavilion, shops, restaurants, regular entertainment, an indoor swimming pool, and a floating casino. The resort was so popular it remained open every summer until 1938.

Despite the Hotel del Coronado's success and San Diego's obvious touristic

Insiders' Tip

Benjamin Harrison was the first U.S. president to visit San Diego, in 1891. He was treated to a reception at the Hotel del Coronado and a rally at Horton Plaza.

The Star of India, *the world's oldest active sailing ship, rests in San Diego Harbor.* PHOTO: DALE FROST,
COURTESY OF THE PORT OF SAN DIEGO

appeal, city leaders held fast to the notion that San Diego's fortunes were inextricably linked to the railroad.

That coveted rail line, the San Diego & Arizona Railroad, finally became a reality in 1919. And it was Spreckels who guaranteed the financing.

An Exposition and a War

If early city leaders had one fault, it was their failure to recognize the value of San Diego's natural attributes: its climate and its deep-water harbor. No railroad and no piece of land would positively influence the city's future in the way those two features did.

To celebrate the opening of the Panama Canal, San Diego hosted an exposition from 1915 to 1916, which lured thousands of tourists. They marveled at the city's arid natural beauty and mild weather. And when they went home, they told their friends about this newfound paradise. They came back—in droves. Then, when Congress declared war on

Germany in 1917, San Diego was remembered because of its strategic importance during the Spanish-American War. The army set up Camp Kearny, the navy took over North Island on Coronado, and the marines established their recruit depot just to the north and across the bay from the naval base. The military was here, and it never left. In that brief span, between 1915 and 1917, San Diego's future as both a tourist mecca and a military town was decided.

The Panama-California Exposition drew thousands of visitors from all over the country. Located in what is now the heart of the city—Balboa Park—the exposition gave birth to the park's most beautiful buildings. By the early 1920s Balboa Park had become the site for the world-famous San Diego Zoo. (Be sure to read all about the history of the zoo in our Balboa Park chapter.) Founded by Dr. Harry Wegeforth with animals left over from the exposition, it was funded in large part by Ellen Browning Scripps, also a major benefactress of Scripps Institution of Oceanography in La Jolla.

In 1937, with funds advanced by the Works Progress Administration, actors Pat O'Brien and Bing Crosby co-founded the Del Mar Racetrack, a lure for locals and for bored Hollywood denizens. With attractions such as the racetrack, Balboa Park, and the Hotel del Coronado resort, as well as pristine beaches and the gambling houses just across the border in Tijuana, San Diego soon became impossible to resist. The Los Angeles film colony discovered the beauty and energy of its neighbor to the south, and quickly made San Diego a regular daytrip. Tourists from other parts of the country found a myriad of reasons to winter or summer here.

San Diego's leaders finally conceded that maybe there was life beyond the railroad. Real-estate speculation proved to be a hard habit to break, though. It remains the sport of choice for many San Diegans even today.

The Aerospace Industry and Another War

In 1927, in an old building that once housed a fish cannery, a small aircraft company was working frantically to finish constructing a special airplane. Ryan Airlines, co-owned by aviation pioneers Claude Ryan and B. F. Mahoney, began regular flights between San Diego and Los Angeles in 1925 and had a sideline division for aircraft construction. What they were constructing then, a plane Ryan built in just 60 days, was the *Spirit of St. Louis*. Soon after, Charles Lindbergh made his historic flight from New York to Paris and planted the seeds for San Diego's budding aircraft industry.

Following closely behind Ryan and Mahoney was Major Reuben H. Fleet, who moved his Consolidated Aircraft Corporation from New York to San Diego. With mergers, his company eventually would become Convair, and then General Dynamics, a giant in the U.S. defense industry and one of the largest employers in San Diego. Fred Rohr, a metal smith who had worked on the *Spirit of St. Louis,* formed his own aircraft company, which is still located just south of the city limits in Chula Vista. Rohr Industries also would become one of San Diego's largest employers, and now has branches and subsidiaries all over the country.

World War II was rapidly approaching, and the aircraft industry thrived, fed by defense contracts. Already a dominant presence in San Diego, the military increased dramatically as war loomed on the horizon. The army set up two new camps, Camp Callan near La Jolla and Camp Elliott on Kearny Mesa. Not to be outdone, the navy purchased Camp Pendleton for a marine base. (San Diego's largest *rancho* in the days before U.S. annexation, Camp Pendleton is a 133,000-acre parcel stretching north from Oceanside all the way to the Orange County line. Today this is the only undeveloped coastal land between San Diego and Los Angeles.) The navy also installed its 11th Naval District headquarters here, as well as the Naval Training Center (now closed) and the Miramar Naval Air Station, the latter now also operated by the U.S. Marines.

Traditional Mexican music and costumes give a special flavor to San Diego's cultural scene.

PHOTO: COURTESY OF SAN DIEGO CONVENTION AND VISITORS BUREAU

Consolidated Aircraft fared well during the war. More than 2,000 PBY Catalinas, a twin-engine flying boat, were manufactured by Consolidated and used extensively by American and British air forces. They proved their value time after time. A Royal Air Force Catalina tracked the *Bismarck* for nine days and nights until the British sank the German sub. A U.S. Navy Catalina spotted a Japanese submarine lurking at the entrance to Pearl Harbor.

At the war's end, many active-duty military personnel stationed in town decided to stay. The population boomed to over 330,000, and San Diego enjoyed a post-war prosperity throughout the 1950s.

A New Direction

Peacetime had its price, and those who paid were in the aircraft and aerospace business. The industry suffered a severe decline that threatened the economy of the entire city. Economic experts around the country were predicting that San Diego was about to bust once again. But seasoned locals scoffed. They knew the history of their town, and that history was a long tale of booming and busting. This time they realized that the key to prosperity lay in looking in a different direction.

Dr. Jonas Salk, developer of the polio vaccine that bears his name, opened the Salk Institute for Biological Studies in 1963. Located in scenic La Jolla, it has become a world-renowned research facility specializing in molecular and cellular biology and neuroscience. Around the same time, the University of California San Diego opened its 1000-acre campus, also in La Jolla. The origins of the university lie with Scripps Institution of Oceanography, which had long been a member of the University of California's statewide system. Saturated with scientists, the institution needed larger facilities not only to enhance its own capabilities but to also attract the best research scientists in the world.

The military was firmly in place, even in peacetime, and tourists kept coming in greater numbers every year. Real estate values were ebbing and flowing just as they always had. And now with the establishment of a world-class research facility and a science- and engineering-based university, the groundwork was firmly in place for San Diego's new course. It was almost as if the city could anticipate the explosion of high-tech and biotech that was about to rise to the top of the world's research and manufacturing industries. When that explosion came, San Diego was ready.

High-Tech, Biotech, and Brain Power

The 1980s and 1990s saw an influx of high-tech and biotech companies that was beyond the wildest dreams of industry pioneers. Pharmaceutical companies, biotech researchers, and electronics and telecommunications companies make up the bulk of the newcomers, and more are coming. One telecommunications titan, Qualcomm Inc., has made its intentions perfectly clear. It started here, and it's here to stay. Co-founded by Dr. Irwin Jacobs, a former professor at UCSD, Qualcomm is bent on integrating into the community.

San Diego is prospering as we begin the new millennium. Although the military was downsized under President Clinton, defense is still among San Diego's top industries, along with manufacturing and tourism. Surprisingly, agriculture is also among San Diego's four most important industries. Avocado groves and fields of flowers, strawberries, lettuce, and tomatoes are a familiar sight in the northern reaches of the county, although agricultural lands are shrinking rapidly as the population expands.

The icing on the cake of San Diego's prosperity is its growing enclave of higher learning. Known by locals as the "alphabet soup," UCSD (University of California, San Diego), SDSU (San Diego State University), USD (University of San Diego), and CSUSM (California State University, San Marcos) head the list of prestigious institutes. Gaining in stature is Point Loma Nazarene University, a high-quality liberal arts college situated on the bluffs of Sunset Cliffs, overlooking the ocean. Added to this collection of four-year universities is an impressive array of community colleges. The result is a stunning production of brain power. (See our Higher Education chapter for more details.)

The majority of graduates stay in San Diego once they finish school. No surprise there; it's a hard place to leave. Nearly 30 percent of San Diego adults hold college degrees, more than any other major U.S. city. We're proud of our eggheads. They

The historic Gaslamp Quarter is a great place for dining, entertainment, or shopping.

PHOTO: BOB YARBROUGH, COURTESY OF SAN DIEGO CONVENTION AND VISITORS BUREAU

are a generation of movers and shakers who are well prepared to lead us in the twenty-first century.

The Flavor of San Diego

The image many Easterners have of San Diego is blond surfer boys and even blonder girls in bikinis languishing under palm trees on the beach. Granted, most inhabitants take advantage of the beach as often as they can, but they do have jobs. Plus, palm trees don't grow well in sand.

San Diego is a city that constantly contradicts its small-town image. It was host to the 1996 Republican Convention and also to a presidential debate that same year. Two Super Bowls have been contested here, with a third slated for 2003. San Diego is home to a first-rate opera company, dozens of theaters, and even more superb art galleries.

The city has a large and diverse ethnic population that is well reflected in its neighborhoods. Cultural events and festivals regularly celebrate the heritage of a multitude of ethnic groups. Its proximity to the Mexican border has naturally resulted in a well-established and growing Hispanic community. Of course the city was Mexican before it was American, and Hispanic traditions and culture can be seen in buildings public and private, place names, and cultural events.

Although San Diego prides itself on being a modern, cosmopolitan city (seventh largest in the country), it still clings tenaciously to its roots. Its Spanish and Mexican heritage runs deep. The pace is a little slower than in most big cities, and San Diegans are more often identified as laid-back than hard-driven. Most believe they have found the best of all worlds. The industries of the future are already here. Educational opportunities abound. And then there's that weather.

Cabrillo could see it. So could Vizcaíno, de Portolá, and Father Serra. Alonzo Horton and John Spreckels figured it out, too. Paradise lies here sandwiched between the mountains and the ocean in a place called San Diego.

Hotels and Motels

Reservations
San Diego County
  Beaches and Mission Bay
  Coronado
  Downtown/Gaslamp Quarter
  La Jolla/Golden Triangle
  Mission Valley
  Point Loma/Harbor and
    Shelter Islands
North County Coastal
North County Inland
East County
South Bay

It didn't take San Diego's founding fathers too long to figure out that their city by the bay had the potential to become an irresistible destination for visitors. Along with the first buildings in downtown San Diego—the general stores, saloons, and rooming houses—came places for guests to hang their hats. And as increasing numbers of tourists targeted San Diego for their vacations, hotels began to spring up to accommodate them.

Today there are hundreds of places from which to choose, everything from a bare-bones motel on the sand to a luxurious, fully appointed hotel designed to cater to your every whim. If your idea of a room is only a place to hang your clothes and grab a few hours sleep, you'll find it here. But if you plan to spend a lot of time in your room or enjoy the touches of luxury that only top hotels can offer, you'll find that too. You need only decide what best fits your style and budget.

Even though San Diego is a year-round destination for visitors, it does have a high season during the summer months. Summer is when you're least likely to find your first choice in accommodations unless you plan ahead. The good news is that there are so many hotels and motels spread throughout the county that you can almost always find an available room, even on short notice. Even during Super Bowl week in 1998, when hotels were sold out a year in advance, rooms were available here and there. If you're the spontaneous type who likes to pack a bag on Friday night and see what you can find once you arrive, chances are a nice room will be waiting for you somewhere in the county.

Your choice of accommodation depends on your plans. If you're visiting friends or relatives, it makes sense to book a room close to their neighborhood. If hiking and nature walks are high on your itinerary, you might look at facilities in the East County or North County Inland to be near the foothills and local mountains. If sun and sand are your first priority, you would naturally want to investigate beachside hotels and motels.

If you plan to do it all—sightseeing, shopping, dining, the beach, and nightlife—you can stay just about anywhere in the county, although it's best to stay close to freeway entrances for easy driving. If you're without a car, though, we recommend that you check out some of the more centrally located facilities in North County Coastal, downtown San Diego, or Mission Valley, so you can take advantage of the bus system, the Coaster, and the San Diego Trolley for transportation.

Whatever your idea of the perfect holiday may be, this chapter includes a good cross-section of available accommodations. Each facility is described to give you an idea of what makes it unique and desirable. We also list special amenities such as workout rooms or business centers. If the hotel has a great restaurant, we mention it.

Hotels and motels frequently change management companies and affiliations. Don't be surprised if you call one of our listings and the facility has a different name. If this happens, be sure to ask if the accommodation has undergone any significant changes. Remember too that the quality of chain hotels can vary from city to city. What might be an outstanding hotel in your city might be a little less desirable someplace else. Read our descriptions carefully, and we promise to steer you in the right direction.

We've divided this chapter into our usual regional designations: Central San Diego, North County Coastal, North County Inland, East County, and South Bay. For your convenience, San Diego has been further divided into the areas most visitors target in their search for a hotel or motel. Bed-and-breakfast inns and vacation rentals are covered in separate chapters; campgrounds and RV parks are noted in our Recreation chapter.

Price Code

Prices are based on one night's stay for two people during summer months. Keep in mind that room rates can be somewhat lower during winter months. San Diego's 10.5 percent hotel tax is not included in these rates.

$	$50 to $100
$$	$101 to $150
$$$	$151 to $200
$$$$	$201 and higher

Reservations

It's always a good idea to make your reservations as far in advance as possible, especially if you have your heart set on a specific facility or part of the county. If you're planning a beach vacation and decide to take your chances when you get here, you might find yourself spending much of your time commuting to the beach from a hotel in an outlying area. Beach accommodations typically fill up far in advance of summer months.

When you make your reservation, most facilities require a major credit card to hold your reservation. Should you decide to cancel, policies vary, so be sure to inquire when you make the reservation. Most require a specified lead time for cancellation to avoid a charge to your credit card. Unless we designate otherwise, all listings accept major credit cards.

Be sure to ask about check-in and check-out times too. Most check-in times are around 3:00 P.M., and checkout is usually around 12:00 P.M. If those times don't fit with your schedule, ask about early check-in or late checkout. Many facilities are happy to accommodate your plans for no extra charge or offer to store your luggage, but some will charge extra fees if you're too early or hang around too long after checkout time.

Also keep in mind that most of the hotels and motels we list here offer smoking and nonsmoking rooms. If this is important to you, be sure to specify your preference when making your reservation. If you can't bear the thought of leaving your pet at home while you're vacationing, you may be in luck. Many hotels and motels these days are putting out the welcome mat for furry guests. We've noted those facilities that do accommodate pets along with any restrictions or special policies. In accordance with federal law, all hotels have accommodations for the disabled. Just be sure to specify your needs to the reservations clerk.

San Diego County

Beaches and Mission Bay

Best Western Blue Sea Lodge $$–$$$
707 Pacific Beach Dr., San Diego
(858) 488–4700, (800) 780–7234
www.bestwestern.com
At the Blue Sea Lodge you can choose from 100 luxury oceanfront rooms or standard rooms with private balconies or patios. Some rooms feature sunken tubs and skylights. Start your morning with coffee on the patio by the oceanfront pool and hot tub, which has direct access to the beach. Then spend the rest of the day sightseeing, swimming, or strolling along the beach boardwalk.

No restaurants are on site, but dozens are within 4 or 5 blocks. If eating in is more your style, ask about suites with kitchens. A few are available.

A nighttime view of the San Diego skyline is the backdrop to this busy marina. PHOTO: JAMES BLANK, COURTESY OF THE SAN DIEGO CONVENTION AND VISITORS BUREAU

Catamaran Hotel $$$
3999 Mission Blvd., San Diego
(858) 488–1081, (800) 422–8386

Long a fixture in the beach area, the Catamaran has 312 rooms with unparalleled access to both the beach and the bay. All rooms and suites are decorated in cool greens and pinks. Most rooms have a refrigerator, and all have a balcony or lanai.

The Catamaran has a water sports center on the bay and a fitness center. Two authentic sternwheeler boats cruise Mission Bay nightly from the Catamaran, offering cocktails and dancing. The Cannibal Bar on the premises is a San Diego favorite for live music and dancing. The Atoll Restaurant serves breakfast, lunch, and dinner daily, including an award-winning Sunday brunch.

Crystal Pier Hotel & Cottages $$$–$$$$
4500 Ocean Blvd., Central San Diego
(858) 483–6983, (800) 748–5894
www.crystalpier.com

These Cape Cod–style cottages on the Crystal Pier in Pacific Beach may be the most romantic lodgings in the county. The surf swirls around the pilings under the pier, lulling you to sleep in a comfy double bed or on the futon couch in the living room. The cottages have full kitchens and one or two bedrooms. They also have private decks right over the water. There are only 26 units, and they book up months in advance. There's a two-night minimum stay in winter, three nights in summer. Insiders consider them one of the best hometown escapes imaginable.

Dana Inn $$
1710 W. Mission Bay Dr., San Diego
(619) 222–6440, (800) 445–3339

An excellent choice for families, the Dana Inn has casual rooms perfect for sandy bodies and wet towels. Rooms facing the pool are best for those who don't mind the sounds of splashing and screaming. Those facing the bay and street are quieter. The hotel has a water sports center, tennis courts, shuffleboard, and Ping-Pong—plenty to entertain the whole family—and it offers shuttle service to Sea World.

All rooms have refrigerators and coffeemakers. Room service is offered, or you can enjoy family dining at the Red Hen Country Kitchen restaurant on the premises. There is a laundry room on the premises.

San Diego Hilton Beach & Tennis Resort
$$$$
1775 E. Mission Bay Dr., San Diego
(619) 276–4010, (800) 445–8667
www.hilton.com

The San Diego Hilton is an oasis of palm trees and sand with a mirage-come-true in the form of beautiful Mission Bay right alongside the hotel. The Mediterranean-style resort has 357 rooms. Standard guest rooms have courtyard and garden views; suites have expansive bay views.

Activities galore await you at the San Diego Hilton. Take a walk down to the bay, which is just steps away, or play tennis on the lighted courts. Maybe you'd like to swim in the hotel's huge pool or hot tub—both have a bay view. The excellent activity center has bikes, catamarans, and other water toys for rent. Cavatappi, which serves all meals, has outdoor seating.

San Diego Paradise Point Resort
$$$–$$$$
1404 W. Vacation Rd., San Diego
(858) 274–4630, (800) 344–2626
www.paradisepoint.com

For the best combination of luxury and a beach vacation, the Paradise Point Resort is a great choice. The 462 lanai guest rooms

have a variety of layouts, and all have patios and a spectacular garden, lagoon, or bay view. Studio and one-bedroom suites are also available.

The resort is perfect for quiet strolls where you'll find surprises at every turn: lagoons with water lilies, fountains, waterfalls, bridges, and botanical treasures. For more active pursuits, try one of six pools (one has a swim-up bar), or swim and sunbathe on the mile of sandy beach surrounding the resort. Tennis, sailing, volleyball, and bicycling are there for the taking, and an 18-hole putting course will help you refine your stroke. Paradise Point also has a fully equipped fitness center and spa.

The Dockside Restaurant serves dinner nightly, and be sure to stop in at the Barefoot Bar, a legendary hangout for Insiders. Also on the premises is the Village Cafe, which is open for breakfast, lunch, and dinner daily. Baleen, the gourmet restaurant, serves seafood with an Asian flare. Small pets are welcome at Paradise Point for a one-time $20 fee. Guests must sign a damage waiver.

Sea Coast Palms Inn **$**
4760 Mission Blvd., San Diego
(858) 483–6780, (800) 554–6555
www.seacoastinn.com

The 50 rooms and suites at Seacoast offer few frills, but for proximity to the beach, it can't be beat. It's located 1 block away from the beach boardwalk and Pacific Beach, one of San Diego's most popular beaches.

Rooms and suites all come equipped with king-size beds; suites have microwave kitchenettes. The rooms are comfortable, clean, and air-conditioned. The facility itself is in the heart of the beach-area business district and has dozens of restaurants and shops within a 5-block radius.

Coronado

Best Western Suites Coronado **$$**
275 Orange Ave.
(619) 437–1666, (800) 780–7234
www.bestwestern.com

One of the best values in Coronado, the Best Western's 63 rooms and suites offer comfort and convenience to all of Coronado's attractions. The Old Ferry Landing, with its shops and restaurants, is a 10-minute walk away, and the downtown village of Coronado is about 6 blocks in the other direction.

All the rooms and suites are decorated in a contemporary style, and some have a view of the quiet courtyard in the middle of the hotel. Government and military travelers especially appreciate the Best Western Coronado because it's close to North Island Naval Air Station. Also available for guests are on-site laundry facilities and a complimentary continental breakfast. The streetside balcony rooms are excellent viewing stations for Coronado's Fourth of July parade.

Crown City Inn $–$$
520 Orange Ave.
(619) 435–6750, (800) 422–1173

One of the nicest features of Coronado is that it's a small island, jam-packed with things to do. And the Crown City Inn is right in the middle of it all. Walk 5 blocks in one direction and you'll find beautiful beaches. Five long blocks in the other direction brings you to San Diego Bay and the Old Ferry Landing.

The inn itself has 33 rooms, including a few one-bedroom suites. If you're not in the mood for a day at the beach, relax by the pool in the courtyard, or catch up on your laundry at the on-site facilities. The inn's Cafe Bistro, open for breakfast, lunch, and dinner, is known for its good French/American cuisine. You're welcome to bring the family pet for an additional $8.00 per night.

Hotel del Coronado $$$$
1500 Orange Ave.
(619) 522–8000, (800) 468–3533
www.hoteldel.com

Don't let The Del's 674 rooms lead you to believe you'll get lost in a maze of structures and people. Despite its size, The Del has created a comfy, cozy, and luxurious atmosphere that will make you feel like its most treasured guest. All the rooms in the main building have been painstakingly restored and are one of a kind in their decor. Rooms in the Ocean Tower combine the grandeur of the past with the conveniences of the present and a sense of quiet privacy. No matter where you choose to stay, you'll be overwhelmed by the surrounding beauty of the Pacific Ocean and the beautifully landscaped grounds of the hotel.

Guests need not stray far from the hotel to enjoy all the elements of a true Southern California vacation. Within the hotel are two restaurants and two lounges, and many more are just a few blocks' stroll away. You can enjoy tennis on The Del's oceanside courts or golf at the nearby Coronado Golf Course. The Del has its own boathouse from which all sorts of water activities can be enjoyed: sailing, fishing, and whale watching, to name a few. Round out your day with a few laps in one of the heated pools and a therapeutic massage in The Del's spa, the most luxurious on the island. And of course, the hotel has its own shopping arcade, which is sure to provide you with the perfect memento of your stay. The Prince of Wales restaurant (see our Restaurants chapter) is consistently rated one of the finest in San Diego. Look for the Close-up on the Hotel del Coronado in this chapter for the history of this fascinating landmark. Locals have traditionally chosen the hotel's Sunday brunch as the setting for their Mother's Day and Easter celebrations. Served in the grand Crown Room, the brunch is a busy, bustling affair yet still feels elegant and special. Make reservations far in advance, and expect to wait in line even when it's time for you to be seated.

Loews Coronado Bay Resort $$$$
4000 Coronado Bay Rd.
(619) 424–4000, (800) 815–6397
www.loewshotel.com

If you're ready to splurge and indulge yourself in the ultimate luxury hotel, the Loews is the place for you. Located on a private peninsula a few miles south of Coronado, its 438 guest rooms and suites all have spectacular views of San Diego Bay, Loews' private marina or one of the sparkling pools. This is a true destination resort (check our entry in Spas and Resorts), so get ready to be pampered.

Everything you'd expect in a resort is here: a full health club, three pools, and five tennis courts. In addition, the Loews has a fully equipped Business Center for those who are combining work with pleasure. On the grounds of the hotel is the divine Azzura Point Restaurant (see our Restaurants chapter for all the scrumptious details), noted for its elegant cuisine and atmosphere. For more casual dining, guests can take advantage of the Market Café for breakfast, lunch, and dinner. If you simply can't drag yourself away from the pool, La Cantina has an outdoor bar and grill. The Café's Sunday brunch is a seafood lover's delight, with gorgeous displays of crab legs, sushi, and marinated seafood salads, as well as carved meats, waffles, and all your brunch favorites. And guests can relax after a long day in the Cays Lounge, which offers evening entertainment and large screen televisions.

Downtown/Gaslamp Quarter

Courtyard by Marriott $$$
530 Broadway, Central San Diego
(619) 530–4000, (800) 321–2211
www.courtyard.com/sancd

The 1927 San Diego Trust and Savings Bank, once a cornerstone of downtown, was uninhabited for several years before Marriott stepped in to revive the ornate building. The hotel's lobby has the original painted ceilings and bank tellers' counters, and the vault is now a meeting room. The 246 rooms are suitably decorated with carpeting and drapes in rich reds and blues. A restaurant and bar take up much of the lobby space.

Embassy Suites Hotel $$$
601 Pacific Hwy., Downtown
(619) 239–2400, (800) 362–2779
www.embassysuites.com

Downtown's Embassy Suites is in an ideal location: slightly removed from the hustle and bustle of downtown, yet close enough to walk to many of its attractions and restaurants. On one side of the hotel, the view is of San Diego's sparkling harbor. The other side offers a view of the stately skyscrapers that populate the heart of downtown. Each of the 337 suites has a living area (complete with refrigerator, microwave, and wet bar), and a separate bedroom and bath. An indoor pool and whirlpool are perfect for unwinding after a long day sightseeing. There's also a full fitness center.

Seaport Village, with its shops and restaurants, is only 1 block away from the hotel (see our Shopping and Attractions chapters for the lowdown on Seaport Village), and the Convention Center is a long 3 blocks away. Allow 10 minutes to reach the center for meetings. Plus, all the shopping, dining, and nightlife of downtown and the Gaslamp Quarter are within a short walking distance.

Children younger than 18 stay for free with their parents.

Hilton San Diego Gaslamp Quarter $$
401 K St., Central San Diego
(619) 231–4040, (800) 774–1500
www.hilton.com

Located directly across Harbor Drive from the Convention Center and near a trolley stop, the Hilton is an urbane, chic hotel. Some of the 275 rooms and suites are designed to resemble artists' lofts, and all are decorated with original art. The rooftop outdoor pool and sundeck overlook the Convention Center. The fitness center has all the latest equipment, and you can jog along Martin Luther King

Insiders' Tip

If you're having trouble securing a reservation or deciding the best location for your stay, call San Diego Hotel Reservations at (858) 627-9300, www.savecash.com. They can usually help you find a room, even during peak weekends and holidays.

Promenade, a linear park that runs alongside the trolley tracks. Take a break from sightseeing to enjoy a bit of pampering at the Artesia Spa. The breakfast buffet at the hotel's New Leaf restaurant is one of the best you'll find in a hotel, and the outdoor terrace seating is tranquil (except when a trolley passes by).

Holiday Inn on the Bay $$
1355 N. Harbor Dr., Downtown
(619) 232–3861, (800) 877–8920
www.sixcontinentshotels.com

The 600-room twin high-rise towers of the Holiday Inn lie at the foot of downtown on the embarcadero, close to everything there is to see and do. Rooms have a view of either San Diego Bay or the city lights and lots of special amenities: voice mail, data ports, and workspaces, to name a few.

Workouts are a breeze in the poolside exercise facility, and a waterfront jogging trail is right across the street. The Elephant & Castle is an English-style pub and restaurant that's open for breakfast, lunch, and dinner and comes equipped with pool tables and dartboards. You can dine in style at the adjacent Ruth's Chris Steakhouse, or grab a sandwich at Hazlewood's Deli. All of Downtown's attractions are a few blocks away, and harbor cruises, the Maritime Museum, the *Star of India,* and the San Diego-Coronado Ferry are right across the street from the hotel. You may bring your pet along, but you must pay a $100 deposit, $75 of which is refundable. Pets are not allowed in public areas.

Horton Grand Hotel $$–$$$
311 Island Ave., San Diego
(619) 544–1886, (800) 542–1886

In 1986 the Horton Grand was built, brick by brick, from two original Victorian hotels in the heart of San Diego's Gaslamp Quarter. Today you can enjoy the elegance of the early-twentieth-century era in this painstakingly recreated hotel. No two rooms are alike, and all are furnished with Victorian draped queen-size beds, antiques, and gas-burning fireplaces.

The Ida Bailey Restaurant is located on the premises, serving breakfast, lunch, and dinner as well as a sumptuous Sunday brunch. High Tea is served on Thursdays, Fridays, and Saturdays, and live entertainment is offered in the Palace Bar on those same evenings. Shopping, restaurants, and nightlife are all within 2 or 3 blocks. Pets that weigh less than 14 pounds are accepted here for a $100 nonrefundable fee.

Super 8 Motel Bayview $
1835 Columbia St., San Diego
(619) 544–0164, (800) 537–9902

Though it's a little off the beaten path, this motel is easy on the wallet. It's located near the Little Italy neighborhood of San Diego (which has several great restaurants), and the nightlife of downtown is a five-minute drive away.

The motel's 136 rooms are clean, contemporary, and comfortable. It has a pool and a spa, and offers a complimentary continental breakfast every morning. Ask for a bay-view room, and your hosts will bend over backward to accommodate you.

Wyndham U.S. Grant Hotel $$–$$$
326 Broadway, San Diego
(619) 232–3121, (877) 999–3223
www.wyndham.com/USGrant

The U.S. Grant has been a San Diego landmark and gathering place since 1910. Ulysses S. Grant Jr. commissioned the Italian Renaissance palace to honor his father, President Ulysses S. Grant. The hotel was quite grand, with an indoor swimming pool and 400 rooms. Several investors have taken charge of the hotel over the years; the Wyndham chain took over in 2002.

As you might expect, the hotel is a study in polished wood and brass. The 280 guestrooms and suites are furnished with antiques and may seem a bit too fussy for some. Others love the classic comfort and elegance. The hotel's Grant Grill has been part of the downtown dining scene for years, and the Grant Lounge is a favorite hangout for Insiders who enjoy live jazz. Across the street from the Grant is Westfield Shoppingtown Horton Plaza Shopping Center (see our Shopping chapter) and the famous Gaslamp Quarter.

Westgate Hotel $$$–$$$$
1055 Second Ave., San Diego
(619) 238–1818, (800) 221–3802

Whether you're traveling for business or pleasure, the Westgate provides an unforgettable experience in luxury. Each of the 223 guest rooms is unique in its design and offers a variety of amenities, including two-line phones and data ports. The rooms are furnished with European antiques.

The Westgate is located in the heart of Downtown, across from the Westfield Shoppingtown Horton Plaza shopping center and the historic Gaslamp Quarter. Candlelight dining can be enjoyed at the hotel's Fontainebleau Restaurant. For more lively entertainment, try the Plaza Bar.

La Jolla/Golden Triangle

Embassy Suites Hotel $$$–$$$$
4550 La Jolla Village Dr., San Diego
(858) 453–0400, (800) 362–2779
www.embassysuites.com

Like its sister hotel in downtown San Diego, the Embassy Suites in the Golden Triangle offers 335 full suites consisting of living room, bedroom, and bath. This is a popular hotel among business travelers, but many visitors enjoy it as well because of its proximity to La Jolla and to University Towne Center, one of San Diego's nicest shopping malls. (Check our Shopping chapter for all the details on UTC.) The mall is within easy walking distance of the hotel and has an abundance of stores, restaurants, and a multiplex theater.

The Coast Cafe restaurant on the premises is open for breakfast, lunch, and dinner, and many top-notch restaurants are within a few blocks. For visitors who plan to do a lot of sightseeing, this is a centrally located spot that's hard to beat. La Jolla is a five-minute drive away, downtown San Diego is 15 minutes south, and North County Coastal's hot spots are 15 minutes north. Children younger than 18 stay for free with their parents.

The Grande Colonial $$
910 Prospect St., La Jolla
(858) 454–2181, (800) 826–1278
www.thegrandecolonial.com

The perfect blend of European ambiance and American hospitality are found at this classy hotel. Its 55 luxury rooms and 20 elegant suites have a French country decor with some antique furniture. Eight of the suites are in a vintage beach cottage set amid flower gardens behind the main building. Rooms at the back of the hotel on the top floors have great views of La Jolla Cove.

A pool is on the premises, and the hotel offers privileges at a nearby health club for its guests. Nine-Ten restaurant is on site, serving breakfast, lunch, and dinner daily. The inn is virtually steps away from La Jolla's numerous fine restaurants, shops, and galleries, so be sure to go exploring. Smoking is not allowed in any of the rooms.

Hotel Parisi $$$
1111 Prospect St., La Jolla
(858) 454–1511, (888) 4PARISI
www.hotelparisi.com

The zen-like ambience of this ultra-chic hotel has made it the darling of celebrities and locals enjoying a special night out. The 20 rooms were designed along feng shui principles and have a beige, cream, and white sleek decor that feels comfortable and soothing. The rooms are located above Victoria's Secret and other shops. Those facing the street can be noisy. There's no restaurant, but nearly every type of food you crave is available within easy walking distance.

Hyatt Regency La Jolla $$$
3777 La Jolla Village Dr., San Diego
(858) 552–1234, (800) 233–1234

Located in the heart of the Golden Triangle, the Hyatt Regency offers all the amenities travelers have come to expect from fine hotels. Eleven acres of lush gardens surround this 400-room hotel, and the architecture and decor reflect the style of architect Michael Graves's version of an Italian palace. The hotel's Aventine Sporting Club is a 32,000-square-foot health spa that's sure to challenge even the most fitness-oriented. And, of course, tennis and a swimming pool are part of the package, too.

The chic Hotel Parisi sits amid cafes and boutiques in La Jolla. PHOTO: COURTESY OF HOTEL PARISI

The hotel is part of the Aventine complex, which includes the sporting club, an office tower, and a restaurant enclave with several trendy eateries. Westfield Shoppingtown University Towne Center (as detailed in our Shopping chapter) is 3 blocks away.

La Jolla Beach Travelodge $
6750 La Jolla Blvd., La Jolla
(858) 454–0716, (800) 578–7878
www.travelodge.com

One of the best bargains in La Jolla, the Travelodge is located outside the village area, but close to Windansea Beach, where you can watch surfing pros ride the waves. The 44 rooms have recently been remodeled and have coffeemakers, irons and ironing boards, and hair dryers. The pool is heated, and there is a hot tub. This is a good choice for those who plan to spend more time out playing than using the hotel facilities.

La Valencia $$$$
1132 Prospect St., La Jolla
(858) 454–0771, (800) 451–0772
www.lavalencia.com

A landmark in La Jolla, La Valencia is the essence of Old World elegance and luxury. Overlooking La Jolla Cove, its 100 guestrooms and suites are custom decorated with a European flavor, and rooms have either a garden or a sweeping ocean view. Fifteen luxurious villas were added in 2001 and have whirlpool tubs, king-size beds, and an abundance of marble and granite accents in the Mediterranean decor. A private butler tends to the villa guests, unpacking their luggage, stocking the wet bar, and collecting the appropriate CDs for the in-room player. It doesn't get much more luxurious than this.

Even though you're just a whisper away from the ocean, the hotel has a heated swimming pool, whirlpool hot tub, and a fitness room with a sauna and massage rooms. There are bicycles for rent, and few rides are prettier than an early morning pedal along La Jolla's coastline.

The Mediterranean Room/Tropical Patio serves breakfast, lunch, and dinner daily. For a more intimate dining experience, try the Sky Room Restaurant on the tenth floor, which has only 12 tables overlooking the cove. Be sure to stop by the

The La Valencia's new ocean villas come with personalized butler service. PHOTO: JEREMIAH SULLIVAN, COURTESY OF THE LA VALENCIA HOTEL

Whaling Bar & Grill for lunch, dinner, or cocktails; La Jolla's Old Guard families tend to think of it as their private club. Nestled right in the heart of the Village of La Jolla, La Valencia is the perfect place to create memories to last a lifetime.

Sea Lodge $$–$$$
8110 Camino del Oro, La Jolla
(858) 459–8271, (800) 237–5211

Step onto the balcony of your room at the Sea Lodge, and you can almost touch the waves. It has become one of California's favorite oceanfront retreats, with its 128 rooms set amid fountains, courtyards, fresh flowers, and ocean breezes. The rooms have a casual, comfortable feeling, so you needn't worry about your wet, sandy beach gear. The architecture is reminiscent of old Mexico, and Mexican antiques are everywhere you turn on the grounds of the hotel.

The Sea Lodge offers an array of amenities: fitness center, tennis, pool and spa, sauna, and volleyball on the beach. The oceanfront Shores restaurant offers breakfast, lunch, and dinner daily. The menu, designed by Chef Bernard Guillas of the Marine Room, offers exceptional cuisine at affordable prices.

Mission Valley

Doubletree $$
7450 Hazard Center Dr., Central San Diego
(619) 297–5466, (800) 549–8010

Located in the heart of Mission Valley's shopping district, the Doubletree has the added bonus of being right across the street from a San Diego Trolley station, which will take visitors to all points of interest in San Diego. The hotel's 300 guest rooms and suites all have mini-bars and PC data ports for those who don't like to be disconnected.

Swim in the indoor/outdoor pool, or get a good workout in the fitness center. Casual all-day dining is available at the

Fountain Cafe, and you can dance the night away at Club Max, the red-hot nightclub on the premises. Enjoy the freshly baked chocolate chip cookie that awaits you on arrival. Pets are allowed and there is no additional charge.

Handlery Hotel & Resort $$
950 Hotel Circle N., San Diego
(619) 298–4135, (800) 843–4343
www.handlery.com

Each of the 222 contemporary rooms at the Handlery provide spacious comfort and a traditional San Diego atmosphere. Guests will enjoy a workout in the fully equipped fitness center and the Swim & Tennis Club. Practice your swing on the hotel's own driving range, or indulge in a game of tennis on one of eight lighted courts. Three swimming pools (including a five-lane lap pool) are waiting to cool you off, and you can reward yourself with a relaxing massage to top off your busy day.

Westfield Shoppingtown Mission Valley and Fashion Valley Shopping Centers (check out our Shopping chapter for details) are nearby, as are movie theaters and tons of restaurants. Or if you prefer to stay close to home, dine at Postcards American Bistro, which serves breakfast, lunch, and dinner daily.

Marriott Mission Valley $$
8757 Rio San Diego Dr., San Diego
(619) 692–3800, (800) 842–5329

Mission Valley can't be beat for its easy access to all of San Diego's attractions, and the Marriott Mission Valley is well situated to take advantage of the best the city has to offer. The 17-story, 350-room hotel has a swimming pool, championship tennis court with night lighting, a health club with a whirlpool and sauna, and a specially designed jogging trail.

Two blocks away are the new Rio Vista Shopping area and Mission Valley Shopping Center, and Qualcomm Stadium is just minutes away by car or trolley. The Gratzi Grill serves breakfast, lunch, and dinner, or grab a snack in Chats Sports Bar or at the Splash Pool Bar. Pets are welcome, but guests must pay a $200 deposit, $150 of which is refundable.

Quality Inn Resort $
875 Hotel Circle S., San Diego
(619) 298–8282, (800) 362–7871

This beautifully landscaped 20-acre retreat has an ideal location, casual elegance, generous amenities, and attentive service. The 202 rooms are family friendly, with lots of room to spread out and relax. Kids will be pleased by the swimming pool and in-room Nintendo, while adults will enjoy the cocktail lounge with pool tables, the whirlpool spa, and the 27,000-square-foot athletic and racquet club.

A 24-hour restaurant is located on-site, and room service is available too. For even more convenience, there's a liquor store and small market. The resort provides complimentary transportation to shopping, trolley stations, and Old Town.

Red Lion Hanalei Hotel $–$$
2270 Hotel Circle N., San Diego
(619) 297–1101, (800) 882–0858
www.hanaleihotel.com

Here's an Insiders' secret: the Hanalei Hotel is one of the best bargains in San Diego County. It's a full-service luxury hotel for a price that fits most budgets. Surrounded by Southern California's signature palm trees and tropical plants, the Hanalei feels like an exotic resort set amid freeways.

The hotel's 416 rooms and suites are fairly standard, and the swimming pool, whirlpool, and fitness center are there to

Hotel del Coronado

Rarely does a mere hotel achieve legendary status, but the Hotel del Coronado has accomplished just that. Built in 1888 in the early stages of the development of the seaside village of Coronado, The Del has maintained a tradition of lavish service in a fairy-tale setting surrounded by mystery and wonder. The grounds sprawl over 26 acres of lush beachfront property, and the hotel itself is an architectural marvel. Some say it is as elaborate and frilly as a wedding cake. Locals have long claimed that Frank L. Baum, who wrote *The Wizard of Oz,* based his design of Emerald City on the hotel's turreted architecture. Actually, the book was written before Baum ever visited Coronado. But he completed other Oz books at the hotel and in a small cottage on the island. His child was even born at the hotel, and Baum is credited with designing the elaborate crown chandeliers that once hung in the hotel's ballroom, aptly called the Crown Room. Everywhere you turn is a nook, a cranny, a gazebo, or an alcove that makes you feel you're uncovering a secret that no one has ever found before.

Two Midwestern builders dreamed up The Del. Back in the 1880s, before Coronado was developed, Elisha Babcock and H. L. Story could see promise in the barren landscape. They spared no money or effort, importing lumber and laborers from San Francisco to help construct their vision. A mahogany bar was built in Philadelphia and delivered fully assembled to Coronado by ship, traveling all the way around South America. Babcock and Story spent a cool $1 million to realize their dream—$600,000 for construction and $400,000 for furnishings—an amount unheard of in those days.

The Del quickly became world famous, and even though it now is more than a century old, it has never sacrificed its old-world charm and elegance.

The hotel has attracted its share of legendary guests. Ten U.S. presidents have stayed at The Del, starting with Benjamin Harrison in 1891. Over the years William Taft, Franklin D. Roosevelt, Richard M. Nixon, Ronald Reagan, and Bill Clinton have all been guests. In 1970 The Del was the site for a state dinner honoring President Richard Nixon and Mexican President Gustavo Díaz Ordaz. The elaborate dinner was held in the Crown Room and was attended by more than 1,000 guests.

But more than just politicians have added their luster to the hotel. Charles Lindbergh was honored at The Del after his historic 1927 flight across the Atlantic Ocean. And in 1920 England's Prince of Wales (who later became King Edward VIII) was an honored guest. It has long been rumored that the Prince met Wallis Simpson at The Del; he later abdicated the throne to marry her. The story is a bit more complicated, and it's not known for sure that they actually met at the hotel. But the romantic rumor lingers.

Hollywood was quick to discover The Del too, and frequently used the hotel grounds and interior for filming movies. Most famous, of course, is the romantic comedy *Some Like It Hot,* filmed in 1958 and starring Marilyn Monroe, Jack Lemmon, and Tony Curtis. Naturally, in 1995, when the Marilyn Monroe postage stamp was released, the only logical place for the unveiling was The Del. More recently, The Del served as the main stage for *The Stunt Man,* starring Peter O'Toole, and it has served as a backdrop for scenes in *Mr. Wrong,* with Ellen DeGeneres, and *My Blue Heaven,* with Steve Martin. There has never been a shortage of fine entertainers, either. During the summers of 1949 and 1950, the flamboyant pianist Liberace entertained in the Circus Room.

For those who have an affinity for the supernatural, The Del does indeed have a resident ghost. Hotel management long hoped that particular legend would die; it now encourages repetition of the story of Kate Morgan, who was shot on a stairway outside the hotel in 1892. It is said that Morgan's spirit haunts room 3312. Some have felt the presence of a ghost in the room Morgan's maid used as well. In fact, the 1972 television series *Ghost Story* was filmed at The Del. If you'd like to add a little adventure to your holiday, ask the receptionist for the haunted room when you make your reservation. Stories of ghost sightings are all just part of the allure.

Today the Hotel del Coronado is as modern as the discriminating traveler demands, but it has never lost its original design and beauty. Thanks to ongoing renovations, the hotel retains the polish of its youth. A recent five-year makeover totaled $55 million. All guestrooms, public spaces, and meeting rooms were refurbished, including the oceanfront ballroom and the Prince of Wales Grill. The beautifully landscaped Windsor Lawn was created to replace the unsightly tennis courts that long marred the view of the ocean from the rooms. A bird cage elevator in the lobby was restored and now has a uniformed operator on duty 24 hours a day. Babcock and Story are honored in a bar and lounge bearing their names. It's a great place for a sunset drink or bedtime brandy.

The hotel's beloved History Gallery—a display of photos along a basement hallway—is gone. We hope the photos will return, since they add to the hotel's charm. The Hotel del Coronado has been designated by Congress as a National Historic Landmark and is dedicated to protecting its architectural integrity. A Heritage Department continually uncovers more details about The Del's fascinating history. Locals insist that the hotel remain the same and strongly protest any significant changes. This is no small task for the owners, when you consider that every modern service and comfort must continually be provided for guests to keep them coming back.

Over the years, even though ownership of The Del has changed hands several times, the owners have never missed a step. The hotel is as beautiful as it was the day it first opened to the public in 1888, and it will continue to be a source of great pride in San Diego for generations to come.

For more than a hundred years, the historic Hotel del Coronado has been a San Diego landmark and a favorite destination for visitors. PHOTO: COURTESY OF HOTEL DEL CORONADO

please the most discriminating traveler. Islands Restaurant serves Pacific Rim cuisine for dinner, and the Peacock Cafe is open daily for breakfast, lunch, and dinner. A $25 deposit will secure accommodations for your small pet.

Town & Country Hotel   **$$–$$$**
500 Hotel Circle N., San Diego
(619) 291–7131, (800) 854–2608

Spread over 40 acres of landscaped grounds, the Town & Country is a San Diego landmark. Amidst dozens of palm trees are two guest-room towers and a sprawl of ranch-style garden bungalows. All together, the Town & Country has 1,000 rooms. It also has an on-site convention center, which makes it a favorite place for small conventions and gatherings of all kinds.

Kick off your shoes and jump into one of four swimming pools, or choose from five restaurants, which offer everything from fine cuisine to casual fare. Also available are barber and beauty services.

Old Town

Best Western Hacienda Suites Hotel   **$–$$**
4041 Harney St., San Diego
(619) 298–4707, (800) 780–7234
www.bestwestern.com

Terraced on a hillside overlooking Old Town State Park is the all-suite Hacienda Hotel. Decorated with handcrafted Southwest-style furnishings, each of the 150 guest suites opens onto a courtyard or a balcony, inviting in those fresh Southern California breezes.

Suites have either one or two queen beds and come equipped with microwave ovens and refrigerators. You can take an afternoon dip here in the pool or hot tub.

When hunger strikes, you need venture no farther than the grounds of the hotel to Acapulco, a casual Mexican restaurant that serves breakfast, lunch, and dinner daily. A fairly good brunch is offered on Sundays, complete with a roving mariachi band to treat you to the ultimate Old Town experience.

Old Town Plaza   **$–$$**
2380 Moore St., San Diego
(619) 291–9100, (800) 905–3319

The price is right and the location ideal at the edge of the I–5 freeway and Old Town. Rooms with either one or two queen beds are available, and all are nicely decorated in an Old California style. Modem jacks are installed in all rooms. Another plus is the on-site guest laundry facility. The pool is heated (it does get cold here in winter). Guests can also enjoy a complimentary continental breakfast, and there are several restaurants nearby.

Ramada Limited   **$$**
3900 Old Town Ave., San Diego
(619) 299–7400, (800) 451–9846,
(888) 298–2054

Located in the heart of historic Old Town, the Ramada Limited combines old California charm with European flair. The inn's 125 guest rooms and six suites are designed to resemble comfortable bed and breakfast accommodations, updated with modern appointments. If you're in the mood for a late-night snack and just don't feel like trekking outside your room, we've got you covered. Each room comes complete with a microwave oven and refrigerator you can stock with goodies.

When you're ready to unwind, there's no better place than the central courtyard with its pool, spa and sundeck. After a day of sightseeing or basking in the sunshine, you can take a five or 10-minute stroll to more than 30 restaurants, which offer everything from casual Mexican fare to fine seafood or ethnic cuisine.

Point Loma/Harbor and Shelter Islands

Best Western Island Palms Hotel   **$$–$$$**
2051 Shelter Island Dr., San Diego
(619) 222–0561, (877) 484–3275
www.bestwestern.com

A common sentiment among visitors is, why come to San Diego if you don't stay on the water? The Island Palms sits beside the blue waters of San Diego Bay and offers a resort-like atmosphere for guests who want to get away from it all and still be close to San Diego's attractions.

The 97-room hotel has a bayside swimming pool and spa, and most rooms and suites have spectacular bay views. If you plan to settle in for a while, take advantage of the oversized suites with full kitchens. The hotel's waterfront restaurant is perfect for dining and unwinding with friends in the lounge. The hotel was renovated in 2001, and all rooms are now non-smoking rooms.

Hilton San Diego Airport Harbor Island $$
1960 Harbor Island, San Diego
(619) 291–6700, (800) 445–8667
www.sandiegoairport.hilton.com

Located on Harbor Island (near the airport), the Hilton's 207 rooms overlook San Diego Bay and the lively marina. Most rooms have a view, either of the city or the bay, and all have balconies or patios.

The Waterfront Cafe offers a breakfast buffet every day and is also open for lunch and dinner.

Humphrey's Half Moon Inn $$$–$$$$
2303 Shelter Island Dr., San Diego
(619) 224–3411, (800) 542–7400
www.halfmooninn.com

A tropical paradise on the bay is the best way to describe the Half Moon Inn on San Diego's Shelter Island. Its 182 rooms and suites are nestled among lush gardens, palm trees, ponds, and waterfalls. Humphrey's Restaurant is on site and in charge of room service.

Guests who visit from June through October are in for a special treat. Humphrey's Concerts by the Bay series (see our Nightlife chapter) takes place right on the grounds of the hotel. Enjoy the evening breezes by the pool or from your balcony while you enjoy music from jazz and pop entertainers such as Ray Charles, Kenny G, Ringo Starr, and more. Kids will enjoy the pool and the continuous Ping-Pong games.

Vagabond Inn Point Loma $
1325 Scott St., San Diego
(619) 224–3371, (800) 522–1555

This is strictly a bare-bones accommodation, but for convenience to Point Loma's fishing docks, it's a gem. Directly across the street are deep-sea fishing boats waiting to take guests on half-day or daylong ocean fishing trips. And for those to

whom fishing is secondary, shopping and many restaurants are within a few blocks.

The 40 guest rooms are clean and comfortable, and the motel is within a 10- or 15-minute drive to most of San Diego's attractions. Pets are welcome for an additional $10 per night.

North County Coastal

Best Western Marty's Valley Inn $
3240 Mission Ave., Oceanside
(760) 757–7700, (800) 747–3529
www.bestwestern.com

Located about 20 minutes east of the heart of Oceanside, the hotel has been an accommodation mainstay since the seventies. There are 111 guest rooms, which are furnished in the modest, practical style of any Best Western. The hotel has a small conference center. There's a pool at the hotel, and dining and shopping are nearby.

Best Western Stratford Inn Del Mar $$
710 Camino del Mar, Del Mar
(858) 755–1501, (800) 780–7234
www.bestwestern.com

One of the best bargains in Del Mar, this hotel is within walking distance of village eateries, boutiques and bookstores, and nifty pubs where you can find some live music. There are 93 rooms, and for days when you'd rather not deal with beach sand, there's a pool. The hotel also has a French day spa offering massages, manicures, and other services.

If you're staying for a week, ask about discounts. The hotel has some rooms with kitchenettes but these are reserved early during both the summer and winter seasons. Book ahead if you want a place to cook.

Carlsbad Inn Beach Resort $$$
3075 Carlsbad Blvd., Carlsbad
(760) 434–7020, (800) 235–3939

This popular hotel is a block from the ocean and only steps away from Fidel's, one the best and most affordable Mexican restaurants in the county (for more on Fidel's see our Restaurants chapter). If you have your heart set on a Carlsbad hotel, make reservations ahead of time. The hotel is popular, especially with families, because of the casual atmosphere. While it's pricey, keep in mind that you're right across a small street from huge, sandy beaches, and within walking distance to the shops and stores and restaurants in Carlsbad, and about 5 blocks from the Coaster station. When you get here you do not need to move the car for the entire vacation. You'll find 60 rooms, some with adjoining rooms and some mini-suites.

There's all you'd expect here, from a pool to rooms with tiny kitchens. Alas, there's no room service, but there are cafes by the dozen in downtown Carlsbad and upscale places for dinner too. If you're carless or like to hike along the famous Carlsbad beach, this is a perfect choice.

Del Mar Hilton $$–$$$
15575 Jimmy Durante Blvd., Del Mar
(858) 792–5200, (800) 445–8667
www.hilton.com

Stay at this Hilton and you can walk to the Del Mar Fairgrounds, including the on- and offsite horse racetrack. It's a popular hotel so if you're determined to stay here during the racing or fair season, make plans well ahead. There are 245 rooms and suites. Some have separate bedrooms and whirlpool tubs. There are meeting rooms and a lounge that invites you to linger. There's a spacious pool and restaurant on site.

Doubletree Hotel Del Mar $$–$$$
11915 El Camino Real, Del Mar
(858) 481–5900, (800) 222–8733
www.doubletree.com

Just east of the ocean communities of Solana Beach and Del Mar, the Doubletree Hotel Del Mar offers 220 luxuriously appointed rooms, oversized and warmly decorated. There are four suites. Rooms come with everything from coffeemakers to two-line phones with modem hookups. Wheelchair-accessible and nonsmoking rooms are available.

Along with that fresh-baked chocolate chip cookie you'll find every night right in your room, you'll be able to relax even if you're visiting on business. Breakfast,

lunch, and dinner are served in the hotel's restaurant and on the patio. There is an exercise room and outdoor pool. Families love the children's playroom and separate wading pool. Within minutes, guests can be splashing in the Pacific or swinging a golf club at one of the many courses in the area. The hotel is near the Del Mar Fairgrounds and racetrack, too. There is complimentary shuttle service within a 6-mile radius of the hotel.

Four Seasons Resort Aviara $$$$
7100 Four Seasons Pt., Carlsbad
(760) 603–6800, (800) 332–3442
www.fourseasons.com/aviara

With 329 rooms, many oversized and all with wonderful views, this is a destination location for anyone who loves luxury. See the Spas and Resorts chapter for details on the resort, including those famous "Four Seasons" beds you may have heard about on the *Rosie O'Donnell* and *Oprah* shows.

There's a championship golf course, two pools (one that's strictly for quiet and relaxation and one that's for family play), poolside lounging, and afternoon tea. Dining in the hotel's restaurants is a delight. There is one four-diamond gourmet restaurant—Vivace—and another extra-nice California Bistro. California Bistro is more casual and is open for breakfast, lunch, and dinner (see our Restaurants chapter); Vivace is open only for dinner.

This is where Insiders come, whether it's for a quiet chat and iced coffee at poolside or a more elaborate event like a romantic second honeymoon. Pets are welcome here at the Four Seasons Aviara, as long as they weigh less than 15 pounds. Guests with pets are required to pay a $100 nonrefundable fee.

Holiday Inn Carlsbad-by-the-Sea $$
850 Palomar Airport Rd., Carlsbad
(760) 438–1442, (800) 266–7880
www.carlsbadholidayinn.com

Close to the highway, close to LEGOLAND California (see our chapter on Kidstuff), close to the Carlsbad Flower Fields (see our Annual Events chapter), close to the Carlsbad Company Stores (see our Shopping chapter), and close to the technology centers of the North County, this comfortable hotel is an obvious choice for many travelers. You can't miss it: A 50-foot Dutch-style working windmill sits atop the buildings. There are 147 rooms.

The hotel is about an hour's drive from downtown San Diego and offers a pool and on-site dining. Remember, directly across the street from the hotel is the not-to-be-missed Bellefleur (see Restaurants) and the quicker eateries in the Carlsbad Company Stores mall. You'll find your favorite fast-food places right in the neighborhood, too.

Inns of America $
751 Raintree Dr., Carlsbad
(760) 931–1185, (800) 826–0778
www.innsofamerica.com

This Carlsbad chain hotel offers few frills, but it's convenient, well maintained, and inviting. There is a pool, and the beach is about a five-minute drive west. If you're a budget-minded traveler, this is your hotel. There's no extra charge for those glorious sunsets you can see from some of the rooms. There's a restaurant on site and good eating choices within minutes in the village area of Carlsbad and in various shopping centers near the hotel. And if you're traveling with your pets, you'll definitely want to stay here as they have a "pets welcome" policy. There's a $10 pet charge, which is due on check in.

L'Auberge Del Mar $$$$
1540 Camino Del Mar, Del Mar
(858) 259–1515, (800) 553–1336
www.laubergedelmar.com

Many people think of L'Auberge as a spa (see our chapter on Spas and Resorts) and they're right. It has wonderful possibilities if you're looking for relaxation; it also has beauty and rejuvenation programs. Yet it's also a convenient and enjoyable hotel located in the seaside village of Del Mar. Be sure to read more about the lovely beaches in Del Mar in our Beaches and Watersports chapter.

There are 120 deluxe rooms and elegant suites; there's a sports pavilion and pool. Along with the breathtaking views of the Pacific, you'll be treated to nearby golf, tennis, horseracing, and, of course, the village's delightful restaurants, sidewalk cafes, boutiques, and bookstores, all within walking distance. (See the entries in our Shopping chapter.)

La Costa Resort and Spa $$$$
2100 Costa Del Mar Rd., Carlsbad
(760) 438–9111, (800) 544–7483
www.lacosta.com

Since the seventies, La Costa Resort and Spa has been known for quality; it continues to be a benchmark for luxury in the hotel industry. The goal for the resort is to maintain privacy while providing every comfort for guests. As a guest yourself, you'll meet visitors from around the globe and those who live in Carlsbad. Insiders know this is a great getaway. The facility offers a range of spa choices (see our chapter on Spas and Resorts) and a hotel's "menu" of incomparable opportunities for recreation and relaxation. Ask about special package offers when making reservations and be sure to treat yourself to a spa experience.

La Costa has two championship golf courses, 21 tennis courts at the La Costa

Sometimes San Diego hotel guests arrive by boat. PHOTO: DALE FROST, COURTESY OF THE PORT OF SAN DIEGO

Racquet Club, five swimming pools, a full conference center, five restaurants, two lounges, walking paths, and of course, the world-class spa. It also happens to be the home of several tennis and golf tournaments.

Motel 6 $
750 Raintree Dr., Carlsbad
(760) 431–0745
1006 Carlsbad Village Dr., Carlsbad
(760) 434–7135
6117 Paseo Del Norte, Carlsbad
(760) 438–1242

Like other Motel 6's throughout the country, this trio of North County Coastal budget hotels is clean and functional. Kids stay free. Ask about AAA and AARP discounts. Pets are welcome at Motel 6's, with no extra charge or special room designation.

If you're going to spend hours outdoors, visiting the local attractions or doing business in the area, then it's tough to go wrong with the basics provided by Motel 6.

Oceanside Marina Inn $$–$$$
2008 Harbor Dr. N., Oceanside
(760) 722–1561, (800) 252–2033
www.omihotel.com

Small (only 64 rooms) and convenient to the marina, this is the hotel of choice for those who motor or sail in for a vacation. There are some rooms with tiny kitchens, many with wonderful views, and in case you don't love walking on the golden Oceanside sand (on one of the best sandy beaches in the area), or playing in the Pacific waves, the hotel has a pool. If you're looking for a romantic getaway, ask about the rooms with fireplaces and balconies.

There isn't a restaurant on site, but dining is close by, and if you're so inclined, you can rent a sail boat or book a fishing trip just steps from your hotel.

Olympic Resort Hotel & Spa $–$
6111 El Camino Real, Carlsbad
(760) 438–8330, (800) 522–8330
www.olympic-resort.com

Located within minutes of Carlsbad's Palomar Airport, this hotel includes 78 oversized rooms, a well-equipped fitness center, two heated pools, and five lighted tennis courts.

There's a restaurant on site and banquet facilities, yet most people don't visit for these reasons. It's the golf right at the hotel that draws in travelers. Yes, a driving range and putting greens are straight out back—barely 50 feet from the hotel. The championship golf courses at La Costa and Four Seasons Aviara are within a five-minute drive.

Best Western Encinitas Inn and Suites $$
85 Encinitas Blvd., Encinitas
(760) 942–7455, (866) 362–4827

Do you need sea breezes? How about great sunsets? How about highway convenience? Then this North County Coastal Best Western is the right choice. It has 94 rooms, some with kitchenettes. There's a restaurant on site and dining within a five-minute drive. Of course, it has the prerequisite pool and lounging features and is especially popular with seminar groups and corporations that use the hotel for retreats and meetings. If you're traveling with your pet and want to stay here, there's a $50 nonrefundable charge and the pet must stay in a portable kennel that you'll need to bring.

Rancho Valencia Resort $$$$
5921 Valencia Cir., Rancho Santa Fe
(858) 756–1123, (800) 548–3664
www.ranchovalencia.com

About 30 minutes from downtown San Diego, Rancho Valencia is elegant and a top choice for spa and resort fans (see our chapter on Spas and Resorts). You'll find upscale touches throughout the resort. The centerpiece is the Hacienda, a restored adobe brick home that was built in the 1940s. There are three suites in the Hacienda, and the entire building is often booked by such luminaries as Bill Gates.

Twenty casitas house the 43 luxurious suites and are scattered around the lush grounds. There are several pools and hot tubs, spa services, 18 tennis courts, and fine dining at the resort's signature restaurant. There are also great hiking and biking trails right out the hotel's door. Be warned, you may become addicted to the ambiance of Rancho Valencia. It's that lovely.

North County Inland

Best Western Escondido $–$$
1700 Seven Oaks Rd., Escondido
(760) 740–1700, (800) 780–7234
www.bestwestern.com

With 100 rooms and a location that's near the highway and the heart of Escondido, this hotel works well for visitors with relatives living nearby. It's about 10 minutes to shopping at North County Faire (see Shopping), 15 minutes from championship golf courses (see Golf), and 20 minutes to the Wild Animal Park (see Attractions).

There isn't a restaurant on site, but many Escondido restaurants are nearby. Ask about the discounted golf packages for your family golfers. Pets under 10 pounds are welcome for a fee.

Comfort Inn $
1290 W. Valley Pkwy., Escondido
(760) 489–1010, (800) 228–5150

Whether you're just passing through or stopping to sample some of North County Inland's fun attractions, the Comfort Inn is a budget-right choice. The 95-room facility has a pool and the amenities that you'd expect at any Comfort Inn throughout the country.

DoubleTree Carmel Highland Resort $$$
14455 Penasquitos Dr., San Diego
(619) 672–9100, (800) 222–8733

Situated just off Interstate 15 in the Carmel Mountain area and about 23 miles north of downtown San Diego, this hotel/resort offers 173 sleeping rooms, suites, two bi-level, and four two-room parlor suites. The rooms are oversized and inviting.

If you need a quiet hideaway, you'll enjoy the hotel. But it's not just for sleeping. The Wild Animal Park, Sea World, and the Zoo are freeway close, and on site you'll find an 18-hole golf course (par 72), five lighted wind-sheltered tennis courts, a state-of-the-art, 5,500-square-foot health and fitness center, and heated outdoor pools. There are also whirlpool spas, steam rooms, and therapeutic massage opportunities.

Holiday Inn Express $$
1250 W. Valley Pkwy., Escondido
(760) 741–7117, (877) 717–5337

The Holiday Inn Express has 86 rooms, many with mini-kitchens, and offers two-room suites to give that extra elbow room often necessary when traveling. Rooms include microwave ovens and refrigerators. There's a free continental breakfast. There's a fitness room, heated pool, and spa. Golf packages can be arranged.

Pala Mesa Resort $–$$$
2001 Old Hwy. 395, Fallbrook
(760) 728–5881, (800) 722–4700
www.palamesa.com

About a 90-minute drive north of San Diego and just off I–15, you'll find one of the area's nicest resorts, where you can leave your hectic city life behind. Pala Mesa Resort has 133 oversized guests rooms and suites clustered in a two-story California ranch-style building that's nearly touching the golf course. Rooms come with well-stocked refrigerators, data ports, and large work desks.

This is the home to Golf University and features an impeccable golf course designed in a classic style that challenges players at every turn. There are four lighted tennis courts, a workout room, dining at the hotel's restaurant, and relaxing at the lounge. Be sure to read more about the golf facilities at this resort in our Golf chapter.

Quails Inn Hotel at Lake San Marcos Resort $$
1025 La Bonita Dr., Lake San Marcos
(760) 744–0120, (800) 447–6556
www.quailsinn.com

Quails Inn Hotel is conveniently located off California Highway 78 in San Marcos, yet once you're settled in one of the 140 over-sized rooms, you'll feel a million miles away from anything as routine as traffic and work. Situated on the shores of Lake San Marcos, Quails Inn Hotel offers a variety of accommodation options, from standard rooms to spacious lakeside accommodations. One- and two-room suites and cottages are available, some overlooking the lake. Room amenities include coffeemakers and hair dryers. The hotel is very popular with those who have retired and provides activities and social mixers for guests who love to mingle.

The hotel is pet friendly too, but there's a $10 per day extra charge when your pet stays with you.

Guests here have access to the 18-hole championship Lake San Marcos Country Club, known for its 6,515-yard, par 72 course. Its third hole is rated one of the toughest in San Diego County. There's also a challenging executive course for those who are perfecting their game. The facility includes a fitness room, canoes, walking and hiking trails, and three restaurants. It's minutes from San Marcos' "restaurant row" where the dining possibilities range from seafood to Mexican favorites (see our Restaurants chapter for more about the choices you'll find).

Radisson Suite Hotel $$
11520 W. Bernardo Ct., San Diego
(858) 451–6600, (800) 333–3333
www.radisson.com

With 174 suites offering beautiful amenities, this work and pleasure hotel, close to Rancho Bernardo's technology hub, is gaining in popularity.

Year after year the hotel receives the Radisson President's Award for quality. In addition to the complimentary full American buffet breakfast, there are complimentary evening cocktails at poolside in the cabana cafe.

For business travelers and for meetings, there's 800-number access, data ports, computer and printer options, and spacious work areas in each room. On the fun side, there's an exercise room, heated pool and spa, nearby golf, tennis, and walking and hiking trails.

The hotel is about 20 minutes from the Wild Animal Park and a half-hour from the mountain hamlet of Julian.

Super 8 Motel $
528 W. Washington Ave., Escondido
(760) 747–3711, (800) 800–8000

Whether you're on a travel budget or just like the convenience of Super 8 motels, this Escondido location is a good choice. The hotel is near the Wild Animal Park, close to the corporate centers of Rancho Bernardo, and blocks from the freeways. This Super 8 is a 75-room hotel that offers AAA and senior discounts. Of course, there's no restaurant on site, but there is a complimentary continental breakfast and guest laundry facility. You'll find all your favorite fast-food restaurants within walking distance; more upscale dining is just minutes by car.

Travelodge $
16929 W. Bernardo Dr., San Diego
(858) 487–0445, (800) 578–7878
www.travelodge.com

This is a thrifty, popular choice for those who are in Rancho Bernardo for business and pleasure (kids stay free with a paying adult). The hotel is freeway convenient. This hotel offers free continental breakfast (there's a restaurant close by) and free cable and HBO in all rooms. Senior discounts are available.

Welk Resort Center $–$$$
8860 Lawrence Welk Dr., Escondido
(760) 749–3000, (800) 932–9355
www.welkresort.com

Welcome to this golfer heaven. Many people select this hotel as a destination spot for that reason alone. Companies and corporations use it for retreats and seminars and families love it for the outdoor attractions, including the golf, swimming, bik-

ing, and walking opportunities.

Pets are welcome here, but you need to know that you and Fluffy will be staying in a "smoking" room. There's a $50 fee, with $25 refundable to you if your stay is "accident" free.

Located in North County Inland, about 45 minutes from downtown San Diego off I–15 and 10 minutes from the city of Escondido, the resort is situated on 600 beautiful acres. There are 132 rooms and suites, many right on the greens. There's a pool, spa, beauty facilities, and a workout room too.

East County

Best Western Continental Inn $
650 N. Mollison, El Cajon
(619) 442–0601, (800) 882–3781
www.bestwestern.com

This AAA, triple-diamond rated hotel makes you feel comfortable. It's a good choice for families who want to stay near the San Diego freeway or who are coming to visit San Diego State University. Golfing buffs choose it since it's close to the East County and San Diego courses. Some suites have hot tubs; some have kitchenettes. There is a honeymoon suite, and there are meeting rooms, too.

Best Western Santee Lodge $
10726 Woodside Ave., Santee
(619) 449–2626, (800) 780–7234
www.bestwestern.com

As with other Best Westerns, this hotel offers good, basic hotel service. There are 46 rooms, a small pool, and you can find restaurants, including the mandatory fast-food kind, nearby.

Comfort Inn-La Mesa $
8000 Parkway Dr., La Mesa
(619) 696–7747, (800) 228–5150

Whether you're just passing through or stopping to sample some of East County's attractions, you'll find the Comfort Inn always clean and hospitable. There's a small pool, and pets are welcome (with a refundable deposit). There are 127 rooms and lower rates are available for weekly stays.

Insiders' Tip

Are you going to visit the area during one of the major holidays? Plan ahead and make your reservations early, especially if you have your heart set on staying right at the beach

Days Inn La Mesa Suites $
7475 El Cajon Blvd., La Mesa
(619) 697–9005, (800) 329–7466

This clean, comfortable, and affordable place is the right fit for travelers who enjoy a suite, rather than a single room. Some suites have mini-kitchens. It's conveniently situated off I-8 and close to San Diego State University. There are restaurants nearby.

Holiday Inn Express-La Mesa $
9550 Murray Dr., La Mesa
(619) 466–0200, (800) 468–4329

With 78 spacious standard rooms and two-room suites, the Holiday Inn Express provides a lot for your money. There's no extra charge for children who stay with adults. The location is convenient to downtown La Mesa, the "Q" (Qualcomm Stadium), and San Diego State University.

The hotel has a pool and a whirlpool and offers a free complimentary breakfast. Ask about the weekly and monthly discounts for those who are staying in East County more than a few days.

Julian Lodge $–$$
2720 C St., Julian
(760) 765–1420, (800) 542–1420

In the heart of this quaint, somewhat touristy village loaded with antiques shops and tempting cafes, the Julian Lodge is a wonderful getaway place. If you're planning to visit during any of the holidays, especially the December ones when there may be snow in Julian, make reservations well ahead, since the Lodge has

only 23 rooms. There's dining and shopping all around the hotel and biking and hiking trails just minutes from the hotel's front door. Breakfast is included in the rate.

La Casa Del Zorro Desert Resort $$
3845 Yaqui Pass Rd., Borrego Springs
(760) 767–5323, (800) 824–1884
www.lacasadelzorro.com

This is one of the jewels of East County. La Casa Del Zorro is a four-star, four-diamond desert resort. Some of the casitas have private swimming pools and some have baby grand pianos. (Be sure to read about this resort in our Spas and Resorts chapter and about the location in our Parks and Recreation chapters.)

Located in the Anza-Borrego Desert State Park, it offers numerous outdoor possibilities from hiking to sunbathing. The hotel is about two hours from San Diego and features 77 two- and three-bedroom casitas; most include fireplaces and individual patios. Pets are welcome here with some restrictions: There's a $100 refundable cleaning fee and an extra $50 per day, per pet, fee. There are only two casitas that are designated for pets and their people, and they are available for smokers and nonsmokers.

You can dine in the hotel's restaurant and get a desert sunset for the asking—check out the stargazing—that's free too. You can sip iced tea or soda (or a more grown-up choice) in the lounge.

The hotel is popular throughout the dry, warm winter months and especially in the spring when the desert bursts with flowers. If you're planning a March or April visit, make reservations ahead of time.

Motel 6 $
550 Montrose Ct., El Cajon
(619) 588–6100, (800) 466–8356
7621 Alvarado Rd., La Mesa
(619) 464–7151, (800) 466–8356

Like other Motel 6's throughout the country, the East County motels are clean and functional. Kids, accompanying an adult, stay free. There are various discounts available, including ones for AARP members.

If you're going to spend your time here visiting the local attractions or doing business, then it's tough to go wrong with the basics, and Motel 6 has them down pat. As with other Motel 6 hotels, your pet is welcome in these two facilities.

Palm Canyon Resort $–$$
221 Palm Canyon Dr., Borrego Springs
(760) 767–5341, (800) 242–0044
www.pcresort.com

Spacious grounds with oodles of hiking, biking, walking, and sunset watching possibilities, this is a perfect choice for a getaway. The hotel has 60 rooms, all have refrigerators and coffeemakers. The adjacent RV park has 132 spaces. Guests at both places have access to the fitness center, pool, and restaurant. The 14-acre complex is situated next to Anza-Borrego State Park, so if you're planning to come to the desert to see Mother Nature's spring flower show, make plans early. All hotels fill up quickly between November and May. Note that there's a three-day notice required on all canceled reservations.

Pine Hills Lodge $–$$
2960 La Posada Way, Julian
(760) 765–1100
www.pinehillslodge.com

An intimate, 18-room hotel that's rustic and attractive, the lodge also serves as Julian's dinner theater. A stay here is popular with those who want to escape from hectic San Diego living and breathe in pine-filled mountain air. This hotel isn't for every traveler. If you need a TV in your room, find another place to stay, since the Pine Hills Lodge doesn't have them. But it does have plays staged in its dining room on weekend nights and offers a theater and overnight stay package for $150 per couple. The dinner is a country-style buffet with barbecued ribs. Some cabins have fireplaces or wood-burning stoves. All are comfy, with down comforters on the beds and wood and wrought iron furnishings that suit the location.

Travelodge El Cajon $
471 Magnolia, El Cajon
(619) 447–3999, (800) 578–7878
www.travelodge.com

This is a thrifty, popular choice of hotel for those who visit the East County. The hotel has 47 rooms and allows pets in some of the rooms. There's a small pool and free cable and HBO in all rooms. There's a free complimentary continental breakfast and there's dining nearby.

South Bay

Holiday Inn Express $
4450 Otay Valley Rd., Chula Vista
(619) 422–2600, (800) 628–2611

For freeway convenience, sparkling clean rooms and proximity to South Bay's attractions, the Holiday Inn Express can't be beat. Furnished in Spanish-southwestern style, the 118 spacious and beautiful rooms make you feel like you're in a bed-and-breakfast inn. A complimentary continental breakfast only reinforces that notion. The inn is located just west of I-805.

Beaches are a 15-minute drive from the inn, but what might impress the kids even more is the fact that Knott's Soak City, with its wave pools and water slides, is just a five-minute drive away. We describe it in detail in our Attractions chapter.

La Quinta Inn $
150 Bonita Rd., Chula Vista
(619) 691–1211, (800) 687–6667

The La Quinta Inn in Chula Vista maintains the high standard that the chain has set nationwide. You can choose from 142 rooms with either a king-size bed or two doubles. The spacious rooms, furnished in contemporary style, offer spacious comfort as well as closeness to all of South Bay's attractions.

When you pry open those sleepy eyes, La Quinta's First Light breakfast is ready for you in the lobby: cereals, fresh fruit, pastries, bagels, juice, and coffee. Or if a Grand Slam is more your style, take a short walk next door to Denny's. Then it's back to the inn for a dip in the refreshing pool. Small pets are welcome here.

Red Lion $
700 National City Blvd., National City
(619) 336–1100

For the business traveler or visitors who simply like to spread out, the Red Lion is an exceptional bargain. It is located just east of I-5 near the border. Each of the hotel's 168 suites has either a city or a bay view. Modern and comfortable, all suites are equipped with computer modems, and all have Internet access.

Laundry facilities are available for guests, as is a complimentary continental breakfast. Or if you're in the mood to lounge around your suite, choose from a full room service menu. Red Lion's central location makes access to beaches and to Mexico just an easy drive. If your favorite family pet does not reach your knees, it's welcome here for a $25 refundable deposit.

Ramada Inn South Bay $
91 Bonita Rd., Chula Vista
(619) 425–9999, (800) 272–6232

If you're visiting family or friends in either Chula Vista or Bonita, you can't go wrong with the Ramada Inn. Located right on the border between the two communities, it's only a few minutes' drive to everything—shopping, golf, and the beach.

Its 97 rooms are comfortable and clean, and a bonus is the casual Love's Restaurant on the premises. It's open for breakfast, lunch, and dinner. Laundry facilities are available on site, and a whirlpool spa awaits your aching bones at the end of a long day.

Seacoast Inn $–$$
800 Seacoast Dr., Imperial Beach
(619) 424–5183, (800) 732–2627

Affordable accommodations right on the sand are hard to find in San Diego County, but the Seacoast Inn is just the ticket. The inn's 24 rooms on two floors either have a beach view or look out over the inviting pool and courtyard. If you

have a large group or are planning a private function, ask about the third floor Penthouse Suite. Rooms have either a king-size bed or two doubles; some have kitchens and dens and private beach decks. Rates range from $55 to $105, depending on the type of room you choose. Naturally, those on the second floor with kitchens, dens, and spectacular ocean views cost the most. There's no restaurant, but most rooms have some kind of kitchen facilities and there are several good restaurants nearby. Pets are allowed and there's no pet deposit. But you do have to pay for any damage.

The Imperial Beach Pier is just steps away for romantic moonlight strolls or to satisfy fishing enthusiasts. This is the perfect place to stay if you're planning to attend the Imperial Beach Sand Castle Contest (described in our Annual Events chapter), so make your reservations early.

Travelodge $
394 Broadway, Chula Vista
(619) 420–6600, (800) 447–8416
www.travelodge.com

Like Travelodges across the country, this one will feel familiar. Its 80 rooms have few bells and whistles, but are dependably clean and comfortable. And if Mexico is high on your agenda, you're in the right place. The international border is less than a 10-minute drive from the motel.

If you are a business person, you'll be happy to know there are computer modems in each room. Complimentary coffee is offered every morning, and although there is no restaurant on site, many fine restaurants are within a few blocks.

Bed-and-Breakfast Inns

San Diego County
North County Coastal
North County Inland
East County

Bed-and-breakfast inns in the San Diego region have a flavor that's strictly Southern California. Each of the bed and breakfast inns has an easygoing ambiance that makes you long to check in and dread saying good-bye. These inns are special, warm, restful, and inviting. They've been chosen because we'd enjoy revisiting them or would recommend them to our closest friends.

These are not the bare-bones accommodations found in some parts of Europe. You know the places: one bath down the hall, "take a number please," and a pint-sized sleeping room where if you sneeze your next door neighbor might respond, "Bless you."

All of the rooms at the bed-and-breakfast inns described in the chapter have private baths, unless otherwise noted. Most have enticing, easy-to-get-to locations, which also happen to be some of our favorites places in San Diego County.

For instance the Victoria Rock Bed and Breakfast Inn, in the East County mountain community of Alpine, receives a few inches of snow each winter. It's an especially sweet spot for a winter-weekend getaway, more so if you plan to drive the extra 20 minutes to the mountains to walk, frolic, or hike in the snow.

The Leucadian Inn by the Sea, in North County Coastal, is so close to the Pacific that you're surrounded with ocean breezes—just the right prescription for even the most ragged spirit. The town that Insiders call Leucadia is actually part of the city of Encinitas. Everything you could want for a relaxing weekend is there and all within walking distance. The town will remind you of a '50s beach and delight you with its many tiny hangouts where you can munch inexpensive fish tacos and its swank restaurants that also offer four-course dinners.

As you look over our listings, keep in mind that it's wise to call and double-check rates and availability of rooms. All of the bed-and-breakfast inns encourage reservations. If you want to book for a holiday, say Christmas or Valentine's Day, we recommend you do so months ahead so you won't be disappointed. Unless otherwise noted, the inns we've included all accept MasterCard, Visa, or cash, but do not accept indoor smoking or pets. Assume too, that children are discouraged, unless we tell you otherwise.

Some of the bed-and-breakfast inns featured here serve a continental breakfast, with plump muffins and fresh juice, along with coffees and teas. It's simple but enough. Others have a full European-style (sometimes called gourmet) breakfast. These are the breakfast feasts of which fantasies are made, that spoil you to the bone while you're enjoying every minute of munching. Some of the inns have in-room eating options too—nice if you'd prefer to have a romantic breakfast on the balcony or in your room. Our entries will tell you what to expect.

In all of the bed-and-breakfast inns we've featured there is a comfortable sitting room,

Insiders' Tip

If you will be arriving late in the day and don't know the area, check the Restaurants chapter for places to eat near your bed-and-breakfast inn. Ask the bed-and-breakfast innkeeper for recommendations too.

Many popular bed-and-breakfast inns are a short distance from a relaxing stroll on the beach.
PHOTO: BOB YARBROUGH, COURTESY OF THE SAN DIEGO CONVENTION AND VISITORS BUREAU

parlor, or library. You may find overstuffed chairs loaded with pillows, lots of reading material, perhaps a puzzle in progress or a stack of board games, maybe a player piano, a decanter of sherry, and some crackers and maybe—but not always—a television. (Some inns only have a television in the main part of the house, but not in individual bedrooms; some don't have televisions at all.)

Even when the bed-and-breakfast inn's parlor is deliciously old-fashioned, it's not unusual to find the rooms decorated in anything from African safari themes to South Seas motifs. Most are typically furnished with antiques and fresh flowers, lovely furnishings, and plump comforters. The morning paper will probably be placed by your door as might a rose or decanter of coffee. Some of the inns have lovingly-placed extras in each of the rooms such as bowls of local fruit or plates of homemade cookies to nourish your inner child.

If you haven't tried a bed-and-breakfast inn and need a few days off or want to stay somewhere unique when you're visiting San Diego, these entries will help you design the perfect getaway.

Price Code

Our prices indicate a one-night double occupancy at high-season rates.

$	Less than $65
$$	$66 to $95
$$$	$96 to $140
$$$$	$141 to $200
$$$$$	More than $200

San Diego County

Balboa Park Inn $$$–$$$$
3402 Park Blvd., San Diego
(619) 298–0823, (800) 938–8181
www.balboaparkinn.com

Does Paris in the '30s appeal to you? What does The Noveau Ritz conjure in your imagination? These are the names of just two of the Balboa Park Inn's 26 uniquely decorated luxury rooms. Host Edward Wilcox welcomes you to the complex of four Spanish colonial buildings that contain a novel assortment of themed rooms and suites. Paris in the '30s has a romantic wood-burning fireplace and a dreamy canopy bed. The Noveau Ritz is decorated in black, gold, and burgundy art deco, with lots of mirrors, a separate kitchen, and a private door to the sun terrace.

Nestled in a quiet residential neighborhood on the north edge of Balboa Park, the inn is a short walk away from the San Diego Zoo, museums, shops, restaurants, and the Old Globe Theatre. And it's just a few minutes' drive from downtown and the Gaslamp Quarter. Fresh fruit, juice, warm croissants, cinnamon buns, and muffins are standard breakfast fare served either in your room or suite, on the sun terrace, or in the peaceful courtyard.

This is one of the rare bed-and-breakfast inns that allows smoking in some of its rooms and also welcomes children. In fact, kids younger than 12 stay free when sharing accommodations with their parents. Cancellations must be made seven days in advance of your scheduled stay.

The Bed & Breakfast Inn at La Jolla
$$$–$$$$$
7753 Draper Ave., La Jolla
(858) 456–2066
www.innlajolla.com

Here is a rare opportunity to stay in an architectural gem that is also a registered San Diego Historical Site. Designed by noted architect Irving Gill, the house was built in 1913 and is one of Gill's finest examples of Cubist-style architecture. The lush, original gardens were planned by renowned horticulturist Kate Session, who was also responsible for planting many of the gardens in Balboa Park.

Get ready to be pampered. Fireplaces and ocean views are available in many of the nine guest rooms in the main house and six in the annex. Fresh fruit, flowers, a glass of sherry, and a terry robe await you upon check-in, and wine and cheese are served as an aperitif every evening. A gourmet breakfast is yours to enjoy in the dining room, on the patio or sun deck, or in your room.

Each room is decorated differently, from the nautically themed Pacific View Room to the Oriental-style Windansea Room, with its rattan furniture. If a splurge is in order, try the Irving Gill Penthouse, a spacious suite at the tip of the house with an incomparable view of the Pacific Ocean.

Elsbree House $$$
5054 Narragansett Ave., Central San Diego
(619) 226–4133
www.oceanbeach-online.com/b&b,
www.bbinob.com

If you're craving a vacation at the beach but still want the homey atmosphere of a bed-and-breakfast inn, Elsbree House is the solution. This Cape Cod house is just 500 feet from the Ocean Beach Pier and public beach and only 2 blocks from the OB business district, with its restaurants and antiques shops.

Innkeepers Katie and Phil Elsbree have created a modern escape to paradise. The six rooms are decorated in country English style. Each has a private entrance and a balcony or patio all to itself, where you can relax with a book or write your own great American novel. In the morning, enjoy a self-serve continental breakfast of homemade bread and muffins, granola, cereal, fruit, and yogurt in the dining room. At sunset, stroll along Sunset Cliffs for a panoramic view of the Pacific Ocean.

The Elsbrees also rent out a three-bedroom condo right by the beach. It can be separated into smaller units. The condo has a full kitchen, big porch, and washer and dryer. Children are welcome, but not

Insiders' Tip

A large number of bed-and-breakfast inns have Web sites where you can pull up information as well as photos of the rooms. For an overview and links, check out www.bbonline.com.

pets. The price ranges from $900 to $1,600 for a week, depending on the number of people and time of year. Ask the Elsbrees, and they'll reveal the secret of Elsbree House: It's the best place to kiss in Southern California.

Heritage Park Bed & Breakfast Inn
$$$–$$$$
2470 Heritage Park Row, San Diego
(619) 299–6832, (800) 995–2470
www.heritageparkinn.com

If you happened to catch a recent issue of *Country Inns Magazine*, you may already know that Heritage Park Inn is San Diego's highest-rated bed-and-breakfast inn. Step across the threshold and you'll understand why. This magnificent 1889 Queen Anne mansion has twelve antiques-filled guest rooms, featuring feather beds, clawfoot tubs, whirlpools, and robes so fluffy you'll loathe to take them off.

Heritage Park is the centerpiece of a collection of Victorian mansions located on a hill above historic Old Town, one of San Diego's favorite visitors' destinations. Peace and quiet are the norm, yet the bustle of shops, restaurants, and the theater are just steps away. It's a great place for a family vacation because of its proximity to Old Town, and children are welcome here. Since 1992 owners Nancy and Charles Helsper have delighted their guests with a full candlelight breakfast, as well as afternoon tea on the veranda. Should you opt for an evening in, classic films are shown nightly in the sitting room.

The Drawing Room, a professionally designed and decorated room, is a romantic fantasy come true, complete with soft colors, lighting, and fabrics and a whirlpool for two. It's so romantic it practically whispers in your ear.

Keating House $$$
2331 Second Ave., San Diego
(619) 239–8585, (800) 995–8644
www.keatinghouse.com

Immerse yourself in 19th-century Victorian luxury. Keating House, a beautifully restored Victorian home (and a San Diego Historical Site), sits proudly in a residential neighborhood full of elegant homes.

Owner Larry Vlassoff has tastefully re-created the splendor of the Victorian era in each of the six rooms in the main house and three in the guest cottage.

A full gourmet breakfast is served every morning in the dining room, and a cozy parlor offers the perfect setting for conversation or the opportunity to curl up in front of the fireplace with a favorite book. Lush tropical grounds surround the house, and several seating areas in the garden and on the front porch allow visitors to drink in the sweet aroma of roses and jasmine and the vibrant colors of bougainvillea, orchids, and jacaranda.

Close to downtown, Hillcrest, and Balboa Park, Keating House is ideally located for the visitor seeking quiet rejuvenation combined with lots of activities.

San Diego Yacht & Breakfast $$$$–$$$$$
Marina Cortez, Harbor Island, San Diego
(619) 297–9484, (800) 922–4836
www.yachtdo.com

Many bed-and-breakfast inns are located near the water, but few can say they're on the water. Picture drifting off to the land of nod while being gently rocked by the tide, and waking up to the glorious sun, water, blue sky, and a full gourmet breakfast. Choose from a luxury yacht, or a floating dockside villa, with space for two to eight guests.

Insiders' Tip
Most bed-and-breakfast inns have a more restrictive cancellation policy than other accommodations. When making reservations ask about the cancellation policy. Sometimes there may be a charge for canceled reservations.

Each guest receives a voucher for a full breakfast at the Marina deli, along with discount coupons for dinner. Or, should the mood strike you, your hosts will arrange to have dinner delivered for a romantic evening on the fantail of your boat. Spacious staterooms have private baths, and all boats have a fully stocked galley, TVs, VCRs, and telephones. Bring the kids along because there are plenty of activities to keep everyone occupied. If you crave water activities, they have a rowboat, paddleboat, and a Boston whaler available. Whale-watching cruises can be arranged.

North County Coastal

The Cardiff-by-the-Sea Lodge $$$–$$$$$
142 Chesterfield Ave., Cardiff
(760) 944–6474
www.cardifflodge.com

You may have read about this bed-and-breakfast inn in *Sunset* magazine, seen it as a prize on *Wheel of Fortune* or heard Insiders talking about it. Overlooking the Pacific in the beach town of Cardiff, this sparkling clean and luxurious inn offers lush gardens and an open-pit fire ring that is high on the rooftop. Imagine roasting marshmallows as you watch the sun shimmering in the west. Yummy, to say the least. These attributes are tough to top.

Owned by Jeannette and James Statser, long-time Insiders themselves, the inn's interior is graced with original art and handcrafted touches. The Southwest Room, for instance, looks like it's straight out of New Mexico with hues of tan, pale pink, and the palest of blues. The crowning glory is the Sweetheart Room and it's Jim's favorite too. Here you'll find hearts everywhere, from the ceiling to the heart-shaped tub for two. Breakfast is simple and good and all homemade—Jim's the chef—with muffins, fruit, coffees, and teas.

All rooms are equipped with queen beds, custom furnishings, oversized baths and showers. There are 17 rooms and a roof garden that's popular for weddings and receptions. Rates here go up during holiday weekends, and you can also expect to pay more for luxury suites or a spectacular view.

Leucadia Inn by the Sea $$–$$$
960 N. Highway 101, Leucadia section of Encinitas
(760) 942–1668, (800) 344–1668

Do whimsical birds, flower leis, and a palm tree right in your room give you a hint that this inn is a bit on the unique side? If so, you're right and the Leucadia Inn by the Sea is making waves. All the rooms have a theme, from the Tropical room (the one mentioned above and the most requested) to the New Orleans suite.

This seaside inn is within walking distance of the Coaster station and a block from the beach. The breakfast package includes a $6.00 certificate at your choice of local eateries.

Pelican Cove Bed and Breakfast Inn $$–$$$$
320 Walnut Ave., Carlsbad
(760) 434–5995, (888) 753–2683

Only 200 yards from the Pacific, the Inn is strolling distance from the antiques shops and fine eateries in the village area of Carlsbad. (If you love to antique shop, be sure to read our Shopping chapter for tips on things to do in Carlsbad.) That would make it nice. But what makes this inn special is the TLC poured on by owners Kris and Nancy Nayudu and the soft luxury and romance of the rooms.

There are only eight of them in this small inn, but each one comes with a fireplace, television, and European (make that fat and fluffy) bedding that surrounds you like a huge hug. Some rooms have spa tubs. The Balboa, with twin beds, is done in lavender florals and green stripes. The Del Mar, an Insiders' favorite, is done in tones of white; staying in this room feels rather like walking in the foam from ocean waves. As a matter of fact the carpet color is called sea foam green. Unlike some other bed-and-breakfast inns, Pelican Cove isn't a frou-frou antiques-strewn establishment. The decor is inviting and uncluttered.

The grounds are studded with flower gardens and trees. There's a sun porch and garden for lounging. The innkeepers make beach chairs, towels, and picnic baskets available for those who can break away from the inn for a day on the beach.

The inn "draws the nicest people," says innkeeper Nancy. "Sometimes they bring us presents." While gifts are not required, compliments are always forthcoming when breakfast is served. "We have a different, hot entree that's included in the full breakfast everyday." On the day one Insider visited the inn, the savory menu included a blended ham and asparagus egg dish, plump blueberry-studded and crunchy nut muffins, scrumptious fruits, and coffee that rivaled that of the best coffeehouse in town.

If that isn't enough, the inn is wheelchair friendly. Be aware that rooms cost more over holiday weekends, so be sure to ask when you call for reservations. There's courtesy pickup at the Amtrak station and Palomar airport. If you're arriving by Coaster, a pickup might be arranged. Ask when you call for reservations. FYI: the Coaster station is about ½ mile north of the inn.

North County Inland

Fallbrook Country Inn $$
1425 S. Mission Rd., Fallbrook
(760) 728-1114
www.pinnaclehotelsusa.com

Popular as a getaway, the Fallbrook Country Inn has a romantic side since it specializes in wedding accommodations. In addition to the graciously appointed bridal suite, the inn offers 28 country-style rooms for family and friends. The garden, a riot of cascading annuals, makes a perfect setting for the ceremony.

All rooms have king- or queen-size beds, cable and color television, spacious baths, and patios. Some of the rooms have kitchenettes.

The inn offers mid-week discounts as well as weekly and monthly rates that are seductive to Canadian visitors (getting away from THAT winter) and Arizonans (cooling off in Fallbrook during THAT summer). Maybe they'll appeal to you too.

You can spend your days lounging pool side, visiting the antiques stores that are aplenty in Fallbrook, or checking out the art galleries and handcrafted jewelry stores that dot the main street of Fallbrook.

East County

Butterfield Bed & Breakfast $$$–$$$$
2284 Sunset Dr., Julian
(760) 765-2179, (800) 397-4262
www.butterfieldbandb.com

Beneath majestic pine and oak trees on a serene hillside that's just footsteps from the historic town of Julian, is the comfortable, inviting Butterfield Bed & Breakfast.

Breakfast is a grand affair with country gourmet served in the Garden Gazebo in the summer and by the crackling hearth when winter sets in.

There are five rooms at the inn. All have televisions, and three have fireplaces. One Insider will not stay at the Butterfield unless she can sleep in the Rosebud Cottage. It's decorated in country decor with a potbelly stove, sitting area, knotty pine ceilings, and a world away from reality.

Orchard Hill Country Inn $$$$$
2502 Washington St., Julian
(760) 765-1700, (800) 716-7242
www.orchardhill.com

Far more than a B&B, Orchard Inn has 22 rooms with deluxe amenities, including a split of wine, Belgian chocolates, and fragrant toiletries. Some rooms have

The award-winning Orchard Hill Country Inn is one of many small inns and B&B's tucked in the mountains around Julian. PHOTO: COURTESY OF THE SAN DIEGO NORTH CONVENTION & VISITORS BUREAU

whirlpool tubs, others have fireplaces, and all have TVs and VCRs (there's a tape library in the main lodge). The rooms have been featured in many decorating magazines. The sophisticated restaurant serves breakfast and afternoon hors d'oeuvres daily and fantastic dinners on Wednesday and Saturday nights.

Rockin' A Bed and Breakfast $$$$
1531 Orchard Ln., Julian
(760) 765–2820
www.julianbnb.com

Just a "piece up the road" from the historical town of Julian, the Rockin' A Bed and Breakfast offers two country-style accommodations. The horse and deer rooms have unique personalities, with private baths and fireplaces. To make a stay extra restful, all rooms feature European-style feather-filled body pillows covered with cuddly comforters. In the parlor and den there's a fireplace, and the rooms open onto a spacious wood deck. Full ranch breakfasts are delivered to the guests'

rooms. Breakfast is a production, real country-style cooking.

Wandering around the grounds is part of the Rockin' A experience. There's a small pond, magnificent oak grove, and an orchard, where you can eat the fruit (in season) straight from the trees. After that strenuous morning you could relax on the deck with Julian apple pie and a cup of hot or cold cider. The Rockin' A is a five-minute drive to Julian's quaint restaurants and shops. After dinner at one of Julian's cafes, you can return to the Rockin' A, sit outdoors, and count shooting stars. Now that's relaxing.

Victoria Rock Bed and Breakfast Inn $$
2952 Victoria Dr., Alpine
(619) 659–5967
www.victoria-rock-bb.com

This bed-and-breakfast inn is small (just four rooms) and Insiders believe that's what makes it inviting—along with the fact that it's in the mountains and off the beaten path. The Victoria Rock Bed and Breakfast

Inn, owned by Darrel and Helga Daliber, is not to be missed if you love staying in intimate inns.

The inn has recently seen major renovations and the rooms are lovely, bright, and fresh. One Insider says his favorite has to be the South Seas room with a strong nautical theme. The room has a full bath as well as an Enchanted Grotto Shower. That's Victoria Rock talk for an 8-foot waterfall/shower.

Another Insider says her favorite place to stay at this inn is the Antique room. It features an oversized four-poster bed, delightful Victorian furnishings, and an early-20th-century ambiance.

Breakfast is hearty and scrumptious. On the day one Insider stayed at the inn, breakfast was the specialty of the house, southwest style eggs Benedict. "This recipe was once a secret but that's not so now since

so many guests have asked for my recipe," says Darrel. Open year-round, smart guests book well ahead for holidays and longer-than-weekend stays.

Insiders' Tip
Some bed-and-breakfast inns have a resident dog or cat. If you're allergic to animals or prefer to stay in an animal-free environment, ask about pets when making reservations.

Spas and Resorts

Go ahead, say the names: La Costa, Cal-a-Vie, the Golden Door. It's impossible to do so without a sigh. These resorts are known here and throughout the world as part of what draws travelers to our region.

Whether you're living here or visiting, the spas and resorts of the San Diego region are diverse, exciting, and accessible. The spas are easy to get to and many are just a short drive from downtown San Diego.

Here in San Diego, some hotels are called resorts and some resorts have fitness and beauty spas on the grounds. In this chapter we've only included those spas and resorts that have special health, beauty, recreation, or relaxation programs and whose main thrust is to nurture the mind and body. These are not places to leave your belongings while you go out sightseeing; they're destinations in themselves—places where time slows, relaxation begins, tensions melt, and you leave your worries behind.

And they are the cream of the crop. Here are the places we'd like to revisit or would suggest to a best friend. In fact, San Diego has some of the most prestigious spas and resorts in the world. If you're looking to relax, rethink fitness goals, revitalize your spirit and play some sports, read on. The spas and resorts in this chapter will give you plenty of opportunities.

The first thing you may notice is that they're all different. Some, like the Golden Door, cater to women (although they do have a few weeks a year when men are invited). Others have incomparable spa and beauty facilities, but do not offer separate healthful or calorie-conscious meals. Some of the spas and resorts included in this chapter have day-spa packages where you can have all the fitness classes and pampering you want and then go back home or to your hotel at day's end.

We've tried to give you an idea about current prices. You may note that we have not used the usual dollar-sign price keys with these entries. This is because some spas charge by the week, others by the day; some include spa services in their prices and some do not. Many offer a multitude of packages, each different and difficult to compare. Nevertheless we've included the charges for typical, popular packages or lodging options, so you can decide which ones are likely to fall within your budget. For even more detailed information, you may want to call the spas to get their brochures and to be put on their mailing lists for upcoming spa-related events. (You might even receive a discount coupon that could make your spa visit even more delicious.)

Be aware that sometimes spas offer two-for-one specials and group discounts (in case everyone in your office or investment club wants to come too). A few of the spas have seasonal packages and there are discounts available. However, here in San Diego it's resort time 365 days a year so don't expect to save a lot by visiting in an off season.

Cal-a-Vie
2249 Somerset Rd., Vista
(760) 945–2055, (866) 772–4283
www.calavie.com

Cal-a-Vie, nestled away in North County Inland, is a sweet refuge from the stresses and strains of modern living. With only 24 guests, and a staff that outnumbers guests, the privacy and pampering are beyond compare. The four-star cuisine is an adaptation of classical gourmet foods, minus the fats. The emphasis is on flavor and the exquisite art of presentation.

The fitness course, tailored for each guest, is invigorating. You'll find classes from aerobics and body shaping to pool activities and stretching. There's a long morning and afternoon hike within the 125-acre landscaped compound. Even the most indulgent guests feel spoiled by soothing European therapies such as massage, body scrubbing, and aromatherapy. A favorite is the seaweed wrap said to promote detoxification and replenish nutrients in the skin.

You'd think all this would be enough, but that's not so. The main objective of Cal-a-Vie is to re-educate guests about the fundamentals of a healthier life style. Evening lectures cover topics such as fitness, nutrition, safe and sane weight loss, and stress management. There's also a class on cooking low-fat, highly delicious food.

Cal-a-Vie has women-only and coed sessions. All sessions begin on Sunday afternoon and end the following Sunday morning. There's complimentary transportation from Lindbergh Field.

The spa offers package plans. The European Plan includes meals, accommodations, all therapeutic treatments, and fitness classes for about $5,395 a week. The California Plan includes meals, accommodations, all fitness classes, and six body treatments for just less than $5,000.

Four Seasons Resort Aviara
7100 Four Seasons Pt., Carlsbad
(760) 603–6800, (800) 332–3442
www.fourseasons.com/aviara

About 40 minutes north of downtown San Diego, just off I-5 at the La Costa Boulevard exit, that spa and resort feeling hits. You feel it the minute you pull into the winding drive and make it up the incline to the white Spanish colonial–style building atop the hill. If you love Four Seasons quality, you'll be gaga over this gem.

The resort features 329 generously sized guest rooms and suites, with prices ranging from $395 for a moderate room to $4,200 for the Presidential Suite with three bedrooms and a view that will knock your socks off. Each upper-story room opens onto a private balcony; ground-level rooms have private, landscaped terraces. All feature the famous Four Seasons bed that movie stars and many regular folks say is the best in the universe.

The grounds are lush, and the adjacent golf course, designed by Arnold Palmer, has been featured in several golf magazines. (See our Golf chapter for the scoop on this aspect of Aviara.) There is a rose garden where plenty of couples have said "I do."

The spa and fitness center are open to registered guests only, so Insiders sometimes register for a night to get that luxurious pampering. Newly renovated and expanded, the spa has 20 indoor treatment rooms where you can enjoy a massage, scrub, or wrap. For a different perspective, try a massage in one of the five outdoor cabanas. One Insider says to be sure to try the clary sage body gommage (50 minutes cost $120) for a gentle loofa experience. Another prefers the avocado body wrap that costs $150 for 50 minutes.

The hair salon is operated by the internationally known stylist Jose Eber. If you'd like to have Mr. Eber coif your hair, make plans ahead of time.

The fitness center is beyond high-tech: Tiny televisions are attached to the treadmills and cardio machines so you won't lose track of CNN while you're racking up the miles.

When fitness and pampering are complete, you can take a dip in one of the resort's two pools, have a healthful and beautiful lunch poolside or in one of the private cabanas, then lounge away the afternoon in the library. "A glass of sherry?" the food server may suggest.

This really is a family place too, with a special Kids for All Seasons program offered during weekends, summer months, traditional school breaks, and holidays.

Guests await their soothing treatments in the peaceful solarium at the Four Seasons Resort Aviara Spa.
PHOTO: COURTESY OF THE FOUR SEASONS RESORT AVIARA

There are supervised outdoor activities like nature hikes and games set around an authentic outdoor teepee, and indoor play in a playroom that features a LEGO station and big-screen TV. Kids for All Seasons is complimentary for kids 4 to 12. Guests pay for the lunches. Children under 4 must be accompanied by a parent. The concierge can also arrange babysitting. Staff members are CPR-certified.

Golden Door
777 Deer Springs Rd., San Marcos
(760) 744–5777, (800) 424–0777
www.goldendoor.com

Town & Country magazine pretty well sums up this spa: "The Golden Door is everything everyone has always said it is—and much, much more."

The Golden Door has been rated as America's number-one spa by numerous spa guides and travel books. If you need some extra TLC and can afford the exclusive pampering, then pick up the phone and reserve your spot now at about $6,000 a week, slightly less in the winter months.

Packing for a stay at the Golden Door is simple because the spa provides everything. It suggests you bring personal basics (like toothbrush, aerobic and hiking shoes, swimsuit, and undergarments); the rest will be waiting for you.

Nestled in 350 acres, including orchards and gardens, the Golden Door provides plenty of room for hiking and other outdoor activities. The formal landscaping here was designed by the famed Takendo Arii. Among the resort's features are three guest lounges, a dining room, indoor and outdoor exercise studios, the Dragon Tree Gym, swimming pools, tennis courts, and plenty of graduated walking trails. Activities are geared to individual guests' requests according to their level of fitness, which is evaluated along with their range of motion, as staff create one-on-one

fitness plans. There's also a customized take-home training program.

The Beauty Court is where you'll find steam rooms, saunas, showers, Swiss hoses, a fan-shaped therapy pool, and sequestered rooms for body scrubs and lulling herbal wraps. There are fitness classes too, taught by well-qualified instructors. These are small classes, (only 39 guests attend the spa each week, and staff outnumber guests four to one) so everyone receives plenty of attention. The clientele include movers and shakers from around the planet and those you see on the big and little screen. In other words, The Golden Door is an exclusive hangout.

For most of the year this is a women-only spa, although there are couples' and mens' weeks. The menu is gourmet and healthful, providing an innovative cuisine that's low in sugar, sodium, and cholesterol yet rich in fiber and good taste. Evening programs might range from cooking demonstrations to lectures.

La Casa Del Zorro Desert Resort
3845 Yaqui Pass Rd., Borrego Springs
(760) 767–5323, (800) 824–1884
www.lacasadelzorro.com

As a relaxation spa, this resort is one of the best; however, you must remember it is in the desert. It does get hot. Fall, winter and spring may be the optimal times to visit. Nonetheless, some Insiders prefer the summer when they relish that dry, hot air and have lots of elbow room at the popular resort.

About two hours northeast of San Diego in East County, La Casa Del Zorro offers you unique surroundings: It's smack dab in the 600,000 acres of Anza-Borrego State Park. Positioned on 42 acres of natural landscape, lush gardens, and waterscapes, La Casa Del Zorro has 77 luxurious and spacious accommodations ranging from rooms and suites to casitas with one to four bedrooms. All rooms come with first-class amenities from coffeemakers and plush bathrobes to a morning newspaper and service bars.

Here in the desert, it's quiet. It can be really quiet at night. That's why this is some Insiders' favorite spot on earth. During the day, guests like to hike or bike the miles of specially designed trails. Afterwards they can watch sunsets the color of rainbow sherbet. At night, in this isolated spot, they can gaze at a sky overflowing with stars. Take along a simple astronomy guide and you'll enjoy your stay even more.

You won't find any specific fitness or beauty regimen here; rather you can choose your own healthy activities. There are six championship night-lit tennis courts and guided desert walking and bicycling tours. If you're a golfer you'll find a couple of courses within quick driving distance, but there's also a nine-hole putting green right on the grounds. The resort also offers shuffleboard, a life-size chess set, and a complete high-tech fitness center.

The resort's spa side is staffed with specialists who offer hair and nail services along with facials (a full facial is $65). You can include a Swedish, shiatsu, or sports massage in your resort package for $85 an hour. Services are a la carte. A casita (a 4-bedroom suite with pool) costs about $880 a night. A standard room is $225.

When you're tired of staring at those stars, there's nightlife at La Casa Del Zorro. At the Fox Den there are special events featuring jazz, blues, swing, and classic musical performances.

La Costa Resort and Spa
Costa Del Mar Rd., Carlsbad
(760) 438–9111, (800) 544–7483
www.lacosta.com

Thirty miles north of San Diego, minutes from I-5, is the 450-acre luxury resort of La Costa. Along with the two 18-hole championship golf courses, a 21-court racquet club, the award-winning restaurants and lounges, you have the Spa.

Covering more than 75,000 square feet, the La Costa Spa is one of the largest spas in North America. There are separate locker and spa facilities for men and women, and co-ed workout rooms providing the finest in weight and cardiovascular equipment. Supervised exercise classes challenge even the most fit.

Knowing the reputation of La Costa Resort and Spa, it's easy to put your health and beauty in the hands of these professionals. With the menu of services, most a la carte, even the most persnickety can find a health and beauty favorite. Be sure to book your treatments at least two weeks in advance of your stay.

Let's start with food: By arrangement you can have a personal consultation for health management, which includes an analysis of your present nutritional habits. You'll get handouts and printouts. Costs for nutritional services range from $99 to $175. If you're serious about turning over a new nutritional leaf, sign up for the supermarket and healthy-eating seminar.

The fitness programs include yoga, water aerobics, and aerobics combined with toning and resistance training. For $65 per 30-minute session, you can have a body-composition analysis and a personal consultation with an exercise physiologist. You can have the services of a personal trainer for a cost of $75 for 50 minutes.

If beauty and relaxation top your list, you'll be interested in the facials, which start at $110 for 50 minutes. Massages (reflexology to shiatzu) start at $110 for 80 minutes.

Ask about the special packages. The price for these is about $420 a night.

L'Auberge Resort and Spa
1540 Camino Del Mar, Del Mar
(858) 259–1515, (800) 553–1336
www.laubergedelmar.com

Have a yen to be treated like you personally own the entire state of California? Then take a closer look at L'Auberge Resort and Spa, in North County Coastal. Located in the heart of Del Mar, one of Southern California's most picturesque coastal villages, the boutique resort offers 120 luxury guest rooms and suites. Rooms are well

Insiders' Tip

Some spas are fancy and people dress up for dinner. Others are more casual. When making reservations, ask about the type of clothing you'll need to bring.

Afternoon Tea (and More) at Aviara

Have you dreamed of quietly elegant afternoons sipping tea and sampling delicate morsels that taste even better than they look?

If the grandeur of afternoon tea is your idea of good living, then the Four Seasons Resort Aviara should be included on your dance card whether you're a registered guest or a visitor. While you might find afternoon tea provided at some teashop in San Diego, Aviara does it with Four Seasons style. We're talking top drawer.

At Aviara, tea comes with a plethora of finger sandwiches, Sultana scones with rose petal jelly (that's to die for), lemon curd and Devonshire cream, delicate pastries, and petit fours. As for the tea, there are plenty of choices, including herbal and fruit infusions and the standards such as Darjeeling, English breakfast, black currant, and Zen.

While you're waiting in the lounge of the Carlsbad resort, allow your mind to contemplate the origins of tea time, an addictive custom. The first afternoon tea was ordered by Anna, seventh Duchess of Bedford, in 1840. Apparently, Anna was tired (or grew hungry) during the long, dull space between meals. One afternoon about four, during her weary, low-energy time, she regally asked something like, "Bring me some tea, bread, butter, and cakes." This refreshing, light meal lifted Anna's spirits and blood-sugar level. Her idea spread like honey on a hot scone. Friends, family, royals, and commoners decided it was the "in" thing and the practice became as English as Buckingham Palace. In 1865, the Aerated Bread Company opened London's first teashop for the public.

Whether you're lingering next to the fountain or lying by the pool, the Four Seasons Resort Aviara is a treat to the senses. Days can be as busy or idle as you like. There's golf, tennis, nature trails, hiking possibilities, beauty and pampering treatments, a well-stocked fitness center, and private cabanas. Everything you need or want is minutes away from your room. PHOTO: COURTESY OF FOUR SEASONS RESORT AVIARA

Just a note for trivia lovers: Afternoon tea is a grand affair with delicate cakes and sandwiches. High tea is the American equivalent to supper, a sturdier meal, and may have been most popular originally with those who lived in the north of England.

Now to return to Carlsbad and the Four Seasons Resort Aviara. Afternoon tea is served daily in the hotel's Lobby Lounge, from 2:30 until 4:00 P.M., and it is deliciously accompanied by a harpist who sets the mood. You can lean back in one of the richly decorated sofas or overstuffed chairs, you can admire the tables decorated in crisp linens, and you can breathe in the fresh rose petals sprinkled around the tables. The view is the focal point, with floor-to-ceiling windows that frame views of the Pacific and the resort's luxurious Palm Courtyard.

Afternoon tea is $18; with the addition of a glass of sparkling wine, port, or sherry the cost is $24.50. Insiders recommend making reservations for afternoon tea, especially during the holidays. The number is (760) 603–3773.

appointed and inviting. Prices range from $250 to $950 for the rooms.

As a guest, you may use the Sports Pavilion featuring the latest in exercise and fitness equipment. You can have a fitness instructor develop and supervise a personal workout plan—or just have the teacher accompany you on a sunrise or sunset walk along the sand, or a vigorous trail hike in Torrey Pines State Park. Additionally, there's golf and tennis nearby. Afterwards, you can choose from a tantalizing menu of massage; skin and body treatments; and hair, nail, and facial treatments. Insiders recommend the exclusive hydrotherapy and body purification programs.

Loews Coronado Bay
4000 Coronado Bay Rd., Coronado
(619) 424–4400, (800) 815–6397
www.loewshotels.com

About 20 minutes south of downtown San Diego, Loew's Coronado Bay Resort has an exquisite location, which is fitting for this exclusive resort on a private peninsula in San Diego Bay.

All rooms include custom furnishings, fully stocked mini bar, two telephones, king-size bathrooms with oversized tubs, and luxury from top to bottom. The bayside villas are truly luxurious, with private decks over the water and bedrooms separated from elegant parlors. Splurge on one of these villas or a room overlooking the marina and you'll feel like you've been transported to an exotic island.

That gives you the basics. Now let's get to the fun stuff—refrigerator raids led by the resort's top chef ($25 for adults and $15 for kids per class), Kung Fu lessons ($15 per person), and yoga ($10 per person). And that's just a sampling. Be sure to take the resort's herb-garden tour; it's free and the beds of flowers and pungent herbs are sure to please and impress you. Free "Dive-in Movies" are shown on a large screen poolside in summer months. Guests float in the pool while watching the films (or lie in lounge chairs when their skin gets all wrinkly).

Guests also have access to bikes and in-line skates, boats, golf, tennis, and the state-of-the-art fitness center with private men's and women's steam rooms. A 9,000-square-foot spa will offer all the latest pampering treatments. Do you want to charter a yacht? Just talk to the concierge. Want a romantic evening? Book a sunset gondola ride around the Coronado Cays, one of the island's most exclusive communities.

The Commodore Kids Club has a supervised program providing entertainment for kids ages four to 12. Activities include arts and crafts, Ping-Pong, board games, and movies. The cost is $50 per child; evening care is $55 per child. As an extra service to you and your children, the management will gladly "kidproof" your room to help keep yours safe and happy during your visit. The accommodations range from $265 for a standard bay-view

Insiders' Tip

Most spas have a non-smoking policy. If you smoke, ask about the restrictions when making reservations.

Accommodations at the Ranch consist of individual Spanish-colonial inspired cottages, most with private patios and fireplaces. The secure grounds are landscaped with lovely gardens. The facility includes six lighted tennis courts, six aerobics gyms, a weight-training gym with advanced equipment, three pools, five whirl-jet therapy pools, and three saunas and steam rooms. There are beauty and skin care opportunities similar to those found at the Golden Door (see above). If you go, be sure to include the Better Breathing class and the African Dance Workout in your schedule.

The question about drinking water was on the mind of one Insider during a visit to the Ranch. The tap water is filtered and fine for drinking. Bottled mineral water is always available too.

The second question most people ask is: How do I get there? If you're coming in from San Diego's Lindbergh Field, a regularly scheduled spa bus can take you to the Ranch. Guests are asked to arrive on Saturday for the seven-day program; the Ranch is about an hour's drive from the airport. During the drive, chipper staff members offer mineral water, snacks, and information on what to expect and what one can expect to accomplish.

Spa packages are for seven days; prices range from $1,500 to $2,700 and are all-inclusive except for Mexican tax and modest charges for special treatments. Ask about special discounted packages, such as the Summer Savings program, and the just-for-couples week for those who want to share new life-enhancing habits.

room to $1,500 for the presidential and hospitality suite.

Rancho La Puerta
Tecate, Baja California, Mexico
(760) 744-4222, (800) 443-7565
www.rancholapuerta.com

Nestled in 3,000 acres of scenic countryside, just 3 miles south of the border, Rancho La Puerta is in a world of its own. Just 150 guests a week visit this valley where hiking trails cross the habitats of the spa's eco-sanctuary.

Unlike some other health and beauty spas, Rancho La Puerta is coed. Yet from its beginning over 60 years ago, it was recognized that men and women require distinct fitness regimens, therapy, and workouts, so there are separate exercise centers, and beauty treatment facilities. Be sure to sample the Kneipp herbal wrap (it will relax even the most Type A overachiever). The Ranch, as Insiders call it, provides multiple facilities for saunas, steams, nude sunbathing, whirlpool, and hot tubs. It also boasts one of the highest ratios of staff per guests of any spa. Ponder that for a moment and you may want to get to a phone to make reservations now.

The feeling throughout the Ranch is one of relaxation and comfort. There are over 60 fitness classes and conditioning programs. There's plenty of pampering. And if you needed any more reasons to consider the Ranch think about this: Rancho La Puerta is the birthplace of spa cuisine, with most of the fresh produce served here coming straight from the Ranch's organic gardens. It's honest food, offered at the peak of flavor. Everything is first-rate and appealing.

Insiders' Tip

Spa Finder, a national network of spas and resorts, can help you find the right one for your needs. You can reach them at (800) 255-7727, www.spafinder.com.

Guests stay in casitas, some with private pools, at Rancho Valencia. PHOTO: JEREMIAH SULLIVAN, COURTESY OF RANCHO VALENCIA

Rancho Valencia Resort
5921 Valencia Cir., Rancho Santa Fe
(858) 756–1123, (800) 548–3664
www.ranchovalencia.com

About 30 minutes and seemingly 3 million light years away from the city of San Diego, Rancho Valencia is elegant and secluded. Located in the North County Coastal area,

All the amenities you could possibly need are available in the Del Mar Suite at Rancho Valencia.

PHOTO: JEREMIAH SULLIVAN, COURTESY OF RANCHO VALENCIA

it is a neighbor to the elite Rancho Santa Fe community and fits in just fine, thank you very much. The resort's Hacienda, a restored adobe brick home built in the 1940s, has hosted countless notables such as Bill Blass, Bill Gates, Merv Griffin, Kelsey Grammer, and Ted Danson. Guests choose from the 43 luxurious suites in 20 casitas spread around the lush grounds; returnees usually have their favorite rooms. Six new casitas opened in 2002. Called the Garden Casitas, these new suites have 40-inch mounted flat screen televisions and other up-to-the-minute details. The complex includes several pools, golf privileges at nearby courses, and fine dining. Some guests return frequently to practice their swings with the pros at the tennis center's 18 Deco-Turf courts.

The spa and fitness programs cover just about every need. The Rejuvenation package includes accommodations, breakfast, an assortment of massages (try the warm-oil massage or the deep-tissue massage), and other spa services along with complimentary use of tennis courts and the fitness center. The two-night package ranges from $1,525 to $1,705 per couple.

A la carte fitness possibilities include a personal bicycle tour led by a fitness instructor for $100. The tour lasts 90 to 120 minutes and rambles through the countryside for 10 miles. Complimentary cross-training bikes are available at the tennis shops.

An Insiders' favorite is the one-night Romantic Getaway that pours on the champagne. You and your lover will be treated to a private breakfast, one-hour Swedish massage for each of you, and a candlelight dinner served fireside in your own suite or the signature restaurant. That package costs

$1,370 to $1,635 per couple. Room rates start at about $450 a night.

You'll find fine dining at the resort and in the village of Rancho Santa Fe. The concierge can arrange for hot-air balloon trips, horseback riding, beach walks, polo lessons, or a day trip to Disneyland. The staff here must be trained in mental telepathy. They seem to know what you need or want even before a request is spoken. Now that's service.

Welk Resort Center
8860 Lawrence Welk Dr., Escondido
(760) 749–3000, (800) 932–9355
www.welkresort.com

Remember the famous band leader? Lawrence Welk loved the area of Escondido where he "discovered" a secluded valley. Once you see the area, you'll understand why he wanted to build a resort here. The air is dry and clear, the breezes are gentle, and why, yes, it's a perfect place to play Welk's favorite sport: golf. Although Welk is gone, his memory and love of comfortable, wholesome living continues in the surroundings of the resort. Today those who remember Welk's bubbling television show enjoy the resort, and even those too young to remember, or have missed the reruns on television, come here to unwind and to play.

Let's get to the specifics: There are two 18-hole courses for players of all levels. The Oaks Par 3 course is ideal to work on your short game, and the famous Foun-

> ## Insiders' Tip
> Day spas are sprinkled throughout the county. Some are located in resorts and hotels. You'll find others by looking at the listings in the Yellow Pages under "Facial-Skin Care."

tains Executive Course is designed by renowned golf course architect David Rainville.

Located in North County Inland, about 45 minutes from downtown San Diego off Interstate 15, 10 minutes from the city of Escondido, the resort is situated on 600 beautiful acres. Room prices range from $89 to $300 per person a night depending on location, and the resort offers shopping, a relaxing fitness center, spas, a beauty salon, pool, and dining possibilities. Insiders agree that the fun of the Welk Resort (above and beyond the golf, in the opinion of some Insiders) is the award-winning live theater where Broadway musicals are performed in casual settings. For further information on the Welk resort, see our entries in the Golf, Arts, and Restaurants chapters.

Vacation Rentals

We're about to let you in on the secret to becoming a real San Diegan, if only temporarily. Whether your stay in San Diego is short, long, or indefinite, one of the best ways to enjoy the true San Diego experience is by living it in a vacation rental. Within minutes of unpacking your bags, you'll find yourself doing the same things the natives do. The only difference is, you don't have to go to work.

Vacation rentals are plentiful and offer a cost-effective way to spend some time in San Diego, especially if you're bringing the whole family along. From a quaint 1940s cottage to a modern, fully appointed condominium to a grandiose house in La Jolla, if you can imagine it, you'll find it.

The vast majority of vacation rentals hug the beach, mainly because that's where most people gravitate. Picture waking up to the sound of the ocean waves gently breaking on the shore and having that first cup of coffee on a deck or patio just steps away from the sand. Or perhaps you're more inclined to be inland a few miles, in the wooded enclave of Rancho Santa Fe, or on the fairway of a world-class golf course.

From Oceanside in North County Coastal to Imperial Beach in the South Bay, you can choose from an array of amenities and price ranges. The primary appeal to staying in a fully furnished house, condo, or cottage, aside from the lower cost, is that you can fend for yourself, and not rely on hotels and restaurants for your needs. It's a much more casual existence. Plus, many people love being absorbed by the local culture, mingling with neighborhood residents, browsing nearby shops, even making the obligatory trip to the local laundromat.

So pack your bags lightly (remember, we're very informal here), bring along your sunscreen, and become a bona fide San Diegan. Imagine lazy days on the beach, a glass of champagne while watching the sunset, a leisurely dinner, and an evening stroll along the water. Then you'll understand why so many people have discovered that a vacation rental is the ideal way to go.

Rental Agents and Independent Owners

Even though most vacation rentals are independently owned, the majority are managed by property management companies. Although you can find beautiful properties that are for rent directly by their owners, unless you have a reliable word-of-mouth referral or good photos that show the interior and exterior, we strongly recommend that you use an established agency. Properties managed by rental agents are uniformly well maintained, the renting agents are completely familiar with the units they are renting, and you will have few surprises. Agents will be more likely to have brochures too, so you can get an idea of what you're renting ahead of time.

One of the benefits of vacation rentals in San Diego is that many of the properties are occupied by their owners at least part of the year. As a result, most are beautifully upgraded and maintained.

Some vacation rental companies advertise their properties only on the Internet, but the ads come complete with pictures and detailed descriptions of the house or condo. This is especially true for rentals in the inland and southern regions of San Diego. A browse around the Internet might be time well spent, particularly if you're looking for something other than beach property. Just search on "San Diego Vacation Rentals," and you'll be overwhelmed by the number and variety of rentals.

Short-term and Long-term Stays

Although shorter stays are usually available during the winter season, most rentals require a minimum of a one-week stay during the summer. Some of the higher-end properties in La Jolla and Rancho Santa Fe, for example, might require a one-month commitment during the tourist season. Long-term stays, usually considered to be for the whole summer, are also an option. If you plan to stay longer than that, you may as well rent privately if for no other reason than to avoid local hotel taxes, which must be collected on vacation rentals.

Rates and Reservations

Not surprisingly, rates fluctuate greatly between the summer and winter seasons. The summer season generally runs from June through September; winter is considered to be October through May. Sum-

Insiders' Tip

Most locals claim to have seen it, but only a lucky few really have. We're talking about the "green flash," a brilliant green light that appears for a split second right at sunset. Watch for it in the western sky over the ocean at the precise moment the sun dips below the horizon.

Insiders' Tip

Rental rates go down when the winter season officially begins at the end of September. However, San Diego has some of its nicest weather in October, when blue skies and warm temperatures are the norm. Book your vacation during October and you'll have your pick of the best properties for the lowest prices.

mertime rates are naturally significantly higher than winter rates, ranging from $600 per week to $3,500, while some winter rates drop by about $300 to $500 per week. So if you'd like to join the ranks of "snowbirds" who flee the harsh winters of the Midwest and the East for a respite in temperate San Diego, you'll probably find some good values.

Keep in mind, too, that quoted rates do not include the required 10.5 percent hotel tax. You will also be required to pay an advance reservation fee and security deposit. Most properties require a 30-day or 60-day cancellation notice to refund the full amount of your deposit. Some will withhold a portion of your reservation fee regardless of how early you cancel.

We highly recommend that you make your reservations well in advance of your visit. Some properties are booked for the summer by January, so the earlier you can make plans, the better.

Kids and Pets

Nearly all rentals welcome children. In fact, most encourage Mom and Dad to bring the kids. San Diego has much to offer the whole family. Most have a limit

Bayfront vacation rentals sometimes include amenities like these catamarans waiting on the beach.

PHOTO: DAVE FROST, COURTESY OF PORT OF SAN DIEGO

on how many people can occupy a property, but they are designed to accommodate as many as possible. Property managers are happy to work with you to make sure your entire group is comfortably accommodated.

For the most part, pets are not allowed. If you're set on bringing Fluffy or Fido along, you might have more luck renting from individual homeowners, most of whom list their properties in the classifieds section of the *San Diego Union-Tribune* or on the Internet. If you play detective and search thoroughly enough, you should be able to find a place willing to host your four-legged family member.

Parking

If there were a way to sugarcoat this issue, we would. But the truth is, parking at the beach is always... well, we'll say, a challenge. Nowhere is that more true than in Mission Beach during the summer. If you're driving into town and considering a Mission Beach rental, a garage or reserved parking space may be one of the amenities you'll wish to place near the top of your list. Even if you're lucky enough to find an overnight parking place on the street, should you decide to go for a drive the next morning, by 10:00 A.M. you will not find another place to park when you return. You'll be forced to park in a lot miles away and shuttle back and forth.

Just in case you're tempted to squeeze your car into a likely spot in one of the alleys, be forewarned. If one of your wheels even kisses the red line that screams "no parking," your car will be towed. And parking enforcement is a constant, vigilant presence in Mission Beach during the summer months. You'll have to pay not only the towing charges but also a painful parking fine. The good news is that even though parking is difficult at best, the payoff is worth it. Most people take it in stride and simply plan ahead. Plus, the other beach areas aren't quite as bad. You might end up having to hike a little, but you should always be able to find something.

Rental Agencies

Beachfront San Diego Rentals
4603 Mission Blvd., Pacific Beach
(858) 483–6116
www.beachfrontsandiego.com
This company handles condo rentals at Capri by the Sea, an upscale beachfront property in Pacific Beach. There are several different-sized units with separate bedrooms and kitchens. The location is ideal, right on a slight cliff over the ocean between Pacific Beach and La Jolla.

ERA Coastal Properties
731 S. Hwy. 101, Ste. 1P, Solana Beach
(858) 793–3600
www.eracoastalproperties.com
ERA specializes in vacation condos and houses from La Jolla north to Oceanside and occasionally offers a property in Rancho Santa Fe or a condo in the Four Seasons Resort Aviara. Included in their territory are Del Mar, Solana Beach, La

Costa, and Carlsbad, areas that are highly sought after for their proximity to the Del Mar Racetrack and North County Coastal golf courses. Most of the properties are high end, but all are exquisitely maintained and appointed to provide a memorable San Diego experience.

Pace Realty
5693 La Jolla Blvd., La Jolla
(858) 454–1123
If you're looking for the ultimate luxury vacation, T. L. Pace Real Estate offers magnificent individual homes for rent in La Jolla, the tony beachfront village that has some of the country's most valuable real estate. You're not likely to find any bargains here, but if you're willing to part with upward of $10,000, you'll get a month in a La Jolla house that is the stuff of which dreams are made.

Penny Property Management
4444 Mission Blvd., San Diego
(858) 272–3900, (800) 748–6704
www.missionbeach.com
Since 1965 Penny Property Management has been helping vacationers find the

Rental cottages and condos are clustered near the shores of Mission Bay. PHOTO: COURTESY OF THE SAN DIEGO CONVENTION & VISITORS BUREAU

perfect beach rental. Specializing in Mission and Pacific Beaches, Penny also has a few hard-to-find rentals in Ocean Beach and La Jolla. All of Penny's booking agents are familiar with each property they rent and can help you find exactly what's right for you, from a no-frills unit to a luxury penthouse in the sky.

San Diego Vacation Cottages
2422 San Diego Ave., San Diego
(619) 291–9091
www.sandiegovacationapts.com

This company handles classic beach cottages in Ocean Beach, a casual community with less traffic and congestion than other areas. The cottages are within walking distance of the beach and are available by the night, week, or month. The company also books charming cottages in Old Town.

San Diego Vacation Rentals
2613 Mission Blvd., San Diego
(619) 296–1000, (800) 222–8281

Like its cohorts, San Diego Vacation Rentals specializes in beach rentals, focusing on Mission Beach, Ocean Beach, and La Jolla. Whether you're looking for a large,

luxury house located right on the beach or bayfront sand, or a secluded cottage tucked away on one of Mission Beach's courts, San Diego Vacation Rentals can help you find a dreamy vacation home.

Restaurants

Central San Diego

Coronado

Downtown/Gaslamp Quarter

Hillcrest/Uptown

La Jolla/Beaches

Mission Valley/Inland

Old Town/Point Loma

North County Coastal

North County Inland

East County

South Bay

The ultimate decision that faces San Diegans most days isn't where to play, it's what to eat. In San Diego County, you're facing nearly 3,000 restaurant choices, from drive-through taco stands to elegant gourmet dining rooms. In this chapter, we've given you an overview of your dining options throughout San Diego County.

Certain areas are culinary hotbeds where you'll find a dozen or more intriguing restaurants sitting nearly door-to-door for several blocks. La Jolla has long been the Insiders' destination for culinary curiosities and excellence. But downtown's Gaslamp Quarter has overtaken all competition. More than 30 restaurants within a 16-block radius offer everything from Irish corned beef and cabbage to paella Valenciana. This long-neglected historic district has become nightlife central for Insiders, who simply spend the night in a Gaslamp hotel rather than driving home a tad inebriated late at night.

San Diego's finest hotels are home to excellent restaurants that are so popular that maitre d's have trouble juggling reservations for hotel guests and locals. Be sure to make reservations in advance at any upscale restaurant recommended in this chapter. Most are extremely popular.

Since San Diego abuts the U.S.–Mexico border, Mexican food is a regional specialty. Local grocery stores sell far more salsa than catsup, and jalapeño chilies, guacamole, and corn chips are among our basic food groups. For the most part, the best Mexican food is found in tiny hole-in-the-wall neighborhood hangouts. If you walk past one that's crowded, you can be sure they serve great tacos, enchiladas, burritos, and huevos rancheros. Some more upscale restaurants are now serving good regional cuisine from throughout Mexico, and a few places specialize in serving premium brands of tequila. Be sure to sample a few fish tacos, a local specialty.

As always, remember that San Diego is a casual place. Very few restaurants have any kind of a dress code. The key phrase seems to be "casually elegant."

However, a few of the top-notch (meaning expensive) restaurants do insist that men wear jackets and that both men and women refrain from wearing shorts or jeans. If such a requirement exists, we'll be sure to mention it. It's not a bad idea to call ahead if you have any doubt, though.

Most restaurants accept reservations except for the ultra-casual places, and we recommend that you make them, especially on weekends. Most also accept all major credit cards; the exceptions are noted. The exceptions are usually small fast-food places that just aren't equipped for credit cards but are certainly worth experiencing. If a restaurant is especially family-friendly, we've mentioned it, but you're likely to see children dining right along with Mom and Dad just about everywhere.

California has tough smoking laws. Smoking is prohibited in all restaurants and bars, unless you're seated in an outdoor patio or terrace. Even then, your fellow diners may object if you light up.

As usual, we've divided the chapter by geographic region, with one slight deviation. Restaurants in the city of San Diego have been further broken down into groupings by neighborhoods for your convenience. Each restaurant has also been identified by its cuisine.

So go exploring and try something new. We know you'll be pleased by what you'll find.

Price Code

Our price code includes the average price of dinner for two, excluding cocktails, wine, appetizers, desserts, tax, and tip.

$	Less than $20
$$	$21 to $35
$$$	$36 to $45
$$$$	$46 and higher

Central San Diego

Coronado

Azzura Point
Loews Coronado Bay Resort $$$$
California
4000 Coronado Bay Rd., Coronado
(619) 424-4000
The decor is sophisticated and exotic, with Venetian-style chandeliers and hand-painted suede and silk drapes. The menu is a study in exquisite delicacies. The service is attentive but not fawning or overly friendly. These are just three of the reasons why Azzura Point is consistently named one of San Diego's top restaurants. Chef de Cuisine Ron Tolle mixes Alaskan king salmon with Peruvian potato hash, muscovy duck breast with fava beans, grilled tenderloin of beef with caramelized onions, roquefort tart and morel mushrooms. You get the idea. His cooking is innovative and highly alluring. Your first time around, you might want to try the Chef's Tasting Menu to get an overview. Then you'll be able to order your favorite entrees with confidence. There's also a vegetarian Herb Garden Menu (drawing from the hotel's fragrant garden). The bittersweet chocolate hazelnut cake with caramel ice cream, chocolate lace, and coffee sauce is enough to make you want to spend the night at the

Loews so you can go back for more. If you want just a sampling of the chef's magic, the adjacent Azzura Point Lounge serves tapas-style hors d'oeuvres. The sommelier has managed to narrow his wine list to just 275 selections; fortunately, he's there to help guide you to the right choice. Dinner is served nightly except Monday.

Chez Loma $$$–$$$$
French/Continental
1132 Loma Ave., Coronado
(619) 435-0661
The finely restored house Chez Loma calls home is a Coronado historical monument, and its award-winning cuisine has received nationwide distinction. The restaurant is broken up into several intimate dining areas that almost make you think you're dining at home—if you have a resident chef who can prepare updated French and Continental classics.

Menus change with the seasons, but some standouts are the horseradish-encrusted Atlantic salmon with smoked tomato vinaigrette. Duck, lamb, seafood, and pasta dishes are also treated to the chef's special touch. A carefully selected wine list complements the menu, and the bar offers premium selections. The early dining special is a great deal. Chez Loma serves dinner nightly. Locals stop by for a glass of wine and an appetizer or coffee and dessert in the enclosed patio, and don't bother dressing up. But you'll want to look a little spiffy if you dine inside.

Prince of Wales Grill $$$–$$$$
Hotel del Coronado
Continental
1500 Orange Ave., Coronado
(619) 522-8496
Deservedly venerable, the Prince of Wales Grill is an airy and elegant oceanfront restaurant that complements all the special qualities of the famed Hotel del Coro-

nado. Floor-to-ceiling windows afford a spectacular view of the Windsor Lawn and the ocean, and the lengthy menu offers equally pleasing fare. Order the chef's selection of oysters with sweet sake sorbet as an appetizer, then settle back, enjoy the live jazz, and study your options. You don't often see roasted Sonoma squab or wild boar tenderloin on San Diego menus; both are excellent. John Dory, a mild fish, is served with divine lobster roe tempura and sweet curry sauce. Naturally, steaks and chops are present, but it's not often your filet of beef comes with truffled potato puree. Men are asked to wear jackets, and reservations are recommended. Dinner is served nightly.

Rhinoceros Cafe $–$$
American
1166 Orange Ave., Coronado
(619) 435–2121
American bistro-style cooking is featured here in this cozy cafe. Choose from steaks, poultry, fresh fish, and shellfish dishes as well as a selection of delicious pasta entrees. Light eaters lean toward the pasta dishes or the herb-sauced poached salmon. A good selection of beer and wine is offered.

The atmosphere is casual, and all menu items are available for take-out. Lunch and dinner are served daily.

Downtown/Gaslamp Quarter

Athens Market $$
Greek
109 W. F St., San Diego
(619) 234–1955
Located in the historic and beautifully restored Federal Building, the Athens Market is a haven for the relaxed dining crowd. Proprietor Mary Pappas offers a comprehensive Greek menu with large portions and high quality. All the traditional favorites are covered, including moussaka and spanakopita, but if you like lamb, don't miss the roasted lamb served here. It's especially nice.

Pappas has a longtime following of legal and financial leaders, along with regular folks who've come to feel like family. There's a full bar that keeps things lively. Dinner is served Monday through Saturday, and the restaurant is open for lunch Monday through Friday.

Bayou Bar & Grill $$
Creole/Cajun
329 Market St., San Diego
(619) 696–8747
Walls adorned with memorabilia of Mardi Gras and music evoking the New Orleans Jazz Festival create a festive atmosphere at the Bayou Bar & Grill. Its Creole/Cajun cuisine has become a favorite of Insiders who keep coming back for such specialties as Mardi Gras pasta, crawfish etoufee, and soft shell crab.

All entrees get the Cajun treatment: Pork chops, duck, and chicken are all standouts in their mildly spicy sauces. Entrees are accompanied by a salad of greens, pecans, and mandarin oranges tossed with a poppy-seed dressing.

Open for dinner daily, the Bayou also has a full bar.

Bella Luna $$$
Italian
748 Fifth Ave., San Diego
(619) 239–3222
For a long while, you couldn't throw a cannoli without hitting an Italian restaurant in the Gaslamp Quarter. Many have come and gone, but the ones that remain are those that have got it right from the beginning. Bella Luna continues to offer the excellent regional food of Capri in its small but chic establishment. The name translates to "Beautiful Moon," and moon-themed artwork covers the walls.

The menu is light and imaginative including lots of fresh seafood and pasta, as well as a tasty breaded veal chop covered with a blend of arugula and fresh tomato. Daily risotto dishes are Insiders' favorites, but if it's available, try the shrimp salad or the tender crepe stuffed with salmon. One specialty always available is the grilled half chicken. Dinner is served nightly.

Alfresco dining is available year-round at sidewalk cafes in the Gaslamp Quarter. PHOTO: ROBERT BRUNI, COURTESY OF THE SAN DIEGO CONVENTION & VISITORS BUREAU

Blue Point Coastal Cuisine $$$
Seafood
565 Fifth Ave., San Diego
(619) 233-6623

You'll feel like you're walking into a San Francisco supper club when you enter Blue Point. With its large wooden booths and dining tables off to one side and a massive bar dominating the other, the mood is elegant and upbeat. In fact, you'll probably be inspired to order one of the dozens of specialty martinis to complement appetizers, which can be ordered at the bar.

Our favorite entree is the Hawaiian ahi, served with wild mushrooms and ginger butter. But you can't go wrong with any of the seafood items here, like crab cakes or catfish, all of which are served with lots of organic vegetables. Dinner is served nightly.

Cafe Sevilla $$
Spanish
555 Fourth Ave., San Diego
(619) 233-5979

The only way to truly appreciate Cafe Sevilla is to go at least twice, because the first time you visit, it's almost mandatory to have the paella Valenciana. This traditional Spanish dish is loaded with clams, mussels, calamari, shrimp, chorizo, and roasted chicken, all cooked in an aromatic saffron rice. When you return, you can enjoy one of the other fine entrees, such as New York steak with Riojo sauce or roasted chicken in garlic sauce.

Should you wish to sit at the bar and make a meal of tapas, which are Spanish appetizers, try a sampling of croquettes of shrimp, mushrooms sautéed in a garlic wine sauce, or fried calamari. If you'd really like to make a night of it, make reservations for the Flamenco dinner show that's winning citywide raves. See our Nightlife chapter for more happenings at Cafe Sevilla. Dinner is served nightly.

Cafe 222 $
American
222 Island Ave., San Diego
(619) 236-9902

Downtown loft dwellers and hip travelers congregate in this wacky cafe for pumpkin waffles, homemade granola, and veggie omelets at breakfast and grilled meatloaf sandwiches for lunch. Regulars tend to linger at the sidewalk tables or inside under the chandeliers made of spoons (you gotta see it to believe it). The food is great, the clientele fascinating, and, if you want to be left alone, there's a huge stack of magazines for your perusal. It's open daily for breakfast and lunch.

Croce's $$-$$$
International
802 Fifth Ave., San Diego
(619) 233-4355

Croce's nearly defies description, as it is much more than a restaurant. It's actually two restaurants, a jazz club, and a sidewalk dining spot. They all flow into one another with an electric mix of great food, divine music, and fun-loving folks. For dining, Croce's is truly an experience; to find out more about it as an entertainment spot, check our Nightlife chapter. Owner Ingrid Croce, widow of legendary singer Jim Croce, opened the first arm of her restaurant when the Gaslamp Quarter was in the early stages of its revitalization. Over the years, the restaurant has spread out into adjacent buildings.

Ingrid Croce, who has authored a cookbook called *Thyme in a Bottle*, is the executive chef. She keeps diners coming back by changing the menu. There's always a chicken dish or two. Try the one with forest mushroom risotto if it's available, or the rigatoni with oven-roasted vegetables. Croce's is open for breakfast, lunch, dinner, and late-night dining daily.

Dobson's $$$
Contemporary American
956 Broadway Cir., San Diego
(619) 231–6771

For power lunches and after-theater dinners, Dobson's is a great choice. Downtown bigwigs know they'll be treated courteously whether they dine in the saloon-style bar downstairs or the upstairs loft dining room. The hands-down Insiders' favorite menu item is the signature mussel bisque with a puff-pastry crust.

You'll also find lots of seafood specialties on the seasonal menu, as well as meats and poultry that mingle French tradition with modern California style. Many go to Dobson's just to hang out at the bar, which is next to a huge front window, affording a view of the constant parade of downtown movers and shakers. Dobson's is open for lunch Monday through Friday and for dinner Monday through Saturday.

The Field $
Irish
544 Fifth Ave., San Diego
(619) 232–9840

The food at this eatery/pub is down-home Irish, corned beef and cabbage being the main menu item. Thick slabs of corned beef that look like prime rib are accompanied by tender, sautéed cabbage. We know that boiled potatoes don't sound too sexy, but give them a try. Combined with the other flavors on your plate, they're a winner.

The interior of the restaurant is furnished with tables, farm tools, and equipment all imported, piece by piece, from Ireland. If you have even a smidgen of Irish in you (as we all do on St. Patrick's Day), you'll feel right at home here. The menu also includes fish and chips and some outstanding breakfast selections. Lunch and dinner are served daily.

Las Cuatro Milpas $
Mexican
1857 Logan Ave., San Diego
No phone

A Barrio Logan mainstay since 1933, Las Cuatro Milpas is a storefront eatery offering authentic Mexican specialties such as chorizo bowls, a spicy Mexican sausage combined with beans and rice. The dangerously fiery salsa concocted on the premises is a mandatory addition to every dish, and the warm tortillas are unlike anything you'll ever find in a supermarket. Over the years the restaurant has expanded its seating into adjacent buildings, which provide plenty of room for family-style eating. But don't be surprised if you find yourself dining on savory pork or chicken tacos in your car or while perched on the curb, because lines often snake out the door and down the street during lunch time.

The specialty of the week is served on Saturdays only, when Las Cuatro Milpas opens at 6:00 A.M. to dish up steaming bowls of *menudo*, a legendary hangover cure. The restaurant is open for breakfast and lunch every day except Sunday. Takeout is available as well as bulk purchases of most menu items. Be sure to bring cash; no credit cards are accepted.

Sushi Deli $
Japanese
828 Broadway, Central San Diego
(619) 231–9597

The plentiful portions and low prices have made Sushi Deli thrive over the decades, despite downtown's ever-changing dining scene. As the name suggests, you'll want to head here for everything from California rolls to raw tuna (sashimi) with plenty of hot wasabi. Most customers know exactly what they want since they've eaten here so often. But first timers need a few minutes to study the extensive menu. The combo platters with a couple of entrees, rice, and salad are a great deal—go for the vegetable tempura or teriyaki beef. It's open Monday through Saturday for lunch and dinner.

Hillcrest/Uptown

Cafe on Park $
American
3831 Park Blvd., San Diego
(619) 293-7275

An American-style bistro, this small and cozy eatery offers hearty breakfasts and lunches daily. Even during the week the cafe is busy from the moment it opens until closing. Breakfast seems to be the standout of the day. You can choose from all the standards—eggs, pancakes, cereals—but they're all prepared with a twist. Eggs are called "scrambles" and are combined with a variety of ingredients, including peppers, onions, chilies, beef, and more.

Most diners are regulars, and most have their favorite dishes, except for one Insider who says his favorite menu item is whatever's in front of him at the time. Imaginative sandwiches, salads, and pasta items distinguish the lunch menu.

Chilango's Mexico City Grill $
Mexican
142 University Ave., San Diego
(619) 294-8646

Mexican fast-food places are never in short supply around town, but few of them feature regional cuisine like Chilango's. Dishes such as pork adobada, lean pork with a rich, sun-dried red chile sauce, is served over thick corn masa patties and topped with pinto beans, guacamole, and crumbled cheese. Or try a *burrote*, a giant flour tortilla burrito stuffed with pollo asado pibil, chicken marinated in tangy sour orange juice, achiote, and spices.

Dining-in facilities are limited to a few tables inside and out, and you'll probably see far more orders to go than to eat in. But if you can dispense with candles and linen, the food makes up for the lack of ambiance. Chilango's also serves breakfast tortas, tacos, and burrotes along with a selection of sweet Mexican pastries. The restaurant is open for breakfast, lunch, and dinner daily and does not accept credit cards.

Corvette Diner $
American
3946 Fifth Ave., San Diego
(619) 542-1001

Music from the '50s, eclectic decor (including a vintage Corvette) and simple diner fare have made this restaurant a family favorite. Burgers, sandwiches, fries, and milkshakes are the mainstays here, and all are first rate. Kids love the Corvette Diner because it's loud and there's lots to look at while awaiting their meal.

Waiters and waitresses are relentlessly cheerful and efficient, and the music eventually creeps into your brain. Your toe will be tapping before you know it. The restaurant is open for lunch and dinner daily.

Karen Krasne's Extraordinary Desserts $
Desserts
2929 Fifth Ave., San Diego
(619) 294-7001

Who hasn't fantasized about skipping dinner and going straight to dessert? This is the place to indulge the fantasy. Owner Karen Krasne, whose sweet creations have been featured in *Bon Appetit*, has carved a niche for those who want to throw caution to the wind and relax with a dessert that's as beautiful as it is tasty. Picture a tender, flaky napoleon, filled with whipped cream and fresh berries, dusted with powdered sugar, and topped with edible flowers.

Or if chocolate is your only idea of dessert, you'll have plenty of choices. Dense chocolate tortes, huge brownies and cookies, and luscious chocolate cakes are yours for the choosing. Tart and sweet lemon tortes awaken the sense buds, and several kinds of buttery shortbread rekindle memories of Grandma's kitchen. Extraordinary Desserts also serves a large selection of coffees and teas, the ideal accompaniment to your sweet delicacy. The restaurant is open to satisfy your sweet tooth from morning to late night daily.

Kemo Sabe $$$
Southwestern/Asian
3958 Fifth Ave., San Diego
(619) 220–6802

As pleasing to the eye as it is to the taste buds, Kemo Sabe grabs your attention as soon as you walk through the door with its unusual collection of sculpture and other art pieces. Even the entrees are works of art—you'll hear lots of oohs and aahs as dishes are placed before diners. And what dishes they are. The perennial favorite is Skirts on Fire, a skirt steak grilled and seasoned with spices that will ignite your senses (and your mouth—but pleasantly).

For appetizers, try the mixed satay, skewers of grilled chicken, shrimp, and steak seasoned with Thai spices and served with a peanut dipping sauce. To complement your dinner, Kemo Sabe's bartender has created a large selection of custom martinis. The Insiders' favorite is the Blue Glacier, a concoction of Bombay Sapphire gin, Skyy vodka, and blue curaçao, with an orange twist. It goes down quite nicely. Dinner is served nightly.

Laurel $$$
Southern French
505 Laurel St., San Diego
(619) 239–2222

Laurel is the number-one favorite with a crowd that keeps coming back for such

Insiders' Tip

Watch for restaurant specials and coupons in Thursday's *San Diego Union-Tribune*. Oftentimes, you'll find two-for-one or early-bird specials that can save you a bunch.

treats as duck confit on garlicky mashed potatoes. Another entree the chef has trouble keeping in the kitchen is the Provençal chicken roasted in a clay pot. Appetizers are unusual—and unusually good—like the Roquefort tart baked on a savory walnut crust.

Service is perfect. The night we visited Laurel, the waiter brought a small sample of wine for us to try that was other than what we ordered simply because he thought we might like it better. He was right, and we were impressed. Desserts are heavenly, especially the warm fruit tarts with caramel ice cream. If you're in the mood for lighter fare but still want the Laurel experience, you can sip and nibble at the spacious bar. Laurel serves dinner nightly.

Mission Hills Cafe $$
Continental
808 W. Washington St., San Diego
(619) 296–8010

Unassuming from the outside, the interior of this casual bistro is graciously appointed with nice linens, beautiful floral arrangements, excellent service, and a varied menu that's sure to please everyone in your party. The restaurant is actually quite large, occupying two rooms that are usually filled, even on weeknights.

The pear Cambozola salad is a delectable lunch entree or an even better way to begin dinner. Baby greens topped with imported Cambozola cheese, a creamy cheese with a tangy, Roquefort-like flavor, are paired with garden-fresh sliced pears and strawberries. Dinner selections include pastas, poultry, seafood, and various meats, including an oven-roasted lamb shank with a house-made tomato garlic sauce. The satiny garlic mashed potatoes served alongside are worth ordering on their own. An excellent wine list offers wine by the bottle or the glass. The cafe is open for breakfast, lunch, and dinner daily.

MiXX $$
Global
3671 Fifth Ave., San Diego
(619) 299–6499

"Cuisine with no ethnic boundaries" is the motto at MiXX, and the eclectic offering of

grill features three cuts that change daily and always get Montana's signature grilling. A cozy, clublike atmosphere envelops you as soon as you walk through the door, and the bar, with its intriguing, artsy light fixtures, is always alive with conversation. Hang around for the divine desserts made on the premises, especially the smooth-as-silk sourdough bread pudding with berries. Montana's is open for happy hour and dinner daily.

Saffron Noodles and Saté/Saffron Chicken   **$**
Thai
3737 India St., San Diego
(619) 574-7737
These side-by-side eateries have the same ownership and serve Thai favorites for take-out or to eat in. Saffron Noodles and Saté offers mouthwatering chicken saté served with jasmine rice, cucumber salad, and peanut dipping sauce. There's also a large selection of noodle dishes served in traditional Thai style, flavorful and spicy. Next door at Saffron Chicken, tender, Thai-style roasted chicken is served with your choice of five sauces and a terrific Vietnamese coleslaw topped with chopped peanuts. There's no seating on this side, but all menu items can be ordered from either restaurant if you're eating in.

Saffron was listed in *USA Today* as one of the ten best places in the country for take-out. Insiders have discovered the place, and it's not uncommon for lines to be a bit long. But it's worth the wait for these savory Thai delicacies. Saffron serves lunch and dinner daily.

entrees gives testament to that philosophy. Upon entering, diners are ushered past a cozy bar area, through the cocktail lounge, which features nightly entertainment, and up a short flight of stairs to the dining room that overlooks the action below.

Standouts on the menu are the salmon with crispy wontons, taquila lime shrimp linguine, and the unusual soups. Don't miss the decadent desserts.

MiXX is open for dinner nightly.

Montana's American Grill   **$$**
American
1421 University Ave., San Diego
(619) 297-0722
Insiders who make it a habit to dine again and again at Montana's do so for one reason. They know their favorite dish will be consistently perfect every time they order it. Owner Francisco "Pancho" Marty has created an ambiance that is a magnet for locals and visitors, and the chef has created a menu that features an innovative combination of flavors.

Many entrees have Southwestern accents, such as the grilled Anaheim chiles with three cheeses and smoked tomato salsa appetizer. For those who like to splurge on meat dishes when they dine out, the mixed

La Jolla/Beaches

Brockton Villa   **$**
Continental
1235 Coast Blvd., La Jolla
(858) 454-7393
Although the food is equally good at lunch and dinner, breakfast is what draws the big crowds to this quaint, century-old beach cottage overlooking La Jolla Cove and the Pacific Ocean. Wander in around breakfast time, put your name on the list, then help yourself to a cup of coffee and a newspaper and lounge around the deck with the rest of the crowd waiting to be seated.

Once you're seated either inside or on the outside terrace, choose from some amazing breakfast dishes, like steamers, Greek-style eggs scrambled with feta cheese, or banana pancakes dotted with big banana chunks. Orange French toast is a keeper, too. The lunch menu features shrimp and chicken salads, and at dinner, don't miss the California seafood stew. Breakfast and lunch are served daily; dinner is served Tuesday through Sunday. The kitchen closes in mid-afternoon, but you can still stop by for coffee, tea, and pastries.

George's Cafe & Ocean Terrace $$–$$$
Contemporary Californian
1250 Prospect St., La Jolla
(858) 454-4244

This is al fresco dining at its best, on a rooftop terrace with an unimpeded view of La Jolla Cove. The California cuisine is also memorable. Lots of pastas are offered, like the fettucine with rock shrimp in garlic Parmesan sauce. Seafood offerings include

a pan-seared king salmon that's served with couscous. Or try the deep-fried prawns accompanied by sweet potato cakes.

The lunchtime menu has great sandwiches and salads, but the star is the quesadilla with spicy-hot Jamaican chicken. The Ocean Terrace is open daily for lunch and dinner, and has late-night dining on Fridays and Saturdays. The cafe sits atop George's at the Cove restaurant, one of the finest dining establishments in La Jolla. Have a special, romantic dinner here if you care to splurge. The cuisine is always exciting, and wall mirrors amplify the view of the sea so no one misses out on spectacular sunsets.

Marine Room $$$$
French/Continental
2000 Spindrift Dr., La Jolla
(858) 459-7222

This treasured restaurant on the sand manages to be both venerable and exciting. It has withstood the test of time and

George's at the Cove is a favorite dining destination for both locals and visiting celebrities. PHOTO: GEORGE'S AT THE COVE, COURTESY OF THE SAN DIEGO CONVENTION & VISITORS BUREAU

been reinvented a number of times over the years to appeal to new generations of diners. In addition to fine adventuresome cuisine, the restaurant is noted for its ocean view. And it's not an ordinary ocean view—it's right on the water. During storms, waves often crash against the triple-thick glass windows facing the ocean, putting on a show of Mother Nature's ferocity.

But back to the food. You could try Scottish smoked salmon with quail eggs or goat cheese brûlée for starters. Then move on to fennel pollen-dusted sweetbreads and Indian spiced scallops. Have you ever tried antelope loin? Here's your chance. Chef Bernard Guillas isn't afraid to experiment, and you'll likely enjoy his inventions. You might want to spend a Sunday morning lingering over brunch. It doesn't matter if the day is sunny or gray, the view will always take your breath away. The Marine Room is open for lunch and dinner Monday through Saturday and brunch and dinner on Sunday.

Sante $$$–$$$$
Italian
7811 Herschel Ave., La Jolla
(858) 454–1315

Sante offers several options for diners: See and be seen in the gracious dining room, or enjoy an intimate tête-à-tête in one of two sidewalk patios or at one of the few tables tucked away in the bar. Wherever you choose to dine, rest assured the chef is determined to make you happy. The fare is classic northern Italian, ranging from antipasti, flavorful soups, bitter salads, and beautifully composed pastas to game, veal, and fresh seafood.

One characteristic that distinguishes Sante is that the chef will happily compose a dish on the spot to suit your taste just in case it doesn't appear on the menu. The night we dined at Sante, we were the fortunate beneficiaries of a spur-of-the-moment, divinely inspired risotto with shellfish. The bar is a comfortable and happy spot for before or after-dinner drinks. Sante is open for lunch Monday through Friday, and for dinner nightly.

Saska's $$
American
3768 Mission Blvd., San Diego
(858) 488–7311

Let's say you've pushed the day into nighttime, it's midnight, and you haven't eaten yet. Where do you go to get dinner other than a "Grand Slam" at Denny's? Since the mid-1950s Saska's has been the solution for late-night diners looking for a steak, a lobster tail, or even a good plate of pasta. Saska's stays open until 2:00 A.M., adding first-rate breakfast items to the menu at 11:00 P.M.

Even if you tend to dine at more conventional hours, it's worth a trip to Mission Beach to experience this legendary restaurant. The food is consistently good, especially the teriyaki steak and chicken, and there's usually a member of the Saska family behind the bar or roaming about to make you feel at home. Saska's serves lunch and dinner daily and brunch on Saturday and Sunday.

Thee Bungalow $$–$$$
Continental
4996 W. Point Loma Blvd., San Diego
(619) 224–2884

Make a point of visiting this longtime resident of Ocean Beach. Owner-chef Ed Moore caters to his customers, who are extremely loyal, changing the menu and prices constantly to adapt to their tastes and moods. One dish that is almost always available is the roast duck, and for good reason. It's superb, as are the fresh fish dishes, innovative soups, and veal creations.

You can dine in the dining room, formal in construction but relaxed in mood, or in the outdoor patio. Watch for value-priced mid-week and early-bird dinners. Thee Bungalow is always trying something different and fun, like the recent recreation of the last meal on the *Titanic*. Dinner is served nightly. Moore took over the restaurant catty-corner to his bungalow in 2002 and created a new cozy place called 3rd Corner. Locals say the cassoulet makes you feel like you're sitting in the French countryside.

Mission Valley/Inland

Adams Avenue Grill $$
Global
2201 Adams Ave., San Diego
(619) 298–8440
Whatever your favorite meal is, you're likely to find it on the menu here. Everything from Thai to Italian to American to Southwest is represented. The mystery is how they all come out so well. The angel hair pasta with roma tomatoes, garlic, basil, and balsamic vinegar is finished with a splash of burgundy that gives this traditional dish a nice twist. Equally pleasing is the Thai salad, a mixture of snow peas, Napa cabbage, and mixed greens tossed with roasted peanuts and a spicy peanut dressing.

Although offered as an appetizer, the Southwest black bean soup served with shrimp and jalapeño quesadilla makes a full lunch. Desserts include a chocoholic's delight, a six-layer fudge cake that's more than a pound per slice. Plan on a trip to the gym if you finish the whole thing. Lunch and dinner are served Tuesday through Sunday.

Kensington Grill $$
New American
4055 Adams Ave., San Diego
(619) 281–4014
The owners bill their restaurant as "New American cuisine," and while we might be hard pressed to define it, we don't care. Whatever it is, it's great. This is a neighborhood restaurant with a large and lively bar on one side and a smallish dining room on the other. A few tables line the sidewalk for outdoor dining.

We strongly suggest you start your meal with a delectable mango and brie quesadilla. It sounds unusual, but it's sinfully good. Then move on to such dishes as pan seared sea bass and meatloaf. You can even get a burger here if you're searching for comfort food. Dinner is served nightly.

Prego $$
Italian
1370 Frazee Rd., San Diego
(619) 294–4700
As you approach Prego through the sunlit courtyard, you'll get the feeling that you're walking into a large Italian villa. Once inside, the sights and sounds of regional Italian cuisine being prepared in the open kitchen will get your mouth watering. Begin with the fresh garlic-rosemary bread baked in Prego's wood-fired oven, then graze through such tasty antipasti as the grilled radicchio, endive, eggplant, and portobello mushrooms accompanied by prosciutto-wrapped goat cheese.

Chicken, seafood, pork chops, and steak all get the Prego treatment, and be sure to ask about the risotto of the day, a creamy arborio rice dish that changes according to the chef's whim. Lunch is served Monday through Friday, and dinner is served nightly.

Seau's: The Restaurant $$
Californian
1640 Camino del Rio N., San Diego
(619) 291–7328
San Diego's own Junior Seau, star defensive back for the San Diego Chargers, opened this restaurant to immediate acclaim. Junior's aim was to have an all-out sports bar that was all things to all people. He's darn well done it, too. Food is not secondary here. It ranges from pizzas, salads, and pastas to sandwiches and grilled fresh fish. And most menu items are quite good, especially the Greek salad, a toss of greens, feta cheese, Greek olives, and tomatoes dressed with a tangy herb vinaigrette.

Of course, baseball, basketball, football, and every other sport on earth is continuously broadcast from TVs placed everywhere. There's a full bar and lounge. Located in Mission Valley Center, Seau's is open for lunch and dinner daily.

Trophy's Sports Grill $
Californian
7510 Hazard Center Dr., San Diego
(619) 296–9600
4282 Esplanade Ct., La Jolla
(858) 450–1400
5500 Grossmont Center Dr., La Mesa
(619) 698–2900
We can't mention one sports bar/restaurant without giving equal space to the

other standout in town. Trophy's predates Seau's, and it has held its own against the young upstart by sticking to its tried-and-true formula. The range of menu items is predictable—pizzas, pastas, burgers, and sandwiches—but you'll find some unusual variations here that are quite good, like the pizza with artichoke hearts and bacon.

Trophy's is a kid-friendly place, providing a place mat and crayons at each table setting. This tends to bring out the kid in most adults, too. Wide screen TVs are in the bar, and smaller ones are sprinkled throughout the rest of the restaurant. Trophy's is open for lunch and dinner daily.

Old Town/Point Loma

El Agave $$–$$$
Nouveau Mexican
2304 San Diego Ave., San Diego
(619) 220–0692
Sipping tequila is an art form here. Once you make your choice from more than 200 varieties, it's served in a miniature carafe and is accompanied by a small glass of sangrita, a cool mixture of tomato juice and lime intended to cool the fire of the tequila.

Moving on to the menu produces even nicer surprises. This is food with a Mexican influence, but there are none of the combo plates with rice and beans typically found in Mexican restaurants. A good way to sample a variety of appetizers is to order the sampler, which includes tiny quesadillas, tacos, and tamales, all with unusual but delicious regional Mexican fillings. The watercress salad is also a star. Peppery watercress is quickly wilted in bacon drippings and served with warm tortillas in which to wrap it. Entrees include a variety of seafood dishes, and chicken with several variations of mole sauces. If you've never tasted mole, we strongly recommend it. It is a complex sauce that combines dozens of flavors and ranges from mild to fiery. Lunch and dinner are served daily.

Bayside restaurants offer scenic views and fascinating atmosphere. PHOTO: DALE FROST, COURTESY OF PORT OF SAN DIEGO

Great Wall Cafe $–$$
Chinese
2543 Congress St., San Diego
(619) 291–9478

Mexican food has long been the dominant force in Old Town, but that's starting to change. One of the most welcome deviations is the Great Wall Cafe, where you can enjoy good-quality Chinese meals on a wide, outdoor terrace that surrounds a rather small indoor dining room. We usually opt for outdoors to sample such treats as minced chicken in lettuce leaves and Szechuan dumplings that are on the spicy side.

If you like a taste of everything, try Buddha's Jump Over the Wall, a hot pot full of meat, seafood, and vegetables. Or if you really want to go all out, we can heartily recommend the Peking Duck. There is a full bar. Lunch and dinner are served daily.

Old Town Mexican Cafe $
Mexican
2489 San Diego Ave., San Diego
(619) 297–4330

No trip to San Diego is complete without stopping for lunch or dinner at "Old Town Mex," as Insiders call it. You'll be hard pressed to tell the locals from the tourists here, because everyone is too intent on the lively conversation and the steaming plates of Mexican food. There's usually a wait, so a good place to hang out (if the bar is full) is on the front sidewalk, where you can watch fresh tortillas being made by hand.

You'll find the usual combination plates of enchiladas, tacos, and burritos, but the dish that keeps everyone coming back is the *carnitas*. You'll understand why when a plate of roasted, shredded, and seasoned pork is placed before you with its accompanying hot tortillas, avocado, onions, tomatoes, and cilantro. Warm chips and salsa are served with every meal. Breakfast, lunch, and dinner are served daily.

Pizza Nova $$
Californian
5120 N. Harbor Dr., San Diego
(619) 226–0268
3955 Fifth Ave., San Diego
(619) 296–6682
945 Lomas Santa Fe, Solana Beach
(858) 259–0666

When the first Pizza Nova opened on the harbor in Point Loma, it didn't take Insiders long to figure out that it served a multitude of purposes. It's a great restaurant for casual dining, for dates, for the whole family, for a quick bite, or for a leisurely meal. Other locations began opening around town, and they all have become fixtures in their respective neighborhoods.

Pizzas are innovative, like the ever-popular Thai Chicken—ginger-marinated chicken breast, green onions, bean sprouts, carrot slivers, cilantro, and roasted peanuts. The chopped salad almost overflows with generous chunks of salami, fontina cheese, turkey breast, and tomatoes. And the sinfully good fettucine with prawns and prosciutto in a garlic cream sauce spiced with crushed red peppers and topped with Parmesan has been a menu mainstay for years.

Pizza Nova is open for lunch and dinner daily. All menu items are available for take-out, and delivery is available. Look for discount coupons in the newspapers.

Point Loma Seafood $
Seafood
2805 Emerson St., San Diego
(619) 223–1109

Enter Point Loma Seafood, make your way to the counter, and prepare to be dazzled by the display of fresh seafood for sale by the pound. Then remind yourself that the same seafood you see before you is the main ingredient in wonderful sandwiches, salads, soups, and platters of fried fish served with coleslaw and french fries. Sushi and ceviche appetizers fly out the door every day, as do the shrimp and crab Louie cocktails.

Favorite sandwiches are the imaginative crab cake sandwich and the squid sandwich on sourdough bread. Several outdoor tables are situated harborside, but they become extremely crowded around lunchtime. So if you have a picnic in mind, this is a great place to stop. Don't miss the large selection of smoked fish. Combine it with some fresh sourdough bread, and you'll have a tasty snack. Lunch and dinner are available daily, but closing hours are early—around 7:00 P.M.

Al's Cafe $
American
795 Carlsbad Village Dr., Carlsbad
(760) 729-5448

Here's an old-fashioned, downtown cafe where you can enjoy breakfast and lunch inside or beneath an umbrella at one of the tables set out on a quiet side street. There are specials served every day. The all-you-can-eat fish and chips (for about $6.00) is a bargain. It's in the heart of downtown Carlsbad.

Angelo's Burgers $
American
621 N. Coast Hwy., Oceanside
(760) 757-5161
1050 S. Coast Hwy., Oceanside
(760) 757-4064
2035 S. Coast Hwy., Oceanside
(760) 967-9911
608 S. Coast Hwy., Oceanside
(760) 943-9115

Angelo's has been a favorite beach restaurant hangout for Insiders since the mid-1970s and continues to serve up great big burgers and mountains of fries for about $4.00. The quality and price are hard to beat. This is a no-frills burger joint (that starts the day with large breakfast burritos and other morning specials). You order at the counter and spread your food on plastic tables. You can dine inside or outside.

The gyros sandwiches are excellent and under $3.00. Hungry for a giant hot pastrami sandwich? Angelo's is your place. Try the homemade onion rings and zucchini strips, deep fried but cooked in cholesterol-free corn oil. Sure, you can't eat this way all the time, but hey, once in a while is fun, and doubly so if you're on vacation, it's the middle of the week, or you need good fast food. All locations are open daily for breakfast, lunch, and dinner.

Bellefleur Winery & Restaurant $-$$$
Californian, Southwestern, and Mediterranean
5610 Paseo Del Norte, Carlsbad
(760) 603-1919

This restaurant is a find and it's convenient too, right off Interstate 5 and Palo-mar Airport Road, in Carlsbad. It's a ½-block walk north of the Carlsbad Company Stores shopping center (see our Shopping chapter).

Service is fabulous. Lunch prices are very modest, but bring your credit card for dinner if you plan to include an appetizer, drinks, dessert, and a cordial or sherry to end your experience. The Happy Hour, from 3:00 to 7:00 P.M. daily, features yummy appetizers and pizzas.

At a recent lunch we had the fresh salmon burger with watercress, lemon pepper aioli, and quinoa salad, all for about $9.00, and the presentation of the ample portions was done with a master's hand. Dinner choices, also luscious and stunning, range from certified Angus beef to sea bass with Maui Onion Risotto. The wine is excellent and priced reasonably for a glass of the Bellefleur Winery brands (which we highly recommend). Bellefleur Winery, for your information, is located in Fallbrook, and has won numerous awards and recognition. This Carlsbad restaurant is open daily, except Monday, for lunch and dinner.

Bully's $$
American
1404 Camino Del Mar, Del Mar
(858) 755-1660

Want a place you can count on every time for good food? Bully's is your answer. This steakhouse has been a tradition in San Diego County since the early 1970s and deserves many repeat visits. They have great steaks, fresh seafood, ribs, succulent

> **Insiders' Tip**
> Do you love wine but hate to pay inflated wine list prices? Most restaurants will allow you to bring your own bottle of wine for a corkage fee. Call ahead for details.

chicken, and plump sandwiches (the burger is immense). But it's the prime rib that draws the repeat crowds. You could order the petite cut, but then you wouldn't have any left over for your essential doggy bag. If you must stick with a salad, go for the classic Caesar salads, either plain or loaded with shrimp or chicken.

Bully's is popular in the summer months, but you can sit outdoors or in the pub and sip and wait. Bully's is open for breakfast, lunch, and dinner daily. There are two other branches, at 5755 La Jolla Boulevard, in La Jolla, (858) 459-2768, and at 2401 Camino del Rio South, Mission Valley, (619) 291-2665.

California Bistro $$$-$$$$
Four Seasons Resort Aviara
Californian
7100 Four Seasons Pt., Carlsbad
(760) 603-6800, (800) 332-3442

You might not expect a hotel's casual restaurant to be one of the top dining spots in the area, but the California Bistro consistently draws diners from throughout the county. It's actually difficult to get reservations for the Friday night seafood buffet, an extravaganza featuring everything from sushi to lobster with drawn butter. The $37.50 tab doesn't discourage seafood lovers. Reserve your table early in the week. The Wednesday night French Buffet Montmarte ($25) is also popular, and it's always a delight to while away the morning at the Sunday brunch ($33 or $40 with champagne).

The regular menu has its highlights as well. Breakfast might start with smoked salmon Benedict, or you could go lighter with rosy papaya and a huge muffin. We highly recommend the honey sunflower toast and the sticky pecan rolls. There's a wonderful buffet available during breakfast ($18.50) and lunch ($19.50) Monday through Saturday.

If you're visiting the California Bistro for lunch, you cannot go wrong with the Bistro chopped salad, Pacific swordfish salad, or the wok fried sweet and spicy prawns with fragrant rice and charred fruit salad. Of course, you might prefer the griddled crab cakes with mango papaya

relish, or the Aviara seafood andouille sausage chowder. The dinner menu always includes a traditional homecooked meal like Mom's Meatloaf, served with green beans, buttermilk-smashed potatoes with gravy, and button mushrooms.

The restaurant's menu is marked with choices that are lower in calories, cholesterol, sodium, and fat, so if you're visiting and enjoying the spa program, you can eat healthy foods. The California Bistro is open daily for breakfast, lunch, and dinner.

Chin's Szechwan Restaurant $$
Szechwan
2959 Madison Ave., Carlsbad
(760) 434-7117
1506 Encinitas Blvd., Encinitas
(760) 753-3903
4140 Oceanside Blvd., Oceanside
(760) 631-4808

While Chin's has a lot of locations, it's a San Diego exclusive and some of the best Szechwan we've had. Actually we were torn about including our favorite Chinese eatery because, by golly, it's already really popular.

The decor is what you'd expect from nearly any Chinese restaurant, but the food is better. Vegetable dishes are hot, crispy, and good. Service is excellent and strangely enough, each time we've been there, seating is possible the moment we walk in the door. Maybe it's just our Insiders' good fortune or because we've come in before the dinner crowd. Chin's has the prerequisite "family" style dinners and early-bird specials, too. Service is excellent. It's open daily for lunch and dinner. You can get take-out if you're headed to the beach or an outdoor concert.

Coyote Bar & Grill $$
American
300 Carlsbad Village Dr., Carlsbad
(760) 729-4695

This hot spot in downtown Carlsbad is mentioned in our Nightlife chapter, but it's more than a place to meet and mingle. Insiders come here for American food with a Southwestern flavor. At lunch, there's the working crowd from nearby offices and the Palomar Airport industrial area. At dinner, it's families and then

Sunset on the coast surrounds diners with the colors of the San Diego evening. PHOTO: COURTESY OF THE SAN DIEGO CONVENTION AND VISITORS BUREAU

couples. The couples often stay for the live entertainment and party atmosphere. Food is grilled over a wood fire. Salads are fresh and lively. You can eat inside or, as we recommend, on the patio. Open for lunch and dinner daily.

Fidel's $
Mexican
3003 Carlsbad Blvd., Carlsbad
(760) 729–0903
607 Valley Ave., Solana Beach
(858) 755–5292

If you've ever fantasized about the perfect Mexican food—hot, fresh, and abundant— Fidel's is your ticket to taste-bud heaven. It happens to be our Insiders' favorite in North County. And we're tough to please when it comes to Mexican food.

The restaurants have been in business since the 1940s and both locations are popular. On a Saturday or Sunday, especially during the summer, you probably will wish that they took reservations; they don't, so have a seltzer or glass of wine on the patio and be patient. You'll be rewarded.

Here's a tip: Come before the dinner crowd. As a matter of fact, come for happy hour (4:00 to 6:30 P.M.) when the drinks are more reasonable and the appetizers plentiful. Lunch prices are affordable and in the $5.00 to $8.00 range; dinner is a bit more pricey, but still easy on the wallet. Ask for the salsa fresca with any meal. It's an explosive combo of onion, chili, cilantro, and tomato and made on the spot just to thrill your taste buds.

Try the tender, piquant carne asada or the Tostada Suprema, which is a massive plate of shredded chicken (or beef) loaded down with guacamole, olives, tomatoes, beans, and lettuce. The Carlsbad location is about 1 block from the ocean, The Solana Beach Fidel's is about 2 miles north of the Del Mar Fairgrounds (see our Attractions chapter). Both locations are open for lunch and dinner and have happy hour and early-bird specials.

Fish House Vera Cruz $$
Seafood
417 Carlsbad Village Dr., Carlsbad
(760) 434–6777

Just 3 blocks from the beach and 3 blocks south of the Coaster station, Fish House Vera Cruz is one of the best seafood restaurants in the county. Fish is grilled to perfection over mesquite wood and is always succulent and fresh. They have a standard menu and catch-of-the-day choices, too. If you're from out of the area, the thought of eating grilled shark might be a bit much. Get over it if you want some really great fish and a great price, because shark is a mainstay on San Diego menus. The *Sopa de Pescado* (a spicy soup loaded with bite-size pieces of delicate fish, tomatoes, carrots, and potatoes) is served with lemon, and is so luscious that the kitchen sometimes runs out.

If you're determined to eat here, come at an off time, such as midafternoon or just before the lunchtime crowd to avoid a long wait. They don't accept reservations. Unfortunately this "find" isn't much of a secret to Insiders. Like its "sister" at 1020 San Marcos Boulevard, San Marcos, (760) 744–8000, the restaurant is open daily for lunch and dinner.

Greek Corner Cafe $$
Greek
1854 Marron Rd., Carlsbad
(760) 434–5557

If you love Greek food, you'll be happy here. The meals, such as the gyros plate for two, are bargains. Most meals are priced in the $10 to $19 range. They have low-fat and vegetarian dishes too. You can dine inside or on the patio. You can't rush this experience because you'll want to savor every bite. It is open for lunch and dinner.

Greek Village $$
Greek
6030 Paseo Del Norte, Carlsbad
(760) 603–9672

At the Greek Village, off Palomar Airport Drive and I-5, specialties of the house and favorites of Insiders are the souvlaki, moussaka, and fettucini ala Greka. You can't go wrong with the gyros platter for only $11.95.

The Greek Village starts serving up food at 10:00 A.M. daily with breakfast choices that include loukaniko and gyros to mundane stuff like a big farm-style breakfast of eggs, bacon, and toast. Lunch is a smaller version of dinner and hot and cold sandwiches. You can dine inside or on the patio. The Greek Village is open daily for breakfast, lunch, and dinner.

Jake's Del Mar $$–$$$
Seafood
1660 Coast Blvd., Del Mar
(858) 755-2002

Here's a classic waterfront restaurant and a sure thing if you're hungry for seafood and atmosphere. The location, right on the ocean, is impossible to beat, and it outshines the food. Take a hint, and call for a reservation or be disappointed with a long wait. It's a good party place and draws in a fun-loving Friday night crowd. After you've partied, stay for the Asian seafood cocktail followed by the tortilla-crusted halibut with avocado/mango salsa. Open for lunch and dinner daily and on Sunday for brunch.

Mille Fleurs Restaurant $$$$
French
6009 Paseo Delicias, Rancho Santa Fe
(858) 756-3085

Here's the benchmark for all French restaurants in the county, and a venerable leader in the romance category. Mille Fleurs, in the upscale area of Rancho Santa Fe, attracts national attention and constantly wins culinary awards. *Food and Wine* magazine has named it one of the top 25 restaurants in the country, and the James Beard House has named Chef Martin Woesle one of the great regional chefs. Owner Bertrand Hug created this cozy cottage restaurant in 1984 and has made it one of the finest French restaurants in the country. Notables, celebrities, and the wealthy gather here when they want superb service and great food. In fact, your chances of spotting visiting celebrities are excellent here. People become hooked on Mille Fleurs and often try to think up special occasions so they can come here to celebrate.

The cuisine is fine dining at its best. The menu changes daily, as Woesle collects his ingredients from gourmet produce farms and other top-notch purveyors. Chances are you'll find sweetbreads,

duck liver, partridge, and other treats you don't normally see on San Diego menus. The extraordinary wine list (with prices to match) makes connoisseurs swoon. Open for lunch Monday through Friday and dinner nightly. Be sure to dress up for the experience. If you come by on a Thursday, Friday, or Saturday night you can join the patrons singing show tunes at the piano bar.

Pacifica Breeze Cafe $$
Eclectic Californian
1555 Camino Del Mar, Del Mar
(858) 509-9147

It's quaint. It has great food. It's popular and it's in downtown Del Mar. You'll want to eat tacos, salads, baked goods, soups, and light entrees on the patio while you sip some home brew. An Insiders' favorite at Pacific Breeze Cafe are the barbecued fish tacos, followed by a margarita. Open for breakfast and lunch daily, the Pacific Breeze is conveniently located in the Del Mar Plaza (see our Shopping chapter).

Pizza Port $$
Pizza
571 Carlsbad Village Dr., Carlsbad
(760) 720-7007
135 N. Hwy. 101, Solana Beach
(858) 481-7332

Insiders' Tip

If you find that evening is approaching and you don't have a dinner reservation, go early. Most restaurants start serving as early as 5:00 P.M., but the dinner crowd doesn't start arriving until about 7:00 P.M. Chances are you'll be able to get a table.

Here's where you'll find praiseworthy pizza that's a cut above the most chi-chi pizzas you've had. Better yet, they brew on-site and provide just the right micro-brewed beer to go with your choice. You can even have your pizza with a whole grain beer crust.

Decor is of the wooden picnic-table variety with big-screen televisions flashing sports, and the music is sometimes loud and the conversation even louder.

Yes, the Pizza Port restaurants are popular. Pizza specials and microbrew choices vary and sometimes they sponsor beer-tasting contests in which the public can participate. The Pizza Port pizzerias are open daily for lunch and dinner.

Prontos' Gourmet Market $
Italian
2812 Roosevelt St., Carlsbad
(760) 434-2644

Here's an eating jewel that's tucked away in the heart of the village of Carlsbad. Once you stop here, you may not want to tell any friends for fear it will become crowded.

Sandwiches are stuffed with meats and vegetables, prices are easy on the wallet, and everything is fresh and tasty. You get choices of breads and side dishes with each sandwich and there are salads too. Most folks take out and get back to work, but there's a shady patio where you can dine outdoors.

Prontos' is open 9:00 A.M. to 6:00 P.M. Monday through Friday. Stop and pick up a prepared meal, like the lasagna, or a sandwich for supper on the way home from work.

St. Germain's Cafe $
European Sidewalk Cafe
1010 S. Coast Hwy. 101, Encinitas
(760) 753-5411

It's impossible to pinpoint a "type" for this quaint cafe set in Encinitas; locals just go there because the food is always wonderful. Here eggs Benedict are served all day long. You can also get Eggs Acapulco (topped with zesty Spanish sauce) and a dozen other breakfast varieties. All food is served with fresh fruit or their yummy cafe potatoes. Belgian waffles, sandwiches, and soups are always good choices, too. Open for breakfast and lunch each day.

That Pizza Place $
Pizza and more
2622 El Camino Real, Carlsbad
(760) 434-3171
1810 Oceanside Blvd., Oceanside
(760) 757-6212

That Pizza Place restaurants are neighborhood pizza eateries (that serve salads and subs too) and have live entertainment on some evenings. Call the numbers above for more information on groups and times. They've been in North County Coastal since 1979 and are proud of the local connection. The places are the gathering holes for community sports teams; they flock in after games. As you might expect the atmosphere is super-casual and no one will notice if your baseball shirt has grass stains on it or your soccer uniform is caked with mud. Why you might even get a round of applause.

The house special pizza is pepperoni, ham, salami, mushrooms, olives, bell peppers, and sausage—you have to ask for anchovies. It's always served up hot and fresh. We think the best things to eat at That Pizza Place are the Roll'N The Dough sandwiches. They're like a pizza burrito. For about $3.00 you can even get the Kitchen Sink, a combination that has about everything on it. If that's not enough, there are special lunch deals, like a small pizza, large soft drink, and a trip to the always-fresh salad bar for about $4.50. You can dine in (with picnic-table elegance) or take it out. The restaurants are open for lunch and dinner daily.

Trattoria Positano $$
Italian
2171 San Elijo Ave., Cardiff
(760) 632-0111

Welcoming and relaxing is the atmosphere of this cafe just a few blocks from the ocean in Cardiff. There's an excellent salad selection; a tangy citrus sauce graces the warm Maine lobster salad priced at less than $13. You'll find seafood, a slew of pasta choices, and vegetarian specialties, too. The decor is California/Italian,

A Seaport Village restaurant at sunset will offer picturesque dining. PHOTO: DALE FROST, COURTESY OF THE PORT OF SAN DIEGO

crisp and clean with great service. Lunch Monday through Saturday; dinner is served daily.

Vivace $$$
International/Californian
Four Seasons Resort Aviara
7100 Four Seasons Pt., Carlsbad
(760) 603–6800, (800) 332–3442

The decor of this popular restaurant is so inviting (some tables have fat easy chairs and sofas rather than straight backed, restaurant-style chairs), you might try to stay forever. When the food arrives you'll be dazzled. It's one of those eating experiences where you can linger over your food, loving the antipasto and appetizers, adoring the soups, diving into the main courses, and cherishing every bite of the dessert. As you make reservations on a beautiful summer evening, ask for a table overlooking the balcony, the lagoon, and the Pacific beyond.

To say that Vivace is a respectable restaurant is like saying a Jaguar is a nice car—this is great stuff. If you're a seafood lover, try the grilled swordfish with roasted fennel or the lobster risotto. It's impossible to go wrong with the lamb osso bucco or veal tenderloin.

Entrees cost $17.50 to about $30.00. All desserts are $6.50. If you have room, try the Warm Bitter Sweet Chocolate Melt over cranberry ice cream. Vivace is open daily for dinner only.

To read more about this resort, please see our chapters on Golf and Spas and Resorts.

North County Inland

Chieu-Anh $$
Vietnamese
16769 Bernardo Center Dr.,
Rancho Bernardo
(858) 485–1231

Chieu-Anh has to be included in a culinary tour of North County Inland because the foods are fresh and combinations unique even for this cuisine. It's tucked into a shopping mall and you might walk past without hardly giving it a second thought, except for the fragrances emanating from the eatery. We love the specialty of feather-light Vietnamese crepe filled with grilled chicken and shrimp. There's a tangy and sour soup with tamarind flavor that's excellent, and the shrimp on sugar cane is a smoky, savory delight. The restaurant is open Tuesday through Friday for lunch and Tuesday through Sunday for dinner.

DiCrescenzo's $
Italian
11627 Duenda Rd., Rancho Bernardo
(858) 487-2776

This is an order-at-the-counter and eat-outdoors place, and it's so popular with the working crowd from the high-tech companies in Rancho Bernardo, you may have to stand in a long line and then get your lunch in a bag. Trust us, it's worth it.

Insiders keep a menu in their desks and call ahead so they can pay and pick up their choices without the wait. Prices are nearly as good as the food. The baked ziti with French bread is just $3.75. The subs, featuring Genoa salami, ham capicolla, mortadella, provolone cheese, and all the other veggie fixings are under $6.00, unless you're picking up one for the whole office that serves 20 people. That sandwich is only $49.95. The menu includes low-fat items, too.

DiCrescenzo's is open for lunch and dinner and what it lacks in atmosphere, it more than makes up for in flavor.

El Bizcocho $$$$
French
17550 Bernardo Oaks Dr., Rancho Bernardo
(858) 675-8500

If you're ready to propose to your darling or celebrate a momentous occasion, book a window-side table at the county's most elegant restaurant, which overlooks the golf course at the Rancho Bernardo Inn. Consistently rated among the top five restaurants in San Diego, El Bizcocho is overseen by Executive Chef Tom Dowling. He's a favorite among local gourmands, who swoon over his foie gras Napoleon, monk-fish with wild mushrooms and black truffles, and roasted duckling carved tableside. El Biz, as locals call their favorite dining

room, has its own sommelier and a wine list valued at over $1 million. The Chef's Tasting Menu is available with wines suited to each of the five courses; it costs $90 with wine and $62 without. The liqueur cart's selection of rare ports may well be worth more than some diners' cars. El Biz serves dinner nightly and a fabulous Sunday brunch ($30). Reservations are essential.

Hot Wok Cafe $
Mandarin and Szechuan
1252 E. Mission Rd., San Marcos
(760) 735-9988

Whether you decide to dine inside or take home the treats, the Hot Wok is popular and gives you plenty of choices and plenty of food.

A special noodle soup for just $4.95 easily serves two. The honey spice shrimp and Szechuan-style egg foo young are two of the popular choices, but as Insiders know, it's nearly impossible to make a bad choice with this much good food. The place is busy and tends to be noisy, so if you're looking for a romantic Chinese place, put out the chop sticks on your own dining room table and order carryout as many do. It's open daily for lunch and dinner.

Lake Wohlford Cafe $
American
25484 Lake Wohlford Rd., Escondido
(760) 749-2755

You could call the decor at the Lake Wohlford Cafe "funky" and not be too far from the mark. The cafe is casual and makes you feel like it's okay to have fun. At this cafe, no one will even notice if you've dripped catsup or eaten the fries with your fingers—you're supposed to, right?

Burgers and fries and lots of American food are on the menu. Call about their special all-you-can-eat catfish dinners. There is live music some nights.

La Paloma Restaurante $$
Mexican
116 Escondido Ave., Vista
(760) 758-7140

When Insiders get into discussions on the best Mexican food in the area (and this is serious business—opinions and chili peppers

El Bizcocho, the fine dining room at the Rancho Bernardo Inn, is considered one of the top restaurants in San Diego County. PHOTO: COURTESY OF THE SAN DIEGO NORTH CONVENTION & VISITORS BUREAU

have a lot in common), La Paloma always wins praise.

Located out of the usual restaurant area, La Paloma serves up fresh, savory, and spicy favorites. Although it's a struggle to name the best choices, we love the shrimp and lobster meat fajitas (at about $16.25), and the *camarones con pollo* cilantro (tender shrimp and sliced chicken breast sauteed in sauce and spices and topped with cheese, avocado, and cilantro).

All meals are served with rice, beans, and tortillas. You can be cautious with tacos and tostadas and burritos (all priced in the $7.00 range); or reckless with *bistec vaquero*, a large steak charbroiled and topped with mushrooms, garlic, and onions; or the Pancho Villa ribs smothered in a zesty barbecue sauce. There are half-price happy hour appetizer specials Monday through Friday in the bar and early-bird dinners Sunday through Thursday. La Paloma is open daily for lunch and dinner and you can dine indoors or on the patio. Choose the patio if you love everything that's great about San Diego.

Mama Cella's Italian Kitchen $$
Italian
16707 Bernardo Center Dr.,
Rancho Bernardo
(619) 613-7770

Do you crave a meatball sandwich? How about a grinder? Or a sandwich that's loaded beyond dripping with eggplant Parmigiana on a bun? Stop in at this no-frills, but great-food Italian restaurant. It's a hot spot with the work-day folks from Rancho Bernardo; the staff is quick and efficient. The pizza selection, according to Insiders, is tops, especially the Toscana (about $16), which includes pesto, mushrooms, cheese, and chicken. Mama Cella's is open for lunch and dinner.

Mr. W's Restaurant $$
American
8860 Lawrence Welk Dr., Escondido
(760) 749-3000, ext. 2129

Some Insiders visit the Welk Resort just to dine with views of the golf course. The restaurant's quality surprised us on some recent visits. Hospitality was warm, food hot and well presented and there's a lavish carved-meat buffet and salad bar (it's available during the dinner theater performances). On the menu you'll find seafood, Angus prime roast beef, and chicken along with international favorites. The restaurant is open daily for breakfast, lunch, and dinner.

150 Grand Café $$
New American
150 W. Grand Ave., Escondido
(760) 738-6868

Cleanly and sparingly decorated in white on white on white, this downtown Escondido venue is the place to show off your glad rags before sashaying over for an evening of entertainment at the Center for Performing Arts, just a stone's throw away. You won't feel uncomfortable, however, in your Dockers or a freshly pressed jean skirt, as the nine-year-old restaurant successfully combines casual with lots of class. In summer choose a sidewalk table; in the winter, the coziest spot is inside under the aquarium-size, shoulder-level, glassed-in fireplace. Whatever the season, you'll be treated to "New American Cuisine," international dishes reinvented with a fresh spin by Chef Carlton Greenwalt. Highly recommended are the watercress salad with a dressing of fresh crème, wasabi, Meyer lemon, soy and honey, and the sweet, tender Atlantic salmon braised with blueberries and wilted spinach, topped with caviar. Cleanse your palette between courses with a complimentary sorbet of lemon grass and ginger, and for dessert, save room for Baked California: avocado ice cream surrounded by a mound of candied-lime meringue with a tequila flambé. The restaurant is open for lunch and dinner daily except Sunday, when it's closed.

Vincent's Sirinos Restaurant $$$
French/Continental
113 W. Grand Ave., Escondido
(760) 745-3835

Reservations are essential for dinner at this cozy dining room overseen by Chef Vincent Grumel. The dining room is unassuming—some say uninspired—but any thoughts that this might be a dull place will end in a flash when you breathe in the fragrances coming from the kitchen, and ultimately onto your plate.

Grumel's specialty is duck, and diners rave about his Canard au Myrtilles and confit of duck. Beef lovers can't miss with the filet mignon with Stilton cheese and a Merlot sauce, and the ravioli stuffed with veal is superb. If you're not into meat, try the pastry Florentine, an overstuffed turnover bursting with spinach, Stilton cheese, and veggies. The eggplant ravioli is also a good option. Vincent's is the perfect place to stop before a concert at the California Center for the Arts. Open for lunch Tuesday through Friday and dinner Tuesday through Saturday.

Wildwood German American Restaurant $$
German-American
1415 S. Mission Rd., Fallbrook
(760) 731-0007

Hungry for bratwurst sausages, dumplings that nearly float into your mouth, and apple strudel nestled in a cloud of whipped cream? If your mouth is watering at these visions, head straight for the Wildwood German American Restaurant. Specialties of German food include breaded pork loin fried crisp and tender in the Wiener schnitzel style, and sauerbraten that is savory and nearly melts on your fork.

The dining room has high ceilings and is decorated with cozy bric-a-brac and candles on the tables. Entrees include crusty wheat bread (hot from the oven), soup, or salad. Ask for the house horseradish dressing if you want to zip up those greens. The restaurant is open daily, except Tuesday, and for dinner only.

East County

The Barbeque Pit $
American
2388 Fletcher Pkwy., El Cajon
(619) 462-5434

Since 1947, the Barbeque Pit has been serving up tender, succulent choices of carved-to-order beef, ham, and rib dinners that bring customers back again and again. Try the chicken, or if you're a hot-sausage fan, you can't go wrong with their spicy choice.

On Friday the specialty is shredded pork, not just on a sandwich, but piled high on a toasted bun. Side dishes include macaroni and potato salads, coleslaw, and French fries. The Barbeque Pit has good grub, the decor is without pretension, and it is open for lunch and dinner.

Barona Casino   **$**
American
1000 Wildcat Canyon Rd., Lakeside
(619) 443–2300, (888) 722–7662

You've read about this casino in our Attractions chapter and here it is again. The casino has a Vegas-style buffet, called the International Buffet. The food themes change often, but what doesn't change is the variety of the spread.

On Mondays it's a taste of Italy. The buffet is open for lunch and dinner. Another restaurant, the Side Court, gives you 24-hour-a-day eating and snacking possibilities. Remember that one must be 18 or older to be present in the casino, even for dinner, after 8:00 P.M.

Dudley's Bakery and Cafe   **$**
American
Calif. Hwy. 78 and 79, Santa Ysabel
(760) 765–0488

The bakery and cafe are East County treasures. To visitors, Santa Ysabel might seem to be smack dab out in nowhere yet Insiders drive from all over southern California for a loaf of Dudley's bread and if they're patient, they wait for a table in the cafe.

You'll want to read about the bakery in our Shopping chapter if you're planning a trip to this part of the county. The food is good enough to warrant the wait you may have on some weekends; it's also a fun stop to or from a Julian outing. Open daily for breakfast, lunch, and dinner. An Insider favorite is the raisin nut bread.

D.Z. Akin's   **$$**
Delicatessen
6930 Alvarado Rd., San Diego
(619) 265–0218

East Coast transplants bemoan the lack of good Jewish delis in San Diego County. You're hard pressed to find a good white-fish platter or chicken-in-the-pot with matzoh balls. That's why Insiders from throughout the county drive east on I-8, past San Diego State, to this deli in a small strip mall. Divine rye bread is piled high with pastrami, tongue, liverwurst, brisket—nearly anything your tastebuds desire. Try the scrambled eggs with lox and onions for breakfast and the tri-salad platter with chopped liver at lunch. You probably won't be able to pass by the bakery counter without buying rugalach, strudel, and eclairs to take home. It's open daily for breakfast, lunch, and dinner. The parking lot is usually packed. Have someone jump out and put your name on the waiting list while the driver waits for sated diners to waddle back to their cars.

Giacopelli's New York Deli   **$**
American
2512 Jamacha Rd., El Cajon
(619) 670–4320

Insiders come here for the hero sandwiches and the mountain-high piles of cold cuts stuffed into a crispy Italian roll. Some say it's the only place in East County where you can get a decent New York–style hot dog (which comes from a cart inside the store). Even if you're not from the Big Apple, you'll like the slowly simmered sauces that include marinara, creamy vodka, and tomato for pasta or a meatball sandwich. Giacopelli's New York Deli is open for breakfast, lunch, and dinner. Call ahead if you want to order and pick up a sandwich.

> ## Insiders' Tip
> Most street-side cafes do not mind if well-behaved dogs are leashed under the tables. But ask before you assume it's okay.

Julian Grille $
American
2224 Main St., Julian
(760) 765–0173

Go for the pie—apple pie, that is, and the pie that put Julian on the map. And be sure to save room after the large servings of American-style choices served at the Grille. This is where the Julian Insiders and visitors eat, and during Apple Days and when the art and photo shows are held, it can be busy. Service is good at the Grille and the food worth the wait.

The Julian Grille is a nice tradition for every trip to the mountain community and it's open for breakfast, lunch, and dinner every day.

La Mesa Ocean Grill $$
Seafood
5465 Lake Murray Blvd., La Mesa
(619) 463–1548

Here's the place if you've been craving lobster in a big way. They're big, sweet, and straight from New England. The whole Maine lobster (served seasonally) includes deviled clam, clam fritters, corn on the cob, red potatoes, and corn bread. The Big Kahuna Fried Fishermen's Plate (about $20) will stuff you with Arctic cod, shrimp, scallops, calamari, crab cake, deviled clam, clam fritters, French fries, coleslaw, and corn bread. You may just want to order one dinner and split it between two. Ask about the daily specials. La Mesa Ocean Grill, a find in East County, is open daily for lunch and dinner.

Mario's de La Mesa $
Mexican
8425 La Mesa Blvd., La Mesa
(619) 461–9390

"This is down-home cooking," say some Insiders after sampling the food at this lesser-known, but wonderful nonetheless, Mexican restaurant. The food arrives in generous helpings, the menu is extensive, and the service is better than home. You can be sure to get smiles with every order here. There's a Don Gallo sauce that is a creamy covering for some of the seafood dishes. It's innovative and downright tasty too. There's a "build your own" taco bar and all the standards you've come to expect from Mexican restaurants. It's open daily for breakfast, lunch, and dinner. On Sunday, it opens for brunch and then heads straight to dinner.

Pinnacle Peak Steak House $$
American
7927 Mission Gorge Rd., Santee
(619) 448–8882

Let's say you're in East County, maybe visiting Summers Past Farms or the casinos (see our Attractions chapter). It hits you. You're hungry for a steak, and not just any steak will do. You want a cowboy-size portion with beans and bread and barbecue sauce that's rich and red. The answer to your need to feed is the Pinnacle Peak, a cowboy eatery where the staff, if necessary, will forcibly take your tie and suit jacket. All the beef (and chicken) choices are grilled to perfection over an open mesquite fire.

If you and a sweetie are lookin' for candles, romantic mushy mood music, and a place where the ostentatious nouveau victuals are no bigger than your thumb, do not, we repeat, do not come to Pinnacle Peak. This is the steak house where the slogan is "beef is our business" and they mean business. Once you see the size of the steaks and burgers, you'll agree that they don't mess around with huge appetites.

The restaurant is a fun experience, a great place for families, and a favorite among residents from all over the county. Pinnacle Peak is open for lunch and dinner every day.

Romano's Dodge House $$
Italian
2718 B St., Julian
(760) 765–1003

This restaurant is just a block off Main Street in downtown Julian. It is an Insiders' favorite, too. There's a classic, Julian-style rustic decor and a fine selection of Italian specialties. Ask about the daily specials and check out the pizza variations. Credit cards are not accepted here, but it is open for lunch and dinner Wednesday to Monday.

Sunday Brunch in San Diego

If you're like most Insiders, you wake up some Sunday mornings with one thought: where shall we go for brunch? San Diego is a big brunch town, and chances are good that your favorite restaurant will have its own version of the weekend ritual. Most include complimentary champagne, and the serving style leans heavily toward buffet, although some restaurants have a special brunch menu. The following list will give you an idea of where some of the best brunches in town are, but don't hesitate to do some exploring. Our price code is the same one we've used throughout this chapter and indicates the cost of brunch for two, excluding cocktails (although some brunches include complimentary champagne), tax, and tip. Most brunches start at 9:00 or 10:00 A.M. and wrap up by 2:00 or 3:00 P.M.

$$$ **Bali Hai**
2230 Shelter Island Dr., San Diego (619) 222–1182

$$$ **Bob's by the Bay**
570 Marina Pkwy, Chula Vista (619) 476–0400

$$$ **Del Mar Hilton**
15575 Jimmy Durante Blvd., Del Mar (858) 792–5200

$$$$ **El Bizcocho**
17550 Bernardo Oaks Dr., Rancho Bernardo (858) 675–8500

Casual dining is interspersed with sublime dinners at the Rancho Bernardo Inn. PHOTO: COURTESY OF THE SAN DIEGO NORTH CONVENTION & VISITORS BUREAU

$$$$	**Hilton Torrey Pines**
	10950 N. Torrey Pines Rd., La Jolla (858) 450–4571
$$$$	**Hotel del Coronado**
	1500 Orange Ave., Coronado (619) 435–6611
$$$	**Humphrey's**
	2241 Shelter Island Dr., San Diego (619) 224–3577
$$$$	**Hyatt Regency**
	One Market Pl., San Diego (619) 687–6066
$$$$	**Loews Coronado Bay**
	4000 Coronado Bay Rd., Coronado (619) 424–4000
$$	**Quails Inn**
	1035 La Bonita, San Marcos (760) 744–2445
$$$$	**Rancho Bernardo Inn**
	17550 Bernardo Dr., San Diego (858) 675–8550
$$$	**Reuben's**
	880 E. Harbor Island Dr., San Diego (619) 291–5030
$$	**Tomatoes**
	4346 Bonita Rd., Bonita (619) 479–8494

Viejas Casino & Turf Club $–$$
Buffet and Food Court
5000 Willows Rd., Alpine
(619) 445–5400

For everything you can expect at this ultra-popular casino, be sure to read our entries in the Nightlife and Attractions chapters. You can also expect casual dining and fine dining, in very easygoing surroundings. Check out the grand buffet (a smaller version of those seen in Las Vegas or Atlantic City). There's also the new China Camp Express for Asian foods and other 24-hour restaurants to make your gaming experience complete. Restaurants are open daily for breakfast, lunch, and dinner.

Village Garden Restaurant & Bakery $
American
8384 La Mesa Blvd., La Mesa
(619) 462–9100

Homestyle cooking with flair is what you'll find at the Village Garden Restaurant & Bakery. Go hungry—this is down-home,

stick-to-your-ribs cooking. Consider the Yankee eggs, served with pot roast at breakfast, or the half-pound bruschetta burger with cheese, garlic, and olive oil. Have a hankering for chicken and dumplings? How about all-you-can-eat fish and chips (served Fridays). The mesquite grill on the terrace is fired up on Thursday and Friday nights in the summer, when diners clamor for the tender baby back ribs. You can dine

Insiders' Tip
Many restaurants can package full meals for take-out service. Call ahead and pick up your order on the way to the beach or an outdoor concert.

inside or on the patio. The eatery is open for breakfast and lunch Monday through Wednesday, and Thursday through Sunday it's open for breakfast, lunch, and dinner.

South Bay

Anthony's Fish Grotto   **$–$$**
Seafood
215 Bay Blvd., Chula Vista
(619) 425–4200
1360 N. Harbor Dr., San Diego
(619) 232–5103
9530 Murray Dr., La Mesa
(619) 463–0368
11666 Avena Pl., Rancho Bernardo
(858) 451–2070

San Diego's Ghio family has established a long tradition of good, reasonably priced seafood at their grotto restaurants. When you enter the grottos, you'll feel you've been transported to an underwater cave, complete with sea animals, coral, and shells. The exception to this decor is the Harbor Drive restaurant, which is open to the bay to take advantage of the view.

Seafood salads are the gems of the lunch-time menu, especially the seafood combo—chunks of lobster, shrimp, crab, and avocado served over fresh greens and topped with Anthony's signature dressing. For more hearty appetites, choose from a variety of fish from both the lunch and dinner menus, including, sole, sea bass, halibut, and swordfish that are grilled, sautéed, or broiled according to your desire. Anthony's is open for lunch Monday through Saturday, and for dinner nightly.

Insiders' Tip

Although it's been a few years since San Diego rationed water (because of the severe drought conditions), you may still have to order water with your meals.

Bob's by the Bay   **$$**
American
570 Marina Parkway, Chula Vista
(619) 476–0400

Bob's is one of the most popular restaurants in the South Bay, and for good reason. The food is consistently well prepared, and the menu features perennial favorites. The grilled shrimp, two skewers of salmon seasoned with citrus and butter, then grilled, is paired with fresh seasonal vegetables and basmati rice—just right for a dinner that's filling but on the light side. Grilled chicken alfredo is another crowd-pleaser—marinated, boneless chicken grilled and served over fettucine with a basil and parmesan cream sauce.

This is a busy hangout for the after-work crowd, too, and a good place to meet friends for a drink before dinner. Bob's is located close to the water in the Chula Vista Marina and is open for lunch and dinner daily.

The Bonita Store   **$$**
Mexican
4014 Bonita Rd., Bonita
(619) 479–3537

If you're searching for a restaurant with strong influences of Baja California and Mexico in the South Bay, look no farther than The Bonita Store (also known as Rockin' Baja Lobster). All the standard Mexican fare is served here, such as combination plates and a la carte tacos, burritos, and enchiladas, but the real treat is the bucket of Baja-style lobster for two.

The bucket includes slipper lobster tails, shrimp, grilled chicken, and carne asada, plus Caesar salad, rice, beans, and tortillas. The atmosphere is party-like and casual. Everyone has fun at The Bonita Store. It's open for lunch and dinner daily.

The Butcher Shop   **$$**
American
556 Broadway, Chula Vista
(619) 420–9440
5255 Kearny Villa Rd., San Diego
(858) 565–2272

As its name implies, The Butcher Shop specializes in beef: prime rib, top sirloin, and just about any other cut that strikes your fancy. Picture a darkened dining room with paneled walls and red fabric booths, a holdover from the days of three-martini lunches in a smoke-filled room.

The restaurant also caters to lighter eaters by offering chicken and fish dishes, but then spoils all your good intentions by serving them with irresistible, giant twice-baked potatoes and piping hot garlic bread. Dinner is served nightly, and lunch is served Monday through Saturday. On Sundays The Butcher Shop opens in the early afternoon for a late lunch or early dinner.

D'lish $–$$
Pizzas, Pastas, Salads
386 E. H St., Ste. 211, Chula Vista
(619) 585–1371
2260 Otay Lakes Rd., Chula Vista
(619) 216–3900
5252 Balboa Ave., San Diego
(858) 277–9977

Whether take-out is on the agenda or you're dining in, D'Lish serves up gourmet salads, pizzas, and pastas with a different but delicious twist. The Caesar salad, for example is made with roasted red peppers

and kalamata olives, a tasty combination of flavors. Another menu favorite is the chicken sun-dried calzone, made with chicken, sun-dried tomatoes, marinara sauce, and sour cream. Or, try the shrimp-scallop angel hair pasta served with red onions, bell peppers, and zucchini.

The atmosphere is casual, with both table and booth seating. A fire pit keeps diners toasty warm on chilly winter nights. The menu may vary slightly at the different locations, and everything on the menu is available for take-out. Lunch and dinner are served daily.

Edelweiss $$
German
230 Third Ave., Chula Vista
(619) 426–5172

If you're a schnitzel fan, Edelweiss is just what the doctor ordered. Try Wiener Schnitzel, Jager Schnitzel, or Holstein Schnitzel. Or if you prefer to jump off the schnitzel bandwagon, sample one of the other authentic German entrees, like sauerbraten or hunter stew. Traditional treats such as potato pancakes and cabbage rolls are quite good, too.

Nightlife

After a hard day playing outdoors, who wants to have more fun? Most of us in San Diego. While the city isn't known for the kind of trendy, chic, and wild nightlife you might find in Hollywood or Manhattan, San Diego's after-hours personality is alive and well.

Here you can choose from a smorgasbord of nighttime pleasures. In this chapter we'll give you the rundown on clubs, bars, brewpubs, and independent coffeehouses. As a note, we didn't list every Starbucks in the county. Just follow your nose to find them or check the listing in the phone book for the closest place for coffee.

We'll steer you clear (by not mentioning them) of those places with questionable reputations and head you toward the ones that can make your trip even better. If there's a cover charge or a specific dress code for a nightspot, we've added that information, but keep in mind, things change.

Since San Diego's population looks young, don't be shocked if you're carded. Club owners and barkeeps have the right to ask anyone for ID at any time. Even if you're in the over-30 crowd, you'll need to carry identification. We have been carded well past college age and said "Thanks very much!"

Remember that in California, there's no smoking in public establishments; to cater to their smoking customers, quite a few bars have installed outdoor patios or rooftop lounges.

While there's plenty to do outside San Diego proper, one of the hottest places to party is definitely the Gaslamp Quarter, in downtown San Diego. To be completed by summer 2002, the House of Blues restaurant and nightclub will offer solid nighttime entertainment along with retail space for those who want to sing the blues—or at least listen to them. Be sure to look for it in the Gaslamp Quarter.

If you're visiting or making San Diego your home, you'll want to browse through the entire section, knowing that to find the right nightlife for you, you may need to drive for a half-hour to find it. That's a small price to pay for a great time.

When we formulated our list, made phone calls, and took field trips (it was a tough job, but someone had to do it), one thing was clear: Clubs, pubs, coffeehouses, and the rest change. One spot might be hot with rock music and then a month later change ownership. The next time you visit you might find a jazz band or a poetry reading or a passle of square dancers. So though we've tried to make our listings as current and accurate as possible, you still might want to make some calls to check on the types of music or entertainment you'll find.

With all the directions and advice out of the way, it's time to introduce our entries and give you the lay of nightlife land. Have fun—it's abundant in San Diego and waiting for you right now.

Nightclubs and Concert Venues

Central San Diego

Barefoot Bar and Grill
San Diego Paradise Point Resort
1404 W. Vacation Rd., San Diego
(858) 274-4630

You can get here by boat, tie up, climb ashore, and start dancing. The Barefoot is legendary in San Diego because of the unusual way some people arrive. Don't worry if you're boatless though; more conventional methods will get you here too. The sound is different every night, from reggae to pop to classic rock to blues. Even though the bar is on the grounds of a resort hotel, you'll find lots of locals of all ages here. There's a cover charge on Friday, Saturday, and Sunday.

The Bitter End
770 Fifth Ave., San Diego
(619) 338–9300
www.thebitterend.com

This classy joint at the corner of Fifth and F Streets is habituated by denizens of the Gaslamp Quarter. In the upstairs lounge there's a rather extensive dress code, including no baseball caps, printed T-shirts, jeans with holes, tennis shoes, or sandals. Once safely up the stairs, you can stake out a coveted plush chair or sofa in front of one of two marble fireplaces; floors are hardwood and the ambiance is comfortable yet elegant. On the ground floor, the long wooden bar gleams and the room is usually packed. For dancing, head to the back of the bar and the Gaslamp Underground, where groups from the '70s, '80s, and today perform weekends and some weekday nights. After 8:00 P.M. on Fridays and Saturdays, when the line of hopefuls stretches around the corner, there's a cover charge of $10.

Blind Melons
710 Garnet Ave., San Diego
(858) 483–7844

This is not a place to dress up. Throw on a pair of jeans and come dance to the sound of the blues from nationally known artists. Jazz musicians are also regularly featured. The cover charge varies according to the notoriety of the band, but it ranges from around $3.00 to $12.00. On weekends the first show usually starts at 4:00 P.M., the second at 7:00 or 8:00 P.M. This is the epitome of a beach bar, so expect the crowd to have a free-and-easy attitude. Although music is the main attraction, there are pool tables and some patrons are always glued to a sporting event on one of several TVs.

Cafe Sevilla
555 Fourth Ave., San Diego
(619) 233–5979

Nibble on Spanish tapas or enjoy a full meal at this trendy restaurant/club in the Gaslamp Quarter. In the downstairs nightclub are dinner shows with a set menu for $30 per person. It's tango on Friday nights; on Saturdays customers are served Spanish paella as the main course as they watch a flamenco dance show. There's dancing every night of the week: Mondays to Latin rock; Tuesday through Thursday to tropical tunes (with dance lessons for the uninitiated). On Fridays Cafe Sevilla hosts a Latin-Euro Dance Club. During the week the cover charge is $6.00 to $8.00; on Fridays and Saturdays it's $10.00. Like most places in the Gaslamp, the age of the crowd varies.

'Canes Bar and Grill
3105 Ocean Front Walk, San Diego
(858) 488–1780

This is a lively spot located in Belmont Park in Mission Beach. On a normal night, the crowd is usually made up of 20-somethings, but special concerts will draw a mixed-age group. Some concerts are open to revelers as young as 18. In addition to concerts, 'Canes has music festivals, local bands, and lots of special activities. The rooftop deck overlooking the ocean offers a nice respite from the activity below. Admission varies according to the event; call for prices.

Cannibal Bar
**Catamaran Resort Hotel,
3999 Mission Blvd., San Diego
(858) 488–1081**

The Cannibal Bar has had some staying power. Trendy hangouts tend to come and go, but this one has been around a while. Live entertainment and dancing are featured Wednesday through Sunday, and the sounds are eclectic: reggae, blues, zydeco, alternative rock, acid jazz, and good old-fashioned rock and roll. There are often cover bands, such as Steely Damned and Pink Froyd. Occasional special concerts are presented, too, for which tickets must be purchased ahead of time. Cover charges fluctuate, ranging from nothing to $10. During the summer months, bands sometimes play on the beach next to the hotel.

The Casbah
**2501 Kettner Blvd., San Diego
(619) 232–4355**

Open daily from 8:30 P.M. to the standard 2:00 A.M. closing, the Casbah is one of San Diego's cutting edge clubs, offering happening young local and nationally known bands. It's a super bargain, as the cover might hover around $10 for the likes of Alanis Morrisette, Ben Harper, The Breeders, and Royal Crown Revue. The club has a smokers' patio and game room with a few pool tables and video games.

The Comedy Store
**916 Pearl St., La Jolla
(858) 454–9176**

What started in Los Angeles has made its way south to La Jolla. First-rate comedians entertain, and sometimes a big name will roll in. Check out the Dreamgirls Revue held weekly, featuring comedy and celebrity lookalikes. If you're an aspiring comic yourself, consider coming for the free "pot luck Sunday," when you can try your act on a captive audience—at least for five minutes. Open Tuesday through Sunday, there's a two-drink minimum nightly and a $5.00 cover charge most nights ($15.00 on Friday and $20.00 on Saturday). Must be 21 to enter.

Croce's Restaurant & Jazz Bar
**802 Fifth Ave., San Diego
(619) 233–4355
www.croces.com**

Croce's has become an institution in San Diego for its fine dining and outstanding entertainment. Owned by Ingrid Croce, widow of singer Jim Croce, the bar features international jazz talents and an occasional appearance by A. J. Croce, son of the legendary crooner. The Top Hat Bar & Grille showcases rhythm and blues and rock on Friday and Saturday nights after 7:00 P.M., but there's live jazz nightly after 8:30 P.M. in the main bar. The whole scene is noisy and exuberant and more fun than you could think up on your own. The cover charge is $5.00 during the week, $8.00 on Fridays, and $10.00 on Saturdays, and it will get you into both the Jazz Bar and the Top Hat. If there's a special event, the cover might be slightly higher.

Dick's Last Resort
**345 Fourth Ave., San Diego
(619) 231–9100**

Granted, this is a chain outfit with a reputation for being slightly uncouth. But take it from us, there's some great music going on here. Talented local bands play every night, and folks of all ages dance, have a beer, throw wadded up napkins at each other by way of introduction, and just generally let their hair down. Give it a try; you'll find all types of music, from rock to pop to salsa to soul every night except Monday. After 8:00 P.M. there's no cover charge.

4th & B
**345 B St., San Diego
(619) 231–4343
www.4thandb.com**

No wonder we're not sure in which category to put it: 4th & B bills itself as San Diego's "multipurpose, multicultural entertainment and special events venue." A wide variety of shows are held here, from the yearly Brazilian Carnival celebration to sit-down concerts featuring well-known rock or blues artists to stand-up Latino comedy. This indoor concert venue has really made its mark on San Diego's music scene. Hot bands as well as legends from the past appear regularly at 4th & B, including Sister Hazel, Sonia Dada, the Squirrel Nut Zippers, Stephen Stills, and Busta Rhymes. Tickets are available at the box office from 10:00 A.M. to 5:00 P.M. or by calling Ticketmaster at (619) 220–8497. You must be 21 or older to get in.

Humphrey's
2241 Shelter Island Dr., San Diego
(619) 224–3577 (lounge and indoor stage)
(619) 523–1010 (box office)
www.humphreysconcerts.com (Concerts by the Bay)

Humphrey's is a comfortable if not terribly exciting bar and restaurant and the place to hear live jazz Sunday evenings throughout the year. More exciting is Humphrey's unique summer concert series. The outdoor amphitheater has a tradition of hosting top-name performers such as David Sanborn, Boz Scaggs, the Indigo Girls, and Harry Belafonte. If you have access to a small boat, you can motor up to the concert site and listen to the music from the water, something that amuses some performers and annoys others. Patrons who prefer a less bootleg approach can purchase tickets through Ticketmaster, (619) 220–8497, or Humphrey's box office, (619) 523–1010. Food, beverages, and cocktails are all sold on site; dinner show packages are a bit pricey and must be reserved in advance.

Insiders' Tip
If you're in town on New Year's Eve, ask about towing companies that will come get you and your car and take you both home—for free. Many taxi companies also provide discounted fares to keep drinkers off the road.

In Cahoots
5373 Mission Center Rd., San Diego
(619) 291–8635

Polish up those boots and get ready for some line dancing and two-stepping. Dancing to DJ-spun country music is what's happening here, and this is a great place for singles of all ages to meet and mix in a friendly, non-threatening atmosphere.

Drink prices are inexpensive, but the main draw is the dancing. The cover charge ranges from $2.00 to $5.00, and there are usually free country dance lessons on Friday and Saturday evenings before things really crank up. The bar has live music usually once a week, so call the above number for a schedule.

On Broadway
615 Broadway, San Diego
(619) 231–0011

Opened in 2001, this large, super-sophisticated nightspot caters to the rich and the famous. Lesser folk can grace the 25,000-square-foot nightclub if they have the cash for expensive drinks and the patience to wait in the line that stretches down the block. In addition to a restaurant serving Euro-Asian cuisine, there's a dance club (open Friday and Saturday), a "chill room" with more tranquil music and even cooler temperatures, and a VIP room for those willing to pay a $35 surcharge to avoid waiting in line. The building was originally built by mogul John D. Spreckels as the Walker Scott Bank Building, and the vault has been transformed into a billiards room.

The Onyx Room
852 Fifth Ave., San Diego
(619) 235–6699

Refined and often full of glamorous-looking 20-somethings, the intimate Onyx Room is housed in a basement-level venue. Decoration of this retro-style lounge is classy, the mood is upbeat, and the lighting both red and subdued. Martinis are the specialty of the house, and there's a dress code: no athletic shoes or sandals, no jeans. It's closed Mondays, but otherwise open nightly until 2:00 A.M. A DJ spins records on Wednesdays and Thursdays, and there's live jazz at least once or twice a week. After 9:30 P.M., you'll pay a cover of between $5.00 and $10.00.

Patrick's II
428 F St., San Diego
(619) 233-3077

When you've got a hankerin' for the blues, look no further than Patrick's II. A mainstay in the Gaslamp Quarter for years (long before this area was even called the Gaslamp Quarter, or was even halfway chic), this is a small club that is usually packed with people of all ages soaking up the blues and soppin' up the brews. Quarters are close, but the crowd is friendly and the music can't be beat. During the week there's no cover charge; on Fridays and Saturdays it's either $3.00 or $5.00.

The Room
909 Prospect St. #150, La Jolla
(858) 459-5010

La Jolla isn't exactly known for its nightlife, which is why The Room is such a find for the young and the restless. The Euro-style dance club usually features dance music on Friday and Latin tunes on Saturday spun by a DJ; on other nights the music varies. There's a $10 cover after 10:00 P.M., and a dress code (no shorts or jeans). Get munchies from the bar, or eat before you come at the adjacent restaurant. There's an afterwork happy hour on weekdays between 4:30 and 7:30 P.M., and live music for dancing Wednesday through Saturday from 7:00 to 10:00 P.M.

Winston's Beach Club
1921 Bacon St., San Diego
(619) 222-6822

This beach-casual club in Ocean Beach features standout bands ranging from reggae and ska to alternative, blues, funk, soul, and acid jazz. The crowd is mixed; you'll see all ages here having fun no matter what type of music is playing. The cover charge ranges from $7.00 to $20.00, depending on the band and the night of the week.

North County Coastal

Belly Up Tavern
143 S. Cedros Ave., Solana Beach
(858) 481-8140

A classic in the county, the Belly Up Tavern has been bringing top performers and newcomer groups to the music scene since the '70s. Ticket prices vary. Music varieties stretch from salsa and ska to bluesy rock and Big Band. The Blind Boys of Alabama, featuring Charlie Musselwhite and other members of the great gospel-blues group, wowed the crowd on a recent Sunday. Call the club's line, noted above, for information, buying tickets over the phone, and subscribing to the Belly Up's newsletter of events.

Concerts Under the Oaks
Quail Botanical Gardens, 230 Quail Gardens Dr., Encinitas
(760) 436-3036

This series of summer concerts presents a range of music from jazz favorites like The American Song Book and Kendra Eskau and Friends to a bluegrass band. This is an early night out (the concerts begin at 6:00 P.M.). Call for a list of upcoming Sunday evening concerts. Ticket prices are $15 for a single concert and light dinner to $40 for the series.

North County Inland

Club Caliente
680 W. San Marcos Blvd., San Marcos
(760) 744-4120

Country music and line dancing not being as popular as they once were, Leo's Little Bit O' Country is now Club Caliente, with live tropical music—salsa, cumbia, and merengue—on Fridays and Saturdays and a DJ the rest of the week. If you've not a clue about salsa dancing, come for the free lessons on Thursdays between 8:00 and 9:30 P.M., or cultivate your cumbia 7:00 to 9:00 P.M. on Sundays. On Wednesdays a DJ spins techno, trends, and mainstream discs. Cover is $10.00 on Wednesday, $8.00 on Thursday, $12.00 on Friday and Saturday, $6.00 Sunday. Closed Monday and Tuesday.

Club Tropics
740 Nordahl Rd., San Marcos
(760) 737–9402
www.clubtropics.com

A hip club with a moderate cover charge, Club Tropics attracts a college-aged crowd and working folks too. You'll be bombarded with music from the '70s, '80s, and '90s, from hip-hop to reggae all the way to old school and Latin tunes, and you can dance on multilevel dance floors or belly up to one of five bars. According to one of the bartenders, this is the place for "hot college babes." So you won't be disappointed, "hot" and "babes" are both in the eye of the beholder and the bartender. (Also, a "Hot College Babe" is an alcoholic drink, so perhaps that's what the bartender meant.) Thursday through Saturday nights feature club and guest DJs who spin the music. Drinks are $1.00 each all night on Thursdays, which is College Night; on Saturdays it's the Harlem Shake dance contest. Doors open at 8:00 P.M.

East County

Dirk's Niteclub
7662 Broadway St., Lemon Grove
(619) 469–6344

Dirk's fun party atmosphere is a big draw for the 35 to 50 age group—you know the people—the ones who remember Buffalo Springfield, Fleetwood Mac, and Sting. And college students who like this vintage music come here too. Dirk's is popular, and the best part is that the classic rock is live on the weekends. Wednesday is karaoke night. Call to find out about upcoming special events such as the 1950s theme parties. Everyone in the East County, from city mayors to college students, gives this club a thumbs-up. There's never a cover charge to get you in the door.

Ox Bow Inn
9816 Campo Rd., Spring Valley
(619) 469–9616

The group attracted to this country-western nightclub is loud and fun and out for a great time. The live music perform-ances on Friday and Saturday evenings start at about 8:30 P.M. The food's worth saving your appetite for, with burgers high on most Insiders' lists. Call for more infor-mation about upcoming performers.

Pine Valley House
28841 Old Hwy. 80, Pine Valley
(619) 473–8708

Love country music? Need some two-step tips? Head east to Pine Valley and enjoy live entertainment every Friday and Satur-day night when this country-style club rocks. Here's where the 50-plus mob gath-ers for a good old time just hangin' out, doing the two-step, or line dancing. This is the denim and boots crowd, but you won't be turned away if you're not wearing appropriate cowboy attire. On some holi-day weekends there are no scheduled per-formances, so if that's important to you, call ahead to see what's being offered.

Sycuan Casino
5469 Dehesa Rd., El Cajon
(619) 445–6002
www.sycuan.com

The Sycuan Casino, in East County's El Cajon, has live entertainment on the

Insiders' Tip

"Car nights" or "cruis-ing nights" are lots of fun for families who love their cars. Muscle cars, hotrods, vintage cars, and Harley David-sons cruise the main streets of Lemon Grove, Escondido, El Cajon, and La Mesa on summer nights, when the streets are blocked off for this purpose. See the Attractions chapter for details.

gaming room floor on Fridays and Saturdays, and schedules name-brand entertainment such as The Doobie Brothers and Roy Clark in its Showcase Theater, although concerts are not held every week. Call or check the Internet calendar for upcoming performances.

Viejas Casino & Turf Club
5000 Willows Rd., Alpine
(619) 445–5400, (800) 847–6537
www.viejasnet.com

As this ultra-popular Viejas Indian Casino says, "We've got more fun," and when you go for entertainment, you won't be disappointed. Of the three major Indian casinos, this is the only one that sells alcohol. Call for the latest lineup and performance times. Shows vary from season to season, but the club often offers blues bands on Fridays after 8:00 P.M. and Big Band music for early evening dancing on Sundays. Neither show has a cover charge, and the DreamCatcher Showroom is renowned for its excellent acoustics.

South Bay

The Butcher Shop
556 Broadway, Chula Vista
(619) 420–9440

The Butcher Shop is legendary around San Diego County for it's top-quality dining. But if you feel like hanging around after dinner, this Chula Vista restaurant offers live contemporary music Wednesday through Saturday from 8:00 P.M. to midnight.

Coors Amphitheater
2050 Entertainment Cir., Chula Vista
(619) 671–3500

This amphitheater adds a much-needed performance venue to the South Bay and to San Diego County. The outdoor theater seats 20,000 (10,000 reserved seats and 10,000 on the grass). You can bring a blanket but no lawn chairs; food and drink cannot be brought but are sold on the premises. Popular entertainers are booked at this modern venue; recent shows featured Sting, Maná, The Dave Matthews Band, Santana, and Phish. Tickets can be purchased at the box office the day of the event only or through Ticketmaster, (619) 220–8497.

Di-mond Jim's Nightclub
773 Third Ave., Chula Vista
(619) 585–7323

Dance to classic rock music every night in this South Bay hotspot. The crowd at Dimond Jim's tends to be of all ages. Dress is casual, and there's no cover charge. A few billiard tables enhance the scene for those looking for a break from the dance floor. Sundays and Mondays are karoake nights, Tuesdays through Thursdays and Sundays there's a DJ; Friday and Saturday nights the music is live.

Bars and Brewpubs

Central San Diego

Coronado Brewing Co.
710 Orange Ave., Coronado
(619) 437–4452

Right in the heart of scenic Coronado is this lively brewpub, which has five varieties of beer on tap. You can lift a pint and have a bite to eat for lunch or dinner. The

Insiders' Tip

If you go bar hopping, make sure to designate a driver. Police units often install sobriety checkpoints (especially during major holidays and on weekends) just inside the Tijuana border and around the city near popular bars, rock concerts, and sporting events.

menu includes casual fare: hamburgers, salads, pizzas, and pasta. Live entertainment pops up occasionally on Saturday nights, but it's a sporadic thing, so call ahead if you need live music to accompany your brew. On Tuesdays kids eat free from the children's menu.

Coronado Island Marriott
2000 Second St., Coronado
(619) 435-3000

If you're looking for a night of jazz, try the La Provence Bar inside this posh resort. Top-notch jazz artists play on Fridays and Saturdays in a decidedly upscale atmosphere. This is where you go when you want to dress up a little, sip a glass of champagne, and feel the romance in the air.

Karl Strauss Brewery & Grill
1044 Wall St., La Jolla
(858) 551-2739
1157 Columbia St., San Diego
(619) 234-2739
9675 Scranton Rd., San Diego
(858) 587-2739
5801 Armada Dr., Carlsbad
(760) 431-2739

One of the first brewpubs to open in San Diego, Karl Strauss's has maintained its quality and reputation through the years. From its first location in downtown San Diego, it now has four locations in the county, all of which have 12 fine brews on tap. There's also a wide menu of casual dining selections, including sandwiches, salads, pastas, and pizzas. This is a great place for after-theater dining. The kitchen stays open until 10:00 P.M. during the week and until midnight on weekends.

Kensington Club
4079 Adams Ave., San Diego
(619) 284-2848

This neighborhood bar has gained some panache, having been discovered by folks outside Kensington. (Still, it opens at 10:00 in the morning, so how classy can it be?) Live entertainment is now being featured on Fridays and Saturdays, and the format varies. If you're really concerned about what you hear, call ahead of time. Or if you feel adventurous, just show up and enjoy

whatever's on the agenda. It may be rock, it may be rockabilly. The cover charge varies from nothing to $10.

The Lamplighter
817 W. Washington St., San Diego
(619) 298-3624

There's a pool table, a full bar, and a neighborhood crowd that couldn't be friendlier at the Lamplighter. Bartenders are exuberant in their attention to customers; some are a show in themselves. But if you want to put on your own show, karaoke starts at 9:00 P.M. nightly except Monday.

McP's Irish Pub and Grill
1107 Orange Ave., Coronado
(619) 435-5280

There's never a cover charge at McP's, and you get a lot for the price of a beer and a burger here. Bands play blues or rock, although there's not a set schedule; Irish music is arranged for special days such as Saint Pat's. This is a favorite hangout of Coronado locals and visitors alike.

The Pennant
2893 Mission Blvd., San Diego
(858) 488-1671
www.thepennantbar.com

Far from fancy, The Pennant is a quintessential Mission Beach bar that has been around forever. Patrons shoot the breeze, watch a game on TV, and generally just hang out in T-shirts and flip flops. The upstairs deck is a godsend on hot summer evenings; smokers enjoy it year-round. The crowd is mixed, from college students to grizzled beach rats to tourists, so everyone fits right in.

Red Fox Room
2223 El Cajon Blvd., San Diego
(619) 297-1313

There was a time when the Red Fox Room was one of the most elegant lounges in town. Its grandeur may have faded a bit, but its popularity has continued over the years. Today it's a piano bar where you can sing along while cozied up with your sweetie in its hallmark red vinyl booths and be assured that your cocktail will be served

Sweet Baby—Here's the Cheathams

Partners in music and marriage, Jeannie and Jimmy Cheatham play in the Kansas City blues style. The two have been producing this feel-good music so long and so well that they're considered legends, both by fans around the globe and by fellow musicians. Jeannie, with her seductive, powerful voice, and Jimmy, a trombone genius, are the cornerstone of their Sweet Baby Blues Band.

Before moving to San Diego in 1978 and selecting the Golden Triangle as a home base, Jeannie and Jimmy did their share of gigs in clubs and concert halls. For a time, they taught at the University of Wisconsin. It was the easygoing environment and climate that pulled the Cheathams to San Diego. Jimmy was soon recruited by UCSD to teach music and Black musical history. "I retired in 1993 with Professor Emeritus status," he says, chuckling. Jeannie can't help but add, "Sure he retired, for about fifteen minutes before the regents realized they couldn't do without him." He can still be found in the classroom he loves.

Jimmy arranges all the music for the band and with Jeannie co-writes some of the songs that have secured their place on the charts and in jazz history. (The Smithsonian recently taped their music to be included in its Oral History of Jazz exhibit.) Asked for a definition of their music, Jimmy says, "It's unrestrained, exuberant, soulful, rollicking, growling, howling, roaring, wicked, virtuous, and wild." Jeannie adds, "It's truthful too." Their songs speak loud and clear about love, friendship, worry, and joy, and in a way that seems downright personal.

Jeannie can remember when she didn't play the piano (she began at five), but knows that life truly began when she did. She began performing and defining her style in the church choir in her hometown of Akron, Ohio. Since those days she's performed with scores of greats, including Sippie Wallace, Big Mama Thornton, Cab Calloway, T-Bone Walker, Diana Washington, and Jimmy Witherspoon. She was featured in the public television special *Three Generations of the Blues,* which won rave reviews from jazz fans and African-American critics throughout the country. Jimmy has played bass trombone with Duke Ellington, Lionel Hampton, Thad Jones, and Ornette Coleman and was musical director for Chico Hamilton.

Each musical success has produced another. *Meet Me with Your Black Drawers On, Back to the Neighborhood, Love in the Afternoon,* and *Homeward Bound* have topped the blues and

La Jolla residents Jimmy and Jeannie Cheatham sing the praises of San Diego at blues and jazz clubs in San Diego and around the world. PHOTO: MEREDITH FRENCH

jazz charts. The band has performed for packed houses at the Long Beach Blues Festival and the Long Beach Jazz Festival, San Francisco Blues Festival, Playboy Jazz Festival, Monterey Jazz Festival, Chicago Jazz Festival, and scores of others. More recently, they performed at KSDS's 50th anniversary party in December 2000, and helped ring in the *real* millennium at Escondido's 2001 First Night celebration.

As Jeannie says, "Music is alive in our souls and it comes out in the songs and melodies." To the benefit of us all.

with panache. The crowd is older during early hours, but as the evening wanes, the age group gets decidedly younger.

San Diego Brewing Co.
10450 Friars Rd., San Diego
(619) 284–2739

If you're serious about beer drinking, this is the place to go. Fifty brews on tap will keep you sampling indefinitely. Talk with the knowledgeable staff about the different varieties, and be sure to try one new to you. Pace yourself with an extraordinary burger or bowl of chili, then sit back and enjoy the sporting events that are broadcast on two big-screen and 12 regular TVs.

Top of the Hyatt Lounge
Hyatt Regency, 1 Market Pl., San Diego
(619) 232–1234

As you step off the elevator and wander into the bar on the 40th floor of the Hyatt Regency Hotel, you might wonder what makes it worth a visit. You'll quit wondering as soon as you look out the window. The Top of the Hyatt Lounge is the best place in San Diego to have a cocktail with a view of the harbor on one side and a view of city lights on the other. The interior of the bar is dimly lit so as not to distract from the glorious sights outside. It's comfortable, romantic, and breathtaking.

Trophy's Sports Grill
7510 Hazard Center Dr., La Jolla
(619) 296–9600
4282 Esplanade Ct., San Diego
(858) 450–1400
5500 Grossmont Center Dr., La Mesa
(619) 698–2900

This homegrown sports bar/restaurant has flourished in all three of its locations, and for good reason. The restaurant itself is good: eats are cheap and quality is high. Plus, you can usually see at least one of the TVs from anywhere in the restaurant. The bar has big-screen TVs along with normal-sized ones, and if there's a game in progress anywhere in the country, it's likely to be on. The lobby of the restaurant is filled with huge collections of sports memorabilia. This is a fun place for families and singles.

Whaling Bar
La Valencia Hotel,
1132 Prospect St., La Jolla
(858) 454–0771

Once an elite hangout for Hollywood types in town for the thoroughbred races at Del Mar, today the Whaling Bar has matured into an elegant gathering place

Insiders' Tip

At the Indian gaming casinos you'll discover dancing and live music, but you may not be able to find a beer. Of the three major casinos, only Viejas serves alcohol. Barona Casino is the largest and most successful Indian gaming casino in California.

for La Jolla locals and visitors. Entertainment is a piano bar, which naturally encourages the singer in us all to join in, and most folks do. A mammoth renovation in the late 20th century restored the bar while retaining its Old World style.

North County Coastal

Coyote Bar & Grill
300 Carlsbad Village Dr., Carlsbad
(760) 729-4695

The age and musical tastes of the crowds who frequent the Coyote change quicker than Dennis Rodman's hair color. Music and people spill out the door, off the patio, and into the parking lot, especially when the weather is perfect—and that happens year-round in San Diego. We've heard that right now it's the baby boomers who are coming for the rock classics. A while back, it was elbowroom only with the college-age crowd.

So call and find out who's playing. For all we know, by the time this book is in your hands there might be string quartets playing at the Coyote. Seriously, the Coyote is a popular hangout with loud music, lots of laughter, and live entertainment on most evenings. On weekdays you can partake of drink and appetizers at happy hour from 3:00 to 6:00 P.M., and karaoke is usually scheduled at least one day a week.

Pizza Port
135 N. Hwy. 101, Solana Beach
(858) 481-7332
571 Carlsbad Village Dr., Carlsbad
(760) 720-7007
www.pizzaport.com

Yes, you'll get pizza but you'll also get some great microbrewed beers with it. The music makes this place feel like party time, even though it's not live. The microbrew choices vary and the pub also has a large selection of imported beers if you prefer something Continental with that garlic and feta pizza. Call for upcoming events such as the microbrew brewing contests.

Tournament of Champions Lounge
La Costa Resort & Spa
2100 Costa Del Mar Rd., Carlsbad
(760) 438-9111

A lounge and gathering spot for visitors and guests of the famous resort (please see our Spas and Resorts chapter for more details), this is normally a quieter nightspot for the 40-and-older crowd. There's live music and the variety changes often.

North County Inland

San Marcos Brewery & Grill
1080 W. San Marcos Blvd., San Marcos
(760) 471-0050

The number of microbrews on tap daily changes, and some Insiders say when the honey-wheat ale is available, get a pitcher because one glass won't be enough. The food is okay, the service is quick and friendly, but Insiders come for the brew.

This microbrewery draws the after-work crowd, students from nearby Cal State San Marcos and Palomar College, and families too.

South Bay

Cafe Lamaze
1441 Highland Ave., National City
(619) 474-3222

Piano bars seem to be making a resurgence, and Cafe Lamaze is no exception.

The Gaslamp Quarter really hums at night. PHOTO: BILL ROBINSON, COURTESY OF THE SAN DIEGO CONVENTION & VISITORS BUREAU

On weekend evenings, sip champagne or your favorite cocktail while listening to the smooth sounds of a variety of pianists, all with their own specialties. But they all like requests, and they'll all encourage you to sing along.

Edelweiss
230 Third Ave., Chula Vista
(619) 426–5172

Come on, admit it. You like accordion music! But how often do you have the opportunity to hear it played seriously and at its best? Here's your chance. Get into the spirit at Edelweiss, formerly the House of Munich, where affable host Franz Dorninger offers up Austrian food and

ambiance and—Friday through Sunday between about 5:00 and 9:00 P.M.—the accordion music of Gordon Kohl. It's a different experience and one well worth trying.

Coffeehouses

Central San Diego

Java Joe's
1956 Bacon St., San Diego
(619) 523–0356
www.javajoes.org

Head to Ocean Beach and this way-cool coffeehouse for live music almost every night (after 8:00 P.M.) but Tuesday. Monday is open-mike night, which always produces some interesting and sometimes surprising entertainment. On other nights there's a wide variety of home-grown talent.

Lestat's Coffeehouse
3343 Adams Ave., San Diego
(619) 282–0437
www.lestats.com

Nightly entertainment is featured here: ska, jazz, acoustic, folk, and even some music from the Middle Ages every once in a while. Monday is open-mike night for aspiring performers looking for an audience.

The Living Room
5900 El Cajon Blvd., San Diego
(619) 286–8434
1010 Prospect St., La Jolla
(858) 459–1187
1018 Rosecrans St., San Diego
(619) 222–6852
2541 San Diego Ave., San Diego
(619) 325–4445
1417 University Ave., San Diego
(619) 295–7911

Although we don't normally recommend chains, each of these coffeehouses is earthy, individual, and truly special. The name says it all. When you walk into The Living Room, you'll feel like you're in your own home. Relax on a comfortable sofa or sit at the polished bar or small tables, perfect for a tête à tête or a few hours of reading or journal writing. Choose from an outstanding selection of coffees and sinfully delicious desserts, from truffles and tortes to shortcakes and scones. There's some light bistro fare as well.

Twiggs Green Room
4590 Park Blvd., San Diego
(619) 296–0616

Something is going on at Twiggs nearly every evening. Most performances are acoustic/folk music, but occasionally a jazz or pop artist or poet will make an appearance too. This is a spacious coffeehouse with lots of room to spread out and get comfortable. Order a sandwich, homemade baked goods, or a wide variety of coffee or teas.

North County Coastal

Esmeralda Books & Coffee
1555 Camino Del Mar, Del Mar
(858) 755–2707

An independent bookstore that sells great coffee, Esmeralda's ambiance encourages you to linger, sip, and buy a smashing selection of books. On the weekends there's live entertainment and highbrow events like poetry readings. (Read more about Esmeralda in our Shopping chapter.)

The store is a popular Insiders' hangout for bibliophiles, local authors, poets, and others who stop in for a browse and conversation. Located in the Del Mar Plaza, it's open seven days a week and stays open until 11:00 P.M. on Friday and Saturday nights.

La Costa Coffee Roasting
6965 El Camino Real, Carlsbad
(760) 438–8160

This is a family-style hangout where people come to mingle, have coffee, and relax, especially after taking in a movie at the

Insiders' Tip

Held each September, the San Diego Street Scene is the second largest music and food festival in the United States. For three days, local and regional talent perform, beginning in the early afternoon, while big-name bands top off the evening. Stages are set throughout the Gaslamp District, and neighborhood clubs get into the act as well.

Sea World's nightly summer fireworks display. PHOTO: BOB COUEY, COURTESY OF THE SAN DIEGO CONVENTION & VISITORS BUREAU

multiplex theater or visiting the branch of the Carlsbad City library right in the same shopping center. There's live entertainment—perhaps a guitarist, cellist, or bluegrass banjo player—on weekend evenings. If you're looking for a coffee-related gift to take back home, there are walls of designer, silly, and fun coffee mugs.

Miracles Café
1953 San Elijo Ave., Cardiff
(760) 943-7924

This homey, somewhat funky coffeehouse offers outdoor seating as well as a cozy fireplace inside. On Sunday mornings you may enjoy the work of a local singer/songwriter on acoustic guitar as you read your paper; on Friday and Saturday evenings there's acoustic guitar or jazz after 7:30 P.M. Every Tuesday is open-mike night.

North County Inland

Metaphor Cafe
258 E. Second Ave., Escondido
(760) 489-8890

Here's a humble place for coffee, perhaps a snack, and comfortable surroundings in which you can enjoy the poetry readings, the jazz jams (including Dixieland jazz bands), and a comedian or two. The Metaphor Cafe alternates between quiet and crowded, and has a refreshing mix of old, young, and families. Things change, but they currently offer open-mike night on Monday.

East County

Cajon Coffee Company
330 N. Magnolia Ave., El Cajon
(619) 588–6376
You can drink your java inside or out on the patio. The Cajon Coffee Company has specialty coffee and a good, plain old cup of brew. It's a nice place to meet friends whether you're on the way to a SDSU game, out shopping, or on the hunt for the perfect antique.

Coffee Merchant
5500 Grossmont Center Dr., La Mesa
(619) 460–7393
Whether you want decaf or the real thing, this is a great little coffeehouse for grabbing a quick cup or hanging out with friends (or a good book). There's a complete espresso and dessert bar and live music every Friday evening, played by a jazz group, perhaps, or a guitarist singing Latino melodies.

Shopping

If shopping is your hobby, passion, indulgence, or sport of choice, San Diego will satisfy you. The area's malls, shops, stores, and districts are huge and eclectic. We think San Diego has about the best shopping on the planet. The choices might even be a bit overwhelming.

So in this chapter, we've included need-to-know shopping information and then presented the best in shopping experiences. As shoppers at heart, we've put a lot of enthusiasm behind the lists we give you in this chapter. The places we've included are the ones we tell our friends not to miss.

Like the malls. Some, like the Fashion Valley Mall in Mission Valley, could easily become an addiction. Like the shopping districts—including Adams Avenue, with its blend of coffee pubs, new and used bookstores, and antiques emporiums. You'll find information on the Carlsbad Company Stores too, where you can find specialty stores from Donna Karan to Ralph Lauren. Although it might be different in your city, here in San Diego County the shopping centers are often a blend of specialty stores like these, national chains such as Sears, and discount stores too, like Marshalls Department Store. Of course, that information is here too.

We've included our favorite stores specializing in resale and consignment clothing, and then added swap meets (and a few flea markets). Half the fun of shopping in these specialty places is that you never quite know what you'll find, and if you'll need it, until you see it.

We've also given you a taste of the antiques stores in the area. Our list is far from a telephone-book tabulation, though. Use it as a basic introduction only. If you're really hooked on antiquing, we recommend that you visit some of the stores and get a newsletter (we'll tell you about that too), which should lead you to even more stores to try. And while you're off on your hunt you might want to scan the listings for other possibilities. If you've traveled the hour and a half to East County's Julian Shopping District, for example, you may find some surprises to take home along with your antiques. This quaint mountain town is heaped to heaven with little shops that sell country accessories, collectibles, and crafts—not to mention fudge, ice cream, apple pie, and apple cider.

Book lovers will find a good sampling of what's available in this area; we've mentioned unusual stores because we're especially fond of them. Keep in mind, though, that the phone book's Yellow Pages can be helpful too, because we couldn't include every possibility.

After organizing all our favorite stores into tidy categories, we discovered something was lacking, so we created a new section. It's called "Unique and Intriguing." Here you will find stores that may tickle your fancy with unusual or hard-to-find offerings, like those little cookies you nibbled in Vienna, the right color chaps for your western-wear outfit, or perhaps a fragrant bouquet of dried herbs. If reading about them appeals to you, they're probably worth the visit, even if they're a ways from the place you're staying.

We've organized this chapter by shopping category; within each of those you'll find the usual regional divisions. So if you're a used-book buyer, hooked on swap meets, or thrill to consignment store buying, then you'll want to look for those categories, see what each of San Diego's regions has to offer, and perhaps hop in your car for one of those long shopping trips Insiders are known to take.

Perhaps, though, all the stores you want to see will be within a few blocks of your hotel doorstep. In either case, with your *Insiders' Guide* in hand, you're ready. Put on your shopping shoes (best make them comfortable), grab your sense of adventure, and head to the stores. You won't be disappointed.

Malls

Central San Diego

Clairemont Town Square Shopping Center
4186 Clairemont Mesa Blvd., San Diego
No phone

Clairemont Town Square is anchored by **Burlington Coat Factory, Circuit City,** and **Michael's,** a giant arts and crafts store. Several fast-food places are sprinkled throughout the mall, and **Acapulco Mexican Restaurant** is nearby, as is the **Outback Steakhouse,** for a sit-down meal and a chance to rest your feet. Also located in the center is the **Pacific Theatres Town Square,** with 14 screens and stadium-style seating.

Fashion Valley
7007 Friars Rd., San Diego
(619) 688–9113

This is San Diego's largest shopping mall, and it underwent a $120 million expansion and renovation at the end of the 20th century. The big department stores are **Neiman Marcus, Nordstrom, Macy's, Saks Fifth Avenue, Robinsons-May,** and JCPenney. And just about every other specialty store you can think of is there, too. Fashion Valley has more than 200 of them, including **Tiffany & Co., Talbots, Gap, Banana Republic, Crate & Barrel, See's Candies,** and many more. **Restoration Hardware** is one of our favorites. It's a hardware store that's enticing to both men and women for its one-of-a-kind reproduction treasures.

Nearly two dozen restaurants, bistros and eateries offer everything from a leisurely meal with wine and cocktails to a quick snack while on the run to the next store. If you're looking for something truly unusual, check out the kiosks located throughout the mall. They offer unique gifts and mementos that are hard to find

elsewhere. If a movie is on your agenda, you can't go wrong with the **AMC Theater** right in the middle of the mall. Eighteen screens and stadium-style seating provide the ultimate movie-going experience.

Westfield Shoppingtown Horton Plaza
Fourth Ave. and Broadway, San Diego
(619) 238–1596

Known for its highly acclaimed architecture and eye-catching color scheme, Horton Plaza is home to more than 140 shops. **Nordstrom, Macy's,** and **Mervyn's** are here as are **bebe, FAO Schwarz, Warner Brothers Store,** the **Disney Store, Victoria's Secret, Ann Taylor,** and **Abercrombie & Fitch.**

Some of our favorite restaurants are inside the mall too, such as the **Panda Inn** for great Chinese food. Or if you're looking for something different, the international food court can't be beat for quick and tasty treats. For entertainment, check out the 14-screen theater or take in a play at the **Lyceum Theatre,** located on street level, one level below the mall's ground floor.

Westfield Shoppingtown Mission Valley
1640 Camino del Rio N., San Diego
(619) 296–6375

Just a hop, skip, and a jump away from Fashion Valley is Mission Valley Center. This is a mall that was in decline until it reinvented itself with the addition of a 20-screen AMC movie theater and a bunch of new stores. It now is one of the most popular malls in the county, especially among teenagers. Besides **Macy's Home & Furniture** and **Robinsons-May** there are more than 100 specialty shops and restaurants. In 2002, **Target** replaced the defunct Montgomery Ward.

Nordstrom Rack, Loehmann's, and **Bed, Bath & Beyond** are the big draw for adults; teens like to shop at **Express,**

A good look at Horton Plaza can take time, so plan for an afternoon or day of shopping. PHOTO: COURTESY OF HORTON PLAZA

Lerner New York, and **Charlotte Russe,** and can be found in **Starworks Arena,** an interactive entertainment center that features virtual reality games and simulations. **Ruby's Diner, O'Nami Japanese Restaurant,** and **Seau's The Restaurant** (check out the latter in our Restaurants chapter) are the main dining spots in the mall, but don't miss the food court that has everything from soft pretzels to fish tacos.

Westfield Shoppingtown University Towne Center
4545 La Jolla Village Dr., San Diego
(858) 546-8858
Having spent $12 million in the late 1990s to create a more parklike setting, UTC has become a place where shoppers are encouraged to slow down and linger. Tranquil touches including grass and fountains are found throughout the mall. You'll find more than 170 stores too, including **Macy's, Robinsons-May, Sears** and specialty stores like **Sephora, bebe, Crate & Barrel, charles david,** and **Ann Taylor. Nordstrom's** big news is that 500 apartments will be built above it by around 2004.

For dining, choose from Chinese, Japanese, Indian, Mediterranean, Mexican, or California bistro cuisine offered by four full-service restaurants. Or sample the variety of treats available in the huge open-air food pavilion. A remodeled ice rink (see our Recreation chapter) guarantees to entertain both kids and adults.

North County Coastal

Del Mar Plaza
1555 Camino del Mar, Del Mar
(858) 792-1555
Found on the corner of Camino Del Mar and 15th Street, the many shops of the Del Mar Plaza open onto a courtyard. Anchored by the restaurants **Epazote, Pacifica del Mar,** and **Il Fornaio,** this mall offers an eclectic array of shopping choices. Here you'll find stores like the **Shoe Cellar** (featuring finer walking shoes), **Del Mar Candle Company,** and **Chicos** (an exclusive line of all-cotton clothes for women). You'll also find the **Harvest Ranch Market** (natural foods and natural health care), and **Esmeralda**

(the wonderful bookstore you may have read about in our Nightlife chapter). If you shop here in the evening, you get an added bonus: The huge balcony outside **Il Fornaio** and **Enoteca del Fornaio Italian,** the adjacent wine bar, faces west and gets a million-dollar view of the sun setting over the Pacific.

Westfield Shoppingtown Plaza Camino Real
2525 El Camino Real, Carlsbad
(760) 729–7927
For some people this mall is the hub for all shopping in North County Coastal. Plaza Camino Real is an enclosed regional mall that boasts more than 140 specialty stores, including those where you'll find upscale women's clothing, shoes, toys, and kitchen gadgets. The anchor stores are **Sears, Robinsons-May, JCPenney,** and **Macy's.**

There are **Walden Books** and **Boot World** as well as more than 21 food specialty shops where you can select everything from pizza to pretzels and a few **Mrs. Fields** cookies to ward off the shopping hungries. There are places to sit and people watch, clothing stores, and accessory boutiques.

North County Inland

Westfield Shoppingtown North County Fair Mall
272 E. Via Rancho Pkwy., Escondido
(760) 489–2332

North County Inland's largest enclosed mall is anchored by **Nordstrom, Macy's, Robinsons-May, Sears,** and **JCPenney.** You'll find 180 specialty shops including **Godiva** chocolates, **Crabtree & Evelyn, Mrs. Fields** cookies, **Lane Bryant, San Diego Padres Clubhouse,** and **O'Nami** Japanese restaurant as well as a food court with everything from pizza to Indian food. Throughout the mall there are plenty of places to sit and people watch—a favorite pastime for those who come along with a true shopper. Parking on weekends can be tricky, but there always seems to be enough.

East County

Grossmont Center
5500 Grossmont Center Dr., La Mesa
(619) 465–2900
Recently renovated and highly spiffy, the Grossmont Center has attracted shoppers from East County and the mountain communities since it was founded in 1965. Currently there are over 100 stores. Anchor stores include **Macy's** and **Target.** You'll find specialty stores that are unique, including **Chic Wide Shoes, Shavers and Small Appliances, Cutler's Cupboard** (a knife store) as well as **Kids R Us, Barnes & Noble,** and a **Cost Plus World Market.**

South Bay

Chula Vista Center
555 Broadway, Chula Vista
(619) 422–7500
Located right in the heart of Chula Vista, this mall is home to **Macy's, Mervyn's, Sears,** and **JCPenney** as anchors. There are more than 100 specialty stores. Shop for men's and women's clothing at **Raya's for Him & Her.**

An **Ultrastar 10 Theater** is in the mall, and so are lots of fast-food places where you can grab a snack.

Westfield Shoppingtown Plaza Bonita Shopping Center
3030 Plaza Bonita Rd., National City
(619) 267–2850
South Bay's only enclosed, climate-controlled shopping center, Plaza Bonita

is anchored by **JCPenney, Mervyn's,** and **Robinsons-May.** More than 130 specialty shops like **Anchor Blue** and **Foot Locker** will keep you shopping for hours. When you need a break, stop in at **Applebee's Restaurant** or one of the many restaurants in the food court.

Discount and Outlet Shopping

Central San Diego

Burlington Coat Factory
3962 Clairemont Mesa Blvd., San Diego
(858) 272–1893
Located in the Clairemont Town Square Shopping Center, you'll find much more than just coats (although there's no shortage of those).

Burlington is one of the largest off-price clothing store in the country, offering fashions for the whole family. Most styles are in season, but in some cases sizes and selection are limited. Additionally, Burlington has shoes, accessories, linens, and baby furniture.

La Jolla Village Square
8657 Villa La Jolla Dr., La Jolla
(858) 455–7550
This almost qualifies as a mall, but it's really a discount shopping center, and a pretty spiffy one, at that. It's a popular shopping destination because of its **Starbucks Coffee,** offbeat fast-food eateries, and 12-screen theater. Mixed in with the leisurely crowd, however, are the power shoppers looking for bargains at **Marshalls, Cost Plus, Linens 'n Things, Famous Footwear, Ross Stores,** and **Crown Books Superstore.**

Shop at **Trader Joe's** for international wines and delicacies.

Loehmann's
1640 Camino del Rio N., San Diego
(619) 296–7776
San Diego's version of this national discount store is located in the east wing of Mission Valley Center (see our entry under "Malls"). Famous for its discount women's designer clothes, it's also a great

place to find bargains on sportswear, shoes, and lingerie. Loehmann's has a good children's department too, and has just recently added a menswear section. Don't forget to check out the back room, where top-of-the-line designer formal wear and more casual duds can be had for deep discounts. Wear your best underwear—fitting rooms are communal.

Nordstrom Rack
1640 Camino del Rio N., San Diego
(619) 296–0143
This is where all those beautiful but pricey clothes from Nordstrom end up. You can get great deals on ladies', men's and children's clothing as well as shoes, accessories, lingerie, and some home decor items. Don't expect the same selection or level of service you'd find at Nordstrom's regular department stores, but the values make it a worthwhile visit. The Rack is located in the east wing of Mission Valley Shopping Center.

Park Valley Center
1550 Camino de la Reina, San Diego
(no phone)
Do you love the clothes at Saks Fifth Avenue but hate spending the big bucks? Then head for **Off 5th** in this new shopping center. It's a beautiful store that is orderly, clean, and inviting, just like the original Saks, but with price tags that are much kinder to your wallet. The shopping center is located just north of and across the street from the giant Mission Valley Center, and also has an **Aaron Brothers Art & Framing** and a **Mikasa** store for china and crystal. Some of the stores are full price, but there are several discount shops and boutiques too.

Shoe Pavilion
4240 Kearny Mesa Rd., San Diego
(858) 492–9833
3337 Rosecrans St., San Diego
(619) 222–6787
In these warehouse-style stores you'll find quality brand-name men's and women's shoes for about half the retail price.

The shoes are displayed on counters with boxes piled up underneath, and it's

Fresh and Fabulous Farmers' Markets

Picture succulent produce, aromatic herbs, and field-fresh flowers. Now put that vision smack dab in the center of a convenient neighborhood parking lot and you'll get a peek at what our area's farmers' markets have to offer.

At all the farmers' markets mentioned you'll find fresh-picked vegetables and exquisite fruits, many cut and offered for sampling. Flowers like the exotic protea compete with familiar roses and perky daisies. Each stall holds something different: herbs or organic eggs, pies, and breads. Some of the markets listed have specialties too, like tamales, wraps, or roasted-on-the-spot peanuts. As you visit them you'll find that each one has a flavor of its own.

Most of the farmers' markets are open for about three hours and are always held outdoors. Although winter rainstorms have been known to put a damper on some farmers' markets, it usually takes a good soaking storm to shut one down.

Remember that the produce found at the farmers' markets is seasonal. If you're visiting in December and looking for vine-ripened strawberries, you may be out of luck. Check that same market between March and June and you'll be impressed by the selection.

It's a good idea to walk the entire market before buying and to bring plenty of single dollar bills to make buying quick and easy.

We've listed the markets by days of the week rather than regions. So if your dinner party is on Thursday and you really need field-perfect squash, mouth-watering melons, and magnificent mushrooms, just find a market that's open that morning, and you'll know which direction to head.

Professional chefs and creative cooks shop for fresh produce at Escondido's farmers' market. PHOTO: COURTESY OF THE SAN DIEGO NORTH CONVENTION & VISITORS BUREAU

SUNDAY: **La Jolla,** Girard Avenue at Genter Street (La Jolla Elementary School), 9:00 A.M. to 1:00 P.M.; **Solana Beach,** 124 N. Cedros, 2:00 to 5:00 P.M.; **Hillcrest** at the DMV parking lot at 3960 Normal Street, 9:00 A.M. until noon.

TUESDAY: **Coronado,** at the Old Ferry Landing, corner of Third Street and B Avenue, 2:30 to 6:00 P.M.; **Escondido** between Grand Avenue and Kalmia Streets.

WEDNESDAY:	**Ocean Beach,** on Newport Avenue between Ebers and Bacon Streets, 4:00 to 8:00 P.M.; **El Cajon,** at The Marketplace, Magnolia Avenue and Main Street, 4:00 to 7:00 P.M.; **Carlsbad,** on Roosevelt Street between Grand Avenue and Carlsbad Village Drive, 2:00 to 5:00 P.M.
THURSDAY:	**Oceanside,** Coast Highway and Pier View, 9:00 A.M. to 12:30 P.M.; **Chula Vista,** Third Avenue at Center Street, 3:00 to 6:30 P.M.; **San Marcos,** Old California Restaurant Row, 1020 San Marcos Blvd., 3:00 to 6:00 P.M.
FRIDAY:	**Rancho Bernardo,** at the Bernardo Winery, 13330 Paseo del Verano Norte, 9:00 A.M. to noon; **La Mesa** at 8500 Allison Street (east of Spring Street), 3:00 to 6:00 P.M.
SATURDAY:	**Pacific Beach,** at Promenade Mall, Mission Boulevard, Reed Avenue, and Pacific Beach Drive, 8:00 A.M. to noon; **Vista** at the corner of Eucalyptus Street and Escondido Avenue (Vista City Hall parking lot), 8:00 to 11:00 A.M.; **Encinitas,** 101 Artist Colony, in the 25 East E Street parking lot, 8:00 to 11:00 A.M.; **Poway** in Old Poway Park, Midland Road between Aubrey and Temple Streets, 8:00 to 11:00 A.M.; **Del Mar,** in the City Hall parking lot at the corner of El Camino del Mar and 10th Street, 1:00 to 4:00 P.M.

strictly self-serve. But friendly salespeople are always glad to answer questions or help you find something special.

Westfield Shoppingtown Mission Valley Center West
**1100 Camino del Rio N., San Diego
(619) 296-6375**
Mission Valley Center's little sister, located just to the west of the main shopping center, has **Old Navy** and **Marshalls,** two discount giants. You'll also find a **Borders Books & Music** and **Just for Feet** athletic shoes. When you're ready to hit the links, stop in at **Golfsmith** for all your golfing equipment and supplies. A giant **Gateway** computer store should fulfill all your techno-wishes.

North County Coastal

Carlsbad Company Stores
**5620 Paseo del Norte, Carlsbad
(760) 804–9000**

Carlsbad Company Stores is a potpourri of some 80 discount outlets, from **Ralph Lauren, Jones of New York, Donna Karan,** and **Royal Dalton** to **Rockport, Tommy Hilfiger, The Gap,** and **Hush Puppies.** North County shoppers who love those exceptional brand names love coming here.

All in all, you can choose from 80 fine stores selling clothing, shoes, outerwear, accessories, and jewelry as well as candy, luggage, and baby accessories.

Should you start fading while you're picking the perfect little black dress or searching out some super-cool sneaks, you'll find chain shops like **Starbuck's,** an Asian fast food restaurant, an old-fashioned malt shop with enormous burgers, and a real California smoothie (juice) bar. Or if you'd like to pop outside, you can find fine dining without even moving your car. Just a short block north is Bellefleur (see our Restaurants chapter), which features fresh and flavorful California-style cuisine and excellent local wines.

On weekends the stores are busy and during the holidays the Christmas decorations are magnificent. There's lots of parking and the mall is wheelchair accessible.

Marshalls Department Store
685 San Rodolfo Dr., Solana Beach
(858) 755-0791

While there are other Marshalls Department Stores in San Diego, many Insiders consider this North County Coastal store to be the best. We're talking primo prices and larger selections, from shorts and T-shirts to business suits.

This store is bigger than the others, for one thing. It stocks higher quality merchandise at the excellent discount prices one expects from Marshalls. Close by are other specialty stores that move in and out of the strip mall. Currently, you'll find an accessories shop, a lingerie store, an office supply store, and a bagel and coffee cafe.

North County Inland

UFO
1120 N. Melrose Dr., Vista
(760) 941-2345

No, you will not find E.T. at this store, but rather great bargains from the Upholstery Fabric Outlet. If you're in the market for fabric or for the accessories it takes to recover or design anything, this is the store. At UFO you'll be tempted by first-class merchandise. Although the sales happen rarely, the clearance table may hold a few finds.

East County

GTM Discount General Store
8967 Carlton Hills Blvd., Santee
(619) 449-4953
663 Broadway Ave., Lemon Grove
(619) 460-2990

This is a discounter with a true no-frills ambiance. These stores specialize in merchandise that's discounted because it's slightly damaged (yet very usable) or because the original store isn't carrying the item any more. Oftentimes you have to look five times before you can figure

Insiders' Tip

Farmers' markets are fun outings for the whole family. If you discover an unusual fruit or vegetable, just ask the vendor for cooking or eating recommendations.

out why the item is in the store. The products come from suppliers such as Costco and 130 other vendors. We've found bargains on everything from beauty aids and stretch pants to pet food and whole bean coffee. Plan on a stop at GTM if you love a deal that feels like a real bargain, especially on items you use every day.

Viejas Outlet Center
5005 Willows Rd., Alpine
(619) 659-2070

Landscaped with massive rocks and rushing water features among bronze statues and structures made to resemble those of an Native American village, this outlet center has a unique look that makes shopping a relaxing affair. There are nearly 60 retail store outlets, including **Casual Corner, Eddie Bauer, Van Heusen,** and **Perry Ellis.** For housewares check out the **Corning Revere Store** and **Linen Barn,** or **Black and Decker** for power tools. Shop for gifts and accessories, jewelry and books, or pop into one of eight footwear outlets. In the evenings around 9:00 P.M. (earlier in winter months) there usually is some form of free musical or laser light entertainment. Those needing a break from the slot machine and bingo at the Viejas Casino across the road duck into **Filippi's Pizza Grotto, McDonald's,** and **Rubio's Baja Grill,** as do shoppers. This is also the home of San Diego's East County Visitors Bureau office, (619) 445-0180 or (800) 463-0668.

South Bay

San Diego Factory Outlet Center
4498 Camino de la Plaza, San Ysidro
(619) 690-2999

Head for the U.S.-Mexico border, but take the last exit before you leave the country (don't worry—plenty of signs will alert you to the fact that the last-chance exit is approaching). What you'll find is San Diego's first factory outlet center and still one of the best. Nearly 40 outlet stores offer outstanding bargains for grown-ups and kids alike. Women will appreciate the outlet stores for **Calvin Klein, Maidenform, Nine West,** and **Georgiou,** while men will be looking for bargains at **Van Heusen, Van's,** and the **Nike Factory Store.** Kids' bargains are found at the **Toy Liquidators Outlet,** and **Oshkosh B'Gosh.** Plenty of discount housewares are available too, as are leather goods, vitamins, fragrances, and cosmetics.

Shoe Pavilion
304 E. H St., Chula Vista
(619) 691-0640

Like its sister stores in Central San Diego and North County Coastal, Shoe Pavilion offers no-frills shopping, but excellent quality, selection, and price in brand-name and designer shoes for men and women. Don't miss the clearance racks, where prices are often as much as 75 percent below retail.

UFO-Upholstery Fabric Outlet
1918 Roosevelt Ave., National City
(619) 477-9341

Even if you have no plans to reupholster any of your furniture, a visit to UFO will change that kind of thinking in a hurry. What seems to be miles and miles of racks of fabric will inspire your creative spirit, and you're sure to find something you can't live without or the perfect fabric to recover Aunt Matilda's antique chaise. UFO, along with its sister store in North County Inland, is an Insiders' secret not to be missed.

Central San Diego

Adams Ave.
Between 30th and 40th Streets

Informally known as San Diego's Antique Row, this stretch of Adams Avenue is filled with antiques stores, art galleries, used-book shops, collectibles, and home furnishings. This is a browser's paradise. As you leisurely stroll from shop to shop, you can take a break at one of the pubs, coffeehouses, or restaurants that are mixed in with the stores.

Be sure to stop in the **Prince and the Pauper** at 3201 Adams Avenue for collectible children's books. **TaTa Lane** (525 Evans Place) for vintage clothing is an Insiders' favorite, as is **Rosie O'Grady's** pub, a longtime fixture at 3402 Adams Avenue.

Bazaar Del Mundo
Juan St., in Old Town State Historic Park, San Diego
(619) 296-3161

Sometimes shopping is more than just shopping—it's an experience. And Bazaar Del Mundo offers an unparalleled experience for the whole family. Enjoy the international sights, sounds, fragrances, and flavors of the Bazaar as you discover treasures from around the world in the 16 shops and five restaurants. **The Guatemala Shop** offers hand-woven textiles, ethnic clothing, and folk art. At **Artes de Mexico** you can find colorful crafts from throughout that country, while **La Panadería** will supply you with typical sweets.

Entertainment is usually on hand, too, in the form of lively mariachis and Hispanic dancers swirling in their colorful costumes. When hunger strikes, sample Southern California's version of Mexican cuisine at **Casa de Pico.** Or if Italian food appeals to you, **Lino's** offers pasta, pizza, sandwiches, and salads.

Ferry Landing Marketplace
1201 First St., Coronado

Not really a mall, not really a neighborhood shopping district, the Ferry Landing Marketplace is nevertheless a fun-filled shopping area. This is the perfect spot for souvenir shopping at places like **Captain Coronado's Trading Company** or the **Coronado Ferry Company.** Fine art can be found at the **Southwestern Indian Den** or the **Art for Wildlife Galleries.**

You can also dine in style at **Peohe's Restaurant** overlooking San Diego Bay and the city skyline.

Gaslamp Quarter
Fourth and Fifth Aves.
Between Broadway and K St., San Diego

Interspersed among the nightclubs and restaurants in the Gaslamp are dozens of unique shops, ranging from the well-known **Z Gallerie** at 611 Fifth Avenue to the **Gaslamp Books, Prints, & Wyatt Earp Museum** at 413 Market Street. Part of the appeal of shopping in the Gaslamp is that the stores are open late on weekends. So after dinner in one of the dozens of restaurants in the Quarter, you can browse leisurely through the shops.

You'll find vintage clothing stores and boutiques that specialize in offbeat fashions. For collectors, art galleries, and rare print stores are abundant. And if you're having trouble deciding what to buy, you might consult one of the resident psychics or palm readers who have set up shop in the Gaslamp.

Hillcrest
Fifth Ave. between Robinson and Washington Sts. and University Ave. between Fourth Ave. and Park Blvd.

A funky and cool collection of shops and eateries lines Fifth Avenue in Hillcrest. You'll find vintage clothing in several shops, including **Wear It Again Sam** at 3822 Fifth Avenue, a San Diego icon for at least a generation. Although timeless bookshops such as the **Blue Door** have fallen prey to the mega-bookstore trend, **Bountiful Books** at 3834 Fifth Avenue, manages to hang on, to the delight of booklovers who love to wander the neighborhood.

Also in this neighborhood, University Avenue between Fourth and Park has tons of resale clothing and furniture boutiques and trendy home furnishing stores tucked among the timeless bars and liquor stores and a few prosperous strip malls. Also here is the Uptown District, where apartments and grocery stores mingle in smart 21st-century fashion with good restaurants and specialty shops such as **Laguna Trends,** which has wonderful gifts as well as stationery, candles, and the like.

La Jolla
Prospect St. and Girard Ave.

La Jolla is famous for its upscale shopping district, and it's hard to argue that there's a better location. Sunshine, the ocean, and streets teeming with happy shoppers combine to make this an out-of-the-ordinary shopping excursion. Here you'll find ultra-trendy boutiques, world-famous clothing designers' stores, art galleries, and just enough offbeat stores to keep things interesting.

One of our favorites is the **Silver Store,** at 7909 Girard Avenue. Silver treasures from dining utensils to tea services to jewelry all can be found here, usually at a discount. You'll find lots of restaurants along both Prospect and Girard, including San Diego's **Hard Rock Cafe,** plenty of casual bistros, and lots of full-service restaurants.

Ocean Beach
Newport Ave., between Sunset Cliffs Blvd. and the beach

Downtown OB is overflowing with antique stores, along with a sprinkling of interesting art galleries, card and gift shops, jewelry stores, and bikini and surf shops (you are at the beach, after all). Often on summer weekends there's a festival or fair happening, complete with craft booths for even more shopping.

Seaport Village
West Harbor Dr. at Kettner Blvd.
(next to the Hyatt Regency San Diego)
(619) 235-4014

We included Seaport Village in our Attractions chapter simply because there's so much to do here: dining, seaside entertain-

Window shopping in La Jolla. PHOTO: BOB YARBROUGH, COURTESY OF SAN DIEGO CONVENTION & VISITORS BUREAU

ment, a carousel for the kids. But we just had to include the 14-acre waterfront zone in Shopping too, because some of San Diego's most interesting stores are here.

Where else can you find a store like the **Captain's Cove,** which specializes in nautical treasures? You'll also find shops selling candles, kites, hammocks, and everything you need to perform magic tricks. There's an **Upstart Crow** bookseller where you can get a great cup of coffee or a pound of beans as well as magazines or books. More than 50 unique stores make up Seaport Village, and for the dedicated shopper, it's a place not to be missed.

North County Coastal

Cedros Avenue Stores and Design Centers
Cedros Ave., Solana Beach

Here you'll find wonderful shops from **Adventure 16** (the outdoor gear and camping specialty store) at 143 South Cedros Avenue to a host of high-end and lower-scale antiques stores. Be sure to stop at **Peck & Peck Antiques** at 241 South Cedros Avenue for that perfect item for your home or office or the folks back home. In the same district you'll find cafes and pubs including **Belly Up** (which is mentioned in the Nightlife chapter).

There are more than 50 storeowners who support one another in the shopping and design center for the North County Coastal area. Parking is mostly on the street, but there are lots places on side streets. FYI: The district is about 3 blocks south of the Coaster train stop in Solana Beach. Check the Coaster schedule to make sure you can get to and from the district at convenient times.

State Street Stores
Between Oak St. and Beech St. on both sides of State St., Carlsbad

If you're looking for an antique, an addition to your baseball-card collection, are just nuts about rare books, or need a good cup of coffee, you'll find it all in this shopping area. Within the 4-block plus shopping district, you'll be treated to about 40 antiques stores, boutiques, and small shops.

Be sure to browse through **DeWitts Antiques and Collectibles** for jewelry and glassware (there are over 50 dealers combined in this store at 2946 State Street and there's a licensed appraiser on-site). Don't miss **Vinge Antiques,** 3087 State Street, where you'll find rugs, books, and paintings along with the usual antique fare.

Mixed among the shops and cafes are boutiques like **Kobos,** at the corner of Carlsbad Village Drive and State Street (2998 State Street). This shop features trendy and sensible beach clothes and California casual sportswear. If you're headed up to North County from downtown San Diego, check the Coaster train schedule to make your trek more enjoyable. The station is right in the middle of this shopping district.

North County Inland

Carmel Mountain Shopping Area
San Diego

If you're traveling on Interstate 15 through the Rancho Bernardo, Carmel Mountain area, there's a shopping district that will fit your basic needs. Take the Carmel Mountain exit and go east. Here's where you find

Insiders' Tip

Specialty shops tend to change ownership and even merchandising direction. If you found trendy sunglasses at a Gaslamp Quarter shop on last year's business trip, the same store may now be focusing on hip electronics. Call ahead if you're seeking a special item or must travel a distance to get just what you want.

a **Marshalls** department store, **Staples, Target, Michael's** (the craft store), **Borders Books and Music,** and a fine selection of chain and fast-food restaurants, including **In 'N Out Hamburgers.**

East County

Julian Main St. Shopping District
Julian

Julian's antique stores are mostly located around Main Street in the downtown area, which is about 5 easy blocks long. That said, if you don't look out the car windows while driving into town you'll miss other stores along Calif. Highway 78 as it winds up to this mountain village.

Be sure to visit some of the antiques stores on Julian's cozy side streets too, such as **Applewood & Co.,** 2804 Washington Street, (760) 765-1185, and **Julian Farms Antiques,** 2818 Washington Street, (760) 765-0250. When you get to town, stop at the Julian Town Hall (on Main and Washington Streets) and pick up an antiques newsletter giving brief descriptions of shops and any specialties. You can also ask about the best places for the famous Julian apple pie and cider, but you may just have to do the sampling yourself. (The truth is, all the pies and cider we've tasted—and we've tried to be fair—are luscious. Be sure to buy enough to take back with you.)

La Mesa Shopping District
La Mesa Blvd. at Spring St.

Sometime in the 1980s store owners along La Mesa Boulevard looked around and decided it was time to spiff things up. And so they did. This shopping district now includes coffee pubs, tidy cafes, inviting boutiques, and antiques shops—nearly 20 at last count—all within the downtown area of La Mesa.

South Bay

Chula Vista
Third Ave., between E and G Sts., Chula Vista

Once a declining business district, Third Avenue has been revitalized and is now the hub of downtown shopping in Chula Vista. Restaurants, an old-fashioned movie theater, a performing arts theater and, most important, lots of shops now line the busy street.

Stop in at **Riviera Bakery** at $315\frac{1}{2}$ Third Avenue for a sweet treat, or if your wedding day is approaching, feast your eyes on the bridal confections at **Bridal World,** 250 Third Avenue. As you amble up and down the pedestrian-friendly street, you'll find card shops, antiques stores, a specialty food market, and a few boutiques, too.

Resale and Consignment

Central San Diego

Dress to Impress
4242 Camino del Rio N., San Diego
(619) 528-9797

If you're looking for a special dress to wear for a formal occasion, Dress to Impress may be your answer. You'll find a large selection of women's formal wear in all sizes both for sale and for rent. Better-quality sportswear, dresses, and suits are also available. The store is open every day but Sunday and Monday, and accepts clothing for consignment by appointment only.

Encore of La Jolla
7655 Girard Ave., La Jolla
(858) 454-7540

Occupying what was once an upscale department store, Encore specializes in way-upscale women's resale designer clothing. All the big labels are here. You might not find the bargain basement prices that you would at other resale and consignment shops, but the selection and quality are fabulous.

Reruns
1015 C Ave., Coronado
(619) 435-5444

Specializing in resale clothing from newborns to teens, this is the spot to take the kids when they bust through the knees of their jeans. Open every day but Sunday.

Wear It Again Sam
3823 Fifth Ave., San Diego
(619) 299-0185

This store is worth a visit just to see the latest finds. Specializing in vintage clothing from the 1900s through the 1960s, there's always something unusual to be found. Quality men's and women's clothing, shoes, and accessories that you haven't seen in years are sure to capture your imagination.

North County Coastal

Always Fabulous
1217 Camino del Mar, Del Mar
(858) 481-8866

From accessories to jewelry, from clothing to shoes, you can select top-of-the-line styles (yes, that have been placed here on consignment) for a fraction of the original cost. As with all resale and consignment shops, the merchandise changes often. Are you after something special or a period piece of clothing? See if a staff member might give you a call when items like you're looking for come in.

Double-Take
731 S. Hwy 101, Solana Beach
(858) 794-5451

Looking for a snappy '60s outfit, a dress first worn in the '20s, or just something really cool? Visit the resale shop and have fun trying on the fashions. This is a great place for accessories and that perfect bit of rhinestone jewelry. The store also features designer brand-name clothing from Liz Claiborne to Carole Little.

Two Sisters Consignment Home Furnishing
616 Stevens Ave., Solana Beach
(858) 755-4558

If you love to browse through collectibles and those nearly antique pieces of furniture you may remember from Mom's or Grandmother's home, this store is a find. Most of the pieces are well within a family's budget.

There's a large supply of home furnishing in nearly perfect condition, and the best part is that consignments arrive daily. (While you're in the neighborhood, check out the Cedros Avenue stores and design center.) It's closed Monday.

North County Inland

Deborah's
1624 E Valley Pkwy., Escondido
(760) 743-8980

This is a huge, one-stop resale store for items for the entire family. In business since 1974, Deborah's has jewelry, shoes, accessories, furniture, household items, toys, and gift items. The store sells only items in very good and nearly perfect condition and has a large supply of department store brands.

The store is open from 9:00 A.M. to 7:00 P.M. during the week. Saturday the store closes at 6:00 P.M. and on Sunday the hours are 11:00 A.M. to 5:00 P.M.

East County

Conceptions
10438 Mission Gorge Rd., Santee
(619) 596-2229

Conceptions offers resale accessories and clothing for babies and children. They purchase gently used clothing and equipment and are always looking for special treasures for baby.

Picket Fences Resale Store
7435 Broadway St., Lemon Grove
(619) 462-7238, (619) 460-3353

A resale shop specializing in children's glad rags as well as women's maternity clothes, the store also sells the necessary accouterments for the new baby, including furniture, strollers, and the like. If you're looking for something special—such as a baptismal gown or a tux for a two-year-old—call ahead, as unique items move quickly.

South Bay

Disabled American Veterans Thrift Store
881 Broadway, Chula Vista
(619) 232-0141

If you're a dedicated bargain-hunter, get ready to dive into the largest of the Disabled Vets' stores. You may have to plow through a lot of stuff before you come upon what you're seeking, but that's half the fun. And there's a ton of quality mixed in with the stuff that might be best classified as "junque." Clothing for the whole family, accessories, and home furnishings are just some of the treasures you'll find. Be sure to check out the collection of silk ties. It's a great way to add to your collection for a fraction of the retail price.

Bookstores

Central San Diego

B Dalton Bookseller
Horton Plaza, 407 Horton Plaza, San Diego
(619) 615–5373
Mission Valley Center, 1640 Camino del Rio N.,
San Diego
(619) 291–1315

B Dalton has been around a long time. Even though it doesn't compete with the superstores in terms of volume of titles, it's a consistently good bookstore with up-to-date stock and friendly salespeople. Plus it has the added benefit of being inside a mall, so it's easy to stop in while you're shopping for other things, too.

Barnes & Noble Booksellers
7610 Hazard Center Dr., San Diego
(619) 220–0175
www.bn.com

With more than 150,000 titles, Barnes & Noble is one of the giants in town. The Hazard Center location is roomy and spread out, and there's a coffeehouse next door where you can spend a few quiet moments with your new book. Part of the special appeal of Barnes & Noble is the huge children's department.

Bay Books & Cafe
1029 Orange Ave., Coronado
(619) 435–0070

Coronado's Bay Books has one of the largest selections of national and international newspapers and magazines to go along with its extensive collection of new

Insiders' Tip

Don't forget to check out the bookstores at San Diego's local universities. Not only do they carry a good selection of books, they also have clothing and other items with the school's name and logo.

books. Best sellers, fiction, mysteries, travel, children's books, cookbooks, and gardening books highlight the collection. You'll have plenty of opportunity to peruse your selection in the reading room or at the espresso bar.

Bookstar
3150 Rosecrans Pl., San Diego
(619) 225–0465
8650 Genesee Ave., San Diego
(858) 457–7561

Owned by mammoth Barnes & Noble, Bookstar is a smaller version of the giant superstores. Don't think for a moment you won't find a huge selection of titles; these stores are just a little smaller and have a cozier atmosphere. The Rosecrans store, for example, is in the old Loma Theater, and still sports the bright blue neon marquee outside. As you move through the store toward where the screen used to be, the floor gently slopes, just the way it did when theater seats occupied the floor instead of bookshelves. Many patrons whisk their purchases next door to the Pannikin coffeehouse and restaurant and begin reading in seats rescued from the adjacent movie house when it was gutted to make Bookstar.

The sales staff at Bookstar is great for helping you locate a title in their computerized inventory. And if what you want isn't in stock, they'll be happy to order it for you.

Borders Books, Music & Cafe
1072 Camino del Rio N., San Diego
(619) 295-2201
www.borders.com

This mammoth 25,000-square-foot bookstore is located in the Mission Valley Center West shopping mall, and like its counterparts across the country, it is a combination bookstore, music store, and cafe.

In addition to carrying more than 200,000 book titles, music selections, and videos, the store features the Borders' Cafe Espresso, where customers are encouraged to sip a cup of coffee while they read their latest purchase.

Something special always seems to be going on at Borders, whether it's a book signing, a live music performance, or a childrens' event. The comfortable interior induces shoppers to hang around and enjoy all the acitivity.

Controversial Bookstore
3021 University Ave., San Diego
(619) 296-1560

Since 1964 this bookstore has been selling just about everything except mainstream books. Spirituality, religion, metaphysics, and wellness are among the popular subjects here. Also offered are new-age music and videos, crystals, jewelry, tarot cards, and other gifts.

Family Christian Store
3231 Sports Arena Blvd., San Diego
(619) 224-2863

Serving the Christian community, this store has a wide selection of religious books, CDs, tapes, and gift items. It's also a treasure trove of church and Sunday school supplies. If there's something you need that is not in stock, the staff is great for handling quick mail orders.

Gaslamp Books, Prints, & Wyatt Earp Museum
413 Market St., San Diego
(619) 237-1492

For that one-of-a-kind find, this is the place. You'll be amazed by some of the old magazines, prints, and books you can find here. Complimenting all the reading material is a nice collection of antiques. And don't miss the **Wyatt Earp Museum**

on the premises. It's a little-known tidbit of history that Wyatt Earp was a saloon owner in the early days of San Diego. This is the kind of place that's discovered by accident—that's how we found it; it's a treasure, and we're happy to share it with you.

John Cole's Book Shop
780 Prospect St., La Jolla
(858) 454-4766

As you enter the front door of this vine-covered cottage, you'll be transported back to a time when book buying was a quiet, leisurely pursuit. Long a mainstay in La Jolla, John Cole's specializes in art books, architecture, travel, cookbooks, fiction, children's books, and books on Baja California. Don't miss **Zach's Music Corner** inside the store, where you'll find CDs and harmonicas.

Upstart Crow Bookstore & Coffee House
Seaport Village, 835 W. Harbor Dr., San Diego
(619) 232-4855

Long before coffeehouses became popular, and eons before anyone thought to combine a coffeehouse with a bookstore, Upstart Crow was doing it, and doing it well. Located right in the middle of the chaotic (but fun) Seaport Village, it's an oasis of calm. You can enjoy a steaming cup of coffee or tea while you're surrounded by stacks and stacks of books, all begging for a reader. Although small, the store has a good cross-section of titles, plenty to keep you occupied.

Wahrenbrock's Book House
726 Broadway, San Diego
(619) 232-0132

No one knows exactly how many books are in Wahrenbrock's—not even the owners. But look around you and you'll surely guess that there must be at least a million. Most of the books are used, but Wahrenbrock's does have some new ones scattered about its three floors. Loosely organized by subject matter, the books offer a browser's paradise. And if you're looking for something specific, ask a staff member. Even with all those titles and no real system to catalogue them, the staff usually knows exactly what they have and where it can be found. If you have a rare book, this is a great place to get an appraisal.

Warwick's
7812 Girard Ave., La Jolla
(858) 454–0347

If a celebrity author comes to San Diego for a book signing, Warwick's is where he or she will likely end up. This venerable bookstore has hosted Norman Schwarzkopf, Margaret Thatcher, Maya Angelou, and Newt Gingrich, as well as lesser-known but equally important persons. Large for an independent, Warwick's carries 40,000 titles along with books on cassette, large print books, maps, and globes. One half of the store is dedicated to gifts and stationery, so chances are you'll find a nice memento in addition to a new book. You're sure to see just as many Insiders shopping here as visitors.

The White Rabbit
7755 Girard Ave., La Jolla
(858) 454–3518

Just as Warwick's is a legendary bookstore in La Jolla, White Rabbit holds its own for its inventory of children's books. With more than 30,000 titles, this is the place to go for that hard-to-find kids' book you've been looking for. The staff is expert in all things literary (kidwise, that is) and will graciously assist you with phone and mail orders. Kids love the weekly story time, too.

North County Coastal

Barnes & Noble
11744 Carmel Mountain Rd., San Diego
(858) 674–1055
12835 El Camino Real, Del Mar
(760) 481–4038
www.bn.com

The Barnes & Noble chain is justly proud of its commitment to customer service. If you need a book, they'll help you find it, and if it's not in the store they'll special order it for you. Since the stores are open all week, they're convenient to visit too. Both have large children's departments, and sometimes have story times or special

kids events. In these locations there are more than 150,000 titles close to your book-loving fingertips.

Bookstar
2500 Vista Way, Oceanside
(760) 721–0706

Bookstar, a sister in the Barnes & Noble bookstore family, is a popular spot for book lovers who like in-store readings and book discussion groups. Kids come for the children's "PJ" story time (with milk and cookies), usually on Fridays from 7:00 to 8:00 P.M. There are special events occasionally, although these are more often held at the Barnes & Noble in Encinitas.

Book Works
2670 Via de la Valle, Del Mar
(858) 755–3735

Book Works has been helping book lovers satisfy their reading needs since the late 1970s. Located at the Flower Hill Center, it offers new and best-selling books, as well as some used ones. It also offers magazines (both foreign and domestic), unusual cards and stationery, English garden statuary, and vintage decorative accessories.

You can also get a cup of coffee or tea next door at an Insiders' cafe paradise, the Pannikin Cafe.

B. Dalton Bookseller
2525 El Camino Real, Carlsbad
(760) 729–5988

Found in the Plaza Camino Real Shopping Mall, this smallish bookstore is high on customer service. You'll find a friendly staff and a well-rounded selection of books and magazines. If you need a good read and you're in the mall, this is the store for you.

Coronet News Stand
111 S. Coast Hwy., Oceanside
(760) 722–3233

This is the place for all your magazine needs; it sells well over 5,000 periodicals, the largest selection in Southern California. This is the place to look if you need an out-of-town or foreign magazine or newspaper. So if you're looking for the latest issue of *Le Monde*, the French magazine *Match*, or the German newspaper *Der*

Spiegel or something more obscure, this is the place. If it's Sunday and you must read an edition of the *Detroit Free Press* or the *Boston Globe* or the *Chicago Tribune*, call the Coronet before dashing up the coast. The store is open from 8:00 A.M. until midnight seven days a week.

Esmeralda Books & Coffee
1555 Camino Del Mar, Del Mar
(858) 755-2707

Besides best-selling books, this independent bookstore offers unique selections, especially in the areas of contemporary fiction, travel, art, design, poetry, travel, and cooking. It also sells children's books. Esmeralda also offers free gift wrapping and will ship your purchases and place special orders. Located upstairs in the Del Mar Plaza (see our listing under "Malls"), it's a great place to come for a cup of coffee, browsing, and, if you like literature, free readings by local and national authors. The store closes at 9:00 P.M. Be sure to read more about Esmeralda in our Nightlife chapter.

Family Christian Book Stores
1842 Marron Rd., Carlsbad
(760) 434-6950

A spacious addition to the chain of Family Christian Book Stores, this Oceanside branch includes religious-oriented books with a strong Christian slant. You'll also find music, videos, and gifts as well as cards. They have a children's book and parenting section and they also carry Sunday school supplies. Closed Sundays.

Heaven on Earth
765 South Coast Hwy, #106 Encinitas
(760) 753-2345

Relocated across the street from its original haunt in the Lumberyard Mall, Heaven on Earth is a metaphysical and spiritual bookstore with tomes on well-known topics like astrology as well as lesser-known ones like Celtic crop circles and sacred altars. It also has a wonderful selection of cards and gifts, including music, jewelry, incense, crystals, and spiritual art.

Paperback Book Exchange
578 Carlsbad Village Dr., Carlsbad
(760) 729-4100

If you love to read and are looking for bargains, you must stop in at the Paperback Book Exchange, which has been doing business in Carlsbad for going on 20 years. This store is just ½ block east of the antiques, cafe, and coffeehouse shopping district of downtown Carlsbad and about 2 blocks south of the Coaster station.

Most of the books have been pre-read (i.e., they're used), and the prices are right. If you're hooked on an author of paperback fiction, call the store to see which titles are in stock, since inventory turns over quickly. They specialize in no particular genre, purveying everything from science fiction and horror to contemporary fiction, historical romance, westerns, and war.

Phoenix Phyre Bookstore
282 N. El Camino Real, Encinitas
(760) 436-7740

This metaphysical bookstore has been in North County Coastal since the mid-1970s. Here you'll find candles, oils, and jewelry along with a fine collection of books on topics ranging from traditional metaphysics to spirituality.

If you simply must know your future or have questions about a specific forecasting technique, you're in luck: There are daily psychic readings and monthly psychic fairs that host guest metaphysical experts. If you're looking for a spiritual piece of artwork (including ones in glass, wood, or pottery), you'll especially enjoy the gallery. Call for a subscription to their quarterly newsletter, which lists upcoming events and readings.

North County Inland

Barnes & Noble
1066 W. Valley Pkwy., Escondido
(760) 738–7168
11744 Carmel Mountain Rd., San Diego
(858) 674–1055
www.bn.com

Part of the fine chain of bookstores found throughout the country, these stores, with their atmosphere of calm, are especially inviting on a hectic weekend. While some bookstores have noisy, boisterous events, here you'll find people who've come to quietly browse, and the staff is happy to have them.

In no time at all, shoppers can be directed to a special book or have it special-ordered. As at other Barnes & Nobles, there's a sizeable selection of children's books and a place for kids and parents to sit and preview the books.

Borders Books, Music & Café
11160 Rancho Carmel Dr., San Diego
(858) 618–1814
www.borders.com

While the address says the store is officially in San Diego, it's really in the Carmel Mountain/Rancho Bernardo/Poway region of the county. To find the store, take the Carmel Mountain Drive exit from I-15 and go east. The store is immense, as you'd expect a Borders to be. It's a busy place with lots going on. If you're the type who loves a cozy, peaceful (read that quiet) bookstore, you won't find your bibliophile heaven here. It can get noisy, busy, and crowded on weekends. The children's area is in the back of the store; this is where the many story-times are held and where parents can sit and read to their little ones. Pick up a newsletter of current events including poetry readings and author book signings.

There's a cafe on site for a cup of tea or coffee and a sweet treat, and no one looks twice if you take the snack to a comfortable reading area.

Cassidy's Books
742 S. Rancho Santa Fe Rd., San Marcos
(760) 727–8640

For book lovers, this is a page-turning paradise. You'll find one of the largest selections of new and used books in the county right at Cassidy's. They carry hard-to-find editions and collector's copies; if they don't have the title you want, they'll start a search and then order it for you. Closed Sunday.

Heritage Books
1785 S. Escondido Blvd., Escondido
(760) 746–6601

In the center of Escondido, this independent bookstore provides book lovers with first editions, rare books, collectable books, and signed editions, as well as a few new books. Heritage both buys and sells, and has a large children's section too. Their slogan is, "We'll search the universe for your books," and although space travel doesn't really come within their realm of service, the staff does give it their best shot. Closed Sunday.

Waldenbooks
200 E. Via Rancho Pkwy., Escondido
(760) 746–4859

Located at the North County Faire Shopping Mall, this Waldenbooks is especially inviting when you've been on a shopping spree. There's a calm atmosphere in the store and the staff is very willing to allow you to browse. They'll special order books too if they don't have them in their large stock.

Ask about upcoming events, including signings by local and national authors.

East County

Barnes & Noble
5500 Grossmont Center Dr., La Mesa
(619) 667–2870
www.bn.com

Located in the Grossmont Center, this Barnes & Noble, like others in the chain, has a real commitment to customer service.

All Barnes & Noble stores are open seven days a week, have large children's departments, and put more than 150,000 titles close to your book-loving finger tips.

Pick up a newsletter to find out about their children's story hour and author book signings. They have special book clubs for seniors and contemporary fiction. It's open Sundays until 10:00 P.M.; other days until 11:00 at night.

Family Christian Store
8227 La Mesa Blvd., La Mesa
(619) 462–9550

This is East County's religious bookstore. Family Christian sells the latest Christian best sellers as well as hard-to-find Christian materials and book titles. The store has a Spanish-language section, a children's section, and a section on parenting. It also sells tapes, videos, and gifts. Closed Sunday.

Romance World
854 Jackman St., El Cajon
(619) 588–5494

If you adore romantic fiction, head to Romance World for oodles of books from authors ranging from Debbie Macomber to Barbara Cartland. Even if you have to make the drive from another part of the county, if you love this genre, you have to visit this store. Here you'll find romance books from the top to the bottom of the shelves. You might get to see one of your favorite authors too, as the store attracts big-name romance authors for signings. Call for an events schedule or to find out what's going on in the store. The staff will special order hard-to-find books.

Yellow Book Road
8315 La Mesa Blvd., La Mesa
(619) 463–4900

This children's and teacher's bookstore attracts people from throughout the county because of its wonderful books and good selection of resource materials for teachers. If the staff doesn't stock what you're looking for, they will get it. There's a newsletter and calendar of events, and they draw in famous children's authors for signings.

South Bay

B Dalton Bookseller
Plaza Bonita Shopping Center,
3030 Plaza Bonita Rd., National City
(619) 267–1294

For the largest selection of titles, this is South Bay's best bet. You're likely to find exactly what you're looking for in this pleasant, well-organized store. Like all B Daltons, this store is open daily and has friendly and helpful sales people.

Family Christian Store
639 Broadway, Chula Vista
(619) 425–4223

Like the other stores in this chain, Family Christian Store serves the Christian community with a wide selection of religious books, CDs, tapes, and gift items. Although they don't carry them in stock, Sunday school supplies can be special ordered.

Gracie's Book Nook
1722 Sweetwater Rd., National City
(619) 474–4464

For the best in bedtime reading material, Gracie's is the place. The "gently read" selection of titles includes mystery, romance, general fiction, true crime, and science fiction. It's always a pleasure to search the shelves for the latest gem to hit Gracie's, and you can't beat the prices. If you're like most Insider bibliophiles, you know what a treat it is to find a great used bookstore, and Gracie's is tops in South Bay in the Towne and Country Plaza.

Antiques

Central San Diego

Adams Avenue Antique Row
Adams Ave., between Texas St. and 40th St., San Diego

You could make a day of browsing through the nearly two dozen antiques shops that stretch along Adams Avenue. Stop in at **Resurrected Furniture** at 2814 Adams Avenue if you're looking for the perfect piece to complete a room. The **Kensington Antique Parlour** at 2938 Adams Avenue is overflowing with a variety of antiques, including toys, jewelry, porcelain, art, and furniture as well as historical items and textiles.

Coronado Antiques & Consignments
1126 Orange Ave., Coronado
(619) 435-7797

Located in the heart of the shopping district in beautiful Coronado, this store is heaven for the antiques shopper. You'll find lots of sterling silver, estate jewelry, and fine porcelains. Coronado Antiques also specializes in American and European furniture, painting, and bronzes. And don't think you won't find those precious decorative arts that charm the soul—they're overflowing with them. The store is closed on Sunday.

D.D. Allen Antiques
7728 Fay Ave., La Jolla
(858) 454-8708

Shopping in La Jolla always results in something special, and nowhere is that more true than at D.D. Allen Antiques. You'll marvel at the antique linens and quilts, or the baskets and beadwork. If figurines are on your list, D.D. Allen has tons of them, along with antique furniture, oil paintings, silver, bronze, crystal, and glass.

House of Heirlooms
801 University Ave., San Diego
(619) 298-0502

This upscale shop is an Insiders' favorite for its comprehensive selection of quality antiques. Among the treasures you'll find here are antique English and American furniture, silver, china, cut glass, brass, and oodles of decorative accessories.

Mission Gallery Antiques
320 W. Washington St., San Diego
(619) 692-3566

If you're a serious antiques collector, you've come to the right place. The Mission Gallery has museum-quality furnishings from the 17th, 18th, and 19th centuries, including such diverse periods and styles as American Empire, rococo, Renaissance revival, Hepplewhite, and Eastlake. You're sure to appreciate the fine American and European oil paintings, silver, porcelain, Persian rugs, and estate jewelry.

Ocean Beach Antique Mall
4847 Newport Ave., San Diego
(619) 223-6170

Dozens of antiques stores line Newport Avenue, some in malls or centers, some standing alone. The **Newport Avenue Antique Mall** has an enormous selection of antiques and collectibles. Whether you're looking for old prints, silver, toys, or dolls, you'll find it all and more here. Just across the street, the warren of antiques stalls filling what used to be **Coronet's 5 and Dime** has an even more intense and overwhelming assortment of merchandise.

Olde Cracker Factory Antiques
448 W. Market St., San Diego
(619) 233-1669

Three floors of antiques and specialty shops await your inspection in this restored warehouse. You're most likely to find collectibles here more often than serious pieces. But as antiques shoppers know, the unexpected treasure can pop up any time, any place. The Olde Cracker Factory has been known to produce many a find. Plus, it's a delightful place to browse. A couple of the mall's 12 shops are closed Monday.

Papyrus Antique & Unusual Shop
116 W. Washington St., San Diego
(619) 298-9291

If you're searching for the trendy but unusual, this is the place for you. Papyrus has a variety of Art Deco, Moderne, Hawaiiana, and early California nostalgia pieces, some of it sitting out on the sidewalk to lure shoppers inside the tiny retail space. You'll also find some interesting jewelry pieces, lighting fixtures, and furnishings. The store is closed Sunday through Tuesday.

North County Coastal

Antique Warehouse
212 S. Cedros Ave., Solana Beach
(858) 755-5156

Under one warehouse roof (perfect when you want to shop for antiques and it's wintry outdoors), this mall has more than 100 shops, and new merchandise arrives daily. If you're on a Cedros Avenue antiques hunt this is a good starting point for your journey.

There's great variety here: shops that specialize in bottles, brass, and Depression glass, and vintage clothing, western gear, and pewter. There's always coffee and refreshments for the weary shopper. Parking and all shops are on ground level. Ask for the warehouse's newsletter which lists upcoming antiques events. They close on Tuesday.

DeWitts Antiques & Collectibles
2946 State St., Carlsbad
(760) 720-1175

One of the many antiques stores lining State Street in Carlsbad, DeWitts is an excellent point of departure for those who love the quest for collectibles, true antiques, period furniture, glassware, toys, and Americana. Among the 50 dealers here you might find Hummels, silver, records, linens, and furniture. Be sure to stop at the other State Street antiques stores (between Beach and Oak Streets), which specialize in everything from Americana to restored lighting fixtures. DeWitts is within 4 blocks of the Coaster train station.

Estate Sale Warehouse
1719 S. Coast Hwy., Oceanside
(760) 433-6549

This store is more on the collectible end of antiques than others, but if you're looking for good quality, used furniture—perhaps

doing a room in sixties retro—then head to Oceanside. You'll find unusual period pieces and truly great prices.

McNally Company Antiques
6033 Paseo Delicias, Rancho Santa Fe
(858) 756-1922

McNally's is the place if you're looking for 18th- and 19th-century furnishings or just love to browse through classic furniture. Here you'll find estate pieces, *objets d'art,* and investment collectibles. They also carry quality items in silver. The store isn't open on Sunday; other days of the week the hours are 10-ish to 5-ish. Really, that's what the sign says on the door.

Vinge Antiques
3087 State St., Carlsbad
(760) 729-7081

Discover their china (lovely tea pots were everywhere during our last visit), Depression glass, and glassware that some of us used in the 1960s and 1970s (which is selling for collectible prices now), and paintings too.

North County Inland

Antique Village
983 Grand Ave., San Marcos
(760) 744-8718

Antique Village has more than 65 stores, and that makes for excellent shopping. You'll find everything from unique collectible garden accessories to glassware collectibles here. And if you love oak and vintage furniture, there's sure to be a piece to tempt you.

This store has the largest selection of antiques in North County Inland. If you're looking for something distinctive and adore the country look, head in this direction.

Hidden Valley Antique Emporium
333 E. Grand Ave., Escondido
(760) 737-0333

Imagine more than 10,000 square feet of antiques shopping. It's here at Hidden Valley Antique Emporium. Currently there are more than 60 shops under one roof, and they have layaway. They're open until 5:00 P.M. on Sunday (other days the hours are from 10:00 A.M. until 5:30 P.M.). Parking can be found along nearby side streets.

Ivy House Antiques & Consignments
3137 S. Mission Rd., Fallbrook
(760) 728–7038

This antiques store specializes in estate sale collectibles so you never quite know what you'll find. During past visits we've seen and been tempted by paintings, fine vintage linen and quilts, Native American items, and Oriental accessories. They also stock furniture and consignment items.

This Old House
30158 Mission Rd., Bonsall
(760) 631–2888

Antiques, dolls, glassware, and oak and Victorian furniture are the stars of this 7,000-square-foot antiques mall. There are more than 50 dealers and that number is growing. Many of the stores specialize in toys and western items. For those antiques shoppers always looking for a clock to add to a collection, this is the place to start. (At our last visit they had an overload of collectible time machines.)

East County

J K Corral Antiques & Specialty Store
2526 Alpine Blvd., Alpine
(619) 445–0315

If you're searching out Western gear, Western collectibles, and other Western furnishings this is the store for you. Insiders rave about the accessories. Perhaps you'll find a Hopalong Cassidy mug or a Roy Rogers lunch box. Perhaps you'll find a more authentic collectible from the real Wild West.

Ramona Antique Mall
872 Main St., Ramona
(760) 789–7816

Quality antiques, furniture, and vintage toys, and this store also specializes in books and jewelry. Call ahead if you're looking for quilts. During a recent visit the store had a large selection.

South Bay

Bush Antiques
460 Third Ave., Chula Vista
(619) 426–2181

A little bit of everything is what you'll find at Bush Antiques. Glassware, linens, books, magazines, kitchenware, and some silver are the headliners. Look a little deeper though, and you're likely to discover some fantastic furniture pieces as well as tons of collectibles. The store is closed Sunday and Monday.

Gibson & Gibson Antique Lighting
(619) 422–2447

Antique Lighting is the specialty at Gibson & Gibson, both originals and reproductions. Does your home need an antique lamp to set off your favorite room? This is the place to find it. Open by appointment only, the store has two warehouses full of fixtures and lamps, and upon learning of your decorating desires, will show you pieces from its vast collections.

Third Avenue Antiques
276 Third Ave., Chula Vista
(619) 476–7222

Is Depression glass high on your list of collectibles? You'll find it in abundance here, along with ceramics, figurines, and furniture. If you're looking for antique costume jewelry, you're sure to find the perfect piece from the large collection at Third Avenue Antiques. Hours are Monday through Friday 10:00 A.M. to 5:00 P.M.; Saturday 10:00 A.M. to 4:00 P.M.

Swap Meets and Flea Markets

Central San Diego

Kobey's Swap Meet
3500 Sports Arena Blvd., San Diego (at the Sports Arena)
(619) 226-0650

Opened in 1980, Kobey's has become San Diego's largest open-air swap meet. Both new and used merchandise as well as many a hidden treasure can be found at Kobey's, and you don't need a fortune to come home with lots of goodies. Clothing, jewelry, collectibles, electronics, fresh flowers, baked goods, and produce are just some of the items to be found. Hot dogs, hot pretzels, and other survival-genre food and beverages are available on the premises. The swap meet is open every Thursday through Sunday from 7:00 A.M. until 3:00 P.M. Admission is 50 cents on Friday; $1.00 on Saturday and Sunday. Children younger than 12 are admitted free.

North County Coastal

Oceanside Drive-In Swap Meet
3480 Mission Ave., Oceanside
(760) 757-5286

The swap meet is held 6:00 A.M. to 3:00 P.M. each Saturday and Sunday, and on holiday Mondays, at this Oceanside location. Treasures to trash are found here and only you can determine what each item or category this merchandise fits into.

There's new and used merchandise, and bargaining is encouraged by many of the regular vendors. This swap meet is said to be one of the biggest in Southern California. Most Insiders agree that it's definitely one of the largest in North County. Admission is 75 cents on Saturday and $1.00 on Sunday. During June there's a "monster garage sale-a-thon" that brings even more sellers and buyers to the location. If you want to participate or go there to buy, call for more information.

Seaside Bazaar
1 block south of Encinitas Blvd. on South Coast Hwy 101., Encinitas
(760) 753-1611

Every weekend for more than 20 years, vendors and shoppers have been coming to this import craft bazaar to sell, buy, and marvel at the merchandise: books, jewelry, and clothing imports from around the world as well as crafts and antiques, collectibles, flowers, plants, and home decorating items. *Sunset* magazine once called it one of the "secret finds along the coast." A secret no more, this North County Coastal sale still offers opportunities to find a bargain if not an outright prize. It's open weekends 10:00 A.M. to 4:00 P.M. year-round. There is no admission fee.

North County Inland

Escondido Drive-In Swap Meet
635 W. Mission Ave., Escondido
(760) 745-3100

The swap meet is held year-round, Wednesday and Thursday, 7:00 A.M. to 4:00 P.M.; Friday 1:30 to 10:00 P.M.; Saturday and Sunday

7:00 A.M. to 4:00 P.M. There are food booths, a farmers' market, and lots of treasures in new and used merchandise. Admission is 75 cents on Wednesday, free Thursday, and $1.00 Friday through Sunday.

East County

Spring Valley Swap Meet
6377 Quarry Rd., Spring Valley
(619) 463–1194

If beauty is in the eye of the beholder, then you may find some beautiful items for sale at this East County swap meet. When you do go, you can never predict what will be there. And isn't that half the fun?

Generally speaking, there's new and used merchandise, antiques, collectibles, farmers' market produce, foods, and stuff that you probably just have to take home. The admission is 50 cents for adults and the vendors are open from 7:00 A.M. to 3:00 P.M. on Saturday and Sunday throughout the year.

South Bay

National City Swap Meet
3200 D Ave., National City
(at the Harbor Drive-in Theater)
(619) 477–2203

Every Saturday and Sunday 50 cents will get you into this swap meet that's primarily of the garage-sale variety. Household items and collectibles are abundant, but you will find some new items, too. Show up early; things usually start rolling by about 7:00 A.M. The swap meet ends around 4:00 P.M. Half a dozen snack bars and food vendors are scattered throughout the swap meet. Be sure to wear a hat and bring your sunscreen.

Unique and Intriguing

Central San Diego

The Black
5017 Newport Ave., San Diego
(619) 222–5498

Back in the 1960s and early 1970s, this was the best-known "head shop" in town. Today it's fun, if only for the sake of nostalgia, to take a trip back through time as you enter The Black, which still sells beads, bongs, incense, psychedelic art, and candles along with calendars, beachwear, and one-of-a-kind items. The Black also has a fine selection of cigars, pipes, and pipe tobacco.

Hillcrest Ace Hardware
1007 University Ave., San Diego
(619) 291–5988

Looking for some nuts and bolts? You'll find them here, along with thousands of things you'd never expect to see in a hardware store. Time after time we hear locals say they stopped into Hillcrest Hardware and had a hard time leaving. There's just so much to look at. Along with traditional hardware items, check out the plants, gift items, antique hardware pieces, and all those other little things you never thought you needed until you saw them here.

IKEA
½ mile west of Qualcomm Stadium on Friar's Rd.
(619) 563–4532
www.ikea.com

It's not unique, because there are IKEA stores around the world. But this massive, endless, and inexpensive store certainly qualifies as intriguing. About ½ mile west of Qualcomm Stadium, this superstore has a huge inventory of everything needed for the home. Styles vary, but most of the furniture—from bedroom to kitchen and beyond—is based on Swedish modern. You'll find Persian rugs, modern and wacky lamps, lots of kitchen accouterments, beds, and office furniture as well as essentials such as wastebaskets and cutting boards. In fact there's so much here that you'll eventually give up and run screaming to the small cafe, which serves hot food as well as coffee, tea, sodas, and soft drinks. Merchandise found on the second-floor showroom can be picked up in the warehouse below; in other departments you just pop the item into your cart.

Horton Plaza, an exciting multilevel shopping area in downtown San Diego, is a must-see for those who really love to shop. PHOTO: COURTESY OF HORTON PLAZA

Museum Shops of Balboa Park
Balboa Park, San Diego

Every single museum in Balboa Park has a gift shop offering distinctive gifts from around the world. You could plan an entire day around nothing but shopping in Balboa Park, especially if you're looking for something a little different.

Books, textiles, jewelry, and ceramics are available at the Mingei International Museum. At the Museum of Photographic Arts you'll find photo kits, cars, posters, and frames. Or how about some sports-related gift items from the San Diego Hall of Champions? See our chapter on Balboa Park for a complete listing of museums and their locations.

99 Ranch Market
7330 Clairemont Mesa Blvd., San Diego
(858) 565-7799

Have you ever wandered into those mysterious, small Asian markets that are stuffed with unusual food items you've never seen before? Imagine that small market expanded to supermarket size, and you'll have an idea of what 99 Ranch is like. It's huge—make no mistake—and if you're seeking an obscure Asian food or ingredient, you'll find it here. Don't miss the fresh fish display, and there are mounds of vegetables, both exotic and pedestrian, to complete your Asian feast. In the front of the store are stalls selling exotic drinks, frozen things, and hot food. Definitely worth a try!

Walter Andersen Nursery
3642 Enterprise St., San Diego
(619) 224-8271

When you step into Walter Andersen's you'll find the usual assortment of trees, shrubs, bedding plants, bulbs, and garden tools—in spades. But what makes this nursery different is the staff. If you need advice, an opinion, or just some conversation about what's growing in your garden, the certified nursery professionals are only too happy to oblige. You'll learn more here in an hour than you would in a month of horticultural study. In other words, these folks know their stuff, and they're glad to share it. Just in case you're looking for something exotic, Walter Andersen has that too, along with many native plants and trees.

The White House Black Market
7927 Girard Ave., La Jolla
(858) 459-2565

Here's an interesting twist—women's clothing and accessories all in shades of white and black. Just walking through this classy store makes you feel like you're shopping for the perfect outfit for an afternoon sipping Bellini cocktails on a terrace overlooking Italy's Lake Como. From casual to dressy, the prices are affordable, and the clothes are adorable. The White House has a store in the Del Mar Plaza shopping center, too (see our entry under North County Coastal).

Whole Foods
711 University Ave., San Diego
(619) 294-2800
8825 Villa La Jolla Dr., La Jolla
(858) 642-6700

Farmers' markets are ideal for picking up organic produce and other goodies, but they're usually open only one day a week. Whole Foods, with a similar selection of freshly picked strawberries and whole grain breads, is open every day. You won't find a larger array of organically grown produce, whole grains, fresh fish, poultry and meats, and herbs and vitamins. Inside the store are **Jamba Juice,** with smoothies and fresh-squeezed everything, and **Mrs. Gooch's Cafe,** where you can enjoy everything from a cup of coffee to a full meal.

> ## Insiders' Tip
> Both Mission Valley and Fashion Valley shopping centers are right on the San Diego Trolley's Blue Line. Make a day of it, and use the trolley to travel between the two.

North County Coastal

Anderson's La Costa Nursery
400 La Costa Ave., Encinitas
(760) 753–3153

Possibly the best nursery and garden specialty store ever conceived, Anderson's La Costa Nursery is far from a secret, although their "secret garden" is not to be missed. This is the place to wander and dream of what your garden can be and then to select perfect plants (that will thrive after they're home).

In addition to plants, trees, and specialty items (such as bromeliads and proteas and huge potted palms) you'll find an enticing collection of wind chimes, bird feeders, statuary, and garden art. The herbs and perennials are worth the drive from all points in the county and in the winter months, you can get David Austin and Old English roses here that are hard to find at other nurseries. Call ahead if you're searching for something special; their knowledgeable staff can answer your plant care questions.

Carlsbad Danish Bakery
2805 Roosevelt St., Carlsbad
(760) 729–6186

If you're visiting the antiques shopping district in Carlsbad, you may want to take a short walk (1 block east and 1 block north) to Roosevelt Street, where you'll find this hidden secret of sweet temptation. The Carlsbad Danish Bakery can offer you a perfect muffin or sweet treat (try the oatmeal cookies and the bran muffins—they're to die for) and a hot cup of coffee or tea.

Their wedding and special-occasion cakes are known as the best throughout North County Coastal. They are beautiful and taste even better. Take home a loaf of their multi-grain bread, too.

This is a popular Insiders' hangout—often packed—so you may have the chance to browse through the offerings before it's your turn at the counter. You can eat here too, inside, or in the fresh air; try coffee and cake at an umbrella-covered table. The bakery choices run out after about 3:00 P.M. and the bakers don't make the same treats every day, so it's best to come early. The bakery is closed on Sunday.

Mary's Tack & Feed
3675 Via De La Valle, Del Mar
(858) 755–2015

This is a horse-lover's and pet-lover's shopping heaven and the best place along the coast if you need a bale of hay or a new set of spurs. Frequented by the upscale residents of Rancho Santa Fe and Fairbanks Ranch, the store is a fun browse and the staff is friendly and knowledgeable on pet-oriented topics.

If you're shopping in Del Mar and have had enough of the designer shops and coffee pubs along the coast highway, head inland about 2 miles for some real-life shopping. Adjacent to Mary's you'll find shops and stands that sell plants, fresh vegetables, strawberries in season, flowers, and country-style collectibles.

Weidners' Gardens
695 Normandy Rd., Encinitas
(760) 436–2194

Two times a year (March 1 to Labor Day and November 1 to December 22), the gardens are open for retail sales; the rest of the year they are open to wholesalers only. This family-owned nursery was formerly called Begonia Gardens, but Mary Weidner changed the name because many thought that was the only flower for sale. In fact, you'll find perfect tuberous begonias of all varieties, from tiny hanging plants to monster-sized specimens, but you'll also find fuscias, impatiens, and other flowers. The nursery sells many new introductions—plants that the public hasn't seen before—and specializes in hanging baskets. Beginning November 1, customers can dig up pansies to their hearts' content: don't wait too long, as they are usually gone in about four days. At Christmastime there's a fine collection of super fresh poinsettias.

North County Inland

G & B Orchids
2426 Cherimoya Dr., Vista
(760) 727–2611, (888) 727–2760

If you're hooked on orchids, you'll have to include this place on any plant-seeking expedition. Here you'll find cymbidiums, oncidiums, phalaenopsis, cattleyas, and dendrobiums by the score. All plants are of premium quality and the helpful staff will tell you what each one requires to keep it happy. They'll also give you plenty of instruction on how to get started in the exotic world of orchids.

S. B. Nickerson Nursery
1761 E. Mission Rd., Fallbrook
(760) 728–8379

S. B. Nickerson's has been called plant lovers' heaven. It's worth a field trip here if you adore plants and all that goes with them. You'll find more than 30 acres of them plus a gift shop. Trust us. If you love to garden you will find something you must have. Be sure to visit the model gardens to get landscaping ideas. The store also sells custom plant baskets, fountains, and indoor plants. This is one of the best gardening stores in North County Inland. Closed Sunday.

East County

Branding Iron
629 Main St., Ramona
(760) 789–5050

An old-fashioned Western apparel and tack store, the Branding Iron has everything from silver bits and spurs to horse blankets and felt cowboy hats. You'll also be tempted with jeans, western clothing, boots, moccasins, and Western collectibles; and if you happen to need some hay or oats for Trigger, you're in the right place too. This is a real Western-wear store and shopping is just part of the experience as you tour the aisles.

Dudley's Bakery
30219 Hwy. 78 and 79, Santa Ysabel
(760) 765–0488, (800) 225–3348

This bakery is a treasure, and while visitors might see it as being smack dab out in nowhere, they have to admit it's busy. In fact, people drive from all over southern California for a loaf of Dudley's bread.

And if you're just going to Julian, it's an absolute "must stop."

The bread is so good you'll want to take some home, but which loaf? There are 17 different types of bread to tempt you, including loaves of bright orange cheddar cheese bread and enormous, $1\frac{1}{2}$ pound rounds of date-nut, sheepherder, or jalapeno bread. Dudley's also has a cafe, which is especially busy during holidays and on weekends. But that's OK. While you wait you can snack on the bread you've bought.

Summer Past Farms
15602 Old Hwy. 80, Flinn Springs
(619) 390–1523

A friendly place where cats tend to wind about your ankles, this nursery attracts gardeners, plant lovers, and those looking for a special gift with an herbal or natural theme. Visit the herbal soap shop and factory, children's garden, vegetable garden, cutting garden, and fragrance garden. The store also holds craft demos and classes. If you're hooked on crafts like wreaths and soap-making, you'll want to call ahead for a brochure (or send a self-addressed, stamped envelope to the address above, including the zip code, 92021, to find out what will be offered during your visit).

We recently attended a free seminar on how to grow, enjoy, cook with, and soothe the body with lavender. These delightful seminars happen throughout the year. Call for their schedule. Check the Sunday "Homescape" section of the *San Diego Union Tribune* for class listings. The shop and gardens are closed on Monday and Tuesday.

South Bay

General Bead
317 National City Blvd., National City
(619) 336–0100

Whether you're looking for a few beads to decorate your favorite jacket, or you need hundreds of beads for that special craft project, you won't be disappointed at General Bead. Choose from among 18,000 items spread out over 3,000 square feet.

Beads of all sizes, shapes, and colors will dazzle you and inspire your creative nature. Closed Mondays, it has abbreviated hours the rest of the week, open only from 11:00 A.M. to 3:45 P.M.

My Bridal Gown
1050 Highland Ave., National City
(619) 474-4025

You'll be overwhelmed by the more than 1,000 designer bridal gowns that this store stocks. Expert bridal consultants will help you select the perfect gown in sizes 4 to 40 for a storybook wedding. If there's something special you have in mind, My Bridal Gown can order direct from the manufacturer at a substantial savings. Your attendants will be delighted by the large selection of bridesmaids' dresses and accessories.

National City Mile of Cars
National City Blvd., between 24th and 30th
Sts., National City

If you're in the market for a new car but are undecided about exactly what you want, drive to National City, park, and start walking. Car dealers line National City Boulevard. Every make and model you could possibly think of is here, so you can test drive all your favorites, without having to visit dealers all over town.

Attractions

Central San Diego

North County Coastal

North County Inland

East County

South Bay

Besides the glorious climate, why do so many people visit and settle in San Diego? Attractions. We have them by the boatload and they're as varied as the county itself.

Sure, we have the places to go and the things to see that you've read about in glossy publications and books. We're justly proud of the famous San Diego Zoo and its "sister," the Wild Animal Park, a 2,300-acre park that's home to 3,000 critters great and small. We love to talk about the history of Old Town, the array of creatures at Sea World, and the San Diego Hall of Champions with its collection featuring numerous sports and a mountain of memorabilia.

As Insiders, we smile when pointing out that attractions in San Diego can mean more than viewing dinosaur bones, marveling at Native American artifact collections, touring working wineries, or even screaming on a roller coaster. These are fun, but there's more.

For instance, there are the museums that are as far from the run-of-the-mill variety as you can get. Take the Surf Musuem in Oceanside where you can learn the history of surfing (it began in 1907), or the Antique Gas and Steam Engine Museum in Vista, where you can see working exhibits of gas, steam, and horse-powered engines. If you're interested in little-known historical sites, it's thumbs up for the San Pasqual Battlefield State Historical Park where the bloodiest battle in the Mexican-American war occurred. Want to visit some lovely gardens? You can't beat the tranquil beauty of the Quail Botanical Gardens. (It's tucked away in Encinitas and even some Insiders don't know its there.)

Now blend this kettle of interesting places with the excitement of casinos, high-energy fun at water parks, and the thrill of roller-coasting at Belmont Park in Mission Beach. Focus on that and then include the things you'll learn at historic sites and the Chula Vista Nature Center and you've taken just a sip of the attractions that are all within an hour's drive of downtown San Diego.

In this hefty chapter we've included our favorite attractions, including the quirky ones, the notable ones, and the ones we always share when best friends come to town. Prices and hours are as current as we can make them. You may want to call ahead, however, in case these have recently changed.

As you browse through this chapter, keep in mind that these activities and not-to-be-missed places may also be described in other chapters. For instance, there is so much to see and do at Balboa Park that you'll find an entire chapter devoted to this jewel of San Diego. Other entries may reappear in Kidstuff or Parks or Nightlife. So to get the most of our chunk of paradise, you'll want to refer to the index to get all the details on your favorites. Like most of our other chapters, this one is organized by geographic region and then by alphabetical listings within each region.

So grab your camera, pack a lunch or some snacks for the road, and let's hit it. There's plenty to do in San Diego and just so many hours in a day.

Central San Diego

Balboa Park
1549 El Prado, San Diego
(619) 239–0512

Balboa Park is truly the heart of San Diego, both geographically and emotionally. You could spend a whole day in the park and barely scratch the surface of all there is to do. Rather than try to cram Balboa Park into a few short paragraphs, we've devoted an entire chapter to an in-depth description of all it has to offer. But just to give you a taste of what you'll find, we'll start with, of course, the world-famous San Diego Zoo. That's a day's expedition all by itself. Another day could easily be spent going through its museums—the Aerospace Museum, the Natural History Museum, the Automotive Museum, and the Model Railroad Museum, just to name a few. The Miniature Railroad and the historic Merry-Go-Round are favorites with the kids, and both adults and youngsters flock to the Ruben H. Fleet Space Theater and Science Center for IMAX films and hands-on exhibits. If you plan to spend the day at Balboa Park, turn to its chapter and we'll give you the whole lowdown, including some tips on scheduling your time.

Belmont Amusement Park
3146 Mission Blvd., San Diego
(619) 491–2988
www.giantdipper.com

Home of the Giant Dipper, one of two remaining antique wooden roller coasters in California, Belmont Park is a small amusement park featuring rides, restaurants, and attractions for the whole family. In the tradition of Coney Island in New York, Belmont Park sits alongside the beach, and the ocean view from the top of the Giant Dipper is spectacular.

Besides the roller coaster, you can enjoy an arcade, Bumper Cars, a Tilt-a-Whirl, the Liberty Carousel, the Sea Serpent ride, a Crazy Submarine, and Baja Buggies. If those seem too much for the young ones, they may enjoy Pirates Cove, a play facility with over 7,000 square feet of tunnels, slides, and a ball pool. Adults and kids will enjoy the arcade game center and CyberStation, which has a collection of the latest electronic games. For the adventurous, the "Trampoline Thing" awaits: a giant trampoline where you can do flips and jumps, all with the guidance of an able-bodied and vigilant assistant.

If you prefer tamer pursuits, take a swim in the indoor Plunge, a nice alternative to the salty ocean. Built in 1925, it's Southern California's largest indoor swimming pool. When you get hungry, stop at the food court, which has numerous fast-food establishments, or enjoy one of the oceanfront restaurants within the park.

Belmont Park's hours are Monday through Thursday, 11:00 A.M. to 8:00 P.M., and 11:00 A.M. to 10:00 P.M. on Friday through Sunday. Admission to the park is free; rides and attractions are priced separately. For good, old-fashioned family fun, try combining a day at the beach with a visit to Belmont Park.

Boomer's
6999 Clairemont Mesa Blvd., San Diego
(858) 560–4211

Like its sister venues in Escondido, Vista, and El Cajon, Central San Diego's version of Boomer's has enough going on to entertain and occupy kids (and Mom and Dad too) for a full day or evening. In addition to the attractions offered by the other centers—miniature golf courses, batting cages, bumper boats, go-carts, and huge arcades—this one also has a laser-runner venue and a Country Fair Fun Zone with amusement park rides. (See the "North County Inland" and "East County" sections for information on other Boomer's.)

Summer hours apply to traditional summer vacation months and school holidays. The park is open daily at 10:00 A.M. and closes at 11:00 P.M. Sunday through Thursday, midnight on Friday and Saturday. Winter hours are reduced, so be sure

harbor during both World Wars. Finally, take a short drive down to the tidepools and check out the shore crabs, bat stars, dead man's fingers, sea hares, and many other fascinating sea creatures there.

The park is open every day from 9:00 A.M. to 5:15 P.M. Admission is $5.00 per vehicle and $2.00 per bicyclist, jogger, walker, or city bus passenger. Keep in mind that the rocks around the tidepools are slippery, and the barnacles can be sharp. Be sure to wear sturdy, non-slip shoes. And remember, collecting marine animals, shells, or rocks is prohibited by federal law.

The Computer Museum of America
640 C St., San Diego
(619) 235–8222
www.computer-museum.org

Computer geeks should not miss this new museum, which houses more than 200 computer-related icons, including such relics as the Apple Lisa computer, the first marketable modern PC. Other not-to-be-missed pieces are the Royal Precision LGP-30, a rare computer representing the end of the vacuum-tube era (it originally sold for $50,000) and the Commodore PET 2000-8, one of the first competitors to the Apple II, boasting an all-in-one-combination monitor, CPU, and keyboard. Check out KPBS's microwave transmitter, recently removed from its home atop Mt. Laguna when the public television station upgraded to digital broadcasting. The museum is free; hours are Tuesday through Sunday 10:00 A.M. to 5:00 P.M.

Dave & Buster's
2931 Camino del Rio N., San Diego
(619) 280–7115
www.daveandbusters.com

Designed with adults in mind, this interactive video game facility has a bar and restaurant, but the chain now admits children. The Mission Valley venue, open Sunday through Tuesday 11:00 A.M. to midnight and Wednesday to Saturday 11:00 to 1:00 A.M., boasts more than 200 games, and it's easy to drop a wad of cash in a big hurry.

to call before you go. The various attractions are priced separately, or purchase an all-day wristband: $23 for bigger kids, $13 for smaller fry. Every Tuesday and Thursday, play unlimited video games for $10.

Cabrillo National Monument
1800 Cabrillo Memorial Dr., San Diego
(619) 557–5450

High above San Diego Harbor, at the tip of the Point Loma peninsula, is the Cabrillo National Monument. The monument commemorates the 1542 landing of Juan Rodríguez Cabrillo in what is now San Diego and acknowledges that he was the first European to set foot on the west coast. After stopping at the visitor center, which has information about the park, exhibits, and films, make a beeline to the Old Point Loma Lighthouse for a trip back in time. Your tour of the lighthouse, built in 1854, will remind you of the days of sailing ships and oil lamps. Back when it was a working lighthouse, its light could be seen 39 miles out to sea.

Once you've taken in the panoramic views of the harbor from the lighthouse, stroll along the 2-mile bayside trail that descends 300 feet through the cliffs and is surrounded by native sage scrub, prickly pear cactus, and yucca. It passes remnants of the defense system used to protect the

Gaslamp Quarter
Between Fourth and Sixth Aves.,
below Broadway, San Diego
(619) 233-4691

No matter what you're seeking—dining, entertainment, history, or shopping— you'll find it in the Gaslamp Quarter. Covering an area of more than 16 blocks, the Quarter was named for the gas lamps that lit the evening sky in the late 19th century.

By day, stroll through the district and go back in time to the days when lawman Wyatt Earp operated three gambling houses and the area was a thriving red- light district. Drink in the beautifully restored Victorian houses, including the William Heath Davis House, the Gaslamp's oldest surviving structure. Browse among the antiques shops, art gal- leries, boutiques, and specialty shops.

By night, join the crowds who fill the streets as the gas lamps begin to glow. Take in a lively happy hour or enjoy fine dining at one of more than 70 restaurants serving a variety of cuisines: Italian, French, Spanish, Greek, Asian, and even Californian. After dinner, have a cup of coffee or tea at one of the many coffee- houses that dot the area.

Then the fun begins. Choose from Dix- ieland jazz, hip hop, country, or Spanish flamenco in the clubs and cabarets that have made the Gaslamp one of Southern California's finest entertainment centers. If you're looking for nightlife in San Diego, you won't be disappointed by the Gaslamp Quarter.

Old Town State Historic Park Visitor Center
4002 Wallace St., San Diego
(619) 220-5422

No visit to San Diego is complete without a day spent where California began. Even Insiders frequently feel the need to redis- cover their roots in historic Old Town, where there's always a fiesta in progress. It was on a hill overlooking this site that Father Junipero Serra established his first mission in 1769, and it was here that the fledgling city took hold.

The park includes a main plaza, where Kit Carson was among those who raised the first American flag in 1846. Surround- ing the plaza are historic buildings, including the Mason Street School (San Diego's first schoolhouse) and La Casa de Bandini, now housing a popular restau- rant. Two of San Diego's other original adobe structures, La Casa de Estudillo and La Casa de Machado y Stewart, have been restored and are open to the public.

On the streets leading to the plaza are surprises galore: a professional theater, artisans, galleries, and shops with old- fashioned wares. When the aroma of restaurant delicacies proves irresistible, choose from dozens of fine restaurants that offer the best in Mexican and interna- tional cuisine. Enjoy live mariachi bands and traditional dancers everywhere you turn. And if you're looking for even more excitement, don't miss the Whaley House, an officially designated haunted house.

Free historic walking tours are offered daily at 2:00 P.M. from the Visitor's Infor- mation Center at 4002 Wallace Street, just across from the western edge of Old Town Plaza. The tour includes many of the museums and historic buildings, includ- ing the Seeley stables, the Blacksmith Shop, and the Dentist Shop. If you prefer a self-guided walking tour, pick up a booklet for $2.00 at the Visitor's Center.

While you're out walking, be sure to tour Heritage Park Village, a collection of

> ## Insiders' Tip
>
> Contact the San Diego County Vintners Associ- ation (www.sdcva.org) for information on area wineries, many of which offer tastings and tours. For the phone numbers of individual wineries, contact the San Diego Convention and Visitor's Bureau at (619) 232-3101.

restored Victorian homes that were moved to their current site at the edge of Old Town in the early 1970s.

Finally, if you're searching for the perfect gift to take home, don't miss the Bazaar del Mundo, a clutch of international shops in a beautiful garden setting. Plan to spend the better part of the day in Old Town to fully enjoy the food, fun, and history of old San Diego. The park is open every day except Thanksgiving and Christmas, from 9:00 A.M. to 5:00 P.M. Admission is free.

San Diego de Alcalá Mission
10818 San Diego Mission Rd., San Diego
(619) 281–8449

In 1769, when Father Junipero Serra established the first of 21 missions at what is now Presidio Park, it must have seemed an idyllic spot overlooking the valley and the sea. In just a few years, however, the need for a better water supply and the lack of local Indians to convert prompted the move to the present location in Mission Valley, where today it is a favorite visitor attraction as well as an active parish church.

Completely restored in 1931, the mission is truly San Diego's most famous historical landmark. The on-site museum displays artifacts unearthed during archaeological digs over the past several years. It also gives visitors a detailed history of Father Serra's work as well as a chronicle of the early days of San Diego. The serene gardens surrounding the property are a favorite spot for relaxation and contemplation, as is the beautiful chapel. The mission is open daily from 9:00 A.M. to 4:45 P.M. Admission is $3.00 for adults, $2.00 for seniors and students, and $1.00 for children younger than 12. Cassette players are provided for self-guided tours.

San Diego Maritime Museum
1492 N. Harbor Dr., San Diego
(619) 234–9153
www.sdmaritime.com

Immerse yourself in San Diego's exciting maritime history by touring a collection of three historic ships docked along the picturesque embarcadero. The 1863 *Star of India* is the oldest actively sailed square-rigged ship in the world. Aboard the ship you can learn about its colorful history of collisions, mutiny, dismasting, and entrapments. The 1898 ferryboat *Berkeley*, which steamed around San Francisco Bay

You can still attend church services at San Diego's historic Misión de Alcalá. PHOTO: JAMES BLANK, COURTESY OF SAN DIEGO CONVENTION AND VISITORS BUREAU

in its glory days, is about to enter drydock for some much-needed structural repairs. During its time, the *Berkeley* was used to evacuate survivors of the 1906 earthquake and ensuing fires. Last but not least is the 1904 *Medea,* one of three surviving great steam yachts. It saw service in both World Wars, under three navies and six national flags.

The floating maritime museum exhibits the history of each boat, demonstrations of nautical skills, maritime art, and interactive activities for children. Hours are 9:00 A.M. to 8:00 P.M. daily. Admission is $6.00 for adults, $4.00 for juniors 13 to 17, and $3.00 for children 6 to 12. Children younger than 6 are admitted free.

Seaport Village
849 W. Harbor Dr., San Diego
(619) 235-4014
www.spvillage.com

Nestled at the foot of San Diego's skyline along the embarcadero, Seaport Village is one of San Diego's premier sites for dining, shopping, entertainment, and sightseeing. Four restaurants provide views of San Diego Bay as well as outstanding continental cuisine. Or if you're in the mood for something a little more casual, sample an international treat at one of more than a dozen eateries situated throughout the village—everything from Chicago hot dogs to an authentic Italian cappuccino.

If shopping is the order of the day, you'll find handcrafted gifts, original art, souvenirs, toys, and fashions are among the unique items awaiting your scrutiny. The kids are sure to head for the restored 1890s Looff carousel, and they will delight at the ongoing parade of mimes, clowns and street performers. Then stroll along the boardwalk for an up-close view of the embarcadero, or hop aboard a horse-drawn carriage for a romantic and scenic tour of the area.

Shops are open from 10:00 A.M. to 9:00 P.M. from September through May, and until 10:00 P.M. during summer months. Admission to the village is free.

Sea World
Sea World Dr., 1 mile west of I–5, San Diego
(619) 226–3901
www.seaworld.com

Although some folks find the sight of marine mammals leaping and cavorting on command distasteful, Sea World does play a part in marine conservation, and when possible rehabilitates injured or sick whales or other fauna and returns them to the wild. However, their main business is entertainment, and there are lots of impressive attractions and exhibits to thrill both children and adults in the 190-acre park. At the Wild Arctic attraction you can journey to the frozen North on a simulated 400-mph jet helicopter expedition. When you land you'll find yourself eye-to-eye with polar bears, beluga whales, walruses, and harbor seals. Or visit the Manatee Rescue attraction or the interactive dolphin habitat. How about a trip to Rocky Point Preserve, home to bottlenose dolphins and Alaskan sea otters? And don't forget the favorite thrill of all: seeing Shamu, the Killer Whale, perform. Afterward, visit "Shamu Backstage," an interactive killer whale experience. The sea lion and bird shows are also impressive, and a big hit with kids and adults.

Sea World features five shows and more than 20 exhibits for the whole fam-

A group of children are entertained by a local juggler at Seaport Village. PHOTO: DALE FROST, COURTESY OF THE PORT OF SAN DIEGO

ily. Beginning Memorial Day 2002, the park presents the "Pets Rule" attraction, in which shelter-adopted pets (including dogs, birds, cats, and even a small pig) perform zany antics to the apparent bewilderment of their human co-stars.

Park hours vary; it opens at 9:00 or 10:00 A.M. and closes anywhere between 6:00 and 11:00 P.M. Call ahead for the current schedule. Admission, which includes almost all shows and attractions, is $43 for adults and $33 for children 3 to 11. Children 2 and younger are admitted free.

Stephen Birch Aquarium-Museum
2300 Expedition Way, La Jolla
(858) 534–3474
www.aquarium.ucsd.edu
Have you ever been eye to eye with a fish bigger than you? Here's your chance to get up close and personal with more than 3,000 native fish from the cold waters of the Pacific Northwest to the balmy seas of Mexico and the South Pacific. The largest oceanographic museum in the country, the Stephen Birch Aquarium-Museum gets you as close to ocean life as possible without getting wet. The aquarium-museum is part of world-renowned Scripps Institution of Oceanography and is dedicated to educating the public about marine science.

Kids especially enjoy the re-created tide-pool on a plaza overlooking the coastline and the interactive oceanographic museum with its hands-on exhibits of seawater recycling, global warming, and earthquakes. Also part of the aquarium-museum is a specialty bookshop featuring a wide selection of educational gifts, books, and souvenirs. Hours are 9:00 A.M. to 5:00 P.M. daily, except New Year's Day, Thanksgiving Day, and

Insiders' Tip
If you're planning a visit to the tide-pools, check the tide tables before you go. Low tide is the optimum time for an up-close look at the vast array of marine creatures.

Underwater wonders delight the eye at the aquarium. PHOTO: BOB YARBROUGH, COURTESY OF SAN DIEGO CONVENTION AND VISITORS BUREAU

Christmas Day, when the museum is closed. Admission for adults is $8.50. Seniors 60 and older are $7.50, students (with ID) are $6.00, kids 3 to 17 are $5.00, and children under 3 are free.

Whale Watching
H&M Landing, 2803 Emerson St., San Diego
(619) 222–1144
Hornblower Cruises & Events,
1066 N. Harbor Dr., San Diego
(619) 686–8700
Islandia Sportfishing,
1551 W. Mission Bay Dr., San Diego
(619) 222–1164
San Diego Harbor Excursion,
1050 N. Harbor Dr., San Diego
(619) 234–4111
Seaforth Sportfishing,
1717 Quivira Rd., San Diego
(619) 224–3383

Every year, visitors and locals have the opportunity to experience the excitement of seeing one of the largest creatures on earth, the California gray whale. Between December and March an estimated 25,000 of these magnificent creatures pass San Diego as they leave their feeding grounds in the Bering Sea for their calving grounds in the lagoons of Baja California, 5,000 miles to the south. Theirs is the longest migration of any mammal on earth.

Most whale-watching cruises are two to three hours long and have comfortable indoor and outdoor seating. Commentary by experienced captains and naturalists accompany each tour. Food and beverages are available on most tours, but amenities and prices vary from company to company. Be sure to call ahead for information and reservations.

North County Coastal

California Surf Museum
223 North Coast Hwy., Oceanside
(760) 721–6876
www.surfmuseum.org

"Don't wait for the tide to come in, come over to the California Surf Museum," is the slogan of this slightly offbeat and wonderfully fun museum. Located at the top of the Oceanside pier, this attraction is a must for surfers and surfer wannabes, too. The goal of the museum is to preserve surf lore and legends of California and the Pacific Rim. There's a gift shop with surf stuff you just might have to buy.

You'll find colorful displays and photos that chronicle surf history, and learn trivia—did you know surfing began in 1907? The featured surfing legend changes every six months. Through photos, clothing, and memorabilia, you'll find out about surfboards, surfers, surfing records, surf clothing, and possibly more than you thought possible about boards. For instance you'll see redwood and mahogany "planks" from the 1930s, hollow wood boards, and boards constructed from balsa, foam, and fiberglass.

The museum is open Thursday through Monday 10:00 A.M. to 4:00 P.M.; closed major holidays. During the summer months, the museum is also open on Tuesday and Wednesday from noon to 4:00 P.M. Admission is free; donations are suggested.

Carlsbad Flower Fields
Palomar Airport Rd. and Paseo Del Norte, Carlsbad
(760) 431–0352

This annual event is greatly anticipated by half the population of San Diego and the surrounding areas. The six-week flower show between March and mid-May is breathtaking. You'll see acres of ranunculas in brilliant whites, yellows, oranges, pinks, and reds. There are also rows of mixed colors.

Plan to stay at least an hour. You can pick up makings for a picnic from the coffee cart and on-site catering service. Adult admission is $5.00; children 3 to 10 pay $3.00; seniors pay $4.00. Purchase bouquets, tubers, and flower-field boutique items at the gift shop on the grounds.

Heritage Park Village and Museum
220 Peyri Rd., Oceanside
(760) 433–8297

This attraction is situated on land that's now part of the San Luis Rey Mission and it celebrates the beginning of the city of Oceanside, one of the oldest incorporated cities in San Diego County. Walking down the main thoroughfare of Heritage Park Village is like walking down Main Street in the old American West. Kids especially enjoy it. A small-fry Insider recently said, "It's just like a movie set."

Local fishing charters arrange visits to the sheltered bays of Baja California during the annual whale migrations. PHOTO: GENE WARNEKE, COURTESY OF SAN DIEGO CONVENTION AND VISITORS BUREAU

A visit to the Carlsbad Flower Fields will brighten anyone's day. PHOTO: COURTESY OF SAN DIEGO CONVENTION AND VISITORS BUREAU

You'll stroll by the first general store, the Portola Inn, a blacksmith shop, and livery stable. Along the way you'll also pass by Oceanside's original city jail, Libby School (the first public school), and the newspaper office. And you'll also see Mrs. Nellie Johansen's house, built in 1886 and moved to Heritage Park in 1976 through the efforts of the Friends of Heritage Park Village and Museum. Guided tours are available by arrangement, and the entire area can be reserved for special events, including weddings. The grounds are open 9:00 A.M. to 4:30 P.M.; the buildings are open for visitation Sundays only, from noon to 4:30 P.M. Call for special tour information. Admission to the park is free.

LEGOLAND California
One LEGOLAND Dr., Carlsbad
(760) 918–5346
www.legoland.com

Home of the only educational amusement park devoted to those ever-popular LEGO BRICKS, this is a not-to-miss experience for kids and parents. Here you won't find that thrill-a-minute excitement of Magic Mountain and Disneyland; the excitement here is a different kind and every bit as good.

Open since March of 1999, the park is about 40 minutes north of San Diego in Carlsbad, on a 128-acre hill overlooking the ocean. (Take the Cannon Road exit off I-5.)

LEGOLAND is a mix of education, adventure, and fun designed for kids 12 and younger and their parents. It took over 30 million LEGO blocks to build the models and displays here; 20 million alone were used in Miniland. Be sure to kneel down and get close to them—many displays have "hidden" design elements that will make you and your kids laugh out loud.

LEGOLAND has six theme areas, each leading easily into the next. **Village Green** includes an opportunity to drive your own Jeep on an African safari; you'll see life-size LEGO giraffes, zebras, lions, and other wildlife. A boat ride takes you through storybook adventures (be sure to look for Little Red Riding Hood carrying something you'd never expect to see in Red's hands). In **Fun Town,** kids drive real electric cars and earn their official LEGOLAND driver's license at a Driving School. There are also kid-size LEGO helicopters (yes, kids pilot them) and Skipper School where you can captain real boats.

At **The Ridge,** you can enjoy the Sky Cycle, where you pull yourself up to the top of a tower for an overhead view of the park, and then free-fall down to the ground. (No, there are no jerky, scary crashes; they're all controlled, easy landings.) At **Castle Hill,** there's a fun Dragon roller coaster, a royal joust, and a chance for kids to enjoy a treasure hunt before moving over to the Hideaway to climb balance beams, walls, and curvy slides. In **Imagination Zone,** families are invited to play with LEGO toys (little ones can start with the larger-sized DUPLO blocks). Older kids can test out LEGO's latest innovations in this area. This is where they can build and program cutting-edge computerized LEGO blocks into robots. The last area (and the favorite of these Insiders) is **Miniland** where you'll see reproductions of American landmarks. You can get up close by walking around Miniland or by taking the Coast Cruise grand tour.

There are more than 25 specialty shops and carts, and open air restaurants where you can get everything from a quick snack or salad to a sit-down dinner of ribs and chicken. The park prides itself on fresh, wholesome foods that will enhance the experience.

The park is open daily in summer; closed Tuesday and Wednesday in winter. Adult admission is $40, and $34 for children 3 to 16. Seniors 60 and older pay $29. Parking is $3.00 for cars, $8.00 for campers. If you plan to visit the park and want to stay close by, we recommend you make hotel reservations in advance. And take our advice: Wear comfortable shoes, use sunscreen and bring a hat. Also, take your time; remember, you can come back.

(For more details, be sure to read about LEGOLAND in the Kidstuff chapter.)

Misión San Luis Rey de Francia
4050 Mission Ave. and Rancho del Oro Dr.,
Oceanside
(760) 757-3651
www.sanluisrey.org

Of the 21 California missions, this is probably the least known and one of the prettiest. It was founded in 1798 as the 18th in the string of missions that dot the state.

Strolling through the grounds, church, garden, and museum you'll be treated to early artwork, historical artifacts, and Native American historical displays. Be sure to visit California's first pepper tree and the *lavanderia,* or laundry area, used by the mission Indians and settlers. It's across the road from the main site. You can also visit the mission cemetery, which dates back to 1798 and is still being used by members of all faiths.

Worship services are held at the mission; the holiday masses often draw families of all denominations. Admission to the museum is $4.00 for adults, students pay $1.00, and children 7 and under are free; families pay no more than $12.00. Hours are 10:00 A.M. until 4:30 P.M. daily. The gift shop and bookstore is worth a visit, or come for Saturday's 5:30 P.M. mass.

Oceanside Harbor
Harbor Dr., Oceanside

This is the quintessential California pleasure harbor. Here you'll see beautiful boats, restaurants dotting the waterfront, and sailors, strollers, in-line skaters, and artists all capturing their own vision of fun.

Insiders' Tip

The Flower Fields in Carlsbad draw BIG crowds, including organized groups, tour buses filled with visitors, and lots of people from Southern California. To avoid the crushing traffic, visit before noon on a weekday during the blooming season, usually from March to Mother's Day.

The harbor is used by more than 900 pleasure crafts and sport-fishing boats. Unlike other ports, the boats are visible from the two-lane road that hugs the harbor. You'll find fine restaurants to simple fish-and-chips hangouts and shops that sell everything from shell wind chimes to upscale clothing.

Insiders visit the harbor for a leisurely walk and to admire the sunset. Families and working folks picnic on the grass and share lunch with the ever-present, ever-hungry flock of seagulls.

Oceanside Pier
West end of Mission Ave., Oceanside

The pier is a popular fishing, meeting, and whale-watching spot for Insiders and visitors alike. At its current length of 1,942 feet it is one of the longest wooden recreation piers on the West Coast.

A license is required to fish from the beach; no license is required to fish from the pier, where there's a bait shop. If you don't catch any, you might stop at Ruby's, a '50s-style restaurant that's drawing interest from around the county. This outing is easy on the wallet, as there's no admission fee.

Quail Botanical Gardens
230 Quail Gardens Dr., Encinitas
(760) 436-3036
www.qbgardens.com

In the midst of developments, Quail Botanical Gardens is a favorite nature retreat for Insiders. Ask five people about their favorite parts of the garden and you'll receive five different answers. There's a tropical area, desert display, seasonal "English" plantings with walls of cascading annuals, and an orchard with tree specimens, including guava, macadamia nut, and loquat. You'll see cork oak, the bird garden that attracts birds and butterflies, and a large display of local plants used by Native Americans for food and medicine.

There are guided tours by arrangement and self-guided tours available with the user-friendly brochures found at the trailhead. There's also a bookstore/gift shop and a small attached nursery, which sells plant starters. The plant sales, scheduled throughout the year, are a hit in the community. Recently, Quail Gardens has become a popular place for garden weddings, so your visit might just include a bit of romance.

The Garden is open daily from 9:00 A.M. to 5:00 P.M.; the shop is open from 10:00 A.M. to 4:00 P.M. Adult admission is $5.00; seniors pay $4.00; children 5 to 12 pay $2.00.

North County Inland

Antique Gas and Steam Engine Museum
2040 N. Santa Fe Ave., Vista
(760) 941-1791
www.agsem.org

Located about an hour's drive from downtown San Diego, this is California's only museum devoted to early engines and early-20th-century farm equipment. If you want to see what early farm life was like, this is the place. Located on more than 40 acres, most in cultivation, the museum collects and displays working, historical gas-, steam-, and horse-powered equipment. Period displays include a blacksmith shop, gristmill, country kitchen and parlor, steam-operated sawmill, and small, gas-powered train.

Fairs are held the third and fourth weekends of June and October, with demonstrations of how the engines and apparatus on site actually work. During these events the family will enjoy food, crafts, and music.

The museum is open 10:00 A.M. until

4:00 P.M. daily. Admission is $3.00 for adults, children 5 and younger are free.

Bates Nut Farm
15954 Woods Valley Rd., Valley Center
(760) 749–3333

At Bates Nut Farm, you'll find nuts. That's a given, but you'll also find an 8-acre park and farm zoo and special events.

Insiders enjoy the shaded park for family picnics—especially popular for Mother's Day and the 4th of July. Kids of all ages adore the pumpkin patch, which is open from September until Halloween. At the patch you can walk out into the field to pick the perfect pumpkin—or two or three or four. Pumpkin picking is a wonderful family sport—but it can become terribly crowded on the weekends preceding Halloween, when there are live bands and craft shows. Later in the year Bates is the place for Christmas trees, too.

The grounds also include a nostalgic country gourmet food store and a "Farmer's Daughter" gift shop. Cultural events and arts and crafts fairs are held throughout the year. Admission is free.

Blue Sky Ecological Reserve
14644 Lake Poway Rd., Poway
(858) 679–5469

A wilderness area that's managed jointly by the Department of Fish and Game and the City of Poway, Blue Sky Ecological Reserve is located on Espola Road, about ½ mile north of Lake Poway Road.

The reserve offers hiking, guided mountain and wildlife walks, campfire programs, and even an Owl Prowl. (See the Parks chapter for more details on these special events.) Call for reservations for programs and a list of upcoming events, many well suited for school-age children. Admission is free and donations are welcome.

Be sure to bring along your own water when visiting the reserve since there are no drinking-water facilities.

Boomer's
830 Dan Way, Escondido
(760) 741–1326
1525 W. Vista Way, Vista
(760) 945–9474

> ## Insiders' Tip
> At local attractions, food can be pricey and not always the most nourishing. Consider packing a picnic or stopping at one of the less expensive restaurants listed in the Restaurants chapter.

Take your choice of locations; all are great family fun. And while they charge separately for activities during the week, weekends are priced right. On Saturday and Sunday general admission is $21.00, and those who stand less than 57 inches get in for $13.50.

Call for times since the various venues keep different hours. Generally, they're open from about 11:00 A.M. until 10:00 P.M., while the Kids Country Fair attraction closes earlier.

So what can you do at Boomer's? How about playing on miniature golf courses, or riding the bumper boats, or trying your luck in the batting cages? You'll also find go-carts, huge arcades, the Kids Country Fair, a giant maze, and at the Vista center a place for laser tag. For kids the Vista center also includes Kidopolis, a soft play area that really tickles small-fry imaginations.

Cruisin' Night
Grand Ave. between Center City Pkwy.
and the Grand/Valley Pkwy. Split
Escondido

Every year between May and September, the city of Escondido shuts down Grand Avenue in the early evening for the weekly Friday night cruise. Like its counterparts in El Cajon, Lemon Grove, and La Mesa, Escondido becomes a meeting place for car enthusiasts from throughout the county, and even beyond. They converge on Broadway and contiguous streets to show off their muscle cars, hot rods, and even their Harleys and to check out what the "competition" is driving. The restau-

Insiders' Tip

Although the "big three" in Indian gaming are Sycuan, Viejas, and Barona casinos, smaller reservations also have casinos. These include Pala Casino, (760) 742-2268, in Pala; Pechanga Entertainment Center, (909) 695-7410, in Temecula; and the new Golden Acorn Casino, (619) 938-6000, in Campo. Each offers slots, games, and dining facilities.

rants do a brisk business, and there's always at least one local band playing. It's a great way for locals and visitors to cruise and enjoy Escondido's quaint older section of town.

Deer Park Winery and Auto Museum
29013 Champagne Blvd., Escondido
(760) 749–1666
www.deerparkwinery.com

Don't let the name mislead you. This is a fun outing and a great place for a picnic. And if you're a car lover, definitely add this attraction to your social calendar.

Deer Park Winery and Auto Museum can be found next to Lawrence Welk Resort, which is 45 minutes north of downtown San Diego on I-15. At the winery and museum, you'll be surrounded by 15 acres of vineyard, orchards, grape arbors, gazebos, and shady oaks inviting you to linger. But don't linger too long, since you'll want to visit one of the country's largest collections of vintage convertibles and Americana, including hundreds of Barbie dolls, neon car-dealership signs, old-time TVs and radios, and vintage wine-making equipment in addition to the vintage autos.

Free wine-tastings (for adults) are offered Thursday through Monday 10:00 A.M. to 5:00 P.M. Admission to the museum is $6.00 for adults and $4.00 for seniors; children 12 and younger get in free.

Escondido Historical Society's Heritage Walk and Grape Day Park
321 N. Broadway, Escondido
(760) 743–8207

Besides nature, you can enjoy a bit of history in this downtown park, which is lovely, shady, and the home of some of Escondido's historic buildings. On a typical Sunday you'll find lots of Insider families here.

The Escondido Historical Society maintains the buildings, which you can visit. So come see the city's first library, a barn with a windmill, a Victorian house, the 1888 Santa Fe Railroad depot, a railroad car, and the model train. You can also visit a working blacksmith shop.

There is no entry fee and buildings are open Thursday through Saturday from 1:00 to 4:00 P.M.

Palomar Observatory
Highway of Stars (off Calif. Hwy. 76),
Palomar Mountain
(760) 742–2119

When you wish upon a star and desire to learn more about the heavens above, you might want to visit this observatory owned and operated by the California Institute of Technology. It's a working observatory so there's no peering through the huge 200-inch Hale telescope or taking a nighttime star tour. What you do get is a self-guided tour, an educational video, and a visit to the gallery dome to see the telescope.

The facility is open daily (except Christmas Eve and Christmas) from 9:00 A.M. until 4:00 P.M. The gift shop, jammed with star- and galaxy-related stuff, is open weekends only from September to June, with extended summer hours. There are hiking trails, and here on the top of the mountain there are great views in all directions. You'll want to pack a picnic since there's no restaurant in the area. Be aware

A cheetah poses for visitors at the "Heart of Africa" in the San Diego Wild Animal Park.

PHOTO: COURTESY OF SAN DIEGO'S WILD ANIMAL PARK

that in the winter Palomar Mountain may get snow, so if you're planning a trip in December or January you may be required to have chains for your car.

San Diego Wild Animal Park
15500 San Pasqual Valley Rd., Escondido
(760) 747–8702
www.wildanimalpark.com

With more than 2,100 acres, this may be the largest, most authentic animal park outside of Africa and worthy of more than one or 10 visits. It's a favorite hangout of Insiders, who buy a yearly zoological society pass and spend many days visiting the animals, the lovely gardens, and the shows.

Included in the entrance fee is a 50-minute monorail ride; this is a great way to start the day. Be sure to bring a sweater if you're visiting in the early morning or in winter; it can be cool and breezy on the monorail. It's worth every goosebump though for the photo and viewing opportunities.

The park is noted for its educational programs, African village, and the higher-than-average birth rate for captive endangered species. Even those who shy away from typical zoos often give the Wild Animal Park a thumb's up. Among the park's latest modifications is a renovated habitat for its 11 Western lowland gorillas. The enclosure, which simulates the habitat of the gorilla's native African savannah, measures nearly 15,000 square feet, giving more room to the animals and making viewing easier for the human visitors.

Winter hours are 9:00 A.M. to 5:00 P.M. (last entrance at 4:00 P.M.); summer hours are extended until 9:00 P.M. on weekends and 6:00 P.M. weekday nights. Admission for people 12 years and above is $26.50, for seniors $24.00, and for those 3 to 11 $19.50; children 2 and younger get in free. Parking is $6.00. Ask about the combination ticket for the Wild Animal Park and the Zoo.

San Pasqual Battlefield
State Historic Park and Museum,
15808 San Pasqual Valley Rd., Escondido
(760) 489–0076

Just down the road from the San Diego Wild Animal Park and a million miles away in focus is the San Pasqual Battlefield. It's a historic park that celebrates those who participated in the 1846 San Pasqual

Giraffe feeding at San Diego's Wild Animal Park is a popular attraction for all ages. PHOTO: COURTESY OF SAN DIEGO'S WILD ANIMAL PARK

Battle, called the bloodiest battle of the Mexican-American War. There's a visitor center, a hiking trail, and the requisite stone marker that describes the historical significance of the area. At the center you'll find an exhibit and video films. In December there's a reenactment ceremony commemorating the battle.

The center is open weekends only, 10:00 A.M. until 5:00 P.M. Admission is free. There are picnic tables and volunteers on staff to answer questions.

The Wave Waterpark
161 Recreation Dr., Vista
(760) 940–9283
www.wave-waterpark.com

It's a strange feeling to put on a swimsuit or grab your beach towel for a day in the waves and then head away from the ocean, but Insiders do it all the time. The Wave Waterpark is a hot place to cool down on any San Diego day from May through September.

This $3.8 million state-of-the-art aquatic park is municipally operated and geared to families. Its attractions include the Flow Rider, four water slides, a Crazy River, a competition pool, and a children's water playground. Admission for those older than 7 is $11.50; it's $8.50 for seniors and kids under 42 inches tall. Children younger than 2 are welcome at no charge. The park is open weekends and holidays only from May 26 to June 3 and from September 1 to October 1 between 11:00 A.M. and 5:00 P.M.; daily from 10:30 A.M. to 5:30 P.M. between June 4 and August 31.

East County

Back to the 50s Car Show
La Mesa Blvd., from Date St. to Grant St., La Mesa
(619) 465–1571

Those in East County know that a visit to the Car Show means a good time will be had by all. Every Thursday starting at about 6:00 P.M., you'll be treated to live music performances and DJs spinning CDs; food vendors; and most important, hotrods, muscle cars, and buffed out motorcycles. Call for information about parking your own hot rod among these beauties.

Barona Casino
1000 Wildcat Canyon Rd., Lakeside
(619) 443–2300, (888) 722–7662
www.barona.com

Grown-up fun is the bill of fare at this Barona Indian gambling center. You can try your luck at more than 2,000 Las Vegas-style slots and gaming tables as well as satellite wagering and high-stakes bingo. If you need another reason to visit, how about the Las Vegas–style buffet and food court? Barona Casino is alcohol-free, air-conditioned, and open 24 hours a day. Scheduled for completion around the end of 2002, a $225 million expansion project, to be called Barona Valley Ranch, will include a new 400-room hotel and restaurant facilities, wedding chapel, 18-hole golf championship course, parking structure, and events room.

Boomer's El Cajon
1155 Graves Ave., El Cajon
(619) 593–1155

See the write-up above for Central San Diego's Boomer's. This venue offers the same games and attractions.

Insiders' Tip

Visit the Downtown Information Center (closed Sunday, 619-235-2222) for maps, literature, videos, and free downtown walking tours. The Information Center is located at the NBC Building, 225 Broadway at Second Avenue.

Costumed dancers perform for visitors at Old Town. PHOTO: BOB YARBROUGH, COURTESY OF SAN DIEGO CONVENTION AND VISITORS BUREAU

Heritage of the Americas Museum
12110 Cuyamaca Dr., El Cajon
(619) 670–5194
www.cuyamaca.net/museum

Set on the campus of Cuyamaca College, this museum attracts some folks who just come for the view. It's located atop a hill that overlooks the entire El Cajon valley area and that's quite a sight on a perfect San Diego day.

The museum is known for its cultural and educational displays, which reflect the natural and human history of the Americas. Don't expect this to be the Smithsonian, but rather a carefully selected collection of minerals and meteorites, fossils, seashells, tribal tools, effigies, baskets, jewelry, and indigenous artifacts. There's a small art gallery too. The museum is open Tuesday through Friday from 10:00 A.M. until 4:00 P.M., Saturdays from noon to 4:00 P.M. Admission is $3.00 for adults; kids younger than 13 are free.

Sycuan Casino
5469 Dehesa Rd., El Cajon
(619) 445–6002, (800) 272–4646
www.sycuan.com

The Sycuan Casino, in East County's El Cajon, isn't just another place for adult fun: It has some unusual gambling games. These include Sycuan Aces, Pai Gow, Caribbean Stud and Video Pull Table Machines. You'll also find satellite wagering, and a 24-hour card room. High-stakes bingo is the biggest draw, right along with the buffet and the restaurants. Call for a schedule of live entertainment. Entrance is free, but you must be 21 to gamble in California, even on Indian reservations.

Viejas Casino & Turf Club
5000 Willows Rd., Alpine
(619) 445–5400, (800) 847–6537

As this ultra-popular casino says, "We've got more fun." They really work at the fun portion, too, and include high-stakes poker, video tournaments, satellite wagering, and Indian blackjack. There's a non-smoking area in the casino, for which non-smokers breathe a sigh of relief. Located on the Viejas Indian Reservation, the club is open 24 hours a day and there's no admission fee. Unlike Barona and Sycuan Casinos, alcoholic beverages are served here, and there's full cocktail service throughout the gaming rooms.

Currently on the premises are four restaurants ranging from the snack-attack style to sit-down and buffet restaurants. Across the street, an outlet center offers shops selling housewares, apparel, gifts, and shoes as well as restaurants such as Subway and Rubio's Baja Grill.

South Bay

ARCO U.S. Olympic Training Center
2800 Olympic Pkwy., Chula Vista
(619) 656–1500
www.usolympicteam.com

One of only three official Olympic Training Centers in the country, the ARCO Center is where Olympic hopefuls train for international competition. Unlike its sister facilities in Lake Placid and Colorado Springs, the ARCO Center is the only year-round warm-weather venue for track and field, kayaking, field hockey, cycling, soccer, archery, and rowing.

Officials at the Training Center like to say that visitors get the "red, white, and blue carpet treatment" when they come for a tour. From the Olympic Path, guests can view the entire 150-acre campus, including the athletes' dormitories, training fields, and tracks. The Chula Vista site has the largest permanent archery range in North America, four soccer fields, an all-weather hockey field, a 15,000-square-foot boathouse, and four tennis courts. In addition to those stellar facilities, the Center provides a 400-meter track, six acres for field events, and a cycling course.

Free tours are offered daily from 10:00 A.M. to 4:00 P.M. Monday through Friday, 9:00 A.M. to 4:00 P.M. Saturday, and 11:00 A.M. to 4:00 P.M. Sunday. Be sure to stop in the Spirit Store, where you'll find a wide variety of Olympic merchandise and memorabilia. Although tours are free, donations are accepted to further the Olympic dream for the Training Center's athletes.

Chula Vista Nature Center
1000 Gunpowder Point Dr., Chula Vista
(619) 409–5900
www.chulavistanaturecenter.org

Did you know that burrowing owls imitate the sound of a rattlesnake to fool potential predators? Hear it for yourself at the Chula Vista Nature Center. Located in the Sweetwater Marsh National Wildlife Refuge, it's one of the few remaining habitats of its

Old Town architecture brings the flavor of south of the border to San Diego. PHOTO: COURTESY OF SAN DIEGO CONVENTION AND VISITORS BUREAU

Transportational Tours

Coach USA Tours San Diego
3888 Beech St., San Diego
(619) 266–7365, (800) 331–5077
www.sightseeingusa.com
A comfortable coach can sometimes be the very best way to take in the highlights of San Diego. Coach USA offers narrated tours on double-decker buses to Old Town, Sea World, Shelter Island, Horton Plaza, Gaslamp, Balboa Park, the Zoo, Little Italy, and other attractions. The best thing about the bus (which costs $25 for adults and $15 for children 5 to 17) is that it's a "hop-on hop-off" service good for a full 24 hours. The best bet may be to start the tour after 2:00 P.M., in which case the ticket is good all of that day and all of the next. You can make several stops the first day and more the next, or take a cruise all around town the first day to see which sites appeal to you most. You can purchase tickets right on the bus, which passes the above-mentioned destinations (as well as others) approximately every 30 minutes. The buses have heat and air-conditioning inside, and of course the open-air top portion is perfect for a perfect San Diego day.

Contactours
1726 Wilson Ave., San Diego
(619) 477–8687, (800) 235–5393
www.contactours.com
This charter service and tour operator has buses for 47 to 58 passengers. Visitors can hop aboard daily sightseeing tours to major San Diego attractions or to Tijuana and other points south of the border. The four-hour city tour costs $25 per adult. Kids are $11 each but one child may attend free with each paying adult.

Corporate Helicopters of San Diego
3753 John J. Montgomery Dr., San Diego
(858) 505–5650, (800) 345–6737
www.corporatehelicopters.com

For a thrilling, bird's-eye view of San Diego, take the tour that adventurous souls swear by: a sky tour over the best of San Diego. Soar past the San Diego skyline in a quiet, jet-powered helicopter. See Old Town and the San Diego-Coronado Bay Bridge as you fly across San Diego Bay. View the beauty of Sunset Cliffs, Mission Bay, and La Jolla. Soon you're safely back on the ground with a never-to-be-forgotten memory. The 30-minute San Diego tour is $135 per person. Other tours are available too, including a Temecula winery tour that lasts three and a half hours, including lunch, and costs $250 per person for a minimum of four passengers. If you have something special in mind, a customized aerial adventure can be arranged.

Harbor Tours
Hornblower Cruises & Events
1066 N. Harbor Dr., San Diego
(619) 686–8700
San Diego Harbor Excursion
1050 N. Harbor Dr., San Diego
(619) 234–4111
See San Diego the way Cabrillo first viewed it—from the water. Both Hornblower Cruises and San Diego Harbor Excursion offer one- and two-hour narrated tours of San Diego's beautiful and diverse natural harbor. Among the many sights you'll see are the U.S. Navy fleet, the *Star of India* sailing ship, the Cabrillo National Monument, the San Diego-Coronado Bay Bridge, and the historic Hotel del Coronado. Enjoy the sights and the sea air from pleasant sun decks or comfortable inside seating. Snacks and beverages are available on board.

Prices for the one-hour tour are $13.00 for adults, $11.00 for seniors and military, and $6.50 for children 4 to 12. Two-hour tour prices are $18.00 for adults, $16.00 for seniors and military, and $9.00 for children 4 to 12. Three-hour dinner cruises are available too, if you'd like to take in the nighttime skyline; cost is $52–$56 per person. Cruise schedules vary depending on the season, so be sure to call ahead for departure times. And even on warm days, the air can get chilly on the water, so it's a good idea to bring along a light jacket or sweater, even in summer.

Old Town Trolley Tours
2115 Kurtz St., San Diego
(619) 298–8687
www.historictours.com
Hop aboard an open-air trolley on wheels and take a leisurely approach to sightseeing. Start your two-hour tour at any of the trolley's stops, including Old Town State Park, the Gaslamp Quarter, Seaport Village, Horton Plaza, Coronado Island, the San Diego Zoo, the embarcadero, or Balboa Park. You can stay on and take a standard two-hour tour, or use the trolley as a means of transportation, getting off at any of the stops to shop, sightsee, or dine. When

you're ready, climb back aboard the next trolley and resume your tour, which is narrated with colorful anecdotes, humorous stories, and historical facts. Call Old Town Trolley Tours for a complete list of their stops or check to see if your hotel has a map. Tour prices are $24 for people 13 and older and $12 for children 4 to 12.

SEAL: Sea and Land Adventure
Old Town Trolley Tours
(619) 298–8687 or (619) 296–0605
Old Town Trolley Tours began operating this new "amphibious adventure" in August 2001. Passengers board a 40-foot-long double-decker bus for a land-and-water tour of San Diego Bay, Sea World, and the Naval Air Station. Narration emphasizes the ecological and maritime aspects of San Diego's history, past and present. Tours last approximately 90 minutes and cost $24 for adults and $12 for children 4 to 12. Kids under 4 are free. You can purchase tickets in advance or at the SEAL booth across from Harbor House restaurant in Seaport Village, where the tours depart.

Slow down the pace and see San Diego. PHOTO: BOB YARBROUGH, COURTESY OF SAN DIEGO CONVENTION AND VISITORS BUREAU

kind on the Pacific coast. A haven for more than 215 species of birds, some endangered, the Nature Center's observation tower provides the perfect venue for watching the birds go about their daily routine.

In addition to birds, a variety of seemingly fierce creatures native to San Diego Bay can be found—and petted. Bat rays and leopard sharks are among the intimidating but harmless water babies awaiting the attention of the curious.

If a bird, bug, and nature walk appeals to you, check with the Nature Center for its schedule. Many such tours and walks are provided to the public.

Hours are 10:00 A.M. to 5:00 P.M. Tuesday through Sunday; it's closed on major holidays. Admission is $3.50 for adults, $2.50 for seniors 65 and older, and $1.00 for juniors 6 to 17. Children younger than 6 are admitted free.

To reach the Nature Center from I-5, take the E Street exit in Chula Vista, and go west to the parking lot.

Free shuttles from the parking lot (near the Baysite/E Street trolley stop) to the facility run about every 20 minutes.

Knott's Soak City USA
2052 Otay Valley Rd., Chula Vista
(619) 661–7373
www.soakcityusa.com

San Diego's newest theme park got off to a slow start in 2000, and it's open only during summer months. But kids don't care; they love the slides and lots of cool, cool water on a hot August day. Knott's Soak City has 17 water slides, a four-story interactive family play structure, and other attractions appropriate for toddlers.

The park is open weekends from 10:00 A.M. to 6:00 P.M. between the beginning of May and Memorial Day and from Labor Day to the end of September. Between those two holidays it's open daily from 10:00 A.M. to 8:00 P.M. Adults pay $22, kids 3 to 11 pay $15. Summer season passes cost $60 for adults and $50 for children. Parking is $6.00.

Kidstuff

Central San Diego
North County Coastal
North County Inland
East County
South Bay

It's not hard to find things for kids to do in San Diego. Most of what makes San Diego special—the zoo, Sea World, Wild Animal Park, the beaches—appeals to kids just as much as it does to adults. Even though kids can have as much fun doing all the things that grown-ups enjoy, there are times when they need something a little different, something that's designed just for them. And that's what we'll help you discover in this chapter.

We've found the special little treats just for kids and given you the lowdown on them all. For kids that like to touch without being chastised, visit the Children's Museum, where they can get their hands on interactive displays geared specifically for the younger set. Or maybe the kids would enjoy seeing a performance by the San Diego Junior Theatre or the Escondido Theater for Families.

Lots of one-time events are staged especially for kids, too, and although we can't ever predict what's coming, we'll tell you where to look to find Frisbee demonstrations, yo-yo clinics, and kids' craft sessions. Some bookstores have story times for kids; we've clued you in on the ongoing ones. Libraries are a good place to check out, too. Most have reading programs for kids ranging in age from toddlers to teens.

A great resource for kidstuff is in the "Calendar" section of *The San Diego Reader*, a weekly tabloid that comes out on Thursdays and can be picked up free at bookstores, libraries, convenience stores, and hundreds of other locations throughout the county. The "Night & Day" section of the *San Diego Union-Tribune* will give you ideas as well.

Things like LEGOLAND and the Children's Museum, designed specifically for kids, are found here, but many of the listings in the Attractions chapter will appeal to children as well as their unpaid chauffeurs.

If an adult's presence is required at a children's event or attraction, we've made note of it. If your child needs to bring along anything extra, we've mentioned that too. Keep in mind, though, that it's always a good idea to phone ahead and get all the particulars. It's nice to touch base with the folks who organize these events; you'll have peace of mind and the kids will know what's in store ahead of time.

Central San Diego

Barnes & Noble Bookstore
7610 Hazard Center Dr., San Diego
(619) 220–0175
www.bn.com

Kids' story time is every Saturday at 12:30 P.M. Special guests like Ms. Frizzle (a char-actor in *The Magic School Bus* book series) make regular appearances with stories, fun, and lots of surprises. Often the program will be repeated in the afternoon for hearing-impaired kids. Sometimes snacks are provided, but if they aren't, try to send something with your child that won't make much of a mess. It's a good idea to send along a favorite toy with younger children (not the squeaky kind, though). There's no cost for admission, but you should call for reservations.

Bookstar
3150 Rosecrans Pl., San Diego
(619) 225–0465

Kids love Monday Night Storytime at Bookstar. Every Monday from 7:00 to 8:00 P.M. a different story is read. Sometimes the subject is animals; sometimes it's the ocean and its many wonders. Snacks are usually provided, and the story time is sometimes followed by a craft activity related to the theme. All events are free, but call Bookstar ahead of time to find out exact times and dates and what's on the agenda.

Boomer's
6999 Clairemont Mesa Blvd., San Diego
(858) 560–4211

We covered the Boomer's located throughout the county in our Attractions chapter. But they're worthy of a mention here, too, simply because kids go wild over the variety of activities they can dive into, such as batting cages, miniature golf, arcade games, go-karts, and amusement park rides.

"Summer" hours apply to traditional summer vacation and school holidays, when the park is open daily at 10:00 A.M. and closes at 11:00 P.M. Sunday through Thursday, midnight on Friday and Saturday. Winter hours are reduced, so be sure to call before you go. The various attractions are priced separately, but all-day passes cost $23 for bigger kids, $13 for smaller fry. Every Tuesday and Thursday, they can play unlimited video games for $10.

Camp Sea World
500 Sea World Dr., San Diego
(619) 226–3834, (800) 380–3202
www.seaworld.com

For preschoolers through high school seniors, Sea World has one of the coolest summer-camp programs around. It's an adventure filled with animals, games, crafts, and learning, and it all adds up to a whole bunch of fun. Camps for preschoolers are designed for children ages 3 and 4 (with parent involvement), and the level of activities and learning experiences accelerate for older kids.

Camp Sea World runs during the morning hours, and there's an extended camp that lets kids stay in the park to enjoy an afternoon of games, shows, and animal attractions. Extended camp ends at 5:00 P.M.

Prices vary depending upon which camp is selected, but generally run about $60 for a three-day morning program for preschoolers and $125 to $150 for a weeklong, half-day program for older children.

Another summertime event popular with kids is the overnight adventure. Children from 5 to 18 years old arrive in the late afternoon and have a pizza party, games, and crafts designed to teach them about marine life. They then sleep in their sleeping bags next to the penguin, manatee, shark, or beluga whale enclosures. In the morning they get a light breakfast, a T-shirt, and a tour of the park before it opens to the public, with the option of spending the rest of the day in the park. The cost is $105 per child.

Children's Pool
Coast Blvd., south of Jenner St., La Jolla

City engineers gave Mother Nature a helping hand when they built a sea wall to partially enclose a natural inlet. The result is Children's Pool, which would more appropriately now be called the sea lions' pool. In recent years, scores of these marine mammals have taken up residence on the sand and rocks, giving kids a close-up look at these amazing sea creatures. Humans, however, are now banned from the beach due to contamination from sea lion waste. And although most kids would change places with the pinnipeds any day, they still get a kick out of watching the social creatures dive from the rocks and roll around in the sand.

Chuck E Cheese's
9840 Hibert St., San Diego
(858) 578–5860
3146 Sports Arena Blvd., San Diego
(619) 523–4385
www.chuckecheese.com

Put on your best game face, Mom and Dad, and prepare for an assault on the senses. Kids absolutely love Chuck E Cheese's for its noise, shows, constant activity, games, rides, prizes, and pizza. The motto is, "It's a magical place where a kid can be a kid." Although it may be a bit much for adults looking for a peaceful meal, the smile on the kids' faces makes it all worthwhile. Large groups are welcome (call in advance), and birthday parties and other gatherings can be arranged ahead of time. Admission is free, and the restaurant is open for lunch and dinner every day but Monday.

La Jolla YMCA Day Camps
8355 Cliffridge Ave., La Jolla
(858) 453–3483
www.lajollaymca.org

La Jolla's YMCA has created a series of traditional and special-interest day camps that run for one-week periods during the summer. For kids who want to learn kayaking, wakeboarding, and water skiing, an intense, five-hours-per-day instruction camp is held at the Mission Bay Aquatics Center. The Harry Potter camp will appeal to confirmed muggles and future wizards alike, with a week's worth of magic arts, crafts, and YMCA-style quiddich lessons.

Dozens of other camps are available too, including cooking, mountaineering, ice-skating, arts and crafts, and more. There's something for any kid between 3 and 17. Prices vary, beginning at $99 and running to several hundred dollars for a one-week session. YMCA members get a discount on camp fees.

Marie Hitchcock Puppet Theater
2130 Pan American Rd. W., Balboa Park,
San Diego
(619) 685–5045

Named for San Diego's original Puppet Lady, who charmed local kids for decades with her amusing puppet acts, the Marie Hitchcock Puppet Theater is now home to the San Diego Guild of Puppetry. It's a group of professional and amateur puppeteers who perform year-round at the theater, staging marionette, shadow puppet, and hand-puppet performances. Occasionally the Guild will stage a ventriloquist act, too. The theater also hosts traveling shows that produce a variety of events.

It's a small theater—only 230 seats—so it's a good idea to get there a little early to get the best seats. No refreshments are sold during performances, and food isn't allowed in the theater. Shows usually run about 30 to 45 minutes. Tickets are available at the theater on the day of the performance; no advance reservations are required. Show times are 10:00 and 11:30 A.M. Wednesday, Thursday, and Friday; 11:00 A.M., 1:00 P.M., and 2:30 P.M. on Saturday and Sunday. Admission for adults is $3.00; children 3 to

---

Insiders' Tip

Many communities and local churches have Easter egg hunts where kids search for candy eggs and have lots of fun—most of the time for free. Look for the lineup of these events in your local community newspaper or call the local parks and recreation department.

---

17 are charged $2.00. Children 2 and younger are admitted free.

Mission Valley YMCA Day Camps
5505 Friars Rd., San Diego
(619) 298–3576
www.missionvalleyymca.org

For kids who think the X Games are the hottest thing going, here's their chance to get some firsthand experience with extreme sports. Campers ages 12 to 15 can participate in X-treme Teen skating. Campers of all ages can join one of a variety of other camps, including cheerleading/dance, marine life, oil painting, salsa/latin dancing, woodworking, wake boarding, and laser tag.

The cost of the camps vary depending on the chosen activity, ranging from $95 to $405.

Nighttime Zoo and Wild Animal Park Adventures
Balboa Park and Escondido
(619) 234–3153
www.wildanimalpark.com

Held at the San Diego Zoo and Wild Animal Park, the park adventures happen in the evenings when the animals are most active (they choose to snooze during the afternoon's heat). During the summer the facilities stay open late for special educational and kids' programs, and continuing shows. The trams run and humans can wander the grounds until 10:00 P.M. throughout the summer. Stroller and wheelchair rentals are available. Pack a picnic dinner to eat at any of the wonderful sites. There are lockers you can rent where you can store supper and extra gear; it may be cool in the evenings. Admission ranges from $12 to about $20; discounted admission is available for children, seniors, and active military. (Also see the listing under "Roar and Snore," below. And be sure to read more about the zoo in our chapter on Balboa Park.)

San Diego Junior Theatre
Casa del Prado Theatre
1800 El Prado, Balboa Park, San Diego
(619) 239–1311 (information)
(619) 239–8355 (box office)
www.juniortheatre.com

Since 1948 the San Diego Junior Theatre has provided kids 3 to 18 with classes in acting, voice, dance, and other specialties like intro to improv, dialects, and stage makeup. One- or two-week class sessions are offered during the summer, and once-a-week sessions of 10 weeks are available during the rest of the year.

Students 8 or older who have taken or are currently enrolled in Junior Theatre classes are eligible to audition or be part of the stage crew for the five or six productions given every year in the Casa del Prado Theatre. Recent productions have included such hits as the musical *Oliver* and Shakespeare's *Comedy of Errors*.

Even if the kids aren't interested in classes, the productions themselves are always crowd-pleasers, enjoyed by children and adults alike. Ticket prices range from $5.00 to $8.00 for children younger than 14 and seniors and from $7.00 to $10.00 for adults. Class prices vary widely depending on the type of class and the age of the child, but the usual fee is between $95 and $120. Call the above numbers for current class schedules and ticket prices.

Summer Sports Camps
University of San Diego
5998 Alcalá Park, San Diego
(619) 260–4593, (800) 991–1873, ext. 2
camps.sandiego.edu

The University of San Diego Sports Camp program is dedicated to providing a unique athletic experience tailored to the individual needs of each camper. The emphasis is on personalized instruction and increased performance. One- and two-week sessions in day or resident programs are offered to children ages 6 to 17. Camps focus on skills in baseball, basketball, softball, swimming, soccer, volleyball, tennis, and water polo. Overnighters stay in dormitories on the beautiful USD campus. Costs range from $120 to $625 per week.

Children 6 to 12 can attend day camps: Team Sports, Wet & Wild, or All-Sports. Team Sports Camp offers general skill instruction in competitive sports, including soccer, tennis, basketball, baseball, softball, volleyball, and football. All-Sports Camp combines team sports and "lifetime sport" activities such as Frisbee, golf, street hockey, and archery as well as recreational games and activities. Wet & Wild Sports Camp offers introductory instruction in snorkeling, lifesaving, water safety, surfing, springboard diving, water polo, and competitive swimming. Half-day camp costs $120 a week; full-day costs $200.

At the Heart of Africa in San Diego's Wild Animal Park, amazing African animals thrill on-lookers.

PHOTO: COURTESY OF SAN DIEGO'S WILD ANIMAL PARK

With mom helping, this toddler is getting a first-time view through the telescope. PHOTO: DALE FROST, COURTESY OF THE PORT OF SAN DIEGO

Zany Brainy
1520 Camino de la Reina, San Diego
(619) 291–9500
10661 Westview Pkwy., San Diego
(858) 547–8700

More than just a toy store, Zany Brainy is event central for kids age 3 to 12. Special programs and demonstrations are going on all the time, such as performances by children's recording artists or magic shows. Kids might learn how to do tricks with yo-yos, master the art of Frisbee throwing, or make cookies or Valentine's Day cards. All special events are free, and most are scheduled on Wednesdays, Fridays, and Saturdays. Call the store for the latest lineup and times.

North County Coastal

Carlsbad Children's Museum
300 Carlsbad Village Dr., Ste. 103, Carlsbad
(760) 720–0737
www.museumforchildren.com

Busy small hands are welcome at the museum. It's just for kids. Located near the beach and Carlsbad's State Street shopping district (see our Shopping chapter), it delights children ages 2 through 12 with interactive exhibits that change often.

Here kids can create crafts and experiment on computers at various activity centers. The Fishing Boat sparks imaginative play, and so does the Castle Play where kids can dress up and act out medieval fantasies. At the Kids Market children can learn the workings of a supermarket, including a conveyor belt that works.

Did you know that in "real" grocery stores—just like at the Kids Market—the conveyor belt is moved along by a switch on the floor? Accompanying the kids to this museum might be a good educational experience for you too.

During the traditional school year, call ahead, since hours are limited. In the summer the museum is open between 10:00 A.M. and 5:00 P.M. There's a $4.00 admission fee; children younger than 2 get in free.

Cole Library
1250 Carlsbad Village Dr., Carlsbad
(760) 434–2870

Kids are king at the Cole Library. Along with a huge collection of books, videos, and tapes, there are reading programs and story hours for toddlers and preschoolers. After-school activities from magic workshops to cultural activities are free and fun. There are lots of arts and crafts programs designed to please even the most particular child. It's fun for the whole family to gather together to watch family-oriented films on the last Thursday of each month at 6:00 P.M., when kids are invited to wear their pajamas and bring a pillow.

The library sponsors teen book clubs and the incredibly popular (for the last 27 years!) summer reading program. Do like the Insiders: Park off Elmwood Street, just east of the library, in the unpaved parking lot. Stop in for a program and newsletter that details the free activities.

Chuck E Cheese's
2481 Vista Way, Oceanside
(760) 439–1444

If you and the kids need a shot of intense family fun, steer the car to Chuck E Cheese's. It's a restaurant like no other because here kids really are encouraged to be kids. You'll get pizza and soda and then the family can wrap it up with plenty of activity and excitement.

Insiders' Tip
In early spring issues of *San Diego Parent* and *San Diego Family Magazine*, you'll find listings of summer activities and camps for kids. If your offspring have their hearts set on a special camp, make reservations early.

No one has to be quiet or use proper manners here—the noise and enthusiasm level is always on full blast. Call ahead if you're bringing a big group or planning an event.

J.W. Tumbles
292-A N. El Camino Real, Encinitas
(760) 942–7411
www.jwtumbles.com

An activity center and gym strictly for kids, J.W. Tumbles offers kid-style fitness and exercise programs and classes. The staff here, too, can help you create great birthday parties. Every other Friday from 5:30 to 9:30 P.M. is Kids Night Out. Parents can drop off children from ages 3 to 10 for supervised activities (from coloring to games) and fun theme parties. The food that's available runs along the pizza and soda line. The cost is $20 per child for the four hours, slightly more for nonmembers. This activity is popular with both kids and parents, so reservations are recommended.

LEGOLAND California
One LEGOLAND Dr., Carlsbad
(760) 918–5346
www.legoland.com

Devoted to those ever-popular LEGO BRICKS, this theme park is most appropriate for smaller children. The park is wholesome fun for kids and their parents, with no scary breath-snatching rides and nothing that will make even the youngest have bad dreams.

It took more than 30 million LEGO blocks to build the models and displays here; 20 million alone were used in Miniland, the heart and soul of this 128-acre theme park, which is divided into six theme areas. Village Green includes an opportunity to drive your own Jeep on an African safari; you'll see life-size LEGO giraffes, zebras, lions, and other wildlife. A boat ride takes you through storybook adventures. In Fun Town, kids drive real electric cars and earn their official LEGOLAND driver's license at a Driving School. There are also kid-piloted LEGO helicopters as well as Skipper School boats. Waterworks offers kids a place to play with water and is best on a hot summer day. There's also DUPLO for younger guests, a puppet theater, a magic theater, and a snack shop.

You can then move on to the Ridge, LEGO maze, and Sky Cycle, where you cycle your way around in a zany people-powered car. The way it's planned, this self-propelled ride will take you up Kid Power Tower. At the top—guess what?—you can experience the exhilarating "free-fall" to the bottom. (Parents: This is all very safe and won't scare even the youngest child.) Too cool? You bet.

There's more child-oriented pleasure in Castle Hill (for medieval scenes and encounters) and the popular Imagination Zone. In addition to the rides and family fun, there are restaurants throughout the park that actually serve fresh, healthy foods. The park is open daily between Memorial Day and Labor Day; closed Tuesday and Wednesday the rest of the year. Adult admission is $40, and $34 for children 3 to 16. Senior admission (for those older than 60) is $29. Parking is $3.00 for cars, $8.00 for campers.

Best photo ops for the park? From the Garden Restaurant near Castle Hill, on the promenade heading into the Imagination Zone, and anywhere in Miniland.

Insider tips for this park are simple. Wear a hat or sunscreen (or both) and your most comfortable shoes, and rent a storage locker for extra jackets, the LEGO purchases you'll have to make, and (if you have one) the diaper bag.

San Diego County Fair, The Del Mar Fair
Del Mar Fairgrounds
2260 Jimmy Durante Blvd., Del Mar
(858) 792-4252
www.delmarfair.com

Even though we've mentioned this huge fair in the Annual Events chapter and you can read the details there, please don't think of it just as an adult attraction. It's truly kid-style fun.

Pre-fair tickets and family passes can make the fair more affordable. In past years, we've saved about $20. During the three-week event, one day is specially designated for kids—and they get in free. When you're at the fair, pick up a free listing of events for the day. Some

favorites with kids, in addition to the food and the midway rides, are the collection contests, the animals, the horse shows, and the special events like sheep shearing and herding demonstrations.

There are free shuttles available from various locations in the county. Admission is $8.00.

Remember lots of things happen year-round at the fairgrounds—including plenty of kids' events. Do like Insiders and call the 24-hour event hotline at (858) 793-5555 to get the scoop on what's happening right now.

Silver Bay Kennel Club Dog Show
Del Mar Fairgrounds,
2260 Jimmy Durante Blvd., Del Mar
(858) 792-4252

Grown-ups (along with dog breeders and handlers) go to the show to see the competition. Kids love it to see how working dogs work, the pampered pooches compete, and the demonstrations. All animal-loving kids, future vets, and children with incredible curiosity (and what kid doesn't have that) talk about this premier dog event for years. Kids can get up-close to elite canines (with permission from the handlers please) before and after competition times.

There is no admission fee for this event that happens each February. If your kids love dogs, keep a watch at pet-food centers and in the newspaper for other dog shows around the county. Show dates change each year, so watch the paper or call the fairground's info line.

(Be sure to check out our Annual Events chapter for other free, kid-oriented

Insiders' Tip

Most libraries have a summer reading program for children. Call your local branch and see what fun your kids can have with books.

LEGOLAND is one of San Diego's newest theme parks. PHOTO: M. J. GOLDSTEIN, COURTESY OF SAN DIEGO CONVENTION & VISITORS BUREAU

things to do, from rodeos to toys shows, that happen at the fairground year-round.)

YMCA
200 Saxony Rd., Encinitas
(760) 942–9622
1965 Peacock Blvd., Oceanside
(760) 758–0808

The Y has been an important source of kidstuff throughout the county for years. Its varied programs are well supervised, age-specific, and lots of fun. Choose to have the kids experience horseback riding, surfing, skating, crafts, gymnastics, or a dozen other fun camps and workshops. There's a popular skateboard park and a BMX dirt jump park for beginner to advanced bike riders at the Encinitas Y. There are also classes and sporting teams for parents and teens as well as family campouts. Call for prices, locations, and a current schedule; Y members receive a discount on events and trips.

North County Inland

Bates Nut Farm
15954 Woods Valley Rd., Valley Center
(760) 749–3333

At Bates Nut Farm, kids can be kids as they discover and touch farm animals. There are wonderful places to let the smaller set run as you put out a picnic lunch. In the fall, plan a trip here to pick a pumpkin. Bates fields will be blanketed with bright orange, plump pumpkins. You might want to bring along a wagon as you go out to find your own. (You'll be disappointed if you don't bring your camera; the snap shots are sure to make the aunts, uncles, and grandparents smile.)

At Christmas, you can select the perfect tree at Bates Nut Farm, and while you're there, you might want to take a horse-drawn hayride too. For many families that's become a holiday tradition.

The look on this carousel rider's face tells the whole story . . . it's loads of fun. PHOTO: DALE FROST, COURTESY OF THE PORT OF SAN DIEGO

(Mom and Dad will enjoy the craft shows that are scheduled during the fall and December holidays. Parents will also like the gourmet foods found at the Bates general; after all this fun you'll need some healthy snacks.)

See Attractions for a full idea of what's in store for kids and grown-ups at Bates Nut Farm.

Blue Sky Ecological Reserve
Espola Rd., ½ mile north of Lake Poway Rd., Poway
(619) 679-5469

If you have curious kids who love everything that has to do with the outdoors then you'll want to take a trip to Blue Sky Ecological Reserve. Be sure to read the entry in the Parks chapter.

The reserve's 700 acres of wilderness are located about 20 minutes from I-15. For those who haven't had a chance to see what San Diego County might look like without freeways, houses, and cars, it's an eye opener. Please remind the kids; it might be a new concept for them.

At the reserve you might spot a coyote, deer, fox, or snake. It's recommended that you always stay on the paths. There are birds in abundance. Bring drinking water since this is a wilderness area. There are special kids' tours and guided tours and an information kiosk with a display of plants and animals that are native to the area. Call for details and to receive a free newsletter.

Boomer's
830 Dan Way, Escondido
(760) 741-1326
1525 W. Vista Way, Vista
(760) 945-9474
www.boomersparks.com

Take your choice of locations and then turn to our Attractions chapter to read about all the fun your kids can have here. Wristbands cost $22 for bigger kids, $13 for kids 58 inches tall or shorter. At each Boomer's, you'll find activities from miniature golf to bumper boats to a giant maze. At the Vista center there's Kidopolis, a soft play area that really stimulates small-fry imaginations. Hours are Monday through Thursday 11:00 A.M. to 10:00 P.M.; Friday 11:00 A.M. to midnight; Saturday 10:00 A.M. to 11:00 P.M., and Sunday 10:00 A.M. to 10:00 P.M.

California Center for the Arts
340 N. Escondido Blvd., Escondido
(800) 988–4253
www.artcenter.org

Families will find lots to do at this cultural center right off I-15 in downtown Escondido. You'll find Education at the Center, which features art and acting classes and other related programs for both kids and adults. Call for a current program of activities and pricing information.

On Sundays throughout the year you and the kids will be treated to Theater for Families. Kids get to meet the artists before and after the show. The shows are just an hour long, accommodating a kid's attention span and need to get up and move. Kids can also do hands-on art projects, participate in the after-show entertainment, and buy snack foods like popcorn, ice cream, and soda.

Programs and plays here are by top performers who specialize in children's productions. Insiders and visitors have been recently treated to the San Diego Chamber Orchestra's Carnival Concert, featuring music from shows such as *The Wizard of Oz*, *Snow White and the Seven Dwarfs*, and *The Sorcerer's Apprentice*. Shows like the Super Scientific Circus use magic and mime, boomerangs, and beach balls to make science fun, while Luma Theater of Light is a fantastic display of color and light set to eclectic music. Tickets cost about $10; call for reservations and seating.

Chuck E Cheese's
624 W. Mission Ave., Escondido
(760) 741–5505
www.chuckecheese.com

There's fun aplenty at this kids-oriented restaurant that has foods and activities for kids. This restaurant is probably the one most requested by the 7 and younger set, and plenty of teens go there, too. If you and the kids need a shot of intense fun, steer the car to Chuck E Cheese's.

Palomar College Programs and Workshops for Kids
Palomar College Community Services
1140 W. Mission Rd., San Marcos
(760) 744–1150, ext. 2702
www.palomar.edu/community

Palomar College's Community Services office offers three-hour memory power, study skills, and spelling-improvement courses as well as beginning drawing classes, the latter once a week for five Saturdays. Cost is $39 for the one-day courses and for the beginning drawing course.

Roar and Snore Camp Over
San Diego Wild Animal Park, 15500 San Pasqual Valley Rd., Escondido
(760) 738–5049
www.wildanimalpark.com

Although you'll meet other adults who go on this once-in-a-lifetime camp, there are plenty of families. For kids and parents who love animals, it's a memory in the making. Attendees have an early dinner before taking a guided nighttime walk to see some of the park's fantastic creatures. Afterwards there's more entertainment in the form of African stories, animal programs, campfires, and live music. Crawling into their sleeping bags, kids will thrill to the nighttime noises of wild animals as they feed, play, and generally go about their nocturnal activities. After an outdoor breakfast, campers can take a tram ride around the park and are free to spend as much time as they like at the park that day.

> ## Insiders' Tip
> A day spent in the backcountry parks can be tons of fun. Just make sure you check with park rangers or officials to get a heads-up on any hazards such as poison oak, rattlesnakes, bobcats, or ticks.

The camp happens on Friday, Saturday, and some Sunday evenings in summer only; call for reservations and a recommended equipment list. Costs are $126 for those 12 and older and $106 for children 8 to 11; children under 8 are not permitted. See our chapters on Attractions and Balboa Park for more details.

The Wave Waterpark
161 Recreation Dr., Vista
(760) 940–9283
www.wave-waterpark.com

This is a wet and wild adventure for kids and parents. Be sure to read all about it in the Attractions chapter, then come sample the fun at this $3.8 million, state-of-the-art, municipally-operated family aquatic park. It's open from May through September. If you're interested in swimming lessons for the kids, it's wise to reserve a space ahead of time.

The attractions include the Flow Rider, four water slides, a Crazy River, a competition pool, and a children's water playground. Admission for those older than 7 is $11.50; it's $8.50 for seniors and kids under 42 inches tall. There's no charge for kids 2 and under. The park is open weekends and holidays only from May 26 to June 3 and from September 1 to October 1 between 11:00 A.M. and 5:00 P.M., and daily from 10:30 A.M. to 5:30 P.M. June 4 to August 31.

YMCA
1050 N. Broadway St., Escondido
(760) 745–7490

You can depend on the Y for quality year-round fun. There are summer day camps, overnight campouts, classes, crafts, and good wholesome fun when you participate in the Y programs. For youngsters in the 10 and older group there are youth events, and the Y has after-school programs too.

When you call for details and a current schedule, ask about family camping experiences, such as those at Lake Sequoia. Call for prices, information, and a current schedule of events. Y members receive a discount on the programs.

East County

Boomer's El Cajon
1155 Graves Ave., El Cajon
(619) 593–1155
www.boomersparks.com

In our Attractions chapter, you'll find all the details about this great activity center. Here you'll find old- and new-fashioned fun: miniature golf courses, batting cages, and bumper boats, as well as go-carts, an arcade with the latest video games, the Kids Country Fair, and a giant maze.

Cuyamaca Rancho State Park
Calif. Hwy. 79 between Hwy. 78 and I–8, eastern San Diego County
(760) 765–0755
www.cuyamaca.statepark.org

If you're a camping family and love to explore, this state park should be on your must-do list. You and the kids will be treated to wilderness areas, a museum with Native American artifacts and more than 100 miles of walking and equestrian trails. Some of the trails are easy walks, perfect for smaller children; others are more challenging.

The wilderness area covers more than 25,000 acres in East County, including heavenly wildflower meadows, Green Valley Falls, and the ruins of a gold mine, the Stonewall mine. There are two developed

Two smiling girls find something to pose with . . . the ranunculus flowers in Carlsbad. PHOTO: CECE CANTON

campgrounds with group campsites and cabins. There is even an equestrian campsite. You'll want to look at the Parks chapter for a full overview of this natural adventureland and of other parks throughout the county that have special kids programs. Most programs are seasonal and change themes often.

Chuck E Cheese's
5500 Grossmont Center Dr., La Mesa
(619) 698–4351
www.chuckecheese.com
Okay, so it's loud inside. Okay, kids run around a lot. And that's more than okay if you and the kids need to laugh, get wild, and have some fun. Kids need time out of their stress-filled days too, and Chuck E. Cheese is often the right prescription. This La Mesa restaurant is a carbon copy of others—same pizza, soda, and fun. This is a popular place for pint-sized sports teams.

As with other Chuck E Cheese's, kids run wild and parents know from the noise alone that their children are having fun. If you're new in the community, this is a great place to meet other families.

J.W. Tumbles
2522 Jamacha Rd., El Cajon
(619) 670–6212
See the write-up under "North County Coastal," above. This location offers the same activities for kids up to 10 years old.

Mother Goose Parade
W. Main and Chambers Sts., El Cajon
(619) 444–8712
The parade is usually held the last weekend in November and really gets the family in the mood for holiday fun. The parade begins at 12:30 P.M. on West Main and Chambers Streets and continues east on Main to Second Street then north on Second to Madison. This is an old-fashioned children's affair with lots of local turnout. You'll see floats, clowns, bands, equestrians, civic leaders, and representatives of charitable organizations. There's no admission fee. Be sure to bring

lawn chairs or blankets for sidewalk sitting. Bring your own lunch or buy food from vendors, then try some of the peanuts or candy for sale. You'll be able to buy banners and toys here too.

YMCA
8881 Dallas St., La Mesa
(619) 464–1323
7733 Palm Ave., Lemon Grove
(619) 667–2955
8669 Magnolia Ave., Santee
(619) 449–9622

The Y is more than just a great place to workout—it's a kidstuff favorite with important learning programs, child care resources, summer classes, and camps that are run on age-specific levels. The Y could be your best resource if you're looking for family fun throughout the county. Call a location that's close for programs and outings, costs, and information. Y members receive a discount on camps and programs.

South Bay

Border View YMCA Day Camp
3085 Beyer Blvd., Suite A-103, San Diego
(619) 428–1168

Like most YMCA camps, this is a traditional day camp that offers 10 one-week sessions during the summer months. It's designed for children ages 5 to 12 and includes arts, crafts, sports, swimming, and field trips to other locations and attractions around the county that have maximum "kid appeal." The weekly cost ranges from $80 to $120.

Chuck E Cheese's
1143 Highland Ave., National City
(619) 474–6667
www.chuckecheese.com

This is a carbon copy of the other Chuck E Cheese's kids' restaurants in the county. You'll notice that they've popped up in every one of our regions, and for good reason: kids absolutely love them. For more information, see our entry under Central San Diego.

Fun-4-All
950 Industrial Blvd., Chula Vista
(619) 427–1840

Fun-4-All is open Monday through Thursday from 10:00 A.M. to 11:00 P.M.; Fridays, 11:00 A.M. to midnight; Saturdays, 9:00 A.M. to midnight; and Sundays, 9:00 A.M. to 11:00 P.M. Miniature golf is $5.25 for adults and $4.25 for children younger than 12. Bumper Boat rides are $3.50 for the driver and $1.50 for passengers. A dollar will get you 18 pitches in the batting cage and a free bat and helmet to use.

Knott's Soak City USA
2052 Otay Valley Rd., Chula Vista
(619) 661–7373

Something about waterparks is irresistible to kids, so when you toss out the idea of a day at Knott's Soak City, the suggestion is sure to be met with cheers and shouts of approval. Even if adults don't like to admit it, they get a kick out of waterparks, too. It must be that combination of warm sunshine, cool water, and knowing your kids are having an excellent time.

We've covered Knott's Soak City in detail in our Attractions chapter, so we'll just give you the basics here.

You'll find body slides, tube slides, a giant wave pool, a four-story interactive family play structure, and a scaled-down structure for younger children.

Plenty of refreshments are available from a variety of snack bars and specialty food booths. The park is open weekends 10:00 A.M. to 6:00 P.M. between the beginning of May and Memorial Day and from Labor Day to the end of September. Between those two holidays it's open daily from 10:00 A.M. to 8:00 P.M. Adults pay $22; kids 3 to 11 pay $15. Summer season passes cost $60 for adults and $50 for children. Parking is $6.00.

Balboa Park

San Diego is famous for its natural attributes—the sparkling beaches, the curving harbor, the imposing ocean bluffs, the blooming desert. It's also noted for its manmade landmarks, such as the Hotel del Coronado, the San Diego-Coronado Bay Bridge, and Sea World. But the best combination of San Diego's natural and manmade attributes is on display at Balboa Park.

Most San Diegans believe that Balboa Park was born during the Panama-California Exposition, held in 1915 and 1916 to celebrate the opening of the Panama Canal. But the seeds of the park were planted—literally—in 1892. Kate Sessions, a noted horticulturist, leased 30 acres of Balboa Park from the city to use as a nursery. In exchange, she agreed to plant 100 trees a year in the park for the next 10 years. It was Sessions who set the standard for the landscaping in the park, which today has vast displays of exotic and drought-resistant plants and trees.

The manmade attributes of the park came later. San Diego's leaders hired some of the finest local and national architects to construct the buildings for the Panama-California Exposition. A cantilevered bridge was constructed over a deep canyon as the entryway to the exposition, leading to the Spanish-Colonial style California Building. The building's 200-foot-high California Tower, topped with yellow and blue tiles, has become one of San Diego's most endearing landmarks.

Some buildings were restored for the California Pacific International Exposition in 1935 and 1936, and others were added to the park. This often rushed and confused approach resulted in a melange of styles, from Beaux Arts to Baroque to Spanish Renaissance. Somehow, the combo worked. These historic buildings make Balboa Park an architectural museum of sorts. Many have been lovingly reconstructed and renovated to house some of the city's finest museums.

At the conclusion of the first exposition, Dr. Harry Wegeforth, a local physician, gathered together a few animals left from various exhibits to start a small zoo. His prescient act led to the formation of the San Diego Zoological Society and the world-famous San Diego Zoo. From those beginnings grew Balboa Park as we know it today, the jewel in the crown of San Diego's attractions.

The park is not something you can absorb in a day. Like a rich dessert, it's better savored at a leisurely pace to fully enjoy its lavishness. The zoo alone can take up the better part of a day. You need another day to see and appreciate the rest of the park. As you read this chapter, you will probably choose the sights that match your interests. But we recommend that you try not to stick too closely to a strict agenda. It's inevitable that you'll get distracted by something. Besides, that's half the fun.

In this chapter we'll describe the zoo, museums, gardens, and other attractions so you can get an overview and see what appeals to you. The park is spread out over 1,200 acres, and even though that sounds enormous, most everything is within an easy walk of any place you park. (Parking in all lots, by the way, is free.) Should you get tired of walking, just hop on the free Balboa Park Tram that runs continuously from 9:30 A.M. to 5:30 P.M. daily. Tram stops are located throughout the park as well as in outlying parking areas.

Loads of places to picnic are scattered throughout the park, and it's a great way to take a midday break from all the activity. One prime spot is the grassy area surrounding the Moreton Bay fig tree, which was planted in 1915. Located beside the Natural History Museum, this magnificent tree has been a favorite of generations of children who have climbed over its gnarled roots and swung from its lofty branches. If lunching al fresco isn't your style, there's no lack of spots that provide food and beverage, from hot dog stands to The Prado, a gourmet restaurant.

The park is loaded with art museums and a noteworthy theater. These are covered in greater detail in our Arts chapter. We'll include some references to attractions with particular appeal to kids, which are also included in our Kidstuff chapter.

Balboa Park is located in the heart of the city, just north of downtown San Diego. It's accessible by auto or by Metropolitan Transit bus. From Interstate 5 north or south, take the Pershing Drive exit and follow the signs to Balboa Park. Once you're there, a good place to start is the Visitors Center, located in the House of Hospitality building at 1549 El Prado, (619) 239-0512. Friendly receptionists can answer questions, give you maps, and steer you in the right direction if you get turned around.

Many of the attractions—the gardens in particular—don't have an actual street address. Signage pointing the way to just about everything is excellent in the park, but it's a good idea to carry a map showing exact locations of the various plazas and buildings. Most hotels have Balboa Park maps and they are also available at the Visitors Center. So carve out a day or two from your schedule, gather up the family, and don't forget your *Insiders' Guide*. Art, science, culture, history, animals, bugs, and botany all await.

Alcazar Garden/Palm Canyon
Located adjacent to the House of Charm

Patterned after the gardens of Alcazar Castle in Seville, Spain, Balboa Park's version is distinguished by its ornate fountains and colorful Moorish tiles. It's a beautifully symmetrical garden, with individual areas bordered by boxwood hedges and planted with more than 7,000 annual flowers for a year-round vibrant display.

Just across the road and behind Alcazar Garden is Palm Canyon, a tropical oasis of more than two acres graced by 450 palm trees representing 70 species. Most prominent in the canyon are Mexican fan palms that date back to the early 1900s.

Both Alcazar Garden and Palm Canyon are open daily, and there is no admission fee.

Botanical Building and Lily Pond
North side of El Prado, between Timken Art Museum and Casa del Prado
no phone

Walking down El Prado, the main pedestrian mall in the park, you can't miss the reflecting lily pond. What you'll notice first are the creamy white lilies and lotus flowers floating on the surface of the 193-foot by 43-foot pond. Then you might spot a turtle or two sunning themselves on the lily pads, or bright orange koi swimming amongst the lilies. It's hard to imagine that the pond was used as a therapy pool during World War II for injured sailors sent over from nearby Balboa Naval Hospital.

A little less striking from the outside, but glorious on the inside, is the Botanical Building that sits behind the pond. At 250 feet long by 75 feet wide and 60 feet tall, it was the largest wood lath structure in the world when it was built in 1915. Inside you'll find more than 2,100 specimens of tropical plants and trees, along with changing seasonal flowers. Orchids, lilies, plants, and flowers you never dreamed existed all await your admiration as you meander along the shaded paths. The

Insiders' Tip
Just in case you think you may miss out on shopping while you're discovering Balboa Park, guess again. Every museum has an expansive gift shop stocked with items related to the museum as well as gifts with general appeal.

This little girl, like most small visitors, likes the horses used by the mounted police who patrol the 1,200 acres of Balboa Park. PHOTO: DAVID KINNEV

Botanical Building underwent extensive renovation in 2001 and 2002. Workers replaced over 70,000 lineal feet of redwood lathe to restore the building's grandeur.

The Botanical Building is open daily, except Thursday and on city holidays, from 10:00 A.M. to 4:00 P.M. Admission is free.

Carousel and Miniature Railroad
Park Blvd. and Zoo Pl., behind the Spanish Village Art Center
no phone

Built in 1910 and imported from New York, the "merry-go-round" has been a park fixture since 1922. Its menagerie of animals were hand carved by European craftsmen. It's one of the few remaining carousels in the world where you can still go for the brass ring and win a free ride.

From mid-June through Labor Day the carousel operates from 11:00 A.M. to 6:00 P.M. every day. The rest of the year it opens on Saturday, Sunday, holidays, and during school vacations from 11:00 A.M. to 5:30 P.M. Tickets are $1.25; children younger than a year old ride free. Adults should plan to accompany smaller children.

Next door to the carousel is the miniature railroad. The $1/5$-scale locomotive takes a three-minute, $1/2$-mile ride around 4 acres of Balboa Park. It's a replica of the General Motors F3 diesel, which pulls the Santa Fe's Super Chief. Adding to the atmosphere is the conductor in a railroad cap and overalls who not only shouts "All aboard" but also serves as engineer for every ride.

The Miniature Railroad runs on Saturday, Sunday, and school holidays from 11:00 A.M. to 5:00 P.M. Admission for "children 1 to 99" is $1.25; children younger than a year old ride for free. Kids younger than 5 must ride with an adult.

Centro Cultural de la Raza
2125 Park Blvd.
(619) 235-6135

Located just south of the Pepper Grove picnic area, the Centro Cultural de la Raza is an internationally recognized art space that hosts exhibitions and performances showcasing Latino/Chicano artists. The building itself is a work of art. Stroll around the

perimeter of the circular building and you'll see that the exterior is one long mural depicting themes from Mayan, Native American, and Chicano cultures.

For more information about the Centro Cultural de la Raza, please see the entry in our Arts chapter. There you'll find greater detail on its exhibits, community outreach programs, and special performances. The Centro is open Thursday through Sunday, 12:00 P.M. to 5:00 P.M. Admission is free.

Hall of Champions
2131 Pan American Plaza
(619) 234-2544
www.sandiegosports.com

Uniforms, trophies, photographs, and other memorabilia from San Diego's sports stars adorn the walls of the Hall of Champions museum. The jerseys of baseball legend Ted Williams are here: the ones he wore when he belted his first homers for the Padres' Pacific Coast League team, and ones he donned in his more famous days with the Boston Red Sox. You'll also find items representing boxing great Archie Moore, tennis star Maureen Connolly, Bill Walton of basketball fame, the Chargers' Dan Fouts, and many others. Local talents from Over-the-Line (see our Spectator Sports chapter for the lowdown on this homegrown sport), golf, the Holiday Bowl, swimming, and horse racing are all honored too.

The Hall of Champions is open daily from 10:00 A.M. to 4:30 P.M. Admission is $4.00 for adults, $3.00 for children 17 and under.

Children have been enjoying this carousel since 1912. PHOTO: COURTESY OF BALBOA PARK ADMINISTRATION

House of Pacific Relations, International Cottages
Pan American Rd. W.
(619) 234-0739

Founded in 1935, the House of Pacific Relations is an organization dedicated to fostering cooperation and understanding among its international groups. More than two dozen countries are represented in the organization, and most of them have their own cottages in Balboa Park. The cottages are furnished and staffed by members of the respective groups and present exhibits that showcase their history, culture, and traditions.

Cottages are open on Sundays from 12:00 to 5:00 P.M., at which time group members, dressed in traditional costumes, are present to welcome visitors and answer questions. Adjacent to the International Cottages is the Hall of Nations, which also has international exhibits. Groups that do not have cottages rotate their exhibits in the Hall of Nations.

On Sundays from March through October, special Lawn Programs are held on the outdoor stage in the cottage area at 2:00 P.M. Members perform ethnic songs and dances and serve food native to their country. Programs last one hour. Admission is free to all House of Pacific Relations events (except films); donations are gratefully accepted.

Inez Grant Parker Memorial Rose Garden/
Desert Garden
Located across Park Blvd., opposite the
Natural History Museum

Stopping to smell the roses has never been sweeter. This stunning, award-winning garden shows off more than 2,200 rose bushes in 178 varieties. Peak bloom time is during April and May, but some of the roses bloom clear through December. If you're in the mood for romance, the Rose Garden is the most popular wedding spot in Balboa Park.

With the heady fragrance of roses still lingering, walk a few yards north and visit the two-and-a-half-acre Desert Garden. Kate Sessions, the horticulturist who was largely responsible for turning Balboa Park into a botanical wonder, was fascinated by drought resistant plants. The Desert Garden displays many of the specimens Sessions introduced to the park, as well as succulents and other drought-resistant varieties from around the world.

The Rose Garden and the Desert Garden are open daily, and admission is free.

Japanese Friendship Garden
Located between the House of Hospitality and the Spreckels Organ Pavilion
(619) 232–2721

Peaceful and serene describe the atmosphere once you pass through the massive wooden gates at the entrance to the Japanese Friendship Garden. Funded by a grant from the San Diego Art and Culture Commission, the garden was built as a tribute to San Diego's sister city of Yokohama. The garden demonstrates the sister cities' shared values of beauty in nature, respect in friendship, and hopes for the future.

Exhibits within the garden change monthly, displaying Japanese art, folk crafts, and Japanese culture. The Friendship Garden is open Tuesday through Sunday from 10:00 A.M. to 4:00 P.M. Admission is $3.00 for adults, $2.00 for seniors 65 and older, and $2.50 for disabled persons, military, students, and children 7 to 17. Children 6 and younger are admitted free. The garden is open free of charge on the third Tuesday of every month.

Marie Hitchcock Puppet Theatre
Pan American Plaza
(619) 685–5045

Named for San Diego's original "puppet lady," the Marie Hitchcock Puppet Theatre has been charming local kids and their moms and dads for decades. The San Diego Guild of Puppetry, a group of professional and amateur puppeteers, performs year-round with marionettes, hand puppets, and ventriloquists. For more information, see our entry in the "Kidstuff" chapter.

Show times are 10:00 A.M. and 11:30 A.M. Wednesday, Thursday, and Friday; 11:00 A.M., 1:00, and 2:30 P.M. on Saturdays and Sundays. Admission for adults is $3.00, and for children 3 to 17 is $2.00. Admission is free for children 2 and younger.

Mingei International Museum
1439 El Prado, House of Charm
(619) 239–0003
www.mingei.org

Many cultures are adopting the word "Mingei" to mean "art of the people." The San Diego Mingei International Museum is dedicated to furthering the understanding of art of all cultures of the world. The goal is to open a window to a broad view of the creative potential of all people.

The Mingei Museum displays indigenous arts and crafts of unsurpassed beauty. Frequently changing exhibitions present

Insiders' Tip
If you plan to spend more than a day or two discovering Balboa Park, you may want to purchase a "Passport to Balboa Park." The $21 passport is valid for a week and allows entrance to 12 museums (a $62 value). Passports can be purchased at the Visitors Center in the House of Hospitality building, (619) 231-1640, or at any participating museum.

essential art forms, such as ceramics, textiles, baskets, pottery, toys, furniture, and other objects of daily use. Numerous videos are also available for viewing at the museum, including *American Expressions of Liberty: Art of the People, by the People, for the People.*

The museum is open Tuesday through Sunday from 10:00 A.M. to 4:00 P.M. Admission is $5.00 for adults and $2.00 for students and children 6 to 17. Admission is free for children younger than 6. Admission is free for everyone on the third Tuesday of each month.

Model Railroad Museum
1649 El Prado, Casa de Balboa, Lower Level
(619) 696–0199
www.sdmodelrailroadm.com

Check out the largest operating model-railroad exhibit in America. More than 24,000 square feet of model train exhibits await your delighted observation. It's a toss-up which attraction kids love more: the train exhibits or the interactive Toy Train Gallery, where they (and you too) can play engineer.

Along with the visually impressive model trains is an in-depth exhibit that details the colorful history of railroads in the American Southwest.

The museum is open Tuesday through Friday, 11:00 A.M. to 4:00 P.M.; Saturday and Sunday, 11:00 A.M. to 5:00 P.M. Admission is $4.00 for adults, $3.00 for seniors, and $2.50 for students and military. Children younger than 15 are admitted free when accompanied by an adult. The first Tuesday of the month is free admission day for the Model Railroad Museum.

Museum of Man
1350 El Prado (under the California Tower)
(619) 239–2001
www.museumofman.org

San Diego's fine anthropological museum is filled with treasures of the ages. In 1915 the Smithsonian Institution gathered a collection of artifacts and physical remains that were displayed at the Panama-California Exhibition. After the exhibition the collection became the Museum of Man, and today it holds more than 70,000 items, each one a symbol of cultures from ancient times to the present.

Replicas of spectacular Maya stelae, stone walls covered with symbols of Maya gods and historical events, stand at the museum's entrance. The arts of San Diego's indigenous Kumeyaay peoples are displayed in a permanent exhibit, as are artifacts from indigenous groups from throughout the Southwest. Ancient hunting spears, ceramic vessels, and delicately woven textiles are just a few of the objects on display. Kids can dress up as pharaohs and their subjects at the interactive Children's Discovery Center's Discover Egypt exhibit.

The Museum of Man is open daily, except Thanksgiving, Christmas, and New Year's Day, from 10:00 P.M. to 4:30 P.M. Admission is $6.00 for adults, $3.00 for children 6 to 17, and free for kids 5 and younger. Everyone gets in for free on the third Tuesday of every month.

Museum of Photographic Arts
1649 El Prado, Casa de Balboa, Upper Level
(619) 238–7559
www.mopa.org

If you're like many Insiders, your photo treasures are limited to the occasional lucky snapshot. But we all appreciate those who have the talent to create spellbinding works of art with the camera. Some of the best are on display at the Museum of Photographic Arts, one of the country's first and finest museums dedicated exclusively to photography.

Insiders' Tip
Ranger tours are scheduled for noon on Wednesdays and 11:00 A.M. on Sundays. Experienced rangers give you historical insight into the Prado, along with the history of the two expositions held in the park. Meet in front of the Visitors Center.

The California Tower of the Museum of Man rises above the park. PHOTO: JAMES BLANK, COURTESY OF SAN DIEGO CONVENTION AND VISITORS BUREAU

Tours

Explore the exotic horticulture, the architectural beauty, and the historical wonders of Balboa Park by taking one of several free tours. Meet in front of the Botanical Building at 10:00 A.M. on Saturdays, except those falling within the holiday break from Thanksgiving through mid-January. No reservations are necessary, but tours are canceled if it's raining or the group is fewer than four people. All walking tours are easy paced and last about one hour. For more information, call the Park and Recreation Department at (619) 235–1121.

History Walk—First Saturday

This tour blends a little bit of everything: history, architecture, and horticultural delights. You'll meander up and down the 2-block El Prado area while your tour guide describes the history and architecture of the various buildings. You'll also get background information on some of the many botanical specimens for which the park is noted.

Palm Walk—Second Saturday

Delve into the world of palm trees. Learn about their structure, growth, and landscape value as your guided tour takes you into Palm Canyon, where a huge collection of palm specimens awaits your inspection.

Tree Walk—Third Saturday

Famed horticulturist Kate Sessions made sure Balboa Park had a vast array of exotic trees. Your guide will introduce you to many of these rare beauties. You'll see some in the Botanical Building and many others that have been planted over the years, all within a few blocks walk.

Desert Walk—Fourth Saturday

Kate Sessions was also devoted to cultivating drought-resistant plants. See the wide variety of American, African, and Baja California desert plants as you tour the Desert Garden across from the Natural History Museum.

Tour del Dia—Fifth Saturday

Explore the Palisades area, where the California Pacific International Exposition was held in 1935 and 1936, and learn about its historical and horticultural roots. Like the other tours, this is a short walk that's equivalent to a few blocks.

Changing exhibits display critically acclaimed historical and contemporary work by some of the world's most celebrated photographers. In addition to its exhibits, the museum offers lectures, workshops, and occasional film series. If you'd like more insight into exhibits, a guided tour is included with your admission on Sundays at 1:00 P.M. The museum is open daily from 10:00 A.M. to 5:00 P.M.; Thursday until 9:00 P.M. Admission is $6.00 for adults and $4.00 for students, seniors, and military; children younger than 12 are admitted free when accompanied by an adult. Admission is free to all on the second Tuesday of every month.

Natural History Museum
Plaza de Balboa
(619) 232–3821
www.sdnhm.org

When its new glass-fronted wing opened in 2001, the Natural History Museum became an exciting and dynamic institution with cutting-edge exhibits and programs. The museum was one of the backers of *Ocean Oasis*, an extraordinary film on Baja California and the Sea of Cortez that debuted at the Smithsonian in 2000. The film is now shown on a giant screen within the museum several times daily and is just one of many new exhibits in the 21st-century research and educational institution.

The museum traces it roots back to 1874, when a group of amateur naturalists formed the San Diego Society of Natural History. The Balboa Park museum opened in 1933 and captured the imaginations of its visitors with exhibits on paleontology, ecology, and mineralogy for decades.

In 1991, the museum took on a new approach to education with a commitment to a strong focus on the binational region of San Diego and Baja California, Mexico. A Biodiversity Research Center of the Californias was established, and the first exhibit to open in the new wing was called Natural Treasures Past & Present. The exhibit features fossils and live snakes and lizards collected in the region. Kids may be more excited by the replica of a dinosaur dig and mineral collection in the Kid's Habitat and the full skeletal casts of a Tyrannosaurus Rex. New exhibits will continue to open as the old halls are remodeled.

Hours at the Natural History Museum are 9:30 A.M. to 4:30 P.M. daily. Admission is $5.00 for adults, $4.00 for students, seniors, and military, and $3.00 for children 6 to 17. Children younger that 6 are admitted free. The museum is open free of charge on the first Tuesday of every month.

The Old Globe Theatres
Located behind the Museum of Man
(619) 239–2255
www.theglobetheatres.org

For more than 60 years the Old Globe Theatre has been presenting Shakespearean classics as well as contemporary plays and musicals. The Old Globe and its sister theaters in the Old Globe complex, the Cassius

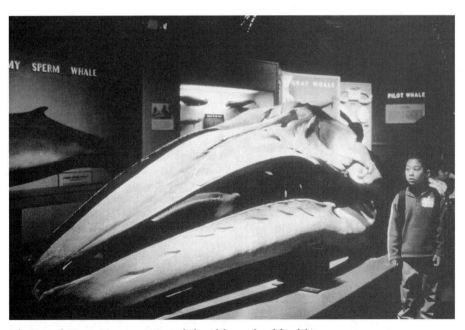

The Natural History Museum captivates kids with larger-than-life exhibits. PHOTO: UMA SANGHVI, COURTESY OF THE SAN DIEGO CONVENTION & VISITORS BUREAU

Carter Centre Stage and the Lowell Davies Festival Theatre, are nestled in a grassy enclave behind the Museum of Man. Visitors love strolling around the grounds and touring the Old Globe, which is a replica of the original Old Globe Theatre in London.

For more information about the Old Globe and its Tony Award–winning productions, please see the entry in our Arts chapter.

Pepper Grove

Pepper Grove is the perfect spot for a picnic. Lots of shady trees and wide, grassy areas give you the choice of eating in the shade at a picnic table or spreading out on the grass to bask in the sunshine.

Located behind the Reuben H. Fleet Space Theater (to the south of the theater), Pepper Grove is a great place for kids to burn off excess energy. It has three separate play areas with swings, climbing equipment, and interactive structures. A parking lot is conveniently located right next to the area.

Reuben H. Fleet Space Theater and Science Center
Plaza de Balboa
(619) 238–1233
www.rhfleet.org

If you've never experienced an IMAX film, you're in for a treat. The space theater surrounds viewers with sound and with sights projected onto a giant domed screen. Here you can see IMAX films such as *Everest*, the story of the tallest Himalayan peak and one of the world's greatest climbing adventures.

The Exhibit Galleries in the Science Center contain more than 70 hands-on displays. Put your hands on the Lightning Globe and become a link in an electrical circuit. Find out how your heart works, or test your reaction time and coordination skills. All exhibits are science-related and highly entertaining for both kids and adults.

The Theater and Science Center are open from 9:30 A.M. to 5:00 P.M. daily. Evening hours vary with the season. Show times vary, but there usually is a show every hour. Ticket prices for Space Theater shows (which includes entrance to the Exhibit Galleries) are $11.50 for adults 13 and older, $9.50 for seniors 65 and older; and

$8.50 for children 3 to 12. Admission to the Science Center Exhibit Galleries only is $6.50 for seniors and adults 13 and older and $5.50 for children 3 to 12. Children younger than 3 are admitted free. Everyone is admitted free to the Science Center on the first Tuesday of each month.

San Diego Aerospace Museum
2001 Pan American Plaza
(619) 234–8291
www.aerospacemuseum.org

Have you ever wondered what it was like when the Wright Brothers made the first powered flight? You can relive that thrilling day in history at the San Diego Aerospace Museum, along with other landmark events and innovations in the history of aerospace. See the Spad, the Nieuport and the Albatros from World War I, and the Spitfires, Zeros, and Hellcats from World War II.

The Aerospace Museum's collection has aviation memorabilia and more than 65 foreign and domestic aircraft, including present-day spacecraft. Don't forget to visit the International Aerospace Hall of Fame, which honors aero-engineers, pilots, and aviation industrialists.

The museum is open daily (except Thanksgiving and Christmas) from 10:00 A.M. to 4:30 P.M. Admission is $8.00 for adults, $6.00 for seniors 65 and older, $3.00 for children 6 to 17, and free for children younger than 6. Active-duty military members are admitted free too, and admission is free for everyone on the fourth Tuesday of the month.

San Diego Automotive Museum
2080 Pan American Plaza
(619) 231–2886
www.sdautomuseum.org

The automobile holds such fascination for Americans that it has become integrated into our culture, our way of life, and our technological advances. Along with automotive memorabilia, the San Diego Automotive Museum exhibits exotic road cars, the historic Model-A, gas-guzzling muscle cars, and luxurious Rolls Royces.

The on-site restoration facility gives visitors a glimpse of restoration tech-

Airplane buffs happily spend hours checking out the planes at the San Diego Aerospace Museum in Balboa Park. PHOTO: COURTESY OF THE SAN DIEGO CONVENTION & VISITORS BUREAU

niques. The research library, which is open to the public, contains rare publications, photos, and vintage films. Museum hours are 10:00 A.M. to 4:00 P.M. daily. Admission is $7.00 for adults, $6.00 for active-duty military and seniors, $3.00 for children 6 to 15, and free for children younger than 6. Admission is free on the fourth Tuesday of each month.

San Diego Historical Society Museum
1649 El Prado, Casa de Balboa, Upper Level
(619) 232–6203

San Diego's history is rich with tales of townspeople determined to turn a town into a city. Despite numerous obstacles and bumps in the road, our dedicated founding fathers persevered. This museum traces the city's development from 1850 to current times with displays of historical photos, costumes, and artifacts.

The museum is operated by the San Diego Historical Society, which also makes its research archives available to the public. History buffs spend hours in the archives, poring over photos and documents from the early days of San Diego.

Research archives are open Thursday through Saturday from 10:00 A.M. to 4:00 P.M., and the fee for using the archives is $5.00; $1.00 for students. The museum is open Tuesday through Sunday from 10:00 A.M. to 4:30 P.M. Admission is $5.00 for adults; $4.00 for seniors, students, and military; and $2.00 for children 5 to 17. Children younger than 6 are admitted free. Admission is free to all on the second Tuesday of each month.

San Diego Museum of Art
1450 El Prado
(619) 232–7931
www.sdmart.org

The San Diego Museum of Art has something for everyone: Italian Renaissance collections, Spanish and Dutch Old Masters, American art, 19th-century European paintings, and numerous other collections. Besides these permanent holdings, the museum holds year-round special exhibits too, such as the Jewels of the Romanov, Faberge Eggs, and a special collection of Monet's works. We describe the museum in detail in our Arts chapter.

Hours are from 10:00 A.M. to 6:00 P.M. Tuesday through Sunday and until 9:00 P.M. on Thursday. Admission prices are $8.00 for adults; $6.00 for seniors 65 and older, young adults 18 to 24, and military, $3.00 for children 6 to 17, and free for children 5 and younger. Admission is free on the third Tuesday of every month.

San Diego Zoo
2920 Zoo Dr.
(619) 234-3153
www.sandiegozoo.com

The world-famous San Diego Zoo was founded in 1916, at the close of the Panama-California Exposition, by an enterprising local physician, Dr. Harry Wegeforth. He gathered a collection of about 50 animals, some of which had been used during the exposition, and some that were part of various local menageries. Today the zoo contains more than 4,000 rare and endangered birds, mammals, and reptiles from 800 different species.

More than just a place where animals hang out, the zoo has long been dedicated to animal research with the goal of preserving endangered species. And you won't find any tigers or polar bears sitting listless and bored in cages. Enclosures and open spaces have been created to replicate the animals' natural habitats. Visit Tiger River, Sun Bear Forest, Scripps Aviary, Gorilla Tropics, Hippo Beach, and Polar Bear Plunge, and you'll see what we mean.

The Children's Zoo, located inside the zoo itself, is a favorite of the kids (and Mom and Dad too). Giant tortoises, goats, and other gentle critters roam freely around the Children's Zoo, giving kids the opportunity for some hands-on interaction. Several animal shows are staged throughout the day in the main zoo showcasing predators and prey from around the world.

Another must-see is the Giant Panda exhibit. Shi Shi and Bai Yun are here from China as part of a cooperative effort between the United States and China to study pandas and help raise funds for their protection. Shi Shi and Bai Yun are the only pair of giant pandas in the United States.

When you get hungry, choose from a wide range of snacks and all-American favorites at stands located throughout the zoo. Or dine in style at one of several full-service restaurants, including the Albert's Treehouse Cafe and the Flamingo Cafe. Picnic areas are also located in convenient spots around the zoo, and you're welcome to bring your own lunch with you. Lockers are available if you're not in the mood to tote your gear till lunchtime.

The zoo is open every day of the year from 9:00 A.M. until 4:00 P.M., with extended hours during the summer, usually until 5:00 P.M. or 6:00 P.M. Admission includes the Children's Zoo and all the animal shows. Prices are $19.50 for ages 12 and up, $11.75 for children 3 to 11, and free for children 2 and younger. Deluxe Admission includes a bus tour and Skyfari aerial tram ride, and is priced at $32.00 for adults and $19.75 for children 3 to 11.

Spanish Village Art Center
1770 Village Pl.
(619) 233-9050

Constructed in 1935 for the California Pacific International Exposition, the charming collection of buildings was meant to depict a picturesque village in Spain. At the conclusion of the exposition, a group of dedicated artists established the village as an arts center. Its only departure from that designation was during World War II, when the U.S. Navy used the village for temporary barracks. Today the center offers the creations of more than 50 artists, many of whom use the buildings as both studios and galleries.

Thirty-five individual studios house artists working in a variety of media: oil, watercolor, ceramics, sculpture, jewelry, wood carving, glass, photography, and enamel. You can shop or just browse among the one-of-a-kind items every day except New Year's Day, Thanksgiving, and Christmas from 11:00 A.M. to 4:00 P.M. Admission is free.

Spreckels Organ Pavilion
Pan American Rd. E.
(619) 702-8138

John D. Spreckels, one of San Diego's founding fathers, presented the city with a gift on New Year's Eve in 1914, just before the beginning of the Panama-California Exposition: a beautiful pipe organ and a grand pavilion to house it. The organ has been in almost continuous use since that time. It contains 4,518 pipes ranging in size from more than 32 feet long to about the size of your little finger.

Year-round organ concerts are presented to the public on Sunday afternoons from 2:00 to 3:00 P.M. Special summer performances are held on Monday nights from mid-June through August at 7:30 P.M. Even if there's no concert scheduled for the day you're in the park, be sure to inspect the pavilion and its stunning architecture; it's located at the south end of Plaza de Panama. Admission to all concerts is free.

Timken Museum of Art
1500 El Prado
(619) 239-5548

The Timken Museum of Art is devoted to the preservation of European and American paintings from the early Renaissance through the 19th century. Among its exhibits not to be missed is a collection of beautiful Russian Icons.

Like Balboa Park's other art museums, we cover the Timken in greater detail in our Arts chapter. Insiders refer to it as San Diego's "jewel box for the arts."

Hours are from 10:00 A.M. to 4:30 P.M., Tuesday through Saturday, and 1:30 to 4:30 P.M. on Sunday. Admission is free.

Zoro Gardens
Between the Reuben H. Fleet Space Theater and the Casa de Balboa

Zoro Gardens were a favorite attraction during the California Pacific Exposition of 1935-1936. Why? Because the gardens were the site of a nudist colony. The chief of police, however, insisted that the women wear brassieres and G-strings, and that the men wear loincloths during daylight hours when visitors were likely to wander in.

Today there are no nudists, but the gardens are an inviting and usually cool spot for a break during your exploration of the park. The winding paths travel far back into the canyons and pass by beautiful plant and floral specimens. There is no admission charge.

Annual Events

Lots happens in San Diego, and on nearly every weekend you'll be faced with choices of what to attend, participate in, or watch. Yeah, it's tough but somebody has to have fun.

Our goal with the list is to bring San Diego's special fun to you. We've included plenty of free events and festivals from the Mother Goose Parade to the Rancho Santa Fe Rummage Sale (the primo sale of the year) to the Mainly Mozart Festival. We've also tried to blend the expected events with the unusual, notable, and eccentric ones, such as the Over-the-Line Tournament and the Pegleg Smith Liars Contest. If there's an adult-only aspect, we've included that; where it's family fun, we've stressed that too.

Typically, the outdoor events include food booths, or you can pack a snack. We've listed the current fee or cost, if it's known. We also let you know when the event is free.

Remember when looking at the calendar of events that we've organized this chapter by months rather than region. Keep in mind that you'll want to call to double check locations and times, or to verify prices. Some phones are handled by volunteers. Try to call during normal work hours.

Many communities have mini-events and cultural activities that are big news for neighborhoods but are too small to be listed here. If you've just moved into the San Diego area and wonder what's happening, ask an Insider or call the city's parks and recreation office, senior citizen centers, or the public library. Events, athletic tournaments, community picnics and concerts are also often listed on bulletin boards.

We've tried to make it easy for you to use this list, by ordering events chronologically. If an event happens in the beginning of any month, you'll find it among the first listings; if it's at the end of the month, you'll find it listed last.

January

San Diego Marathon
The starting line is near Plaza Camino Real shopping center, 2500 El Camino Real, Carlsbad
(858) 792–2900

This 26.2-mile marathon draws runners, walkers, and watchers from around the country. Last year the number of participants exceeded 8,000. This is a three-day weekend event with Friday activities featuring a golf tournament and Saturday activities including a Keebler Kids Marathon and a health expo, food, vendors, and activities. The actual marathon is on Sunday and begins in Carlsbad near Plaza Camino Real shopping center. Call for entrance fees, which vary; Saturday activities and watching the marathon are free.

Local Authors Exhibit
San Diego City Public Library
820 E St., San Diego
(619) 236–5800

This is an important event for Insiders and also for visitors who are interested in local authors. There are some best-selling writers among our literary crowd. The month-long exhibit and author readings highlight the best the county has to offer. Call for library hours, information on readings, and, if you're a writer, information on submitting your work. Admission to the readings is free.

Penguin Day Ski Fest
De Anza Cove at Information Center, Mission Bay
(619) 221–8901

During this ski fest, you won't see any of the penguins from Sea World; however, you will see brave (read that daring) water-skiers race around Mission Bay (no wetsuits allowed), and lots of people swimming and skiing in chilly ocean water. It's kind of crazy to be going in the water in winter, but that's where the fun comes in. The ski fest is from 9:00 A.M. to 1:00 P.M. Call for details if you want to enter (watch-

With miles of immaculate beaches, San Diego's construction isn't limited to bricks and mortar.

PHOTO: THORN VOLLENWEIDER

ing is free). There is always a party afterwards where you'll find food booths and places to picnic.

Martin Luther King Jr. Day Parade
County Administration Bldg. to Seaport Village
885 Harbor Dr., San Diego
(619) 262-4646

School marching bands and homemade floats parade along Harbor Drive to commemorate Dr. Martin Luther King Jr. The festivities continue with an award ceremony and a festival with exhibits, dance demonstrations, and food vendors.

Robert Burns Supper
Town & Country Hotel
500 Hotel Circle N., San Diego
(619) 234-3525
www.oblaw.com

The Robert Burns Club of San Diego holds this annual event in honor of Scotland's national bard. The traditional banquet includes haggis; the entertainment includes pipe bands and Scottish dancing. Tickets are $45.

Whale Watch Weekend
Cabrillo National Monument
1800 Cabrillo Memorial Dr., San Diego
(619) 557-5450

The monument atop Point Loma is one of the best places to spot California gray whales spouting and breaching in the ocean. The park celebrates the whales' arrival with special exhibits, films, and lectures. The park is open every day from 9:00 A.M. to 5:15 P.M. Admission is $5.00 per vehicle and $2.00 per bicyclist, jogger, walker, or city bus passenger. The pass allows entrance for seven days.

Rose Pruning Demonstration
The Inez Grant Parker
Memorial Rose Garden/Desert Garden,
across Park Avenue from the Natural History
Museum, Balboa Park, San Diego
(619) 235-0512

Sponsored by the San Diego Rose Society, this demonstration at Balboa Park's rose garden will teach you the how-tos and what-fors of growing gorgeous blooms.

The event is held from 9:00 A.M. to 1:00 P.M. Rose Society members and volunteers trim, clip, and coddle the more than 1,300 bushes found in the Park's knockout rose garden. Volunteers are encouraged to participate in the fun. Usually held toward the end of January, depending on the weather, the event is free. Call the society for the specific Saturday when the event is held.

Teddy Bear, Doll and Toy Festival
Scottish Rite Temple, 1895 Camino Del Rio South, San Diego
(760) 434-7444
You'll find everything imaginable at this weekend festival for professional collectors and those who appreciate the world populated by teddy bears, dolls, and toys. With 200 or more vendors, this semi-annual event (it's in August too) is in its fortieth year. Admission is $5.00.

February

Anza-Borrego Desert Wildflowers Season
Anza-Borrego Desert State Park, Borrego Springs
(760) 767-4684 (for an events message),
(760) 767-4205 (to speak with a park volunteer)
www.anzaborregostatepark.org
When spring comes to the desert the colors are breathtaking. It's a short blooming season and worth the drive. If you haven't visited Anza-Borrego "for the flowers," as Insiders say, then do not pass go until you've done so. Pack your camera, sunscreen, and sense of wonder. Flowers do not bloom on a strict schedule so should rains come early, the blooms will too. A call to the park's visitor center can give you the status of the blooms. There are plenty of roadside opportunities for viewing the flowers, but if you love nature and flowers, you'll want to visit the information center at the park too. There's a $5.00 fee to enter the park beyond the visitor center, add various charges for camping. See our Parks and Recreation chapters if you're a hiker or camper and want more information about outdoor opportunities at the park.

San Dieguito Half Marathon
Lomas Santa Fe and Highland Dr.,
San Dieguito County Park, Rancho Santa Fe
(619) 298-7400
www.kathylopezevents.com
This race is half the size of the San Diego Marathon and more do-able for less determined runners. The race, which begins at 8:00 A.M., is held each February and goes through the San Dieguito County Park and surrounding community. There are hills so it can be a challenge. If you're not up to running, then do like plenty of other Insiders and walk it for a workout. Spectators can cheer for free. Call for entrance fees.

International Dance Festival
Balboa Park Club Building, Balboa Park, San Diego
(619) 286-0355
The fair is free; however, you'll want to bring some money since the ethnic clothes and pottery, especially the coffee mugs, are treats for any shopper. And there's plenty

Dancers perform during the Pacific Islanders Festival, one of many cultural events in San Diego.

PHOTO: BRETT SHOAF, COURTESY OF THE SAN DIEGO CONVENTION & VISITORS BUREAU

of food—from traditional American to exotic ethnic fare. The weekend event features more than 1,700 folk dances from all over the world. Some groups invite festival-goers to join in the dancing.

Jamboree by the Sea
Del Mar Fairgrounds, 2260 Jimmy Durante Blvd., Del Mar
(858) 792–4252

There's so much fun to squeeze in that this event lasts for three days. You'll marvel at the skill, the precision, and the energy of the dancers. Come and watch them square, clog, and round dance—it might encourage you to join the fun. This is an enjoyable family event and there's no charge for visitors.

Buick Invitational of California
Torrey Pines Municipal Golf Course
11480 N. Torrey Pines Rd., San Diego
(619) 281–4653, (800) 888–BUICK
www.torreypinesgolfcourse.com

San Diego's Torrey Pines Municipal Golf Course shines during this all-star golf competition. The best of the best play at this PGA event, which attracts more than 100,000 spectators. The tournament was especially exciting in 2002, since the course was remodeled with new challenges for the golfers. Ticket prices are $19 on weekdays and $25 on weekends. Call to verify ticket prices and availability, and plan to walk a ways from the parking locations. For more information about this event, check out the entries in our Spectator Sports and Golf chapters.

Chinese New Year Celebration
Third Ave. and J St., San Diego
(619) 234–4447, (619) 234–7844

Go for the festival and stay for the fun with this celebration that presents the many cultures of China. There are traditional dancers, martial arts demonstrations by pros and students, cultural information, craft booths, and food. The tea sets are especially worth a second look. The event is held for two days. Remember that Chinese New Year doesn't always happen in February. Free admission.

Cupid's Carnival
Spreckels Park, Seventh and C Sts., Coronado
(619) 522-7342

If it's romance you're looking for, head elsewhere. This is a high-intensity, giggling children's carnival that never goes out of style. It's Valentine fun for the family in this kidstuff event held annually on Coronado. There's a kissing booth, play area, games of chance (for a quarter a try), and an ice-cream sundae making event. The carnival is free.

San Diego International Auto Show
San Diego Convention Center,
111 West Harbor Dr., San Diego
(800) 345-1487

More than 32 domestic and foreign manufacturers roll out their newest and fastest and sleekest vehicles. You'll see auto design exhibits, cars of the future and past, and exotic street machines too. Admission is $9.00 for those 14 and older; children 13 and younger enter for $5.00. There are discounts for seniors and the military. Sunday is Kid's Day, with special activities. Check newspapers, car dealers, chain supermarkets, and local restaurants for discount coupons for adult admissions to this event.

Mardi Gras in the Gaslamp
Gaslamp Quarter, San Diego
(619) 233-5227

The Gaslamp Quarter hosts this parade and festival, which features music, food, and entertainment that might make you feel like you were in New Orleans. The parade, which starts at Fifth Avenue and K Street, begins in the late afternoon; however, the fun doesn't stop until the wee hours. The parade is free. Call the Gaslamp Quarter Association for details on the venues.

Silver Bay Kennel Club Dog Show
Del Mar Fairgrounds, 2260 Jimmy Durante Blvd., Del Mar
(619) 588-0507

This is a premier dog event that usually takes place the last weekend in February, although you'll want to call to confirm the dates. The Silver Bay show attracts more than 2,500 canine contenders vying for Best in Show (that's what the top dog is called). Judging begins about 8:30 A.M. on Saturday and continues through Sunday as dogs in various categories compete for titles and trophies. At any given time, there may be as many as 20 different competitions going on in the three huge indoor facilities. If you're a dog lover, this is the place to find everything you need for your pooch, from doggie hats to the latest in dog foods and canine treats. Be sure to catch the herding demos and dog obedience competitions as that's where training shines. The show is a family affair, and admission is free. So if you're wondering what's just the right breed for you and the kids, you can research your question nose-close to these beautiful dogs.

Vietnamese Tet Festival
2160 Ulric St., San Diego
(858) 268-1204

This festival will delight you with children's ethnic-costume contests, savory and satisfying foods, and dancing. There are traditional games, martial-arts demos, crafts, and folk music. It's a multi-day festival. Call the number above for dates, admission, and times.

Insiders' Tip

Flower shows are held monthly at Balboa Park's Casa del Prado. Call (619) 239-0512 for information; there is no admission fee. One Insider's favorite show is the spectacular Mother's Day event featuring epiphyllums. (What's an epiphyllum? Look it up—it's worth knowing about.)

Marine Gear Swap Meet
The Marina at Chula Vista,
550 Marina Parkway, Chula Vista
(619) 691–1860

Calling the oars and crafts crowd: This is the boat and watersport-related swap meet of which dreams are made. What can you expect? A humongous parking lot heaped with good, used items. Here you'll find generators, compasses, scuba stuff, captain's hats, and other stuff a boater can't live without. There are plenty of interesting objects for boating-gear collectors too. It's billed as a great day for the seafarer. There are shows in June and October as well, but this is the biggest. Admission is free, but if you have stuff to sell, you'll need to call for pricing to rent a space.

Ocean Beach Kite Festival
4741 Santa Monica Ave., San Diego
(619) 531–1527

This is a build-it-yourself festival filled with the magic known as kites. There are prizes, a parade, food booths and demonstrations, and of course the kite-flying competition, held on the nearby beach. Come fly your own; walk it along in the parade. Or just come for the sight of them: triple-deckers, Japanese kites, fish-shaped kites, and all manner of imaginative homemade flyers. This is great family fun and it's free for everyone.

Saint Patrick's Day Parade
Sixth Ave., San Diego
(858) 268–9111
www.stpatsparade.org

If you've seen *Riverdance* and loved the high-stepping Celtic dancers, you'll have a treat here watching experts and novices kick up their heels. The parade also features marching bands (including ones carrying bagpipes) and civic volunteers from Rotary members to dogs for the blind (and the people who train them).

After the event there's an Irish festival. It's held in Balboa Park and you needn't be Irish to have a great time. There's plenty of food and that traditional St. Pat's day brew. Try one of the Irish varieties. Or if

Insiders' Tip

If you're looking for events at the Del Mar Fairground (and something is always happening there), call (858) 792-4252 to reach the box office. Call (858) 793-5555 for a 24-hour event hotline or visit www.delmarfair.com for information on monthly events and upcoming concerts.

you're a hearty soul, you can sip a beer that's been "greened" just for the special day. There are drinks for the kids too. This is fun for the whole family. The parade and festival are free; food prices vary.

MS Walk
8840 Complex Dr., Ste. 130, San Diego
(858) 974–8640

The walks are held in various locations in Carlsbad and San Diego, and proceeds go to the Multiple Sclerosis Society. They're a great family activity for a worthy cause. Last year's participants included babies in strollers, folks in wheelchairs, and well-mannered family dogs (with leash, collars, poop bags mandatory). The 5K and 10K give you a chance to meet people, do some good, and even get a T-shirt—provided your collected pledges total at least $95. (Should you or your group raise $5,000, there's a Macy's gift certificate for $400 that comes your way—yes, you still get the T-shirt.) If you're new in town and want to get involved, the Society is always looking for volunteers. On the day of the walk alone, scores are needed for registration, to look after the rest stops, hand out T-shirts, and clean up, too. Call the MS society for locations, pledge levels, dates, times, and sponsorship information.

Fred Hall's Fishing, Boat and RV Show
Del Mar Fairgrounds
2260 Jimmy Durante Blvd., Del Mar
(805) 389-3339

Fishing addicts swarm to this well-known show, where they get to test out the latest gear, shop for bargains on fishing line and lures, and brag about their catches. Many a boat lover finds his or her dream boat here. Although owners are known to say a boat is merely a hole to pour money into, they can't resist the new models. If you're a landlubber, you'll want to climb into a few souped-up recreational vehicles to fuel your fantasies.

April

Spike and Mike's Classic Festival of Animation
Museum of Contemporary Art
700 Prospect St., La Jolla
(858) 459-8707

This film festival will tickle your funny bone and give you a new appreciation for the art of animated film production. The series, different each year, showcases prize-winning short films from around the world. Before the films were famous, we saw the now internationally acclaimed Wallace and Gromit films right here, and still feel like we "discovered" them. You might get to view a soon-to-be-classic too. Most of the festival's films have a PG rating; the R-rated ones screen late. Call ahead for the schedule, and if you're concerned about the ratings, ask about the content of the program. The program runs for four weekends. For more information on this event, see our The Arts chapter.

Schooner Cup Regatta
Harbor Island and Shelter Island, San Diego Bay
(619) 233-3138

The largest schooner race on the West Coast and the largest charity regatta in America, it's the weekend of weekends for anyone who loves the spray of the sea. The race, held during the beginning of the month, raises funds for the Navy/Marine Corps Relief Society (providing help for military personnel and military dependents in time of personal need). After the race, there's a party that rocks the Voyager Room of the Kona Kai Continental Resort. The course begins at Reubens on Harbor Island, turns around at Point Loma and at the San Diego Bay. Watching the event is free; call for information if you want to participate in the event.

Surfing Contests
Varying locations, San Diego beaches
(619) 223-7017

The South Coast Surf Shop, in San Diego, knows where and when you'll find these monthly competitions. You can also check with the local parks and recreation office or watch for notices in the newspapers. If "surf's up" is important news to you or you simply want to admire the skill and daring of surfers, then call for more info. Watching the event is free.

Flower Fields of Carlsbad
Palomar Airport Rd. and I-5, Carlsbad
(760) 431-0352

Insiders say that this event is not to be missed and with a six-week time slot (Mother Nature's in charge of the actual dates), you should be able to admire the awesome flower fields. The ranunculus, in shades too startling to describe, is the star in this explosion of colors. Months before the blooming season, growers stagger their plantings so that the flowering cycle stretches for a six- to eight-week period. And those flowers stretch for acres. You can catch a glimpse of the fields driving north on I-5 or by visiting the Carlsbad Company Stores (see our Shopping chapter). But we

Insiders' Tip

When going to an outdoor event, don't forget to apply sunscreen or wear a hat. Even on cloudy days, those San Diego sunrays are abundant.

The Carlsbad flower field "blooming" is an annual affair that attracts visitors. PHOTO: CECE CANTON

recommend, no, urge you to stop and pay the small entrance fee ($5.00) to walk the fields. Camera buffs will want to pack extra film, and gardeners will want to visit the garden store for bulbs and bouquets. Picking flowers is strictly prohibited, as these are commercial fields. This is a perfect activity for the family.

Easter Egg Hunts
Carlsbad (760) 602–7517
Coronado (619) 522–7342
Fallbrook (760) 728–5845
Oceanside (760) 435–3388
Poway (858) 679–4366
Santee (619) 258–4100

The hunts are scheduled in many communities throughout the county. There may be games and hat-making contests too. They are usually open and free for all egg and candy hunters younger than 10. Check with your local parks and recreations departments for details, times, and dates.

Gaslamp Quarter Easter Hat Parade
Fifth Ave. and L Sts.,
Gaslamp Quarter, San Diego
(619) 233–5227

Come and stroll the Gaslamp in your Easter bonnet for this annual event that's family fun. There are hat-making activities for children and adults at 11:00 A.M. The parade starts after the hats are made and runs from Fifth Avenue and L Street and continues along Fifth to the Horton Grand Hotel. There's an Easter egg hunt and treats for children. The event is free.

La Jolla Easter Hat Sidewalk Promenade
Prospect St. and Herschel Ave., La Jolla
(858) 454–2600

Flower bouquets teeter atop bonnets during this elegant (and sometimes silly) promenade through the fashionable streets of La Jolla. The ladies take their chapeaux seriously—you're sure to see some outrageous creations.

San Diego Crew Classic
Crown Point Shores, Mission Bay, San Diego
(858) 488–0700
www.crewclassic.org

Championship rowing teams from the United States, Canada, and Europe have been competing at Mission Bay in this popular event since 1973. Crowds line the shores along the route, often gathered under flags representing the universities or organizations in the competition. It's a great way to spend the day outdoors listening to bands, checking out picnic layouts, and cheering on our team. Admission is $5.00 for anyone over 12 years of age. There is a fee for preferred parking—go early, since the lots fill quickly.

Pegleg Smith Liar's Contest
Anza-Borrego Desert State Park, Borrego Springs
(760) 767–5555

Like telling tall tales? Enjoy twisting the truth just a bit? You'll be delighted with the elaborate lies contestants create for this annual contest. Participants must make up a tale about lost gold, the desert, and colorful characters and spin it for the rapt audience. The event takes place in the evening and is free.

Adams Avenue Roots Festival
Adams Ave. at 35th St., San Diego
(619) 282–7329

Folk, jazz, and blues musicians perform on a half dozen outdoor stages during this venerable event. The Adams Avenue neighborhood is known for its ethnic diversity, cluster of antiques shops and bookstores, and colorful, funky attitude. The festival is family oriented, with plenty of games and activities for kids. Admission is free.

Coronado Flower Show Weekend
Spreckels Park, Coronado
(619) 437–8788

The residents of this genteel community take great pride in their gardens and even have a competition for the best front-yard gardens every spring. The flower show is a must for gardeners; it's said to be the largest such show on the West Coast. Individual blooms, floral arrangements, and plants undergo strict scrutiny before receiving a ribbon—it's enough to make amateurs green with envy. The weekend-long event includes a book sale, an art show, and a lineup of classic cars.

ArtWalk
Kettner Blvd. and India St., San Diego
(619) 615–1090
www.artwalkinfo.com

This two-day art fest has become San Diego's premier arts event. It takes place in Little Italy near downtown and includes visual and performance arts displays at galleries, studios, and other venues along the boulevard. Hundreds of artists participate in the event, which began in 1984. Kids are encouraged to participate in art workshops, and music performances and food stands add to the festivities. Admission is free.

Avocado Festival
Main St., Fallbrook
(760) 728–5845

Do you make a guacamole that has friends begging for the recipe? Would you like to taste avocado ice cream? Have you ever wondered if your child could be the next Little Miss or Mr. Avocado? Then don't miss this family-oriented outdoor street fair in downtown Fallbrook, which features recipe contests, booths selling arts and crafts, music, and lots of food—everything from ribs and potato salad (with chunks of avocado in it, of course) to burgers smothered in avocado and yes, even avocado ice cream. (Some say it's a tasty treat. We've never gotten up the gumption to try it.) Of course, there's plenty of guacamole too.

The fair includes an organic farmer's market, art show, and antique aircraft display. And, least we forget, the Avocado Olympics that features such "sports" as pit spitting, avocado pit croquet, and the ever-popular avocado bowling competitions (all in good fun).

Are you aware that San Diegans eat more of it than any other county in the country? Be sure to check out the guacamole recipe in this chapter's Close-up. The event is usually held on a Sunday in mid-April, but call for dates. With no admission, it's high time you attended this event.

Rose Society Annual Show
Balboa Park Club, Balboa Park
(619) 239–0512

Does a Double Delight or Queen Elizabeth rose that's blooming in your garden have what it takes to be Queen of the Day? Call for entry info, times, and rules. Spectators can watch as roses are judged by category, form, and even fragrance.

Before or after the show, be sure to walk around the rose garden, which will be at peak bloom. Call for directions to the location at the park. Admission is free.

Lakeside Western Days and Rodeo
Calif. Hwy. 67 N. and Mapleview, Lakeside
(619) 561–4331
www.lakesiderodeo.com
Whoa baby, this much-anticipated event is locally known as the granddaddy of western fun. Visit it and you'll know why. The two-day celebration includes performances by nationally known western music groups and lesser-known ones too, and by school bands. There's a parade, booths, crafts, clothes, and food. According to Insiders who don boots and cowboy hats, this is the county western event of Southern California. General admission is $8.00; reserved seating is $10.00; kids younger than 12 are admitted free of charge.

May

Vista Garden Club Show/Plant Sale
1200 Vale Terrace Dr., Vista
(760) 724–7656
One Insider thinks this plant sale is the best-kept secret in North County—until now. Normally held near the beginning of May, the plant sale and flower show run from 1:30 to 5:00 P.M. on Saturday and from 10:00 A.M. to 5:00 P.M. on Sunday. Along with houseplants, you may be tempted with bonsai trees, cactus plants (which may be in bloom), and potted rose bushes. There are plants at prices for every gardener and the staff is helpful so bring your landscaping questions along. There's no charge for admission to the event.

Carlsbad Spring Faire
Grand and State Sts., Carlsbad
(760) 931–8887
This event is billed as the biggest and best arts and crafts faire in Southern California (some say the world). The Faire satisfies your expectations with arts, crafts, T-shirts, collectibles, antiques, books, tools, and gourmet foods. Then it takes you a step further with its size. If you miss it,

don't despair. There's another Faire in November. The entire village area of Carlsbad is closed to traffic and crowds mingle through the displays. There is no admission fee. Parking can be tricky, so be prepared to walk to the faire. There are free shuttles from Plaza Camino Real shopping center and the Carlsbad City Library.

Cinco de Mayo
Various locations throughout the county, including:
Old Town State Historical Park, San Diego
(619) 291–4903
Grape Day Park, Escondido
(760) 432–2893
The Gaslamp Quarter, Fifth Ave., Downtown
(619) 233–5008
Oceanside Pier Ampitheater, Oceanside
(760) 761–1140
Christmas Circle, Borrego Springs
(760) 767–5555
Cinco de Mayo is a Mexican national holiday commemorating the battle in which Mexican troops defeated the invading French military in 1862. Although it isn't Mexico's most significant holiday, it is celebrated with great fanfare throughout San Diego. Our heritage shines during this May celebration, and just about everyone turns out. Most celebrations occur during the weekend closest to May 5, so don't be thrown if the event doesn't coincide with your calendar. Look for Latin dancing for kids and adults, Mexican foods, and activities for the family. Some festivals feature arts and crafts. Old Town's includes folkloric ballet performances and mariachi bands. Admission is usually free.

Portuguese Festa
2818 Avenida de Portugal, San Diego
(619) 223–5880
The reds and greens of the flag, the huge scarlet swirling skirts of the traditional dancers, and the chords of the fado (a traditional Portuguese song) are what will stick in your memory. That and the aroma and taste of the foods you can try here. You'll not find hot dogs and burgers—and that'll suit you well. You might want to start with *caldo verde* (a green cabbage and spicy

Avocados: A Mainstay of San Diego–Style Eating

Do you know that San Diegans eat more avocados than any other regional group in the United States? If you love the shiny, sometimes bumpy green and glorious avocado, you know why. They're good in and on about everything that Insiders serve.

In case your school didn't teach Avocado 101 here's a primer so you can increase your avocado IQ:

Avocados are native to Mexico. Hernando Cortez, the Spanish explorer and adventurer, discovered them in Mexico City in 1519. Montezuma II, the Aztec emperor, treated the avocado like a treasure, and according to legend it was offered as a gift to the Spanish conquerors. Much later in 1848, a year before gold was found at Sutter's Mill, Henry Dalton planted avocado trees in Southern California. In 1911 Carl Schmidt traveled to Mexico and brought back other avocado varieties.

Schmidt, like others who first began farming the avocado, had some setbacks. His first grove was hit hard by the frost of 1913, and only one variety survived. Schmidt called it the Fuerte, the Spanish word for vigorous and strong, and it is still known by that name today. About the same time Rudolph Hass discovered the Hass (it rhymes with "moss") avocado. The Hass and Fuerte, along with the Zutano, Bacon, Pinkerton, and Reed varieties, are the most popular with today's avocado growers and eaters.

Avocados are persnickety and need some pretty fine conditions to produce. Luckily, in San Diego, we have what it takes. Here avocados prefer living near the coastal strip (not more than 50 miles from the ocean) that stretches from San Luis Obispo to the Mexican border. Depending on the variety, trees have been known to grow from 20 to 60 feet tall. Some well-tended, mature trees bear from 200 to 300 of the fruits a year. Some large Mexican trees have produced over 3,000 in a season.

The Hass variety has a thick, pebbly skin that turns purplish-black when ripe. You'll find this one in the store nearly year-round. The smoother varieties, such as the Fuerte, do not change color when ripe. The "greenskins" are ripe when they yield to a gentle pressure and are available from November to April. And yes, each variety has a special flavor.

Even today in our high-tech society, avocados need to be harvested by hand using avocado shears called clippers. The fruits move from the picking stage to the packing stage and cold storage within hours. They'll hang out in cold storage either at the packinghouse or in trucks until they reach your supermarket.

Because avocados seem creamy, exotic, and tempting and are often more expensive than other produce, they're sometimes considered a luxury. Living in San Diego, however, we're treated to the best of the crop and often at incredibly low prices, especially when we get them at farmers' markets.

More avocados are eaten in the San Diego region than in any other part of the country.
PHOTO: CALIFORNIA AVOCADO COMMISSION

Insiders eat avocados in soups, spreads, guacamole dip, on sandwiches, on bagels, and straight from the shell.

PHOTO: CALIFORNIA AVOCADO COMMISSION

Along with the thought that avocados are just for special occasions, they've been given a bum rap in the nutritional department. Get it straight: They have no cholesterol; they're low in sodium and saturated fat and loaded with fiber and nutrients, such as vitamins B6, C, E, and potassium. It's the cheese, sour cream, and other ingredients that many add to the fruit that make avocados dangerous for dieters. Avocado can be used as a healthy substitute for toppings such as butter, cream cheese, and cheese, and in dips and spreads. Doing so you can get that creamy, green goodness taste with none of the cholesterol.

Okay, you're convinced—now you agree with Montezuma and most of the people who live in our county. Avocados are worth their weight in gold and are far more attainable. But what do you do when you bring avocados home and they're so hard you could break a window with them? It's simple. To ripen the fruit, place it in a fruit bowl at room temperature for a week. Or as Insiders suggest, place the fruit in a paper bag with an apple to speed the process. Either way, check the ripening process every few days.

To prepare avocados, cut lengthwise around the large seed and rotate the halves to separate. Remove the seed by sliding the tip of a spoon gently beneath it and lifting it out. To peel, place the cut side down and remove the skin with a knife or your fingers.

Eat the fruit when ripe. After opening, sprinkle lemon juice on it to avoid browning and refrigerate it in an airtight container for 2 to 3 days.

Fallbrook's Avocado Days
First-Place Guacamole Dip

Competition was keen in a recent Fallbrook's Avocado Days Guacamole contest. Here's the first-place winning recipe entered by Bruce Taylor.

    4 ripe Hass avocados
    4 green onions, chopped
    1 tablespoon finely chopped cilantro (Chinese parsley)
    2 tablespoons lime juice
    Salt to taste

Peel and blend avocado until it is as chunky or smooth as you prefer. Blend in other ingredients. Eat immediately or cover and refrigerate for up to four hours. It tastes best when made with San Diego–grown avocados.

sausage soup) then move on to a hearty fish stew; be sure to save room for rice pudding with Port, *doces de ovos* (egg sweets), or *cauacos* (a hard, sweet biscuit). Billed as one of San Diego's longest-running ethnic events, there's a parade, crowning of the Festa Queen, dancing, music, and Portuguese foods that tempt any appetite. The festa is held in Point Loma, home to many families of Portuguese fishermen. Admission is free; the event is usually held in May, but do call for the exact date.

International Gem and Jewelry Show
Del Mar Fairgrounds, 2260 Jimmy Durante Blvd., Del Mar
(858) 792-4252

The local San Diego Gem and Jewelry Association sponsors this sparkling three-day event. Gems and jewelry are sold here at a variety of prices. So you can come just to look and learn or you might want to buy something too. Kids love the geodes, the lumps of golden-colored amber, and the highly polished quartz that feels so smooth to the touch. They often come home with a handful of stones from the 10-cents-a-stone bins. Adults go for the uniquely designed bolos, necklaces, and rings studded with turquoise, jade, garnets, and collectible stones.

Kids love the show, and since there's no admission cost, it's a fine family outing. Call for dates and times since they vary.

Annual Rummage Sale
Avenida de Acacias, Rancho Santa Fe
(858) 756-4101

Sponsored by the Rancho Santa Fe Garden Club, this isn't your parent's idea of a rummage sale, but of course, you'd expect more from one of the county's premier communities. If you're a true bargain hunter you'll be in buyer's heaven. As with any rummage sale, early birds get the best selection. The three-day sale, held the first Thursday, Friday, and Saturday in May, begins at 9:00 A.M. and continues throughout the day. Proceeds are earmarked for charities, scholarships, and upkeep of the walking and hiking trails in Rancho Santa Fe. Admission is free.

Humphrey's Concerts by the Bay
2241 Shelter Island Dr., Shelter Island, San Diego
(619) 523-1010
www.humphreysbythebay.com

Call or check local entertainment sections of the newspaper for a current list of concerts. Tickets sell out early so it pays to plan ahead. The concerts are outdoors, wonderful (read that romantic) on a balmy evening. They run through the summer. You'll see big name performers like the Beach Boys and lesser-known local celebrities too. The recent season included performances by George Benson, Gordon Lightfoot, Travis Tritt, the Del McCoury Band, and Peter Frampton. Ticket prices vary. Call for the times and prices of upcoming events. (See our Nightlife chapter for further information.)

Roar and Snore Camp Over
San Diego Wild Animal Park,
15500 San Pasqual Valley Rd., Escondido
(760) 718-3050, (800) 934-CAMP
www.wildanimalpark.com

Not only will you talk with the animals, but you'll get to sleep up close to them with this special series offered by the Wild Animal Park. Costs range from about $105 for adults to about $85 for kids 8 and older. There are hikes, instructional programs, campfires, and al fresco dining (including a vegetarian choice). Bring a sleeping bag for the tent accommodations. This is a not-to-be-missed San Diego experience for all animal lovers. The camp happens on Friday, Saturday, and Sunday summer evenings only; call for reservations and an equipment list.

June

Indian Fair
Museum of Man, Balboa Park, San Diego
(619) 239-2001

Representatives from American Indian groups throughout the country assemble at the Museum of Man annually. The fair includes dances, arts and crafts displays (bring your wallet), and ethnic food vendors. The museum has a large collection of American Indian artifacts; combine a visit to the museum with the fair. Admission is charged.

A Taste of Gaslamp
Gaslamp Quarter restaurants, Downtown
(619) 233–5227
www.gaslamp.org

Downtown's historic district is packed with excellent restaurants. In fact, it may be the most diverse dining district in San Diego. Many of the finest restaurants participate in this annual event, where hungry diners pay $20 to sample the specialties of several fine chefs. This is a happening event, so get there at 5:00 P.M. when the tasting begins. It runs until 9:00 P.M., when the crowd mobs the Gaslamp's nightspots for further revelry.

Greek Festival
3655 Park Blvd., San Diego
(619) 297–4165

Are you hungry for gyros and moussaka? Are you amazed by the skill and precision of traditional Greek dancers? This annual event, sponsored by Spyridon Greek Orthodox Church, gives you plenty to celebrate even if you can't claim Greek heritage. Be sure to check out the Greek imports and crafts. It's free to attend this event, which takes place at St. Spyridon Church.

San Diego County Fair
Del Mar Fairgrounds, 2200 Jimmy Durante Blvd., Del Mar
(858) 792–4252, (858) 793–5555 (24-hour event hotline)
www.delmarfair.com

This may be the biggest county fair you've ever attended, but don't let the scope and size put you off—there's old-fashioned fun to be had. The three-week event draws top country and rock 'n' roll musical performers, but hometown talent is also a big draw. There are baking contests, hobby displays (you've got to see the lint collection!), woodworking prizes, weirdest vegetable competitions, kids' events, and even wine and microbeer competitions.

What is the most popular event with the crowds? With the 10 and younger set it's the midway rides and the animal displays (4H is active in San Diego). Teens enjoy the vendors, the carny games and competitive events sponsored by schools and clubs. The 20-and-older group appreciate all of the above along with displays, landscape exhibits, flower shows (you've got to see the roses), and food. The cinnamon buns are huge (and scrumptious) and the roasted corn on the cob is a bit of heaven. Food is pricey; pack a lunch or eat before you go and then buy treats. Free shuttles are available from various locations in the county. Single admission is $9.00. Here's an Insider tip: Watch the newspaper for a schedule of concerts and events.

The Jewish Community Center Festival of New Jewish Plays
Lawrence Family Jewish Community Centers
Mantel Weirs Eastgate City Park,
4126 Executive Dr., La Jolla
(858) 457–3030

A distinguished series of staged readings of new plays explores the Jewish experience. The festival offers a dynamite array of drama, comedy, and music with discussions following each performance so that participants can become part of the creative energies. Prices range from $100 for four performances to $12 for single performances, depending on the featured actors and on seating.

Mainly Mozart Festival
Various locations in San Diego and Mexico
(619) 239–0100

You've just gotta' love Wolfgang or forget going to this outstanding series of chamber music and piano concerts. The musical performances are sublime, to say the least, and are held in various locations throughout San Diego and Mexico. Ticket prices vary so call for dates and availability as the festival books up fast. (To read more about Mainly Mozart, see The Arts chapter.)

Pala Mission Fiesta
Pala Mission Rd., U.S. Hwy. 76, Pala
(760) 742–3317

Help celebrate our Native American heritage with this little-known festival of Corpus Christi. The fiesta is held on the grounds of Mission San Antonio de Pala and it includes dancing, food (a pit barbecue and Indian fry bread are not to be missed), and wonderful music. The fiesta is an outstanding, wholesome experience especially for the fourth grader in the family who studies California's rich heritage.

Chili Cook-Off in San Marcos
2200 Sycamore Dr., San Marcos
(760) 744–1270

This event is hot stuff and draws over 10,000 people to the Walnut Grove Community Park in the North County Inland community. It's a family event which includes entertainment—like those square dancers burning off calories before the chili is ready—and demonstrations, too. You might see folks making chili wreaths or designing ceramics with southwestern motifs. The food booths here sell everything from chili-flavored beef jerky to chili-flavored candy (a taste that has to be acquired, we believe). It's all hot fun, nonetheless. Bring your wallet, because you can buy one of those chili pepper wreaths, and chili pepper plants, and other chili pepper concoctions. Of course, you've got to be there for the chili competition, which is serious business. The cook-off runs from 10:00 A.M. to 6:00 P.M. Admission is free.

Dr. Seuss Run/Walk for Literacy
Balboa Park and Seaport Village
(858) 792–2900

With benefits going to the San Diego Council on Literacy even the Cat in the Hat would join this event. The 8K run is in Balboa Park; the 1-mile Fun Run is held at Seaport Village. There is a fee to run/walk the race. Spectators see it all for free.

Scottish Highland Game & Gathering of the Clans
Brengle Terrace Park, Vista
(619) 645–8080
www.sdhighlandgames.org

Do you love the music and energy of *Riverdance*? Do you adore the sound of bagpipe music? Do you think that shortbread should be one of the four food groups? Do you have a Scottish ancestor or two on your family tree? If you've answered "yes" to any of the questions above, then this event is for you. There are bagpipers and Celtic music, highland dancers, and sporting competitions. There are imports and crafts from Scotland. And Scottish food too—don't miss the haggis (there's even vegetarian haggis for the non-meat eaters). An additional highlight is the sheep dog competition, where the dogs follow a set of whistle commands as they herd flocks of sheep. Saturday features the Highland Dance Competition. Admission is charged. The Games are usually held in June or July.

July

Fourth of July Fireworks and Parades
Various locations
Marina View Park, Chula Vista
(619) 691–5140
Old Town, San Diego
(619) 291–4903
Coronado Beach, Coronado
(619) 522–7342
Oceanside
(760) 966–4530

Several communities hold Fourth of July celebrations featuring everything from parades to street fairs to surfing contests to fireworks displays. Naturally, each town claims to have the best festivities, but we think Coronado takes the prize.

Insiders' Tip
What's the Fourth without fireworks? Insiders think those at the Oceanside Pier in Oceanside, Ocean Beach, and Ferry Landing Marketplace in Coronado are the best in the West.

The lights of the Del Mar Fair brighten the night sky. PHOTO: DIANNE SLEZAK, COURTESY OF THE SAN DIEGO CONVENTION & VISITORS BUREAU

The parade (which starts at 10:00 A.M.) is followed by U.S. Navy air and sea demonstrations (the parachuting is awesome), a concert in Spreckels Park, and fireworks over Glorietta Bay.

Check with your local parks and recreation department for what is happening on our nation's birthday. The newspapers and TV news programs also list the times and places of major fireworks displays.

Del Mar Thoroughbred Horse Racing
Del Mar Fairgrounds
2260 Jimmy Durante Blvd., Del Mar
(858) 755–1141, (858) 792–4242

The mid-July through mid-September season is anticipated by locals and visitors alike, because these races bring the country's most illustrious horses and jockeys to San Diego. The venue is billed as the place where the "turf meets the surf," and from the grandstand you'll know why: The Pacific is the track's neighbor. The view is spectacular—it's often so clear you'll think you're seeing all the way to Hawaii. (Actually, what you're probably seeing is San Clemente Island.) Down on the track you'll be seeing the likes of the famous racehorse Cigar running his heart out.

This is the track Bob Hope, Bing Crosby, and other celebrities used to flock to in the 1940s. Today, you'll see the elite movers and fashionable shakers of San Diego. (Lots of Insiders go to the track to people watch as well as watch the ponies.) There's on-track wagering, and with a bet as low as $2.00 you can experience the thrill of the race. The events start at 2:00 P.M. General admission varies depending on special events, promotions, and coupons. Check the newspaper for special deals. Concerts are held on the infield after the races on Friday nights. See our Spectator Sports chapter for more information on the races.

Over-the-Line World Championships
Fiesta Island, Mission Bay, San Diego
(619) 688–0817

The big networks wanted to put this annual event on television so that all of America could watch the fun. The hitch? The competitors would have to clean up one of their traditions: X-rated team names. "No way," said the Old Mission Beach Athletic Club, which sponsors the beach softball fest. Therefore, the adult-oriented event can only be seen in person. But you'll hear a lot about it at local nightspots, on radio, and in the press. Admission is free. To read more about the Over-the-Line competition, see the entry in our Spectator Sports chapter.

U.S. Open Sand Castle Competition
911 Grove Ave., Imperial Beach Pier,
Imperial Beach
(619) 424–6663

This competition makes any sand architect marvel. The two-day event includes a parade at 10:00 A.M. on Saturday. The kids' competition starts at 2:00 P.M. with all children winning prizes. Sunday is the day for serious professional and amateur competition; pre-entry for the competition is required. Sure it's sandy fun, yet consider that prize money is awarded for the sand structures, with $5,000 to the best in the professional competition. About 200,000 visit the free spectator event so parking can be at a premium. With fireworks beginning at dusk on Saturday, it's a wonderful weekend at the beach that will truly spark your imagination.

> ## Insiders' Tip
> Heading to the Del Mar Fairgrounds for the county fair? Traffic jams can be unpleasant, but there are alternatives. You can take the Coaster or one of the free shuttles. Watch the schedules, which can be found in the local newspapers. Some days kids and seniors need not pay admission fees.

Thoroughbred horse racing brings plenty of fast-paced excitement to the Del Mar Fairgrounds.

Lesbian and Gay Parade and Festival
Fifth Ave. at Laurel St., Hillcrest, San Diego
(619) 297–7683
www.sdpride.org

San Diego's large and powerful gay community comes out en masse for this celebration of diversity. Events include a 5K run and walk and an elaborate parade complete with bands, floats, and outrageous costumes. The festivities then move to Marston Point in Balboa Park at 6th Avenue and Juniper Street, where revelers enjoy live bands, great party food from various stands, and a general sense of happy camaraderie. The parade usually takes place at the end of July.

August

Obon Summer Festival
Vista Buddhist Temple,
150 Cedar Rd., Vista
(760) 941–8800

This classical Japanese festival features the dances (odori) and displays of taiko (the incredible Japanese drums) along with ethnic foods and crafts. The festival is usually held between the end of July and the middle of August and begins about noon on Saturday and Sunday and continues to 8:00 P.M. The admission to this perfect outing is free.

Acura Tennis Classic
Costa del Mar Rd. and El Camino Real, Carlsbad
(760) 438–5683

San Diego's premier women's professional tennis event comes to North County at the La Costa Resort and Spa. Past lineups have included superstars Venus Williams, Martina Hingis, Monica Seles, and Steffi Graff. The nine-day event draws in excess of 70,000 spectators, including celebrities, movie stars, and notable Insiders. Tickets range from $16 to $35 for individual days, with packages going for between $35 and $350. There is a charge for parking. See our Spectator Sports chapter for more information on this event.

Ringling Brothers and Barnum and Bailey Circus
San Diego Sports Arena, 3500 Sports Arena Blvd., San Diego
(619) 224–4171

The Big Top doesn't get any better than this and draws kids of all ages. Be sure to see the Parade of the Animals, in which animals and performers walk down the city's streets from the Old Town Station (you can get there by taking the trolley or the Coaster) to the Sports Arena—a short walk but a thrilling spectacle. The parade is held the day before the circus begins. Seat prices at the circus are about $9.00.

World Body Surfing Championships
Oceanside Pier and Beach, Oceanside
(760) 435–4014

Tried riding waves only to end up eating sand? Watch the pros use their fins to chase the wave's crest and ride atop the foam to shore. Body surfing is more exciting than board surfing for amateurs. After watching the show, you feel like you too can get atop a wave without being dragged under. The show begins at 7:00 A.M. and runs until about 6:00 P.M. Admission is free.

Annual Julian Weed Show and Art Mart
Julian Town Hall, Main St., Julian
(760) 765–1857

A weed is a weed is a weed when it's in your garden, but in this show a weed might be a work of art. Come see how the pesky plants can be arranged to delight the senses. Yes, arranged as one would a bouquet. The two-week event, held from 10:00 A.M. to 4:00 P.M. daily, includes a show of San Diego artists, so in addition to admiring weeds, you can also feast your eyes on paintings and sculpture, and ceramics and weaving and photography. Of course, you can always buy a slice of Julian's famous pie at this and all events that take place in Julian. Admission is free.

Midnight Madness Fun Bicycle Ride
County Administration Bldg.
1600 Pacific Hwy., Downtown
(619) 645–8068

Don your jammies and sneakers and hop on your bike for this 20-mile midnight ride through downtown San Diego—surely one of the strangest bike rides you'll ever enjoy. Local bike groups and shops support the ride and can provide specifics. You must apply to participate in advance of the ride, which usually takes place in mid-August.

Julian Fall Apple Harvest
Throughout Julian
(760) 765–1857

San Diegans are accustomed to appreciating the small signs of seasonal changes. The best place to feel like you're in the crisp fall air is in the mountain town of Julian, where apples grow in abundance. The festival includes pie baking contests, concerts, crafts fairs, and other events scheduled on weekends throughout September. Just driving through the mountains is a joy. Take along your hiking boots and hit the trails outside town to see trees with gold and red leaves.

Street Scene
Gaslamp Quarter, between 3rd and 7th Aves.,
San Diego
(619) 557–8490
www.street-scene.com

Downtown San Diego's Gaslamp Quarter turns into the biggest street fest imaginable with this three-day production that includes the most diverse collection of music, food, and performances in California. We're talking Fun and grownups (family activities are scheduled for Sunday). The music is loud and plentiful. It runs the gamut from rap to rock, from cool jazz to hot zydeco. Food options range from fish tacos to Louisiana gumbo. The crowds are overwhelming as music fans gather around the stages. Get there early and arrange a meeting spot so you don't lose track of your companions. Take a Coaster commuter train or trolley to make parking a non-issue. Be sure to check the schedules before you buy a ticket because timetables can change. If you're a serious music lover, book a hotel room downtown so you can take in the entire fest.

Grape Day Festival and Parade
Grape Day Park, Grand Ave., Escondido
(760) 743–8207

Come celebrate the Annual Grape Day Festival and Parade with fun for the whole family, especially since this event is free. Celebrated on the first or second Saturday in September, it goes from 9:00 A.M. to 5:00

P.M. There's a tour of the historical sites at the park, creative cooking (with grapes of course), and performances by local Bluegrass and Country groups. One year we tapped our toes to the "Texas Toothpicks" and then sat in awe at the Ballet Folkorico de Cristo Rey dance group. You'll find mountains of food choices, free grapes, and plenty of kid and adult entertainment.

Día de la Independencia
Old Town State Historical Park,
Old Town, San Diego
(619) 296–3161

Old Town celebrates Mexican Independence Day, September 16. (Mexican Independence Day actually begins at 11:00 P.M. on September 15 and continues throughout the next day.) You'll be treated to lots of music, dancers performing traditional steps, and even a salsa-tasting contest. The mariachi bands are incredible, so wear your dancing shoes. Other cities and neighborhoods also celebrate this festival; check with your local parks and recreation department. Admission is free. Call to see exactly on what day the celebration will take place.

Thunderboat Races
Mission Bay, San Diego
(619) 225–9160

This event is technically called San Diego's Bayfair World Series of Powerboat Racing on Mission Bay. Insiders call them the Thunderboat Races. The excitement happens during a three-day weekend, usually in the middle of the month. The viewing is best at Crown Point, Fiesta Island, and Vacation Island. And yes, the boats are

Insiders' Tip

All during the month of October, kids 11 and younger can visit the zoo for free. On Zoo Founders Day, October 5, everyone is admitted free.

loud and fast. The event includes the Thunderboats (the world's fastest boats), Formula 1 boats, unlimited lights, and drag boats. There are food booths and vendors. Check on the shuttles to get to the races from offsite locations and parking will be easier. (For more details, see the entry in our Spectator Sports chapter.)

Rosarito-Ensenada 50-Mile Fun Bicycle Ride
Call for official starting location
(619) 424–6084
www.rosaritoensenada.com

The annual Fall Baja cycling event attracts more than 8,000 riders of all skill and age levels. Starting at 10:00 A.M. from Rosarito Beach the route runs south along the two-lane free (libre) road to the finish line. The end point is in Ensenada, Baja California where there's a fiesta. Entry is $19; the T-shirt is an extra $10.

October

Marine Corps Air Station Miramar Air Show
Miramar Marine Base, San Diego
(858) 577–1000
www.miramarairshow.com

This is an aviation expo that excites the entire family. Parking and admission are free. There are displays and performances that will snatch away your breath, including flights by the Blue Angels. There's a twilight show on Saturday. Special seating in the grandstand and box seat area can be reserved by calling (619) 220–8497.

Oktoberfests
Various locations

Come celebrate fall with German-related festivals that happen in many of San Diego's cities. Some charge for entrance, but at others it's the food that carries a price tag. Insiders say the best Oktoberfest is at the German-American Club in El Cajon (located at 1017 South Mollison Street), (619) 442–6637.

Western Regional Finals Championship Rodeo
Lakeside Rodeo Grounds, U.S. Hwy. 67 and
Mapleview Ave., Lakeside
(858) 292–0092

The championship full-scale, seven-event rodeo features top riders from 11 western states. The events include calf roping, barrel racing, saddle bronc riding, bull riding, team roping, bareback riding, and steer wrestling. There's also mighty fine western grub, foot-tapping music, and wholesome, cowpoke fun for the whole family. Dust off your boots and get to Lakeside for the Championship Rodeo. General admission is $8.00, reserved seating $11.00; kids younger than 12 are admitted free.

Mum Festival at the Wild Animal Park
San Diego Wild Animal Park,
15500 San Pasqual Valley Rd., Escondido
(619) 234–6541
www.wildanimal.org

Shades of gold, red, and burnt umber collide in bursts of color from the fall chrysanthemums that crowd the park during this annual botanical celebration. It's billed as the largest mum festival in the West and once you see it, you'll agree. Admission is about $26.50 for adults and includes the tram ride through the park.

Halloween Festivals and Haunted Houses
Various locations throughout San Diego County
Gaslamp Quarter, San Diego
(619) 231–3611
The Scream Zone, Del Mar Fairgrounds, Del Mar
(858) 755–1161

Almost every community in San Diego celebrates Halloween with fun houses, haunted houses, and activities such as pumpkin-carving contests and pin-the-tail-on-the-pumpkin games. Most of the activities are free. Adult Insiders like the Gaslamp Quarter's The Frightmare on Market Street. Tickets are about $20 and there's a costume contest, gourmet food booths (and fun food too), and plenty of partying in the clubs and restaurants in the Quarter. Kids prefer the Fairgrounds' Scream Zone, which is open throughout the month. The 25-room haunted house is filled with frights, and the midway rides take care of any other screams waiting for release. Call your local parks and recreation department for what's happening in your neighborhood.

Rodeo time means barrel racing and this rider is going for it. PHOTO: THORN VOLLENWEIDER

November

Fall Village Faire
State St. and Grand Ave., Carlsbad
(760) 434–8887
Similar to the Carlsbad Spring Faire (see May for details), this faire has a holiday flavor. It features Christmas crafts, decorations, and oodles of holiday gift-giving ideas. There's a certified organic farmers' market that sells perfect produce. The market is normally found near the intersection of Grand Avenue and Carlsbad Boulevard. Some Insiders go late in the afternoon when the vendors may be interested in doing some dealing. Others swear it's best to be there right at 8:00 A.M. when it starts.

There's no cost for admission. Other communities, including the Gaslamp District and University Heights, hold fall fairs.

Tecate/Score Baja 1000
Ensenada to La Paz, Baja California
(818) 225–8402
www.score-international.com
This is an annual off-road race for cars, trucks, and motorcycles, and it is much anticipated in the dirt-racing community. According to Insiders, this isn't the famous Dakar off-road race; hey, but it's treacherous nonetheless. The race covers the roughest terrain on the Baja California Peninsula and if you've ever driven in the area or flown over it, you know it's

Hot-air balloons are a colorful addition to the blue skies around San Diego. PHOTO: BOB YARBROUGH, COURTESY OF THE SAN DIEGO CONVENTION AND VISITORS BUREAU

desolate. There's an entry fee for racing folks; viewing is free. The race starts early in the morning in Ensenada and attracts thousands. At the end in the city of La Paz, there's a fiesta and rowdy party that some parents might consider to be R-rated.

Mother Goose Parade
W. Main and Chambers Sts., El Cajon
(619) 444-8712
www.mothergooseparade.com

El Cajon's chamber of commerce sponsors this parade, which is usually held the last weekend in November. It begins at 12:30 P.M. on West Main and Chambers Streets and continues east on Main to Second Street then north on Second to Madison. This is an old-fashioned childrens' affair with lots of local turnout. You'll see floats, clowns, bands, equestrians, civic leaders, and charitable organizations represented. There's no admission fee, so bring your lawn chairs or blankets for sidewalk sitting, and some cash for the food, peanuts, toys, banners, and candy.

Annual Festival of Lights
Bazaar del Mundo, Old Town, San Diego
(619) 296-3161

The Bazaar del Mundo kicks off the holidays with this annual celebration that happens the weekend after Thanksgiving. It's a holiday tradition for many Insiders who especially enjoy the performance of dances from around the world. The Nativity scene is lighted and remains on display through New Year's Day. It's free and many families make the annual visit to get into the holiday spirit.

December

Christmas on the Prado Balboa Park
(619) 239-0512
www.balboapark.org

Balboa Park twinkles, glistens, and shines during the holidays. This weekend-long celebration, usually held at the beginning of the month, includes carolers, a candlelight procession, ethnic food and crafts stands, and general holiday merriment. Admission

to the museums is free after 5:00 P.M. Stock up on goodies at the museums' shops.

Old Town Holiday in the Park and Candlelight Tours
Old Town State Historical Park, San Diego
(619) 220-5422

Walk through the historic districts of San Diego, view the holiday period decorations, and listen to stories about the early days of Old Town. The Las Posadas reenactment of Mary and Joseph's search for shelter is held mid-month. There's entertainment, caroling, and refreshments. Old Town's shop owners decorate their stores, and most are open late during the tours.

Boat Parades of Lights
Various harbors

The parades feature boats of all shapes and sizes decorated for the holiday season. To get the best view of the Mission Bay Christmas Boat Parade, Insiders suggest watching it from Crown Point, on the east side of Vacation Island. For Oceanside's Boat Parade, anywhere in the harbor is perfect. For San Diego's, the best views are at Seaport Village and Harbor Island. If you want to enter your boat, call or contact the local parks and recreation office or chamber of commerce. Remember to wear a jacket. It can be breezy and cool on December evenings. Most parades start about 7:00 P.M.; watching is free.

Holiday Parades and Celebrations
Various locations

Escondido's annual Christmas Parade begins at Escondido High School and runs along Broadway to Grape Day Park. Bring the family to see floats, cutest twin contests, local public servants riding the route and waving to the crowd, and plenty of horses and high school bands. This is an old-fashioned parade where families wave to the parade participants and neighbors meet and mingle. Ocean Beach has a parade and tree festival too. The parade there goes down Newport Avenue and includes every children's organization in the community. At the end of Ocean Beach's parade, there is a holiday festival and community tree

Seaport Village is often the venue for fireworks displays and seasonal festivals. PHOTO: COURTESY OF THE SAN DIEGO CONVENTION & VISITORS BUREAU

lighting. All are free events. For more information, contact the cities' chambers of commerce or park and recreation offices.

Great American Train Show
Del Mar Fairgrounds,
2260 Jimmy Durante Blvd., Del Mar
(630) 834–0652

This is a model railroad traveling show that comes to San Diego just once a year. It's a mandatory event for anyone who loves trains. You'll see train layouts on display, trains for sale, trains to operate, train gadgets, and gizmos and train-related clothing. Adult admission is $5.00; kids 12 and younger are admitted free.

Wild Animal Park's Festival of Lights
San Diego Wild Animal Park,
15500 San Pasqual Valley Rd., Escondido
(760) 796–5615
www.wildanimalpark.com

Nairobi Village, the main shopping and eating area of the park, is even more appealing with sparkling holiday lights. The festival, which occurs the week before Christmas, features free children's activities from face painting to craft making to sliding and playing in Snow Hill. (The park has snow hauled in for the event.) There are carolers, programs, and educational shows featuring live animals. Adult admission is $26.50. Children 3 through 11 pay $19.50. There is a $6.00 parking fee.

Holiday Bowl
Qualcomm Stadium, 9449 Friars Rd., San Diego
(619) 283–5808

The Holiday Bowl, held in late December, features a football face-off between nationally ranked teams from the Big 12 and either the WAC or the Pac 10. Begun in 1978, the Holiday Bowl has earned a reputation for close games. This is a popular event in San Diego, so get your tickets early; they range in price from $29 to $50. (Read more about the Holiday Bowl in our Spectator Sports chapter.)

First Night Escondido
Downtown Escondido near the California
Center for the Arts, Escondido
(760) 739–0101
www.firstnightescondido.org

This is a G-rated New Year's Eve event, so you can celebrate with the family. It's a no-alcohol event where you buy a button (that's your ticket) for $10—less if you buy it before the event. The ticket allows you inside the roped-off performance areas and gives you access to all the fun. There's something for everyone, from steel bands and chamber music to mariachi bands and acrobats. There's lots of food too—everything from pizza and hot dogs to foot-long sandwiches, ribs, and chicken. Insiders always save room for the strawberry cheese cake and gourmet coffee. First Night begins at 6:00 P.M. and goes until the midnight fireworks. Proceeds from the admission support the arts community. Call your local parks and recreation department for other First Nights in the area.

The Arts

It's a common complaint among visitors to San Diego and even among some locals that San Diego is bereft of culture. Take it from us—that may have been true 25 years ago, but it simply isn't the case any longer and hasn't been for some time. Once an idea is established, however, it's hard to convince folks otherwise. So we'll just let San Diego's fine arts establishments and performers speak for themselves. You'll soon see that no matter what region of the county you're visiting, you'll find an abundance of galleries, museums, classical music performances, theaters, and much more.

In North County Inland, Escondido, for example, has its own California Center for the Arts. And small but distinguished theaters are found throughout the county. Within the city of San Diego, everything you could possibly look for in the arts is somewhere to be found.

During its season, the San Diego Opera features internationally renowned singers like Viveca Geneaux and Cecilia Bartoli. The Old Globe Theatre in Balboa Park, modeled after the original in London, not only continues with its cornerstone of Shakespearean plays, but has also presented everything from Molière to Mamet, from *Electra* to *Damn Yankees*. The La Jolla Playhouse has established itself by premiering several plays that have gone on to Broadway.

Around the county are hundreds of art galleries where you can find paintings, prints, and sculptures by emerging as well as established artists. In the East County are a myriad of galleries featuring Western art from the likes of Olaf Wieghorst and Remington; in La Jolla and North County you'll find African, Aboriginal, Scandinavian, Indian, Chinese, and Egyptian art—just about any type that piques your interest.

Traveling troupes have discovered that San Diego audiences enthusiastically embrace touring performances such as Broadway reviews/revues, ballet, and ethnic dance shows like *Riverdance* and *Stomp*.

The film scene has started to emerge in San Diego, too, and several film festivals have sprung up in recent years. San Diegans have long enjoyed the Latino Film Festival and Spike & Mike's Classic Festival of Animation. In 1998 the San Diego International Film Festival was added to the mix. All draw filmmakers from all over the world, giving locals the chance to learn more about the history of filmmaking and to see some off-the-beaten-path movies.

San Diego has also begun to attract a growing enclave of writers. Victor Villaseñor, author of the best-selling *Rain of Gold*, is a native of Oceanside, in North County Coastal. Joseph Waumbaugh, author of *The Onion Field* and numerous best-selling novels, has adopted San Diego as his hometown, and scores of lesser-known but highly successful writers pen their works from somewhere around the county.

You can see that San Diego indeed is no slouch when it comes to the fine arts. With unlimited time and an unlimited budget, you could be out every evening attending a play, a concert, a musical, or an art film. So when someone bemoans San Diego's lack of cultural accouterments, you can just smile knowingly and head to the opera while the uninformed spend another night in front of the tube.

In this chapter we'll give you a comprehensive description of all San Diego has to offer in the way of arts. We'll tell you where the best clusters of galleries are, where the best art-film houses are, and how to get discount tickets. Like everywhere else in San Diego, dress tends to be on the casual side, even for nighttime performances of the symphony and the opera. Although only the most daring wear jeans to these events, tuxedos and full-length evening gowns are nearly as uncommon, and most patrons of the arts choose comfortable and casual yet elegant clothing.

For current listings of performances, festivals, and special gallery shows, check the "Night and Day" section of the *San Diego Union-Tribune* or the "Calendar" section of the free *San Diego Reader,* which can be picked up in convenience stores, libraries, and bookstores all over the county. Both come out on Thursdays.

Classical Music

Central San Diego

La Jolla Chamber Music Society
(858) 459–3728
www.ljcms.org

All year long the La Jolla Chamber Music Society presents classical music ensembles featuring national and international musicians. Different series now stretch throughout most of the year, including the Revelle Series, which presents such notables as violinist Hilary Hahn and the Beaux Arts Trio in the Museum of Contemporary Art's Sherwood Auditorium. The Celebrity Series, staged at downtown San Diego's Civic Theater, brings together the world's most distinguished musicians and orchestras. The less expensive, more informal Discover Series showcases talented newcomers. In August the 19-day Summerfest, also held at the Sherwood Auditorium, dazzles music lovers with a series of daily concerts, workshops, and exhibitions. Call for information on the individual series and their lineups as well as ticket prices.

Mainly Mozart Festival
(619) 239–0100
www.mainlymozart.org

The title of this festival spells it out: It's mainly a series of performances of the works of Mozart, but it also includes his 18th-century contemporaries, Baroque composers of the late 17th century, and the romantic masters of the early 19th century. Since 1988 the festival has successfully bridged the gap between the winter concert season of San Diego's primary performing arts groups and the major summer events. Many of North America's finest musicians are showcased every June in the All-Star Orchestra,

led by artistic director and conductor David Atherton. Performances are held throughout the county and across the border in Tijuana.

Even though the bulk of the performances are held in late spring, the festival has expanded in recent years to include special events year-round, such as the Spotlight Series held during the winter. For the most current performance schedule and to order tickets, call the number listed above. Ticket prices range from $30 for a single concert to $100 for a four-concert series.

San Diego Civic Youth Orchestra
4330 La Jolla Village Dr., Ste. 330, San Diego
(858) 484–9635

Gifted young musicians make up the San Diego Civic Youth Orchestra, a group dedicated to studying and performing the world's great orchestral works. Each year the organization embarks on an international tour to perform in music festivals around the world. Here at home, they delight and entertain audiences around

Insiders' Tip

For half-price, day-of-performance tickets to local shows, check out the Times Arts Tix Booth on the southwest corner of Horton Plaza, half a block from the Lyceum Theater. Or call (619) 497-5000 for a list of each day's half-price shows.

the county with performances of such works as Tchaikovsky's *Nutcracker Suite,* Beethoven's *Symphony No. 5,* and John Williams's *Star Wars.*

Performances are held in various venues throughout the county, including the California Center for the Arts, Copley Symphony Hall, and Spreckels Theater.

The season runs year-round. Call (858) 484–9635 for the current schedule.

San Diego Master Chorale
4455 Federal Blvd., Ste. A-098, San Diego
(858) 672–7664
www.sdmasterchorale.org

Originally founded as the choral arm of the San Diego Symphony in 1962, the Master Chorale split off into an independent organization in 1979. Consisting of around 100 of San Diego's finest singers, the chorale produces its own concert season and joins other organizations occasionally for collaborative efforts. Frequently the chorale will join the San Diego Opera and the San Diego Symphony for special performances.

The group performs all around San Diego County in a variety of settings, from churches to outdoor stages. The repertoire includes a broad scope of music from master choral works to modern songs and show tunes. For information about the chorale's schedule, visit the Web site or call (858) 672–7664.

San Diego Opera
1200 Third Ave., Ste. 1824, San Diego
(619) 232–7636

There's little middle ground with opera: you either love it or hate it. But if you happen to be on the fence, we strongly suggest you take in a performance of the San Diego Opera; we suspect it'll make a convert of you. Since 1965 the San Diego Opera has been steadily maturing into a major community asset for San Diego. With General Director Ian Campbell at the helm since 1983, the character of the opera has evolved beautifully. Fiscally conservative and artistically daring, Campbell has led the opera to a point where its financial status is sound and its performances are a combination of the classics and the contemporary.

Campbell promises at least one con-

temporary opera each season, such as Gershwin's *Porgy and Bess,* André Previn's *A Streetcar Named Desire,* and Catán's *Rappaccini's Daughter,* the first Mexican opera ever to be performed in San Diego. Balancing out the new and unusual are the standard opera war-horses like Puccini's *Madam Butterfly* and Verdi's *Aida.*

Five operas are performed during the season, which runs from January through May. Information about subscriptions and tickets to individual performances are available by calling (619) 570–1100 or by stopping by the Civic Theatre box office. Ticket prices for individual operas range from $31 to $105. The opera performs in the Civic Theatre at Third Avenue and B Street in downtown San Diego.

San Diego Symphony
Copley Symphony Hall, 750 B Street, San Diego
(619) 235–0804
www.sandiegosymphony.com

Mired in bankruptcy, the San Diego Symphony ceased performing for a couple of years but was revived in time for the 1998 Summer Pops season. Many of the symphony's original musicians returned, and under the leadership of Jung-Ho Pak, the symphony's artistic director and principal conductor, the future looked bright. Financial woes abruptly vanished in January 2002 when Qualcomm CEO Irwin Jacobs and his wife Joan announced a $120 million endowment, the most significant donation ever awarded a symphony orchestra by an individual. Half of the money will benefit the symphony now, with the second installment to be endowed upon the philantropists' deaths.

The symphony produces several subscription concert series during its primary season from October through May, with performers such as Burt Bacharach, Dave Brubeck, Mark O'Connor, and Yo-Yo Ma. Formats range from the traditional pieces of the Masterworks Series to family-oriented concerts around the holidays and the Light Bulb Series, in which more unusual multimedia pieces are performed. Concerts are also presented at The California Center for the Arts, in Escondido.

The Summer Pops are always an Insiders' favorite, featuring such productions

The San Diego Opera performs in Escondido's Center for Performing Arts as well as downtown San Diego's Civic Theatre. PHOTO: KEN JACQUES, COURTESY OF SAN DIEGO CONVENTION & VISITORS BUREAU

as Beatlemania, Truly Tchaikovsky, and Broadway, Just Off Broadway. The venue for the Pops is at downtown's Navy Pier, at Harbor Drive south of Broadway. Ticket prices for the above events range from $10 for gallery seating to $70 for a champagne table and can be purchased through Ticketmaster at (619) 220-8497 or at the Symphony Hall box office at (619) 235-0804.

San Diego Youth Symphony
Casa del Prado
1650 El Prado, Balboa Park, San Diego
(619) 233-3232
www.sdys.org

Founded in 1945 the San Diego Youth Symphony provides talented young musicians with the experience and discipline necessary for performing at a professional level. Musicians are between the ages of 7 and 25, and the 350 or so members come from all over San Diego County and Baja California.

The Youth Symphony performs in various locations around San Diego, sometimes breaking the ensemble into just strings or just winds. Occasionally the group will join with the San Diego Master Chorale for a special concert. Whatever is on the agenda, these talented youngsters are always a delight to hear. Check the Web site or call (619) 232-3232 for updated schedule information.

Starlight Theatre
2125 Park Blvd., San Diego
(619) 544-7827
www.starlighttheatre.org

This organization has been delighting its patrons for decades with such easy to digest performances as *Hello Dolly*, *Camelot*, and *Seven Brides for Seven Brothers*. All shows are held in the Starlight Bowl Amphitheater in Balboa Park, where you'll see lots of families picnicking on the grassy areas in the park before the show. Once the performance begins, be prepared for one of the quirks peculiar to Starlight Bowl. It's right under the flight path to San Diego International Airport, so every time a plane comes over, performers will freeze the action until the plane has passed and the actors can be heard once again. This happens 30 to 40 times during the performance, and kids especially get a kick out of watching for incoming planes and guessing when the action will freeze.

Ticket prices range from $16.50 to $41.50 and can be ordered by calling (619) 544-7827. Bring a cushion or a blanket to sit on—the hard seats may become uncomfortable. It tends to get somewhat cool in the evening, so be sure to bring a sweater or light jacket, too.

North County Coastal

San Diego Chamber Orchestra
2210 Encinitas Blvd., Ste. M, Encinitas
(760) 753-6402, (888) 848-7326
www.sdco.org

Established in 1984, the San Diego Chamber Orchestra's mission is to provide San Diego with a resident chamber orchestra of impeccable professional talent. The group performs music composed for smaller orchestras of 35 to 40 musicians, and it stages concerts in dozens of venues around the county, including the Museum of Contemporary Art, Fairbanks Ranch Country Club, and the California Center for the Arts, Escondido.

Single ticket prices range from $10 to $70; VIP packages are available that include special seating and perks like champagne. Find out where the Chamber Orchestra is performing by calling (760) 753–6402.

Dance

Central San Diego

City Ballet School & Company
941 Garnet Ave., San Diego
(858) 272–8663
www.cityballet.org

San Diego's City Ballet is a nonprofit corporation that has been producing high quality ballet performances and outreach presentations since 1993. Each August the company offers free performances in the Organ Pavilion in Balboa Park, and, of course, the traditional *Nutcracker* is a must-see at Christmas time. City Ballet tends to stay with the familiar, staging such ballets as Shakespeare's *A Midsummer Night's Dream*. The venues vary as do ticket prices, but most tickets are in the $19 to $29 range.

City Ballet also has a strong educational program that provides training for professional and pre-professional dancers. Its "Discover a Dancer" program provides free ballet training for inner-city children in San Diego.

Malashock Dance & Co.
3103 Falcon Street, Suite J, San Diego
(619) 260–1622
www.malashockdance.org

A small company of dancers is led by its founder, John Malashock, a former principal dancer with Twyla Tharp in New York. The company maintains rehearsal and teaching studios in Balboa Park. Its mission is to advance the art and experience of modern dance through creative self-expression.

Malashock has an active year-round schedule, performing all over San Diego County, including fall performances at Balboa Park's Old Globe Theatre. Call the number above for a current schedule of performances and for ticket information.

Film Festivals

Central San Diego

San Diego-Baja California Latino Film Festival
Mann Hazard Center 7
7510 Hazard Center Dr., San Diego
(619) 291–7777
www.sdlatinofilm.com

This event is presented annually in late February or early March by the Centro Cultural de la Raza. Latino filmmakers, writers, and actors are showcased in a series of short and feature-length films. The goal of the festival is to make the mass audience aware of talented Latinos who are making commercially successful films. Special guests have included noted filmmakers such as Moctezuma Esparza and actors Edward James Olmos and Joe Mantegna. Tickets for each screening are $8.00. Festival passes for from 11 to 100 screenings can be purchased for $70 and include such perks as VIP seating, free event T-shirt, and no waiting in line. These packages can be purchased online or by calling or writing the San Diego Latino Film Festival 2002, c/o Media Arts Center San Diego, 2039 29th St., San Diego, CA 92104, (619) 230–1938. Individual tickets can be purchased at the theater box office on the day of the screening.

San Diego International Film Festival
Price Center Theater, 9500 Gilman Dr. (UCSD campus), La Jolla
(858) 822–3199
www.sdiff.com

After screening films the previous year at Hazard Center, in 2002 this film festival returned to its roots at UCSD, this time at the renovated Price Center Theater, which seats 500 and now can project DVDs and videos as well as 35mm films. This festival gives movie-lovers a chance to see non-commercial live-action and animation features and shorts in many genres, from comedies and kids' movies to documentaries and dramas. Many are foreign films that have not been optioned by U.S. distributors, so they are otherwise unavailable to San Diego audiences. Filmmakers will talk about their films before or after some screenings, most of which will start at 7:00 P.M.; if it's a double feature, the second flick starts at 9:00 P.M. Tickets cost $8.00 for the general public, $5.00 for students with ID, and $80.00 for the series. Although the 2002 festival screened in the first two weeks of April, the schedule varies; call or check the Web site for program information.

San Diego Jewish Film Festival
(858) 362–1348

More than 40 films from nearly a dozen countries—including features, short subjects, and documentaries—are shown in this February festival. Some films examine the Holocaust, but other topics are art, the family, and women's rights; post-film discussions are held after each event. Screenings take place at various venues. In 2002 these were expanded to include two theaters of the Ultrastar chain—the Creekside Plaza 10 in Poway and the La Costa 6 in Carlsbad—in addition to the AMC La Jolla 12 and the Mann Hazard Center Theater in Mission Valley. Admission costs $10; series passes are $90.

Spike & Mike's Classic Festival of Animation
Museum of Contemporary Art
700 Prospect St., La Jolla
(858) 454–0267

Do you picture Porky Pig and Elmer Fudd when you think of animation? Do you associate animation with Saturday morning in front of the television with a bowl of Trix? Then you're in for a treat and an education at this festival. It's a combination of low-tech and high-tech. Some of the films, such as Don Hertzfeldt's *Lily and Jim,* take you back to the early days of animation, when cels were individually drawn by hand. Jan Pinkava's Oscar-

winning *Geri's Game,* on the other hand, utilizes the latest in computer technology. Screenings are held in the evenings, and the festival runs from September through mid-November. Tickets are $7.00 at the box office or $6.50 through Ticketmaster at (619) 220–8497.

Galleries

Central San Diego

The Artists Gallery
7420 Girard Ave., Ste. 200, La Jolla
(858) 459–5844
www.artists-gallery.com

Many exceptionally talented artists call San Diego home, and the Artists Gallery is a favorite showcase. Owner Georgeanna Lipe, La Jolla's most noted watercolorist, offers the work of more than 30 artists in this cheerful and colorful gallery. Original watercolors, oils, mixed media, and sculpture are all available. The gallery is open Tuesday through Saturday from 10:00 A.M. until 5:00 P.M.

Chuck Jones Studio Gallery
2501 San Diego Ave., San Diego
(619) 294–9880
www.chuckjones.com

Animation is the cornerstone of this gallery, which features original work by such legendary artists as Chuck Jones, animator of Warner Brothers characters like Bugs Bunny and Daffy Duck, as well as the art of Dr. Seuss and Walt Disney. Fine art by internationally acclaimed photographers and artists such as Phil Borges and Sid Avery is also displayed. The gallery is open Sunday through Wednesday from 10:00 A.M. to 6:00 P.M., and Thursday through Saturday from 10:00 A.M. to 8:00 P.M.

Cosmopolitan Fine Arts
7932 Girard Ave., La Jolla
(858) 456–9506
www.cosmopolitanart.com

La Jolla boasts many fine galleries, and Cosmopolitan is an Insiders' favorite. The gallery specializes in contemporary French impressionist and post-impressionist paintings by Cortes and his contemporaries. The fabulous plein air work of Dutch artist Cornelius Roos is also featured, as is the Russian Vladmir Pervuninksy, who paints in the rich Moscow style. Hours are Sunday through Thursday from 10:00 A.M. until 5:00 P.M., Friday and Saturday 10:00 A.M. to 6:00 P.M.

Debra Owen Gallery
354 11th St., San Diego
(619) 231–3030

Should you wish to take home a true representation of artwork from the area, Debra Owen Gallery is the place to visit. It is well recognized as a showcase for emerging artists from Mexico and the Californias. Exhibitions change frequently and feature both trained and self-taught artists, and the gallery is especially noted for finding and establishing new talent. Hours are from noon to 5:00 P.M. Thursday through Saturday, and from 10:00 A.M. to 3:00 P.M. on Sunday. The gallery shares the restored ReinCarnation building with Sushi Performance Theater.

Michael J. Wolf Fine Arts
363 Fifth Ave., Ste. 102, San Diego
(619) 702–5388

It's essential to stop in at this wonderful small gallery when visiting the Gaslamp Quarter. Among their most endearing and enduring artists is Josue Castro, whose paintings and sculpture are imbued with the luminous colors of his native Mexico. Although his imagery is contemporary, the artist gets inspiration from cultures such as the Zapotecs of Oaxaca, whose culture was cutting edge in sixth century Mesoamerica. Others in the international cadre of emerging artists include Anne Bachelier of France and Fabio Calvetti of Florence, Italy. The gallery is closed Sunday and Monday.

Scott White Contemporary Art
7661 Girard Ave., Ste. 200, La Jolla
(858) 551–5821

Formerly the Soma Gallery, this upscale La Jolla gallery offers contemporary painting, sculpture, and photography by such internationally recognized artists as William Glen Crooks, James Renner, and Carol Hepper. Special exhibitions are ongoing, with opening receptions the first night of each exhibition. Hours are from 9:00 A.M. to 5:00 P.M. Tuesday through Saturday.

Spanish Village Art Center
1770 Village Pl., Balboa Park, San Diego
(619) 233–9050
www.spanishvillage.com

Spanish Village is a unique, concentrated collection of 41 studio/galleries that display the work of local artists. Many of the artists are on site, creating their work as you watch.

You'll find artwork in a variety of media, including oil, watercolor, ceramics, sculpture, jewelry, woodcarving, glass, photography, and enamel. There's no admission to Spanish Village, and it's open every day from 11:00 A.M. to 4:00 P.M.

Stephen Clayton Galleries
1201 1st St., Ste. 111, Coronado
(619) 435–6474

Lithographs by contemporary artists such as Red Skelton and Boulanger are the

Insiders' Tip

La Jolla-based Art Tours offers interesting albeit expensive ($179 per person) oil painting expeditions to some of San Diego's most scenic locations, including Coronado, La Jolla, Balboa Park, Torrey Pines, and Mission Bay. All supplies, instruction, and a picnic lunch are provided during the five-hour outing. For details contact the company at (888) 459-5922 or www.arttoursinc.com.

specialties at this gallery. You'll find both lithographs and original art by Hessam and lithos and serigraphs by children's author Dr. Seuss. In addition to lithographs, you'll find a nice selection of modern sculpture. Hours are Sunday through Thursday 10:00 A.M. to 7:00 P.M., Friday and Saturday 10:00 A.M. to 9:00 P.M.

North County Coastal

Art & Accents
312 S. Cedros Ave., Solana Beach
(858) 755–0062

To say that this gallery has wonderful pieces of art and the perfect accents for your abode is an understatement. You could be like us and find you really can't get a certain bronze sculpture or ceramic piece off your mind. You'll be tempted here by work from nationally recognized artists and local ones too. Choose from Venetian glass, paintings, and fine Italian ceramics such as Vietre, Cottura, and Mamma Ro. The store is open daily from 10:00 A.M. to 5:00 P.M. and is in the center of the Cedros Shopping District. (See our Shopping chapter for more on this area.)

Enchanted Gallery
2650 Via De La Valle, #230, Del Mar
(858) 792–6704

This truly is an enchanted gallery featuring the fine art of jewelry designers and acclaimed artists. You'll be treated to extraordinary sculptures and paintings. In addition, the store offers mineral and crystal specimens for sale. The gallery is open Monday through Saturday 10:00 A.M. to 7:00 P.M. and Sunday noon to 5:00 P.M.

North County Inland

Archives of Escondido, Inc.
431 N. Escondido Blvd., Escondido
(760) 747–8973

Maintaining some of the same inventory as the previous owners of J&J Gallery and Framing, this gallery has paintings, prints, lithos, etchings, serigraphs, posters, and sculpture, specializing in traditional media and subject matter and selling mainly local artists. Home and business design services

are available. The gallery is open Tuesday through Friday from 9:00 A.M. to 5:00 P.M. and Saturday 10:00 A.M. to 5:00 P.M.

Escondido Municipal Gallery
142 W. Grand Ave., Escondido
(760) 480–4101

The shows at this intimate gallery change focus often so it's worth stopping in to browse when you're in the neighborhood. At a recent exhibit there was an all-media exhibition of two- and three-dimensional art by local artists. Each show has a different theme. The gallery is open Tuesdays through Saturdays, 11:00 P.M. to 4:00 P.M.

Poway Center for the Performing Arts
1598 Espola Rd., Poway
(858) 748–0505

The gallery at the Center exhibits the work of new and established artists. A recent exhibit included the inaugural show of the North County Printmakers of San Diego. The gallery is open Monday through Friday 9:00 A.M. to 4:00 P.M. and Saturdays 11:00 A.M. to 3:00 P.M.

East County

Art World–Western Heritage Gallery
1266 Broadway St., El Cajon
(619) 440–1041, (800) 269–8081
www.4westernart.com

According to Insiders who love Western or wildlife art, this is the primary gallery in Southern California. Many people travel from Los Angeles to visit it. More than 50 artists are represented here, including Bev Doolittle, G. Harvey, Mark Martensen, Frank McCarthy, and many more. The store also carries numbered and fine-art prints and limited editions. The gallery is open Monday through Friday from 10:00 A.M. until 6:00 P.M., and Saturday from 10:00 A.M. until 4:00 P.M.

Julian Fine Art and Photography Shows
Julian Town Hall,
Main and Washington Sts., Julian
(760) 765–1857

If you love art and want some fun, too, be sure to see the various fine art and photography shows you'll find in Julian. Call the number above for information on the usually-free shows held at Julian's Town Hall (and be sure to read our Annual Events and Shopping chapters for more about Julian). Many artists, ceramists, weavers, and photographers live in the area. Some have shows from time to time but you can often see their work at various local shops and stores.

El Cajon Art Association
1246 E. Main St., Ste. 113, El Cajon
(619) 588–8875

More than 200 East County artists belong to and show at this cooperative art gallery. Although the media are nearly always two-dimensional, there's a wide range of styles and themes to be found in the 11 exhibits shown each year. The gallery has three juried shows per year and offers life drawing and watercolor classes. It's open Wednesday through Saturday 11:00 A.M. to 4:00 P.M.

South Bay

Frame Gallery
305 3rd Ave., Chula Vista
(619) 422–1700

If you're a seeker of collectibles, this is the place for you. It would be hard to find a larger assortment of collectible figurines anywhere else in the county. If Snow Babies get you going, they're here in abundance. So are Disney figurines and tons of plates. The gallery also has several autographed prints of sports figures and Hollywood celebrities. A complete framing service is offered, too. Hours are from 10:00 A.M. to 5:30 P.M., Monday through Friday, and from 10:00 A.M. to 5:00 P.M. on Saturday.

Museums

For a more comprehensive list of museums, see the Balboa Park chapter.

Central San Diego

Mingei International Museum of Folk Art
1439 El Prado, Balboa Park, San Diego
(619) 239–0003
www.mingei.org

The word "Mingei" is used transculturally for "art of the people." Thus, traditional and contemporary folk art, craft and design representing the many cultures of the world are the focus at the Mingei Museum. You'll see exhibits such as "Dolls—Mirrors of Humanity," which showcases more than 200 objects, including an 18th-century dollhouse and a parade of dolls in vehicles of all kinds. All permanent and changing exhibits portray the essential arts that are satisfying to the human soul.

In the planning stages is a new North County satellite on Grand Avenue in Escondido, just down the street from the California Center for the Arts. The new facility will have a multimedia education center as well as a 5,000-square-foot exhibition gallery for displaying some of the museum's 12,000-piece collection. The museum is open Tuesday through Sunday from 10:00 A.M. to 4:00 P.M. Admission is $5.00 for adults and $2.00 for students and children 6 to 17. Admission is free for children younger than 6.

Museum of Contemporary Art
700 Prospect St., La Jolla
(858) 454–3541
1001 Kettner Blvd., San Diego
(619) 234–1001
www.mcasd.org

Insiders' Tip

A great introduction to the San Diego art scene is the yearly Open Studios Tour, held each September. Self-guided tours allow lookie-loos and prospective buyers access to the studios of more than 50 artists. Call the Convention and Visitor's Bureau at (619) 232-3101 for details.

Both locations of this museum have a long-established reputation for thought-provoking exhibitions as well as highly regarded permanent collections, both can truly be labeled "cutting edge." For those who want to understand contemporary art, docent tours are free. Among the most interesting of recent exhibits are the 2002 retrospective of Wolfgang Laib's installations at the MCA La Jolla, in which the artist evokes a spiritual consideration of nature using organic objects of simple beauty such as beeswax, milk, pollen, and rice. Also at the La Jolla MCA, the Edwards Sculpture Garden and surrounding area have been improved with pieces from the collection that have been awaiting exhibition space, including works by Niki de Saint Phalle, Judith Shea, and Roman de Salvo. Temporary sculptures and installations can be found there as well.

Lectures and commentaries are frequently scheduled, too. Both locations are closed Wednesdays. The downtown museum is free and open year-round Thursday through Tuesday from 11:00 A.M. to 5:00 P.M. The La Jolla museum is open Friday through Tuesday 11:00 A.M. to 5:00 P.M., Thursday from 11:00 A.M. to 8:00 P.M. During the summer it's open weekdays (except Wednesday) until 8:00 P.M. Admission there costs $4.00. Both locations have worthwhile gift and book shops and offer many lectures, films, and community events.

Museum of Photographic Arts
1649 El Prado, Balboa Park, San Diego
(619) 238–7559

Photography is one of the more intriguing art forms, and the Museum of Photographic Arts consistently displays stunning examples of the work of some of the finest international photographers. In addition to its permanent collection, changing exhibitions highlight the museum's dedication to displaying outstanding photography. MoPA puts on approximately six shows a year.

A recent exhibition was *Double Vision: Photographs from the Strauss Collection.* In this show, works by 71 artists from the collection of Ted and Joyce Strauss were assembled, juxtaposing traditional black-and-white photographs

such as those of Man Ray and hand-colored images by Hans Bellmer with postmodernist works by artists such as Cindy Sherman. After a one-year expansion and remodel, the museum reopened in March 2000. Renovations include additional gallery space, a print-viewing room and 25,000-volume library, and the 238-seat Joan & Irwin Jacobs Theater, where art films are screened regularly. The museum is open Monday through Sunday 10:00 A.M. to 5:00 P.M.; Thursday until 9:00 P.M. Films are generally shown Tuesday, Wednesday, and Friday evenings, but double-check current show times. Admission is $6.00 for adults and $4.00 for seniors, students, and military.

San Diego Museum of Art
1450 El Prado, Balboa Park, San Diego
(619) 232–7931
www.sdmart.org

This venerable museum has a respectable permanent collection consisting of Italian Renaissance, Spanish Old Masters, American art, 19th-century European paintings, and 20th-century paintings and sculpture. There's also a gallery dedicated to California Art.

It's the traveling exhibitions that draw the big crowds, though, and recent years have seen the Jewels of the Romanov visit the museum, as well as a huge collection of Fabergé eggs. Another memorable show was *Monet: Late Paintings of Giverny from the Museé Marmatton,* an exhibit of 22 paintings by the famous French impressionist.

Hours are from 10:00 A.M. to 6:00 P.M. Tuesday through Sunday and Thursday 10:00 A.M. to 9:00 P.M. Admission prices are $8.00 for adults; $6.00 for seniors, young adults 18 to 24, and military; and $3.00 for children 6 to 17. Children 5 and younger are admitted free.

Timken Museum of Art
1500 El Prado, Balboa Park, San Diego
(619) 239–5548

Known locally as San Diego's "jewel box for the arts," the Timken Museum is devoted to its select collection of European and American masterworks, which includes a small sampling of beautiful Russian icons. The Putnam Collection

San Diegans find art wherever they look, even at the airport. PHOTO: COURTESY OF THE PORT OF SAN DIEGO

within the museum spans five centuries of art, from the early Renaissance through the 19th century. You'll see the works of artists such as Veronese, Bruegel, Cezanne, Clouet, Rembrandt, and Reubens.

American artists are well represented, too, including Bierstadt, Copley, Heade, and others. This is an outstanding small museum that's known nationwide for its critically acclaimed, tasteful, and well-lit setting for viewing its collection. The hours are from 10:00 A.M. to 4:30 P.M. Tuesday through Saturday, and from 1:30 to 4:30 P.M. on Sunday. Admission is free.

North County Coastal

Carlsbad Children's Museum
300 Carlsbad Village Dr.,
Ste. 103, Carlsbad
(760) 720–0737
www.museumforchildren.org
Found in the Village Faire Shopping Centre, this museum has interactive exhibits and also exhibits of art by children and children's artists as well as activities for kids 2 through 12.

During the traditional school year the hours of operation are limited, so call ahead. In the summer the museum is open daily between 10:00 A.M. and 5:00 P.M. There's a $4.00 admission fee for adults and children 2 and older.

Oceanside Museum of Art
704 Pier View Way, Oceanside
(760) 721–2787
Located in the historic Gill Building, which was the old Oceanside city hall in the '20s, the museum features local and international art. Its rotating exhibits include pottery, sculpture, paintings in watercolor and oil, and mixed media installations that sometimes include the work of local weavers. The museum is open Tuesday through Sunday 10:00 A.M. through 4:00 P.M.; Sunday noon to 4:00 P.M. Admission is $3.00 for adults and $2.00 for children, seniors, and military.

North County Inland

The Visual Arts at the California Center for the Arts
340 N. Escondido Blvd., Escondido
(760) 839–4120
www.artcenter.org

An always changing group of exhibits are on display here. Recently there was an exhibition of 20th-century still-life paintings from the Phillips Collection with work by artists Pablo Picasso, Georges Braque, Stuart Davis, and Georgia O'Keeffe.

With your ticket to a performance at the Center, you can visit the museum for free. Otherwise, ticket prices are $5.00 for adults and $3.00 for children 12 and older and students with identification. It's open Tuesday through Saturday 10:00 A.M. to 5:00 P.M. and Sunday noon to 5:00 P.M. It's free the first Wednesday of every month.

Performance Venues

Art Film Houses

Central San Diego
Hillcrest Cinemas
3965 Fifth Ave., San Diego
(619) 299–2100

This five-theater complex tucked away in the Village Hillcrest Shopping Center shows first-run foreign films and independent American films. The theaters are on the small side, lending a cozy atmosphere to the experience, but the amenities are modern and first-rate.

Ken Cinema
4061 Adams Ave., San Diego
(619) 283–5909

Old-style theaters are rapidly falling by the wayside since the tidal wave of multiplex cinemas began taking their place. The Ken remains, however, and manages to hang on and to draw crowds to its retrospectives and special showings. For instance, the theater has shown a retrospective of Kurosawa films, a series of Humphrey Bogart thrillers, Monty Python collections, and all the Godfather movies. A recent hit was the "Sing-a-Long Sound of Music," in which theater-goers were encouraged to join in singing with Maria the governess and the Family Van Trapp. Classics are favored here, and there's always something interesting or provocative showing.

North County Coastal
La Paloma
471 S. Coast Hwy. 101, Encinitas
(760) 436–7469

Inaugurated in 1928 as a silent movie house with a wonderful organ, La Paloma is now the place for watching art films and viewing wild, weird, or funny classics. Don't expect high brow stuff at this beach-town film house; most of the films are on the contemporary side of classic. For instance, if you must see the 1960s surf classic *Endless Summer* on the big screen once again, La Paloma is the place. La Paloma also hosts various community events and programs.

Cultural Centers

Central San Diego
Centro Cultural de la Raza
2004 Park Blvd., Balboa Park, San Diego
(619) 235–6135
www.centroraza.com

Murals that cover the exterior walls of this institute of Mexican, Chicano, and indigenous arts and culture depict the historical and mythological roots and traditions of these cultures. Both traditional and experimental forms of visual and performing arts are presented in the classroom/workshop space, including film screenings, literary presentations, and numerous workshops, such as African drumming, video production, and still photography. Admission is free, but donations are gratefully accepted.

San Diego Concourse Convention and Performing Arts Center
Third Ave. and B St., San Diego
(619) 570–1100

This is a grand title for what actually is pretty much restricted to the Civic Theatre. Although the Concourse gets heavy use by conventions and trade shows, the performing arts are intelligently confined to the theater, which has the acoustics and the ambiance the Concourse does not. From January through May, the Civic Theatre is the exclusive home to the San Diego Opera. But once the opera season is over, watch out! Everything from *Beauty and the Beast* to *The Fully Monty* and *Jesus Christ Superstar* has made an appearance at this gracious and graceful theater. If there's a popular Broadway production to be seen, chances are good that it will show up at the Civic Theatre.

As the holidays approach, you can take it to the bank that a traveling performance of *The Nutcracker* will turn up, and this is where you'll find the rare ballet that comes to town. The theater holds just under 3,000 people, but the seats in the upper regions virtually demand binoculars. So if you have your heart set on seeing a special concert or show, get your tickets early. Tickets can be purchased at the box office at the Concourse or by calling Ticketmaster at (619) 220-8497.

Simon Edison Centre for the Performing Arts
Old Globe Theatre, Cassius Carter Centre
Stage, Lowell Davies Festival Theatre, Located
behind the Museum of Man in Balboa Park
(619) 239-2255

Insiders' Tip

Art museums in Balboa Park offer free admission one day every month. The Museum of Photographic Arts offers free entry on the second Tuesday. Visits to the San Diego Museum of Art and Mingei International Folk Art Museum are free on the third Tuesday. Admission is always free at the Timken Museum of Art.

Beautifully situated in Balboa Park, this complex consists of three theaters, including the Tony Award–winning Old Globe Theatre. The other two are the 225-seat Cassius Carter Centre Stage, which is a theater-in-the-round, and the 625-seat Lowell Davies Festival Theatre, an outdoor venue used between July and October.

The three theaters stage performances ranging from the traditional Shakespearean classics to world premieres such as *Getting and Spending* and *Paramour*. Christmastime always brings something to please the young ones, like *How the Grinch Stole Christmas*. Ticket prices range from $20 to $50 and can be purchased at the box office or by calling (619) 239-2255.

Spruce Street Forum
301 Spruce St., San Diego
(619) 295-0301
www.sprucestreetforum.com

Grants and individual donations support this gallery and performance venue. Gallery hours are Friday and Saturday 1:00 to 6:00 P.M., and the exhibits cover the gamut of artistic expression. Musical performances also vary widely, from classical music to experimental and jazz and beyond. Most of the concerts are inexpensive, and the gallery exhibits are free.

North County Coastal

Oceanside Museum of Art
704 Pier View Way, Oceanside
(760) 721-2787

Located in the old Oceanside city hall, the museum sponsors dance and musical performances, including chamber music concerts. Admission prices vary. At a recent performance of the Alouette Trio, an evening of works by women composers of the Romantic Era such as Clara Schumann and Rebecca Clarke, admission was $10 per person. Performances are usually held in the afternoon. The museum itself is open from 10:00 A.M. to 4:00 P.M. Tuesday through Sunday.

The Old Globe Theatre in Balboa Park, modeled after the original in London, has presented everything from Molière to Mamet, from Electra to Damn Yankees. PHOTO: COURTESY OF SAN DIEGO CONVENTION AND VISITORS BUREAU

North County Inland

California Center for the Arts
340 N. Escondido Blvd., Escondido
(760) 738–4138, (800) 988–4253
www.artcenter.org

Will it be *Cats, The Music Man, Oklahoma, The Nutcracker,* or Shirley Bassey, The Los Angeles Guitar Quartet, or a taping of Michael Feldman's *What Do You Know?* The performances at the California Center for the Arts run the gamut from serious to knee-tapping fun. The world-class arts center is located on a 12-acre campus and includes fine educational programs. Designed by the late renowned architect Charles Moore, it includes a 1,538-seat concert hall, a 408-seat theater, and a full-service conference center. In December 2001, philanthropist Edna Sahm pledged $663,000 dollars to the center, bringing its total endowment to nearly $1 million.

The theater brings troupes from around the globe to the inland community and brings Insiders and visitors from around Southern California to enjoy the varied programs. There are musical theater and Broadway shows, classical productions, dance, and music from around the world, holiday programs, jazz and big band shows, and family theater. (See our Kidstuff chapter.) Prices vary from about $10 to $70. Call or check the Web site for current programs.

Poway Center for the Performing Arts
1598 Espola Rd., Poway
(858) 748–0505
www.powayarts.org

This cultural center provides live stage and musical performances for Insiders and visitors. Programs are varied and include plays you can attend with children, chamber music, Broadway-style reviews, and even performances by the San Diego Opera and the New Shanghai Circus, with its dramatic and elegant acrobats. This center seats 800 people, but it's a popular venue, so be sure to make reservations early for popular programs. Call for a schedule of upcoming events. Ticket prices depend on the performance and seating location.

Theaters

Central San Diego

Horton Grand Theatre
444 Fourth Ave., San Diego
(619) 234-9583

Located in the heart of the Gaslamp Quarter, this small theater continuously presents crowd-pleasing plays that more often than not are held over. It's a fairly small theater but is comfortable and elegant. A case in point is *Triple Espresso: A Highly Caffeinated Comedy*, which was brought back by popular demand and has been running, although not consecutively, since 1998. The theater is within a few blocks of all the Gaslamp's restaurants and clubs, so a performance can easily be combined with dinner and after-theater entertainment.

La Jolla Playhouse
La Jolla Village Dr. at Torrey Pines Rd., La Jolla
(858) 550-1010
www.lajollaplayhouse.com

This distinguished theater, founded by actors Gregory Peck, Dorothy McGuire, and Mel Ferrer, is constantly on the cutting edge of world premier plays and musicals that have a habit of finding their way to Broadway. Several Tony Award–winning plays have debuted here, including Roger Miller's *Big River* and The Who's rock opera *Tommy*. Classics are never ignored at the La Jolla Playhouse, however, and recent seasons have included such venerable plays as the Pulitzer Prize–winning *Our Town* and Michael

Ondaatje's *The Collected Works of Billy the Kid*. For the detailed history of the La Jolla Playhouse, be sure to read the Close-up in this chapter.

Lamb's Players Theatre
1142 Orange Ave., Coronado
(619) 437-0600
www.lambsplayers.org

The history of the Lamb's Players Theatre is one of extremes. It started out in a Quonset hut in the East County and now occupies a historic theater in Coronado. Along the way it has grown into San Diego's third-largest theater organization, behind the Old Globe Theatre and the La Jolla Playhouse. Its resident acting company stages performances year-round, including plays like *A Man For All Seasons, The Survivor*, and *Godspell*. Beginning in the 2002 season, the playhouse is hosting Singles Night Out, a venue for singles to meet others who share their passion for plays at an after-performance appetizer buffet at the Costa Azul Restaurant.

Mystery Cafe
Imperial House Restaurant
505 Kalmia St., San Diego
(619) 544-1600
www.mysterycafe.net

Insiders' Tip

A wonderful venue for concerts and other performances is the grounds of the historic San Luis Rey Mission. Receptions are sometimes held before or after a performance. See our Attractions chapter for more information on the mission, and call (760) 757-3651 for a schedule of performances.

La Jolla Playhouse

This is a story of three Hollywood actors who were at the peak of fame and fortune in their film careers, but still longed for the purity of the stage. Gregory Peck, Dorothy McGuire, and Mel Ferrer had dreams of opening a playhouse to bring live theater to California, where it was sadly lacking, and much to the good fortune of San Diego, they chose La Jolla.

Peck had grown up in San Diego and attended local schools. So it was only natural that he would return to his roots. With the financial support of David Salznick and a solid core of local theater-lovers, the La Jolla Playhouse opened its first season in 1947 in the auditorium of La Jolla High School. The first production starred Dame May Whitty in *Night Must Fall,* a play in which she had been triumphant in both London and Hollywood. It was a great success and quelled all doubts about the threesome's venture. The future of the La Jolla Playhouse looked bright.

Peck himself performed in three plays at the La Jolla Playhouse during the next few years. Ferrer acted in three, as well, and McGuire in six, among them Tennessee Williams' *Summer and Smoke* and Oscar Wilde's *The Importance of Being Earnest*. In 1997 a new production of that same play opened the 50th anniversary season of the La Jolla Playhouse, and Peck and Ferrer were in the audience.

The early days of the Playhouse were filled with remarkable performances by notable actors including Jennifer Jones, Groucho Marx, Charlton Heston, and David

Neil Patrick Harris (left) and Christian Mena (right) sing in the West Coast premiere of Rent *at the La Jolla Playhouse.*

PHOTO: JOHN JOHNSON

Niven. La Jolla quickly became a playground for the stars, and after each opening night the three founders could be found carousing with the likes of Desi Arnaz and Lucille Ball in the Whaling Bar at the La Valencia Hotel.

The Playhouse occupied La Jolla High School's auditorium for 18 seasons. Production ceased after the 1964 season for a number of reasons, the biggest being economic. It would take 19 years before the Playhouse presented another play; however, the dream of a La Jolla Playhouse never died. As early as 1954 local supporters were raising funds for the construction of a new theater, but that feat wasn't accomplished until 1982, when construction was completed on the current La Jolla Playhouse. Supporters were able to enlist the aid of UCSD's Dr. Roger Revelle, and as a result, the new Playhouse found a home in the Mandell Weiss Theatre on the campus of the university, where it remains today.

Under artistic director Des McAnuff, the La Jolla Playhouse reopened in 1983 with Peter Sellars' production of *The Visions of Simone Machard,* which was later distinguished by the *Village Voice* as one of the 10 best regional theater productions of the 1980s. But it was the 1984 production of *Big River* that started the real buzz about the Playhouse. With its score by Roger Miller, *Big River* went on to Broadway and won seven Tony awards.

This was just the beginning of a tradition of Broadway-bound productions making their debut at San Diego's homegrown theater. *A Walk in the Woods* followed a few years later and quickly made its way to Broadway. So did Frank Galati's adaptation of *The Grapes of Wrath*.

But the real test of McAnuff's genius came in 1993, when playgoers gathered on a summer evening in July, anxiously awaiting the debut of The Who's groundbreaking rock opera *Tommy*. It was wildly successful among both the traditional playgoers and rock fans. Naturally it went on to Broadway, and the next year *Tommy* won five Tonys, including one for McAnuff. But those weren't the only Tonys San Diego felt pride in that year. During that same award ceremony the Playhouse received the Tony given annually to an outstanding regional theater.

That same year McAnuff stepped aside and passed the torch to Michael Greif, whose 1997 production of *Rent* garnered a Tony nomination for Best Director. After less than a half-decade of experimenting with theater in other venues, McAnuff returned to the Playhouse, much to the delight of longtime fans.

But it's more than just a charismatic and innovative director that endears the Playhouse to its patrons. Education and outreach programs help inspire future actors, directors, and even playgoers. Every summer kids in second through ninth grade study acting, movement, improv, and stage combat with professional actors in the Young Performers program. High school students can participate in even more demanding five-week courses. Internships are offered each year in disciplines from costume development and wardrobe to electrical technician and production. The "Pop Tour" brings theater to schools and libaries in communities where many people may have not experienced, or regularly experienced, live theater.

It has been 50 years since three actors with a germ of an idea started the La Jolla Playhouse. And each year, San Diegans take more and more pride in the quality of productions at the Playhouse. The 2002 season included four world premieres—with contributions from José Rivera, Heather McDonald, Geoff Hoyle, and Charles L. Mee—and a new production of Molière's clever classic, *Tartuffe*. The combination of classics, popular musicals and plays, and groundbreaking productions has put the little theater on the national theatrical map.

Serious patrons of the arts might sniff haughtily at the idea of dinner theater, but sometimes ya just gotta do it. And the Mystery Cafe at the Imperial House is one of the best. Audience participation is not only encouraged, it's expected, and plenty of laughs are guaranteed.

The long-running *Murder at the Café Noir* entertained guests with its hilarious blend of mystery and red herrings; another performance, *The Catskills Conspiracy*, is billed as "*Dirty Dancing* meets *Dragnet*." Along with the performance, a four-course meal is served.

San Diego Repertory Theatre
79 Horton Plaza, San Diego
(619) 544–1000
www.sandiegorep.com

Two subterranean theaters house the San Diego Repertory Theatre, the 550-seat Lyceum Stage, and the 270-seat Lyceum Space. The season runs from autumn through spring, and the performances are eclectic: musicals, dramas, and comedies. Many are fairly well known, and Shakespeare makes at least one appearance each year, although often with modern staging. The Rep stages a two-week run of *A Christmas Carol* every December, presenting a different version each year. Community-based festivals include February's Kuumba festival, showcasing local African-American performers, and in June, The Lipinsky Family San Diego Jewish Arts Festival, with concerts and plays by international Jewish artists.

Sushi Performance Gallery
320 11th Ave., San Diego
(619) 235–8468
www.sushiart.org

Since 1980 Sushi has gained national acclaim as an adventurous alternative performance art space. Whoopi Goldberg got her start here, and feminist performance artists Karen Finley and Holly Hughes have appeared too. Most evenings you can just show up and be assured of getting a ticket, and the dress is always casual. Sushi's performances require an open mind; most are edgy and thought provoking.

Theatre in Old Town
4040 Twiggs St., San Diego
(619) 688–2494
www.theatreinoldtown.com

An indoor, amphitheater-style house, the Theatre in Old Town presents familiar, favorite plays and often musicals. Outside shaped like a huge barn, the venue is actually intimate, with just 250 seats wrapping around the thrust stage, ensuring easy viewing for all. Whether it's *Forever Plaid, Beehive,* or another show, this theater is worth a visit. The atmosphere is relaxed and casual, and all of Old Town is right outside the door.

North County Coastal
North Coast Repertory Theatre
987D Lomas Santa Fe Dr., Solana Beach
(858) 481–1055
www.northcoastrep.org

You might see a drama, comedy noir, or, as often is the case, classics like *Auntie Mame, Fiddler on the Roof,* and *Our Town* in this 194-seat theater. The theater is intimate, elegant, and comfortable, and you can come as casually dressed or as gussied-up as you choose. Thursday through Saturday performances start at 8:00 P.M. On Sundays there are shows at 2:00 and 7:00 P.M. Call or check the Web site to see about "off-night" performances such as those presented recently by the UCSD Gospel Choir.

North County Inland

Avo Playhouse
303 E. Vista Way, Vista
(760) 726–1340 X1523 (information)
(760) 724–2110 (for tickets)

The 382-seat Avo Playhouse was recently renovated and now proudly supports the live-theater addicts of our communities. It is the winter-season home of the Moonlight Amphitheater, mentioned below. It's also an important North County venue for youth and community productions. You can get a schedule by calling the ticket number above.

Moonlight Amphitheater
1200 Vale Terrace Dr., Vista
(760) 724–2110

An outdoor theater in North County Inland, the Moonlight Amphitheater produces musicals, comedies, and dramas that you can watch under the stars. Nearing its 30th anniversary, the theater has recently produced *The Music Man, The King and I, How to Succeed in Business Without Really Trying,* and *Grease.* There is some seating, but if you plan to sit on the grass, bring low lawn chairs only or blankets and pillows. Lots of Insiders bring picnic suppers or, if they're coming from work, fast food. Call for an upcoming schedule and to get on the mailing list.

Patio Playhouse Community Theater
201 E. Grand Ave., Escondido
(760) 746–6669
www.patioplayhouse.com

The Playhouse is a not-for-profit, volunteer organization presenting a range of live performances in comedy, drama, mystery, and musicals. There are seven different shows presented each year and three youth theater shows. For the kids in the family, there are plays such as *Puss & Boots* and for adults such entertainment as Frank D. Gilroy's drama *The Subject Was Roses.* Call or check the Web site for a schedule of events and ticket prices.

Welk Resort Center
8860 Lawrence Welk Dr., Escondido
(760) 749–3448, (888) 802–7469

In our Spas and Resorts chapter we covered the relaxing things you can do at the Welk Resort Center, but there's a whole lot more than spa-ing and golfing here. The Welk Resort's production team offers such classic shows as *Showboat, Carousel, Guys and Dolls,* and *Singing in the Rain* as well as mystery dinner theater and Broadway-style dinner theater. Each week there are about five matinees and three evening performances, and both are available with lunch or dinner buffet or for the performance only. Prices range from $30 to $45.

East County

Christian Community Theater
1545 Pioneer Way, El Cajon
(619) 588–0206, (800) 696–1929
www.cctyt.org

The theater presents productions that the entire family will enjoy and often there are children's classics on the live theater "menu." The Christmas programs are especially popular and many Insiders make attending them a family tradition.

East County Performing Arts Center
210 E. Main St., El Cajon
(619) 440–0395
www.ecpac.com

Built in the 1970s by the city of El Cajon and the Grossmont-Cuyamaca Community College District, the 1,142-seat theater

---

Insiders' Tip

Each spring, the San Diego Museum of Art presents *Art Alive,* a fabulous show in which artists and gardeners interpret paintings and sculpture from the museum's collection using flowers, ferns, moss, and anything green or growing.

Artistic inspiration comes easily with spectacular scenes like the San Diego de Alcalá mission.

PHOTO: CECE CANTON

continually lost money until acquired by the Arts Center Foundation in 1997. Since then the concert and performance venue has been revamped, with a new state-of-the-art sound system, stage curtain and carpeting, and heating and air-conditioning systems. Recent programs have included the musical review *Tommy Tune,* a concert by the Boston Chamber Music Society, and a performance of Celtic music in celebration of Saint Patrick's Day. Seats in all price sections are wheelchair accessible.

South Bay

Onstage Playhouse
Park Village Theatre, 291 Third Ave., Chula Vista
(619) 422–7787
onstage.itgo.com

If you like to get up close to the stage and see every little thing that's going on, try one of Onstage Productions' fine plays. The theater is intimate—only 60 seats— and sitting so close to the stage, you could almost believe you're part of the play. The quality of the plays is excellent. Recent productions include Neil Simon's *Barefoot in the Park* and William Inge's *Bus Stop.* Call or check the Web site for the current schedule and ticket reservations.

> ## Insiders' Tip
>
> At the foot of the San Diego-Coronado Bay Bridge, at the intersection of National Avenue and Crosby Street on the San Diego side, is Chicano Park. Within the park, Chicano artists have painted the abutments of the bridge with murals representing their history and social concerns. The result is an internationally acclaimed public art project.

Parks

Central San Diego

North County
    Coastal

North County Inland

East County

South Bay

In this chapter you'll find parks where you can have lunch, fly kites, take a walk, discover a nature center, or have a wonderful family outing. As in other chapters of the book, we've divided the material into regions and then listed those entries alphabetically. Of course our list isn't exhaustive; if you're looking for a neighborhood park, check the Yellow Pages of the phone book for a complete listing of parks in your region. If you want to visit a beach park, check out the sites listed in our Beaches and Watersports chapter.

Although we mention some wilderness areas in this chapter, you'll want to see our Recreation chapter if you want to know about other ones and the serious hiking, biking, climbing, and other rugged activities that happen in them. Further camping possibilities are listed there too.

Besides the smaller parks listed here, where people can jog after work or picnic at lunchtime, we've included some national forests and large regional parks and preserves too, and we've sometimes narrowed in on certain areas within them. Cleveland National Forest, for instance, takes up a major section of the East County, and offers some superb places to picnic, camp, walk, and hang out. Since Cleveland National Forest is huge, we haven't just said, "Head east, friends." Instead we've done some of the scouting for you and selected parks within the area that are special, such as Palomar Mountain State Park and Cuyamaca Rancho State Park.

But large or small, all the parks here offer outdoor fun for adults and are just right for families too. If you're visiting with children, though, remember safety precautions. It makes sense to watch small fry when they're playing at the tot lots and running through campgrounds and picnic areas. Whether you're hiking alone or with another person, it's wise not to roam into unfamiliar and isolated areas after dark. Pets, on 8-foot leashes and with a responsible owner, are normally welcome in county parks, but not in all city parks. They must be attended at all times, and it might be smart to call to find out if Fido is welcome. Or you can check the signs you'll see posted at most park entrances.

We've included special information to make your park visits more enjoyable. For example at Blue Sky Ecological Reserve you might see vultures and foxes, but you won't find drinking fountains. You'll need to bring your own water. At Laguna Mountain Recreation Area, you can reserve a place for some thrilling nightlife—if you're into stargazing. Star parties are held during the summer months. When there are specific hours of operation or if the park has unusual restrictions, we've noted that.

Laws against picking wild flowers, removing plants, and tampering with archaeological artifacts or the animal and natural features from state, county, and city parks are strictly enforced.

Some parks let you reserve picnic areas for parties and reunions. For some camping areas, the reserved list is long. It's always sound advice (in our popular county) to make park reservations well in advance of the date you plan to visit. See the Close-up in this chapter for phone numbers of major camping locations and the individual parks for more details.

Wait no more. Pack a lunch; grab a hat. Now let's head out and explore San Diego's parks.

Phone Numbers for Major Camping Locations

San Diego County Parks:
(858) 694–3049; (877) 565–3600 for reservations; www.co.san-diego.ca.us/parks

California State Parks:
(858) 642–4200 information; (800) 444–7275 for reservations;
cal-parks.ca.gov

National Park Service:
(619) 557–5450 information; (800) 365–2267 for reservations; www.nps.gov

U.S.D.A. Forest Service:
(858) 673–6180 Cleveland National Park; (877) 444–6777 National Forest Recreation Reservations; www.fs.fed.us

Central San Diego

Kate O. Sessions Memorial Park
5115 Soledad Rd. and Loring St. in Pacific Beach, San Diego
(858) 581–9927

Named for famed horticulturist Kate Sessions, this 79-acre park is a tranquil spot overlooking Mission Bay. During summer months it's an ideal location for picnicking, especially for those who want to avoid the traffic and congestion of the beach areas but still want to take advantage of those ocean breezes (which, by the way, make this a favorite spot for kite-flying).

For those who crave a hike, a 2-mile trail, lined with coastal sage scrub and other native plants and trees, winds its way through the park and up and down a canyon. If you prefer something less challenging, there's also a paved walking path—perfect for walking off that big picnic lunch. This is a well-equipped park with plenty of picnic tables, barbecues, playgrounds for the kids, and rest rooms.

Marian Bear Memorial Park
Accessible from either Regents Rd. or Genesee Ave., south off Calif. Hwy. 52, San Diego
(858) 581–9952
www.sannet.gov/park-and-recreation/parks/marbear2.shtml

One of the nicest things about San Diego is that it has maintained so much open space within its urban areas. Marian Bear Park is a 466-acre expanse of woodland and trails that runs the length of San Clemente Canyon. You'll feel like you've left the city far behind as you make your way through the dense live oak trees, sycamores, willows, and tons of native grasses and shrubs.

Hikers will enjoy the 7 miles of trails, and mountain bikers are welcome to use the park's maintenance roads. You'll often see mountain bikers practicing their moves here. This is a peaceful spot for a picnic, and there are lots of picnic tables to accommodate you.

Miramar Reservoir
10710 Scripps Lake Dr. off Scripps Ranch Blvd., San Diego
(619) 668–2050
www.sannet.gov/water/recreation/Miramar.shtml

Do you like to just get out and walk? So do many Insiders, and Lake Miramar is one of the most popular places for walkers, joggers, and skaters. The distance around the perimeter is just under 5 miles, which makes for a perfect workout, whether you're strolling, running, or on wheels. Plus, the hiking trails around the lake provide the opportunity to feast your eyes on lots of native vegetation and waterfowl.

The lake is a good spot for game fishing, too, and you're likely to reel in rainbow trout, largemouth bass, sunfish, and channel catfish.

Plenty of picnic areas are available, as are concession stands and rest rooms. The lake closes for 30 to 60 days each fall, generally in October.

Mission Bay Park
2688 E. Mission Bay Dr. (visitor center), San Diego
(619) 221–8901

As this is technically classified an aquatic park, we'll cover Mission Bay Park more thoroughly in our Beaches and Watersports chapter. But we also mention it here because it offers more than just watersports.

What was once a stretch of mud and marshlands began its transformation into Mission Bay Park in 1960. At 4,600 acres, it's the largest facility of its kind the world created by dredging, filling, and landscaping. The park and picnic areas are used for volleyball, softball, kite flying, and horseshoes. The 27 miles of bayfront and 17 miles of oceanfront beaches are probably the county's most popular place for bicycling, skating, jogging, or just strolling along and people watching.

Facilities are extensive and varied—boat rentals, docks and launches, beaches, picnic tables, fire rings, rest rooms, and play-

grounds for the kids all make the park perfect for whatever recreation you have in mind. Even if you plan no more than a snooze on the grass while listening to the seagulls and the water lapping on the shore, you can't go wrong with Mission Bay Park.

Mission Trails Regional Park
1 Father Junipero Serra Trail, San Diego
(619) 668–3275

Imagine this: 5,820 acres of open space with nearly 50 miles of hiking and biking trails—right in the middle of San Diego. Add to it the highest point within the city of San Diego, Cowles Mountain (read about what a great hike this is in our Recreation chapter), and stone outcroppings for rock climbers. Mission Trails Regional Park even has its own lake—Lake Murray—and it's open year-round for fishing on Wednesdays and weekends.

An impressive Visitor and Interpretive Center provides all the sights and sounds to be found within the park with videos, photography, and interactive exhibits that describe the geology, history, plants, and animals found in the park. The best spot for picnicking within the park is around Lake Murray, and the paved trail around the lake is ideal for jogging and walking.

Presidio Park
Taylor St. and Presidio Dr., San Diego
(619) 692–4918

This is the site of Father Junipero Serra's first mission in California, and it's where San Diego was born. Although the mission was moved to a new location a few years after it was built, a museum now stands on top of the hill where it once stood. Surrounding the museum is a beautiful, tree-filled park with gently sloping grassy hills.

The museum itself is worthy of a visit; it's a visual history lesson of the beginnings of San Diego. But if you're just looking for recreation and a picnic, this is a fantastic spot that's easy to get to and close to everything. Plenty of picnic areas are available, and pitch-and-putt golf course is within the park for those looking to work on their short game. A newly refurbished rec center offers indoor basketball, volleyball courts, and a gym.

Tecolote Canyon Natural Park
Tecolote Rd. off I-5, San Diego
(858) 581-9952
www.sannet.gov/park-and-recreation/parks/
tec/te1.shtml

For the explorer, this is one of the best parks in town to while away the hours, absorbing the quietness, and observing native plant and animal life. Hiking trails meander back and forth across Tecolote Creek in this 970-acre park, and you'll wander through wooded glades of willows, live oaks, and sycamores.

Tecolote has a nature center (open only sporadically) featuring exhibits on canyon ecology, natural history, and Native Americans. The nature center also offers lectures and guided walks through the park. This park isn't set up for picnicking, but if you bring your lunch along with a blanket to spread out, the undeveloped atmosphere can't be beat. Sturdy shoes or hiking boots are recommended.

North County Coastal

Guajome County Park
3000 Guajome Lakes Rd.,
Oceanside
(858) 565-3600, (877) 565-3600 (toll-free in
San Diego County)

To find this 599-acre park, exit Interstate 5 on Mission Avenue in Oceanside and drive about 7 miles east. Nature trails ramble for miles through the lush wilderness here. There are equestrian trails too. The marsh area is popular with serious bird watchers and the lakeshore is a well-liked fishing spot. You'll find camping available in 35 RV sites (with showers for campers). There are plenty of picnic and barbecue areas along with a play area and convenient rest rooms. Near the parking lot is an information kiosk that has brochures about the area. Nature tours and walks are held periodically; call for times and dates.

San Elijo Lagoon Ecological Reserve
2710 Manchester Ave., Encinitas
(858) 565-3600, (760) 436-3944
www.sanelijo.org

> ## Insiders' Tip
>
> Love the outdoors? Want to make new friends? The County of San Diego Department of Parks and Recreation is eager for reliable volunteers to run programs and become docents. Call (858) 694-3049 for more information.

There are nearly 300 different species of birds that can be seen at this North County Coastal reserve. One Insider recently spotted egrets, blue herons, coots, and an array of ducks. This is one of the county's best-preserved wetlands. The 900-acre reserve has more than 5 miles of walking trails that wind through chaparral and marshes. Depending on the season, you'll see ferns and wildflowers.

Docent-led nature walks are held every second Saturday of the month at no cost. The walks begin at 9:00 A.M. Call for starting points and routes.

Torrey Pines State Reserve
N. Torrey Pines Rd.,
1 mile south of Carmel Valley Rd., San Diego
(858) 755-2063
www.torreypine.org

This is the sanctuary for the Torrey pine, one of the rarest plants in the United States. On the 2,000-acre reserve you could count more than 4,000 of these once-endangered trees, but it's far more fun to visit the indigenous plant garden surrounding the interpretive center and wildlife museum. In the spring and early summer, you'll find native wildflowers mixed among the sage and chaparral-loving plants. Nature walks are held on weekends and holidays at 10:00 A.M. and 2:00 P.M.

The reserve is open daily from 8:00 A.M. to sunset. Dogs are not allowed and picnicking and trail bike riding are prohibited.

Families picnic in beautiful, beachside parks. PHOTO: DALE FROST, COURTESY OF PORT OF SAN DIEGO

North County Inland

Blue Sky Ecological Reserve
Espola Rd., .5 mile north of Lake Poway Rd.,
Poway
(858) 679–5469

A wonderful addition to the "outback" parks in the county, Blue Sky Ecological Reserve has 700-acres of wilderness. There's a mixture of chaparral, riparian woodland, and coastal sage scrub that gives off a wonderful aroma when warmed by the San Diego sun. The area is home to coyote, deer, foxes, and snakes of many varieties. For the bird watcher, of special note might be gnatcatchers, vultures, and hawks.

In this reserve and other parks be sure to walk on the trails and sit on benches rather than rocks and fallen logs. This is snake country and rattlers, while not aggressive, are dangerous when surprised.

Drinking water isn't available at the park, which is open during daytime hours. Bikes, horses, and vehicles are prohibited in the reserve. Near the parking lot is an information kiosk with a display of native plants and animals. Guided nature walks are offered on weekends at 9:00 A.M.; call for information and reservations.

Lake Hodges
20102 Lake Dr. off Via Rancho Pkwy.,
Escondido
(619) 668–2050
www.lakehodges.net

The 1,234-acre shoreline park on Lake Hodges is a popular place for walking, boating, bike riding, and picnicking. While not for the small-sized people in your family, Insiders recommend the 15-mile trail for the long-distance walking family. The trail passes through open grassland to marshlands, making it a wonderful place to see birds and other wildlife. According to those Insiders who love to fish, the lake is teaming with largemouth bass, crappie, and catfish. Motorboat and rowboat rentals are available and there's a sailboat launch if you bring your own. Swimming isn't allowed in the lake.

The area is open March through October on Friday, Saturday, and Sunday from sunrise to sunset.

Lake Poway Recreation Area
Lake Poway Rd, off Espola Rd., Poway
(858) 679-4343

Lake Poway is a 35-acre recreational area that's popular in this youthful community. There is a 60-acre reservoir for boating and fishing, and it's stocked with trout in the fall and winter and catfish in the summer. Nonmotorized boats are available for rental Wednesday through Sunday year-round (no private boats are allowed). There are two playgrounds for the younger set. There are picnic areas, a nature trail, and a concession stand that's open year-round. The eight campsites have running water and rest rooms; there is no vehicular access, and campers must hike about a mile to the campsite.

Los Penasquitos Canyon Preserve
Black Mountain Rd., west from I-15,
Rancho Penasquitos
(858) 538-8066
www.penasquitos.org

The reserve is about 3,700 acres and you'll find woodlands, scrub oak, and chaparral. There are walking trails, but bikes are allowed only on the service roads. Depending on the season, some of the trails may be closed; the preserve is open from 8:00 A.M. to sunset daily.

Within the park are remnants of San Diego County's first Mexican *rancho*. The adobe structures, built between 1825 and 1862, can be toured Saturdays at 11:00 A.M. and Sundays at 1:00 P.M. They are located at the end of Canyonside Park Driveway, off Black Mountain Road. Call (858) 484-7504 for more information

Palomar Mountain State Park
19552 State Park Rd., Palomar Mountain
(760) 742-3462, (800) 444-7275 for camping reservations
www.palomar.statepark.org

As you reach the fork in S-7, one way leads to Palomar Mountain State Park and the other takes you to the national forest and the observatory. The sign is clear but the choice may be hard. This picnic, walking, and camping area is popular year-round, but nicest in spring and fall. In winter, the snow brings San Diegans in droves. Be sure to bring chains during the winter if you head toward Palomar Mountain for some fun in the snow. You may not be allowed to drive up to the top without them.

At the park you'll find some rambling walking trails. The Doane Valley Nature trail is about a 3-easy-mile walk; most of it is on flat ground. The hike to the observatory, according to the self-guided trail markers, is about 4 miles with some climbing. Therefore, this isn't the right trail for tiny people in your family, but kids older than 10 will probably love the challenge. Request a trail brochure from the ranger station staff as you drive into the park.

For those who love to picnic, you'll find eating areas and camping spots with barbecues. Many Insiders picnic on Thanksgiving and Christmas, and the outings have become family traditions. There are also developed campsites. Speaking of picnics and camping, become "bee" wary. The bees and yellow jackets (a hungry, hazardous wasp) can be a serious fun-deterrent during the late summer and fall when they swarm around campgrounds and picnic areas. They can be frightening and dangerous for small children and the family pooch. Be alert for swarms and bring along insect repellent.

The observatory and visitor center at the end of County Road S-6, are open from 9:00 A.M. to 4:00 P.M. daily throughout the year. The park is open from dawn to dusk. (Find out more about them in

---

Insiders' Tip
Frequent visitors to San Diego's regional parks can purchase a parking pass. Good for any park or recreational area with a $2.00 parking fee, the $25.00 pass lasts a year from date of purchase and can be transferred from one vehicle to another.

San Diegans enjoy a great day in the sun at Mission Bay Park. PHOTO: COURTESY OF SAN DIEGO CONVENTION AND VISITORS BUREAU

our chapter on Attractions.) There's a small gift shop that's open daily and an adjacent bakery and vegetarian restaurant.

East County

Anza-Borrego Desert State Park
Borrego Springs
(760) 767–4684 (for an events message),
(760) 767–5311 (to speak with a park volunteer)
www.anzaborrego.statepark.org

There are more than 600,000 acres of desert within this State Park for camping, picnicking, walking, biking, and hiking. Here you'll see plants from the silver cholla and jumping cholla (a prickly cactus that will earn your respect if you mess with it) to the agave (or century plant) and indigo bush (with its cobalt blue flowers). There's wildlife too, from big jackrabbits to bigger coyotes—and four species of rattlesnakes.

It's a paradise for naturalists of all ages. See our Attractions chapter for details about the wildflowers which bloom here in late winter or early spring and turn the desert into a breathtaking burst of exotica. If you're bringing kids with you, get each one a "disposable" camera and let them snap their favorite flowers. When the photos are developed, see if they can identify the flowers and plants in their snapshots.

At the park, you'll find 110 miles of trails (remember to take water—carry some with you and leave more in your car). Borrego Palm Canyon has 117 developed campsites, five group sites, and a hiking trail that leads to an oasis of palms and shaded pools that's always unexpected even if you've hiked the park 20 times. Tamarisk Grove has 25 developed campsites. Call the park and ask to have the latest newsletter sent or scout out books on the park at bookstores and libraries. The more you read about the region, the more you'll understand why it's important to respect the delicate ecosystem of our deserts.

If you're adventurous, there are primitive campsites here and there throughout the park that are given out on a first-come, first-served basis.; backcountry camping is allowed by permit. Remember, you'll need to pack in your water and pack out the trash. The equestrian camp has 10 sites and a corral. The visitor center, located 1 mile west of Borrego Springs on West Palm Canyon Drive is a great place to begin your visit. Watch a slide show, visit the labeled cacti and succulent garden, and get a map of the park. It's open from 9:00 A.M. to 5:00 P.M. October through May; weekends and holidays June through September. There's a $5.00 day use fee.

Cuyamaca Rancho State Park
Calif. Hwy. 79 between Hwy. 78 and I-8,
eastern San Diego County
(760) 765-0755, (800) 444-7275 (camping reservations)
www.cuyamaca.statepark.org

This is a state park that's worth visiting again and again, whether you come for a short walk or plan to disappear for a while in the wilderness. Horses, mountain bikers, and hikers share more than 100 miles of paved and unpaved roads; trails are for humans only. The wilderness area covers 25,000 acres in East County including heavenly wildflower meadows, Green Valley Falls, and the ruins of a gold mine, the Stonewall mine. There are two developed campgrounds with 166 units, group campsites, and cabins. Equestrian campsites accommodate both groups and families.

Lake Cuyamaca is popular for fishing, boating, and bird watching. Playing on the shore is allowed, but swimming isn't. Motorboats, paddleboats, and rowboats are rented throughout the year. During the summer, canoes and kayaks are available. Call (760) 765-0515 for rental information and reservation. The park has a museum too, displaying Native American artifacts; it's open 10:00 A.M. to 4:00 P.M., with extended hours in summer. Call for park hours.

Laguna Mountain Recreation Area
County Rte. S-1, 6 miles northeast of Pine Valley
(619) 445-6235 (for information),
(619) 473-8547 (for the information center)

Located within the Cleveland National Park, you'll find 8,600 acres of recreation area with more than 70 miles of trails. Included is part of the Pacific Crest Trail, where every turn presents Kodak opportunities.

The visitor center has information on safety, hiking, and campfire programs along with the summertime star-gazing parties. The center is open Friday 1:00 to 5:00 P.M. and weekends from 10:00 A.M. until 5:00 P.M. (weekends only in winter). There are several hundred developed camping sites, some open year-round, others only during the summer months.

Insiders' Tip

Mountain lions (a.k.a. cougars) are found in some San Diego wilderness areas. There you should avoid hiking alone, especially at dawn and dusk, when the big cats tend to hunt. If you see a cougar stalking you: MAKE EYE CONTACT; act large and menacing, raising your arms and yelling; pick up small children but avoid crouching. Don't let the lion get behind you.

Lake Morena County Park
Lake Morena Dr., off Calif. Hwy. 94,
or Buckman Springs Rd., off I-8, near Campo
(858) 694-3049

Part of the Cleveland National Forest, which stretches through San Diego County and into Orange County, Lake Morena is a lakefront park that covers about 3,250 acres. The terrain is rocky foothills with scrub oak and chaparral. Here you'll find part of the Pacific Crest Trail that excites hikers of skill. You'll also find easy walking trails for young kids.

If you're into camping, this is a choice park. There are 86 developed campsites, 58 with RV hookups, and 2 campsites for disabled campers. There are scores of picnic areas. Due to low water levels, the primitive campsites at the northern end of the park are closed indefinitely.

If you're into fishing, call the "fish report hotline" at (619) 478-5473 for the latest report. Fishing is popular here, and bass, bluegill, catfish, crappie, and stocked trout crowd the lake—at least that's what we've heard from those who love the sport.

Enjoy a hike to see the varied habitats around San Diego. PHOTO: BOB YARBROUGH, COURTESY OF SAN DIEGO CONVENTION AND VISITORS BUREAU

There's a rowboat launch and motor and rowboats are available for rent. The park is open daily from just before sunrise to just after sunset.

Santee Lakes Regional Park
9040 Carlton Oaks Dr., Santee
(619) 596–3141
www.santeelakes.com

Popular Santee Lakes Regional Park offers a profusion of picnicking, jogging, lounging, boating, and fishing opportunities around a chain of seven lakes. There's a developed campground with 172 sites with RV hookups, a general store, a swimming pool, and rec center along with a laundry room. To add to the fun there are horseshoe pits, volleyball courts, and a large playground. Kids will immediately take to the places to fly kites, throw a softball, and enjoy the San Diego weather. Dogs are not permitted in the day use area. A wheelchair-accessible fishing pier and a children's playground are currently being developed around Lake #4.

South Bay

Sweetwater Summit Park
Summit Meadow Rd. off San Miguel Rd., Bonita
(858) 694–3049
www.co.san-diego.ca.us/parks

If your idea of the perfect day at the park includes hiking or horseback riding, Sweetwater may be the place for you. Its 580 acres of open space and trails include more than 36 miles of hiking and equestrian trails that run along the Sweetwater River and the southern shore of the Sweetwater Reservoir. If that's not enough, a 4-mile paved bicycle and equestrian trail runs from the western end of the park to San Diego Bay.

Sixty developed campsites are in the park (see our chapter on Recreation for more camping information), and picnic sites are available. Sweetwater is a wilderness park that is dedicated to preserving the area's riparian habitat and grasslands.

Tijuana River National Estuary Research Reserve
301 Caspian Way, Imperial Beach
(619) 575-3613

A bird watcher's delight, this 2,500-acre salt marsh reserve boasts more than 300 species of migratory birds. See them for yourself as you wander along 4 miles of trails that cross the reserve. There's a visitor center that has exhibits on local ecology and the species of birds you're likely to see. The center also offers guided nature walks on weekends.

Winter is the best time to see migratory waterfowl; in springtime acres and acres of chaparral-covered hillsides are blanketed with colorful wildflowers, putting on a display that only Mother Nature could create. The visitor center is open daily.

Insiders' Tip

If you're a bird watcher, don't miss the Kendall-Frost Marsh Reserve in Mission Bay Park. More than 100 species of waterfowl can be seen. The Reserve is at the north end of Crown Point Drive, between Lamont and Olney Streets.

Recreation

Looking for something to do? You won't have to look far—San Diego is famous for its abundance of recreational activities, both indoor and outdoor. The perception that locals and visitors spend much of their time in pursuit of recreation is no myth. From bicycling to bowling to hang gliding to inline skating, the opportunities are almost endless. So numerous, in fact, that we've devoted entire chapters to watersports and golf. In this chapter we'll cover everything else and give you enough information to get you started on your favorite sport.

We'll tell you where the nicest bike paths are, and where to find the county's best hiking and walking trails. If being airborne appeals to you, we'll direct you to places where you can hook up with a hot-air balloon or a hang glider. And we promise to keep earthbound enthusiasts busy but safely anchored.

Part of the appeal of San Diego is that you can combine relaxation with fresh air, exercise and a ton of fun. We encourage you to try something new while you're in town. Rent a pair of inline skates and glide around Mission Beach. Once you have the hang of it and can direct your attention elsewhere, you'll discover that this is one of the best sports in the world for people watching. Or join an impromptu game of volleyball at the beach or in any of the county's many parks.

A couple of good sources for organized (and usually free) hikes, walks, bicycle tours, and many other activities are Thursday's "Night and Day" section of the *San Diego Union-Tribune* and the *San Diego Reader*. The *Reader* also comes out on Thursdays and is distributed free at record stores, bookstores, drug stores, and many other businesses throughout the county. They both have comprehensive listings of things to do around town. Whatever you decide to do, keep in mind that safety precautions aren't just for kids. Use common sense and heed the advice of professionals. And even when the temperature is mild, don't forget your sunscreen.

Ballooning
Bicycling/Mountain Biking
Billiards
Bowling
Camping
Climbing
Hang Gliding
Hiking
Horseback Riding
Ice Skating
Laser Tag
Martial Arts
Paintball
Racquetball
Skating/Skateboarding
Tennis
Volleyball
Walking

Ballooning

Ever since the movie *Around the World in 80 Days* focused attention on ballooning as a mode of transportation, the fascination for those brightly colored, soaring globes has held steady. If you'd like to quietly glide through the sky above San Diego, several balloon companies are eager to make your dream come true.

California Dreamin' Balloon Adventures
2153 Woodland Heights Glen, Escondido
(800) 373-3359
www.californiadreamin.com

Soar high above the earth on a sunrise ride over the wine country in Temecula or a sunset ride over Del Mar. Riders receive a photo and certificate at the conclusion of the ride. The sunrise ride is $128 per person and includes a continental break-

Several North County companies offer ballooning adventures. PHOTO: REED KAESTNER, COURTESY OF SAN DIEGO CONVENTION & VISITORS BUREAU

fast and champagne mimosa; the sunset ride ($138 per person Monday through Friday, $148 per person Saturday and Sunday) includes champagne.

Skysurfer Balloon Co.
1221 Camino del Mar, Del Mar
(858) 481–6800, (800) 660–6809

Sunrise balloon rides in Temosa's wine country include a picnic breakfast upon landing. Sunset coastal excursions in Del Mar offer on-board champagne. Rates are $135 per person Monday through Friday, and $145 per person on Saturdays and Sundays.

Bicycling/Mountain Biking

Whatever your pleasure—gentle, flat surfaces or more challenging hills and terrain—you'll find it somewhere around town. Designated bike paths are clearly marked on many San Diego streets, and great off-road trails are located throughout the county. One of the best street rides is along the coast, from Mission Beach north to La Jolla. It hugs the shoreline for most of the way, but when it does veer inland for a block or two, you'll be treated to a peek at some magnificent homes. For mountain bikers, the Iron Mountain trail in East County is a moderately difficult favorite. Trailheads are located on California Highway 67 at Poway Road and Calif. 67 at Ellie Lane.

Bicycles can be rented at several locations; we've listed a few below, along with Gravity Activated Sports, a company that guides thrilling organized tours. Rental rates vary, but you usually can rent a cruiser for $6.00 per hour. Full-day rates range from $20 to $38. Mountain-bike rentals are usually a few dollars more. Most bike shops provide maps that highlight street bike paths and off-road trails all over the county, or you can pick up a map at the Caltrans office at 2829 Juan Street, San Diego, (619) 688–6699. Remember, bicycle helmets are recommended for all and required by law for children younger than 18.

Bike 101
211 N. Highway 101, Solana Beach
(858) 793–5431

Bike 101 specializes in mountain bikes that can be ridden either off-road or on the street. Rentals are available by the hour or by the day.

Bikes and Beyond
1201 First St., Coronado
(619) 435–7180

Beach cruisers and mountain bikes can be rented by the hour, half-day, or full day. The shop is located in the Ferry Landing Marketplace. A wide variety of cycles is available for adults and kids.

Bike Tour San Diego
509 Fifth Ave., San Diego
(619) 238–2444

This shop specializes in hybrid bikes (a cross between a road bike and a mountain bike) and mountain bikes. Also available for rent are hard-to-find mountain bikes with front suspension. Free pick-up and delivery are offered, and all bike rentals come with roadside assistance, locks, helmets, and maps.

Gravity Activated Sports
16220 Calif. Hwy. 76, Pauma Valley
(760) 742–2294, (800) 985–4427

GAS is famous for the "Palomar Plunge" a 16-mile, 5,000-foot guided bicycle descent that includes a tour of the Palomar Observatory, bike and equipment rental, lunch, T-shirt, photo, and certificate of achievement. The cost is $80 per person. Also ask about their cycling wine country tours, the desert descent, and off-road tours.

Mission Beach Club
704 Ventura Pl., San Diego
(858) 488–5050

A fixture in Mission Beach for decades as Hamel's, Mission Beach Club still rents a full range of bicycles and mountain bikes for the whole family. Its turreted, castle-like building is located right across from Belmont Amusement Park in Mission Beach.

Mission Bay is the perfect place for a leisurely family bike ride. PHOTO: BRETT SHOAF, COURTESY OF SAN DIEGO CONVENTION & VISITORS BUREAU

Bicycle Clubs

For organized cycling adventures, we suggest you contact one of the following clubs:

North County Cycle Club
P.O. Box 127, San Marcos, CA 92069
(760) 471-2239
Three groups make up the membership of NCCC: The Cruisers, who are laid back and like to enjoy the scenery while they ride; The Roadies, who are fast, intermediate to advanced riders who like to pick up the pace a little; and The Spokey Dokes, who are the mountain bikers of the group. All three sections schedule regular rides.

San Diego Bicycle Club
P.O. Box 80562, San Diego, CA 92138
(858) 495-2454
www.sdbc.org
This is the oldest bicycle club in San Diego and has members of all ages. Its focus is on racing, and members are trained by experienced cyclists that have both racing and coaching backgrounds. The club organizes several races throughout the year.

San Diego Bicycle Touring Society
P.O. Box 1941, Chula Vista, CA 91912
(619) 332-6215
Geared mostly for the bicyclist who likes distance, this club offers some challenging rides. Members schedule weekly Tuesday evening and weekend rides that take place in locations all over the county.

Billiards

The game of billiards has been enjoying a resurgence in recent years, a fact borne out by the increasing number of billiards parlors in San Diego. Plus, you can usually find a table or two in many bars around the county. But for pure, uninterrupted billiards, we recommend you visit one of the facilities devoted primarily to the game.

Joltin' Joes
717 N. Escondido Blvd., Escondido
(760) 743-7665

With a full sports bar, grill, and 26 pool tables, you can't go wrong here. Rates range from $6.00 per hour for daytime hours during the week to $10.00 per hour for weekend nights.

Pacific Q Billiards Club
1454 Encinitas Blvd., Encinitas
(760) 943-9929
www.pacificq.com

Play pool on 13 gorgeous tables for $4.50 per player, per hour, up until 7:00 P.M., Sunday through Thursday. After 7:00 P.M., the price is $4.50 per player, per hour, and $6.50 on Friday and Saturday. Domino's Pizza delivers from next door, and the bar itself serves very basic pub grub, as well as more than 70 brands of beer.

Society Billiard Cafe
1051 Garnet Ave., San Diego
(858) 272-7665

In addition to 15 regulation pool tables, Society Billiard Cafe has a bar that serves cocktails, beer, and wine from around the world. Pizza, salads, and sandwiches can be enjoyed at the on-site restaurant, which also has patio dining. Rates range

Insiders' Tip

The Bible of the San Diego outdoor enthusiast is Jerry Schad's *Afoot & Afield in San Diego County*. Providing incisive information about nearly every inch of the county, Schad describes trail length/difficulty, terrain, suitability for kids, dogs, mountain bikers, etc. Further insight can be found in the outdoorsman's weekly column in the *San Diego Reader*.

from $5.00 per hour during the day to $12.00 per hour on weekend nights.

Bowling

One sport that never goes out of style is bowling. San Diego has several bowling alleys where you can enjoy a leisurely game or two, or if league play is more to your taste, all alleys provide that, too. Prices vary considerably from facility to facility and depend on the day of the week and the time of day. You can bowl a lane for as little as $2.00 or as much as $8.00 per person, per hour. Most facilities have discounts for seniors and kids, and some offer special events with music, disc jockeys, and laser lights on weekends. Be sure to call in advance to find out prices and lane availability.

AMF Eagle Bowl
945 W. San Marcos Blvd., San Marcos
(760) 744-7000

Forty lanes with automatic scoring make AMF Eagle Bowl a modern, up-to-date facility. If you're looking for something a little different, try Extreme bowling on Friday and Saturday nights (9:30 and 8:00 P.M., respectively; $4.50 per person or $22.00 per lane, up to 6 people). Classic rock 'n' roll plays, the house lights go off, and the black lights go on while pins and balls go all glowy and weird. You'll find a snack bar, lounge, and pro shop on the premises.

Brunswick Premier Lanes
845 Lazo Ct., Chula Vista
(619) 421-4801

Brunswick Premier has 48 lanes, a pro shop, a cocktail lounge, a snack bar, and a Pizza Hut Express. This is a busy facility, so reservations are highly recommended (weekdays only; on weekends it's first come, first served). There are bowling leagues for kids and seniors, too.

Kearny Mesa Bowl
7585 Clairemont Mesa Blvd., San Diego
(858) 279-1501

Forty lanes provide ample opportunity for bowling on even the most crowded days. A sports bar with satellite television is a popular hangout, as is the snack bar and video arcade. The fully stocked pro shop has everything you'll need in the way of equipment.

Mira Mesa Lanes
8210 Mira Mesa Blvd., San Diego
(858) 578–0500

Mira Mesa Lanes is a relatively new bowling facility with 44 modern lanes and an automatic color scoring system. On the premises is everything you'll need to make your bowling day a complete experience: a sports bar, snack bar, well-stocked pro shop and video arcade. On Fun Fridays ($14 per person) from 10:00 P.M. to 1:00 A.M., a DJ spins records and colored lights create a disco effect.

Parkway Bowl
1280 Fletcher Pkwy., El Cajon
(619) 448–4111

Parkway Bowl has long been a family entertainment center in East County. Its 54 lanes include 28 that are equipped with bumpers just for kids—which means no gutter balls. All lanes have automatic scoring, and the facility has a pro shop, bar, and snack bar. Prices here are reasonable, and the lanes stay open on Friday and Saturday until 3:00 A.M. On Monday through Friday from 8:30 A.M. to 6:00 P.M., adults pay just $2.00 per person.

Surf Bowl
1401 S. Coast Hwy., Oceanside
(760) 722–1371

If bowling by the sea appeals to you, the Surf Bowl is the place. With 32 lanes, a snack bar, and lounge, you'll find everything you need for an enjoyable afternoon or evening at the lanes. The on-site pro shop is fully stocked for all your equipment needs, too. Try to arrive about an hour before the 10:00 P.M. start of Extreme Bowling ($12 per person) on Fridays and Saturdays to grab a lane.

Camping

Is your idea of camping truly roughing it with just a tent and few essentials? Or do you prefer a more upscale form of camping, say, in an RV or a park that has all the luxuries of home? Whatever your heart's desire, San Diego has the perfect campsite for you.

We have listed private and government campgrounds pertaining to the county or within state parks and national forests, all with as many or as few amenities as necessary to satisfy the adventurer in you. Here we give you a sampling of some of the area's best and most popular campgrounds. You may want to check some of the camping sites described in our Parks chapter, too. But if you want an in-depth listing of the dozens of sites throughout the county, contact the county's parks and recreation department at (858) 694-3049, www.co.san-diego.ca.us, or the state's parks and recreation department at (800) 444-7275. Or look for camping guides and books at your local library or bookstore, especially those listed as "Insiders' Tips" on these pages. Most but not all campgrounds accept advance reservations and dogs. Rates change frequently, so be sure to check for current prices.

Agua Caliente County Park
39555 County Rte. S2
(877) 565–3600 (reservations),
(858) 694–3049 (information)

Heaven in the desert is the best way to describe Agua Caliente. Two naturally fed mineral pools are the main attractions here. One is a large outdoor pool kept at its natural 96 degrees; the other is indoors, heated, and boasting Jacuzzi jets. The 140 campsites accommodate tents or RVs with full or partial hook-ups. In addition to miles of hiking trails, there are a children's play area, horseshoe pits, and shuffleboard courts to amuse kids and adults. Campsites rent for $14–$18 per night, and reservations can be made 12 weeks in advance. Closed between Memorial Day and Labor Day.

Campland on the Bay
2211 Pacific Beach Dr., San Diego
(858) 581–4260, (800) 422–9386
www.campland.com

Every campsite at Campland comes with a beach, a bay, and a rollicking good time.

Spending time on or near the water is a popular San Diego pastime. PHOTO: DALE FROST, COURTESY OF PORT OF SAN DIEGO

Right on the shores of Mission Bay, this private campground has nearly 600 spaces; almost all have fire rings. Tent sites offer water and electricity (summer rates $53 midweek; $67 on weekends); 420 RV sites have full hookups (pay according to location and season: $57 to $110). Campers can enjoy a wide range of equipment and activities, including two Jacuzzis and heated pools, showers, picnic tables, a large playground, a recreation room, and tons of water activities; bikes and rollerblades can also be rented. A full-time rec director organizes Ping-Pong tournaments, bingo, line dancing lessons, etc. Primitive sites ($30 to $40 weekends) open only when the rest of the camp is full. At the other end of the spectrum is the Supersite ($160 to $185), a private site overlooking the bay with a Jacuzzi, washer and dryer, telephone, landscaping and lawn furniture, gas grill, and cable TV. Reservations are accepted up to two years in advance.

Laguna Campground (Cleveland National Forest)
3 miles northwest of Mount Laguna, off County Rd. S1
(619) 445–6235 (for information),
(877) 444–6777
www.reserveUSA.com (for reservations)

Camping in the Laguna Mountains is back-to-nature with just the basics, but a more beautiful and peaceful spot would be hard to find. The federally owned Laguna campsite has 103 tent and RV sites. There are no hookups, but there's a sanitary dump station about 4 miles away at Buckman Springs. You will find running water, primitive toilets, barbecues, fire rings, and picnic tables, as well as access to the Laguna Rim and a portion of the 2,627-mile Pacific Crest Trail, which stretches between the borders of Canada and Mexico. Rates are $14 per night. Open year-round.

From North County, take Highway 78 east through Ramona toward Julian; turn right (east) at a stop sign after 4 blocks and turn right on Highway 79; follow to the junction with S1 (Sunrise Highway); turn left. It's about 5 miles to the campground. Heading east on I-8, take the Sunrise High-way (S1) exit; the entrance is about 3 miles north of the Laguna store and post office.

South Carlsbad State Beach
5 miles south of Carlsbad, via County Rd. S21
(760) 438–3143 (information)
(800) 444–7275 (reservations)
www.reserveamerica.com

This is a rare campsite set on the beaches of Carlsbad and perfect for those who wish to combine camping with water sports. Surfing, fishing, or simply swimming are all right at your feet here.

The site includes coin-op laundry, convenience store, showers, rest rooms, fire rings, and picnic tables. The campground has 220 tent or RV sites (no hookups), all $12 per night. Reservations can be made up to seven months in advance.

Sweetwater Summit
Off Summit Meadow Rd., Bonita
(858) 565–3600

Sixty campsites accommodate tents, RVs, and horse trailers. Several sites have horse corrals, and all have water and electricity. Horse trails galore are the main attraction here. Other amenities include rest rooms, showers, barbecues, picnic tables, and a large group area.

As with all county parks, reservations are accepted up to 12 weeks in advance. Rates are $16; for horses, add $2.00 to the fee. To get to the campground take Bonita

Insiders' Tip
Are you an amateur photographer? Capture some of San Diego's most beautiful images at Mission Trails Regional Park. The dramatic stone outcroppings are captivating subjects for shutterbugs.

Road east until it becomes San Miguel Road. Turn left on Summit Meadow.

Climbing

Indoors or outdoors, rock climbing is quickly becoming the sport of choice for many locals and visitors alike. Indoor facilities are available for climbing, lessons, and equipment purchase or rental. For outdoor climbing, we highly recommend you take advantage of an organized climb, especially if you're a newcomer to the sport or unfamiliar with the area. Outdoor climbing areas are abundant throughout San Diego County, but you can't go wrong with the recommendations and guidance of professionals.

Adventure 16 Outdoor and Travel Outfitters
4620 Alvarado Canyon Rd., San Diego
(619) 283–2374
www.adventure16.com

The travel experts at Adventure 16 specialize in group climbs all over the county. This is also a great place to get top-notch instruction in the art of rock climbing. Outdoor clothing, gear, and boots are available for purchase or for rent.

REI Recreational Equipment
5556 Copley Dr., San Diego
(858) 279–4400
www.rei.com

In addition to offering clothing, gear, and boots for purchase or rental, REI has a small indoor climbing wall for enthusiasts to get a quick (and free) taste of what rock climbing is like. It's open, however, Friday evenings and Saturday mornings only.

Solid Rock
2074 Hancock St., San Diego
13026 Stowe Dr., Poway
992 Rancheros Rd., San Marcos
(619) 299–1124
www.solidrockgym.com

This indoor climbing facility has three locations, all offering 30-foot, seamless, textured climbing walls and a multitude of apparatus for practicing techniques such as bouldering, top-roping, and lead climbing.

Hours are Monday through Friday 9:00 A.M. to 9:00 P.M., Saturday and Sunday, 11:00 A.M. to 7:00 P.M. Day passes can be purchased for $10.00, Monday through Friday before 5:00 P.M. After 5:00 P.M. and on weekends, a day pass is $4.00. Children 16 and younger are always charged $10, $12 on weekends. Lessons are available but are not required of inexperienced climbers.

Vertical Hold Climbing Center
9580 Distribution Ave., San Diego
(858) 586–7572
www.verticalhold.com

This center has an indoor 17,000-square-foot climbing wall and welcomes beginners to advanced climbers. Beginning climbers are required to take instruction. Hours are from 11:30 A.M. to 9:00 P.M. Monday through Friday, 10:00 A.M. to 10:00 P.M. Saturday and 10:00 A.M. to 8:00 P.M. Sunday. Day passes are $12.

Insiders' Tip
If you plan to test your skills at one of San Diego's indoor climbing facilities, morning hours are the least crowded time. By early afternoon, there may be more climbers around you than you want to contend with.

Hang Gliding

Hang gliding, or paragliding as it is frequently called, is as close as you can get to flying without actually having wings. For the thrill of a lifetime, soar above the beautiful Torrey Pines coastline and enjoy unparalleled stillness and serenity while navigating either a hang glider or paraglider. All fliers must have an advanced license to soar on their own, but you can experience the thrill right away by taking a tandem flight with a licensed pilot.

Glider enthusiasts like to hang glide off the Torrey Pines cliffs. PHOTO: COURTESY OF SAN DIEGO CONVENTION AND VISITORS BUREAU

Torrey Pines Gliderport (Air California Adventures)
2800 Torrey Pines Scenic Dr., La Jolla
(858) 452–9858
www.flytorrey.com

Located at the historic landmark Torrey Pines Glider Port, Air California Adventures offers training courses ranging from beginner to advanced. The three- to four-day beginner course ($795) teaches the basic skills necessary to fly under direct instructor supervision. To achieve the next level, where solo flights are permitted, you'll need an instruction packet costing a total of $1,300. For a one-time thrill, try a tandem flight. No instruction is necessary—you glide with an experienced pilot. The cost is $150 for a 20- to 30-minute flight.

Hiking

We proudly declare that there is no better place in the world than San Diego for hiking over a variety of terrain, from mountain to desert to coastal trails. While we may be overstating the case just slightly, if you're a dedicated hiker, you will not be disappointed here. If you'd like to meet new friends and prefer to hike with a group, check Thursday's *San Diego Union-Tribune.* It usually has a long list of organized hikes from which you can choose.

If you prefer the solitude of hiking on your own or selecting your own location, we'll highlight a few of the best hikes here. For comprehensive maps and lists of hiking trails, check with any sporting goods store or bookstore. Be sure to pack lots of water and sunscreen, and if you're planning to make a day of it, include a picnic lunch and some basic first-aid supplies. San Diego does have its share of dangerous critters too, so be alert for rattlesnakes (even on the coast) and mountain lions.

Cuyamaca Rancho State Park
10 miles northeast of Alpine
(760) 765–0755
www.cuyamaca.statepark.org

If diversity in hiking is what you're after, this park is the ticket, with more than 100 miles of hiking trails: along streambeds and through pine-oak forests, meadows, and sagebrush. The park is bisected by Highway 79, and a variety of signed trails depart from parking lots along the road. One of the most rewarding, moderate hikes is a portion of the East Side Trail. Some climbs await you, but the reward is an unequaled scenic vista. This trail is not marked well in some places, so we advise you to get a map from the ranger station before you set out. The trail length is 4.7 miles, and it should take you about two hours. As always, be sure to take more water than you think you'll need. To get to the trailhead, take I-8 east to Calif. 79, turn left (north), and drive about 4 miles to a large parking lot on the right.

Los Peñasquitos Canyon Preserve
10 miles north of downtown San Diego
(858) 538–8066
www.penasquitos.org

Hike through oak trees and lush meadows on this 6½-mile trail before descending to the canyon floor where you'll be surrounded by giant boulders. During winter and spring, a stream forms small waterfalls between the boulders, making this a perfect spot for a picnic. You'll hike up a canyon for a while before returning to the grove of oaks and the main trail back to the parking lot. The hike takes about 2½ hours. To get to the trailhead, take I-15 north to Mira Mesa Boulevard. Turn left (west) and travel ½ mile to Black Mountain

Road. Turn right and drive to the parking lot, which is 1 mile ahead on the left.

Mission Trails Regional Park
1 Father Junipero Serra Trail, San Diego
(619) 668–3275

Mission Trails contains almost 6,000 acres of hiking, mountain biking, and equestrian trails that meander through mountains, valleys, and lakes. Guided hikes depart from the Visitors/Interpretive Center on Wednesdays, Saturdays, and Sundays, usually at 9:30 A.M., and from the park's only campground on the second and fourth Saturdays of the month at 8:30 A.M. One of the best hikes in the park (no guide is necessary) is to the top of Cowles Mountain. At 1,591 feet, it's the highest point in the city of San Diego. To reach the trailhead from the coast, drive east on I-8 to Mission Gorge Road, then turn left (north). Drive 5 miles to Golfcrest Road and turn right (south). Head up the hill for 1 mile to the parking lot on the left. You'll hike up a series of switchbacks to the top of the mountain, a 3-mile hike. The views are spectacular.

San Elijo Lagoon Ecological Preserve
Encinitas, North County Coastal

This is an easy 4-mile hike that you can stretch into a two-hour stroll. Once you leave the parking lot, you'll make a series of right turns until you pass underneath the freeway. Turn left (south) and follow the trail that travels alongside the lagoon. Signs along the way will point out some of the endangered species that inhabit the preserve. At the end of the trail is a lovely view of the Pacific Ocean. To get to the trailhead, take I-5 north (from the city of San Diego) to Manchester Avenue. Turn left (east) onto Manchester and drive ¼ mile to a small dirt parking lot just across from the entrance to the preserve.

Horseback Riding

Grab your cowboy hat, pull on those boots, and climb on a horse for a different view of San Diego. Whether you prefer riding on the beach or in the wilderness, both are available for short rides of one hour or longer rides up to a full day.

These horses will be taking visitors for rides in the Cuyamaca Mountains. PHOTO: THORN VOLLENWEIDER

Adventures on Horseback
24928 Viejas Blvd., Descanso
(619) 445-3997
www.adventureonhorseback.com

Located in the Cuyamaca Mountains in San Diego's East County, Adventures on Horseback offers wilderness rides from 90 minutes up to four hours, with full day and overnight trips by special request. The rate for a 90-minute ride is $40; a two-hour ride is $55; a three-hour ride is $75 and includes beverages. If you ride for four hours the fee is $125 and includes a picnic lunch. Call for reservations.

Happy Trails
12115 Black Mountain Rd., San Diego
(858) 271-8777

See nature at its most pristine from atop a horse as you ride into the Los Peñasquitos Preserve. Guided rides are offered seven days a week; cost is $35 for one hour, $65 for two.

Sandy's Rental Stable
2060 Hollister St., San Diego (in the South Bay)
(619) 424-3124
www.sandysrentalstable.com

At Sandy's you'll be fitted with a saddle and introduced to your horse as soon as you arrive. Absolute beginners to experienced riders are welcome. Several riding tours are offered, but the most popular are the three-hour beach ride for $60 per person and the one-hour river trail ride for $30 per person. No reservations are necessary.

Ice Skating

Hard to imagine ice skating in San Diego? Believe it or not, it not only exists, it thrives. Several local skating rinks have public hours for amateur skaters to test their skills gliding across the ice. Remember, even in summertime it can get chilly inside the rinks, so dress appropriately.

Ice Chalet
4545 La Jolla Village Dr., San Diego
(858) 452-9110
www.icechalet.com

Located in the University Towne Center mall, Ice Chalet offers public ice skating seven days a week. If you need lessons, teachers are on hand to help get you upright and moving forward. The rink is available for private parties too, in case you're looking for someplace unique for your next gathering. Because the rink is located in the UTC shopping mall (see our Shopping chapter), there's the added benefit of a food court surrounding the rink, and parents can shop while kids skate. Rates are $9.75 per person, including skate rental. There are youth and adult hockey leagues as well, and hockey lessons for future Wayne Gretskys. Public hours vary from day to day, so be sure to call ahead.

Iceoplex
555 N. Tulip St., Escondido
(760) 489–5550
www.iceoplex.com

This modern facility in North County Inland has public skating, as well as individual and group lessons for ice hockey, adult and youth hockey leagues for men and women, camps, and hockey clinics. Join a pickup hockey game most days of the week, or form your own team. Figure skating lessons are available. Private activities that can be scheduled include broomball (easygoing "hockey" where kids in tennis shoes hit a soft ball) and "snow days," where groups of 10 or more play on the ice and in piles of snow and later warm up with cocoa and cookies. There's a pro shop and pizza parlor on site as well, and two lap pools, a gym, whirlpools, and saunas. The cost for skating any day or evening session is $9.75, including skate rental.

San Diego Ice Arena
11048 Ice Skate Pl., San Diego
(858) 530–1825
www.sdice.com

This skating rink offers public skating every day and most evenings. Hours change from day to day, so call ahead for current hours. A complete sport shop is on the premises, and both individual and group lessons in figure skating and hockey are offered. Skating rates are $6.00 per person; skate rental is $2.50. Group activities range from Christian Music Night to swing parties and activities for local school children and Girl and Boy Scouts. This is the best spot in the county to learn to play hockey.

Laser Tag

Advanced technology has created new and innovative ways to play, and nowhere is that more true than in a laser-tag venue. Laser tag is an interactive adventure that combines computer technology with action-oriented team play. Players don a special pack and take a laser-pulse phaser into intricately designed play areas where they score points for their team by "tagging" opposing team members.

All ages are welcome, but players should be at least 7 years old to get maximum enjoyment from the game.

Laser Storm
9365 Mission Gorge Rd., Santee
(619) 562–3791

Players receive a brief introduction to the game, put on lightweight vests and headsets, then enter a futuristic arena with phasers in hand. The object here is to seek, find, and deactivate opposing team members and their base station. The arena is full of barriers, strobe lights, police beacons, sentries, roboscanners, and many more obstacles to add to the fun and the challenge. Games last for approximately 10 minutes, and the cost is $3.50 per person for the first game and $2.50 for subsequent games.

Laser Storm is generally open from noon to 5:00 P.M. Monday through Friday, and from 7:30 to 10:00 P.M. in the evenings. However, times may vary; call ahead for details.

Imperial Beach Pier is a great place for fishing, strolling, and ocean-viewing. PHOTO: DALE FROST, COURTESY OF PORT OF SAN DIEGO

Ultrazone
3146 Sports Arena Blvd., Ste. 21, San Diego
(619) 221–0100

Laser tag at Ultrazone starts in the Briefing Room, where players get specific game and equipment instruction, learn safety rules, and are divided into teams. Once inside the 4,000-square-foot arena, players are confronted with a fog-filled, UV-black-lit environment crammed full of mazes, passageways, ramps, and obstacles on several levels.

The game typically lasts for about 15 minutes, and the cost is $7.00 per game. Hours are from 4:00 until 11:00 P.M. Monday through Thursday and from 2:00 P.M. until 2:00 A.M. on Friday. Saturday hours are from 10:00 P.M. until 2:00 A.M., and Ultrazone is open from 10:00 A.M. until 11:00 P.M. on Sundays. During summer months, starting time is at noon during the week.

Martial Arts

If mastering one of the many martial arts piques your interest, you'll find no shortage of schools or disciplines tailored to your unique desires. From judo and karate to tae-kwan-do and Thai kickboxing, you'll find a huge variety of studios and classes. We've listed a few studios here that cater to the whole family, mainly to get you started. If a particular discipline interests you but isn't mentioned here, never fear. It's bound to be taught somewhere in San Diego. If you call any of the numbers listed below, you're likely to get a good referral. Class rates vary widely depending on the level of instruction and number of classes.

International Self Defense Center
12657 Poway Rd., Poway
(858) 748–5829
www.isdc.net

This 4,000-square-foot facility was established in 1967 and offers classes in Shaolin kung fu, kempo, karate, jiu jitsu, aikido, kickboxing, tai chi, and meditation. By studying these arts students develop confidence, peace of mind, strength, and flexibility. The arts of concentration, courage, and patience are all taught with a sense of humor. Self-defense classes exclusively for

San Diego Marathon

Imagine this: It's a perfect early morning winter's day in San Diego. That means the sun is out and it's in the high 40s or low 50s, but sure to jump 20 degrees by lunch. The scene could be tranquil; however, with over 8,000 people warming up, stretching, and psyching up to compete in this event, all is far from serene.

The annual San Diego Marathon is the second-oldest marathon on the West Coast. Begun in the late '50s by the San Diego Track Club, it was originally run from Oceanside to Mission Bay. It moved to North County in December of 1990.

Change is constant in San Diego, and usually brings improvements. This new race was no exception. When the current organizing company, In Motion, Inc., was hired to orchestrate the event, it turned into a not-to-be-missed happening that continues to score high marks with runners, watchers, and supporters.

When In Motion moved the race to North County Coastal in 1990, it increased its national exposure and changed the race into more than a recreational activity. It's a community event now. (FYI: In Motion, Inc. is owned and run by Insiders: Lynn Flanagan and her daughters, Ellen Flanagan and Christine Flanagan Adams.)

The marathon is held in the middle of January. If you'd like details for the next run, call In Motion at (858) 792–2900 or watch the local press. The company also coordinates a fitness-training program for those interested in running but who might not be in shape. The 25-week regimen is designed to help everyone, regardless of age or fitness level, to participate in the race—and have some fun too.

Even if you don't run, there are still exciting things to do at the three-day All About Fitness Expo, which is held in conjunction with the race. The expo is free. It's a big deal and thousands come to see the latest in exercise equipment, tasty healthy foods—including energy bars and smoothies—and meet some local celebrities, from the mayor to the winners of previous years' races. Keep in mind that this isn't just a San Diego marathon or a three-day program—it's a West Coast event.

All the races (there are choices) start and end at Carlsbad's Plaza Camino Real shopping center at El Camino Real and Marron Road, about 40 minutes north of downtown San Diego. You can find it by driving north on Interstate 5, then following Highway 78 east about 1 mile.

The featured event is the marathon (26.2 miles) where runners run northern San Diego's coastline. Lynn Flanagan, founder of In Motion, Inc. explains: "The marathon, and half marathon, are run on a gently rolling out-and-back course along the ocean. All marathon events are run on

Racers of all stripes compete in the San Diego Marathon. PHOTO: COURTESY OF IN MOTION, INC.

a closed course with safety provided by the Carlsbad Police Department." Mother Nature supplies perfect days.

The half marathon is recognized as one of the fastest races of that distance in the United States, and Lynn says that it draws the very best field of American runners competing for the $1,000 purse. The Marathon Relay, which offers 25 different divisions, including law enforcement, military, non-profit, financial, and medical, is open to five-member teams. Southern California's businesses and civic clubs always participate in this event, which draws lots of cheering supporters of the various teams. Children 12 and younger are winners no matter how they place in the Keebler Kids Marathon Mile. Wheelchair competitors compete in the marathon too. Many of the events are covered by national television, including ESPN, and magazines such as *Outdoor Life.* The local press and TV crews are always on the spot.

There's a marathon run for everyone. Most exciting? The one in which you are entered. PHOTO: COURTESY OF IN MOTION, INC.

The San Diego Marathon is good for San Diego. The organization helps local non-profit associations find ways to use the marathon for fund-raising, and programs like the Special Olympics, Blind Recreation Center, the Autism Association, and Volunteers on Probation have done so. The 2002 sponsor list included Kaiser Permanente, Albertson's, BMW, Gatorade, NBC/Channel 7, *Runner's World,* and New Balance.

Schedule of Events

Thursday
San Diego Marathon Golf Tournament

Friday
All About Fitness Expo   3:00 to 7:00 P.M.

Saturday
5K Run/Walk   8:00 A.M.
All About Fitness Expo   8:00 A.M. to 6:00 P.M.
Keebler Kids Marathon Mile   9:30 A.M.
Albertson's Carbo Dinner at LEGOLAND   4:30 to 7:00 P.M.

Sunday
Walk start, marathon   5:30 A.M.
Early marathon start   6:30 A.M.
Half marathon start   7:00 A.M.
Wheelchair start   7:25 A.M.
Marathon start   7:30 A.M.
Marathon Relay   7:30 A.M.

women are now offered. The facility has free weights and a bag room for unlimited punching practice.

Twin Dragons Kenpo
6924 La Jolla Blvd., La Jolla
(858) 454–5413

All styles and all ranks are welcome at Twin Dragons for classes in karate, boxing, grappling, and Thai kickboxing. Since 1969 this state-of-the-art studio has given classes for adults and children. In addition to boxing-ring and bag training, video training is provided in each of the offered disciplines. Martial arts supplies are also available on-site.

White Dragon Schools
191 El Camino Real, Ste. 212, Encinitas
(760) 944–7272
225 N. Magnolia Ave., El Cajon
(619) 441–1144
7127 University Ave., La Mesa
(619) 461–2760
5953 Balboa Ave., San Diego
(858) 277–7557

Since 1985 the instructors at White Dragon Schools have been teaching men, women, and children the arts of Yang tai chi, Chinese kickboxing, and choy li fut for health, self-defense, and discipline. The classes are designed to be fun and to improve self-confidence and mental attitude. The four facilities are large and fully equipped, and private lessons are included at no extra cost.

Paintball

Here's a treat for those looking for something a little different. Paintball has taken firm root as a game filled with fun, thrills, and strategy. Players seek out opponents with the intent of eliminating them with a brightly colored blob of paint. Come alone, bring a friend, or organize a group, and get ready for a unique experience.

Camp Pendleton Paintball Park
Camp Pendleton, Oceanside
(800) 899–9957

Paintball competition consists of two teams playing the classic "capture the flag" game in an outdoor park. The staff is always on hand to assist you with equipment needs, explanation of the rules, and general tips to enhance your paintball day. The Marine Corps Base park is open to the public (bring proper identification) Saturdays and Sundays from 9:00 A.M. to 4:30 P.M. or on weekdays for prearranged private parties only. Guests must be 10 years or older, and those younger than 18 must have signed parental consent to play. Admission is $12; equipment rental packages are $28.

Mr. Paintball
25320 Lake Wohlford Rd., Escondido
(760) 737–8870
www.mrpaintballco.com

Owner Mr. Paintball (otherwise known as Stan Burgis) likens the sport to the cops-and-robbers games we played as kids. Mr. Paintball emphasizes safety while ensuring that participants have a good time. Folks can play either on outdoor fields or inside.

Paintball can be played on weekends from 8:00 A.M. to 4:30 P.M. Full-day admission is $39, including equipment and lunch (calzone and soda).

Racquetball

Although racquetball isn't the rage that it once was, there are still dedicated players who hit the courts with regularity. Some fitness centers and clubs have racquetball courts and will allow the public to play without purchasing a membership. But your best bet is to try one of the public courts listed below. They charge a per-person rate for one hour's play, but if the courts aren't busy, you can keep playing for no additional charge.

American Athletic Club
2539 Hoover Ave., National City
(619) 477–2123

Rates range from $7.00 to $8.00 per person depending on the time of day. The club has six courts and is open Monday through Friday from 6:00 A.M. to 10:00 P.M., Saturday from 7:00 A.M. to 6:00 P.M., and Sunday from 8:00 A.M. to 2:00 P.M.

La Mesa Racquetball
4330 Palm Ave., La Mesa
(619) 460–3500
www.lamesaracquetball.com

Racquetball can be played on nine courts here, 365 days per year. The courts are open from 9:00 A.M. to 11:00 P.M. Monday through Friday, and 7:00 A.M. to 10:00 P.M. Saturday and Sunday. Rates range from $6.50 to $8.50 per person. An added bonus in case you push yourself too hard is the on-staff chiropractor.

San Diego Workout
1010 S. Santa Fe Ave., Vista
(760) 724–6941
409 W. Felicita Ave., Escondido
(760) 871–6600
2010 Jimmy Durante Blvd., Del Mar
(858) 481–6226

Three racquetball courts are available for public play at this facility, and reservations are accepted up to a week in advance. Rates are $10 per person per hour for nonmembers. Hours are 5:00 A.M. to 11:00 P.M. Monday through Thursday, 5:00 A.M. to 9:30 P.M. on Friday, 6:00 A.M. to 5:00 P.M. on Saturday, and 7:00 A.M. to 5:00 P.M. on Sunday.

Skating/Skateboarding

As in most cities, the popularity of skating and skateboarding seems to be in direct proportion to the intolerance for the sports. The city of Del Mar, for example, discourages skating and skateboarding wherever it can within the city limits. Both are also prohibited in Balboa Park, but for good reason. There's always such a large group of people milling about that combining wheels with slow-moving feet would be a recipe for disaster.

Never fear, however. We'll get you rolling safely and legally in some of the best spots in the county. Do it on your own, or join an organized skate to meet new friends and discover new skating places.

Coronado Skate Park
Tidelands Park, Coronado
(619) 522–7342

Skaters pay a yearly fee of $10 (which includes first session equipment rental and entrance fee) to skate at this smooth new park just across the bridge in Coronado. Summer hours are Monday through Friday 9:00 A.M. to dusk; during the school year the outdoor park opens at 1:00 P.M. Year-round weekend hours are Saturday and Sunday 9:00 A.M. to dusk. Helmets, knee pads, and elbow pads are required; wrist guards are recommended. This equipment as well as skateboards can be rented on site. Call ahead for session hours, as these change frequently. Cost is $3.00 to $5.00 per session.

Mission Bay Park

Miles and miles of paved (and wide) walkways are shared equally by walkers, joggers, skateboarders, and skaters. Choose from the beach or bayfront boardwalk or the pathway that meanders from the beach all the way around the various bays and inlets that make up Mission Bay Park. There are no restrictions here, except for an 8-mile-per-hour speed limit on the boardwalk.

Robb Field Skate Park
Sunset Cliffs Blvd. at W. Point Loma Dr.,
San Diego
(619) 525–8486

Forty thousand square feet of outdoor skateboarding bliss can be purchased for $5.00 per day at the eastern end of Robb Field, in Ocean Beach; yearly passes cost just $30. Kids under 18 need a permission form signed by a parent to use the facilities. Hours are Monday to Friday 10:00 A.M. to dusk; weekends 9:00 A.M. to dusk.

Temecula Skate Park
42569 Margarita Rd., Temecula
(909) 695–1409

Temecula Skate Park may be a bit off the beaten path, but skaters and skateboarders flock to this park designed and built especially for them. Plentiful bowls, lifts, and jumps will test your skills and challenge even the most talented daredevils on wheels. For the complete lowdown on this one-of-kind park, see the Close-up in our Daytrips chapter. Hours are Monday through Friday from 1:00 P.M. until 9:30 P.M., Saturday from 10:00 A.M. to 9:30

P.M., and Sunday from 1:00 P.M. until 6:30 P.M. The entrance fee is $5.00 for non-residents.

Tennis

Looking for a game of tennis? You're in luck. Many hotels have their own courts, but if yours doesn't, you'll find quite a few public courts throughout the county. Here we list the most centrally located within our five regions.

Balboa Tennis Club
2221 Morley Field Dr., San Diego
(619) 295-9278
www.balboatennis.com

This tennis center at Morley Field (part of Balboa Park) has 25 courts (19 are lighted) and is open from 8:00 A.M. to 8:00 P.M. weekdays and from 8:00 A.M. to 6:00 P.M. on weekends. An all-day individual permit is $5.00. Courts are assigned on a first-come, first-served basis, except for members, who can schedule their games ahead. The best time to get a court is between 11:00 A.M. and 5:00 P.M.

Coronado Tennis Association
1501 Glorietta Blvd., Coronado
(619) 435-1616

Eight courts, three of them lighted, are available on a first-come, first-served basis. Play is free, and courts are open from dawn until 10:00 P.M.

George E. Barnes Tennis Center
4490 W. Pt. Loma Blvd., San Diego
(619) 221-9000
www.tennissandiego.com

Twenty hard courts and four clay courts are available for public play daily. Adult walk-on prices are $5.00 for the day for hard courts and $7.50 for clay during the day (add $2.00 after dark for lighted courts); children 18 and younger play for free. Courts are open Monday through Saturday 8:00 A.M. to 9:00 P.M., Sunday 8:00 A.M. to 8:00 P.M.

La Jolla Tennis Club
7632 Draper Ave., La Jolla
(858) 454-4434

The courts never close here, so if you can see, you can play. The lights, however, do go off at 9:00 P.M. No reservations are accepted for the nine courts; play is strictly on a first-come, first-served basis. Previously free, the facility now offers memberships: $85 a year permits unlimited daily access to the courts. Nonmembers pay $3.00 if accompanied by a member or $5.00 on their own. Two full-time pros give lessons and clinics for adults and juniors and organize round-robins and outings to the U.S. Open and other tournaments.

Lake Murray Tennis Club
7003 Murray Park Dr., San Diego
(619) 469-3232
www.lakemurraytennis.com

Ten newly resurfaced courts are waiting for players. A fee of $5.00 allows non-members all-day play; members pay a small annual fee but play for free. Call ahead to make reservations. Hours are 8:00 A.M. to 10:00 P.M. Monday through Thursday, 8:00 A.M. to 8:00 P.M. Friday, and 7:00 A.M. to 8:00 P.M. on weekends. There's an on-site pro shop, and the club sponsors round-robins and tournaments throughout the year.

Southwestern College Tennis Center
900 Otay Lakes Rd., Chula Vista
(619) 421-6622

This is a small tennis center with 14 courts located on the campus of Southwestern College. Although courts are sometimes in use for classes or clinics, there's no charge for play. Check at the pro shop for current open-play hours. The courts are staffed by four tennis pros, and group and private lessons are available for beginning, intermediate, and advanced players, be they juniors or adults. Clients as young as four can begin honing their skills. Clinics, skill development sessions, and match play are available. Courts are open from 9:00 A.M. to 6:00 or 7:00 P.M., and play is on a first-come, first-served basis.

San Diego's sunny, mild climate gives little excuse to be a couch potato. PHOTO: BRETT SHOAF, COURTESY OF SAN DIEGO CONVENTION & VISITORS BUREAU

Volleyball

Volleyball in San Diego is a big deal, especially beach volleyball. Newcomers and visitors will notice, however, that it's not a particularly well-organized sport. Most games consist of groups of friends who set up a net and start playing when the mood strikes them. If you happen to be at the beach or at one of the county's parks and see a game in progress, chances are you can join in. But the best way to assure a game is to organize it yourself.

About a mile south of Belmont Park, in South Mission Beach, there are 17 permanent sand courts. In Ocean Beach, players bring their own nets to affix to permanent poles.

Two organizations sponsor tournaments and other events throughout the year: the California Beach Volleyball Association (www.cbva.org) and West Coast Beach Volleyball (www.wcbv.com, 858-509-9228).

One way to meet others who share an interest in the sport is to sign up for lessons. Or if you're really serious about your volleyball, there's a coed league in Poway that plays indoor volleyball once a week (see the information that follows).

Beach Volleyball Classes
(888) 742-4763

Classes are held at Ocean Beach every week from 6:00 to 7:30 P.M. Beginners and intermediates meet weekly between April and September. Call for information and registration. The seven-week class is about $100, and classes fill up, so make your reservation early.

City of Poway Parks and Recreation
12320 Meadowbrook Ln., Poway
(858) 679-4343

The city of Poway Parks and Recreation Department sponsors four-on-four coed volleyball league play. Teams consist of six players and must have at least two women. The registration fee is $52 for Poway residents, a bit more ($59) for outsiders. Call for the current schedule; venues and times change quarterly.

Walking

Sometimes there's a fine line between walking and hiking, but for those who truly love to stroll around city streets or even take an easy nature walk, hundreds of spots exist for both.

The beauty of walking is that, other than a good pair of shoes, no special equipment is needed, no reservations are required, and you can do it just about anywhere. If you like to confine your walks to paved sidewalks, no prettier place can be found than the walkway around Mission Bay, or the coastal streets and walkways in La Jolla. But any neighborhood in the county will provide the requisite fresh air and exercise.

Some prefer walking as a solitary pursuit, others like to walk with a friend or a group. If an organized walk sounds like it might be of interest to you, check out one of the many walking organizations listed below. You'll have your pick of organized nature walks, neighborhood walks, backcountry walks or any other kind of walk you can possibly imagine. And you'll have the added pleasure of making new friends.

Encinitas Walkers
(760) 634-3165

Every Monday, Wednesday, and Friday this group meets at Starbucks Coffee in the Lumberyard Shopping Center, 947 South Coast Highway 101, Encinitas, leaving promptly at 7:30 A.M. Different 4-mile walks are scheduled for every meeting. Dogs on leashes welcomed.

Gaslamp Quarter Walking Tours
410 Island Ave., San Diego
(619) 233-4692

Combine exercise with a little bit of history as you take a two-hour guided walking tour through San Diego's historic Gaslamp Quarter. Prices are $8.00 for adults and $6.00 for seniors and students. Tours depart at 11:00 A.M. every Saturday.

La Jolla Walking Tours
910 Prospect St., La Jolla
(619) 292-2221
www.lajollawalkingtours.com

At 10:00 A.M. every Saturday, La Jolla Walking Tours offers a two-hour guided tour that combines exercise with stories of La Jolla's history and famous residents,

Speedwalkers get their workout along one of the many harbor walkways. PHOTO: DALE FROST, COURTESY OF THE PORT OF SAN DIEGO

past and present. Some tours highlight shopping and include lunch at a nice restaurant; prices vary, so call for information. Reservations are required.

Sierra Club
3820 Ray St., San Diego
(619) 299–1744

The Sierra Club offers a number of hikes in different locations throughout the county. Interested individuals are invited to the club orientation at 7:00 P.M. on the second Wednesday of each month at the Tierrasanta Recreation Center, 11220 Clairemont Mesa Boulevard, San Diego.

Walkabout International
835 Fifth Ave., San Diego
(619) 231–7463

Walks are scheduled almost every day of the year by this well-known group. Call for the current schedule of events.

Insiders' Tip

Look for *Walking San Diego* by Lonnie Hewitt and Barbara Moore. If you're a dedicated walker, this is a great book that tells you where to go to get away from it all and what to do when you get there.

Beaches and Watersports

What's the first thing everyone, including locals, thinks of when they think San Diego? Beaches, of course. Long stretches of tan sand, sparkling blue ocean, sunny days basking in the warm California sunshine with your toes buried in the sand—all these images float through the minds of those hankering for sun and surf. Guess what? It's no myth. Those magical beaches do exist, and we're about to give you the skinny on each and every one of them. Even better, there's never a fee to use any of San Diego's beaches, just an occasional parking charge.

For those of you who want to interact with the blue Pacific, but prefer a little more activity than just dreaming away the day with maybe a splash in the water to break things up, we also have a whole bunch of watersports you can enjoy. We'll show you where to rent jet skis, surfboards, scuba equipment, and more. If fishing is what sends you to nirvana, we'll point you to the best piers and sport-fishing expeditions. We'll give you the scoop on licensing requirements and where to get your equipment. We'll even tell you what fish you can expect to reel in.

Picture yourself sailing across the smooth waters of Mission Bay in a kayak or a sailboat. You can even rent powerboats and take the whole family water-skiing. Or try something new and rent a wind surfer. With just a short lesson, you can be sailing across the water with nothing but a sail and a surfboard to move you along. And don't think you need to bring a lot of stuff with you. Virtually everything you need, from basic equipment like a boat to wetsuits and life jackets, is either easily rented or comes as part of a package.

Now we have a few words of caution for you. The Pacific Ocean can be deceptive. It looks calm and beautiful, but it can pack a wallop. Even the most serene lake or swimming pool has its dangers, so we urge you to bring your common sense along and take the advice of a couple of longtime beach rats: If you plan to go in the water, know how to swim. If you're not a swimmer, don't you dare go in the pool or ocean past your ankles. Rip currents in the ocean are hard to spot and can get ahold of you before you know what's happened. A rip current is sort of like a narrow but very powerful river that's heading back out to sea. They tend to form in the deepest points along the ocean floor, pulling everything with them as they flow seaward. Even the strongest swimmers have a healthy respect for rip currents.

If you're in a boat, always wear a life jacket and make sure all children wear them, too. Should a mishap occur, you won't have time to put one on, so you're well advised to just keep it on at all times.

If you heed some simple guidelines about rip currents and other potential dangers, though, you should have no problem. First and foremost, whether you're swimming in the ocean or a pool, be sure it's protected by a lifeguard, and pay attention to all warning signs, especially those regarding rip currents. Lifeguards can spot them and will post red flags where they have formed. That's a clear signal to avoid swimming in that area. Should you get caught in a rip, swim parallel to the shore in either direction until the pull of the current subsides. Then you can swim in to shore.

Lifeguards advise you to swim with fins. They use them; you should, too. Also, never swim when you've been drinking. Alcohol impairs your judgment and your physical capabilities. Avoid using things like Boogie Boards or rafts as swimming aids if you're a weak swimmer. You shouldn't venture any farther with a raft than your swimming ability would normally take you. Finally, if you get into trouble, simply wave your arms. Lifeguards recognize this as a distress signal whether you're in the water or on the shore. You'll get immediate attention.

In addition to heeding safety tips, you'll need to follow the few rules and regulations that exist to make going to the beach a pleasure for everyone. The permissibility of alcoholic beverages varies from beach to beach. Most don't permit alcohol at all, but some will allow it between certain hours. Signs are posted at all beaches advising you of current regulations. Bottles are never permitted on beaches, so bring your beverages in cans or in plastic. Fires can be built in provided fire rings only, and many beaches have them. Never bury coals in the sand—they don't go out for hours, and some unsuspecting beachcomber may stumble upon them and end up with a bad burn.

You might expect that San Diego overflows with marinas since we spend so much time in and on the water. And although there are quite a few, they're mostly private. You can rent a temporary slip at a hotel marina if you're a guest, but arrangements should always be made in advance. Vacant slips are hard to find, so we don't advise that you sail into town and expect to find a marina to accommodate you.

Now that we've given you the heads up on how to stay out of trouble, let us urge you to throw caution to the wind and explore all the possibilities that coastal life has to offer. And remember, you don't have to have any special knowledge or skill to take advantage of most watersports. Experienced captains are always on hand to pilot a boat for you, or to take you on a tandem windsurfer, or teach you to water-ski. But if that sounds like just too much activity, then do as we do. Grab a beach towel, some no-brainer summer reading, lots of sunscreen, and hit the sand. You'll feel remarkably mellow at the end of the day.

We've listed the beaches in geographical order, from north to south, and have tried to point out the characteristics and quirks that distinguish each. We've included a few that don't have lifeguard service or facilities such as rest rooms, but do have something special that tends to attract locals. Just be advised that these aren't places to take the kids. Watersports are listed by activity, with a description of the sport along with where to go to get the necessary equipment.

So put the sightseeing aside for a day and head to the water.

Beaches

San Onofre Surf Beach
I-5 and Basilone Rd., San Onofre

This is one of the most popular surfing beaches along the coastline in San Diego County. Insiders call it "Trestles" and it's known around the world for truly cool surfing. Many people say it's the best surfing spot in the entire state.

Once you exit the freeway (at the Basilone Road exit), follow the blue signs for beach access and parking. There's a $3.00 entrance fee to park your car. The north end of the beach has a wide, sandy shoreline that's good for walking, swimming, and sunset watching. The south end is more narrow and covered with large beach stones—here's where the surfers hang out. The beach is walkable for about 4 miles in either direction. The beach has lots of rest rooms, cold showers, running water, some picnic tables, and fire rings. Shade is limited. There are public phones near all the rest rooms. There is no lifeguard on duty; for emergencies, you'll have to call 911.

Oceanside Beaches
Oceanside

You can locate the Oceanside beaches by simply driving west on most of the Oceanside city streets. Oceanside beaches all have wide sandy shores, which are great for lounging, picnicking, sunbathing, and yes, even swimming. Surfing is especially good between Tyson Street Park and the Oceanside Pier, just south of Mission Avenue.

Pacific Street runs all along the ocean in Oceanside and there's beach access between Wisconsin Avenue and Morse Way. There is free and metered parking, with handicapped spaces provided. Parking is at a premium, however, so be prepared for a walk to the water during the summer months and especially on the Fourth of July when beaches are busy.

Buccaneer Beach, 1506 South Pacific Street, is popular with families because of its wide sandy shore. The YMCA brings the summer surf-day campers here for lessons (see our Kidstuff chapter for other activities at this beach). The beach is patrolled 24 hours a day by police, and there are lifeguards at Buccaneer too. The beach has picnic tables, barbecues, some shade, and a public telephone.

Just south of Buccaneer Beach is a popular surfing place with a width that varies with the seasons and the tides. Parking is scarce and illegal parking will nearly guarantee you a ticket. There's no lifeguard on duty here.

Eaton Street, at the south end of Pacific Street, fronts the gated community of St. Malo. Security guards at the St. Malo discourage entry; however, all beach below the high-tide line is public, so you can still walk through without fear of trespassing.

Carlsbad Beaches
Carlsbad

The beaches begin south of Buena Vista Lagoon. Carlsbad City Beach, the first of the string we present here, has some sand at high tide; at low tide, it's a wide and popular spot for surfers rather than walkers and swimmers. There are no facilities at the north end of this beach, which is open from 6:00 A.M. to 11:00 P.M. daily.

To access the beaches where there are facilities and lifeguards, you can walk the beach steps down from Ocean Street, Christiansen Way, Grand Avenue, or Carlsbad Village Drive straight to the sea. After Carlsbad Village Drive stops at the ocean, turn left to Ocean Street and then merge into Carlsbad Boulevard. Here

A crowd gathers to watch the beach artists perform their magic during the annual Sand Castle event on Imperial Beach. The Imperial Beach pier reaches out to the ocean in the background. PHOTO: COURTESY OF SAN DIEGO CONVENTION AND VISITORS BUREAU

you'll find street parking (although it's at a premium) and flights of stairs to reach the sand. Beach access signs, indicating how to get to the water, are everywhere. The Carlsbad beaches, by the way, are only about 3 blocks west of the Coaster station. So if you'd like to visit this community's water and sand and would rather not drive north, check the Coaster's schedule.

Whatever you decide, be sure you're wearing comfortable shoes, either to walk from the station or from that parking place wherever you may find it (at least most parking is free).

There are cold-water, open public showers at Christiansen Way and Tamarack Avenue and rest rooms, telephones, and lifeguard stations all along the shore. You'll see fire rings along the beaches as well. Where Tamarack Avenue ends at the Pacific Ocean there is a public parking lot. You can't, however, expect to find a spot on beautiful sunny days.

Directly above the beach is the well-maintained Carlsbad Seawall, a 4-foot-high barrier between the cliffs and the sea. It was built to help maintain the integrity of the cliffs since erosion and generations of ground squirrels, who also love beach life, have weakened the earth. You can stroll on the walk that follows the seawall.

Or, at street level, there's the popular beach-view sidewalk for strolling, skating, jogging, or briskly walking from Carlsbad Village Drive all the way to Cannon Drive—a good 5-mile trek. Lots of folks who work in Carlsbad take brown bag lunches, or buy fast food, and eat at the tables along the beach. Lots of folks walk here in the evenings—including many Insiders with leashed canine companions. (Dogs are not allowed on the lower level of the seawall walkway and you will be ticketed if you don't scoop up after a pet's potty stop.) At the street level, there are picnic tables and benches, and there's some shade too.

South Carlsbad State Beach
Poinsettia Dr. and Carlsbad Blvd., Carlsbad

To reach this state beach, exit Interstate 5 at Poinsettia and drive west. There are no day use facilities here. It's a popular beach

Insiders' Tip

Overnight parking is prohibited at most beaches, and your car will be ticketed or towed away. Camping is allowed at a few state beaches, and reservations should be made many months in advance of your stay. For information on California State beaches contact the state office at (916) 653-6995, (800) 444-7275, or www.parks.ca.gov. To make reservations for camping contact ReserveAmerica, (800) 444-7275, www.reserveamerica.com.

campground and those who want to camp here make reservations months in advance. Even in winter it's nearly always full. From the campground, there are eight exits to the narrow pebbled beach. There are lifeguard towers. Surfing is supposed to be outstanding.

At the campground there are rest rooms, tables, fire rings, shade, and a food store.

Beacon's Beach
Encinitas

Exit I-5 at Leucadia Boulevard and head west, then follow the "Beach Access" signs toward Diana Street. Beacon's Beach has a small parking lot that's open from 6:00 A.M. until 10:00 P.M. There is a public telephone and a steep path down to the heavily pebbled beach. There are no lifeguards. This is a surfers' beach and parking is often a problem since it's so limited. Insiders park legally where they can find a place and walk a number of blocks to the beach.

Children search for sea anemones in tidepools during low tides. PHOTO: BRETT SHOAF, COURTESY OF THE SAN DIEGO CONVENTION & VISITORS BUREAU

Moonlight State Beach
Encinitas

Exit I-5 at Encinitas Boulevard and drive west. There is parking on C Street and Third Street. This is one of the nicest beaches in North County: a place where kids can run and parents can play. There are rest rooms, public phones, a snack bar, showers, fire rings, and picnic tables. Moonlight State Beach is a popular swimming beach with lots of wide sandy areas that make walking fun. This beach is about a 5-block walk from the commuter train station.

Swami's
Encinitas

Just below Sea Cliff County Park, where First Street and Highway 101 merge, is Swami's. There are rest rooms, tables, barbecues, and public telephones at the park on the bluff. Above the beach is a romantic sunset-watching spot and an excellent place to whale watch during the winter months. To get to the surfing beach—no sand, just pebbles—there are stairs. Swami's is known worldwide as an excellent surfing beach and is best left to the pros. It's a dangerous place for casual swimmers or amateur surfers, since the seasoned surfers are more interested in riding their waves than looking out for swimmers.

San Elijo State Beach
Cardiff

Just south of Swami's is San Elijo State Beach. There's a campground here and facilities from showers to snack foods; there's a $3.00 charge if you want to park in the campground. There is limited street parking along Highway 101. You'll find the stairs to the beach at the campground, too. It's another San Diego pebble beach so you'll need to wear sneakers unless your feet are tough. San Elijo State Beach is locally known as "Cardiff Pipes." There are lifeguard stations.

Tide Beach
Solana Beach

You can reach this sandy beach by exiting I-5 at Lomas Santa Fe Drive. Drive west past First Street (which in places may be marked Highway 101) to Acacia Avenue. Turn right to Solana Vista Drive and you'll see the sign for Tide Beach. Parking is limited. There is a lifeguard tower and a wide shoreline that's good for walkers. There is a large reef just offshore that's perfect for snorkelers (if the surf is calm). It's also a great spot to look for sea creatures in the tidepools when the tide is low.

Fletcher Cove
Solana Beach

Just south of Tide Beach, you'll notice this one has sand; there's a parking lot at Plaza Street and South Sierra Avenue. Fletcher Cove, also locally known as Pill Box Beach, is popular with fitness walkers and families. The beach is open between 6:00 A.M. and 10:00 P.M. There are rest rooms, showers, telephones, and fire rings.

Dog Beach
Del Mar

Insiders started calling it Dog Beach because you can let Fido off the leash

Insiders' Tip

One of our favorite beach activities is absolutely free. It's called tidepooling, and it involves clambering about on wet rocks looking for sea creatures in pools of water left by the receding tide. You can find starfish, sea anemones, hermit crabs, and other critters at tidepools at Ocean Beach, Tourmaline, La Jolla Cove, Moonlight, and any beach with a rocky shoreline.

here, and the name stuck. Exit I-5 at Via de La Valle and turn right on Hwy. 101. There's roadside parking; handicap access is difficult since you'll be crossing dirt paths and must hike up and down some cliffs. Look for the beach access signs. Dog Beach is found between Via de La Valle and the San Dieguito River. The area is also called "Rivermouth."

Insiders sometimes forget to explain a few things about Dog Beach. As much fun as it sounds, not all dog owners bring friendly, kid-loving pets to the beach. If you're planning a family outing, talk to the kids about dog safety before you hit the sand. Make sure your canine companion is current with all vaccinations, isn't aggressive, and doesn't infringe on others. Then you can hope that others do the same.

Del Mar Beaches
Del Mar

The beaches in Del Mar are wide, and wonderful for family times, beach walking, and swimming. The Del Mar beaches are typical of postcard photos friends and family have sent you when they've visited San Diego. The beaches are open 24 hours a day. The central lifeguard tower is staffed between 9:00 A.M. and 8:00 P.M.; additional towers add staff as beach use demands. There are no fire rings or tables here, but portable barbecues are permitted. Parking is always at a premium.

Above Del Mar Beach is Seagrove Park with a tot lot, picnic tables, benches, grassy picnic areas, and places to spread a blanket, but no other facilities. This is a popular, brown-bag lunchtime area for those who work in Del Mar. There's metered parking and controls are enforced.

Good news in Del Mar—there's disability access. There are two special beaches where wheelchairs are kept at the main lifeguard station, and many beach entrances are wheelchair accessible.

Torrey Pines State Beach
Del Mar

Exit I-5 at Carmel Valley Road and turn left at Torrey Pines State Beach. There is some roadside parking, but you'll have to climb over some rocks to reach the sand. There is a parking lot with a $2.00 entry fee where you'll have access to rest rooms and public telephones. There's beach access from the parking lot and no fee for visitors on foot.

Here's where you'll find the entrance to Torrey Pines State Beach, a 1,750-acre park with picnic tables, walking trails, sandy and pebbled beaches, and rest rooms. Along the beach are lifeguard towers. Picnics are permitted on the beach, but not in the wildlife preserve area.

Unique along the coastline is the Torrey Pines State Beach underwater park. It is protected and maintained for marine research and enjoyment by scuba and snorkel divers.

Black's Beach
Torrey Pines

Black's Beach is famous (or infamous) as San Diego County's nude beach. Actually, the nudity is not legal, but officials look the other way. The access to the nude area involves a climb down a steep path from the Torrey Pines Gliderport at 2800 Torrey Pines Scenic Drive. You can also reach the clothing-optional area by walking south along the sand from Torrey Pines State Beach. There are no facilities or lifeguards.

> **Insiders' Tip**
>
> Several beaches have a supply of large-wheel sand chairs for beach lovers with disabilities. They are available on a first-come, first-served basis at the main lifeguard towers at Coronado City Beach, Imperial Beach, La Jolla Chores, Ocean Beach, South Mission Beach, Oceanside, and Torrey Pines State Beach.

This smiling fisherman's catch has the attention of a group of children. PHOTO: DALE FROST, COURTESY OF PORT OF SAN DIEGO

La Jolla Shores Beach
La Jolla

La Jolla Shores is a favorite hangout for teenagers and families. It's a wide, sandy beach nearly a mile long, with a gently sloping ocean floor. Waves are usually fairly gentle—just the right size for those who want a taste of wave action without being bowled over every time a set rolls in. Separate water areas are reserved for swimming and surfing. Rest rooms and showers are located 100 yards north and south of the main lifeguard tower, which is staffed daily. Kellogg Park, a nice grassy area for those who don't like sand in their peanut butter and jelly, is located behind the tower.

To get to La Jolla Shores, take La Jolla Village Drive west from I-5 south, or Ardath Road from I-5 north. Follow the signs to Torrey Pines Road and head south. Turn right on La Jolla Shores Boulevard and left on Camino del Oro to the beach. A free parking lot runs the length of La Jolla Shores, but it fills up quickly during summer months. Then you're on your own. You can park on adja-

cent streets, but you will probably end up with a big hike ahead of you. It's a good idea to drop your companions and all your gear at the beach if the lot is full, then only one of you has to make the trek from car to beach.

La Jolla Cove
La Jolla

To reach La Jolla Cove, follow the directions for La Jolla Shores, but continue on Torrey Pines Road to Prospect Street. Turn right and follow the road to Coast Boulevard. The cove is in the 1100 block. Swimming, snorkeling, and scuba diving are the activities permitted at the cove. It's a north-facing cove and has unusually coarse sand, but water visibility is usually excellent, sometimes as much as 30 feet, which is why so many divers and snorkelers frequent the waters here. Grassy Scripps Park is immediately adjacent to the cove and is a fine place for a picnic. Lifeguards are on duty year-round, and a public rest room with showers is located in Scripps Park. This is a great place to bring the family, especially the little ones who might be overwhelmed by big waves. Come early, though: parking is limited to what's available on the street.

Marine Street Beach
La Jolla

This is a local's hangout for those who like to toss Frisbees, sunbathe, and scuba dive. From La Jolla Boulevard, the main street that runs north/south through La Jolla, turn west on Marine Street and drive to the foot of the street. Parking is limited to what's available on adjacent streets. The drawback to Marine Street Beach is that there are no facilities and no lifeguard service. Perhaps it's the isolation that draws people here, but Insiders know there's something else, too: a wicked shore break that challenges even the most experienced body surfers. If rough and tumble in the waves sounds like a day in heaven, this may well be the ideal spot for you. Otherwise, you might prefer to stick to one of the more conventional beaches.

Windansea Beach
La Jolla

Windansea is both a swimming and surfing beach distinguished by its sandstone rocks that take the place of sand. It offers a secluded and scenic atmosphere for sunbathing; swimming and surfing are a bit more of a challenge, and this is not a recommended place for diving. To reach Windansea, turn west off La Jolla Boulevard to Neptune Place, and park wherever you can find a spot on the street.

Like Marine Street Beach, Windansea has a shorebreak, a condition on steep beaches that produces hard-breaking surf right at the shoreline. Experienced swimmers and surfers know to take care while entering and exiting the water to avoid injury. Lifeguards are present only during the summer months.

Bird Rock
La Jolla

Take Bird Rock Avenue west off La Jolla Boulevard and drive to the end of the street to find this unusual beach. Bird Rock is not a beach for swimmers or sun-

bathers, but surfers, divers, and bird watchers love it. Conditions for both surfing and diving are usually top notch, but the big draw is the beach's namesake: Bird Rock. It's a huge boulder that sits right off the coast and plays host to scores of visiting sea birds. Bring your binoculars. No facilities or lifeguard staffing is available at Bird Rock. Parking is limited to what's available on the surrounding streets.

Tourmaline Surfing Park
Pacific Beach

No swimming is allowed at this designated surfing park, but surfers flock to Tourmaline in droves. Turn west off La Jolla Boulevard onto Tourmaline Street and head for the large parking lot. Surfers love the year-round reef break, and there's enough room for novices to practice without being overrun by more seasoned surfers. There's a nice picnic area for those who'll be staying shoreside, and rest rooms and showers are conveniently situated in the park.

North Pacific Beach
San Diego

This mile-long beach stretches south from Tourmaline Surfing Park to Crystal Pier,

> ## Insiders' Tip
> Many of San Diego's beaches lose their sand during winter storms and become rocky and difficult to walk on. At some beaches, such as the popular Moonlight Beach in Encinitas, sand is trucked in every spring to replenish the beach. At others, such as Ocean Beach, the sand is piled into berms to prevent flooding during winter high tides, then smoothed out in spring.

Palm trees and soft breezes grace this evening paradise. PHOTO: COURTESY OF SAN DIEGO CONVENTION AND VISITORS BUREAU

which is located at the foot of Garnet Avenue, the main drag through Pacific Beach. To reach the beach, take the Grand Avenue/Garnet Avenue exit from I-5 and drive west to the beach. It's a beach that's protected by high cliffs, and it has separate water areas for swimming and surfing. Lifeguards staff the beach from spring break through the end of October. Scuba diving is not recommended here because of the heavy use by surfers and sailboarders, and also because there just isn't too much undersea life in this area. Rest rooms and showers are located at the foot of Diamond Street and Law Street on the south end and at Tourmaline on the north end. You can park either in the Tourmaline lot or on nearby residential streets.

Pacific Beach/Mission Beach/South Mission Beach
San Diego

A continuous 2 miles of sand bordered by a cement boardwalk stretches south from Crystal Pier, at the foot of Garnet Avenue, to the channel entrance to Mission Bay. It's

the busiest and most popular beach in the county during the summertime. People-watching is a preferred activity, and the boardwalk provides plenty of it. Joggers, walkers, inline skaters, skateboarders, and bicyclists combine to form a never-ending parade of entertainment. The beach itself has separate water areas for swimming and surfing. Lifeguards staff the main lifeguard towers at the foot of Grand Avenue in Pacific Beach, West Mission Bay Drive in Mission Beach, and Avalon Court in South Mission Beach. During the summer months, additional lifeguards staff seasonal towers that are sprinkled along the beach. Public rest rooms and showers are located on all three beach areas.

Alcohol is permitted on the beach between 8:00 A.M. and 8:00 P.M., but not on the boardwalk. There is much debate among local politicos and those who own homes near the beach about the wisdom of allowing alcohol here. Some feel it lends to the general rowdiness, others say it's their right to quaff a few cold ones while sunbathing on the sand. The issue has not been resolved. Be sure to read the signs posted along the beach, and don't carry alcohol in your cooler if it's not permitted—you can be ticketed. Scuba diving is not recommended here because there's not much underwater sea life and the water is usually crowded with swimmers and surfers. To reach any of these beaches, walk along any of the streets west from Mission Boulevard, but don't bother trying to park there. You're best off heading for the lots along south Mission Boulevard, by Belmont Park. Get here early. Once the lots are full, the police block off vehicle access to the beach except for residents.

Mission Bay Park Beaches
San Diego

More than 4,600 acres make up Mission Bay Park—half water and half land. The park has 27 miles of shoreline, 19 of which are sandy beaches. To find Mission Bay, take the West Mission Bay Drive exit from I-8 west and follow the signs—they're plentiful and easy to follow. You'll see just about everything here: power boaters, sail boaters, rowers, water skiers, picnickers, joggers, and even swimmers. The many coves and inlets provide scenic spots for a day at the beach, and the gentle bay is

often preferred by families with small children. Lifeguard staffing usually begins around spring-break time, and continues on the weekends until summer, when it becomes daily. After summer, weekend staffing continues until the end of October. Between November and spring break, there's no lifeguard staffing on any of Mission Bay's beaches. Rest rooms and showers are liberally sprinkled throughout Mission Bay. A bonus is that most of the swimming beaches have large parking lots.

Ocean Beach
San Diego

A wide, sandy beach, O.B. is populated mostly by locals and visitors who are staying in the area. Drive west on I-8 until the freeway ends at Sunset Cliffs Boulevard. Follow Sunset Cliffs Boulevard to Newport Avenue. Turn right, and park in the large lot at the Ocean Beach Municipal Pier or in one of the auxiliary lots along Abbott Street. Surfing is especially popular just north of the pier, and there are separate water areas for swimming. The main lifeguard station is staffed year-round, and additional stations are set up during the summer.

Heavy surf crashes over the seawall at Children's Pool in La Jolla. PHOTO: CECE CANTON

At the north end of Ocean Beach, separated by a long rock jetty, is Dog Beach. Dog owners are allowed to let their pets run free on the beach. Their owners are a congenial group who strive to keep the beach clean. Keep in mind that even though disposal facilities are provided, some people do not pick up after their dogs. Dog Beach has become something of a local legend; the owners and their pets even march together in the Ocean Beach Christmas parade. If you're traveling with a dog, be sure to let it have its day at the beach here.

Rest rooms and showers are located at the foot of Santa Monica Boulevard and Brighton Avenue.

Sunset Cliffs Park
San Diego

Take I-8 west to Sunset Cliffs Boulevard and follow it until you see an impressive sight: towering cliffs with surf pounding at the base. This is one of the best spots in San Diego to watch a sunset; every Insider has a pile of Sunset Cliffs snapshots. Staircases at the foot of Bermuda Avenue, Santa Cruz Avenue, and Ladera Street lead down to small, secluded beaches from which you can surf, scuba dive, and swim. Novices are best off staying on top of the cliffs, however. The surf can be rough here, and swimmers can find it hard to get back to shore without crashing into rocks. Life-

guard rescues are common here, and residents in the area are accustomed to hearing the blare of sirens as lifeguards and ambulances rush to the scene. It's important to note that the cliffs are soft and continuously eroding, so mind the warning signs and use only specified approaches to the beaches. A few parking lots are sprinkled along the cliffs; otherwise, street parking is usually easy to find. There are no lifeguards or other facilities.

Coronado City Beach
Coronado

Aside from being one of the prettiest beaches in San Diego, long, wide, and sandy, there's some romance attached to Coronado Beach, too. It's the Hotel del Coronado that lends the romance, and rightfully so. It's hard to feel less than royal when you're sunbathing with the grand hotel as a backdrop. This is a great family beach with lots of room to spread out. Crowds are well behaved and the beach is always spotlessly clean. Fishing, swimming, and surfing are all given separate water areas, and nearby Sunset Park is a large grassy area for picnickers and Frisbee throwers. There is a wheelchair ramp leading down the sand almost to the water line. Once you're on the island of Coronado, take Orange Avenue west to the beach, and park wherever you can find a spot on residential streets. Plenty of lifeguards and rest rooms are provided.

Silver Strand State Beach
Between Coronado and Imperial Beach

From Coronado, take California Highway 75 south to the signs that point the way to the beach. From Imperial Beach, take the Palm Avenue exit from I-5 and drive west until it veers north to Silver Strand Boulevard. Silver Strand State Beach has something unique in San Diego: clamming. It's typically an East-Coast activity, but you should be able to dig up some of the tasty mollusks at Silver Strand. Also look for the tiny silver shells for which the beach was named. They cover the 2 miles of shoreline on the narrow spit of land between the ocean and San Diego Bay. There are facilities galore here: picnic areas, rest rooms, lifeguard stations, and RV camping.

Imperial Beach

Imperial Beach is a vast, sandy beach that's popular with swimmers, surfers, and boogie-boarders. It's also home to the annual sand-castle competition (see our Annual Events chapter for more details on this ultra-fun event), which draws a ton of people every August. The Imperial Beach Pier, at the south end of the beach, is a favorite with folks who like to fish. Grassy picnic areas are available, as are rest rooms and year-round lifeguard service. Drive west on Palm Avenue from I-5 until you reach the ocean. Parking is tight, as it is at most beaches, but you should be able to find something either in one of the lots or on nearby residential streets.

Watersports

Freshwater Fishing

Freshwater fishing is a popular hobby with lots of Insiders and visitors, and there are several lakes that have rental boats available. The popular fishing lakes are regularly stocked with rainbow trout, catfish, and other popular catches. All anglers over the age of 8 must have a California state fishing license and a freshwater fishing permit.

At **Lake Miramar,** Scripps Lake Drive off Scripps Ranch Boulevard, Central San Diego (619-668-2050), you can fish for rainbow trout, bass, catfish, and channel catfish.

Lake Murray at Mission Trails Regional Park, 1 Father Junipero Serra Trail, Central San Diego (619-668-3275), is open Wednesday, Saturday, Sunday, and major holidays between November and Labor Day for fishing.

Lake Poway Recreation Area, Lake Poway Road off Rancho Bernardo Road, Poway (858-679-5466), has a 60-acre reservoir for boating and fishing. Fishing and boating are allowed Wednesday through Sunday from sunrise to sunset. The lake is stocked with rainbow trout weekly from November through mid-May, and with catfish in the summer months.

Lake Morena County Park, Lake Morena Road, off California Highway 94,

Dads enjoy teaching their kids how to fish off local piers and fishing boats. PHOTO: BRETT SHOAF, COURTESY OF THE SAN DIEGO CONVENTION & VISITORS BUREAU

or Buckman Springs Road, off I-8, near Campo (858-694-3049), has a "fish report hotline" at (619) 478-5473. Fishing is popular here, and bass, bluegill, catfish, crappie, and stocked trout crowd the lake. There's a rowboat launch, too.

Guajome County Park, Guajome Lakes Road, near Mission Avenue, Vista (858-565-3600), gives you the chance to fish and picnic or bird watch all in the same developed park and wildness area. The park is nearly 600 acres, with trails. The lake has shore fishing and is popular with kids from the area.

Lake Cuyamaca, Highway 79 between Highway 78 and I-8 in eastern San Diego County (760-765-0515), has year-round trout fishing, along with smallmouth bass, channel catfish, bluegill, and sturgeon. The 110-acre lake is an angler's delight, populated by fans of both fly-fishing and boat fishing. Free fishing classes are offered every Saturday at 10:00 A.M.

Be sure to read our Parks chapter for information on all the lakes that have fishing, boating, and watersporting possibilities. If you prefer to cast your line in the ocean, see this chapter's section on Sport Fishing.

Wherever you go, you are required to have a California State Fishing License. A resident sport fishing license costs $30.45.

A nonresident license costs $81.65. The license is good from January through December; it's not good for a year from the date you purchased it. You may also need special permits for catching certain fish. A two-day sport fishing license costs $11.05 and allows you to fish in fresh and salt water. For up-to-date information on licenses, call the California Department of Fish and Game at (916) 227-2244. Most bait and tackle shops and sport fishing outfitters sell licenses. There is a $250 fine for fishing without a license. You may fish from piers without a license or if you are 16 or younger.

Kayaking/Canoeing/ Wave Riding

One of the best ways to experience San Diego's waterways is in a kayak or canoe. Be sure to check posted signs before putting your vessel in the water; boating regulations vary. Boating is not allowed in certain wildlife preserve areas, including Buena Vista Lagoon and Batiquitos Lagoon in Carlsbad.

Aqua Adventures Kayak School
1548 Quivera Way, Central San Diego
(619) 523–9577, (800) 269–7792
www.aqua-adventures.com

This full-service center offers kayak rentals, sales, and tours. The fee for a full-day kayak rental is $35, and the shop has a frequent-renter program with reduced rates. Rentals include lifejackets, and the shop has a selection of wetsuits you can rent for an additional fee. You can also arrange for kayak instruction and take advantage of the ocean and river kayaking trips and tours, including trips to Baja.

California Water Sports Rentals
4215 Harrison St., Carlsbad
(760) 434–3089

Located at Snug Harbor Marina in North County Coastal, this store provides everything you need for a watersporting good time, including instruction on use and safety.

You can rent kayaks and canoes for $12 to $18 an hour. You can rent Wave Riders for $50 to $75 for an hour, and the equipment can be shared with up to three people. When you rent motorized equipment, you'll also be shown a seven-minute safety and instructional video. They like having first-timers come to Snug Harbor Marina and make sure there are plenty of instructors on the beach for additional help. You can also take classes on these sports at the marina. Snug Harbor also has a pro shop, snack bar, and picnic tables.

Carlsbad Paddle Sports
2780 Carlsbad Blvd., Carlsbad
(760) 434-8686
www.carlsbad.paddle.com

For paddle sports and kayak fun, Insiders use this store, which is more than a place to rent equipment. Knowledgeable staff here provide instruction, lead adventure trips, and can tell you about local paddling possibilities. They sponsor paddles at the La Jolla sea caves and in Oceanside harbor. If you need equipment, it's $45 for an eight-hour kayak rental.

The adventure trips to Catalina and Baja aren't just for the adventurous; the staff is well qualified to instruct even novice kayakers. The trip to Catalina Island includes everything from wetsuit to kayak, food to tent; you just bring a sleeping bag. No, you don't kayak across the rough Pacific to Catalina, but take the ferry out of San Pedro, near Los Angeles. The actual paddling is about 6 miles of kayaking. The cost is $340 per person.

The trip to Baja is less expensive, although you must bring everything you'll need (except the kayaks, which are provided). The paddling trip is about 8-miles long and costs $175 per person. Participants meet at a designated spot on Baja's western coastline. For Baja or any of the treks, you'll want to follow the checklist the store gives you when you pre-register.

REI-Recreational Equipment Inc.
5556 Copley Dr., San Diego
(858) 279-4400
www.rei.com

If you don't want to transport your kayak to San Diego or if you want to try the sport without buying one, REI is your ticket. It's $60 to rent an ocean kayak for one day. For those who are not members of the REI association, there's a security deposit of $150. Membership costs $15. The store's savvy staff reminds you to reserve a kayak if you want it for a holiday weekend. The store also has a full line of outdoor accessories for sports from camping to biking, and rents lots of other equipment. See our Recreation chapter for more about REI's climbing wall.

Resort Watersports
Catamaran Hotel, 3999 Mission Blvd., Pacific Beach
(858) 539-8696
Bahia Hotel, 998 W. Mission Bay Dr., Mission Beach
(858) 539-7696

For rentals of watersporting equipment and lessons, Resort Watersports is a one-stop shopping and outfitting emporium. Single and double kayaks range from $17 to $20 for an hour's rental. There is a discount if you want to rent them for a day. The staff shows you how to use the equipment and then lets you get out on the bay or ocean. Call first to reserve equipment since this is a popular shop.

Windsport
844 W. Mission Bay Dr., San Diego
(858) 488-4642

This is a full-service kayaking and windsurfing shop where you can buy and rent kayaks. They also have kayaking accessories from lifejackets to designer sunscreen. The price for a sit-on kayak is $13 for an hour, $36 for four hours and $45 for a full eight-hour day. You'll get some basic instructions from the craft-smart staff before they set you free to paddle the bay. If you'd like further instruction on other kayaks, a two-hour private lesson is just $60. Be sure to call ahead to rent or arrange lessons.

Sailing and Power Boating

San Diego is a sailor's dream come true. You can sail on San Diego Bay or just around Shelter and Harbor Islands. You can sail up and down the coastline and never lose sight of land. You can head for Catalina, the Channel Islands, or even Hawaii (as long as you know what you're doing).

You can also sail on some of our local lakes. Lake Hodges, at Lake Drive off I-15

and Via Rancho Parkway, Escondido (760-735-8088), has a small boat launch and a boat-rental concessionaire. There's a shady picnic area, parking, and tiny grocery stores in the area should you forget to bring lunch. (See our Parks chapter for more places to boat and sail on our lakes.)

Many marinas have sailboats to rent, and depending on the size and length of time you'll be on it, they are priced accordingly. If you want to sail around San Diego Bay you can get a 14-foot Capri for as little as $18 an hour. Visitors and Insiders rent the boats for a few hours to see the city from a different viewpoint and experience the joys of being on the water.

With the small, two-person sailboats, you may be restricted to the bays and marinas and will be asked to show that you're competent with the boats before you leave the dock. There's usually a security deposit required when you rent a boat. For larger sailing crafts, you may have to take a test cruise with an instructor (for a fee), and only then will you be able to set sail. Many of the sailboat rental companies have sailing clubs and lessons. Local parks and recreation offices in coastal

Sailing the harbor at sunset can be a memorable experience. PHOTO: JAMES BLANK, COURTESY OF THE SAN DIEGO CONVENTION AND VISITORS BUREAU

Several California gray seals come ashore during heavy surf at La Jolla. PHOTO: CECE CANTON

communities like Oceanside will have sailing and other watersport classes, too.

Harbor Sailboats
2040 Harbor Island Dr., San Diego
(619) 291–9568
www.harborsailboats.com

You don't have to take lessons here to get into a sailboat. You will have to show you know what you're doing though when a staff member checks you out before untying the mooring ropes. Prices range from $60 for four hours on a 22-foot Capri to $475 for a full day aboard a 411 Beneteau. If you're headed to San Diego and have made up your mind to sail, just call and reserve a craft. Remember that over holiday weekends (and we're talking Thanksgiving and Christmas, too) and the summer months, boat availability may be limited. By renting boats here, you get yacht club discounts and instruction for all levels and can enjoy other club and cruising experiences. There's a pool, deli, and restaurant on site at the Harbor Island Sailing Club.

Resort Watersports
Catamaran Hotel, 3999 Mission Blvd., Pacific Beach
(858) 539–8696
Bahia Hotel, 998 W. Mission Bay Dr., Mission Beach
(858) 539–7696

As mentioned above, Resort Watersports is the place to rent everything from kayaks to wave runners. They also rent powerboats (a 16-foot powerboat will cost you $65 for an hour, $195 for four hours). They rent sail boats too. The Capri sailboats, 14-, 18-, and 22-foot lengths, range from $18 to $35 for an hour and there's a savings if you want to rent in four-hour periods. Call to reserve boats and for more information.

Scuba Diving

San Diego has some excellent locations for scuba diving, if you don't mind cold water and wetsuits. In fact, some of the earliest divers perfected the sport in San Diego's waters. Divers from the Scripps Institute

Insiders' Tip

If you decide to visit the beaches in Del Mar and Ocean Beach, where dogs are permitted, keep in mind that dogs are dogs. Some dogs are friendly and some dogs are not. And there are irresponsible beach-goers who "forget" to clean up after Fido. You may have to watch where you step, sit down, or play in the sand. If you are not a dog lover, head to another of our area's fine beaches.

of Oceanography have photographed incredible underwater sights here, and there is a strong and enthusiastic scuba community. As is common everywhere, you must be a certified diver to get your tanks filled and to dive legally with local operators. If you're in town for a week or so, you can get certified in as little as four days and then be able to discover and explore the fascinating underwater world. However, even though the intrepid diver can find lots of interest in local waters, most novice scuba divers head elsewhere. The water here tends to be cold most of the year, and a consistent surge can keep things murky underwater. Sometimes visibility is limited to a foot or less.

Once you're a certified diver, the best spots for diving are La Jolla Underwater Ecological Reserve and the kelp beds off Point Loma. You're likely to see California's state fish, the tiny but brilliantly colored orange Garibaldi, as well as countless varieties of large fish. Keep in mind that if you're diving in any ecological reserve, it's prohibited to remove anything—even a shell. Look, but don't touch.

La Jolla Cove is beautiful and has become a popular beach for swimming and sunning. PHOTO: COURTESY OF SAN DIEGO CONVENTION AND VISITORS BUREAU

Boat diving is also popular here; you can choose from half- and full-day trips to the Coronado Islands in Mexico or trips around local waters. Safety is a big issue with scuba diving, so always remember what you've been taught: Dive with a buddy and observe all the safety rules your instructor has pounded into your head.

The Diving Locker
1020 Grand Ave., San Diego
(858) 272–1120
www.dininglocker.com

Since 1959 the instructors at the Diving Locker have been teaching the skills of scuba to thousands of would-be divers. Lessons start at around $150 and include four pool sessions, four classroom sessions, and five ocean dives. Students are required to provide their own mask, snorkel, gloves, and booties. The Diving Locker also offers certified divers full equipment rentals for $35.

Ocean Enterprises
7710 Balboa Ave., San Diego
(858) 565–6054
www.oceanenterprises.com

This excellent dive shop offers all levels of PADI certification courses starting at about $150. They run several specials throughout the year at reduced rates. The shop is a diver's delight and displays all the latest gear in the brightest neon colors. They also offer rental gear and boat dives.

San Diego Divers Supply
4004 Sports Arena Blvd., San Diego
(619) 224–3439

For $99 plus the cost of materials (which brings the price up to about $160), San Diego Divers Supply offers a four-week certification class for new divers. You'll learn the basics in pool classes and on an ocean dive. Once certified, the store can fill all your equipment needs at a deep discount. Rental equipment is available, too.

Water Education Training
4122 Napier St., San Diego
(619) 275–1822, (866) 261–7716
www.getwetscuba.com

This PADI facility offers several levels of scuba instruction, beginning with an open-water certification class starting at $250. Boat dives are also offered by W.E.T., for $65 you can dive for a half-day off Point Loma or La Jolla. They also offer boat dives to several sunken ships and artificial reefs in the area.

Snorkeling

If the time and expense involved in full scuba certification put you off, try snorkeling. With just a mask, snorkel, and fins, you can explore the underwater world for as long as you wish. You can even learn to dive below the surface, holding your breath and then resurfacing and blowing the water out of your snorkel with ease. There's much to be seen that's close to the surface and the shore of the beach, and equipment is easily rented or purchased. All sporting goods stores sell snorkeling equipment. If you're serious about the sport, it's nice to have your own mask that fits well. You can even get a mask that matches your eyeglass prescription if need be.

Insiders' Tip

Water contamination is a serious problem at San Diego's beaches, unfortunately. Contamination is most common at Mission Bay, Ocean Beach, and Imperial Beach. Keep an eye out for signs warning swimmers to stay out of the water, and follow their advice. You may see some hard-core surfers ignoring the signs, but their bravado often results in ear infections and other illnesses.

The best place by far for snorkeling in the county is La Jolla Cove, where there are rarely any waves or strong currents. At most other beaches, you'll need to check the waves before trying to breathe through a snorkel without having it fill with water. There are good snorkeling spots at Tourmaline Beach, Sunset Cliffs, and Bird Rock.

O.E. Express
2158 Avenida de la Playa, La Jolla
(858) 454–6195
www.oeexpress.com

This is the closest place to La Jolla Cove where you can rent or purchase snorkeling equipment. Daily rental rates are $5.00 for a mask and snorkel and $5.00 for fins. O.E. Express also offers full scuba training and equipment.

Play It Again Sports
1401 Garnet Ave., San Diego
(858) 490–0222
8366 Parkway Dr., La Mesa
(619) 667–9499
9969 Mira Mesa Blvd., San Diego
(858) 695–3030

If you're in the market to purchase snorkeling equipment (or any watersport equipment, for that matter) this is a great place to check out. The store specializes in new and used equipment, and you can find everything from a mask to a wetsuit here, all at a big discount.

Sport Fishing

Most sport fishing boats operate year-round in San Diego, regardless of the weather. The waters off San Diego are home to albacore, yellowfin and bluefin tuna, marlin, shark, yellowtail, barracuda, bonito, calico bass, sand bass, halibut, and rock cod. There are specific seasons for the various types of fish. The best season is from May to October. If you have your heart set on catching a big tuna, ask if they're in the nearby waters before forking over the money for a trip. The sport fishing companies we've included offer half- or full-day excursions, along with overnight trips. Before deciding on an expedition, consider what's included in the price, such as gear and food. Other factors are impor-

It's a great day for families in the sun on a Mission Bay beach. PHOTO: COURTESY OF SAN DIEGO CONVENTION AND VISITORS BUREAU

tant too, like how the boats are equipped, the number of passengers they carry, the facilities on board, the size of the boats, and the experience of the crew. You must have a California Fishing License even when going out with a charter boat. Most bait and tackle shops and sport fishing outfitters sell licenses. A two-day sportfishing license costs $11.05 and allows you to fish in fresh and salt water. There is a $250 fine for fishing without a license. See the Freshwater Fishing section for further information on fishing licenses.

Fisherman's Landing
2838 Emerson St., San Diego
(619) 221–8500

Charter boats are available with Fisherman's Landing for one-day, two-day, or long-range trips lasting several nights. The captains will head for whatever type of fish is in the waters and do their best to make sure even novices catch something. The cost of a one-day trip on a 65- to 95-foot boat, which leaves at night and returns the next evening, ranges from $135 to $175; gear rental is extra. Equipment is available for purchase.

H&M Sportfishing
2803 Emerson St., Central San Diego
(619) 222–1144

H&M offers half-day and longer trips. Their half-day trips stick close to shore and are a good option for those trying fishing for the first time. Tackle sales and equipment rental are available. The cost of renting rods for a short trip is about $15 to $29. The cost of a half-day trip is $35 to $65; the fishing permit is not included.

Point Loma Sportfishing
1403 Scott St., Central San Diego
(619) 233–1627
www.pointlomasportfishing.com

This outfit arranges fishing trips on several different charter boats. They offer nearly every type of fishing you might want, from short, inexpensive trips to long-range trips lasting 16 days or more. One-day of deep-sea fishing costs $90 for adults and $75 for children under 16. A

Insiders' Tip

For an up-to-the-minute surf report for the entire coastline, call Encinitas Surfboards at (760) 753-0506.

two-day trip (which gives you a better chance of catching big fish) costs about $365 and includes a bunk or a cabin and meals. Longer trips cost anywhere from $300 to $5,000.

Seaforth Sportsfishing
1717 Quivira Rd., San Diego
(619) 224–3383
www.seaforthlanding.com

Seaforth has half-day, full-day, and twilight trips and is conveniently located at Mission Bay Park. The company has tackle and bait for sale and equipment can be rented. Specialty trips include shark and rock cod in season, and this company fishes the waters off the Coronado Islands. For the partial-day trip, 6:30 A.M. until 4:00 P.M., the cost is $43 for adults and $33 for children 15 and younger. For the two-day sports fishing trip, 10:00 P.M. until 10:00 P.M. the following day, the cost is $135 to $175 per person and includes sleeping accommodations but not food.

Surfing

San Diego County has world-renowned surfing beaches, including Trestles, Windansea, and Swami's. These are the premier spots to ride big waves when the surf is high. If you're visiting and have to see the sport San Diego-style or are into the surfing scene, check out these beaches and the surfers by the pier at Ocean Beach or at Tourmaline Beach. See this chapter's "Beaches" section for information on these and other surfing spots. We also have some pretty cool surf shops. Following are a few Insiders' favorites.

The Beach Company
1129 S. Coast Hwy., Oceanside
(760) 722-2578

The surf shop prides itself on its large selection of merchandise, lots of it at unexpected and wonderfully affordable prices. They want to make the sport affordable for everyone. The store carries surfboards, body boards, and wetsuits. They also sell swimwear, sportswear, and footwear, including those surfer-style soft leather boots imported from Australia. In addition, should you have ding problems, they have a technician right at the store who can help. Just bring in your board, and they'll offer you a quote for repairs.

California Surf-n-Sport
617 Pearl St., La Jolla
(858) 454-4580

Smack dab in the middle of La Jolla's upscale shopping district (see our Shopping chapter), this wonderful store is for you if you're California dreamin' of surf paraphernalia. They have surfboards (and buy used ones), wetsuits, clothing (with all the right labels), and body boards. If you're already going shopping or dining in La Jolla, step inside, and you'll be certain to find the right outfit to make your San Diego stay truly cool.

Emerald City Surf Shop
3126 Mission Blvd., Ste. G, San Diego
(858) 488-9224
1118 Orange Ave., Coronado
(619) 435-6677
www.ecboardsource.com

Insiders swear that Emerald City Surf Shops have the best prices on brand-name surf gear, so some trek from outlying areas to come to the stores. The Mission Boulevard store is in Mission Beach and is located near the roller coaster in Belmont Park (see our Attractions chapter). The Coronado store is just 1 block north of the famous Hotel del Coronado (see our Hotels chapter). Emerald City is also a store for buying wave boards and other surf and watersport supplies.

Hansen's
1105 1st St., Encinitas
(760) 753-6595
www.hansensurf.com

Hansen's is the place to come for all the fashion-conscious surf lines of clothing and watersport accessories. That said, many Insiders think of Hansen's as "too touristy." They still come here, though, during sales and if they need something the other stores just don't have. The store carries body boards, water skis, wetsuits, new and used surfboards, and in-line skates too. The store is about 2 blocks north from Swami's (see our "Beaches" section in this chapter) so after you have the right gear, you can hit the waves or watch those who know what they're doing. If you want the surf report in Encinitas, you can call (760) 753-6221.

Longboard Grotto Surf Shop
978 N. Hwy. 101, Encinitas
(760) 634-1920

Want to browse and buy at a store that real surfing Insiders come to? Then Longboard Grotto is it. The store has been selling longboards and books, videos, and memorabilia on surfing and the sport for 20 years. It's fun and funky and an experience whether you've moved here or are cruisin' the coast.

Ocean Snow Surf Shop
1016 W. Valley Pkwy., Escondido
(760) 747-7873
www.oceansnow.com

This store in North County Inland is the place to find everything from tips on the best surfing spots and the newest suggestions on sunscreen to wetsuit wearing recommendations and yes, even surfboards, too. Ocean Snow Surf Shop has been a

---

Insiders' Tip

Be aware that some beaches are "surfing only" beaches during specific hours of the day. Check the signs as you enter the beach area.

Kayaking is one of the best ways to enjoy the peaceful beauty of San Diego's bays. PHOTO: BRETT SHOAF, COURTESY OF THE SAN DIEGO CONVENTION & VISITORS BUREAU

mainstay of the area since 1980 and can supply your clothing and sports needs with quality logo brands.

Offshore Surf Shop
3179 Carlsbad Blvd., Carlsbad
(760) 729–4934
Offshore Surf Shop can outfit you in everything from a perfect-fit wetsuit to reef sandals and shoes. Yes, they sell new and used surf boards. If you're looking for something special, say an antique long board, put in your request here. The store has a full line of men's and women's beachwear from shorts to logo T-shirts and bathing suits. They can also tell you about the surf along Carlsbad State Beaches. Call for the surf report before you head to the coast.

South Coast Surf Shop
5023 Newport Ave., San Diego
(619) 223–7017
www.southcoast.com
This is your place to find out about upcoming surfing contests and buy surfing and water gear and other equipment.

The store also has surf and sports clothing and sometimes has used equipment for sale. It's an Insiders' place to hang out and talk about surfing too.

Sun Diego Surf & Sport
Fashion Valley Mall, 7007 Friars Rd., San Diego
(619) 299–3244
North County Fair Mall, 272 E. Via Rancho Pkwy., Escondido
(760) 489–2332
These surf shops in malls are a stretch for Insiders who are devoted to serious surfing. Many shun them as gauche, others as too commercial. But these same folks also admit that the stores have a place in the county.

So if you find yourself far from the beach and at the mall and say you need some surf wax, a T-shirt, or want the latest copy of a surfing magazine, stop in. The stores have equipment that goes beyond surfing, namely snowboarding and skateboarding merchandise. They have an extensive line of apparel for kids, men, and women too, and if you're looking for truly cool sunglasses, Sun Diego can help you out.

With the luxury of some palm trees for shade and the Coronado Bridge in the background, this group is enjoying one of the many "perfect" beach days that San Diego is famous for. PHOTO: COURTESY OF SAN DIEGO CONVENTION AND VISITORS BUREAU

Surf Rider Board Shop
1909 S. Coast Hwy., Oceanside
(760) 433–4020

If you're looking for surf gear, shoes, and accessories, Surf Rider always offers a big selection of top-quality merchandise, including the designer labels you may be looking for. They have a fine selection of long boards and also rent them for $12 for a half day, $18 for a full day. There's a $250 security deposit on the boards and they do take major credit cards for merchandise and the deposit.

Witt's Carlsbad Pipelines
2975 Carlsbad Blvd., Carlsbad
(760) 729–4423

If you were to create a surf shop for a movie set or television show, you'd build it just like Witt's. It's a bit crowded, loaded with surf stuff and all of the staff has that truly–San Diego surf look down pat, including the warm friendly smiles. If you're from a part of the country or world that doesn't have surf shops and you want to see the ultimate example, head to Witt's and take some snapshots of the store to show the folks back home. This could be one of your favorite memory-making experiences.

At Witt's you'll find Insiders shopping and talking about surfing. It's a welcoming, low-key place with a dedication to service. No surfing question is too basic and no one will laugh if you can't figure out how to get into a skin-tight wetsuit. They want you to succeed at the sport and while the more upscale stores might sell you unnecessary stuff, at Witt's you can depend on solid advice.

Two Insider tips: Witt's has great sales every spring and fall. And Witt's offers trade-ins on surfing stuff. If you've outgrown your board or wetsuit or want to trade up, Witt's can make you a tidy deal on new gear. Just ask.

Swimming

Swimming isn't limited to just beaches; you can get a pool fix at any number of public and municipal pools around the county. Or you might enjoy spending a day at one of the two water parks in the county, Knott's Soak City in Chula Vista or The Wave Waterpark in Vista (check our Attractions chapter for all the details). Many health and fitness clubs have pools that are open to the public for a small fee. And if you're staying at a hotel, you probably need venture no farther than a few steps outside your room. Just in case you want to swim with the locals, though, we'll give you some options.

Municipal pools offer swimming lessons for all ages, from toddlers up to adults, in groups or individually. Lessons start at around $28 per child for ten group lessons and go up from there, depending on age and type of lesson. Recreational swimming hours vary from pool to pool, so be sure to call before you go. At San Diego pools, admission is $2.00 for adults and $1.50 for children younger than 16. Admission prices for pools in other cities around the county are indicated separately. The San Diego municipal pools listed here are the ones that are open year-round. For a complete listing of San Diego pools, call the Swim Hotline at (619) 685–1322.

San Diego Municipal Pools

Allied Gardens
6707 Glenroy St., San Diego
(619) 235–1143

Bud Kearns Memorial Municipal Pool
2229 Morley Field Dr., San Diego
(619) 692–4920

Clairemont
3600 Clairemont Dr., San Diego
(858) 581–9923

Swanson
3585 Governor Dr., San Diego
(858) 552–1653

Tierrasanta
11238 Clairemont Mesa Blvd., San Diego
(858) 636–4837

Vista Terrace
301 Athey Ave., San Ysidro
(619) 424–0469

The steady ocean breezes make the bay a great place to learn to windsurf. PHOTO: DALE FROST, COURTESY OF PORT OF SAN DIEGO

North County Coastal

Carlsbad Community Swim Complex
3401 Monroe St., Carlsbad
(760) 434-2860

Designated hours for lap swimming and recreational swimming are offered here; call for the schedule, which tends to vary because of special events. Admission is $2.00 for adults who are Carlsbad residents, $3.00 for adult nonresidents and $1.00 for children 17 and younger.

North County Inland

Woodland Park Aquatic Complex
671 Woodland Pkwy., San Marcos
(760) 746-2028

Operated by the city of San Marcos, this pool has a 50-foot water slide as well as a water basketball hoop. Admission is $2.00. Call for public swimming hours.

East County

Fletcher Hills Pool, 2345 Center Pl., El Cajon
(619) 441-1672

Public swimming hours are available every day, but tend to vary and are scheduled around lessons. Admission is $1.50 for adults and $1.00 for children 3 to 17.

South Bay

Parkway Pool, 385 Park Way, Chula Vista
(619) 691-5088

You can get your laps in here or merely splash around if the spirit moves you. Admission is $1.50 for adults, $1.00 for seniors and children ages 6 to 17.

Water-Skiing/Jet-Skiing/ Windsurfing

One reason that San Diego is a watersport paradise is that you have choices. You can jet ski, water ski, and windsurf in the ocean, on our bays, or in many of the local lakes. Check with the rangers, however, if you're entering state or community parks and before you put the boat in a lake. Some lakes may allow sailing but not jet skiing, so ask first. For information on rental equipment see our listings under "Kayaking and Wave Riding."

Monkey Sea Monkey Doo Rentals
1551 Shelter Island Dr., San Diego
(619) 222-9625

Monkey Sea Monkey Doo Rentals is the exclusive Sea Doo jet boat rental company in San Diego. If you want to rent a jet ski for two for eight hours the price is as low as $30 per hour. For one hour, it's $60, and they do have other rates depending on how long you want to ski.

Golf

"It's five-star golf," say avid players about the courses in San Diego. That's why championship golf tournaments are held here and why golfers throughout the country drag along their clubs when they're headed to our fair city.

For duffers there are plenty of courses where one can have fun, enjoy the sport, and keep some self-respect intact.

In this chapter, we'll give you the goods on the good places to play. As you look over the listings, be aware that these aren't the only places in the county. The Yellow Pages of your phone book will give you a full listing.

What you have here are the ones we like and recommend to friends and family. And we've included all the extraordinary ones, like Oaks North Golf Course, the ultimate executive course located in Rancho Bernardo. In each case we've tried to sketch out what makes them especially worthy of inclusion—what makes them winners.

If there's an extra cost for the cart, or something special you need to know, like a dress code, we've added that. Most of the courses here have driving ranges and putting greens. However, we haven't repeated those under the driving range category. The driving range entries are strictly that, except for Surf & Turf in Del Mar, in North County Coastal, with its miniature golf area. Here you can play a really short game and it's also fun for the shorter crowd (the kids in our families).

Like restaurants and shopping districts, golf courses sometimes change with time. For instance, one course in North County Coastal had a reputation for well-maintained fairways and manicured greens and for years before developments spread up the coast, it was the only place to play north of Del Mar. Then the owners sold it. Now, rumor has it, when it rains more than a teaspoon, the dry fairways become mudville. So it's smart to call to make sure you'll get what you expect and to verify the greens fees, too.

We've divided our chapter into public golf courses, executive courses and driving ranges, with entries under each category following our usual geographic order. At all of the courses and ranges, you can rent clubs and at most you have to look clean and casual. At the Four Seasons Resort Aviara, for instance, you'll want to spiff up a bit more, since this is an upscale course.

We've omitted those country club and resort courses where you need to be a member or guest to play. Keep in mind, however, that at courses connected to hotels, like the one at the La Costa Resort and Spa in Carlsbad, you can get great golf-package deals.

If you're determined to golf when visiting San Diego, if you want to play at a popular time or if you're traveling a distance, call ahead. Some courses, like Torrey Pines, which hosts the PGA tour, hold tournaments. We provide phone numbers so you can get the scoop and be sure you'll get a tee time.

San Diego's many golf courses are popular year-round. PHOTO: BOB YARBROUGH, COURTESY OF SAN DIEGO CONVENTION & VISITORS BUREAU

Golf Courses

Central San Diego

Balboa Park Municipal Golf Course
2600 Golf Course Dr., San Diego
(619) 570–1234 (reservations), (619) 239–1660 (pro shop)

First opened in 1915, Balboa underwent a comprehensive renovation in 1999. Located in the heart of Balboa Park, it has spectacular views of the San Diego skyline and the Blue Pacific from many of the holes. Seemingly short at 5,801 yards from the white tees, the par 72 course can reach out and bite you when you least expect it. The bulk of the first nine climb in and out of a canyon while the back nine has some new holes that require pinpoint accuracy.

The signature sixth hole is a par 3 that requires you to sail your tee shot over a ravine filled with ball-eating brush. If you hedge your bets and blast one over the green, 193 yards away, you'll have to chip back up from a swale beneath the green. This is a good course for straight hitters

with lots of patience. A driving range with mat tees will get you warmed up, as will a putting green and chipping area. The venerable clubhouse overlooks the 1st and 18th holes. Greens fees during the week are $33; on weekends the fee is $38. A special twilight fee of $19 takes effect at 3:00 P.M. from November through March and 4:00 P.M. from April through October. City residents pay a discounted fee if they carry a resident card, which can be purchased for $12 at the course. The resident greens fee is $20 during the week, $22 on weekends, and $11 for twilight play. Golf cart rental is extra: $21 during the week and $23 on weekends. There are no restrictions on walking.

Coronado Municipal Golf Course
2000 Visalia Row, Coronado
(619) 435–3121 (reservations),
(619) 435–9485 (pro shop)

This is one of the most underrated courses in the county, mainly because it can be tricky getting a tee time, so lots of golfers don't even try. But if you're persistent, you'll be pleasantly rewarded. A beautiful new clubhouse opened in 1997, and the

9th and 18th holes were rebuilt soon thereafter. But the course's greatest claim to fame is that on June 10, 1996, President Bill Clinton shot a 79 here, breaking 80 for the first time in his golfing career.

The par 72, 6,317-yard course is flat and open, and it stays in the shadow of the San Diego-Coronado Bay Bridge for most of the front nine. Still, you'll face two par 5s within the first four holes, so keep your driver polished. A couple of ponds guard the 8th and have been known to swallow many an errant ball. The approach to the 8th is long and requires accurate shooting to avoid the ponds. Fortunately, the back of the green slopes down to hold those shots from far back in the fairway.

Greens fees are $20 for everyone, every-day. Cart rental is $14 per person. The twi-light rate is $10, with cart rental going down to $10.

Mission Trails Golf Course
7380 Golfcrest Pl., San Diego
(619) 460–5400

Nestled in a canyon at the foot of stately Cowles Mountain, Mission Trails has under-gone considerable renovations in recent years, bringing much-needed improvements to this popular course. Most of the greens have been resodded, resulting in a putting surface that's a bit more predictable than in years past. It's a par 71, 5,603-yard course that has lots of ups and downs in the fairly rugged terrain.

The signature hole is the 16th, the longest par 4 on the course. It's noted not so much for its difficulty—it's a not-too-daunting dogleg right—but for the beauti-ful view of Lake Murray as you approach the green. If you're walking, keep in mind that the climb to the 18th green is a steep one. Greens fees are $22 Monday through Friday and $32 on weekends. Cart rental is $12 per person. The course also has a 28-station driving range and putting, chip-ping, and sand practice areas.

Riverwalk Golf Club
1150 Fashion Valley Rd., San Diego
(619) 296–4653

Reopened in the spring of 1998 in the heart of Mission Valley, this centrally located course was formerly the Starlight County Club course. Three nine-hole courses combine to produce the par 72, 6,156-yard Mission/Presidio course, the par 72, 6,033-yard Mission/Friars Course, and the par 72, 6,277-yard Presidio/Friars Course. Presidio is longer and straighter than Mission and is favored by brute-force hitters. Mission has several doglegs and lots of water, so accurate golfers tend to fare well here. Friars has long, undulat-ing fairways that tend to produce unex-pected bounces. Thirteen of the 27 holes are protected by four lakes and the San Diego River. If you can distract yourself from your game for a few moments, you'll appreciate the beauty of the waterfalls, wildlife, and wetlands flora that are all over the course.

The second hole on Mission is a short par 4 with a dogleg left and a narrow land-ing area. It calls for precision shots. Slice it, and you're in the water. Hook it, and your ball will be bouncing among the cars driving by on Fashion Valley Road. Greens fees include a cart and are $76 Monday through Thursday, $86 on Friday, and $96 on weekends. Residents get a $23 price break. Call the pro shop for a litany of twi-light, super twilight, and evening rates. You can walk, but the greens fee will be the same as with a cart. There's a two-sided,

Insiders' Tip

Most golf courses have already switched to soft spikes only. If your golf shoes still have metal spikes, consider changing before you show up at the golf course ready to play. Otherwise, you can easily get them changed in the pro shop before you tee off.

Golfers enjoy a game played next to the water's edge. PHOTO: COURTESY OF SAN DIEGO CONVENTION AND VISITORS BUREAU

lighted driving range with practice greens adjacent to the course.

Torrey Pines Golf Course
11480 N. Torrey Pines Rd., La Jolla
(619) 570–1234 (reservations),
(858) 452–3226 (pro shop)

When the PGA makes its tour stop at Torrey Pines in February of each year for the Buick Invitational, millions of television viewers across the country are awed by the splendor of the course with its emerald green fairways and stunning views of the towering cliffs and the ocean beyond. As a result, when visiting golfers find their way to San Diego, playing Torrey is a must. We won't lie to you—it's hard to get on, but not impossible. For those who manage to get a tee time, it's an experience of a lifetime.

Divided into two courses, the North and the South, it's a day of golf that can bring even seasoned golfers to their knees. Most prefer to play the tougher South Course, mainly because that's where the pros play the last two rounds of their tournament. This course was completely redone by Rees Jones in time for the 2002 Buick Invitational, to the tune of $3.3 million. According to Scott Simpson, a San Diegan

who won the 1998 Buick Invitational on the course, "It's a much prettier course because of the holes they moved closer to the ocean, and it will definitely be tougher." Simpson also approved of the styling of the greens and bunkering, which have been vastly improved. The course was made longer, too, now 6,885 yards but still par 72.

Until the remodel, many golfers preferred the par 72, 6,326-yard North Course, with a tricky par 3 overlooking the ocean as well as a view south to downtown La Jolla. Once you recover from the splendor of the view, the hole itself is waiting to humble you. The green slopes from back to front and is guarded by bunkers on both sides and in front. Shoot over the green and kiss your ball bye-bye. It'll be gone forever in a sharp, brush-covered dropoff.

Greens fees have gotten a bit complicated since renovation of the South Course. Weekday rates for those 18 holes are $85 for visitors, $65 for county residents, and $40 for city residents. (San Diego residents need a $12 photo ID card.) North Course rates are $65 for visitors, $50 for county residents, and $29 for city residents. Add $15 on weekends; cart fees are $32. Twilight rates are available after 2:00 P.M. The driving range and practice facilities are top-notch.

North County Coastal

Four Seasons Resort Aviara Golf Club
7100 Four Seasons Point, Carlsbad
(760) 603–6900

Here's the only Arnold Palmer-designed course in San Diego County and it's also considered one of the longest and toughest. Golfing Insiders say it's one of the best, too. But with this much beauty to surround you it really doesn't matter if you're playing the finest game ever. Every hole has a panoramic view of the mountains, the lagoon, and the azure Pacific.

The 18-hole course has been featured in *Golf Digest* and *Golf* magazines as one of the top courses in the United States. There are four sets of tees measuring 5,007 yards to 7,007 yards. This allows golfers of various abilities to enjoy the play. The course is open to all, but the driving range and practice facility is available for guests only. Greens fees range from $175 to $195 and include a cart. You can reserve a tee time up to six days in advance.

The signature hole is the 18th, a par 4. When asked about the hole, Arnold Palmer said, "A picturesque finishing hole with a wide fairway." Then he added this Insider's tip: "Direct the tee shot towards the fairway bunkers away from the lake. The shot to the fairway is visually exciting with the rock and waterscape highlighting the approach." For a complete look at all that happens at this resort (beyond playing where Palmer plays), check out our Spas and Resorts and Restaurants chapters.

Remember this is a lavish resort. If you stroll into the pro shop in cutoffs and flip-flop sandals, you'll be reminded that upscale golf attire is required.

Call the resort for information on golf and spa package deals.

North County Inland

Castle Creek Country Club
8797 Circle R Dr., Escondido
(760) 749–2877 (information),
(760) 749–2422 (pro shop)

If your idea of a good game of golf is to play on a course that has big trees, beautiful fairways, and flawless greens, then Castle Creek Country Club is your course. Castle Creek's golfers come here to play golf and have fun.

It's a par 72, 6,400-yard, 18-hole course, and the signature hole is number 14. To make this one, without losing balls or adding a lot to your score, you'll be expected to drive over a creek, hit to the right and then make it over a small lake. Oh yes, don't forget that there's a huge oak tree guarding the hole.

Challenging and fun, Castle Creek's greens fees are about $43 for the 18-hole course midweek; $56 for weekend play, including cart rental. You can reserve a tee time up to 14 days in advance of your game time. There's a driving range, putting green, pro shop, and snack bar near the first hole.

Doubletree Carmel Highland Resort
14455 Penasquitos Dr., San Diego
(858) 672–9100 (reservations),
(858) 485–4145 (pro shop)

You can see the course from Interstate 15 in the Rancho Bernardo, Carmel Mountain area of San Diego. There's a short-game practice area, nicely maintained and always very green, and the 18-hole par 72, 6,428-yard championship course. The signature hole is number 5; it's a long par 5 that twists slightly.

If you're an early bird, greens fees before 9:00 A.M. are only $33, after that it's $55 Monday through Thursday, $60 on Friday. Saturday, Sunday, and holidays it's $75 and all greens fees include the cart.

Insiders' Tip
Would you love to play golf in Mexico? Look over our South of the Border chapter for some suggestions on challenging courses.

Golfers from around the world enjoy Torrey Pines Golf Course for its challenge and scenery.

The convenience of this course makes it popular for the seniors, so it may be busy during the workweek. Just call ahead if you have weekday flexibility because you'll most likely need a reservation. Golf packages are available through the resort.

Pala Mesa Resort
2001 Old Hwy. 395, Fallbrook
(760) 728–5881, (800) 722–4700

Tucked away in Fallbrook, just off Interstate 15 in North County Inland, Pala Mesa is considered one of the best truly traditional courses in the county because of the stately trees and manicured greens and extensive fairways. Lots of seniors and those with weekday flexibility come here Monday through Friday.

The course is lush and especially delicious, we think, in the fall when the trees hugging the fairways change colors. Pala Mesa has rolling fairways, edged with pines and sycamores and a challenge at every turn. The mountain views are spec-

tacular on the 6,502-yard course. It's a par 72 with a 131 slope. It's also home to Golf Digest School so if you need a few tips or some advice on that swing, you can reserve time with an instructor.

The signature hole is the 11th because of the view. You get a 360-degree panorama portrait of the area. Don't be shy about admiring it. If you have room for a camera in your golf bag, it's worth taking one along to take this shot back home.

Greens fees are $70 Monday through Friday and $90 weekends and holidays. Twilight fees are substantially less but vary by season. A golf cart is required and included in the price; the dress code is enforced.

San Luis Rey Downs
31474 Golf Club Dr., Bonsall
(760) 758–9699, (800) 783–6967

This par 72 course measures 6,750 yards, and while the overall length isn't that long, it is formidable. For duffers, the better word might be difficult. It's not that the course isn't beautiful—it is. You see, there are large trees dotting the fairways and many other hazards. There are also wonderful ocean breezes... wonderful when your opponent is at the tee and you've already placed your ball on the green.

Monday through Thursday, fees are $32; the shared cart is $10 for each player. Friday green fees are $34; Saturday, Sunday, and holiday fees are about $62, including the cart.

The signature hole is the 15th. It's long and narrow and deceptive. Just when you think everything is perfect, a caboose gets in your way. Yes, a train caboose is on the golf course with a resort sign attached. With the wonderful breeze your ball could be swept straight at that obstacle. Trust us on this one.

East County

Carlton Oaks Country Club
9200 Inwood Dr., Santee
(619) 448–4242

Carlton Oaks Country Club has a challenging 7,088-yard course designed by Pete Dye. This is the course where Curtis Strange hit a 1-iron to the 18th and made eagle to win the NCAA individual title and assure Wake Forest of the team title.

There are tinkling creeks, clusters of tall trees, and a strategically undulated peninsula fairway. Carlton Oaks greens fees Monday through Thursday are $55; Friday, $70; weekends and holidays, $80. Cart included. There are package deals that include lodging, breakfast, and dinner with prices that could entice you; call for information.

The signature hole here is the 12th, a par 3 that's on an island. (Take extra balls if you play like we do!) There's also a driving range, full-service pro shop, and cafe to make your day complete.

Singing Hills Resort
3007 Dehesa Rd., El Cajon
(619) 442–3425

Once family owned and operated, Singing Hills was recently acquired by the Sycuan band of the Kumeyaay Indian tribe. The course is spread over gently rounded fairways and hugged by rugged mountains. There's a choice of three 18-hole courses, two 18-hole championship courses, and an executive course, offering golfers of all abilities challenging and fun play.

You may have already seen Singing Hills on ESPN. It has been the site of numerous PGA, LPGA, and SCGA championships, in addition to hosting the School of Golf (for women, juniors, and seniors). The courses were designed by Ted Robinson.

Greens fees here are inexpensive: $15 any day for the Pine Glen course; $37 to $45 for Willow Glen or Oak Glen (weekdays and weekends, respectively). Shared carts are available for $11; ask about golf packages. The course is busy on weekends, so call ahead to reserve a tee time.

This is a sunny course so you may want to wear a hat and use sunscreen. East County can be warm in the summertime so pack a bottle of water in your golf bag.

Steele Canyon Golf and Country Club
3199 Stonefield Dr., Jamul
(619) 441–6900
www.steelecanyon.com

The 27-hole championship golf course in this golf community was designed by Gary Player. When you play it you'll feel Gary's respect for the game and his appreciation for nature.

The Canyon Ranch course requires strong shot-making abilities over breathtaking elevations; the signature 5th hole is elevated—and we're talking high up. The

Insiders' Tip

Try walking on at some of the more popular courses like Torrey Pines and Balboa. Singles and even twosomes can usually get a game with a minimum wait because of cancellations and no-shows.

Ranch Course winds through the fields of a working ranch and it's the 3rd hole, called Parachute, that's the challenge. Again, here you'll be challenged with the elevation. The Meadow Course meanders along the valley floor with woodlands and streams surrounding you. You might spy rabbits and lots of birds. For the Meadow course, it's the 6th hole that most remember. Here you must hit the ball over a deep ravine to make it to the green. The Canyon course is 3,206 yards; the Ranch course, 3,205 yards; and the Meadow course is 3,273 yards, with six different combinations of play for all types of players.

There's a practice facility including a target-oriented driving range and two large putting greens. Monday through Thursday the greens fee is $65, Friday it is $75, and on the weekends and holidays it's $85. Late weekday is a bargain for this course at about $40. There's no extra charge for carts. You can reserve starting times in advance, paying extra to reserve eight days ahead or more. Softspikes are required, and there's a dress code: no cutoffs, short shorts, T-shirts, or tank tops. Clubs can be rented at the well-stocked pro shop.

South Bay

Bonita Golf Club
5540 Sweetwater Rd., Bonita
(619) 267–1103
www.bonitagolfclub.com

Most of the fairways are lined with trees at this South Bay course, which is scenic if you hit straight, but trouble if you hook or slice. It's a fairly short par 71 course at 5,832 yards, so concentrate on accuracy rather than long drives. Watch out for water, too. The Sweetwater River meanders through six holes, and a large pond comes into play on another two. Bunkers are sparse, thankfully.

The signature 13th hole presents a couple of choices, both of them doubtful. It's a par 5 dogleg left that has both the river and a big pond to contend with. If your tee shot is too short, you just might have to lay up short of the river on your second shot. Conversely, if you blast your drive into the stratosphere, you're likely to plunk it into the pond.

Warm up on the driving range, putting green, and chipping/sand practice area that are all set around a large clubhouse with a nice sports bar and restaurant. Greens fees are $22 on weekdays and $43 on weekends. Carts are an additional $12 per person. Twilight golf is $15 during the week and $22 on weekends.

Chula Vista Golf Course
4475 Bonita Rd., Bonita
(619) 479–4141

Former PGA star Billy Casper helped design this municipal course in the early 1960s. It's short on trees and pretty flat, but don't let the lack of scenery fool you. It's a par 73 course that plays longer than its 6,186 yards. Only a few holes don't have water to bedevil you, and the last three holes on the back nine are straight into the wind, which is usually strong in the afternoon.

The par 4 6th is the toughest hole on the course. The wind comes in from the west and has a habit of knocking your drives down to a conveniently located bunker. Second shots demand a long iron or fairway wood to reach a skinny little green that has bunkers on both sides.

A nice grass-tee driving range is on the grounds, as is a putting green and chipping/sand practice area. Greens fees are $21 on weekdays and $28 on weekends. Carts are $12 per person extra. Twilight fees are $12.50 during the week and $15.50 on weekends. Chula Vista residents with an $8.00 annual ID card receive discounted greens fees.

Eastlake Country Club
2375 Clubhouse Dr., Chula Vista
(619) 482–5757

At first look, you might think the computer-equipped carts at Eastlake are little more than a gimmick. But once you get used to the information you can get at the push of a button, you may well be hooked. Screens on every cart provide exact distances to the pin, along with helpful hints about the idiosyncrasies of each hole. They can't help your swing, though, so that part is up to you.

The par 72, 5,726-yard course has fairways that are lined with nearly 2,000 young trees, six lakes, three waterfalls, and dozens of sand traps. Most holes have bunkers placed right about where your drive should land. Approaches are narrow but clear, with bunkers guarding either one side or the rear of the green. It's usually the par 3s that are the sticklers, and the 12th at Eastlake is one of them. A head wind can play havoc with your tee shot, and water laps right at the putting surface. It's also protected by a couple of bunkers to the right and directly behind.

Greens fees are $50 Monday through Friday, $65 on weekends, and include the computerized cart. Twilight golf (after 2:00 P.M.) is $25 on weekdays and $35 on weekends; carts cost an additional $8.00. A luxurious three-building clubhouse complex offers all the after-golf amenities, and there's a grass driving range, two chipping/sand practice areas, and two putting greens.

Executive and 9-Hole Courses

Central San Diego

Balboa Park 9-Hole Course
2600 Golf Course Dr., San Diego
(619) 570–1234

If you're too short on time or talent to tackle the main course at Balboa, the nine-hole is more than adequate as a second choice. It underwent a renovation at the same time the main course did, and the effort actually improved a course that was already too much fun. It's a par 32, 2,175-yard course that has some of the same hazards as the big course—big trees and bunkers.

Most fairways are lined with trees, and errant shots can easily end up in the next fairway over on the several holes that are adjacent, going up and back. Players tend to be accepting of this, and it's probably

An aerial view of Torrey Pines Golf Course shows the place where famous golfers have challenged the game. PHOTO: JAMES BLANK, COURTESY OF SAN DIEGO CONVENTION AND VISITORS BUREAU

one of the few places where you look ahead and behind before you hit the ball. This is a good course for walk-ons in the late afternoon. Greens fees are $18 every day; $7.50 with a $12 resident card.

Mission Bay Golf Course
2702 N. Mission Bay Dr., San Diego
(619) 490–3370

This is the only course in San Diego that has lights for nighttime play. It's a fun course with 18 holes that stretch into a par 58 of 2,719 yards. Each nine has seven par 3s and two par 4s. The best is saved for last, with the 18th being the longest hole on the course at 291 yards.

If you play at night, our best advice is to hit it straight. The lights are bright, but should you wander too far from the fairway, you'll probably have some trouble finding your ball because the lights are aimed at the tee boxes and the greens. Greens fees are $16 on weekdays and $18 on weekends. Most everyone walks on this course, but a few carts are available for those with disabilities. You can also play nine holes for a discounted rate of $11 during the week and $13 on weekends after 2:00 P.M.

Presidio Hills Pitch & Putt
4136 Wallace St., San Diego
(619) 295–9476

A nine iron and a putter are all you'll need to navigate this charming pitch-and-putt course in historic Old Town. You'll see veteran golfers out here working on their short games, and the course is designed to test even the best. It opened in 1932 and has all

---

Insiders' Tip

Check out www.golfsd.com for course information, greens fees, and other useful information about San Diego County courses.

---

par 3 holes ranging from 45 to 100 yards. Just in case you don't think you'll be challenged, wait until you get to the 17th hole, which requires a tee shot over an extremely tall and wide tree to reach the green.

This is a good place for kids (and grown-ups) who are just learning the game, too. Greens fees are $10 every day. No reservations are necessary, and it's fairly easy to walk on and tee off within a few minutes. There's a nice snack bar on the course that's housed in one of the oldest adobe structures in Southern California.

Tecolote Canyon Golf Course
2755 Snead Ave., San Diego
(858) 279–1600

Designed by Robert Trent Jones Sr. and Sam Snead, this course is widely known as one of the toughest par 3s in California. You might not pull every club in your bag, but we guarantee you'll be challenged. The course is in a narrow canyon with swirling winds that make club selection a creative sport. Four par 4 holes range from 299 to 339 yards, and the total yardage is 3,161 on the par 58 course.

The fun starts at the 1st hole, where you tee off from the top of a cliff to the green below. It's a feel-good hole that's easy and gives you false confidence for the rest. By the time you get to the killer 11th, you'll have figured out that this is no walk in the park. The 299-yard, par 4 11th begins at the farthest point of the course, and lots of trees and the edge of the canyon provide trouble on the right. Most lay up short of the creek that runs through the fairway, then play a 9-iron up to the green, which is guarded by a trap.

Greens fees during the week are $18 to walk and $30 to ride. On weekends it's $23 to walk and $33 to ride. There's a lighted driving range with half grass and half mat stations, a practice putting green, and a small chipping area.

North County Coastal

Emerald Isle
660 El Camino Real, Oceanside
(760) 721–4700

Emerald Isle is billed as North County's "most challenging executive course," and it's the hills that get your attention if you're walking the course with its full 18 holes. Emerald Isle is a comfortable, unpretentious place to play and where you can have family fun. If you've never been into mingling with the Rolex watch crowd or you're a beginner, Emerald Isle could become your favorite.

Prices are right here. On weekdays, it's $16 before 2:00 P.M. and weekends $20 before 2:00 P.M., after which the price drops a few dollars. Carts are $18 for two people. There's a putting green, spacious driving range, and snack bar. Emerald Isle's staff offers instruction, whether you need a few tips or a series of lessons with the pro.

Rancho Carlsbad
5200 El Camino Real, Carlsbad
(760) 438–1772

This executive golf course, "Rancho" as it's known by Insiders, is right off El Camino Real, near LEGOLAND California (see our Kidstuff chapter), the Carlsbad Flower Fields (see our Annual Events chapter) and shopping (see our Shopping chapter). It is an Insiders' favorite. Not that many people frequent it so you'll rarely have to wait long, even if you don't call ahead to reserve a tee time.

While executive courses usually don't have signature holes, we like the 9th. There's a long narrow fairway and the green is elevated. Should you hit the ball way out in the rough on this hole, remember you're playing in the backcountry and watch where you step. Snakes have been known to think that the brush adjacent to the 9th is their home.

There's a shady putting green and a driving range (buy your tokens for the ball machine at the pro shop). You can browse through the pro shop and visit the snack bar. You can eat on the patio. The entire package here is wrapped in mature trees with plenty of shade even on warm days. If it's been raining or looks like a storm's on the way, call to make sure Rancho is open. On wet days management closes the course to avoid destroying the fairways. It's $13.50 during the week and $16.50 on weekends to play a round on the full 18-hole, par 56 course. After 2:00 P.M. it's $13.50 to play as many holes as you want. This course is tucked out of traffic and it's quiet.

North County Inland

Lake San Marcos Executive Golf Course
1556 Camino Del Arroyo Dr., San Marcos
(760) 744–9092

Lake San Marcos has flat, inviting fairways that make play, especially for the less experienced, a whole lot of fun. It's popular with seniors who enjoy the perfect weather and gentle breezes in San Marcos.

A par 58 course, Lake San Marcos can be busy as there are always tournaments going on. The price is right, too. It's $18, but only $13 after 2:00 P.M. every day of the week. Golf carts are available every day for $18 for riders.

Oaks North Golf Course
12602 North Oaks Dr., Rancho Bernardo
(858) 487–3021

This is it: our Insiders' favorite executive course. Actually there are three 9-hole courses that easily add up to a pleasurable day out.

Oaks North is stunning with long and short fairways that make it fun for experienced golfers (you see lots of them) and duffers, too. There is a dress code here—you'll need to wear nice shorts or khakis and golf shirts (or shirts with collars). The prices range from about $30 during prime play time to about $12 for 18 holes in the late afternoon. A cart will cost you $8.00 extra per person, and unless you always

These golfers are taking advantage of the beautiful San Diego clime. PHOTO: BOB YARBROUGH, COURTESY OF SAN DIEGO CONVENTION AND VISITORS BUREAU

get a cart when you golf, forego it here. The walk is worth the price of admission.

Call ahead to reserve a tee time. There's a snack bar and shaded patio for an after-golf iced tea or soda or beer.

Welk Resort Center
8860 Lawrence Welk Dr., Escondido
(760) 749–3225, (800) 932–9355

Hidden away in the lushness of the foothills and about an hour's drive from downtown San Diego, the courses here delight avid players and novices too. Surprisingly, the cost of playing at the resort can be reasonable. For instance, at the Fountains and Oaks executive courses, the fees are less than $20 to walk and play after 4:00 P.M. on weekdays and include the cart. Of course the fees are significantly higher on weekends and during prime play times.

Every hole is beautiful and with the warm, sunny days of summer that last well into the evening, you might be wise to play late in the afternoon. Some of the fairways are steep, but they make for a good bit of exercise if you're walking the course.

The yardage, designed by David Rainville, is 1,837 at the Oaks and 4,002 at the Fountains. If you want a golf getaway, call about golf packages. Some include lodging at the resort (see our Spas and Restaurants chapters) and unlimited golf with a cart to play either course.

South Bay

National City Golf Course
1439 Sweetwater Rd., National City
(619) 474–1400

This is a quick-play par 34 nine, and many golfers play around twice, completing a full round in about four hours. It's a narrow canyon course that can be lots of fun for straight hitters. Those who lean left or right are in for some creative second shots. The fairways are very narrow, especially on the only par 5, the 525-yard second. Water comes into play on three holes.

Greens fees are $9.00 for nine holes; $15.00 for 18 on weekdays. Weekend fees are $12 for nine and $19 for 18 holes. Carts are $10 per person.

Driving Ranges

Central San Diego

Sorrento Canyon Golf Center
5605 Carroll Canyon Rd., San Diego
(858) 642–0181

This is the newest of all the golf ranges in the city of San Diego, and it's got a lot of perks, like 74 stations on two levels. All stations have both a mat and a little plot of grass that's replaced every few days. In addition to the tee stations, there's an 18-hole, par 58 grass putting course with distances ranging from 35 feet to 114 feet. It's $5.00 to play the putting course.

Buckets are $4.00 to $12.00. You can also work on your short game at a 75-yard chipping-practice area. Facilities include a golf shop, lockers, deli, and a club-repair shop. The lighted range is open from 9:00 A.M. to 9:00 P.M.

Stadium Golf Center
2990 Murphy Canyon Rd., San Diego
(858) 277–6667

When this range first opened, passersby thought aliens had landed because the lights were so bright and visible from such a distance. What evoked images of E.T. in some is a benefit to those who use the range because you can see just where your shots land, even in the dead of night.

With 48 mat tees and 24 grass tees, there's rarely a problem finding an open tee here. The landing area is long and grassy and has seven target greens. One of the nicest features is the 10,000 square-foot bent-grass putting green that's available for play (along with the chipping and sand practice areas) for $3.00. Bucket prices range from $6.00 for 45 balls to $16.00 for 225 balls.

North County Coastal

Carlsbad Golf Center
2711 Haymar Dr., Carlsbad
(760) 720–4653

The Carlsbad Golf Center in Carlsbad is tucked behind a hill and a strip shopping center right off Calif. Highway 78. Exit at El Camino Real. You might not know it's there until you're past the exit. Call for directions if you don't have a good map because the location is extra nice; it's worth going out of your way to find this driving range.

The center is big, with more than 100 stations where you hit the ball off imitation grass. It's rarely crowded—we know because we've been here a lot. (Hey, we were doing research for the book and someone had to see if we could recommend it to you.) There's a well-stocked pro shop, and the range also has tournaments. You can arrange for lessons here, too.

The putting green is of the plastic-turf style. It's well maintained but might disappoint someone who seriously wants to practice his or her short game. We find it fun nonetheless. Six dollars will get you a big bucket of balls. Get the tokens in the pro shop.

Olympic Resort Hotel & Spa
6111 El Camino Real, Carlsbad
(760) 438–8330

Here's a driving range for the serious golfer and anyone who wants a challenge. At Olympic Resort Hotel & Spa there are 48 deluxe stations. There's a practice bunker and four—count 'em—four putting greens. You can also arranged for PGA instructions and take advantage of video lessons on state-of-the-art equipment. Down side? The range is situated so that in the late afternoon or early evening (depending on the time of year) you're hitting straight into the sun. So for about an hour you'll

---

Insiders' Tip

The private course at La Costa Resort and Spa earned one of *Links* magazine's 50 Best of Golf Awards for its dedication to the preservation of golf played with caddies.

need sunglasses, or simply schedule your practice session for another time.

Surf & Turf Driving Range
1555 Jimmy Durante Blvd., Del Mar
(858) 481–0363

Surf & Turf is easy to get to. Just exit Interstate 5 at Via De La Valle in Del Mar and head toward the ocean. Make the first left turn onto Jimmy Durante Boulevard. You can't miss it. The range is across from the Del Mar Fairgrounds. The staff here offers individual and group lessons. The range is lighted and open daily from 7:00 A.M. until 9:00 P.M.

If you're from a part of the country that has lush, green driving ranges and you come here in the summer, you might be surprised. While the stations have astro-turf, from about June through October, you'll be hitting balls into dirt.

Keep in mind that when the horses are running (during racing season) and during the four weeks the Del Mar Fair is being held, traffic can be unpleasant. If you're uncertain of what's happening at the fairgrounds or the track, call the driving range about traffic conditions before you set your sights on hitting golf balls here. If you want to play some strictly-for-laughs golf after hitting a bucket of balls, Surf & Turf has a place to play miniature golf, too.

North County Inland

Thunderbird Driving Range & Training Center
26351 N. Centre City Pkwy., Escondido
(760) 746–0245

Conveniently located right off I-15 (take the Deer Springs Road exit), the Thunderbird is well lighted and popular. The downside is that the highway traffic can be noisy.

There's a pro shop and snack bar. A large bucket of balls will cost you $6.00.

East County

Fletcher Hills Golf Range
1756 Weld Blvd., El Cajon
(619) 449–6311

Fletcher Hills is popular with golfers who live in East County and can get there during the daylight hours. You see, there are no lights so they sell the last bucket at 7:00 P.M. in the summer. In the winter, it closes earlier. A large bucket of balls will cost you $7.00.

South Bay

All Golf
540 Hollister St., San Diego
(619) 424–3213

Located just off I-5 in the South Bay, the 48 hitting stations here are half grass and half mat. The landing area is grassy, and target flags and yardage markers are sprinkled throughout. A bonus is a nice chipping course with nine holes ranging from 30 to 70 yards. Buckets of balls are $5.00 and $7.00. The range is lighted and is open from 8:00 A.M. until 9:00 P.M. daily.

Bonita Golf Center
3631 Bonita Rd., Bonita
(619) 426–2069

Rent a bucket of balls and swing away on this lighted range that has 30 grass tees and 18 mat stations. The first 175 yards of the range have small target areas that are marked by flags for those accuracy shots. If you just want to swing away and see how far you can drive, distance markers are placed beyond the target areas.

Next to the pro shop is a putting green and a large sand/chipping practice area. If you bring your own balls, it's $4.50 per hour to use the practice facilities, but if you rent a bucket, it's free. Balls rent for $3.00 for a small bucket of 30, $4.50 for 60, and $6.50 for 100. Hours are 8:00 A.M. to 8:00 P.M. daily.

Spectator Sports

San Diegans have a reputation for being fair-weather fans—literally and figuratively. Whether or not that reputation is deserved is up for debate, but the fact is that professional sports teams struggle at times to generate sustained interest among local fans—unless, of course, the team is in the hunt for a championship. If the Padres or the Chargers are having a dismal season, chances are that more than a few Insiders will look elsewhere for entertainment, mainly because there's so darn much to do here. Why waste an afternoon or evening watching the hometown boys turn in yet another lackluster performance when you could bask on the beach or sip champagne at an outdoor concert by the bay?

That said, don't think for a moment that we don't appreciate our sports teams. Scores of rabid fans attend every home game (and many away games, too) simply out of sheer devotion and loyalty, regardless of the standings. And when the team is winning or an out-of-town superstar is making an appearance, tickets can be hard to come by.

In addition to the standards—football, baseball, hockey, golf, tennis, and auto racing—San Diegans are blessed with a couple of oddball (but highly entertaining) sports spectacles. Among them is Over-the-Line, a three-person-per-team softball game invented by some local beach guys who believed that running the bases interfered too much with their beer drinking. From that inauspicious philosophy was born a game that now is celebrated every summer in a two-week tournament that draws players and spectators from all over the world and somewhere along the line has earned some actual credibility.

The X Games have been to San Diego twice, bringing along such extreme sports as sky surfing, bicycle stunt riding, and the downhill luge. Everyone hopes they'll be back for future meets. Another repeat performer is the Super Bowl. In 1998 both the event itself and its weeklong festivities were so successful that the NFL Super Bowl will be back in 2003.

Although San Diego does not have an NBA basketball team at the moment, there is no lack of exciting sporting events to fill the gap. Thunderboats—high-speed racing boats—roar across Mission Bay in an annual competition, thrilling onlookers with their death-defying speeds. A short trip south of the border is all you need to see the ancient and historic sport of bullfighting. And the beautifully renovated Del Mar Thoroughbred Club plays host to the sport of kings every summer.

We'll fill you in on them all in this chapter. Some sports are annual events; some are held during a regular season. We'll give you dates, ticket prices, and venues, all you have to do is make up your mind what appeals to you most. You're likely to find a sporting event to watch on any day of the year. And if it's a nice day, which it usually is, ignore the lure of the beach. The sun will be out at the stadium, too, and we guarantee you'll have a great time.

Qualcomm Stadium
9449 Friars Rd., San Diego
(619) 641–3131
www.ci.san-diego.ca.us/qualcomm

Home games for Padres baseball, Chargers football, and San Diego State University Aztec football are all held at Qualcomm Stadium. Located in Mission Valley, the stadium is just north of Interstate 8, between Calif. Highway 163 and Interstate 15. Parking is a hefty $6.00 per car for Padres and Chargers games, $5.00 for Aztec football games and $7.00 for all other special events, so we strongly urge you to carpool. Bus service to home games is provided by North County Transit, (800) 266–6803, and San Diego's Metropolitan Transit, (619) 233–3004. If you taxi your way in, rest assured that you'll find one waiting for you following the game in the stadium parking lot. One of the best ways to get to Qualcomm is by way of the San Diego Trolley. The trolley departs from locations all over town and takes you right to its station in the stadium parking lot, just a short walk from the gate.

Bottles, cans, and liquid containers are not allowed inside the stadium. The exception is baby bottles and containers with formula. Food may be brought into the stadium, but since 9/11, coolers and large backpacks are prohibited, and bags and purses are subject to inspection at the gate. Smoking is not allowed in any of the seating areas or in the field-level concourse. Smoking is permitted in the plaza, loge, and view concourses.

Tailgating is a popular way to kick off a game. Gather your friends, some food, and drink, and have an impromptu party in the parking lot. Just remember that tailgaters must confine themselves to their own parking space.

Baseball

San Diego Padres
Qualcomm Stadium, 9449 Friars Rd., San Diego
(619) 280–4636
www.padres.com

May 27, 1968, was an exciting day for baseball fans—San Diego was awarded a National League franchise, the San Diego Padres. Now in its fourth decade as a major league team, the club has amassed some statistics that have little to do with hits and runs: The Padres have seen four owners and 15 managers over the years. And it was 1975, seven years after the team's inception, before the club climbed out of the cellar.

It took another eight years of fluctuating between fourth place and last before everything clicked. In one memorable season, in 1984, the Padres soared. Not only did they beat San Francisco to win their division, they came back from an early deficit in the National League Championship Series to snatch the pennant away from the Chicago Cubs. The beleaguered Padres were going to the World Series!

No matter that the Series proved to be anticlimactic—the Pads dropped four of five to the Detroit Tigers—they had made it to the big show. Never was a city more proud of its team. Winning seemed almost irrelevant. It's a good thing, too, because subsequent years brought more of what fans were used to. The team dropped to third place in their division the following year, then fourth, and then last, a position they seemed almost comfortable with.

Days of glory finally returned, though. In 1994 John Moores and Larry Lucchino bought the team, and a new and better era began. The quality of the team improved dramatically with the acquisition of play-

Baseball action gets intense when the San Diego Padres take the bat. PHOTO: THORN VOLLENWEIDER

ers such as Ken Caminiti, Steve Finley, Wally Joyner, Greg Vaughn, and Kevin Brown, who joined veteran slugger Tony Gwynn. And by the dog days of summer 1998, the Padres had returned to the World Series, only to suffer an even more ignoble fate than before—being swept by the New York Yankees. After that season, all the aforementioned players (with the exception of Gwynn) moved to other teams. So the Padres are once again rebuilding.

Perhaps San Diegans remain true to the Pads because the club is really involved in the community. Owners and players fund the Padres Scholars program, giving $5,000 scholarships to talented but financially challenged seventh-grade students. Through 2001, more than 200 students have received more than $1 million for college tuition. The Little Padres Parks program will build or refurbish 60 youth baseball fields across the region. And through the Cindy Matters Fund, the club has donated $650,000 to the UCSD Pediatric Oncology Research Center since 1987 to honor the memory of a young Padres fan who lost her life to cancer.

The Padres' history includes such notable players as Randy Jones, Rollie Fingers, Gaylord Perry, Ozzie Smith, Steve Garvey, Gary Sheffield, and Fred McGriff. More than a dozen Gold Glove Awards belong to Padres' players (five to Tony Gwynn alone), and the team boasts three Cy Young Awards for pitching. But history doesn't win today's pennants, and Tony Gwynn, whom local sports writer Nick Canepa calls "the greatest pure ball-striker of his generation," is history as well; he retired at the end of the 2001 season. Fortunately the franchise's future looks bright. With quality ownership, young but talented players, and loyal, exuberant fans, it's easy to believe that division championships, league championships, and that elusive World Series championship will soon grace the Padres' record books.

The big news these days is the construction of a new baseball-only ballpark, a joint venture by the Padres and the city of San Diego. Construction on the site, just east of downtown's Gaslamp Quarter, was begun not long after voters approved the project in 1998, but came to a grinding halt soon thereafter as one lawsuit after another was filed. In January 2002, a judge threw out the 16th lawsuit, paving the way for bond sales and the resumption of construction. Developers now hope to have the new stadium ready by April 2005. And even most of those who opposed a new downtown ballpark are by this time ready to see it made a reality.

Ticket prices range from $6.00 to $28.00 for individual games. Season tickets start at $100 and are available in 20-game, part-season, and full-season packages. Tickets may be purchased at Gate F in the stadium. Call (888) MY-PADRES for information on season ticket packages or (877) FRIAR-TIX for single-game tickets.

Football

Holiday Bowl
Qualcomm Stadium, 9449 Friars Rd., San Diego
(619) 283-5808
www.holidaybowl.com

For more than 20 years the Holiday Bowl has featured a football face-off between nationally ranked teams from the Big 12 and either the WAC or the Pac 10. Since its inauguration in 1978, the majority of games have been won by a margin of one touchdown or less, and most have been decided in the final two minutes. It's no wonder the Holiday Bowl has earned a

The San Diego Qualcomm Stadium: site of the 2003 Super Bowl. PHOTO: THORN VOLLENWEIDER

reputation as America's most exciting bowl game.

The hometown San Diego State Aztecs made an appearance in the Holiday Bowl in 1986 and put on one of the best shows ever. The Aztecs held off the Iowa Hawkeyes until the final four seconds, when an Iowa field goal gave the team a one-point edge over the Aztecs and a final score of 39 to 38.

Holiday Bowl tickets are available in advance by calling the Bowl ticket office at (619) 283–5808. Ticket prices range from $46 to $52. The game is held in late December.

San Diego Chargers
Qualcomm Stadium, 9449 Friars Rd., San Diego
(619) 280–2121
www.chargers.com
The histories of the San Diego Chargers and the Padres have followed an eerily parallel course. Just as the Padres are not frequent contenders in the World Series, the Chargers have made it to the Super Bowl but one time, in 1995. And like both the Padres' World Series contests, the Chargers faced a powerhouse opponent

in the Super Bowl—the San Francisco 49ers—and were soundly trounced.

The loss didn't totally squelch the enthusiasm of fans, though. Game day always finds a sea of blue-and-gold-clad aficionados who are ever loyal to their beloved "Bolts." (The Bolt refers to the streak of lightning on the Chargers' uniforms.) After two terrible seasons under head coach Mike Riley (with 11 straight losses in his second year of coaching, and 9 straight to end his third and final year), fans are looking forward to new leadership under Marty Schottenheimer, who signed in January 2002.

Team members have shown a devotion to San Diego by diving headfirst into charitable ventures. Charger Champions scholarship funds, charity golf tournaments, and Junior Charger Girls are just a few of the ways in which players give back to the community. Earlier Chargers players such as Lance Alworth, Rolfe Benirschke, and Dan Fouts set the example, and today players Junior Seau and quarterback Doug Flutie have established their own foundations in support of the San Diego community.

Loyal Chargers fans in their team colors make sure their cheers are heard. PHOTO: THORN VOLLENWEIDER

Number 55, Junior Seau, pumps up his teammates both before and during the game. PHOTO: BOB YARBROUGH, COURTESY OF SAN DIEGO CONVENTION AND VISITORS BUREAU

Whether the Chargers are having a winning season or not, you can always count on sellout crowds whenever their perennial nemesis, the Oakland Raiders, are in town. One step below the Raiders in terms of rivalry are the Denver Broncos. But whomever the team is playing, the excitement is unparalleled.

Individual home game tickets are available at the Chargers' ticket office, Gate E at the stadium, or by calling Ticketmaster at (619) 220-8497. Prices range from $34 to $72. For information on season tickets, call (619) 280-2121. Season ticket prices range from $240 to $650.

San Diego State University Aztecs
Qualcomm Stadium, 9449 Friars Rd., San Diego
(619) 283-7378
www.goaztecs.com

Many Insiders, but especially SDSU alumni, are just as loyal to the Aztecs football team as they are to the Chargers. Home games commonly draw more than 40,000 fans to the Q (as Qualcomm Stadium is often called) to cheer on the team led by head coach Tom Craft. Prior to the opening of Qualcomm Stadium in 1967, San Diego State played its games in Aztec Bowl, located on campus, or in Balboa Stadium downtown. Neither facility was large enough to hold the masses clamoring for tickets, so the move to Qualcomm was a welcome one.

The Aztecs competed in the Western Athletic Conference until the end of the 1999 season against teams such as UNLV, BYU, Air Force, and Wyoming. After that, the Aztecs split off with several other members of the WAC to form a new conference called the Mountain West Conference. Despite their less than illustrious performance in this conference, the NFL draft does keep an eye on SDSU, and players such as Fred Dryer, Willie Buchanon, and Marshall Faulk have gone on to greater glory in professional football. Tickets to home games range in price from $7.00 to $27.00; SDSU students with ID receive a discount. Tickets are available at Gate G in the stadium or at the SDSU ticket office on campus.

This young sports fan knows how to add enjoyment to his game-day activities. PHOTO: BOB YARBROUGH, COURTESY OF SAN DIEGO CONVENTION AND VISITORS BUREAU

Auto Racing

El Cajon Speedway
1875 Joe Crosson Dr., El Cajon
(619) 448–8900
www.cajonspeedway.com

Choose from a heap of racing events: NASCAR, Spec Trucks, Grand American Modifieds, Stock Cars, and Destruction Derbies, to name a few. The Cajon Speedway is a 3/8-mile track on 40 acres adjacent to Gillespie Field Airport in El Cajon. The track has turns banked to 18 degrees for great racing. Regular race events include a Trophy Dash, Heat Races, Semis, and four Main Events.

Mid-March through mid-October is the racing season. Ticket prices for adults are $10.00 for the east side, $9.00 for the west side. Children 6 to 12 get in for $3.00; kids younger than 6 are admitted free when accompanied by an adult.

Parking is $1.00. The parking lot opens at 5:00 P.M. Qualifying begins at 5:15 P.M., and the first race is at 6:45 P.M.

Bullfighting

El Toreo de Tijuana
Blvd. Agua Caliente at Blvd. Cuauhtémoc, Tijuana
Plaza Monumental
Playas de Tijuana, Tijuana
(619) 232–5049

If you have an appreciation for the ancient sport of bullfighting, head south of the border to one of two bullrings in Tijuana. Dating back to 2000 B.C., bullfighting is a combination of ritual and mortal combat, pitting man against beast in a graceful but deadly battle. El Toreo de Tijuana and Plaza Monumental present some of the world's leading matadors.

Bullfights are generally held between May and September, but not every Sunday. Tickets are available in San Diego through Five Star Tours, Santa Fe Train Depot, 1050 Kettner Boulevard, which is by far the easiest way to arrange the excursion. Five Star adds a $5.00 service charge to the price of the ticket and also offers bus transportation, $14.00 per person round trip. Ticket prices vary based on the fame of the matador and other factors, but generally cost $11.00 for general admission (nosebleed seats in the sun), to around $40.00 (plus $5.00 service charge if booked in San Diego) for reserved seats.

Golf

Buick Invitational Golf Tournament
Torrey Pines Golf Course, 11480 N. Torrey Pines Rd., La Jolla
(858) 570–1234

The annual PGA Tour men's tournament makes its way to Torrey Pines every February for a week of special events topped off with the 4-day professional competition. Sponsored by the local Century Club, this is the only PGA Tour event held on a municipal course—and a more beautiful one would be hard to find. Beautifully manicured fairways and greens are located on the bluffs above La Jolla, and the views are spectacular.

Crowd favorite Tiger Woods took the championship in 1999 and hometown favorite Phil Michelson outpaced the field in 2000 and again in 2001. Both of them love this tourney.

Practice rounds are held Monday and Tuesday, a Pro-Am featuring local and national professionals is Wednesday, and the competition runs from Thursday

Insiders' Tip

Try one of Rubio's famous fish tacos while you're attending a game at Qualcomm Stadium. Available on the concourse of the Plaza, these delicacies are pure Southern California.

through Sunday. For exact dates of the tournament and to order tickets, call the Century Club at (619) 281–4653, or Ticketmaster at (619) 220–8497. Advance season badges can be purchased for $65 in advance and $75 at the gate. Single-day tickets during the week are $20 in advance, $25 at the gate.

Hockey

San Diego Gulls Hockey
San Diego Sports Arena, 3500 Sports Arena Blvd., San Diego
(619) 225–9813
www.sandiegogulls.com

If you enjoy watching one of the fastest games in professional sports, then Gulls ice hockey is for you. The San Diego Gulls play in the South Division of the West Coast Hockey League, and have consistently made the finals in the Taylor Cup Championship series.

The season runs from October through April; the playoffs run into May. Ticket prices range from $11.00 to $17.50, and are available at the Sports Arena Box Office or by calling Ticketmaster at (619) 220–8497.

Horse Racing

Del Mar Thoroughbred Club
Del Mar Fairgrounds, 2260 Jimmy Durante Blvd., Del Mar
(858) 793–5533, (858) 755–1141
www.dmtc.com

Bing Crosby and his Hollywood buddies envisioned a horse palace by the sea where they could play all day and party all night, and thus was born the Del Mar Thoroughbred Racing Club. Bing was there to greet the first fan through the gate on July 3, 1937, and even now, each racing day begins with a recording of Bing singing, "Where the surf meets the turf in old Del Mar." The track is still a favorite of Hollywood celebs, as well as families, singles, and crusty-voiced race bet veterans. The racing runs from mid-July through early September.

> **Insiders' Tip**
>
> At the races, everyone has a unique wagering technique, including betting on the jockey's silks. To learn more sophisticated techniques, attend Del Mar's free handicapping seminars, weekends between 12:30 and 1:15 P.M. For more fun, don't miss "donut days," Saturday mornings in August. For two hours beginning at 8:00 A.M. you can grab a free OJ, donut, and coffee as you watch the thoroughbreds work out.

Some of racing's top California-bred horses have set records at Del Mar, including Bertrando and Best Pal, and one of the sport's all-time favorite jockeys, Willie Shoemaker, holds the records for most wins all-time and in one season. The track's most exciting day ever was in 1996, when the mighty Cigar attempted to break Citation's 16 consecutive wins record, only to be upset by an unheralded horse.

Races are held daily except Tuesdays. First post is at 2:00 P.M., except on Fridays, when first post is at 4:00 P.M. General admission is $4.00; reserved grandstand seating is $5.00. Clubhouse admission is $7.00; another $5.00 gets you a reserved seat. You can also have a meal at restaurant tables, well placed in front of season boxes. Special events and jazz concerts (usually on Wednesdays) take place at least once a week on the infield after the last race. Parking costs $3.00 to $7.00.

Hydroplane and Power Boat Racing

Thunderboats Unlimited
Mission Bay Park, San Diego
(619) 225–9160
www.bayfair.com

Since 1964 Unlimited Hydroplanes and other classes of powerboat racing have been held on Mission Bay. The stars of the spectacle, three-ton monster Unlimited Hydroplanes, bring thrills and chills to spectators with their rooster-tail-spewing power. Also, you'll see Drag Boats, Formula Ones, Super Stocks, Unlimited Lights, and many more boats on the water. East Mission Bay's Bill Muncey Course is named for the sport's all-time greatest star, who was instrumental in bringing Unlimited Hydroplane racing to San Diego.

Nighttime fireworks, demonstrations by Navy SEAL teams, and performances by the Sea World Beach Band entertain spectators between and after races. Kids will love the in-line skating, skateboard demonstrations, and interactive games and rides.

Three racing venues are used during the September event: East Vacation Isle, Fiesta Island, and Crown Point Shores. Your ticket is good for all three locations, and shuttles run continuously between them. Tickets for a three-day pass are $35 for adults, $15 for children 7 to 12, and free for children 6 and younger. Single-day tickets, sold only to adults, are $20 for Friday, $25 for Saturday, and $30 for Sunday (no single-day tickets are sold to children). Three-day pit passes are $25; single-day pit passes are $10 for Friday, $15 for Saturday, and $20 for Sunday. Children younger than 4 get in free. Preferred three-day parking is $30; single-day is $10 for Friday and $15 for Saturday or Sunday. Three-day general parking is $20. To order tickets, call (858) 225-9160.

Motocross Racing

Carlsbad Raceway
6600 Palomar Airport Rd., Carlsbad
(760) 727–1171, (760) 722–6639

The county's only motocross track is home to a series of races for all classes: beginner, novice, intermediate, and expert. Races are scheduled at various times throughout the year, usually in a series of eight races spread over three or four months. Admission is $12. Gates generally open at 10:00 A.M., practice starts at 11:00 A.M., and racing starts later in the day; times vary by event, so call ahead for information about upcoming races. A catering truck is located at the racetrack, or you can bring a lunch with you.

Polo

San Diego Polo Club
14555 El Camino Real, Rancho Santa Fe
(858) 481–9217
www.sandiegopolo.com

For pure primal excitement, nothing compares to the thrill of eight mounted riders thundering downfield in pursuit or defense of a goal. The object of polo is to move a ball through the goal in six periods of play called "chukkers." Each chukker is seven minutes long, and there are no time-outs except for injuries or penalties.

The San Diego Polo Club holds its matches on Sundays from June through September. Pre-match festivities include picnics, tailgating, polo demonstrations, kids' activities, and complete food and beverage service. Spectators have one responsibility—during the intermission between the third and fourth chukkers, fans are asked to make their way to the field and

Insiders' Tip

If you plan to attend OMBAC's Over-the-Line Tournament, remember the organizers' safety motto: No bowsers (dogs), bottles, or babies.

Hard-hitting excitement reigns in this Del Mar polo game. PHOTO: BOB YARBROUGH, COURTESY OF SAN DIEGO CONVENTION AND VISITORS BUREAU

stomp down the divots unearthed by the ponies. It's a great tradition and a chance to meet other polo aficionados, too.

Matches begin at 1:30 and 3:00 P.M. Admission is $5.00.

Sand Softball

Over-the-Line World
Championship Tournament
Fiesta Island, Mission Bay, San Diego
(619) 688–0817
www.ombac.org

The Old Mission Beach Athletic Club (OMBAC) consists of a group of friends who organized in 1954, mainly to sponsor beach volleyball. From the beginning OMBAC has been most famous for Over-the-Line, a game invented by its members. Three players per team compete on a rectangular field with a triangle at its tip, pointing toward the batter. The spot where the base of the triangle abuts the rectangle is "the line." The object is for the batter to hit the ball over the line without being fielded by the opposite team. In keeping with OMBAC's philosophy of maximum pleasure with minimum effort, no base running is involved.

Now evolved into a major tournament, this annual ritual occurs every second and third weekend in July, and tens of thousands of fans flock to Fiesta Island to watch it. One of the signature characteristics of the tournament is the team names. Entrants are encouraged to be as creative as possible, and the result is a collection of names that are bawdy at best and downright crude at worst. This is not an ideal event for kids, but for people-watching, lots of sunshine, and an interesting game, it can't be beat.

Hot dogs and soft drinks are sold at the tournament, but you're welcome to bring your own food and drink. Bottles are not permitted, although there's no ban on booze. The tournament runs from 7:00 A.M. to dusk, and admission is free. Parking on the island isn't permitted during the tournament, but you can catch one of the shuttles that run continuously between Fiesta Island and Mission Bay High School along East Mission Bay Drive, or the South Mission Bay route that connects to Belmont Park. (Traffic getting to those spots can still be hairy, so take public transportation if you can.) Be sure

Few sports are as physically demanding as two-man (or woman) sand volleyball. PHOTO: THORN VOLLENWEIDER

Tony Gwynn, San Diego Padres

It's summer. You're a Padres fan, so you're at the ballpark, with your bag of roasted peanuts and your significant other. You know you should be happy, but you're not. Because it's the bottom of the first inning, and the number-three batter is about to move into position. But it's not Mr. Padre, because Tony Gwynn retired on October 7, 2001.

Tony will be sorely missed by the fans. He flirted with batting .400 a couple of times, one of the few players in modern baseball to approach the milestone last achieved by San Diego native Ted Williams more than 60 years ago. He's the all-time club leader in batting average, hits, runs, doubles, triples, stolen bases, RBI, and games played. On top of those achievements, he holds eight batting titles (a National League record), and five Gold Glove Awards for defensive excellence and has been voted to the All-Star Game 15 times. One thing is certain, Tony Gwynn is the most beloved Padre in the history of the team.

But it isn't just his killer stats that have made him a hometown hero. There's no posturing with Tony, who was always as open and cheerful with reporters grilling him for details about a game full of bloopers as with youngsters seeking an autograph. And throughout his major league career he has been committed to working within the community, particularly with disadvantaged children. Along with a dozen charitable organizations to which Tony has dedicated his time and considerable energy, he and his wife, Alicia, established the Tony and Alicia Gwynn Foundation, which funds organizations supporting needy children. During the off-season, Tony always spent a good chunk of time teaching his craft to kids from around the country at the San Diego School of Baseball.

One thing San Diego sports writers often mention is Gwynn's impeccable work ethic. Despite his slow, easy grin and large frame, he never spends much time resting—at least not resting on his laurels. Throughout his career, he was invariably the first to arrive at the ballpark on game day, and he spent the time taking extra batting practice, not schmoozing. When spring training rolled around, he arrived long before many of his colleagues came rolling in.

That commitment will serve him well in his post-retirement position. Beginning in 2003, the 41-year-old future Hall of Famer will begin his new career as head coach of San Diego State University's baseball team. He'll replace head coach Jim Dietz, who coached Tony when he played for the Aztecs nearly 25 years ago.

So fans of baseball and of Tony Gwynn don't have to worry about their hero buying a retirement home in Florida or Palm Springs. Mr. Padre is here to stay, at least for a few more years—and we're betting that it will be longer than that. So if you want to see Tony in action, just head for the Aztec's new state-of-the-art ballpark. It's called Tony Gwynn Stadium.

Future Hall-of-Famer Tony Gwynn. PHOTO: COURTESY OF SAN DIEGO PADRES

to bring a beach chair or towel, a small cooler, a hat, and sunscreen.

Soccer

San Diego Sockers
San Diego Sports Arena,
3500 Sports Arena Blvd., San Diego
(858) 836–4625
www.sockers.com

The San Diego Sockers returned to the tiny World Indoor Soccer League (WISL) in 2001. They won the regular season, but there were only five teams in the struggling league. The WISL will join the Major Indoor Soccer League (MISL) beginning in the 2002–2003 season to form a larger, nationwide indoor league. The season is slated to run October through April, although the details are still being worked out. Like other U.S. indoor soccer teams, the ten-time world champions have some great personnel from all over the world. Now they just need a fan base big enough to support the sport.

San Diego Spirit
University of San Diego's Torero Stadium,
5998 Alcala Park, San Diego
(619) 692–9872
www.sandiegospirit.com

Women's soccer in the United States got an enormous boost when the U.S. team won the Olympic silver medal in 2000 in Australia. Since then names like Joy Fawcett, Julie Foudy, and Shannon McMillan spring easily to the lips of little girls in San Diego, among the Spirits biggest fans. All three of these stellar players, luckily for us, are now members of the San Diego Spirit, one of eight teams in the new WUSA (Women's United Soccer Association), formed in 2001. The regular season runs from April through August, 2001 ticket prices ranged from $10 to $16; season tickets cost $110 to $270 for 10 home games.

Tennis

Acura Tennis Classic
La Costa Resort and Spa, Costa Del Mar Rd.,
Carlsbad
(760) 438–5683
www.acuraclassic.org

Every summer the women's professional tennis tour stops in La Costa, in San Diego's North County Coastal region. The tournament attracts top stars and the excitement is nonstop. Held on the grounds of the posh La Costa Resort and Spa, this is professional tennis at its best.

The end of July or the first week in August is the usual time for the tournament, but call the box office at (760) 438-5683 to get the exact dates. Tickets range in price from $20 for practice rounds to $40 for the finals. It's best to purchase your tickets as far in advance as possible, as they usually sell out early. Tickets are available at the box office at La Costa Resort or through Ticketmaster at (619) 220-8497.

College and High School Sports

San Diego State University's athletic teams are competitive, although they can't hold their own against football teams such as Arizona State or the University of Illinois. The Aztecs basketball team is improving, however, and fans hope that recently acquired head coach Steve Fisher will pull the team together. He definitely has the experience and the wherewithal, as, before becoming an Aztec in 1999, his University of Michigan team won nine post-season tournaments, including three trips to the NCAA championships. The Cox Arena, inaugurated in 2000, is the new home of the Aztec b-ball team. For information about all SDSU sporting events, check out www.goaztecs.com.

Insiders know that USD's Toreros (www.usdtoreros.com) tend to shine in

Over-the-Line was invented right here in San Diego. PHOTO: THORN VOLLENWEIDER

football, basketball, baseball, volleyball, and soccer. The Tritons of UCSD compete on a national level in a number of sports, and Point Loma Nazarene has strong athletic teams, too.

Let's not forget our community colleges. Their intercollegiate sports can be every bit as competitive as their four-year counterparts. And for the ultimate sports experi-

ence, go to a high school game. With more than 60 county high schools, all of which have sports programs, you're sure to find a game of some kind on just about any day of the week. This is sports in its purest form, and the rivalries between teams are intense. Remember, these youngsters are the superstars of tomorrow. Join the parents, faculty, and boosters at any high school game.

Daytrips

The Deserts

Orange County

Temecula

Temecula Wine Country

Why leave the San Diego area even for a daytrip? That's a good question.

We have nearly a never-ending supply of places to see and things to do right here in our amazing county. But folks here do want to get out and about. They like to visit the desert communities, Disneyland, San Juan Capistrano mission, and Temecula's wine country. It's fun to explore.

We selected the trips for our Daytrips chapter using two simple principles: 1) they had to be ones we'd recommend to friends and family, and 2) they had to be doable in one day.

We thought about including Los Angeles, but it's really far from doable. It takes a good three hours to drive there from downtown San Diego, and more frustrating hours trying to find your destination in gridlock traffic. That's not the way to spend an enjoyable day. If you want to see Los Angeles, drive up—you'll need a car once you get there since public transportation is nearly nonexistent. Spend a couple of nights in a hotel, see the sights, then drive back to San Diego. You'll be thrilled to get back to our relatively clean air and free-flowing traffic.

You can reach the desert communities of Palm Springs, Rancho Mirage, and Indio in about two hours, so it's possible to go there for the day. Traffic is normally light, compared to that of Orange County and Los Angeles. The desert scenery is gorgeous. And you'll be treated to the sight of snow-covered mountains in winter atop Mount San Jacinto and the electricity-generating windmill farm near the Palm Springs exit from I-10. So get a map, gas up the car, and get ready to explore Southern California.

The Deserts

Whether you go for the hot display of spring flowers or the hotspots of shopping, eating, golfing, and celebrity watching in Palm Springs, the desert communities are perfect daytrips. Many Insiders go to the desert cities when it's cool and damp along the coast. Some prefer to visit during the summers when there are great deals on tennis, golf, and food packages.

Anza-Borrego Desert State Park
200 Palm Canyon Dr., Borrego Springs
(760) 767–5311 (the park),
(760) 767–4205 (visitor center)
www.parks.ca.gov

Every year about 600,000 visitors travel to the park to camp, enjoy desert hikes and walks, and see the spring flowers. (Please see our chapter on Annual Attractions and Parks for more tips.) At the park's visitor center—the best place to start—you'll find information and brochures about the area. The center holds naturalist's talks, fossil programs, garden walks, nature

Insiders' Tip

For special values on accommodations, attractions, and events in the desert communities, call year-round for a *Hot Summer Values* brochure, from the Palm Springs Visitor and Information Center at (800) 347-7746.

hikes, campfire programs, and activities for "junior" rangers. The visitor center is open daily from October through May, 9:00 A.M. to 5:00 P.M. During the summer, the center is open weekends and holidays only. There's overnight camping and other options at the park too. Be sure to see our entry in the Parks chapter for more information on Anza-Borrego.

The Desert Cities
Palm Springs Desert Resorts
Convention and Visitors Bureau
69-930 Hwy. 111, Suite 201, Rancho Mirage
(800) 417–3529
www.desert-resort.com
City of Palm Springs Visitor and Information Center
2781 N. Palm Canyon Dr., Palm Springs
(760) 778–8418, (800) 347–7746
www.palmsprings.com

A fashionable resort city, Palm Springs is known worldwide for celebrities, perfect winter temperatures, and endless golf greens. Once considered the playground for the rich and famous, today Palm Springs and the desert communities such as Palm Desert, Indio, and Rancho Mirage have transformed themselves into family areas.

And yes, there are still plenty of celebrities who make their homes here. Golf, tennis, and spa packages abound at the hotels and resorts, and during the winter "snow birds" flock to the areas from colder climes.

From San Diego, you reach the desert towns by traveling north on Interstate 15 and connecting with Calif. Hwy. 60 or Interstate 10. The 60, as Insiders call it, is a winding mountain road in some places, but a safe drive nonetheless. Whatever choice you make, just head east and you'll be heading in the right direction. The trip from San Diego is about two hours and traffic is hardly ever heavy.

For shopping fun while you're in the area, don't miss a stop on I-10 about 17 miles west of Palm Springs at the **Cabazon Outlet Stores** (909-922-3000). Here you'll find a rest stop (rest rooms and food) blended with outlet shopping that Insiders say is the best in the area.

For the mildly adventurous types, photo enthusiasts, and the outdoor guy or gal, the **Palm Springs Aerial Tramway** is a must-do when you're in the desert. Kids love it. Call for hours of operation as they change depending on the season, (760) 325-1391. To take the tram, exit I-10 at California Highway 111 and head toward Palm Springs. Exit again at Tramway Road and follow the signs. The entrance is about 3 miles up the road toward the mountain. Once the admission fee is paid (about $21 for those 13 and up; about $14 for kids 3-12), you'll board the tram, which transports passengers 2.5 miles from Valley Station in Chino Canyon (at an altitude of 2,643 feet) to and from Mountain Station (at 8,516 feet) at the east edge of Long Valley. The trip in an enclosed, hanging gondola isn't the proper jaunt for those who avoid heights or are uncomfortable in enclosed areas. If you love scenery from a bird's eye view, this is a spectacular way to see the mountains and the entire Coachella Valley below. On any blistering summer's day, you can leave Palm Springs in 100-degree-plus weather and feel a chill on top of the mountain. At the summit you'll find a cafeteria, observation area, picnic spots, museum, gift shop, and snack bar along with walking and hiking trails.

Once you're back down in the desert, you can take a celebrity-spotters bus tour (760-770-2700) with **Palm Springs Celebrity Tours.** The two- to five-hour tours start at $23 for adults and $10 for students. (You can call ahead for reservations and they're recommended during the popular winter season and during the film festivals.)

You can shop along **Tahquitz Way,** with stores such as Gucci and Saks beckoning you inside. And from ice-cream parlors to chic dining establishments, you can choose a place to satisfy your daytripping appetite. You can take in a museum, too. **The Palm Springs Desert Museum** (101 Museum Drive, 760-325-0189) has exhibits on Western and contemporary art and the human and natural history of the Coachella Valley. Call for dates and performance information; the museum holds events from drama to dance in the Annenburg Theater. General admission is $7.50.

If you can't resist the golf courses, play a round at **Indio Municipal Golf Course** (760-347-9156, 83-040 Avenue 42). Fees are $10. Another choice is **The Golf Center at Palm Desert** (760-779-1877, 74-945 Sheryl Drive), where course fees are $16.

Just east of Palm Springs in Palm Desert is the **Living Desert Zoo and Gardens** (47-900 Portola Avenue, 760-346-5694, www.livingdesert.org). Here visitors can take a self-guided tour of the grounds and learn about the more than 400 animals representing 150 different species such as coyotes, bighorn sheep, zebras, and cheetahs. Hours are seasonal, so call ahead. General admission from September 1 through June 15 is $8.50 for adults, $7.50 for seniors 62 and older, and $4.25 for children 3 to 12. Summer rates are $6.50 for people 13 years and older, and $3.00 for children 3 to 12.

Orange County

Orange County—all of it—is filled with daytrips for anyone who wants to explore. In this section, we're giving you a taste of what you'll find in Orange County. You may also contact the Anaheim/Orange County Convention and Visitor Bureau at (714) 765-8888, (888) 598-3200 or www.anaheimoc.org.

Graceful palms stand watch along coastal highways and through surrounding areas. PHOTO: BOB YARBROUGH, COURTESY OF SAN DIEGO CONVENTION AND VISITORS BUREAU

Good Golly Miss Molly—They're Grinding

And they're thrashing and getting some air. Yep, you guessed it. These folks are on skateboards and happily involved in a sport that's growing by the second.

Once you tell your kids about this daytrip to Temecula, just over 80 miles from downtown San Diego, be prepared to be pestered until you actually make the trek north on Interstate 15. It's worth the drive to see this model skateboard park and perhaps even try your own luck at the sport. You can rent safety equipment when you arrive, so the excuse, "Gee, honey, I don't have a helmet," won't cut it here.

Temecula's skateboard park is located at Rancho California Sports Park and shares space here with ball fields, places for inline skating, and a roller hockey rink. It's open to kids of all ages, seven days a week. Weekday hours are 4:00 until 9:30 P.M. Saturday hours are 10:00 A.M. to 9:30 P.M., and on Sunday it's open from 1:00 until 6:30 P.M.

The park features challenging areas for beginners and special times for anyone who has yet to learn to balance on a skateboard. Those who are really good at the sport will just have to try it to believe the air they get flying off a ramp.

There are bowls, lifts, and jumps to sample, a fun box and one area that looks like a pyramid with a flat top. A favorite is the Embarcadero steps, a series of cement stairs that resemble those that might lead down from a building. Each obstacle holds a thrill for skaters who live and breathe the tricks and maneuvers that sometimes make a parent's heart stop.

Kevin Thatcher, skateboard guru and an editor for the skateboarding magazine *Thrasher* was one of the park's designers. His patience paid off during the process and he was impressed when he finally skated the park on its opening day—June 27, 1996.

Flying off a ramp, negotiating stairs, and catching "air" from a side-wall are part of the fun at the spectacular Temecula Skate Park. PHOTO: COURTESY OF CITY OF TEMECULA

"It's bad, rad, gnarly, and groovy. . . . It should provide a lot of thrills, definitely. It's far and away better than any facility in America."

Why the excitement about an acre that's covered with cement shaped into hills and valleys and vaguely resembling a swimming pool that's been drained? That answer requires more questions, starting with: Is skateboarding illegal in your home-town and on your city's sidewalks? If you've said yes or have seen warning signs pro-hibiting skaters, you're not alone. But imagine for a minute outlawing baseball? Or soccer? Imagine telling fitness walkers to get off the hiking trails or face a fine?

The concept is hard to envision, yet that's what has happened to skateboarders in many cities, including ones here in San Diego County. Thatcher and other advo-cates of skateboarding continue to remind us that in most areas, skateboarders are treated like lowlife hoods. Many communities have forbidden the sport, yet provide no alternatives. Temecula is one of a small handful of communities that had the fore-sight to find a solution.

In the spring of 1993, the City of Temecula heard pleas from skaters and skate-boarders who wanted to practice their sport. While some store and business owners screamed that they wanted skating enthusiasts run out of Dodge, other citizens in this progressive area knew the truth: What skateboarders lacked was a safe, well-run venue. It took time and lots of planning, but public opinion and soil were turned. What emerged was the Rancho California Sports Park.

It cost about $300,000 to build the one-acre skating utopia. It costs another $62,000 for annual upkeep; these costs are easily offset by fees.

The park has been enormously successful, judging by the skate park's mountain-ous pile of waivers (each skater must sign one), and by the park's growing reputation. City officials from around the country have toured the facility. Herman D. Parker, deputy director of Temecula's Community Services Department, says, with a good measure of pride, that "there's even been interest in the park from planners in Lon-don, England."

Julie Pelletier, Temecula's recreation superintendent, points out one of the unique factors in the park's success: "Many cities have opened parks, but they are not manned. We have a staff of seven." Pelletier also mentions other reasons the skate park is so popular: "A lot of professional skaters live in Southern California." She adds that the park draws not only kids but lots of adults too. "It really caters to all ages," she says. Whatever explains it, the park has become a mecca for beginners and pro skaters alike.

And the rules don't drive them away either. Of course there are some—that's to be expected. You must sign a waiver form. Temecula residents with proof of residency must pay an annual $1.00 fee and a $2.00 entrance fee for each session. (A session lasts about two hours.) Non-residents must pay a $5.00 entrance fee. All skaters younger than 18 must have a parent or guardian sign an information form or waiver to use the facility. Parents of skaters who live in Temecula must visit the park in per-son to fill out the form. Children younger than 7 must be accompanied by an adult.

While spectators can't enter the park while skating is occurring, there are plenty of grassy areas. It's fun just to watch and marvel at the skill and balance of those who put on skates or ride skateboards. There's a snack bar outside of the rink, rest rooms, an equipment rental service, a tot lot, and plenty of parking. On holiday weekends be prepared to wait for a turn. Only 35 skaters are allowed at a time.

No bicycles, food, or drink are allowed in the park and any skirmishes between skaters are dealt with promptly. But these disputes rarely happen. And broken bones?

There have been a few, but the bad injuries are kept down since all patrons must wear appropriate safety gear (wrist guards, elbow pads, kneepads, and helmet) that is in good condition. Skateboards and skates must be in good condition, too.

The park fulfills the dreams of skaters of all ages. The roller hockey rink accommodates state-of-the-art league play for in excess of 2,000 youths per year. That's quite an accomplishment since only a short time ago these youngsters had nowhere to play but parking lots and public streets. Now rather than practice their sport on the blacktops of malls and public roads, the skaters can enjoy a safe, well-supervised, and challenging place to participate in their sport.

For more information on the Temecula Skate Park, call (909) 695–1409.

Remember when driving in Orange County, it's well worth avoiding the freeways during peak commuter times and to find alternative routes if possible. Carry a map, should there be a snag in traffic. Listen to the radio channels that give traffic updates, too. Doing so will make your daytrip a snap.

Crystal Cathedral
13280 Chapman, Garden Grove
(714) 971–4000
www.crystalcathedral.org

It's not worth driving all the way to Orange County just to see this, but if you're in the neighborhood you may want to stop by for the sheer amazement of seeing this masterful piece of architecture. It was designed by famed architect Philip Johnson.

The Cathedral resembles a four-pointed star with 10,000 panes of glass covering the weblike, translucent walls and ceiling. The tickets for the pageants of "The Glory of Christmas" and "The Glory of Easter" (the two internationally known events) sell out long before the seasonal performances. Call well ahead for reservations if you have your heart set on seeing these.

If you attend the performances, you'll be treated to music that seems to echo from heaven. Some of the "actors" are live animals that, well, play animal parts in the programs.

Visitors are welcome at the cathedral Monday through Saturday 9:00 A.M. to 3:00 P.M. Sunday hours for the Christian, nondenominational worship are 9:30 A.M. and 11:00 A.M. There is an evening service at 6:00 P.M.

Disneyland
1313 S. Harbor Blvd., Anaheim
(714) 781–4565
disneyland.disney.go.com

Space Mountain, Frontierland, and the whole new Tomorrowland are just a sample of the fun that's in store at Disneyland. The theme park is as much Southern California as oranges, surfers, and blue-sky days. The park is about 90 miles north of San Diego and there are signs to get you to Disneyland displayed on I–5 at Katella Avenue in Anaheim.

Insiders and visitors from around the country make this wonderful family tradition part of their vacation plans. It's open every day, with more than 60 major attractions, 50 shops, and 30 restaurants, from sit-down places to snack-food walk-up counters.

The newest addition to the Disney Resort is California Adventure, a stone's throw from the original park. The park is divided into six Golden State districts: Condor Flats, Bountiful Valley Farm, Pacific Wharf, Bay Area, Grizzly Peak Recreation Area, and Golden Vine Winery. Some of the more popular rides are Grizzly River Run (better experienced during the warm summer months since you will get quite wet on the final plunge) and Soarin' Over California, which uses state-of-the-art technology to combine suspended seats with a spectacular surround-style movie. Riders literally "soar" over California's picturesque sights.

A recent development at the park is an ingenious service called FASTPASS. This newest brainchild of the Disney folks allows visitors to "save" their place in line for some of the more popular rides. With some minimal attention to scheduling, you can drastically reduce your time spent waiting in lines. The attractions that offer the FASTPASS service are listed on the map provided when you enter the park. You simply slide your admission ticket into a FASTPASS machine and a paper will pop out with the time when you can come back and (usually) walk right on the ride. This service is available at both Disneyland and California Adventure.

Wedged between Disneyland and Disney's California Adventure is a new shopping and entertainment complex called Downtown Disney, (714) 300-7800. There is no charge to enter, and with ample parking, it's a good choice for grabbing a bite to eat and relaxing after a day at one of the parks. The AMC Theaters offer love-seat-style stadium seating and surround sound, while the ESPN Zone has two floors and 35,000 square feet of interactive entertainment, dining, and 175 TV monitors broadcasting different sporting events. Downtown Disney has ten eating establishments offering everything from Voodoo Shrimp (at the House of Blues) to tapas (at the Latin-style Y Arriba Y Arriba). If the kids are with you, be prepared to be dragged into the LEGO Imagination Center; they will surely want to check out the giant dinosaur built entirely of LEGOS, together with the hundreds of LEGO toys and products for sale.

Adult admission to Disneyland and Disney's California Adventure is $43 for

Insiders' Tip

When visiting amusement parks with children, remember that for safety reasons some rides prohibit youngsters who are less than 40 inches tall. Call ahead for restrictions if you're traveling with small ones.

each park; children age 3 to 9 pay $33 for each park. Park hours vary, so call ahead, but both are open daily and hours are extended during the summer.

Knott's Berry Farm and Knott's Soak City USA
8039 Beach Blvd., Buena Park
(714) 220-5200
www.knotts.com

Knott's Berry Farm is a fun family theme park that celebrates California and the West. There are six areas: Old West Ghost Town, Indian Trails, Wild Water Wilderness, Fiesta Village, The Boardwalk, and the world-famous Camp Snoopy (home of the Peanuts gang).

Within the park are 30 shops and restaurants. Here you can buy that fabulous Knott's boysenberry jam and lots of other Knott's jams too. Gift baskets—nice to take back home with you—are also available. At the not-to-be-missed Mrs. Knott's Chicken Dinner Restaurant you can sample some of that famous delicious fried chicken. Park hours vary, so call or check the Web site before you go To get to the park, which is about 90 minutes from San Diego, drive north on I-5, then take California Hwy. 91 west to the Beach Boulevard exit, then head south. Unlimited-use tickets are $40 for adults and $30 for seniors 60 and older and children 3 to 11.

Next door to the amusement park is Knott's Soak City USA, a water-themed park sure to keep the tykes entertained all day. Open daily from June 3 through Labor Day and weekends only during May and September, it has high-speed slides, inner tube rides, and tube slides (probably best avoided by those claustrophobic sorts). There is also a large pool where "tidal" waves are generated every 15 minutes. The Sparkletts® Sunset River gently floats folks of all ages down a leisurely ride on oversized inner tubes. Admission is $21.95 for adults and $14.95 for children 3 to 11.

Mission San Juan Capistrano
31522 Camino Capistrano, San Juan Capistrano
(949) 234-1300
www.missionsjc.com

Padre Junipero Serra founded this mission in 1776 and every year the swallows migrate to the grounds on Saint Joseph's Day,

Driving through Anza-Borrego Desert during the springtime, you may be thrilled to see the desert in bloom. PHOTO: COURTESY OF SAN DIEGO CONVENTION AND VISITORS BUREAU

March 19. The swallows are not aware that humans try to clock their arrival and flock to see the birds coming back. Depending on weather conditions throughout the world, the birds may arrive early or late, but visitors come nonetheless.

Padre Serra's Chapel at the mission is the oldest building, still in use, in the state. For youngsters in the fourth grade who study California history, the trip to the mission is sometimes the most impressive field trip of the year.

On the 10-acre grounds you'll see the Serra Chapel, padres' quarters, the cemetery, and the Great Stone Church. There are often crafts demonstrations and various festivals.

The mission is within walking distance of the Amtrak train station depot in San Juan Capistrano, and many Insiders take the train and a picnic lunch for a day at the mission. If you're driving, exit I-5 at the California Hwy. 74 exit and drive west, following the signs to the mission. Admission is $6.00 for adults, $5.00 for seniors, and $4.00 for children. The mission is open daily from 8:30 A.M. to 5:00 P.M. except for Thanksgiving, Christmas, and Good Friday. Within a few blocks of the mission, there are boutiques, cafes, antiques shops, and bookstores.

Movieland Wax Museum
7711 Beach Blvd., Buena Park
(714) 522–1145
www.movielandwaxmuseum.com

The Movieland Wax Museum, about 90 miles from downtown San Diego and 1 block north of Knotts, lets you get up close and personal with the stars from movie-making history. Since the early 1960s, the museum has been documenting the world of film by adding celebrities to their wax collection. Currently, there are more than 300 figures including replicas of Julie Andrews, John Wayne, Bette Davis, Tom Selleck, Michael Jackson, and Mike Meyers as Austin Powers. At the museum, you'll see sets from *Star Trek, Bonanza, The Wizard of Oz,* and *The African Queen.* The museum hours vary. Admission is $12.95 for adults, $10.55 for seniors 55 and older, and $6.95 for children 4 to 11. To get to the museum, drive north on Interstate 5 to Buena Park,

Insiders' Tip

Heading to the desert region in February? Add the National Date Festival in Indio, in Imperial County, to your "to do" list. The festival features camel and ostrich races and Arabian Nights musical pageants. Call the Indio Chamber of Commerce at (760) 347-0676 or (800) 444-6346 for more information and the specific dates.

taking California Highway 91 west. Exit on Beach Boulevard.

Temecula

Temecula is a favorite daytrip. Head north on I-15 past Escondido. You may want to stop along the way at one of the many farmers' stands filled to the brim with fresh vegetables and fruits. You can pick up plenty of healthy snacks for the day. You'll see these as you exit I-15 at California Highway 76, going either east or west. Just 6 miles farther along the interstate, you'll find the valley of Temecula in Riverside County.

Temecula and Rancho California are fast-growing, family communities. For the daytripper, the area is a treasure trove of possibilities. Be sure to read this chapter's Close-up about the famous skateboard park that's located in this sprawling community.

Antiques Shopping District

Old Town Temecula along Front Street may be as close to heaven as any antiques hunter could imagine without going through the pearly gates—at least that's what some Insider antiques lovers say. In a

Cattle graze near Julian in a quiet pasture setting. PHOTO: COURTESY OF SAN DIEGO CONVENTION AND VISITORS BUREAU

multi-block area, you'll find more than 20 stores. The city spent $5.2 million on improvements in this area in 1998, adding wooden sidewalks and old-fashioned benches. The area also has family-style restaurants and specialty food spots.

Temecula Skate Park
42569 Margarita Rd., Temecula
(909) 695-1409

This model skate park is a favorite among serious and fun-loving skateboarders and in-line skating enthusiasts of all ages and abilities. The park consists of a competition 64-foot diameter bowl with ramp entry and a 10-foot-wide apron that connects the upper bowl with a street plaza skate area. In the street area are the pyramid, fun box, curbs, ramps, stairs, and a 20-foot handrail.

Don't fret if you've forgotten your safety equipment—you can rent everything you need. See the Close-up in this chapter for more details.

Temecula Wine Country

Temecula Valley Vintners Association
(909) 699-3626, (800) 801-9463

When in Temecula, do like other visitors do and take the wine country tours. Call the Vintners Association at the phone number above for a map or call one of the wineries mentioned below for directions.

This is southern California's largest wine-producing area, and within the valley of Temecula you can visit more than 12 wineries, each offering samples of their distinct products.

According to the vintners, this is perfect wine country because of the combination of geography, micro-climate, and well-drained soil. The 1,500-foot elevation and cool summer nights add to the grape-growing and wine-making magic.

The wineries range in size from one that produces about 1,000 cases a year to large-scale wineries with production exceeding 100,000 cases each year.

The following are just a sampling of the wineries you'll discover in Temecula.

Baily Vineyard & Winery
33440 La Serena Way, Temecula
(909) 676–9463

This vineyard and winery produces award-winning wines available primarily at the tasting room. Open daily 10:00 A.M. to 5:00 P.M., there's a picnic area, a gift shop, and special events. Baily Vineyard & Winery is known for its Chardonnay, Muscot Canelli, and Riesling.

Hart Winery
41300 Avenida Biona, Temecula
(909) 676–6300

This winery specializes in handcrafted, barrel-aged red wines and dry, full-bodied white varieties. Tasting is available daily from 9:00 A.M. until 4:30 P.M. There's a cost of $2.00 per person and it includes a winery logo glass you can take home. Hart Winery, according to in-the-know Insiders, does an excellent Fene Blanc, and the Barbera and Merlot are outstanding.

Van Roekel Vineyards & Winery
34567 Rancho California Rd., Temecula
(909) 699–6961

This vineyard and winery is the newest in the area, and has already developed premium wines. Tasting is daily from 10:00 A.M. to 5:00 P.M. There's a picnic area and a shop that sells gourmet cheeses, deli items, and a wide selection of wine-related gifts. You'll want to taste and of course bring home Van Roekel's Chardonnay, Chenin Blanc, and Syrah Rose.

South of the Border

¡Bienvenido a Mexico! Most visitors to San Diego (and most locals, too) sooner or later end up south of the border. Even though they are warned that Tijuana hardly represents the "real" Mexico, the idea of visiting a foreign culture proves a powerful lure. Added to that lure is the fact that the U.S.–Mexico Border is only a 20-minute drive from downtown San Diego, which makes for an easy daytrip or after-dark excursion. Many Insiders make regular forays to **Tijuana** for an evening on the town. Fine dining is abundant, and Tijuana has several nightclubs that are popular among revelers of all generations, but especially the young.

Beyond the border city of Tijuana lie the resort towns of **Rosarito Beach** and **Ensenada.** Either can be visited as a long daytrip, or relax a little, visit both, and spend the weekend. With much smaller populations (Tijuana is Mexico's fourth largest city) and decidedly less congestion and crime, Rosarito and Ensenada are worth the extra effort to get there. A popular getaway for Hollywood stars during the '30s and '40s, Rosarito Beach has grown from a tiny enclave and suburb of Tijuana to a strip of restaurants, hotels, and shops fronted by a seemingly endless stretch of beach. Ensenada itself is more attractive than Rosarito and has more of a town feel. Although bathing or surfing beaches there are found only north or south of town, several successful fishing fleets are based at the town's bustling port.

Between Tijuana and Ensenada are some favorite stops. One is **Puerto Nuevo,** once a collection of humble if compelling lobster shacks, which in recent years has evolved into a more formal enclave of restaurants. If many of the spruced-up venues now accept credit cards, and a few savvy entrepeneurs have opened hotels in the vicinity, the menu hasn't changed at all: It still consists of boiled and broiled lobster, refried beans, rice, and baskets of hot tortillas. A few miles north of Puerto Nuevo is **Foxploration** (Free Road to Ensenada Km 32.8, Popotla, 661-614-9499). Emerging from the set of the major motion picture *Titanic,* filmed in 1997, the theme park has a film set, wardrobe room, and other areas that show how films get made. There's also an outdoor stage, food court, and shopping arcade. Closed Tuesdays and Wednesdays in summer and Mondays also in winter. Admission is $12.00 for adults and $9.00 for children 3 to 11.

Golfers head for **Bajamar**, the posh resort overlooking the sea between Tijuana and Ensenada, or **Real Del Mar**, just a few miles south of the border. The golfing is good at both courses and the facilities are first-rate. Folks who are serious about their fishing go south to Ensenada or southeast, to **San Felipe** on the eastern coast of the Baja California Peninsula. Boats depart regularly from San Felipe in search of record-breaking marlin, swordfish, yellowtail, and sailfish in the Sea of Cortez.

Tijuana is the city that draws the most visitors, though, and there's no shortage of attractions. Shopping, dining, and cultural performances and exhibits all await the intrepid explorer. We'll introduce you to the highlights in this chapter and give you lots of tips for planning your trip and finding things to do once you get there. Most places south of the border accept American dollars and major credit cards in addition to the Mexican peso. If credit cards are not accepted at an establishment, we've made a note of it.

Getting There and Getting Back

The border crossing at San Ysidro (at the southern end of Interstate 5) is open 24 hours; the Otay Mesa crossing at the eastern end of Interstate 905 is open daily from 6:00 A.M. to 10:00 P.M. Travelers crossing the border into Mexico are usually waved through with few, if any, questions. When you return to the United States whether walking or driving, you must stop for inspection by U.S. Customs and Immigration officials. Usually you will be asked a few questions, like your place of birth, where you've traveled, and what you're bringing back with you, but occasionally drivers will be asked to stop for a secondary inspection. It's a fairly rare occurrence and only happens if customs inspectors suspect you might have exceeded your permissible duty-free articles or are attempting to smuggle contraband.

Driving

If your idea of a trip into Mexico is a leisurely expedition, stopping here and there, without a set agenda or time schedule, then you should drive. A word of caution, however. Driving in Tijuana is not for the weak of heart. Traffic is usually heavy, street signs and directions are often in short supply and are in Spanish, and the driving habits of exhuberant locals may be disconcerting to first-time tourists. Tijuana is also chock-full of traffic circles. Getting stuck in one can be frustrating and disorienting. Just remember to bear right and follow the counterclockwise flow of traffic; if possible it's best to keep moving. Also, watch for one-way street signs, which are numerous. If you're used to driving in large foreign cities such as Rome or Paris, Tijuana will be a piece of cake. If the prospect sounds a little intimidating, you might be better off taking taxis or signing on with a tour group.

Should you decide to drive, take I–5 south to the San Ysidro border crossing. From I–805, drive south to I–905, and go east to the Otay Mesa border crossing. The

San Ysidro crossing is recommended for easiest access to downtown Tijuana; Otay Mesa is generally used for access to Tijuana's international airport. Once across the border and into the downtown Tijuana area, you'll find plenty of pay lots (recommended) and on-street parking. Most shopping centers offer free parking. You can also drive all the way to the border, park in one of several security-guarded lots, and walk across. The fee ranges from $2.00 to $3.00 for half an hour, but tops out between $6.00 and $10.00 for 24 hours.

If you're driving a rental car, be sure to check with the rental agency to see if they allow their cars to be driven across the border. Of the larger rental agencies, Avis, Budget, and Enterprise do allow travel into Mexico. But policies change, so be sure to check ahead of time.

Insurance

This is important. Be sure to purchase Mexican auto insurance before you cross the border. Mexican authorities recognize insurance policies issued only by companies licensed to transact insurance sales in Mexico. If you're involved in a traffic accident while in Mexico, a Mexican insurance policy will pave the road to resolution. The laws are different in Mexico, where you're presumed guilty until proven innocent. If it's determined that you are at fault, and you don't have a Mexican policy, you will be expected to pay for the damages on the spot. If you can't, you'll be taken to jail. In any case, you might end up in jail while the whole thing is sorted out, even if you are not at fault. Having Mexican auto insurance will prevent this from happening. To purchase insurance (and to drive in Mexico) you'll need your valid driver's license and current vehicle registration.

Mexican insurance policies are available through the Auto Club of Southern California and from a number of companies that have set up shop near the border; there signs are clearly visible when you take the last U.S. exit off I–5. Several companies will sell you a daily or yearly policy by phone, including Kemper México (P.O. Box 744, Temecula, CA 92593; 909-506-4444) and

Dancers perform in traditional Aztec Indian costumes. PHOTO: BOB YARBROUGH, COURTESY OF SAN DIEGO CONVENTION AND VISITORS BUREAU

Sanborns (210 North International Boulevard, Hidalgo, TX 78557; 956–843–8747, www.sanbornsinsurance.net).

Alternative Transportation

Public transportation is a highly recommended method for a trip across the border. The San Diego Trolley Blue Line goes all the way to the San Ysidro border crossing for a fare of $2.25, then you can walk across the border and catch a taxi for the short drive into town. Or you can join the crowd of people who enjoy walking into town, an easy stroll of less than a mile. A typical taxi fare from the border or for a drive within town runs about $6.00 to $7.00. You might be able to negotiate a lower fare, but be sure to establish what the fare will be before you take off.

Greyhound Bus Line (120 West Broadway, 619-239-3266, 800-231-2222) also has frequent service from downtown San Diego to its station in downtown Tijuana. Bus transportation to Tijuana airport or to attractions anywhere between Tijuana and Ensenada can be arranged through **Five Star Tours** (1050 Kettner Boulevard, San Diego; 619–232-5049). From the last U.S. trolley stop or from the Border Station Parking & Visitor Information Center (next to San Diego Factory Outlet Center) at the last U.S. exit off I-5, big red **Mexicoach** buses charge $1.00 per person each way to deliver passengers to the other side of the border. They run every 15 minutes, daily, between 9:00 A.M. and 9:00 P.M.

One of the easiest ways to navigate Tijuana and regions beyond is by joining a tour group. You can sign up for half-day, full-day, or even overnight tours to Tijuana and beyond, and leave the worries of driving to the tour company. Here are two companies that offer South-of-the-Border tour packages.

Coach U.S.A. Tours San Diego
3888 Beech St., San Diego
(619) 491–0011
www.coachusa.com
Formerly Gray Line, Coach U.S.A still offers half-day Tijuana tours to the heart of Tijuana's shopping district. Reorganizing at press time, they are unsure of fees to be charged for this service, or whether tours to Ensenada will be offered. Check their Web site for current information.

San Diego Scenic Tours
2255 Garnet Ave., Ste. 3, San Diego
(858) 273–8687
www.sandiegoscenictours.com
Tour guides have been entertaining folk since 1993 with the history and culture of Tijuana. You'll have plenty of time to shop and take in the sights along Avenida Revolución, the city's main shopping street, to have lunch at one of many fine restaurants in the area, or simply sit and enjoy mariachi music while sipping a frosty margarita. Food and drink are not included in the tour price. Both full- and half-day tours are available, with prices starting at $26 for adults and $14 for children 3 to 11.

More Travel Tips

Citizens of the United States and Canada do not need tourist cards if traveling within 100 miles of the U.S. border. However, if the length of your stay exceeds 72 hours or you plan to journey beyond Ensenada or San Felipe, a tourist card for each traveler is required. Tourist cards can be obtained in the United States from Mexican consulates or Mexican tourism offices, the Auto Club of Southern California, and most travel agents. Travelers must fill in the necessary information and have either a valid passport or a certified

Insiders' Tip
If you drive south of Tijuana, you'll soon encounter toll roads. The fares total around $6.50 from Tijuana to Ensenada; you can pay in U.S. currency or Mexican pesos.

Going south of the border? Some visitors take in a bullfight when they are in Mexico. PHOTO: COURTESY OF SAN DIEGO CONVENTION AND VISITORS BUREAU

birth certificate. It's always a good idea to keep identification and proof of citizenship with you while traveling in Mexico (driver's license, military ID, passport, or birth certificate).

English is spoken most everywhere in Tijuana, but knowing a few Spanish words can be helpful, especially *por favor* (please) and *gracias* (thank you). Don't be afraid to try a few words from your Spanish-English dictionary. You'll endear yourself to the locals. And remember that a smile is the universal language.

Tijuana and the border area are duty-free zones, and you can pay for your goodies with U.S. dollars or Mexican pesos. Most of the tourist-oriented shops, hotels, and restaurants accept travelers cheques and credit cards, but be sure to ask. Returning U.S. citizens are allowed up to $400 worth of merchandise for personal use once in every 30-day period. You also are allowed one liter of alcoholic bever-

ages. Keep in mind that most fruit and vegetables are not allowed to cross into the United States.

Now let's clear up some common misconceptions. Yes, Tijuana is a great place to buy fireworks. No, you may not bring them back into the United States. If you are caught, they will be confiscated and you may be subject to a hefty fine.

You've probably also heard about the great deals you can get on prescription medications in Tijuana. You *must* have a valid prescription from a U.S. doctor to bring medications back across the border, and don't plan to bring back more than a two months' supply.

Ready, Set, Go

Now that we've gotten all the caveats out of the way, get ready for a one-of-a-kind experience. Granted, Mexico is not for everyone. Close as it is to San Diego, it's a different country, with its own customs and laws, and different food and language. But open-minded individuals will surely enjoy the experience and most likely return with a precious trinket, a great story, or some other interesting experience to share.

And don't forget to have a margarita for us. Lift your glass and say, *"¡Salud!"* and *"¡Viva Mexico!"*

Accommodations

Should you decide to stay for a spell, several nice hotels and resorts are available where you'll be quite comfortable. Keep in mind that the level of service may not be what you're accustomed to back home, but in all the hotels we recommend, you should be quite comfortable.

Price Code

The price code indicates the cost of accommodations for two for one night excluding tax. Tijuana hotels typically do not have price hikes during the summer season, so the fees quoted are reliable any time during the year.

$	$50 to $100
$$	$101 to $150

Tijuana

Fiesta Inn Vita Spa $
Ave. Paseo de los Héroes 18818, Zona Río, Tijuana
(800) 343–7821, 011–52 (664) 634–6901
www.fiestamexico.com

This hotel has passed through a few hands since its glory days as the Prohibition-era Agua Caliente Spa. After it joined the Fiesta Inn/Fiesta Americana chain in 1995, rooms were redecorated in deep rose, dark green, and other tasteful colors. The lobby restaurant feels a bit exposed and the food is standard international hotel fare, but waiters are generally swift and congenial. Swimming in the pool behind the restaurant makes you feel you've jumped into a public fountain—it's that small and exposed to the view of

restaurant diners. But beyond the pool, you can soak in the mineral waters of the spa's original hot tub, or better yet, take advantage of men's and women's steam rooms, sauna, and Jacuzzi on the second floor. The health spa also offers body wraps, manicures and pedicures, and other treatments.

Hotel Lucerna $$
10902 Paseo de los Heroes, Tijuana
(800) 582–3762, 011–52 (66) 34–20–00
www.hotel-lucerna.com.mx

Authentic Mexican atmosphere combines with modern amenities to make the Hotel Lucerna an Insiders' choice. It has 168 rooms and nine suites, and features a sunken lobby, an open-air cafe, and a courtyard garden. The hotel's swimming pool is in the midst of the garden and is surrounded by palm trees. In addition to the cafe, there's a French restaurant, a cocktail lounge, and a nightclub. Rooms have double, queen, or king-size beds, cable television, and fully appointed baths. The more expensive rooms have a courtyard view. This hotel is geared toward business people, and rates therefore are considerably reduced on weekends.

Rosarito

Rosarito Beach Hotel & Spa $–$$
Blvd. Benito Juarez, Rosarito
(800) 343–8582, 011–52 (661) 612–1106
www.rosaritobeachhotel.com

This is the place to stay in Rosarito Beach. Made famous in the '30s and '40s by legions of Hollywood stars and other glamour pusses escaping the constraints of Prohibition, the resort has expanded and become more plebeian but retains much of its original charm. Most of the 280 rooms and suites have been renovated over the years and are modern and efficient, if somewhat small, with standard hotel decor. Rooms are available in beachfront lowrises or in the tower. The upper floor ocean view rooms are the most expensive.

The hotel sits on Rosarito's long, creamy-sand beach; there are also two pools, one with a slide and shallow pool

Shopping is the sport of choice for many who come to Mexico. Here, a shopper admires some embroidery on Avenida Revolución in Tijuana. PHOTO: COURTESY OF SAN DIEGO CONVENTION AND VISITORS BUREAU

that caters to kids. Singles barhop among the three watering holes or relax in one of the three Jacuzzis. Play tennis or racquetball, billiards, or Ping-Pong. In a '30s mansion next door is the Casa de Playa Spa. It's a full-service European-style spa that offers massages, herbal wraps, saunas, and hot tubs. Chaberts restaurant, specializing in both steaks and French cuisine, is a dignified, stately restaurant where chandeliers, plush Middle Eastern carpets, massive oil paintings, and lovely table linens will make you want to don your finest apparel. Much more casual, and with terrific food, is the hotel's Acteza bar-restaurant.

Ensenada

Estero Beach Resort Hotel $–$$
On Highway 1, 6 miles south of Ensenada
(800) 762–2494, 011–52 (646) 176–6235,
(646) 176–6230
www.hotelesterobeach.com

This is truly an Insiders' favorite. Tennis, horseback riding, and boating are just some of the activities to occupy your time while at Estero Beach. Located on a long estuary (for which it's named), this is a good spot for birding. There's a playground and large pool for the amusement of children and adults. A 15-minute drive from the shops and restaurants of Ensenada, this is a good bet for those who like staying put and enjoying the beach and hotel amenities.

The resort has 108 rooms and suites, which are modern and well maintained. Rooms in the Palenque wing are more expensive than those in the Tikal wing, but are a better choice. Suites are in a two-story building that fronts the ocean. Also available are cottages with kitchenettes and patios that are popular among honeymooners. Both double and queen-size beds are available. A restaurant is also on the premises.

San Felipe

San Felipe Marina Resort $$
Carretera San Felipe–Aeropuerto,
San Felipe
(800) 291–5397, 011–52 (686) 577–1568

Just a little south of town is this ever-expanding complex of hotel rooms, time-shares and condos. Sixty hotel rooms are available, and all are decorated in a Mexican-Mediterranean style with white-tiled floors and woven rugs. Lots of folk-art accents adorn the rooms, and they all have balconies or patios, most with views of the Sea of Cortez.

Visitors have their choice of the beach or two pools, one of which is indoors and is a popular hangout on cool days. Next door is an RV campground, and plans are in the works for a 100-slip marina.

Attractions

People often forget that Tijuana is a major city, and as such has developed a number of worthy attractions over the years. When you've had your fill of shopping and dining, check out some of the attractions that are unique to Mexico or at least uncommon elsewhere.

Sporting Events

El Toreo de Tijuana
Blvd. Agua Caliente at Blvd. Cuauhtémoc, Tijuana
Plaza Monumental
Playas de Tijuana, Tijuana
(619) 232–5049 (San Diego)

If the ancient sport of bullfighting intrigues you, two bullrings in Tijuana present some of the world's top matadors. Dating back to 2000 B.C., bullfighting is a combination of ritual and mortal combat, pitting man against beast in a deadly battle in which the humans enjoy better than 100 to 1 odds.

Bullfights are held between late May and the end of September, but not every Sunday. Tickets are available in San Diego through **Five Star Tours** (Santa Fe train depot, 1050 Kettner Boulevard, 619-232-5049) which is by far the easiest way to arrange the excursion. Five Star adds a $5.00 service charge to the price of the ticket and also offers bus transportation to the event at $14.00 per person round trip. Bullfight ticket prices vary based on the fame of matador and other factors, but generally cost from $11.00 for general admission (nosebleed seats in the sun) to around $40.00 (plus $5.00 service charge if booked in San Diego) for good reserved seats. Box seats for up to four people are situated at ground level for up-close viewing of this deadly spectacle.

Caliente Race Track
Blvd. Agua Caliente and Tapachula, Tijuana
011–52 (664) 633–7300, (619) 231–1910 (in San Diego)

Some folks deplore greyhound racing, while others contend it is no crueler than horse racing. Whatever your personal feelings, greyhounds run year-round at this former hippodrome. If you prefer the ponies, satellite wagering is available for all major North American thoroughbred racetracks as well as for football, baseball, hockey, and soccer contests. Greyhounds run nightly at 7:45 P.M. and on Saturday and Sunday at 2:00 P.M. General admission is free. Turf Club seating is $5.00, which includes a $5.00 betting voucher.

L.A. Cetto Winery
Cañón Johnson 2108 and Ave. Constitución
011–52 (664) 685–3031

An interesting outing just a short walk from downtown is a tour and tasting at the L.A. Cetto winery. Here you can sample (and purchase) sparkling and sweet wines, reds and whites, as well as brandy and tequila. The shop has accoutrements for the wine-lover, including glasses with the winery's logo in gold. Individuals can tour without an appointment (although we suggest calling ahead); groups of 10 or more should call for an appointment. Tastings cost $2.00 for four samples, but you can taste more! Choose the vintages

that most interest you or let your guide introduce you to something new. Hours are Monday to Friday 9:30 A.M. to 6:30 P.M., Saturday 10:00 A.M. to 5:00 P.M.

Museums

Tijuana Cultural Center
Paseo de los Héroes and Avenida Independencia, Tijuana
011–52 (664) 687–9600

For a little bit of Mexican history and culture, stop in at this modern complex. The newish California museum (closed Mondays, $2.00) features archaeological, historical, and craft displays, all labeled in English as well as Spanish. Other salons have changing exhibits, and an OMNIMAX theater (closed Mondays, $3.50) has films in both Spanish and English. The 1,000-seat performing arts theater offers a variety of musical and dramatic performances.

Wax Museum
Calle 1 near Avenida Revolución, Tijuana
011–52 (664) 688–2478

Some travelers cannot visit a new city without seeking out the local wax museum, and the one in Tijuana is worth a look-see, if typically weird and even a bit scary for children. Mixed in with the standard representatives of Hollywood (Marilyn Monroe, Madonna) are figures from Mexican history such as Emiliano Zapata and Benito Juárez. International historical standouts are featured, too. You can get nose to nose with the likes of Mahatma Gandhi and Mikhail Gorbachev. Hours are from 10:00 A.M. to 8:00 P.M. daily. Admission is $2.50 for adults, $2.00 for children 6 through 12, and free for children younger than 6.

Fishing

Fishing South of the Border has traditionally had a mystique attached to it that's hard to explain. Truth is, the fish bite no better down south than they do off the coast of San Diego, but that doesn't stop hordes of fishermen from packing their tackle and catching a boat in the quest for a record-breaking yellowtail.

In the border zone, Ensenada and San Felipe are the two hot spots. San Felipe is about 120 miles south of San Diego on the eastern Baja California peninsula. You can sign up for a variety of fishing expeditions including daytrips, extended-trip charters or just to go out for a few hours and back again. Fishing trips that last only for a day or less are best arranged on-site. Prices are up to the individual captain and are usually negotiable.

For longer trips, **Fisherman's Landing** (2838 Garrison Street, San Diego, 619-221-8500, www.fishermanslanding.com) will help you make your arrangements in advance. The longer trips are up to six days on vessels large enough to provide a good level of comfort for die-hard seekers of that trophy fish. Almost everything you might need is built into the cost of the trip, including fishing gear, meals, and a Mexican fishing license. The cost of such trips vary widely, beginning at $200 for a two-day adventure. Many varieties of fish inhabit the waters on both sides of the Baja peninsula; you're likely to hook tuna, halibut, sea bass, and, with great luck, the elusive marlin.

Golf

San Diegans are serious about their golf. From the occasional hacker to the smooth swinger with a low handicap, golfers jump at any chance to play, and that includes forays South of the Border.

Bajamar Ocean Front Golf Resort
K-77, Ensenada Toll Rd.
(800) 342–2644, 011–52 (646) 155–0151

Between Rosarito Beach and Ensenada is this Insider's favorite golf resort. It's about a 50-minute drive from the border, and golfers often stay for a day or two to take full advantage of the links-style courses. Three nine-hole courses combine to provide different challenges. The par 71 Lagos to Vista Course is 6,968 yards with a 74.9 rating and a 143 slope.

The rugged Baja California coastline provides an incomparable setting, and you'll undoubtedly see a few road runners

sprinting through the fragrant desert lavender. It's a tough course, and the brutal rough tends to swallow balls. Bring lots of them—one Insider lost 20 in one round. Hole number 11, a par 4, 500-yarder, has a waterfall and a large lake sheltering a green that doesn't seem to have any flat spots. Most golfers feel that a par on this hole is as big an achievement as a hole in one.

Bajamar has a putting green and a driving range. Both men's and women's locker rooms are huge and nicely outfitted. The clubhouse has a pro shop, a restaurant, and a bar in an observation tower with a 360-degree view. A luxury hotel and condos make up the balance of the resort, and special golf/accommodations packages are available. Greens fees include a mandatory cart and are $65 Monday through Thursday and $80 Friday, Saturday, Sunday, and holidays. Reduced rates are offered for late afternoon play.

Real Del Mar Golf Resort
K-19.5, Ensenada Toll Rd.
(800) 662–6180, 011–52 (661) 613–3401
www.realdelmar.com.mx

Just 12 miles beyond the border crossing, Real Del Mar is another outstanding course down south. Like Bajamar, Real Del Mar overlooks the ocean and is a challenging course with seven lakes and 50 bunkers. Its looks are deceptive; it seems benign, but the course will reach out and bite you when you least expect it. Its fairways are narrow, and some of the greens are elevated on pedestals. If you miss one, you've got your work cut out for you. The par 3 18th consists of an immaculately appointed tee box and a beautiful green—and nothin' but agua in between. Making par on this one is cause for a post-round celebration.

Facilities include a putting green and driving range, luxury clubhouse with men's and ladies' locker rooms, sauna, and gym. Should you decide to stay for a few days, the luxurious Marriott Residence Inn at the golf course offers a complete European-style spa, tennis courts, swimming pool, and jacuzzi. The par 72 course is 6,403 yards of manicured fairways and greens, with a rating of 70.5/131 slope. Greens fees are $59 Monday through

Terrific items and great bargains in Tijuana make shoppers return again and again. PHOTO: BOB YARBROUGH,
COURTESY OF SAN DIEGO CONVENTION AND VISITORS BUREAU

Thursday ($35 after 1:00 P.M.) and $69 ($40 after 1:00 P.M.) Friday, Saturday, Sunday, and holidays. Tee times are available one month in advance.

Nightlife

Locals South of the Border love their nightlife. So do the hordes of Americans who regularly cross the border just for a taste of something different. You'll find everything from rock bands to traditional Mexican mariachi music. Cover charge, if any, varies according to the day of the week, time, and if there's live entertainment. The drinking age in the border zone is 18. Remember that it's against the law to drink alcoholic beverages on public streets.

Tijuana

Baby Rock Disco
Paseo de los Héroes and Ave. Diego Rivera, Tijuana
011–52 (664) 634–1313

From the outside, Baby Rock appears to be a gigantic grouping of boulders. Once inside, you'll find a modern dance floor and loud, loud, loud rock music. This obviously is a favorite among the younger set, but don't be surprised to see a fair number of older party-lovers dancing the night away. Dress up! No slackers are allowed in this chic nightspot. Open Thursday through Sunday after 9:00 P.M., the serious party people don't show up until midnight.

Señor Frog
Pueblo Amigo, Paseo de los Héroes between Puente de México and Ave. Alfonso Reyes
011–52 (664) 682–4962
www.senorfrogs.com

Above this super popular restaurant is a happening bar, where roving waiters speak perfectly inflected English and DJs often broadcast from the dance floor. It's loud and open and seems to be equally popular with young Americans cruising for fun, Mexican couples on first dates, and groups of friends relaxing after work. Drinks are expensive and not particularly

fine; you're paying for the ambiance. Drink in the restaurant downstairs for a more relaxed although still lively evening.

Rosarito

Papas & Beer
Ave. Eucalipto and Ave. Mar Adriático
011–52 (661) 612–0444

Open daily from 11:00 A.M. 'til 3:00 A.M., and longer when there's serious partying to be done, this 47,000-square-foot venue is right on the sand and open to the stars. There are many different areas, from the ocean view "lounge" to the underground "womb," where a Gothic mood prevails. Geared toward young people, it is an amazing site that most anyone can enjoy—at least for one quick drink.

Ensenada

Hussong's Cantina
113 Avenida Ruiz, Ensenada
011–52 (646) 178–3210

You cannot go to Ensenada without stopping in at the legendary Hussong's. It has been an institution in the seaside town since 1892, and even though its hype is bigger than its reality, it's still a great party bar. If you want a table, be sure to arrive by early afternoon, and be prepared to dodge a raucous crowd. It's fairly tranquil in the afternoon and early evening, but as the night heats up, both mariachi and ranchera music are played nonstop.

Restaurants

Dining South of the Border offers many pleasant surprises. Of course, it's easy to find eateries that offer the familiar combo plates of enchiladas, tacos, and burritos. Beyond that, we'll show you where to find traditional treats from all regions of Mexico as well as some cosmopolitan venues offering both Mexican and international fare. You'll also be happy to find that a full gourmet meal can be enjoyed for a price that might bring you an appetizer and a cocktail in the States. Toss caution to the wind and try something new and unusual.

Price Code

Prices given indicate the cost of dinner entrees for two, excluding beverages, tax, and tip.

$	Under $15
$$	$16 to $30
$$$	$31 to $40

Tijuana

El Potrero $–$$
Blvd. Salinas 4700 at Blvd. Agua Caliente, Tijuana
(664) 681–8082

Stained glass windows with Mexican scenes entertain diners in this casual eatery with superb food. The menu describes each dish in detail, which is great because these are not the tacos and enchiladas foreigners are most accustomed to. In addition to steaks prepared in various styles and served with baked potato, there are wonderful hearty soups, a variety of salads, and a wide range of appetizers. Mexican business people come for power breakfasts, but it's great any time of day.

La Fonda de Roberto $$
Blvd. Cuauhtemoc Sur Oriente 2800 Colonia América, Tijuana
011–52 (664) 686–4687

A mainstay in Tijuana for many years, La Fonda offers an array of appetizers and entrees with regional flair. Try the house specialty, *chiles en nogada*. Large chiles are stuffed with beef and pork along with a mixture of nuts, raisins, fruits, and spices. The chiles are then fried and served with a walnut sauce.

La Fonda's appetizers are hard to resist. Tiny corn tortillas are served with a spicy cactus salad or stuffed with a variety of meats and chiles. The restaurant serves lunch and dinner Tuesday through Sunday.

La Mansión de Quetzal $
Esteban Cantú No. 2630, Tijuana
011–52 (66) 86–33–51

This unique restaurant offers traditional regional dishes from the nine different Mexican states. You can create an entire meal that might come directly from a kitchen in Veracruz, or you might sample courses from a combination of cuisines from, say, Yucatán, Campeche, and Michoacán. The star of the menu is a fork-tender, double-layered beef filet, stuffed with Oaxacan cheese and mushrooms and surrounded by an avocado sauce that could make you swoon. From Campeche you might try the coastal coconut-fried shrimp served in a cantaloupe bowl. Another standout is a spicy lamb dish served with nopal cactus from Tlaxcala.

Salads and desserts are equally intriguing, like the flaky *buñuelos* from Tlaxcala that are covered with cinnamon and sugar and served with a plum sauce. The restaurant serves breakfast, lunch, and dinner daily.

Rosarito Beach

Mariscos de Rarito Vince's $–$$
97-A Blvd. Benito Juarez, Rosarito Beach
011–52 (661) 612–1253

Lobster fresh from coastal waters is what draws hungry diners to this popular restaurant, especially lobster served Mexican style, grilled and presented in the shell. Other seafood specialties are offered, too, including a grilled fish of the day. Large portions and exceptionally fresh fish make this a favorite with locals as well as visitors, despite the plastic cutlery.

The restaurant also has a deli for those looking for a meal on the go. Lunch and dinner are served daily. Credit cards are not accepted.

Ensenada

El Rey Sol $$–$$$
1000 Avenida López Mateos, Ensenada
011–52 (646) 178–1733

Imagine a combination of French and Mexican cuisine. Hard to picture? Let us assure you that the result is worth a trip to Ensenada. This is a family-run restaurant that opened in 1947. The dining room is decorated in old European style, with stained glass windows, massive drapes, and heavy oak furniture.

Seafood, poultry, and beef dishes with a French flair are all served with appetizers, and the traditional Mexican dishes are outstanding—like the *machaca*, a mixture of dried beef, onions, pepper, and eggs. Breakfast, lunch, and dinner are served daily. Reservations are recommended, as it's a popular place.

Shopping

Shopping is the sport of choice for most visitors who cross the border, for a couple of reasons. First, the area's duty-free status provides savings (usually slight, although occasionally substantial) on imported merchandise such as perfumes, jewelry, cosmetics, leather goods, watches, and apparel. Second, shopping for Mexican arts and crafts, curios, and souvenirs in downtown Tijuana, Rosarito Beach, and Ensenada is just plain fun. You'll find some unique objects from the heartland of Mexico as well as striped blankets; leather jackets, wallets, and purses; silver jewelry by the ton; and designer knockoffs. Shopkeepers expect you to bargain, so sharpen up your negotiating skills and wrangle yourself a good deal.

Tijuana has several shopping plazas, although their appearance and percentage of occupancy seem to rise and fall like the tide at San Felipe. (In case you haven't yet been to San Felipe, that's way up, way down, and of course, somewhere in the middle.) Here, one does not negotiate the retail price, but you'll still find that prices for some goods are lower than they are in the United States.

Before you go overboard, though, remember your $400 per-person duty-free maximum. Most stores, both in the shopping centers and downtown areas, are open from 10:00 A.M. to 9:00 P.M. daily.

Tijuana

Avenida Revolución,
between Calles 1 and 8, downtown Tijuana

This is the oldest tourist shopping street in Tijuana and is usually a first stop for visitors. Both sides of the street are lined with shopping arcades, curio shops, and apparel stores. The street is crowded with bars and eateries in addition to the shops, and revelers of all ages flock to Avenida Revolución simply because it's so much fun.

Don't neglect the streets surrounding Avenida Revolución. They all are popular shopping areas, and if you expand your radius of reconnaissance by just a block or two, you'll find shops selling Mexican arts and crafts, home furnishings, and clothing.

Avenida Revolución can be reached on foot by following the pedestrian walkway starting just beyond the border crossing and leading straight to the downtown shopping area, where Avenida Revolución is the main street. It's a mile-long walk, and it's very common to see folks walking from the border rather than driving or taking public transportation.

Plaza Río Tijuana
Paseo de los Héroes between Aves.
Cuauhtémoc and Independencia, Zona Río,
Tijuana
011–52 (664) 684–0402

This is a shopping center located within the Río Tijuana area, near several nice hotels and nearly across the street from Pueblo Amigo. Several major Mexican department stores anchor the center, and you'll find lots of specialty stores, informal restaurants, and a multiplex movie theater.

Rosarito

Shopping in Rosarito used to be almost exclusively for home furnishings of wrought iron or rustic wood, but today a

from wrought iron, willow, and specialty woods. If you're looking for fine art, sculpture, and innovative jewelry, peruse the work of a myriad of artisans at **Galería Giorgio Santini** (Carretera 1, Free Road to Ensenada, Km 40, 661–614–1459, www.giorgiosantini.com). Closed Wednesday, this gallery is located near Foxploration, between Rosarito and Ensenada.

Ensenada

greater variety of merchandise can be found. Rosarito's shopping is found along one street—Benito Juarez—which is the main street through town. At the south end of town is the Rosarito Beach Hotel, which has several shops of its own. Here you'll find duty-free imports, arts and crafts, clothing, and items from Guatemala.

For more shopping, follow the main street south, out of town, and you'll wander into a huge marketplace that features curio shops, pottery, and cement statuary and fountains. As you stroll along the street, you'll see many furniture shops that display locally crafted pieces made

Seventy-five miles south of the border you'll find yet another kind of shopping experience. Ensenada is a pretty port city with several classy boutiques hidden among the souvenir stands and shops selling T-shirts and silver jewelry. Although more diverse than Rosarito Beach, most of Ensenada's shopping is along the main street—Boulevard López Mateos—and it's just a block from the waterfront. One of the town's nicest shops is located here: two-story **Bazár Casa Ramírez** (Calle López Mateos 496, 646–178–8209), which offers a wonderful collection of arty bric-a-brac.

Neighborhoods and Real Estate

After a few days in San Diego, visitors and newcomers inevitably reach the same conclusion—San Diego is nothing but a very big small town. Insiders just nod their heads and smile. That's what pleasantly distinguishes San Diego from other big cities. Even with a population of nearly 2.9 million countywide, San Diego has somehow managed to hold on to its small-town flavor while enjoying the advantages of a major metropolitan city. Most everything you would look for in New York or San Francisco is here: theater, opera, museums, first-class restaurants, and vibrant nightlife. But the sense of community that you find in smaller cities is here too. And nowhere is that sense of community stronger than in the neighborhoods.

San Diegans appreciate and enjoy all the cultural and entertainment opportunities available to them, but they place even more value on life within their neighborhoods. Community pride is fierce. Almost without exception, neighborhoods within both the city and county limits have planning groups to monitor growth and plan activities. Residents care very much about what happens down the street and around the block.

Over the decades, each neighborhood within San Diego County has developed its own unique characteristics. Take Poway and Rancho Bernardo, for example. Both are located in North County Inland; in fact, they're very close to one another. But they could hardly be more different. Rancho Bernardo is an interesting combination of high-tech industry, golf courses, and retirement communities. Poway, on the other hand, has a strong working-class population that focuses its energy on local festivals, politics, and public school issues.

Farther south, in Central San Diego, is the neighborhood of Mission Hills. With its stately mansions and high-ticket real estate values, it makes a strangely genteel neighbor for adjacent Hillcrest, a buzzing, active neighborhood with a highly concentrated gay population. Somehow it all works, though.

Then there are the neighborhoods that have cute quirks. Burlingame, for example, a tiny area in North Park, is distinguished by its red concrete sidewalks—the only community in the entire county to sport such a feature. Birdland has a quirk of a different sort. Tucked away between Linda Vista and Serra Mesa, all its streets are named after birds: Hummingbird Lane, Peacock Drive, and Nightingale Way, to name a few.

We'll take you through the individual neighborhoods, region by region, so you can get an idea of the variety of lifestyles, architectural styles, and just plain old standout features—and there are many. You'll surely find something that appeals to you. Just keep in mind that in the city of San Diego alone there are more than 100 separate, identifiable neighborhoods. So we'll group many of them together and give you an idea of the characteristics of the general area.

One of the best ways to get a good idea of what an individual neighborhood is like is to attend one of its annual festivals or celebrations. Check out the listings in our Annual Events chapter or pick up a community newspaper in a neighborhood library, coffeehouse, or convenience store. You'll undoubtedly find a parade, block party, or arts festival that will give you the feel for what the area is like. Chat with the locals. You're sure to get an earful.

Real Estate—A Tale of Boom and Bust

The history of the real estate market in San Diego is one of excess. Either the market is booming and prices are excessively high, or housing prices have gone bust and buyers can snatch up a property for well below market value. Rarely is moderation the name of the game.

We seem to be smack in the middle of another boom period, where prices go through the ceiling, bidding wars break out whenever a property hits the market, and buyers are forced to put together some creative financing to purchase even the most modest property. Right now housing prices are seeing double-digit increases, seemingly overnight. But interest rates are still low, which is a strong motivator for many buyers to find some way to wiggle into their dream house.

Here's the scary part: The median price for a single-family resale home in San Diego County is about $274,000. That's a daunting figure, we know. And it's the main reason San Diego habitually makes the least-livable city lists that come out periodically. The cost of living otherwise is quite affordable. It's that darned real estate that makes you swallow so hard.

The good news is that bargains can still be found if you're willing to be a little flexible in terms of neighborhoods and amenities. Many young families are buying homes in some of the older neighborhoods in the county and restoring the homes to pristine condition. As more and more people catch on to the idea, revitalized neighborhoods are emerging from older, more rundown ones, and whole communities are being reborn.

Outlying areas are growing rapidly too, as folks move farther away from Central San Diego in search of more affordable housing. Traditionally, housing costs in North County Inland, East County, and the South Bay have been somewhat easier on the wallet than those in North County Coastal and some of the prime areas in Central San Diego. This adds a bit of a commute to the mix, but city planners are committed to making that commute as easy as possible. Currently their main focus has been on North County routes into the city. Freeways are being widened and ways to increase usage of special commuter lanes are being tested.

The rental market seems to rise and fall with real estate values, and right now rental units are at a premium. They also are on the expensive side. The average monthly rent for a one-bedroom apartment in the county is more than $800. Ouch! But again, do your homework, and you should be able to find a nice place in the neighborhood of your choice. Some of the best units for the best value are listed in the classifieds by their owners. Just be prepared to make an immediate decision and have cash in hand for first and last month's rent, plus a security deposit.

As we introduce you to the various neighborhoods throughout the county, we'll also try to give you an idea of housing prices. Aside from a few communities like Rancho Santa Fe and La Jolla, where home prices always have more digits than you want to know about, most neighborhoods have a wide range of prices. Modest cottages can usually be found right around the corner from some pretty impressive houses in most neighborhoods.

We'll steer you toward some good resources too that will help you find a house, condo, apartment, or whatever your heart desires. Real estate brokers are abundant, and we'll give you the heads-up on some of the best resources for finding an agent. We'll also list home buyers' and apartment guides to help make your search easier.

Central San Diego

Beaches: Pacific Beach, Mission Beach, Ocean Beach

Beach life is different. It's special. It requires forbearance—forbearance for the tourists in the summer, the inflated housing prices year-round, and the damp air that sometimes settles in, threatening to never leave. But as soon as the sun pokes its head through the clouds, all the challenges of beach life are forgotten, and the benefits are abundantly clear.

The three beach areas in Central San Diego are so different they may as well be on three different planets. Those who live in **Pacific Beach** are generally twenty-something career people in search of fast times and the club scene, and they have minimal housing requirements. Apartment complexes are seemingly everywhere and are the residences of choice for this crowd. Sprinkled amongst the younger set, however, are residents who have called PB home for years. They have the same pride of ownership and community spirit that you would find elsewhere, but they also have an affinity and tolerance for the exuberance of their youthful neighbors. Together they add up to more than 42,000 residents, making Pacific Beach by far the most densely populated beach community.

A half mile or so inland in Pacific Beach is where many homeowners have found housing prices that are within reach, and a lifestyle that still qualifies as beach living. Single-family homes range from about $225,000 on the far east end of PB to $1.5 million for beachfront houses or for some of the stately homes in the hills. Condos range from $125,000 for a one-bedroom unit to $400,000 for something with a few more bells and whistles.

Mission Beach is a tiny isthmus only 2 blocks wide between bay and beach, and it stretches south from PB to the jetty at the mouth of the San Diego River. The vast majority of cottages, apartments, and condos in Mission Beach are rentals. This is where the college crowd settles in during the winter and vacationers rent during the summer months. A few hardy souls have made Mission Beach their permanent home, but you'll find few families here. As in PB, housing prices range from $225,000 for a small, run-down fixer-upper cottage to well over $1 million for beachfront property.

Ocean Beach is another story. Its northern edge is the southern jetty across the channel from Mission Beach, and it continues south to Sunset Cliffs and Point Loma. Sometimes called the Haight-Ashbury of San Diego, OB was an enclave for hippies and flower children during the late 1960s and early 1970s. Many of the erstwhile hippies stayed on, bought houses, and raised their children here. Other beach-

lovers have been in Ocean Beach for several generations. Still more newcomers have found it to their liking and have settled in, resulting in a population of more than 13,000. Still, much of the flavor of the community is reminiscent of that interesting generation of 30 years ago, only these days in a much more refined sense. The public beach in OB is one of the best in the county, and the downtown village in the community boasts dozens of excellent antiques stores, casual restaurants, and one-of-a-kind boutiques.

Housing prices in OB used to be among the best bargains for beach communities, mostly because much of the neighborhood is in the flight path for jets taking off from Lindbergh Field. But OB prices have risen dramatically in the past few years, ranging from $186,000 to $230,000 for condos, and $350,000 to $750,000 for single-family homes. A lot of quality lies in between, so those who crave the beach existence can usually find something that matches their expectations and their budget. Rental prices in all beach areas tend to be a bit higher than in other parts of San Diego, averaging about $900

The San Diego Convention Center attracts thousands of visitors to downtown. PHOTO: BOB YARBROUGH, COURTESY OF THE SAN DIEGO CONVENTION & VISITORS BUREAU

for a small studio or one bedroom apartment. You can find them cheaper, but bear in mind that the lower the rent, the lower the quality of the rental. College students don't seem to have a problem with a dearth of amenities, but the older crowd might find rental life too much like roughing it.

Downtown and Golden Hill

Fifteen years ago few people lived **Downtown** except for the poor who couldn't find housing elsewhere, down-on-their-luck transients, and drug dealers who inhabited the streets and seedy flophouse hotels that populated the area. A lot has changed, and now downtown boasts a number of ultra-modern high-rise condominiums, townhouses, and artists' lofts. Buyers are flocking to the downtown area because massive redevelopment projects have resulted in several hip and trendy neighborhoods, fine restaurants, shopping, theaters, and clubs. Plus, many appreciate the convenience of being able to walk to work or take a quick trolley ride to offices outside the downtown area.

The area's appeal continues to increase, and so do housing prices. Detached single-family housing is nearly nonexistent, and the median price for condos is $324,500. Lofts are somewhat less expensive and have become quite popular; more and more seem to be springing up every day. Even though loft prices are somewhat less than the pricey condos, they're pretty much bare bones. You usually get walls and plumbing, the rest is up to you.

Just to the east of Downtown is **Golden Hill,** a community of mostly single-family homes developed in the early days of San Diego. Many of the homes are stately Victorian gems from the early-20th century, and some have been beautifully refurbished. Like Downtown, Golden Hill has seen a period of blight, but is rapidly recovering. Much of it borders Balboa Park and the park's golf course, so it features some outstanding scenic properties.

Housing prices are still very affordable in Golden Hill. The median price for houses is $175,000. Condos are mostly in the $75,000 to $125,000 range. Many of the houses are in need of some TLC, but smart buyers are snapping them up, recognizing that Golden Hill is one of the up-and-coming communities in San Diego.

Kearny Mesa, Serra Mesa, Birdland

Although designated as three separate neighborhoods, **Kearny Mesa, Serra Mesa,** and **Birdland** are so similar that they often are thought of as one. They do have their distinctions, though. There's no mistaking when you're in Birdland, for all the streets have an ornithological designation. Serra Mesa overlooks Qualcomm Stadium and has a couple of brain-teasing street names: Unida Place and Haveteur Way (sound them out—you'll get it). And **Kearny Mesa** is the location of the first major business district in San Diego outside of Downtown. So they do have their distinguishing features, but the housing remains much the same from area to area: mostly modest tract houses that have nevertheless been well maintained and upgraded over the years to accommodate growing families. Houses cost between $175,000 and $275,000; condos range from $85,000 to $160,000.

Eastern: Tierrasanta, Allied Gardens, Grantville, Del Cerro, San Carlos

Tierrasanta's development began in the late '60s, and it is a glowing success story. Located across Interstate 15 from Kearny Mesa, it has matured into an eye-pleasing community that focuses on families. The schools are great, housing prices have stayed within reach, and an amazing number of first-time buyers have stayed in the area rather than moving to bigger houses elsewhere. Houses are priced from around $200,000 to $400,000, and condos range from $175,000 to $275,000.

Southeast of Tierrasanta are **Allied Gardens, Grantville, Del Cerro,** and **San Carlos,** another group of communities that share common characteristics. Del Cerro is slightly more upscale than the others, featuring more custom homes with more floor space. But the solidly built tract homes in Allied Gardens, Grantville, and San Carlos have held their value over the years. Grantville was one of the first neighborhoods in San Diego because of its proximity to Misión San Diego de Alcalá. It once consisted of dairy farms, but along with Allied Gardens and San Carlos was fully developed in the mid-'50s and '60s. Now the neighborhoods are welcoming back children of the original homebuyers. This generation is either buying their parents' homes or ones nearby, a testament to the appeal of the community and its affordability. The median price for houses is $293,000, and condos go from $100,000 to about $160,000.

Many Del Cerro homes are distinguished by their glorious views of Mission Valley and beyond. On clear days the ocean, 10 miles to the west, is easily visible. As a result, housing prices are quite a bit higher than in neighboring communities, starting at about $200,000 and going as high as $750,000.

La Jolla and Torrey Pines

It seems as though everyone has heard of **La Jolla.** From Omaha to Orlando, folks have heard tales about the beauty and opulence of the seaside village that some say is like Beverly Hills—only with a view. Some, however, are surprised to learn it is part of Central San Diego, and many La Jollans wish its location were an even better-kept secret. Residents are close-knit and protective, and they fiercely guard the natural beauty and mystique of their neighborhood.

Although Jolla is not a word found in the Spanish dictionary, the word "joya" means jewel, and the two words are pronounced the same. That's close enough for the 38,200 or so residents who inhabit the palm tree-lined hills and shores of La Jolla village. The jewel by the sea it is, and a more appropriate description would be hard to find. La Jolla sits squarely on top of some of the most valuable real estate in the United States. Million-dollar homes are the rule rather than the exception. And if a view of the blue Pacific comes with the house, the price tag goes way up. To lucky residents, no amount of money is too great to have the opportunity to settle in what inarguably is one of the most glorious spots on earth.

The San Diego trolley carries commuters between Downtown and their homes in East County.

PHOTO: ANDREW HUDSON, COURTESY OF THE SAN DIEGO CONVENTION & VISITORS BUREAU

For visitors (and many residents, too) it's the downtown village that draws them to La Jolla. Prospect Street and Girard Avenue, the two main streets in the village, are crammed with art galleries, chi-chi boutiques and trendy (but fabulous) restaurants. Insiders know souvenirs can be found in La Jolla, but you'll have to search if you're looking for the ubiquitous snow globe with a surfer and a starfish in it. Trinkets to remind you of your trip to La Jolla are more likely to require currency with Ben Franklin's face rather than Abe Lincoln's.

The beaches are the stuff dreams are made of and offer a little something for everyone. La Jolla Cove is a treasure trove for snorkelers and scuba divers, and the fun sands of La Jolla Shores are a favorite of families.

Monetary considerations aside, just look at faces of residents as they sip their coffee and mimosas and nibble their croissants on a restaurant deck overlooking La Jolla Cove on any Sunday morning, and you'll understand that they believe they're living in heaven. And if heaven is a place where the most controversial political issue of the day is whether the townspeople should install parking meters or not, then La Jollans are right to guard their secret well.

The hillsides around La Jolla have exploded with growth, and there's barely a bare spot of dirt anywhere. Still, newcomers manage to construct their dream homes on tiny parcels or by destroying the previous owner's idea of architectural excellence. About 20,000 people live on the outskirts of the village on quiet residential streets and in jam-packed clusters of condos or townhouses.

Just to the north of La Jolla is **Torrey Pines.** The campus of the University of California at San Diego is in Torrey Pines; so are many of the high-tech and biotech companies that are becoming such a significant force in the local economy. Many professors and scientists spend their daylight hours in Torrey Pines, and then take a short drive down the coast to their homes in La Jolla.

The two communities are inextricably linked. The "town and gown" atmosphere is an integral contributor to La Jolla's social

scene, and the educational and scientific community in Torrey Pines is heavily dependent on the generosity of its La Jolla benefactors. Drive south along Torrey Pines Road and you can almost feel the waves of brain power exuding from UCSD. Then as soon as Torrey Pines Road turns into La Jolla Boulevard, you can sense the luxury and see the beauty of this stunning oceanfront community.

Housing prices in both neighborhoods will make most people wince. A simple, tiny condominium can go for $300,000. Start adding such amenities as bedrooms, and you'll be pushing $500,000. The median price for houses is a whopping $915,000.

Mid-City East: Kensington, Talmadge, Normal Heights, North Park, College Area

Atop a long mesa overlooking Mission Valley lie the neighborhoods that make up the mid-city area of San Diego. Rich in history and even richer in modern-day personality, these communities are home to San Diegans who enjoy a sense of neighborhood, but savor the proximity to urban amenities, too.

Kensington is one such neighborhood. Developed in 1910 by a Canadian expatriate, it was named for the famous London borough. A stroll down the sidewalks of today's Kensington reveals the developer's original intent: Stately English Tudor houses are plentiful. The twist is that they are intermixed with houses sporting San Diego's traditional Spanish architecture, white walls, red tile roofs, and all. Strangely enough, the result is an appealing combination of the two styles, and the well-manicured landscaping attests to current owners' neighborhood pride.

Across the canyon from Kensington is its sister community of **Talmadge.** Silent film stars and sisters Norma, Constance, and Natalie Talmadge lent their name to the subdivision and were further rewarded for their generosity by having individual streets named for them. Norma, Constance, and Natalie Drives are the main streets that take you through this well-kept, quiet area. Real estate agents know that people who live in Kensington and Talmadge are rigorous defenders of their neighborhoods and are vocally active in

Craftsman-style homes are abundant in San Diego's older neighborhoods. PHOTO: THORN VOLLENWEIDER

local politics. Kensington's housing prices are slightly higher than those in Talmadge, ranging from $200,000 for a small fixer-upper to $1 million. One factor that may tend to inflate that range is that several bona fide mansions dot the northern rim of Kensington's mesa. Condos are much more reasonable, starting at around $90,000 and topping out at about $200,000. In Talmadge the range is from $200,000 to $400,000 for houses, and condos are about the same as in Kensington.

West of Kensington and Talmadge are the neighborhoods of **Normal Heights** and **North Park.** Housing tends to be more affordable in both areas, ranging from $75,000 to $350,000 for houses and $65,000 to $200,000 for condos. Both neighborhoods have suffered periods of neglect. The neighborhoods are rebounding, though, and many of the houses are remarkable. Along with the standard array of Spanish styles are some of the best examples of Craftsman cottages in San Diego. Many have been refurbished, many more are awaiting a dedicated owner to restore them to their original glory.

North Park and Normal Heights are in the early stages of redevelopment, but there is no doubt that the two neighborhoods have huge potential. That's why savvy homebuyers are taking advantage of the real estate bargains now, before prices start to climb.

Finally, there is the **College Area,** called so because it's home to San Diego State University. This area too is an older San Diego neighborhood, but, like communities to the west, is seeing an influx of younger families seeking good quality, affordable housing. The presence of the university helps maintain the value of the surrounding neighborhoods and is seen by most as a community asset. The cost of a home in the College Area ranges from $130,000 to $400,000, while condos sell between $75,000 and $175,000.

All the mid-city neighborhoods are good places for families. And community pride has generated a new wave of restaurants, local watering holes, coffeehouses, and retail shops.

Mid-City West: Mission Valley, University Heights, Hillcrest, Mission Hills, Middletown

Mission Valley, named for San Diego Mission de Alcalá, is a valley that runs east-west between two overlooking mesas. Bisecting the valley is the San Diego River. The valley has very few single-family homes (one of the few in the neighborhood sold for $5.5 million in 2001), but it does have plenty of apartments and condominiums that attract buyers who appreciate the central location. The San Diego Trolley runs through the valley, and Mission Valley and Fashion Valley shopping centers are a stone's throw from one another and right on the trolley line. The median price of condos in the neighborhood is $155,000, and apartment rental rates average $900 for a one-bedroom unit.

Hillcrest and **University Heights** are right next door to each other and are similar in housing styles. The difference is that University Heights is strictly residential, while Hillcrest is one of San Diego's hippest commercial districts. The village area of Hillcrest is almost a miniature Gaslamp Quarter, with fabulous restaurants, way-cool shops, and trendy clubs. Hillcrest also has a large gay population that has been instrumental in revitalizing the area. Pride of ownership is clear as you drive down the streets of both Hillcrest and University Heights. Immaculately maintained houses and yards show off their owners' efforts. Many Craftsman-style houses dot the streets of the two neighborhoods and can still be purchased without having to win the lottery. The median price of houses is $442,000, and condos range from $150,000 to $400,000.

Mission Hills is an old neighborhood that has never endured a downturn. The beautiful houses, many of which were built at the turn of the 20th century, maintain their original elegance. Second- and third-generation families keep returning to Mission Hills, and they do so for a number of reasons. First is its beautiful location, of course, overlooking Mission Bay and Presidio Park, the site of the original mission founded by Father Serra. Second is its central location. Tucked above the intersection of I–5 and I–8, it's close to everywhere. Third is its proximity to Hillcrest. It may seem an odd juxtaposition to have a predominantly gay neighborhood right next to a stately, old-money community, but the two intermingle beautifully.

Housing prices are high in Mission Hills. Single-family homes range from $350,000 to upwards of $1 million. Condos range from $200,000 to $500,000.

Rounding out Mid-City West is **Middletown.** Originally called Little Italy, this is where the Italian community laid its roots. Today, Little Italy is undergoing a fantastic renaissance as entrepreneurs develop condominium and office buildings beside venerable pizza parlors. Little Italy has become a Downtown neighborhood (it's just a few blocks from Broadway and on the trolley route). The prices for condos in new developments in the neighborhood start at about $340,000 and go as high as $800,000. New live/work lofts rent for $950 to $1,500 a month. The neighborhood has become quite desirable, and families who have held on to the small homes on residential streets have seen their values double and triple in the past couple of years.

Northeastern: Mira Mesa and Scripps Ranch

Mira Mesa is a bedroom community of tract houses that began to develop in the late 1960s. It provided a much-needed source of affordable housing for young families, especially military families in search of off-base living quarters. The neighborhood has stood the test of time and is still a haven for families. Schools, shopping centers, and restaurants have all made their way into Mira Mesa. So much so, that it is nearly a self-contained community. Housing prices remain affordable, ranging from $200,000 to $300,000 and most of the houses are built with families in mind: lots of bedrooms, baths, and family rooms. Condos range from $85,000 to $200,000.

Just to the southeast of Mira Mesa lies the newer and slightly more upscale neighborhood of **Scripps Ranch.** Housing prices are substantially higher than in Mira Mesa, from $225,000 to $600,000 for houses, and from $150,000 to $350,000 for condos. But you're purchasing more square footage and more atmosphere. Nestled among eucalyptus trees, the community has a kind of country flavor, and yet it's commuter close to downtown San Diego. The houses are tract homes, as they

La Jolla's Mediterranean-style village is graced by the beauty of the La Valencia Hotel. PHOTO: JEREMIAH
SULLIVAN, COURTESY OF THE LA VALENCIA HOTEL

are in Mira Mesa, but are bigger and have many more amenities. Plus, the entire community is within walking distance of Lake Miramar, which has jogging and bike trails around the perimeter. Many Scripps Ranch homes have a view of the lake too. It's a serene setting, and you can't help feeling you're someplace much farther away from the bustle of the city.

Northern: Linda Vista, Clairemont, University City, Sorrento Valley

To the east of I–5 are the long-established communities of **Linda Vista** and **Claire-mont.** So long-entrenched is Linda Vista that it has the distinction of being the home of the first shopping mall in the United States. Small in comparison to the mega-malls we're familiar with today, it nevertheless put the tiny community on the map. Today Linda Vista is known for its most prominent neighbor: the University of San Diego.

Surrounding much of Linda Vista is Clairemont, which comprises the neighbor-hoods of Bay Ho and Bay Park too. Large in area and population (Clairemont is home to some 80,000 residents), the area has a melt-ing pot of inhabitants, from young families to retired folks who have been living in the same house for more than 50 years.

Linda Vista and Clairemont can't be considered suburbs, because they're right in the heart of the city. But quiet streets and neighborhood block parties blend right in with the shopping centers, strip malls, and other businesses that all coexist in a wonderful mix of everything that's good about San Diego. Plus, the beach is ten minutes away. Clairemont and Linda Vista both border Tecolote Canyon Park, a nature reserve with oodles of hiking trails and a golf course. Housing prices are rea-sonable in both communities, unless you happen upon one of the Clairemont homes with a panoramic view of Mission Bay and the ocean. Then you're likely to pay upward of $500,000 for a three-bedroom house. But the range for the rest is from $160,000 to $300,000 for houses, and $120,000 to $220,000 for condos.

University City, a slightly more upscale version of Clairemont, is located just to the north. The community is a little newer, and the houses are a little bigger. Other than that, it has the same neighborhood feel that Clairemont boasts. The north end of University City has been taken over by apartment buildings because of its proximity to UCSD. Rental rates are quite high—$1,000-plus for apartments. Housing prices range from $200,000 to $600,000; condos from $100,000 to $325,000.

North of University City is the community of **Sorrento Valley.** Sorrento Valley itself isn't new—it has long been a center for San Diego's high-tech businesses and industries. But it's only recently that housing developments have begun to spring up. Like any new community, it will take time to develop a personality of its own. Houses range from $300,000 to $500,000, and condos start at $175,000 and top out at $300,000.

Point Loma and Coronado

At the tip of the Point Loma peninsula sits the Cabrillo Lighthouse, a monument to the explorer who claimed San Diego for Spain. From the base of the peninsula to its tip are located some of San Diego's prettiest houses and longest-established neighborhoods. One of the most prolific industries in days gone by was tuna fishing, an enterprise started by San Diego's Portuguese community. Most of that community remains ensconced in **Point Loma,** where Portuguese festivals, food, and culture are abundant.

Somewhere along the way others discovered Point Loma too, and took advantage of the hillside properties on either side of the peninsula to build houses that command magnificent, unobstructed ocean or bay views. The biggest drawback to life in Point Loma is the nearby airport. Lindbergh Field's runway is aimed right at the Loma Portal area of the peninsula, and residents endure airplane noise all day long, from 7:00 A.M. to 11:00 P.M. With a little extra soundproofing insulation and the advent of newer, quieter planes, it has become more bearable of late, and most feel it's a small price to pay for the beautiful houses and views.

Across the bay is the neighboring island of **Coronado,** with its 29,000 residents. Technically it's not really an island—it's a narrow spit of land that reaches north from Imperial Beach, near the U.S.–Mexico border. But Coronado residents like the idea of it being an island, and few outsiders are ungenerous enough to disagree.

Coronado may have more retired Navy officers than any other location in the country among its residents. It is home to a large Navy Command Center, and many young enlistees vow to return to the island to raise their families. But it's not just military brass who have discovered the charm of the island. It's an ideal place to raise a family—good schools, low crime, and beautiful beaches are among its attributes. And the downtown village of Coronado is so picturesque it looks like something out of a movie. One-of-a-kind shops, theaters, and restaurants line Orange Avenue, the main boulevard through town.

Coronado and Point Loma have one thing in common: exorbitant real estate. In Point Loma you can still find the occasional fixer-upper to fit your budget, say for $350,000. Houses can easily top $2 million, especially if they have one of those coveted views. The median price for a house in the area is $507,000. Condos are a little more affordable, from $210,000 to $500,000. Bargains are not to be found in Coronado, however. The least expensive house for sale on the island as we write this is $600,000, and the mansions don't seem to have an upper limit. One that was on the market for quite a while (and had the distinction of a presidential visit during the mid-1990s) had a ticket price of more than $7 million. Even condos make you catch your breath, ranging from $499,000 to $4.5 million for a luxury unit in the Coronado Shores high-rise complex.

North County Coastal

Carlsbad and La Costa

Carlsbad and its La Costa district are like fraternal twins, forever joined with similar backgrounds. Yet there's a world of difference in the twins' approach to San Diego living.

Starting with **Carlsbad,** a city of about 70,000, which stretches from the city of Oceanside way down the coast to Encinitas, and inland to Vista, you'll find a family community, blended with small stores and shops. There's a real downtown area in this town. In it you'll find city hall, the main branch of the library, great restaurants (and some beach hangouts and clubs), supermarkets, antiques shops, beauty salons, and all you'd expect in a small town. (If you love to shop for antiques, be sure to read about Carlsbad's antiques district in our Shopping chapter.) There are also the usual downtown office buildings—but they're never more than three stories high—and hotels and motels, from posh resorts to more thrifty establishments.

In addition, Carlsbad offers some tourist attractions. Be sure to read about Carlsbad's LEGOLAND California in our Kidstuff chapter.

The neighborhoods are a mix of ethnic backgrounds and their population is young: The median age of residents is 36 years. With about 70,000 residents (including those in the La Costa section), Carlsbad is a thriving area.

The beach property of Carlsbad includes million-dollar oceanfront homes. New homes in Carlsbad not along the shore are in the $400,000 to $1 million range.

Resale homes to the west of I-5 are sometimes less expensive, but don't count on it. Apartments on that side cost an average of $850 a month for a one-bedroom.

On the east side of I-5, most resale home prices are between $400,000 to over $600,000. These are not custom homes, mind you. They are remodeled or well-maintained sixties' tract houses that once sold for $6,000. Now add an ocean view to this equation, and even if you can only see it by standing on your tiptoes and craning your neck through a second-story window, you can easily add to that figure.

Carlsbad has a nice range of condos. Those found in neighborhoods with apartments sell for about $210,000. But expect to pay way more than that for those with ocean views.

Now let's look at **La Costa,** the area south of Carlsbad and adjacent to the La Costa Resort and Spa. In this upscale area there are condos, some apartments, and lots of family homes.

There are multi-million dollar homes, too. As in Carlsbad, it's not unusual in today's booming real estate market for a house to be sold even before a broker can decide what to put in an advertisement. Because the moment the rumor begins to circulate that a house is up for sale, bids immediately appear. As one Insider recently found out, if you fall in love with a neighborhood, you need to drive around it often, and be prepared to jump in with an offer (with lender info all in place), since Carlsbad and La Costa homes aren't on the market long.

Schools are good in the Carlsbad-La Costa neighborhood, the city government listens to the voters, and crime is lower than in other cities. Air quality (except for a few days in autumn when LA's smog invades the coast) is excellent, and the quality of life makes Carlsbad's neighborhoods desirable. The down side? Those who commute south or east face miles of slow-and-go—and that's on a good day. We're talking gridlock. Carlsbad residents are a resourceful lot, and many take the Coaster, work flex hours, and get jobs closer to home to avoid the grind that can start as early as six in the morning.

Del Mar

Del Mar has a laid-back beach-tourist feel that visitors expect to find when visiting San Diego. Regardless of the time of day, there are people outdoors. Some are walking, jogging, or playing beach sports. Others come out to mingle at the cafes and coffeehouses that are sprinkled through town. When that first group goes back to work or school, the next wave takes its place and the cycle continues until late in the evening. Del Mar is an outdoor town and home to outdoor institutions including a polo club, racetrack, and the Del Mar Fairgrounds where there's something happening outdoors nearly every weekend. (Be sure to read our Annual Events chapter for some of the great things that happen at the fairground.)

Del Mar is only 1.8 square miles and the residents (a number that hovers at about 6,000) like it that way. While some

If it's country hillsides you're longing for, the outlying areas around Julian may be the focus of your home hunting. PHOTO: COURTESY OF SAN DIEGO CONVENTION AND VISITORS BUREAU

Quail Gardens provides an oasis of peace in North County. PHOTO: BOB YARBROUGH, COURTESY OF THE SAN DIEGO CONVENTION & VISITORS BUREAU

of the county's communities have less desirable areas, Del Mar is Del Mar and that means charming. In the section of Del Mar that's found west of I-5, the custom homes are in older neighborhoods with established landscaping and shady twisting streets. East of I-5, past the multistory business offices seen from the freeway, are planned neighborhoods whose homes have red Spanish tile roofs and perfectly green lawns.

Housing prices have soared in this coastal community. The average house in Del Mar, a 20-something-year-old, 2,500-square foot home, costs $1,216,000. A good number of homes have ocean views, which can tack on a cool hundred grand or more to that price tag. Those homes on the beach may be smaller, but alas, still go for the big bucks. The typical Del Mar home is a spacious, custom dwelling with a nice-sized family lot. The community is close enough to the city of San Diego to make the commute tolerable.

There's some apartment living in Del Mar, but you're more likely to find a condo for rent. Rents are in the $1,500-a-month range for apartments. The price of renting a house could easily soar to $5,000 a month, depending on location. The price of condos ranges from $250,000 to $750,000; the median is $450,000.

Encinitas

Encinitas, a city of about 65,000 residences, with its official boundaries incorporating the towns of Cardiff and Leucadia, is half the size of Carlsbad, and enjoys a youthful community spirit. At one time, Encinitas, Leucadia, and Cardiff-by-the-Sea (Insiders just call it Cardiff) were three distinct locales. But in 1986 they grouped together to form the city of Encinitas. Yet, each area strives to keeps its individuality.

Driving north along I-5 from San Diego, you'll first see **Cardiff,** with its older, established family homes set on rolling hills. Most homes in Cardiff have an ocean view (or at the very least relish breezes).

There are schools, supermarkets, sidewalk cafes, and sandy beaches in this town. The overwhelming flavor of Cardiff is casual.

Encinitas, the hub of the community, is filled with the energy of its growing families. It's going somewhere—and just where that is concerns residents. This pristine city strives for a clean and wholesome image that sets it apart from many other beach cities. As with other coastal communities, Encinitas has a downtown with shops, cafes, restaurants, businesses, and specialty stores lining Pacific Coast Highway and along the few blocks on either side of it. Inland, on the east side of I-5, are most of the city's homes, typically in planned communities with shopping centers and strip malls.

If Insiders think that Cardiff is quiet, **Leucadia** could be accused of taking a full-time siesta. It has sleepy neighborhoods with architectural jewels mixed in with simpler homes. There's more elbowroom here too: There are still a few undeveloped lots available should you want to build.

Leucadians are reluctant to promote growth, and take an active part in the decisions that affect their part of Encinitas. Years ago when the city wanted to put in sidewalks on some of the peaceful roads, the voters quickly nixed that. "No change needed," they said firmly. Today Leucadia continues to be a serenely sweet town.

Resale homes in Encinitas, in all three areas of the city, are in the $400,000 neighborhood; new homes in planned communities can be substantially more. Condos are close to the resale homes figure, with the average condo selling for about $275,000. Apartments close to the ocean can rent from $950 to more than $3,000; those without an ocean view are usually in the $1,000 category. Houses and condos in family neighborhoods rent for more.

Oceanside

Oceanside, incorporated on July 3, 1888, was one of the first cities in North County Coastal. It's the largest of the cities, too, with more than 40 square miles within its boundaries and about 160,000 people. Housing prices vary in this ethnically diverse, working-class community.

You may be able to find a tiny, older house, a real *Home Improvement* fan's fixer-upper, for $100,000. A resale home in a family part of town will run about $260,000 and up. Newly built homes in planned developments can exceed $300,000. But don't be misled by these figures. Oceanside's best properties sell for more than $500,000, depending on location, view, and neighborhood. Condos range from $150,000 to the higher figures just cited. There are more rental units in Oceanside than in other parts of North County Coastal due to the military presence in Camp Pendleton. Rent prices vary with location and are somewhat lower than those of Oceanside's neighboring cities.

Oceanside rightfully bursts with pride at all it has to offer. There are well-established parks, big sandy beaches, a respected community college, and a recreation system that brings programs to kids, adults, and seniors. Currently it's trying to shake off that "Oceanside is just another military town" stigma. Whatever it's doing, it's doing it right. More new businesses, enterprises, and manufacturing groups are coming to town and that means more jobs and more families. As we go to press, there's a major beach-area resort in the discussion stage. Clearly, the city of Oceanside is moving comfortably into its new image.

Rancho Santa Fe

The community that Insiders refer to as "the Ranch" doesn't come with a visible price tag. As the cliché goes: If you must ask the price of property in **Rancho Santa Fe,** you may not be able to afford it.

Having said that, we want to add that some of our favorite Insiders live in this community where multi-million dollar homes are the norm, yet we still pal around with them like they are regular folks. That's the nice part of the community; everything is understated. The Ranch has the feel of just another upscale San Diego town. The median price for a home here (we're talking spacious home with plenty of prime property, perhaps a pool and a tennis court—the kind you see in better decorating magazines) is about $1.7

million. Condos, if you can find them, are selling for about $500,000. Rentals here are traditionally handled by agents and can be anything from a condo near the tiny downtown to oversized mansions on oversized lots with matching monthly rental fees.

Streets are tree-lined and inviting. As you drive through the Ranch, you can glimpse mansions tucked behind the lush landscaping. Traffic is regulated and slower than in other cities. Parking can be a challenge, especially during the lunch hours. People know each other and those who work in the Ranch often walk to work and walk at lunch. People meet at the post office often since there is no home mail delivery in the Ranch.

Rancho Santa Fe feels safe and is rather old-fashioned. The downtown is small, with exclusive jewelry shops, clothing boutiques, the usual doctors' and dentists' offices, and a supermarket. You'll find the busy post office there too. The cafes and restaurants are fun to try; menu choices are no more expensive than you'd expect in other parts of the region.

Solana Beach

Solana Beach is hugged by Del Mar and Encinitas. The city seems to have the best of its neighbors' best qualities, plus an added shot of adrenaline. There's energy everywhere. Check out the downtown area along the Pacific Coast Highway: You'll see early-morning, lunchtime, and evening walkers and runners; parents pushing kids in strollers; business people on break and out for a browse; and shoppers claiming prizes in those famous Cedros Street home furnishing stores. (Be sure to read our Shopping chapter for information on the stores in the Cedros Design District.)

This is a family town too, with good parks and schools and recreational activities. Residents in Solana Beach think about the environment—the ocean is their best neighbor—and recycling programs abound. Many residents also opt for a cleaner form of transportation. After one Insider rode the commuter train, the Coaster, during a rainy winter, she reported that more business people seem to get on and off in Solana Beach than at any other station.

The town has an excellent blend of family homes, condos, and some apartment living. The average price for a resale home that's about 20 years old is $750,000. Homes in residential areas away from the beach cost about $579,000. New homes in planned communities average about $600,000. Condos have a wider range since some are built overlooking the ocean and garner bigger price tags. The average condo now goes for about $350,000, if you can find one. Again, it's all in the location. Rentals, if you can find them, average about $1,500 for an apartment or very small home.

North County Inland

Escondido

Escondido seems to have been transplanted from another time. It's a hometown, with a downtown, downtown merchants, and a civic pride rivaling that of any Midwestern community. People live and work in this town that's situated in North County Inland, about an hour's drive (in traffic) from downtown San Diego. That's not saying there aren't those who brave the rush and commute out of Escondido using I-15.

The drive can become a gridlock similar to that found along I-5 along the coastal communities, yet a lot of people who work in San Diego and East County drive in from Escondido daily. While there are express buses that take commuters into San Diego and diamond lanes for carpoolers, there's no commuter train yet.

With the California Center for the Arts, a multi-purpose facility with a multi-story theater, culture is established in Escondido. (Be sure to read more about the center in our Arts chapter.) The center draws big time performers from around the world and audiences from around the county.

Obviously, highbrow opportunities are not lacking, but people like the community fun in this town too. There are parades, arts and crafts fairs, picnics, and historical tours of houses built in the late 1880s, which is about the time the city was incorporated. Back then it was a hub of

Folks who settle in Coronado commute to downtown San Diego across the graceful San Diego-Coronado Bay Bridge. PHOTO: JAMES BLANK, COURTESY OF SAN DIEGO CONVENTION AND VISITORS BUREAU

agricultural activity. Less than ten years ago you could still visit avocado and citrus packinghouses and working orchards within the city limits.

Escondido has a blend of older and newer neighborhoods. You may find smaller houses, family homes, at the low end of the real estate price tag in the $180,000 range and more posh family abodes netting close to $600,000. The range reflects the location. Condos are in the $150,000 range and apartments and rental homes, depending on the location, can be found for between $700 and $2,000.

Fallbrook and Valley Center

There's lots of fresh air in these communities situated about an hour and a half northeast of downtown San Diego. You'll also find working avocado and citrus orchards, people who love horses and dogs, and lots of families who've chosen these communities for the elbowroom. You'll also find some retired folks since golf courses are abundant. See our chapter on Golf.

The cities provide a nice combination of stores, services, and eateries. In both towns, there's a main street and neighbors who still stop and chat. The schools encourage civic pride and there are lots of family activities from Fallbrook's Avocado Days to Valley Center's local art fairs.

Homes in this area are usually custom-built, and situated on hillsides—both communities are known for the views of tree-studded mountains and miles of open backcountry. Most have at least an acre of ground, some quite a lot more. People who want to have horses and other farm critters often move to these communities for the land and friendship of other animal lovers.

The average home is re-selling for about $300,000. New homes are easily $100,000 more. Condos and apartments are limited. There's a general feeling that the real estate market in Fallbrook and Valley Center is about to explode.

Rancho Peñasquitos and Poway

The communities of **Poway** and **Rancho Peñasquitos** (or just Peñasquitos as Insiders call it) are grouped because they are lively, family towns with a younger than average population. If you move to

Peñasquitos or Poway your neighbor might be a doctor who works at Scripps Hospital, a local landscaper with a thriving business, a computer genius who interfaces with colleagues over the Internet, or someone in public service or the military. People and professions blend well in these cities which offer planned communities with tree-lined streets.

Homes in Poway and Peñasquitos are slightly more expensive than those in neighboring communities. Resale homes average about $350,000; Peñasquitos house price tags are about $360,000. New homes in both cities, in well-planned developments, are about $550,000. Condos average about $150,000 and some rental houses and condos go for $800 to $2,000 a month.

There are a few apartments, but most people look for condos and homes in this family-oriented, newly developed area.

Rancho Bernardo

Rancho Bernardo is many things to many people. Seniors think of it as the perfect retirement community, because of its lovely weather, great services, easy freeway access, and super golf courses. Families think of it as a family town. And large corporate entities such as Hewlett Packard see it as the perfect business site. Whatever you name this inland city, you'll find a bucketful of reasons why people live here.

Just off I-15, about 40 minutes north of San Diego, the community stretches out on both sides of the freeway. There are shopping centers, parks and golf courses, excellent medical facilities, and a number of colleges. The University of California, San Diego, has a satellite center in the area.

The range of housing prices is extreme and again depends on location. It tops at $1 million yet can go as low as $290,000 for a small, fixer-upper (if you can find one that someone is selling). The median price is $345,000.

Condos average about $160,000, although there are not that many that go up for sale. You can figure that rental homes and apartments will begin at about $1,000 and skyrocket straight up if you're in the market for a six-bedroom, six-bath home on the ninth green with a back view of a private country club.

San Marcos, Vista, and Bonsall

These "sisters" are happily connected by proximity. To the newcomer they seem to be very much alike, with planned developments, acres of roofs topping lowland and hillside alike, and clustered areas of shops and malls. They are all family towns, where younger people are beginning their lives. Each is unique, however, and that's where your choices enter the picture.

San Marcos is home to California State University, San Marcos. The campus graces one of the hills just off California Highway 78. Having CSUSM in San Marcos will eventually provide the city with that college feeling and cultural activities. Right now everyone in the community is still getting used to saying all those initials—and also to the new civic center, increased traffic, and the change from a rural to a suburban environment.

Home prices in San Marcos average about $250,000 and in planned communities they can top out at about $500,000. Condos run a little less (about $150,000). You'll have to look for houses and condos if you want to rent in this community; apartments are scarce.

Vista is more established than San Marcos. It has older neighborhoods, and if you're a handy person, you might just find a fixer-upper here. The mid-range for resale homes is $225,000; new ones can be in the $400,000 bracket. Condos come with a price tag as low as $180,000. This is still a deal for North County, which is within twenty minutes of the coast.

Bonsall, connected to Vista on the south and Oceanside on the east, is spread out amongst winding roads meandering through groups of custom and owner-built homes. It has the feel of a backcountry town. People stable horse and farm animals, meet friends at the feed store, and then dash to work in their expensive 4X4 or foreign car. Resale prices range from $279,000 to $389,000. You won't find rental apartments or condos here; most dwellings in Bonsall are homes.

East County

Alpine

Unlike the other communities in East County, **Alpine** was a planned community (we're talking the planner of the late 1800s). It started in life as Viejas Stage Stop. The town originated when drivers hauled supplies to the mines in the Cuyamacas and returned with gold destined for San Diego. Farther along, the Butterfield Stage line allowed passengers to get out at the stop and shake off some of the dust. As more people began passing through, more services came to the area.

Today an interstate highway, not a dusty trail, connects Alpine to the cities of San Diego County. There's a cozy downtown with cafes and stores and friendly smiles on peoples' faces. And if you're searching for the perfect glamorous outfit or a fine wine or want to do some serious shopping (as in a huge mall), Alpine now has the Viejas Shopping Outlets, a beautifully designed shopping center near the Viejas Casino.

Alpine became a desirable community in the 1980s as custom homes began rising on the outskirts of town. Today, you can find older, rustic houses for under $200,000, but the median price is around $350,000. You may find a rental home in Alpine, but don't expect to find many condos or apartments.

Julian and Ramona

Julian and Ramona are known for their quiet country, feel-good environments. While some folks live in Ramona and work in San Diego, few if any people commute "down the mountain" from Julian into the urban areas. In these towns you'll find sprawling ranches, quaint custom homes, and plenty of wide-open spaces. That makes the area especially attractive to people who like to spread their wings, and add some horses, hiking trails, and natural habitats to their estates. Houses are normally custom-built. The few condos you can find go for about $180,000.

Julian is known for the western-town atmosphere and not-to-be-missed apple pie. The town is tucked within Cleveland National Forest. It's a favorite community for artists, writers, crafts people, and those who own the local establishments, from bed-and-breakfast inns (there are more than 20 in town) to the pie shops and antiques stores. Folks are friendly in Julian and enjoy knowing they live in a desirable area. When houses come up for resale, they range from $100,000 to $250,000. New custom homes can easily exceed $500,000.

Think of a town in Wyoming, without the really big mountains and all that snow, and you have a romanticized idea of **Ramona**. With its annual dusting of snow and warm, dry summers, it's an ideal location for those who want to get just far enough away from it all. Within town are enough stores, services, and shops for more than the basics of life. Yet if you need something special Escondido or San Diego are where you need to head. The city is over an hour from San Diego, and about 30 minutes from Escondido. Resale homes range from rambling ranch styles that might go for about $250,000 to new custom abodes that cost more than $500,000.

El Cajon, Lakeside, and Santee

The cites of **El Cajon, Lakeside,** and **Santee** are neighbors and have been linked since the founders of Misión San Diego de Alcalá chose this valley area to graze cattle.

In more recent times they were thought of as bedroom communities to San Diego, but that's changed. Now they are thriving as younger families select these cities to put down roots. There's a

Insiders' Tip

Once you've chosen your home, you'll surely want to start redecorating. For tips on hiring an interior designer, contact the American Society of Interior Designer's San Diego chapter at (858) 274-3345 or www.asidsandiego.com. To get a good overview of the traditions in local design, check out the San Diego Historical Society's Showcase home, open for tours in April and May. Call (619) 533-7355 for information.

Jamul, Borrego Springs, and the Desert Communities

Like Palm Desert did twenty years ago, the desert communities—including those of **Jamul** and **Borrego Springs**—could very well boom at any second. However, as some skeptics point out, that feeling has been around for a long time.

Tourists and snowbirds flock to the desert during the mild falls, wonderful winters, and delightful springs. Town people stay year-round and love that hot, dry desert air.

Home prices, when you can find one that's available for resale, are in the $130,000-plus bracket. Those who want to enjoy desert living normally purchase land and build their dream house. As for condos, as one Insider who wanted to find a winter home recently said, "Good luck!" Rumor had it that there was a condo for sale in Borrego Springs—just rumor mind you—and three people made offers and five more were trying to get their financial packets in order so they could do so, too.

La Mesa and Spring Valley

La Mesa and Spring Valley were once considered backcountry by those cosmopolitan settlers of San Diego and people who made homes along the coast. Nowadays, young families, retired people, students, and professionals continue to go east to find their perfect homes.

It's a little-known bit of trivia that **La Mesa** was originally known as Allison Springs. Early settler and rancher Robert Allison purchased a part of the area to graze sheep. Then it was renamed La Mesa Springs, and finally in 1912, when it was incorporated as a city, the name officially changed to what we call it today.

The Native American name for **Spring Valley** was Meti. For a while the mission padres called it the Spanish equivalent to "The Springs of St. George." Finally, early farmer August Ensworth settled in the area. The story goes that he asked his young daughter for the perfect name and Spring Valley was born.

People continue to discover quality of life in East County and there's a good mix of housing here. With luck, one can still find an older home for about $180,000.

feeling of renewed vigor, excitement, and youthful energy. There are plenty of activities for kids and parents coordinated by local parks and recreation centers. There are parades and rodeos (see our Annual Events chapter about the Lakeside Rodeo), Easter egg hunts, and outdoor music, arts, and crafts festivals.

The housing ranges from modest to elaborate; prices follow along that range. You may find a home in a working-class neighborhood for about $190,000 and another that's been renovated right across the street for $300,000. Some Insiders believe that as more people come to San Diego, the reasonable homes will be snapped up before agents even put a sign on the lawn.

You will find condos and rentals in these areas, and these are especially attractive to those needing a place (with an okay commute) close to SDSU. Condos average about $100,000, and apartments, depending on the size, can be found for about $700 a month.

The median house price is $250,000. Condos go for about the same.

Homes in family neighborhoods, near services, parks, and schools, begin at $230,000. New development homes can easily be seen in the $300,000 to $500,000 range.

South Bay

Chula Vista and Bonita

Chula Vista is the second-largest city in San Diego County, with a population of around 153,000. It was originally part of El Rancho de la Nación, a huge area of land in the South Bay that was once part of Mexico but ended up as part of California when it was granted statehood. From the 1890s through the early 1900s it was known as the lemon capital of the world because the world's largest lemon orchard existed there. Nowadays it is a vital, bustling city.

Newcomers and longtime residents of San Diego are gravitating in increasing numbers to the developments in Chula Vista. Prices are usually more affordable, and the master-planned communities offer grand amenities for families. The EastLake development, for example, has a manmade lake, complete with sandy beaches, and a first-rate public golf course. Another master-planned community Otay Ranch, is in the early stages of development and promises to rival the appeal of EastLake. Housing prices vary widely. In the urban area of Chula Vista, prices are as low as $100,000 for a condo and $225,000 for a single-family home. In the outlying subdivisions like EastLake, Rancho del Rey, and Otay Ranch, prices start at $100,000 for condos and go as high as $500,000 for houses.

City leaders lobby hard to entice new industry to Chula Vista, and recent years have seen the opening of a giant water park and an official Olympic Training Center. Both are bringing greater recognition to Chula Vista, as well as an increase in tourism.

Neighboring **Bonita,** an unincorporated area, has a gentrified rural atmosphere complete with horses, stables, and an occasional farm animal. Residents of Bonita prize their detachment from city life and local politics, preferring the peace and quiet of country living. However, the benefits of the city are easily within reach. Chula Vista is just a short drive away. Houses are typically sprawling ranch style, with larger than average lots and swimming pools, that range from $260,000 to $575,000. Condominiums are generally in the neighborhood of $180,000.

Imperial Beach

Imperial Beach is the most southwesterly city in the continental United States. Its motto in the 1940s was "Where the sun and the surf spend their continuous honeymoon." A little outdated today, the motto is still not too far off the mark. Imperial Beach was first settled in the 1880s by a developer who intended it to be a beach resort for residents of the Imperial Valley, a desert community east of San Diego. Though it achieved that status, other people soon discovered its charm, and it now draws visitors from all over.

Today Imperial Beach is home to one at the world's biggest sandcastle contests (see our Annual Events chapter for details), which attracts amateur and professional sandcastle artists from all over the world to compete in the annual event. Beachfront condos sprinkle the shores, and folks from landlocked cities like to make Imperial Beach their home during the summer months. Its proximity to Mexico is a big attraction too. A self-contained, incorporated city, Imperial Beach has its own city council that attends to hot issues of the day. For the most part, though, the community tends to be laid back and casual, a mecca for surfers.

Condos range from $150,000 to $350,000 for beachfront properties. The median house price is $235,000.

National City

National City was the second established city in the county after the city of San Diego. It was founded and developed by the Kimball brothers, Frank, Warren, Levi, and George. The brothers were the purchasers of El Rancho de la Nación, a

La Jolla is an upscale area with expensive homes and condominiums. PHOTO: COURTESY OF SAN DIEGO CONVENTION AND VISITORS BUREAU

26,000-acre plot of land (of which Chula Vista was also a part). They laid out the town, founded a number of businesses and helped establish the olive and citrus industries. The houses the Kimball brothers built for their families were the first genuine houses in the county—the so-called houses in Old Town, in San Diego, weren't much more than four adobe walls with a crude roof. Some of the lovely mansions later built by the Kimballs still stand today.

Today National City is a working-class town, with many of its residents employed by nearby National Steel and Shipbuilding Company. The city is also noted for its Mile of Cars, a large concentration of auto dealers.

Houses are modestly priced and have a median price of $185,000. Condominiums are from $80,000 to $100,000.

San Ysidro, Otay Mesa, and Nestor

San Ysidro and **Otay Mesa** are two southern communities that abut the U.S.-Mexico border. Thus their combined population of 59,000 includes a high proportion of Hispanic-Americans and many businesses that cater to shoppers who cross the border from Tijuana. The history of San Ysidro is unconventional. Most cities have a beginning that leads to a period of development, then a modern incarnation. San Ysidro started and stopped.

It began as a utopian colony founded by William Smythe in the early 1900s. Smythe named the colony Little Landers to reflect his philosophy of life. He believed that his group of land owners needed only enough land to raise food for their families and have a little extra to sell. Their motto was "A little land and a living." The colony was fairly successful until a flood in 1916 wiped out the farms. All that remains of Little Landers today is Smythe Avenue.

Recent years have seen lots of development in San Ysidro and Otay Mesa, both of which boast relatively new housing projects. Houses range from $180,000 to $350,000, and condos are in the $80,000 to $175,000 range.

Nestor is a community of just under 17,000. It, too, began as a farming community, only its residents were mostly Japanese. The Japanese farmers pretty much disappeared, though, during World War II when most were placed in internment camps. Today Nestor focuses on its schools. Its middle school and high school are invariably among the first to come up with new programs to stimulate young minds and encourage a love of learning. And community service is as deeply ingrained in residents of Nestor as is getting out of bed in the morning.

The median house price is $213,000, and the median condo price is $142,000.

Shopping for a Home

By now you've probably figured out that real estate is of prime value in San Diego. So it should come as no surprise to learn that there are more than 8,000 Realtors, agents, and brokers doing business around town. The commonly held theory is that every single resident of San Diego is either in the business himself or has a brother-in-law, a cousin, or a buddy who is. Many companies are long established with excellent reputations. Others have a tendency to come and go.

If you're relocating to San Diego, we can suggest several ways to select a Realtor to best serve your needs. Probably the safest and most reliable route is to work with one of the national chains. They all have offices in every neighborhood, community, nook, and cranny in the county, and if you call one of the relocation numbers listed below, you'll be hooked up with a Realtor who is intimately familiar with the areas you might be considering.

Otherwise, a referral from a friend is usually reliable. With so many agents from which to choose, it's obviously a buyer's market. So we strongly suggest you interview potential agents. Ask questions, find out about their standard policies and what they can do for you. It doesn't hurt to ask if their commissions are negotiable, too.

National Real Estate Offices

Century 21 National Referral Service
(800) 4–HOUSES
www.century21.com

Since the early 1970s Century 21 has saturated the country with its local offices with the intent of making home buying a happy and satisfying experience for its clients. With 16 offices and nearly 300 agents in San Diego County, Century 21 has become a major force in the real estate industry here.

Century 21 is the world's largest franchiser of residential real estate brokerage offices, thus their agents and brokers receive the very best in training, management, administrative, and marketing support. If you call the number listed above, a friendly representative will provide a referral to a San Diego Century 21 office. The only hitch is that you need to know the zip code of your desired area. Alternatively, you can call any Century 21 office nationwide, and agents will be happy to help you find just the right office to suit your needs.

Coldwell Banker Residential Brokerage
(800) 488–6683
www.coldwellbanker.com

Colbert Coldwell founded his company in 1906 after the San Francisco earthquake, mainly as a result of his disapproval of agents who were taking advantage of vulnerable homeowners. His philosophy was to place the customer's interest above all, and that philosophy remains the driving force behind Coldwell Banker today.

With 13 offices in San Diego County, the company is committed to making the real estate process easier and more accessible for everyone. If you call the number above, you will receive a home price comparison index as well as information about the area of your choice and a referral to a nearby agent.

Coldwell Banker has a long history of integrity, exceptional service, and customer satisfaction.

Prudential California Realty
(888) 888–7356
www.prudentialcal.com

With corporate offices in the North County Coastal community of Del Mar, Prudential California Realty is one of the main real estate players in San Diego. The company has nearly 30 offices countywide with more on the drawing board.

By calling the relocation information number above you can find the right agent to fit your special needs and one who speaks your personal language. You will also receive a free relocation packet that includes details about our region and average home prices. It also provides a good sketch of our neighborhoods.

As one of the perky and helpful information specialists says, "We like to provide counseling as well as home buying data. Our goal is to assist buyers to homes where they feel comfortable." With information like that, Prudential California Realty takes the mystery out of finding the right home for you.

RE/MAX Realtors
(800) 227–3629
www.remax.com

With nearly 25 offices throughout the county, RE/MAX has more than 350 agents in our region. Each agent is determined to serve your needs and support San Diego. RE/MAX people are strong on community involvement and support volunteerism in the communities they serve. The type of involvement for a RE/MAX associate is as varied as the neighborhood he or she lives and serves. One might spend time with a scouting program and another help provide expertise with Habitat for Humanity.

Says Fred Christiansen, president of the RE/MAX Brokers/Owners Association of San Diego County, "Elbow grease is what it takes in today's world. It means rolling up your sleeves and plenty of shoe leather. RE/MAX agents believe that investing in our communities makes our neighborhoods better places to live, work and grow." Founded in 1973, the RE/MAX

weeks. It is broken down by region and features full-color photos of apartment complexes around the county. The guide also has a comprehensive list of amenities and restrictions of each complex (it will tell you for instance, about pet policies). It also includes contact phone numbers and maps. When it comes to driving time, this guide can be a big time-saver.

SanDiegoApartments.Com
2878 Camino del Rio S., Central San Diego
(888) 782–5671

This excellent Web site lists up-to-date rental units throughout the county. They can help you locate roommates and narrow your search to your specific needs. There's also a very informative section of background information on San Diego.

organization sells more property than any other firm with offices worldwide.

Apartment Hunting

Just as you can find magazines to help you buy a home, so can you find guides to help you rent an apartment. Located in the same places as home buyers guides—racks in supermarkets, drugstores, and convenience stores—these free guides will give you an idea of how the rental market stacks up in San Diego County.

Apartments For Rent
9682 Via Excelencia, Ste. 100, San Diego
(858) 530–2295
www.forrent.com

Serving all of San Diego County, *Apartments for Rent* is published every two

Homebuying Magazine

Even if after digesting all our neighborhood descriptions you still feel in the dark about San Diego real estate, a good way to get a feel for what's out there is to pick up one of several free magazines or guides. They all have photos, descriptions, prices, and referrals to real estate agents. Look for the following magazine in racks at the front of most supermarkets and drugstores, and some convenience stores too.

Harmon Homes
9682 Via Excelencia, Ste. 100, San Diego
(858) 874–2459

Broken down into several editions by region, this twice-monthly magazine features resale properties with descriptions and photos. Each property also has a referral to the listing agent.

Education and Child Care

Education is as essential to residents of San Diego County as a healthy dose of outdoor activity. While that might oversimplify our need for it and commitment to it, we're sincerely proud of the opportunities that exist for those in search of knowledge.

Sure, the rare curmudgeon will say the entire system is headed you-know-where and in a you-know-what. But rather than focus on what's wrong with education in San Diego County, parents, teachers, and students find that there's lots that's right.

To give you a quick sketch of our educational system, consider this: There are more than 600 public schools, hundreds of private schools, and scores of community colleges, colleges, and universities (which we describe in our Higher Education chapter). Now factor in the educational programs that range from Platt College's architectural drafting and computer graphic-design classes to the Pacific College of Oriental Medicine's advanced massage and herbology classes, and it won't take any "book learning" to see the diversity of instruction, education, and training San Diego offers.

Education

Public Schools

Under the authority of the San Diego County Office of Education, 6401 Linda Vista Road, San Diego (858-292-3500), there are about 600 public schools, kindergarten through 12th grade. Amazingly, San Diego County has 42 school districts within its boundaries, which teach 470,494 students. And that number grows each year as more people are drawn to our perfect climate.

The breakdown of schools is impressive, too. There are independent study schools, special education schools (a selection that addresses special needs from learning challenges to hearing impairments), alternative schools, and continuation schools for students who learn best outside the traditional high school environment.

Many school districts have gone to great lengths and somewhat extreme measures to improve student achievement. Perhaps the most dramatic (and controversial)

example is the San Diego Unified School District's "Blueprint for Student Success," designed by Superintendent Alan Bersin and Chancellor of Instruction Anthony Alvarado. The focus of this latest approach to learning and teaching is rigorous instruction in reading and writing in addition to expanded training programs for teachers, as well as a low tolerance for mediocrity among both teachers and administrators. This plan was fully implemented in city schools by the 2000-2001 school year. An independent study by the American Institute for Research, reported in the *San Diego Union-Tribune* in February 2002, gave generally high marks to the program's success, while warning that many parents and teachers feel frustrated and intimidated by the rather heavy-handed, rapid implementation of the plan. Another criticism of the literacy-heavy "Blueprint" is that it leaves insufficient time for non-literacy-related subjects and that the teaching models required for its implementation are too rigid.

Issues of control and creativity are resolved by administrators and parents creative and energetic enough to design their own charter schools, public schools that are independently run under the auspices of the school district. The charter school is freed from the obligation of complying with the state education code, for example, and given leeway to do things as it thinks best. Examples include High Tech High, whose name says it all, and Preuss School. Situated on the UCSD campus, Preuss School was formed to reach highly motivated students from lower-income areas in San Diego where students often do not reach their potential.

If you'd like to know more about the public schools in the area in which you're thinking of living, make an appointment with the school's principal or the district's superintendent. And for a listing of public schools in your area, look under "Schools" in the Yellow Pages. You can find a specific school by name in the White Pages of the phone directory.

Each year around two-thirds of all graduating seniors go on to higher education. The number is never exact, since some seniors take classes and work part-time or return to college after working for a year. For a complete look at the opportunities for higher education in San Diego County, be sure to read our Higher Education chapter. Many high school seniors attend our community colleges. Others focus on our excellent colleges and universities, often referred to as "alphabet soup," with school acronyms from CSUSM and USD to SDSU and UCSD.

Quite a number of San Diego's learners seek out other educational arenas, such as the no-cost programs offered by the Office of Education. Nontraditional students seem to be everywhere these days as they learn new skills or retrain in another career. Classes offered by the Regional Occupation Program (ROP) help these students pursue a myriad of educational choices. (Call 858-292-3611, or stop by one of the campuses listed in our Close-up.)

ROP courses are diverse. Sure, they include the expected computer skills and welding, but you can also learn about media production, auto engine performance, cabinet making, the travel industry, grocery operations, dog and cat grooming, international trade, and fashion design. ROP is one of the best educational bargains in San Diego. All classes are free, although some require a small materials fee. Some classes are held during the day; quite a few are evening classes. Lots of San Diego adults and high school students take ROP classes for the joy of learning new things.

Private Schools

In San Diego there are hundreds of private educational opportunities. The choices range from the tiny ones to those with large student bodies and worldwide prestige. As in many other larger cities and regions, the majority of San Diego's private schools focus on specific religious beliefs. For example, nearly every Catholic parish in San Diego has an elementary school, which in turn is affiliated with a Catholic high school. If you're interested in religious schooling for your kids, contact your pastor or the advisor for your church or synagogue. Tuition varies a great deal, according to the size of the facility, its location, courses, and staff.

In addition to those schools with a religious affiliation, there are other well-respected private schools here in San Diego; most can only be described as on the high side of expensive.

Most parents in San Diego County are comfortable sending their children off each day to one of our public schools. Because most of the private schools are out of financial reach for San Diego parents, we give you just a sampling. Check

Insiders' Tip

Nearly one-fifth of San Diego County's high school seniors are taking advanced placement (college prep) courses.

A young San Diego student prepares to board the school bus. PHOTO: CECE CANTON

the Yellow Pages under "Schools" for other private schools.

Army-Navy Academy
2605 Carlsbad Blvd., Carlsbad
(888) 762–2338
www.army-navyacademy.com
The Army-Navy Academy is a distinguished North County Coastal military school. It's located about 4 blocks north and east of the Coaster commuter train station in downtown Carlsbad, and, even more pleasing to students, it sits right on the beach. It is a year-round boarding school. The Academy's students number about 310 boys in seventh through twelfth grades. Students come from every corner of our globe and right from Carlsbad, too. Instruction is diverse and intense, and yes, students wear military-style uniforms. Included in the curriculum is an award-winning ROTC program, honors programs, advanced English as a second language program, and full athletics. The student to teacher ratio is 15:1. Ninety-five percent of the Army-Navy Academy graduates go on to college; many attend military academies like West Point.

La Jolla County Day School
9490 Genesee Avenue, La Jolla
(858) 453–3440
www.ljcds.org
A co-ed school, the respected La Jolla County Day, as it's known to Insiders, has an enrollment of about 1,000 students, kindergarten through 12th grade. This is a college prep school with an emphasis on traditional liberal arts. After graduation, it's likely that its students will go on to notable universities like Harvard, MIT, and Stanford.

Montessori East County Preschool and Kindergarten
10017 Maine Ave., Lakeside
(619) 561–0902
Montessori American
3604 Bonita Rd., Chula Vista
(619) 422–1220
Montessori School of San Diego
1323 W. Spruce St., San Diego (Middletown)
(619) 295–7591

For the younger crowd, Montessori schools are sprinkled throughout the county. All the schools are privately owned, so curricula vary. The Montessori East County Preschool and Kindergarten has 84 students; Montessori American, a preschool and kindergarten only, has 96 students; and the Montessori School of San Diego is a K through third-grade private school with a little more than 100 students.

Vocational and Technical Schools

We'd be lax if we didn't point out some of the outstanding private vocational and technical schools in San Diego. Here are a few to give you a taste of what you can find if you're looking for specialized education. For a complete list of technical and vocational schools, consult the Yellow Pages under "Schools." Remember, if you're looking for technical and vocational programs, review the cost-free possibilities with ROP, mentioned above; ask plenty of questions; and talk to graduates before spending your money.

The Advertising Arts College
10025 Mesa Rim Rd., San Diego
(858) 546–0602
www.taac.edu
Devoted exclusively to advertising, animation, graphic design, and computer arts, TAAC offers traditional four-year MS and MA degrees and three-year associate degrees. Among the more than 60 courses in the curriculum are copywriting; multimedia design; graphic design; and general education classes in sociology, psychology, and ethics.

Many students already have jobs in advertising and want to improve their skills, while others attend to develop a career in the field. Students develop ad campaigns in class, and their work is critiqued by other students and professors. Facilities include fully equipped classrooms, video cameras and monitors, still cameras, audio recording equipment, visualization systems, duplication machines, scanners, printers, and transfer stations.

San Diego Regional Occupation Programs

Escondido Adult School
3750 Mary Ln., Escondido (760) 739–7309

Grossmont Union High School District
924 E. Main St., El Cajon (619) 590–3923

Metro ROP, Revere Center
6735 Gifford Wy., San Diego (858) 627–7208

Oceanside Instructions Center
2080 Mission Ave., Oceanside (760) 439–5738

Palomar Community College
1140 W. Mission Rd. #AA-136., San Marcos (760) 744–1150, ext. 2301

Poway Unified District
13230 Evening Creek Dr. South, Suite 220, Poway (858) 679–2560

Ramona High School
1401 Hanson Ln., Ramona (760) 787–4035

San Diego CCD
8401 Aero Dr., San Diego (619) 388–6851

San Diego CCD South
5415 Imperial Ave., San Diego (619) 388–6851

Vista Adult School
305 E. Bobier Ave., Vista (760) 758–7122

California College for Health Sciences
2423 Hoover Ave., National City
(619) 477–4800, (800) 221–7374
www.cchs.edu

Although based in San Diego County, this is basically a correspondence school for health professionals, especially respiratory-care technicians. It offers 10 different degree programs and is accredited by the Accrediting Commission of the Distance Education and Training Council. More than 10,000 students are enrolled nationwide, and independent study schedules are personalized for each student.

California Institute for Human Science
701 Garden View Ct., Encinitas
(760) 634–1771
www.cihs.edu

The California Institute for Human Science, an accredited university, offers postgraduate degrees in the fields of life physics, comparative religion, and philosophy; human science; and clinical psychology. It provides graduate-level education and training services.

Founded by Dr. Hiroshi Motoyama, the institute's unique offering of graduate programs is designed to prepare the mature student to contribute meaningfully as a professional and a scholar in the emerging global society.

The California Institute for Human Science has daytime, weekend, and evening courses and workshops, many of which are accredited for continuing education units (CEUs) for healthcare professionals.

Coleman College
7380 Parkway Dr., La Mesa
(619) 465–3990
1284 W. San Marcos Blvd., San Marcos
(760) 747–3990

Founded in 1963 to support the budding computer industry, Coleman College has established itself as a resource and cornerstone of private technical education in San Diego. Classes are small, typically about one instructor to 10 or 15 students, often less. The coursework is intensive. Classes are held in the day and evening and start-up cycles occur often. Coleman's innovative curriculum gives career training first so students can become qualified for a computer-related position in a matter of months. Longer programs include those for associates, bachelors, and masters degrees.

Programs include computer information science, computer engineering technology, and computer applications and networks. The college also has a placement service for graduates and those seeking part-time employment while studying.

Contractors Licensing Service
340 Vernon Way, Ste. C, El Cajon
(619) 440–2122
www.licenses4contractors.com

Contractors Licensing Service, established in 1965, provides exam preparation programs for would-be contractors. There are on-campus classes, home-study programs, and even crash-course curriculum. In addition to the educational segment, their services include, but are not limited to, sending in student forms to the state and weekly progress checks with the state to ensure a timely issuance of licenses.

Design Institute of San Diego
8555 Commerce Ave., San Diego
(858) 566–1200
www.disd.edu

This college is devoted exclusively to education in interior design and is accredited by the Foundation for Interior Design Education Research as well as the Accrediting Council for Independent Colleges and Schools. Founded in 1977, the insti-

tute teaches students creative and technical skills, sound business practices, and history of design.

Fashion Careers of California College
1923 Morena Blvd., San Diego
(619) 275–4700, (888) 322–2999
www.fashioncollege.com

Students interested in a career in the fashion industry can obtain a certificate or an associate of arts degree in either fashion merchandising or fashion design here. The curriculum includes internships and study tours to New York and Los Angeles, and as part of the program, students work on fashion shows and other activities in the San Diego fashion industry.

Certificates in either merchandising or design can be obtained in one academic year; associate of arts degrees take two years. Credits earned at the college are accepted at major colleges for the applied arts throughout the country.

Insiders' Tip

In a recent Stanford Achievement Test, the Stanford 9, San Diego County public school students came within 10 percentile points of the national average in virtually all subjects and grades. In California's second largest school district, San Diego Unified, 97 schools were recently awarded $577 million in performance awards because of strong student academic improvement during the 1999-2000 year.

Educational opportunities abound for these San Diego youngsters learning about sea life firsthand at the Stephen Birch Aquarium. PHOTO: COURTESY OF THE SCRIPPS INSTITUTION OF OCEANOGRAPHY, UNIVERSITY OF CALIFORNIA SAN DIEGO

Kelsey-Jenney College
201 A St., San Diego
(619) 233–7418, (800) 734–4625
www.kelsey-jenney.com
Established in 1887, Kelsey-Jenney prepares students for entry-level careers in the business, computer sciences, industry, medical, and legal fields. The instruction is job-oriented, designed to develop the highest level of language, business, and technical skills. Accredited by the Western Association of Schools and Colleges, Kelsey-Jenney offers associate of arts degrees as well as certificates in a variety of practical fields.

Courses may be taken during the day or in the evening at either the downtown campus or the northern campus at 7310 Miramar Road, San Diego. Students are required to complete course work in general studies in addition to their chosen field.

Pacific College of Oriental Medicine
7445 Mission Valley Rd.,
Suite 105, San Diego
(619) 574–6909, (800) 729–0941
www.ormed.edu
As interest in holistic medicine and practices becomes more widespread, folks are pursuing academic knowledge to become practitioners themselves. Accredited by the National Accreditation Commission of Schools and Colleges of Acupuncture and Oriental Medicine, this college offers a wide variety of degree and diploma programs at its San Diego campus. Students can study to practice traditional Oriental medicine or become a holistic health practitioner, massage therapist, massage technician, Oriental body therapist, or Chinese health exercise specialist, among other disciplines.

The college offers flexible scheduling for working adults, and students can take courses during the day or on evenings and weekends. Tours and consultations are always welcomed.

Palomar Institute of Cosmetology
355 Via Vera Cruz, San Marcos
(760) 744–7900
This cosmetology and manicurist school prepares students to pass the State Board Examination and for careers as hair stylists, facialists, manicurists, make-up artists, and cosmetic and beauty product representatives.

Platt College
6250 El Cajon Blvd., San Diego
(619) 265–0107, (800) 225–0613
www.platt.edu
Platt College provides comprehensive, professional education programs and associate of applied science degrees in computer graphic design and multimedia design. In the graphic design program students learn form, color, typography, and the development of design skills. Multimedia is an extension of the graphic design program, in which students apply the technical knowledge and creative skills they've acquired in the integration of text, illustrations, photos, sound, voice, animation, music, and video on computer. The drafting technology and architectural drafting programs combine knowledge of manual drafting and computer-assisted drafting training. One of the college's primary goals is to help students find careers related to their field of study, so they maintain an active placement assistance program for their graduates.

Travel Experts Training School
3505 Camino del Rio S., #220, San Diego
(619) 281–4333
www.travelschool.org
Travel and tourism is one of San Diego's largest industries, although travel agencies have lost business as the Internet is more widely used. Nonetheless, Travel Experts Training School continues to train travel agents, tour operators, flight attendants, airline representatives, and reservationists for the hotel, cruise, rail, and car rental industries. Since 1976 the school has provided the facilities and resources necessary to train students in theoretical knowledge and practical skills in their chosen field.

All faculty members are trained professionals in the field in which they teach. Among the classes offered are world geography, worldwide rail transportation, cruises, airline computer training, and worldwide tours and land arrangements. The school is accredited by the California Council for Private Postsecondary and Vocational Education.

Child Care

Child care is an issue close to the hearts of San Diego residents, and we wish we could tell you we have answers to working parents' quandaries. Like our co-workers in every part of the nation, we're faced with the fact that sometimes there are no perfect choices for the care of our kids. We've tried to provide resources to get you started, however, in your hunt for safe, happy day care and after-school programs, which we assure you can be found in San

Insiders' Tip

The Learning Annex (619-544-9700, www.learningannex.com) provides an eclectic assortment of classes. You'll find classes from the bold (Learn to Strip for your Lover) to the conventional (like Word for Windows™ and Web page design). Catalogs can be found at video stores, many libraries, and retail shops, or by calling the number above. Fees vary.

This youngster is admiring the elephant lights at the entrance to the San Diego Wild Animal Park.

Diego. We've included a couple of special camps for kids, too.

To make child care concerns and questions a bit less overwhelming, we've done part of the legwork for you. Securing appropriate child care for the kids of working parents is a personal issue. You know your child better than anyone, so we haven't composed a list of what we think would be a good choice for child care, day care, or home care. Instead we provide some resources for making choices and mention just a few almost universally accepted facilities you may want to contact.

As you review the choices for child care, whether from the phone book or one of the giveaway magazines found at the grocery store, it's crucial to check references, make impromptu visits, and ask plenty of questions.

If your child requires individualized attention or special medical care, you may want to talk with your pediatrician, healthcare provider, or school district. They may be able to make referrals.

The **San Diego County Family Child Care Association** is another source of information. You can contact them at (760) 736-2598 to get information on providers. To read reports about specific day care centers, call the **California State Licensing Board** at (619) 767-2200.

Religious and academic private schools often have extended day-care programs. A number of YMCAs in San Diego (see our chapter on Kidstuff) provide after-school activities for kids for a fee. You can reach the **YMCA Childcare Resources Service** at (800) 481-2151 or (619) 521-3055, and this organization can also provide recommendations for day care in your area. Some school district elementary schools also provide this service.

Here on vacation or a business trip and need help caring for kids?

If you're wondering how to keep the kids happy and safe while you're doing business and enjoying San Diego, the first step to the care issue may be a talk with the concierge or reservations desk staff member. Often hotels, resorts, and spas have contacts with licensed and bonded babysitters and nannies (see our Spas and Resorts chapter). Some resorts have "camps" with special kid-style activities.

For instance, the **Four Seasons Resort Aviara**, 7100 Four Seasons Point in Carlsbad, (760) 603-6800 or (800) 332-3442, has a Kids for All Seasons program. Supervised activities for children ages 4 to 12 include nature hikes, a kids' pool, croquet, kite-flying, table tennis, and treasure hunts. All of the staff members are CPR certified. Kids are welcome to join activities for the whole day or part of the day. Lunch is billed to the parents' room; otherwise it's a free service. At least one parent must remain on the premises while the child participates. Hours are 1:00 to 5:00 P.M. on school days; weekends and school holidays 9:00 A.M. to 5:00 P.M. Reservations are suggested.

The Commodore Kids Club, at **Loews Coronado Bay**, 4000 Coronado Bay Road, Coronado, (619) 424-4000, also has supervised programs for kids 4 to 12. Activities include arts and crafts, Ping-Pong, board games, and movies. The cost is $50 per child, including lunch; $30 for a half day. Evening care (Friday and Saturday night 6:00 to 10:00 P.M.) facilities are available for $60 per child. The resort's "Generation G" package provides mementos and special rates for people traveling with their grandchildren.

Higher Education

Four-year Universities and Colleges

Law Schools

Community Colleges

Extended Studies Programs

San Diegans took a look around one day and discovered that their recreation-oriented county had quietly turned into a remarkable enclave for higher education. Anchored by three major universities—San Diego State University (SDSU), the University of California at San Diego (UCSD), and the University of San Diego (USD)—the educational scene comprises more than 50 institutions for higher learning. Rapidly gaining in stature are Point Loma Nazarene University and California State University, San Marcos, both of which can be considered major universities themselves. Also multiplying in number are several well-respected business colleges. And finally, dozens of trade, technical, and vocational schools (which we cover in our Education and Child Care chapter) round out the higher education scene. It's really no wonder that so many fine institutions have sprung up in San Diego. After all, it's a piece of cake to draw students. The combination of excellent academics and the San Diego lifestyle is irresistible.

San Diego State University is the granddaddy of them all, established as the Normal School in 1897 by the California Legislature. It moved to its current site on Montezuma Mesa in 1931, where it evolved into the dominant liberal arts university it remains today. Its younger brothers and sisters do not suffer by comparison, though; they enhance its presence with their different focus and programs.

The university community is a crucial component of San Diego's industry. The majority of students stay put after they graduate, and they are the future of the county's business and industry. Working hand-in-hand with the local scientific community, UCSD produces the next generation of high-tech, biotech, and engineering talent so desperately needed. With its first-rate law school, USD keeps the legal community filled with talented lawyers. All the universities are deeply involved in the surrounding community, and they never hesitate to exchange ideas and resources among themselves. For example, the three majors established a library consortium to trade books among their students. When a student at one university requests a book from another, it is usually delivered the same day. This spirit of cooperation makes for a better educational experience for all.

In this chapter we'll give you an Insider's look at the major universities, the up-and-coming institutions, the colleges geared toward working adults, and the excellent community colleges. We'll also talk about extended studies programs affiliated with the universities, where adult students with or without degrees can enhance their knowledge and skills or participate in certificate programs. Unless otherwise specified, all colleges are accredited by the Western Association of Schools and Colleges.

Keep in mind that we're giving you the best-known and most well-established colleges here. Plenty more await you, and if the ones described here don't fill your bill, there almost surely is an institution around town that will be perfectly tailored to your needs.

Four-year Universities and Colleges

Alliant International University
10455 Pomerado Rd., San Diego
(858) 635–4772
www.alliant.edu

The California School of Professional Psychology combined with U.S. International University in 2001 to form Alliant International University (AIU). The nonprofit university has six campuses in California, including one in San Diego County, as well as one in Mexico City and a charter university in Nairobi, Kenya. San Diego's campuses currently serve more than 640 students.

Graduate and undergraduate degrees are available in behavioral and social sciences, liberal arts, education, and business. San Diego campuses offer master's degrees in counseling psychology, organizational psychology, organizational behavior, and psychophysiology and biofeedback. Doctoral degrees are available in clinical psychology, industrial/organizational psychology, consulting psychology, and health psychology.

Among the university's research facilities is the Rehabilitation Research and Training Center for Persons Who Are Hard of Hearing or Late Deafened (RRTC), which, as its name implies, studies and disseminates information about deafness.

California State University at San Marcos
Barham Dr., San Marcos
(760) 750–4000
www.csusm.edu

The new kid on the block in San Diego County, CSUSM opened its doors to students in the fall of 1990 as the 20th campus in the 23-campus California State University system. Nestled in the foothills of North County Inland, the 304-acre campus is home to some 6,500 students who attend one of three colleges: Arts and Sciences, Business Administration, and Education. The university is growing rapidly—by design. Projected student enrollment by the year 2020 is more than 18,000.

The three schools at CSUSM offer 19 majors, 15 teacher-credential programs, and 9 master's degree programs. Of the 190 faculty members, more than 90 percent have a doctoral or terminal degree. The university is just starting to field some athletic teams, beginning with track and field, cross-country, and golf for men and women.

Chapman University
7460 Mission Valley Rd., San Diego
(619) 296–8660
www.chapman.edu

Chapman University is the seventh oldest university in California. An independent liberal arts college, it is composed of the Wilkinson College of Letters and Sciences and six schools: the School of Business and Economics, the School of Communication Arts, the School of Education, the School of Film and Television, the School of Music, and the School of Law.

The university offers more than 40 fields of undergraduate study, graduate study programs and teacher-credential programs in a unique 10-week term format. Geared toward working adults, many classes are offered during lunchtime, evening hours, and Saturdays at its Mission Valley headquarters and five other locations around San Diego. Chapman makes a point of catering to the military population in San Diego and gives credit for military training and experience. About 1,000 students are enrolled in Chapman's San Diego locations.

Christian Heritage College
2100 Greenfield Dr., El Cajon
(619) 588–7747, (800) 676–2242
www.christianheritage.edu

Tucked away at the base of Shadow Mountain in East County's El Cajon, Christian Heritage College has a liberal arts curriculum. Founded in 1970 with a Christian-oriented mission, learning in all CHC's academic programs is biblically focused.

In addition to its halls of learning, the 34-acre campus has playing fields and a swimming pool for intercollegiate and intramural sports for men and women students. Christian Heritage has more than 15 undergraduate academic programs, including Aviation Technology, Sports Medicine, and Biblical Studies to augment the more traditional disciplines. Because of its small student population of approximately 650, individualized attention is the norm. The student-teacher ratio is 15 to 1.

National University
4121 Camino del Rio S., San Diego
11255 N. Torrey Pines Rd., La Jolla
(858) 642–8000, (800) 628–8648
www.nu.edu

Based in San Diego, National University has 26 campuses throughout California, 12 in San Diego County alone. Its enrollment of 25,000 students makes it the second largest private university in California. National offers a one-course-per-month format for both undergraduate and graduate programs, with most classes held in the evenings and on Saturdays. The average age of students is 34. Sixty-eight percent are graduate students and 32 percent are undergraduate students.

Founded in 1971, the university is committed to adult learning in a convenient and practical way. New courses begin each month, so students can enroll at any time during the year. Its headquarters are in Mission Valley, but learning centers and campuses are spread throughout the area, with several located on military bases. Three schools—the School of Business and Technology, the School of Education, and the School of Arts and Sciences—offer more than 45 undergraduate and graduate degree programs and 15 teaching credentials.

Point Loma Nazarene University
3900 Lomaland Dr., San Diego
(619) 221–2273
www.ptloma.edu

The predecessor to Point Loma Nazarene University, Pacific Bible College, was founded in 1902 in Los Angeles. Later moved to Pasadena and renamed in that city's honor, the school was transferred to its current location atop the bluffs of Sunset Cliffs on the Point Loma peninsula in 1973. The Point Loma Nazarene campus spreads over 90 acres overlooking the Pacific Ocean and has an enrollment of more than 2,600 undergraduate and graduate students.

The university, an institution of the Church of the Nazarene, offers liberal arts curriculum in an environment of Christianity in the evangelical and Wesleyan tradition. Undergraduate degrees in 40 major fields of study are available, plus eight graduate degrees. Of its faculty, 80 percent have doctoral degrees. Point Loma Nazarene has a variety of extracurricular activities, including clubs and organizations, fraternities and sororities, campus ministries, and intercollegiate athletics for men and women students. The student-faculty ratio is 15 to 1.

San Diego State University
5500 Campanile Dr., San Diego
(619) 594–5200
www.sdsu.edu

Part of the California State University system, SDSU celebrated its centennial in 1997. Belying its reputation as one of the top party colleges in the country, SDSU's academic excellence is nationally recognized.

It is the largest institution of higher learning in San Diego, with a student population of more than 34,000 and an average student age of 25. Located atop Montezuma Mesa on the eastern edge of the city, the campus occupies more than 4.5 million square feet in 44 academic buildings, including the new 320,000-square-foot Malcolm A. Love Library. Although SDSU is considered a teaching university, it has strong research programs too; at last count faculty members attracted $124 million in research grants and program administration contracts from outside sources.

> **Insiders' Tip**
> If you're planning to attend a San Diego State University football game at Qualcomm Stadium, you can support the team by wearing the traditional Aztec colors: red and black.

Seventy-six undergraduate degrees are offered; there are also 59 master's and 13 joint-doctoral programs. Further emphasizing the university's pursuit of academic recognition is the presence of five multi-disciplinary honor societies on campus: Golden Key, Mortar Board, Phi Beta Kappa, Phi Eta Sigma, and Phi Kappa Phi.

Complementing the academic side of education are the extensive varsity athletic programs. Aztec teams have won national championships in volleyball, track and field, basketball, and football. The new Tony Gwynn Stadium opened for Aztec baseball in 1997, and Aztec basketball has a new home, too, in the Cox Arena, a facility that seats 12,000. In August 2001, the four-story, 130,000-square-foot Aztec Athletic Center opened to house the Hall of Fame, a state-of-the-art weight room, and an athletic training center for women's and men's varsity sports.

Locals flock to the campus for concerts and lectures or to use the library.

University of California, San Diego
9500 Gilman Dr., La Jolla
(858) 534–2230
www.ucsd.edu

San Diego State University may be the most well-known college in town, but there's little doubt that UCSD is the most prestigious. The scenic campus boasts a faculty that includes five Nobel laureates and a former astronaut and has state-of-the-art research facilities. It attracts the highest caliber students too. Approximately 99 percent graduated in the top 10 percent of their high school class, with average SAT scores of more than 1,200.

The university consists of six colleges: Eleanor Roosevelt College, Earl Warren College, Thurgood Marshall College, John Muir College, Revelle College, and the new Sixth College. Open to students beginning in the 2002 fall semester, Sixth College's curriculum will emphasize courses in culture, art, and technology. Ninety-seven undergraduate majors are available along with more than 30 graduate programs. In addition, seven joint doctoral programs are offered in conjunction with San Diego State University.

The student population is about 16,000 in the undergraduate colleges and approximately 2,600 in graduate programs. Students at UCSD average just over four years to acquire a degree, a rarity these days, and the student-teacher ratio is 19 to 1.

The San Diego Supercomputer Center, a research unit of UC San Diego, has a staff

This futuristic structure is the library at the University of California at San Diego. PHOTO: THORN VOLLENWEIDER

of 400 scientists and research personnel dedicated to developing new technology to advance science, including biosciences and environmental sciences for the national scientific community. Because of UCSD's close ties to San Diego's high technology, wireless communication, and biomedical industries, its students have an advantage in securing internships, summer jobs, graduate school positions, and careers. *US News & World Report* ranks UCSD's undergraduate biomedical/biomedical engineering program second in the country, after Johns Hopkins University.

Although athletics are nowhere as important at UCSD as academia, Triton intercollegiate teams have won 29 national championships. Both women and men participate in intercollegiate soccer, track and field, tennis, golf, and other sports. Social, athletic, and leadership opportunities include more than 300 student clubs and organizations.

University of San Diego
5998 Alcalá Park, San Diego
(619) 260-4600
www.acusd.edu

A private Catholic institution, USD sits on a 180-acre hilltop campus overlooking Mission Bay. The university offers a liberal arts curriculum and is known for its commitment to teaching, values-oriented programs, and community involvement. More than 80 undergraduate and graduate degree programs are available to USD's 6,800 students, including doctoral programs in education and nursing. Five schools comprise the university: the College of Arts and Sciences, the School of Education, the School of Business Administration, the Philip Y. Hahn School of Nursing, and the School of Law (see School of Law entry that follows).

The university offers a master of arts program in international relations and has a strong international study program. ROTC and paralegal programs are increasingly popular among USD's students, who also avail themselves of more than a dozen intercollegiate sports along with dozens of club sports and intramurals. Ninety-seven percent of faculty members have a doc-

toral or terminal degree, and the student-faculty ratio is 18 to 1.

Law Schools

California Western School of Law
225 Cedar St., San Diego
(619) 239-0391
www.cwsl.edu

California Western began as a small law college called Balboa Law College in 1924. Located in downtown San Diego. It was accredited by the American Bar Association in 1962 and admitted to the Association of American Law Schools in 1967.

The student population totals more than 700; the student-faculty ratio is 16 to 1. An average of 80 percent of California Western's students pass the bar exam on the first attempt. Among the most compelling of USD's special programs is the California Innocence Project, in which students work with criminal lawyers to seek the release of people unjustly convicted of crimes and currently serving time in prison.

Thomas Jefferson School of Law
2121 San Diego Ave., San Diego
(619) 297-9700
www.tjsl.edu

Founded in 1969, Thomas Jefferson School of Law is a private, nonprofit independent law school whose mission is to provide legal education to a diverse array of students. The campus is located in Old Town and consists of two Spanish-style buildings that overlook San Diego Harbor. In 1996 the law school received provisional accreditation from the American Bar Association, followed by full accreditation in 2001.

Dedicated to individualized instruction, class sizes at Thomas Jefferson average fewer than 30 students. Faculty and administration recognize that law school is a stressful experience, thus they provide maximum accessibility and many support services to help provide students with the necessary skills to successfully complete their course of study.

Special programs include a Judicial Internship Program that permits students to clerk for federal and state judges, and Field Placement Programs that provide opportunities for working with attorneys in public agencies. Thomas Jefferson offers a three-year, full-time or a four-year, part-time program.

University of San Diego School of Law
5998 Alcalá Park, San Diego
(619) 260–4528
www.acusd.edu

Founded in 1954, USD School of Law is accredited by the American Bar Association and is a member of the Association of American Law Schools and The Order of the Coif, the most distinguished rank of American law schools. The law school offers degrees of juris doctor and master of laws. In addition, joint degree programs are available in conjunction with USD's graduate schools: a master of business administration, a master of international business, and a master of arts in international relations.

The student population is approximately 1,100, and both full-time and part-time programs are offered. The full-time program requires three years for completion; part-time students usually need four years of evening study plus one summer to complete the degree.

The Center for Public Interest Law at USD is an academic center for research, learning, and advocacy for the disadvantaged or underrepresented in state administrative proceedings. Likewise, the Children's Advocacy Institute is a legal advocacy and research center that promotes the health and well-being of California's children. The Patient Advocacy Program works to ensure the rights of the mentally disabled; the new Joan B. Kroc Institute for Peace and Justice hosts international symposia and conferences and promotes peace in the nation and the community.

Community Colleges

San Diego's community colleges often serve as an intermediate step between high school and university. They usually offer two-year associate degree programs along

> ### Insiders' Tip
> Campus tours of UCSD are available from Monday through Saturday (except holidays) promptly at 11:00 A.M. Stroll through the peaceful environment surrounded by eucalyptus trees, and be sure to see the extraordinary artwork, such as the mosaic snake pathway that leads to the library, an architectural wonder in itself. Call (858) 534-1935 for tour reservations and important information.

with specialized certificate courses and vocational studies.

Grossmont-Cuyamaca Community College District
8800 Grossmont College Dr., El Cajon
(619) 644–7010
www.gccd.net

The district includes both Cuyamaca College and Grossmont College, which offer custom contract courses for foreign nationals in addition to its traditional programs. The district works with overseas groups to design courses that fulfill their specific educational goals, including English language courses and introduction to American culture.

Cuyamaca Community College
900 Rancho San Diego Pkwy., El Cajon
(619) 660–4000
www.cuyamaca.net

Opened in 1978, Cuyamaca offers a comprehensive curriculum of lower division courses and academic preparation for transfer to any of the California State

University of San Diego

For decades the University of San Diego has been known around town as "that little Catholic college up on the hill." For a long while that was a relatively accurate assessment. It isn't any longer. That little Catholic college has grown up into a major university.

Officially chartered by the State of California in 1949, USD began as the vision of Bishop Charles Francis Buddy. Newly consecrated as Bishop of the Diocese of San Diego in 1937, the bishop visited his friend and colleague, Mother Rosalie Hill, superior vicar of the San Francisco College for Women. He shared with her his dream of inaugurating a Catholic college in his new diocese and hoped that she would join him in his quest.

Mother Hill eagerly accepted the challenge. By 1944 they were surveying sites, finally settling on a stunning piece of property in Linda Vista. The property, situated on a long mesa at the west entrance to Mission Valley, consisted of more than 100 acres overlooking Mission Bay, Old Town, and historic Presidio Hill, where Father Junipero Serra established his first mission in California. Bishop Buddy and Mother Hill named the site Alcalá Park, in honor of San Diego de Alcalá; the university had come one step closer to reality.

The two were committed to building separate colleges for men and women, but agreed that, to provide social interaction, the two should remain close to one another. Mother Hill decided that the architecture should be an adaptation of Spanish Renaissance because of its lasting appeal, its softness of line, and its quintessential California quality. Subsequent structures have remained true to that style, resulting in a campus of unparalleled beauty.

Ground was broken in 1948, and the first classes in the College for Women were held in 1950. The colleges remained separate for two decades but began allowing reciprocal course registration in the late 1960s. Finally, encouraged by Vatican II, they merged in 1972 to become the University of San Diego.

Today USD draws students from around the world who seek superior academics with a strong philosophy of values and ethics. Complementing the academic side of life at USD are intercollegiate and intramural athletic programs, campus ministry, fraternities and sororities, clubs and organizations, and a committed and wide-ranging community outreach program.

During the 1996 U.S. presidential campaign, USD received national exposure when it played host to one of the candidate debates. Those who watched the debate, which was televised live internationally, saw a beautiful campus and a flawless production. The preparations,

Spanish Renaissance architecture is faithfully adhered to in University of San Diego buildings.

however, were far from matter-of-fact. Shiley Theater, the venue for the debate, had to be gutted. New seats were added, air conditioning installed, and at the last minute, the stage was extended to accommodate the debate's town hall format. In the end, all the preparations paid off, and USD got a gold star and national acclaim for its role as the perfect host.

Today the campus's buildings, the plaza, and the fountain are set off by the lush landscaping and a beautiful setting. The bishop's dream is realized; the little college on the hill has become a jewel in the crown of higher education in San Diego.

University or University of California campuses. It also has a variety of technical-vocational, engineering, and other professional programs and general education courses. Study abroad allows students to experience a foreign culture as they study the language; programs are in place for study in Mexico, Central or South America, and Europe.

Cuyamaca College's 165-acre campus is located on a scenic hillside in East County. The college serves about 4,500 students in daytime, evening, and Saturday classes. Afternoon college targets working adults who can dedicate weekday afternoons to general education requirement courses prior to transferring to a four-year school. Community learning classes are free or inexpensive courses for adults, with summer programs for children.

Grossmont Community College
8800 Grossmont College Dr., El Cajon
(619) 644-7010
www.grossmont.net

Like Cuyamaca, Grossmont offers dozens of associate degree, certificate, and transfer programs. In addition to a full range of courses in disciplines from theater arts to international business and computer systems management, students can take advantage of summer or semester-long study abroad programs in Australia, France, and Costa Rica. Students here benefit from academic and vocational support and resources that support and supplement instructional programs. Grossmont also has a community continuing education program and a ROP program.

MiraCosta Community College
1 Barnard Dr., Oceanside
(760) 757-2121, (888) 201-8480
(Oceanside Campus)
3333 Manchester Ave., Encinitas
(760) 944-4449, (888) 201-8480
(San Elijo Campus)
www.miracosta.cc.ca.us

Opened in 1964 to serve the educational needs of North County Coastal students, MiraCosta's Oceanside campus is located on a 121-acre hilltop site with panoramic views of the Pacific Ocean to the west and the mountains to the east. Seventeen miles south is the San Elijo campus, 42 acres above the San Elijo Lagoon reserve. The Oceanside campus has a student population of 6,000, and about 3,000 attend classes at the San Elijo campus. Approximately 1,000 students alternate between the two.

MiraCosta offers freshman- and sophomore-level courses in preparation for transfer to a four-year university. Transfer agreements are established with most California public universities, including UCSD, SDSU, and CSUSM. Also offered are dozens of certificate job-training courses as well as associate of arts degrees.

Palomar Community College
1140 W. Mission Rd., San Marcos
(760) 744-1150
www.palomar.edu

Serving North County Inland, Palomar's 200-acre San Marcos campus houses up-to-date classroom and laboratory facilities, the largest research library in North County, a planetarium, athletic playing

Insiders' Tip

Make a point of visiting the University of San Diego's new Fine Art Gallery, at the Joan B. Kroc Institute for Peace & Justice (on campus at 5998 Alcala Park). It's open to the public Wednesday, Friday, and Saturday from noon to 4:00 P.M.; Thursday noon to 6:00 P.M. Check the university's Web site, www.sandiego.edu, or call (619) 260-2280 for information on current shows.

fields, the Boehm Art Gallery, the 400-seat Brubeck Theatre, a Wellness/Fitness Center, and a 45-acre arboretum. In addition to its phenomenal facilities, Palomar was named by the *Community College Journal* as one of three flagship community colleges in the United States for its emphasis on learning.

More than 27,000 students (mostly part-time) take classes at the main campus and at eight Education Centers throughout North County. Distance Learning is available through internet and TV courses. Students may choose from more than 130 associate degree and certificate programs as prelude to transfer or for vocational preparation. Palomar also offers foreign language immersion programs and travel/study credit courses such as their Art and Photography in Italy and France trip.

San Diego Community College District
3375 Camino del Rio S., San Diego
(619) 388–6500

All three of the colleges in the San Diego Community College District, City College, Mesa College, and Miramar College, have transfer agreements with the University of California, the California State Universities, and other universities and colleges as well.

San Diego City College
1313 12th St., San Diego
(619) 230–2400
www.city.sdccd.net

Occupying four square blocks on the outskirts of downtown San Diego and next door to its namesake, San Diego High School, City College is the oldest community college in the San Diego District. Serving some 15,000 students, the urban campus offers an array of two-year associate degrees and a large number of certificate programs.

The City Knights compete in intercollegiate baseball, basketball, cross country, soccer, volleyball, tennis, and track for men and women. City College is distinguished by its on-campus radio station, KSDS-FM, San Diego's only 24-hour jazz radio station.

San Diego Mesa College
7250 Mesa College Dr., San Diego
(619) 388–2600
www.mesacollege.net.us

Among the largest community colleges in the nation, the 24,000-student Mesa College is situated in the geographic heart of San Diego, in Kearny Mesa. Sprawled over 104 acres, the college offers some 48 degrees as well as certificate programs, and has one of the highest student transfer rates among the 108 community colleges in California.

Special programs include a comprehensive array of allied health programs in dental assisting, medical assisting, physical therapist, radiological technology, health information technology, and animal health technology. New curricula in biotechnology and biochemistry have been introduced, and a $20 million Learning Resource Center, with a library, computer labs, and media facilities, opened in 1998.

San Diego Miramar College
10440 Black Mountain Rd., San Diego
(858) 536–7800
www.miramar.sdccd.cc.ca.us

Opened in 1969 on 140 acres of undeveloped land, Miramar College initially concentrated on law enforcement and fire science training. It has since broadened its curriculum to include general education and computer and transportation technology sciences courses to better serve its student enrollment of more than 10,000. In the works are an athletic and aquatic complex as well as a science and technology center.

Southwestern Community College
900 Otay Lakes Rd., Chula Vista
(619) 421–6700
www.swc.cc.ca.us

The jewel of South Bay, Southwestern College was established in 1961, and construction was completed in 1964 on its 156-acre campus in eastern Chula Vista. Over the years the college has evolved into a facility that serves a diverse range of educational needs for its 17,000 students, including preparation for transfer, pursuit of two-year associate of arts degrees, courses for personal development and job enhancement, and acquisition of new occupational skills.

Specialized programs include hazardous material handling, emergency medical technology, and electronics. Because of its closeness to the U.S.-Mexico border, Southwestern provides special focus on the maquiladora industry (bi-national manufacturing enterprises), importing/exporting regulations, international law, and foreign trade zones.

Extended Studies Programs

All three public universities in San Diego County offer outstanding extended studies programs for individuals pursuing professional certificates, university course credits, professional development, or just general knowledge and information. The mission of extended studies programs is to fulfill the lifelong knowledge and skill-development needs of individual citizens, businesses, and the community at large. Classes are usually geared toward working adults and are held at flexible times during the day, evenings, and weekends.

California State University, San Marcos, Extended Studies
Foundation Classroom Building, CSUSM Campus, San Marcos
(760) 750–4020, (800) 500–9377
www.csusm.edu/es

Among the highlights of CSUSM's extended studies program are community education courses, workshops, and seminars. The American Language and Culture Institute here holds intensive classes for international students wishing to pursue an education at American colleges and universities. At the Open University, students can take regular university classes without going through the formal admission process. In addition, members of the community can take most of the regular college courses through the Open University program without matriculating, when space is available. Cost per unit is the same as for matriculated students.

San Diego State University College of Extended Studies
Gateway Center, 5250 Camponile Dr., San Diego
(619) 594–5152
www.ces.sdsu.edu

San Diego State's extended studies program specializes in professional and executive development and training for some of San Diego's leading organizations. It also offers certificate programs in which participants become recognized specialists in a variety of fields. Unique among extended studies programs is SDSU's program for retired adults.

Located in Rancho Bernardo's Continuing Education Center, this program offers not-for-credit classes such as "Rival Queens of England" and "Harry Potter: Biblical Echoes, Kabbalah and Mysticism." Although geared toward older people, anyone over 18 can attend. The American Language Institute offers intensive English-language courses, currently instructing some 2,500 students from 60 countries. Telecourses and Internet courses are also available.

San Diego State University's Aztec football games draw fans from all over San Diego County.
PHOTO: THORN VOLLENWEIDER

University of California, San Diego, Extended Studies and Public Programs
Extension Complex, UCSD Campus, La Jolla
(858) 534–3400
www.extension.ucsd.edu

In addition to the main extension complex on the UCSD campus, the extended studies program offers classes at several other locations in La Jolla and one in Rancho Bernardo to serve North County residents. Programs at UCSD Extension focus heavily on the telecommunications industry, information technologies, teacher education, applied healthcare, business management, and international languages. In addition to those specialized fields, a wide variety of general courses are available. Online courses are increasing in popularity too.

Health and Wellness

Emergencies happen. Even the best-planned vacation or business trip can be interrupted by a visit to a doctor or hospital emergency room.

When relocating, it's always a challenge to find the right medical assistance. In this chapter we'll provide some help in locating the services you may need. Keep in mind that this chapter is not comprehensive. There are nearly as many healthcare centers in San Diego as there are parks, beaches, and shopping centers. The ones we present are representative of the many options in this area:

According to a study conducted by the Northwestern National Life Insurance Company, San Diego receives high marks on access to healthcare. We have more than 75 healthcare facilities and hospitals in the county, and all our major hospitals have intensive care and critical care units. We also have six specifically designated trauma centers. That means when serious trouble hits, you can be at a trauma center in minutes. In fact, San Diego is one of the nation's leaders when it comes to trauma care. San Diego is unique in that its trauma centers work together with the County Division of Emergency Medical Services to create an efficient system. That system, which coordinates the efforts of physicians, hospital staff, and county health officials, was put together in 1984 and was immediately successful: The county trauma death rate dropped by 55 percent in the first year.

The San Diego Trauma Care System consists of the County Department of Health Services, the Division of Emergency Medical Services, other pre-hospital providers, and six trama centers: Children's Hospital and Health Center, Palomar Medical Center, two Scripps Hospitals, Sharp Memorial Hospital, and UCSD Medical Center.

To say you're in good hands in San Diego is a truism. Insiders take wellness seriously, and the county has small, sophisticated wellness centers and state-of-the-art hospitals. Scripps Hospitals are major research centers and provide some of the best, most innovative care available in the United States. The Scripps HealthCare System is a benchmark for care in the area. Sharp Hospitals are consistently rated number one for care and service in the state.

Our county also offers adequate mental health facilities, alternative medical care, walk-in facilities, and drug- and substance-abuse treatment centers. You'll want to check the Yellow Pages in the telephone directory under your specific need. The sections on home healthcare, mental health, physical therapists, nurses, and nursing registries as well as clinics and care for the disabled will help you find services. In this chapter we've included the major healthcare facilities, including information on mental-health, hospice programs, and alternative care. The hospitals are listed alphabetically by region. The sections on mental health, hospice, and alternative care are a countywide overview.

Hospitals

San Diego

Children's Hospital and Health Center
3020 Children's Way, Central San Diego
(858) 576–1700, (800) 788–9029
www.chsd.org

Opened in 1954, Children's Hospital's mission continues: to "restore, sustain and enhance the health and development potential of children." It is now the region's only designated pediatric trauma center and the only area hospital dedicated exclusively to caring for kids, birth through adolescence. The facility includes Pediatric Intensive Care and Neonatal Intensive Care. Roughly 125 trauma cases are seen per month.

From its 15 outpatient clinics to the hospital in Kearny Mesa, Children's Hospital serves all the communities in the area. It is also active in numerous outreach programs including health education, early intervention and counseling for drug and alcohol abuse, childhood immunizations, child-abuse prevention, and child safety issues. In partnership with other community-based organizations, like the Greater San Diego Chamber of Commerce and the Safe Kids Coalition, the hospital sponsors the Children's Center for Healthier Communities for Children, which links San Diego families with the educational tools and community services they need to raise healthy kids. Children's Hospital also works with local schools, businesses, government, and law enforcement agencies.

The elements of hope and beauty and life are represented in the Leichtag Family Healing Garden, which is designed to provide a blend of integrative wonder and peaceful respite. The garden is available to patients, children, parents, and staff.

Kaiser Permanente Medical Care Center
4647 Zion Ave., Central San Diego
(619) 528-5000, (619) 528-3290 (directions to county facilities)
www.kp.org

Centrally located in San Diego, this medical center serves those who belong to the Kaiser Permanente group. Here and at various other Kaiser facilities in the county, members can access outpatient treatments for anything from addictions to women's health problems. Most patients go to the Zion Avenue facility for any care that requires a stay in the hospital. There are about 400 beds in this large hospital.

Other Kaiser facilities have pharmacies on campus; check the white pages of the phonebook. The one at the Zion Avenue hospital, however, is open seven days a week. This hospital also features a well-staffed emergency facility where patients are treated for life-threatening and non-life-threatening needs.

Scripps Memorial Hospital, La Jolla
9888 Genesee Ave., La Jolla
(858) 457-4123
www.scrippshealth.org

Scripps Hospital has been in its present location since 1964 and now includes a huge array of high-tech medical options and services. Many believe that the Scripps Hospital healthcare system is the finest in the country. It's by far the most extensive health provider in the county. For instance, Kaiser Permanente subcontracts with Scripps Hospitals for various services, such as cardiac treatments and surgical procedures, rather than performing the procedures at their facility. Scripps is also part of the Trauma System. The recently established Scripps Polster Breast Care Center provides comprehensive healthcare and educational services for women. More than 1,700 employees and hundreds of volunteers help Scripps provide the best care. The 372 acute care licensed bed facility is located on a 43-acre campus in the heart of the Golden Triangle area of Central San Diego.

Sharp Cabrillo Hospital
3475 Kenyon St., Central San Diego
(619) 221-3400
www.sharp.com

Sharp Cabrillo serves Central San Diego with a full range of services. Opened in 1958, the 226-bed facility has more than 1,106 affiliated physicians. In 1996 the hospital linked its clinical services with Sharp Memorial. The facility includes a laser eye center, outpatient and inpatient rehabilitation, and a senior resource center.

Insiders' Tip
If you or a family member must go to the emergency room, call ahead to let them know you're coming and the reason for the visit. To find the one nearest you, check the Yellow Pages under "Hospitals."

Sharp Coronado Hospital
250 Prospect Pl., Coronado
(619) 522–3600
www.sharp.com

This 204-bed acute care hospital was established in 1942 and continues to serve the Coronado community. The hospital has four operating rooms, an intensive care unit, and a 24-hour emergency room. It provides obstetrical services, subacute and long-term care, and rehabilitation therapies.

The Motion Center, a state-of-the-art fitness facility, provides therapy and fitness programs for patients, outpatients, and the community. In addition to operating the Villa Coronado skilled nursing facility, the hospital also offers senior services such as skin cancer screening, mature drivers' courses, and health-education classes.

Sharp Mary Birch Hospital for Women
3003 Health Center Dr., San Diego
(858) 541–3400
www.sharp.com

Opened in 1992, this hospital provides services for women in all stages of life. In a single location and with more than 108 licensed acute beds and 61 neonatal intensive care beds, the hospital, which has its own pharmacy, focuses on complete care, including normal and high-risk obstetrics, laboratory, and diagnostic testing for women and infants, and in- and outpatient gynecological care. It is known for its Sharp Fertility Center and the services of the Sharp Perinatal Center, an ambulatory center for women experiencing high-risk pregnancy. The hospital continues to be recognized nationally as one of few similar facilities dedicated to women's care.

Sharp Memorial Hospital
7901 Frost St., Central San Diego
(858) 541–3400
www.sharp.com

With 464 beds, Sharp Memorial on Frost Street is Sharp HealthCare's largest hospital. As one of San Diego's trauma centers, it handles more than 1,000 trauma cases annually. Also a provider of cardiac care, each year it performs thousands of cardiac cauterizations, and hundreds of angioplasties and cardiac surgeries.

Opened in 1955 and staffed by more than 1,100 physicians, it is especially known for outstanding programs in cardiac care, trauma care, cancer treatment, pulmonary care services, rehabilitation, and multi-organ transplantation.

Memorial also offers extensive outpatient care and prevention programs. Its Sharp Senior Health Center offers health groups and services for seniors. Its Web site is an excellent source of healthcare tips.

North County Coastal

Scripps Memorial Hospital, Encinitas
354 Santa Fe Dr., Encinitas
(760) 753–6501
www.scrippshealth.org

This state-of-the-healing-arts hospital joined the Scripps Health system in 1978 with nearly 140 acute care licensed beds available. The hospital's staff includes over 700 trained professionals. You'll also find a caring team of volunteers. The facility provides 24-hour emergency services, intensive care, cancer/oncology, nuclear medicine, occupational medicine, orthopedics, neurology, and an ambulatory surgery center.

Tri-City Medical Center
4002 Vista Way, Oceanside
(760) 724–8411
www.tri-citymed.com

Three years in a row, Tri-City Medical Center in North County Coastal was ranked among the nation's top 100 hos-

Good Numbers to Keep Handy

For emergency or health-related questions and concerns, these phone numbers could help. Crisis lines are operated around the clock.

Throughout San Diego a call to 911 will bring police, ambulance, and paramedic services, most within five minutes.

Accessible San Diego (for travelers with disabilities)	(858) 279–0707
Airport Travelers Aid	(619) 231–7361
Alcohol Anonymous	(619) 265–8769
Border Patrol	(619) 216–4000
Customs, U.S.	(619) 557–5360
Dentist Referral	(800) 917–6453
Doctor Referral	(800) 628–2880,
	(800) 727–4777
Domestic Violence Services	(888) 272–1767
Harbor Police	(619) 686–6272
Highway Patrol (State Police)	(619) 220–5492
Mental Health Hot Line	(800) 660–7537
Poison Center	(619) 543–6000,
	(800) 876–4766
Suicide Hotline	(800) 479–3339
Womens' Resource Center, 24-hour help line	(760) 757–3500

pitals. This 400-bed facility at the Oceanside center includes an around-the-clock emergency room to provide on-the-spot care and dispense life-saving procedures. The hospital's location makes it especially convenient to freeway travelers.

North County Inland

Fallbrook Hospital
624 E. Elder St., Fallbrook
(760) 728–1191, (800) 647–6464
www.fallbrookhospital.com

The Fallbrook Hospital, a 146-bed health-care organization, now operated by Community Health Services, Inc., has served the people of Fallbrook, Bonsall, Rainbow, Deluz, and Temecula Valley since 1950. It provides both high-tech care and loving high-quality caring to North County Inland residents.

The staff calls it "a hospital without walls," since it offers home-health nursing, a hospice program, private home services, and a nurse-monitored walking regimen (part of their Cardiac Rehabilitation program). At the hospital proper, you'll find a women's center and services, a skilled nursing facility, and radiology, oncology, and emergency programs. You'll also find active volunteers who bring a pet-therapy program to patients.

Palomar Medical Center
555 E. Valley Pkwy., Escondido
(760) 739–3000
www.pphs.org

Located in the heart of Escondido this 328-bed acute-care hospital boasts North County's only trauma center. In addition, it has a 24-hour emergency department and the area's first state-of-the-art cardiac,

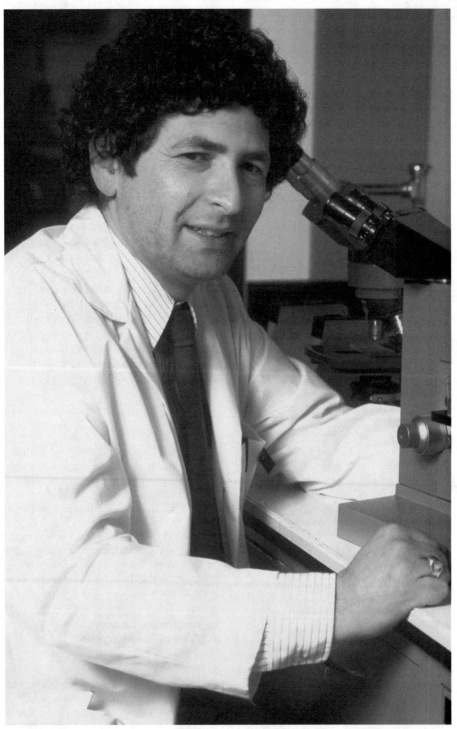

Some medical staff at the University of California at San Diego are involved in ongoing research programs. PHOTO: THORN VOLLENWEIDER

oncology, and general medical/surgical center. The Birth Center offers mothers high-tech medical care in private suites.

This facility is part of the Palomar/Pomerado Health System and shares certain services with Pomerado Hospital. Among them are radiology services, a hospice, and an industrial medicine program. Palomar Medical Center is also a designated Kaiser Permanente emergency center.

Pomerado Hospital
15615 Pomerado Rd., Poway
(858) 613–4000
www.pphs.org

A 107-bed acute care hospital located in the rapidly growing Poway area, this hospital has a round-the-clock emergency center. Along with the fine medical and surgical care, the hospital provides the kind of caring atmosphere not found in some mechanized hospital settings. Pomerado shares a healthcare board with Palomar Hospital; the two facilities share radiology and hospice services, healthcare boards, and an industrial medicine program. This facility is part of the Palomar/Pomerado Health System.

East County

Grossmont Hospital
5555 Grossmont Center Dr., La Mesa
(619) 465–0711
www.sharp.com

Affiliated with Sharp HealthCare, this is the largest and most comprehensive hospital in East County. Grossmont has been serving the community for more than 45 years and currently has more than 500 beds. In addition to acute-care services, it offers cardiac care, women's services, rehabilitation, orthopedics, cancer treatment, pediatric care, mental health services, a hospice program, and hyperbaric medicine. Also, the hospital has a comprehensive sleep-disorder program unique in the area.

The hospital operates the David and Donna Long Center for Cancer Treatment and Cardiovascular Diagnosis, which was the first cancer center in San Diego County. In addition, there's a Senior Resource Center and Women's Health Center on site.

South Bay

Paradise Valley Hospital
2400 E. 4th St., National City
(619) 470–4321
www.paradisevalleyhospital.org

Along with fine general medical care, Paradise Valley offers outstanding service in the areas of cardiology and oncology. Here you'll also find 24-hour emergency and walk-in services and the New Life Family Center. Prospective parents come here for childbirth classes and then to have their babies in a comfortable homelike atmosphere. There is also a nursery. The 237-bed campus also includes a Center for Health Promotion, which sponsors programs to quit smoking, and a walking club. The hospital also offers pediatric services and a transitional-care skilled nursing service.

Scripps Memorial Hospital, Chula Vista
435 H St., Chula Vista
(619) 691–7000
www.scrippshealth.com

Serving people throughout the South Bay, this is another in the string of Scripps Hospitals. Centrally located in Chula Vista on a 13.5-acre campus, a recent 40,000-square-foot expansion added a new 24-hour emergency department, intensive care unit, laboratory, and lobby. There are 173 acute care licensed beds and more than 700 employees. A Level II neonatal intensive care nursery provides short-stay intensive care for low birth-weight babies. The facility joined the Scripps Health System in 1986.

Sharp Chula Vista Medical Center
751 Medical Center Ct., Chula Vista
(619) 482–5800
www.sharp.com

Sharp Chula Vista Medical Center is a comprehensive medical center in South Bay. The hospital offers a variety of services including outpatient surgery, cardiac-care programs and facilities, a certified cancer treatment program, and a full scope of programs for women in all stages of life.

The hospital opened in 1944 and offers high-tech services. The 306-bed center provides 24-hour emergency care, and is equipped with a heliport. A women's and infant's pavilion provides obstetric and gynecological services.

Mental Health Services

Mental health facilities are often included in many of our county's hospitals. In this listing you'll find some that provide comprehensive care. Note that the entries are in a general countywide group rather than listed by geographical area as we've done previously.

One facility, Sharp Mesa Vista in San Diego, includes an involuntary detention center for the care of acutely-ill patients who are judged to be a danger to themselves, a danger to others, or are gravely disabled as a result of a psychiatric illness. Other facilities listed specialize in substance-abuse problems. Note, too, that you'll find emergency numbers and crisis hot lines in the Close-up found in this chapter.

In the phone book's Yellow Pages, you'll find a listing for "Mental Health." When calling, you'll want to ask about the specific services offered and whether your health-care coverage provides for those services.

Sharp Mesa Vista Hospital
7850 Vista Hill Ave., San Diego
(858) 694–8300
www.sharp.com

Sharp Mesa Vista is the largest freestanding psychiatric hospital in San Diego County. The 150-bed facility was opened in 1963 and became affiliated with Sharp Health-Care in 1998. It offers premier psychiatric services with a medical staff of nearly 300.

Treatment programs are designed for specific patient populations including adults, children, and chemical dependents. It shares services with the Navy's adult psychiatric inpatient program, its child and adolescent psychiatry program, and the department of obstetrics.

Immediate-Care Facilities

Walk-in clinics are found throughout the county, and they're an excellent resource for minor injuries and medical problems. Usually found in strip malls and the central areas of neighborhoods, these centers can treat non-life-threatening injuries and illnesses. They will treat anyone, but if you think you may want to use their services, check with your insurance carrier. If you have a life-threatening illness, some HMOs will pay for treatment at a hospital emergency room but not pick up the tab for walk-in clinic treatment. The great advantage with these clinics is that you usually don't have to deal with the long waits that are often a necessary part of hospital emergency room treatment.

We do recommend that you visit a hospital's emergency room if you're in

The climate encourages a healthy lifestyle for San Diegans. PHOTO: JAMES BLANK, COURTESY OF THE SAN DIEGO CONVENTION & VISITORS BUREAU

need of immediate serious medical care. Our hospital emergency rooms provide excellent, state-of-the-art medical services on a round-the-clock basis. There is usually a hospital within 20 minutes of any place you might be in San Diego. No matter what your immediate need, you'll be directed to the level of care you need, often within minutes of your arrival.

Keep in mind that if you do not have insurance or your carrier cannot be billed for the services you require, you'll be required to pay when services are rendered, regardless of whether you go to a hospital emergency room or a walk-in clinic. You'll find listings for walk-in clinics and immediate care facilities listed under "Clinics" in the phone book's Yellow Pages.

Alternative Care

Alternative healthcare isn't everyone's cup of java, yet for those who choose to seek health and wellness in some of the ancient traditions, the choices in San Diego are excellent.

Your best bet when seeking alternative medical care is to ask for referrals from people you know and trust. Remember, you can also call and ask questions about the practitioner's methods, background, and certification.

When making an appointment, discuss the expected treatment and costs in detail, along with possible side effects. It's fair, too, to ask for references.

Most alternative healthcare facilities offer a full "menu" of services. These might include acupuncture, shiatsu, and acupressure techniques. The services may help you quit smoking or provide drug-free solutions to pain or alternative therapies for women's health problems. The Yellow Pages give a complete listing of practioners in the areas of chiropractic, acupuncture, herbology, holistic medicine, Chinese herbal therapies, therapeutic massage, and other treatments. Swedish/circulatory massage, sports massage, and foot reflexology are additional health-wise options you may wish to explore.

The Chopra Center for Well Being
7630 Fay Ave., La Jolla
(858) 551–7788, (888) 424–6772
www.chopra.com

This wellness center was founded in 1995 by Deepak Chopra, M.D, one of the nation's most recognized specialists in alternative healing. The center offers single and multiday programs on all aspects of wellness, medical consultations including the principles of Ayurveda, and a day spa. Chopra has become a media celebrity, and his center attracts clients from throughout the world who want to improve the quality of their lives and their health.

Hospice Care in San Diego

Hospice care has long been a part of San Diego's healthcare picture. Most hospice organizations have in-home services, and several are available for residential stays for terminal illness. The program is open to those whose disease prognosis is measured in months, not years, and who are seeking comfort, not cure. Patients may elect to stay at home or at a licensed facility. Most hospices include medical directors, registered nurses, social workers, the clergy, home health aides, and volunteers. Hospice is a model program, one that never forgets that patients are people.

San Diego Hospice, 4311 Third Avenue, San Diego (619) 688–1600, is a county leader in hospice care and the oldest hospice in the area for persons facing a life-limiting illness.

In North County Coastal, you can contact **Hospice of North Coast,** 5421 Avenida Encinitas, Carlsbad, (760) 431–4100. This program reaches those who prefer care within their homes; however, the staff can coordinate licensed residential care, too.

In North County Inland, Hospice care can be coordinated by **Fallbrook Hospital District,** 624 East Elder Street, Fallbrook, (760) 728–1191, for both in-facility care and at-home hospice assistance.

Also in North County Inland is **Elizabeth Hospice,** 150 West Crest Street, Escondido, (760) 737–2050 or (800) 797–2050. The Elizabeth Hospice team is available to the general public and is a referral for physicians in the county.

Some of the county's hospitals also offer hospice programs and, in addition, there are private hospice plans. The hospitals that provide hospice care include Grossmont Hospital, Fallbrook Hospital, and Tri-City Medical Center.

Retirement

With San Diego's perfect weather, relaxed lifestyle, and great outdoor opportunities, most Insiders take leisure time as seriously as those who choose to retire from full-time employment. We believe that regardless of one's age, San Diego is easy on the body and soul.

Most who retire in San Diego immediately feel right at home here; after all, our seniors are a valued part of every neighborhood. Folks who call San Diego home typically stay here when retirement beckons. Others move from those places where the white stuff accumulates each winter—and we're not talking beach sand. The benefits include the weather and numerous outdoor activities. This is a watersport and golf paradise (just check out our chapters on these topics). The down side of retirement in San Diego is the cost of living. The county is one of the more expensive areas in the United States, yet our senior population continues to increase.

In a recent report it was determined that about 15 percent of San Diego's population is 55 or older. In some neighborhoods, such as Rancho Bernardo, San Marcos, and Rancho Santa Fe, that percentage is considerably higher. In nearly every community in our county there's a comfortable mix of families, singles, and retirees. See our chapter on Neighborhoods and Real Estate to get a feel for the area's communities.

Regardless of age, Insiders love to sit at the marinas and watch the sailboats, picnic at Balboa Park on lazy summer days, and hike or bike in the wilderness areas with cameras slung around our necks. The only real difference is that some of us have to get back to work on Monday and others go out to find more fun.

In this chapter we've identified some opportunities for the 55-plus group. We've included information on senior centers, senior programs, and organizations that offer senior advocacy. We've pointed out some senior publications and given information on how seniors can get any help they need. We have included a smattering of residential options that include multi-level care. These facilities abound in San Diego County, so we've tried to point out some ways you can compare the many choices before you sign on the dotted line.

Senior Living—Housing Options

Choosing the right retirement place can be tricky unless you do your homework. Location is, of course, a chief issue. If you prefer sea breezes to the inland area's dry summertime air, then a coastal home is best. However, as we've noted in the Neighborhoods and Real Estate chapter, it's more expensive to live near the ocean. If family, friends, church or synagogue, and community services are important, take these into consideration.

If your medical insurance plan limits the facilities you can use, you may want to

> **Insiders' Tip**
> In California, senior drivers may be able to get a discount from their car insurance company by participating in the Mature Driver Improvement Program. Ask your car insurance agent about this moneysaving program.

Retirees enjoy spending time at Old Town, exploring historical buildings and fascinating shops. PHOTO: BRETT SHOAF, COURTESY OF THE SAN DIEGO CONVENTION & VISITORS BUREAU

live within a reasonable distance of your doctors' offices and hospitals. Beyond those considerations, you're free to live at the beach or in the desert, mountains, or city and still call yourself a San Diegan.

If you're interested in living in a retirement community or facility in San Diego County, give yourself plenty of time to examine your options and visit the places that sound interesting. San Diego County has several planned neighborhoods designed for above-55 residents. Buying a home in one of these requires many of the same conditions you would consider when choosing a family home, but there are some specific needs you'll want to take into account. As you tour various senior communities, think about ease of access for today and later. Although it might be fun now to dash up a flight of stairs to your two-story condo with a view, five years from now those stairs may become tedious.

When buying a house, condo, town house, or apartment, consider how it might be outfitted for any special equipment needed later in life. Can a ramp be

built by the front steps? Will the bathroom be big enough should a wheelchair be required? Insiders constantly bemoan the amount of bureaucracy involved in acquiring building permits here. Ask about such issues before you buy—you'll save yourself considerable anguish.

If you're looking at a designated retirement home or community, there are other considerations. List the topics you'd like to discuss before visiting with the staff. Be sure to cover the options for ongoing medical care. Ask about activities, both at the facility and off grounds. If you are accustomed to urban living, find out if there are stores and libraries within walking distance and if there is a downtown business district nearby. If you prefer driving, make sure you have easy access to major freeways and shopping areas. Does the facility provide transportation to community programs, including church or synagogue services, along with trips to shopping malls and area attractions? If you'll be in a facility that provides meals, join the residents for a lunch or two. You'll want to know if you'll enjoy your dining companions. Ask for references, and try to talk with both residents and their families. Make a scheduled visit to talk with someone on the sales staff. Then stop by unannounced another time.

Some privately owned rental units throughout the county prefer to rent to seniors; some can help apartment dwellers arrange for rent reduction through HUD. To find senior rental housing, contact the senior centers in the communities you're considering.

As your selection of a retirement home or apartment narrows, think of security. Are you most comfortable in a gated community? Are you interested in having a security officer on site at night? Is on-site medical staff essential? Will you want a multilevel facility (one that provides multiple levels of care) so that skilled nursing care is available when needed? Or do you prefer a community that caters to those interested in independent living?

Finally, consider how much of your current furniture will reasonably fit into your new home. Some communities listed below have furniture rentals available should you want to see what it's like to live in the area before having all your furnishings shipped.

The questions are endless, but they can all be answered. The salespeople at communities are accustomed to answering all sorts of inquiries. Keep going back and asking more questions until you're satisfied that you'll be happy in your new home. The entries below will give you a feel for the types of retirement living options found in San Diego County. Take note: Many facilities have waiting lists.

Brookdale Place of San Marcos
1590 W. San Marcos Blvd., San Marcos
(760) 471–9904, (800) 864–0600
www.brookdaleplaceofsanmarcos.com

Beautifully landscaped grounds and the convenient North County Inland location draw seniors to this community. While most who live at Brookdale Place are independent, the facility also offers assisted-living options—meals, housekeeping, and transportation—as well as staff checks for medication and medical conditions. There

> ## Insiders' Tip
> If you're looking for skilled nursing, assisted living, and multi-stage housing (where one can arrange for full care), pick up an issue of *San Diego Eldercare Directory*, (619) 718-5245. The book lists everything from day care and respite care for adults to in-home solutions and transportation for the disabled.

is a heated swimming pool, spa, walking paths, rose gardens, and a putting green. Beach walks, shopping, cultural events, and movies are favorite outings for the active crowd who live here. The complex, with studio, one-bedroom, and two-bedroom apartments (some facing the courtyard and rose garden) is close to grocery stores and other everyday shopping. Small pets are always welcome. Rents start at about $2,200 a month; this includes housekeeping, activities, and two meals a day.

Chateau La Jolla Inn
233 Prospect St., La Jolla
(858) 459–4451, (800) 452–5652

Chateau La Jolla Inn offers carefree living with an elegant touch that's not grandiose, just comfortable and designed with ordinary people in mind. Choose from studios and one- and two-bedroom apartments and enjoy three meals daily.

This is an independent living complex; however, medical care can be provided on an as-needed basis for long-term residents. There's complimentary limo service, cultural activities, socials, computer room, classes, fitness programs, and loads of

cottages, you'll find apartment-style living in an eight-story tower, assisted-care, and skilled nursing. There's also an adult day care center on site.

The facility is located on 24 garden-like acres with paths and ponds and walkways and gardens. Living options range from a utility studio to a penthouse suite; prices go from about $1,200 a month and up. All of the units come with housekeeping services.

There are various meal options. You'll find 24-hour-a-day security and medical response, transportation, programs, and cultural events. And a friendly staff.

The White Sands of La Jolla
7450 Olivetas Ave., La Jolla
(858) 454-4201, (800) 892-7817
www.scphs.com

A Southern California Presbyterian Home, this exceptional community offers three levels of care, should you ever need the options. We're talking ocean close. This is understated luxury in the finest sense, with lovely rooms, some more pricey and spacious than others. Amenities include housekeeping, delicious meals, and transportation. At the end of Pearl Street in La Jolla, it is also blocks from excellent shops and restaurants. It's an interesting bit of trivia that more than 55 percent of the residents at White Sands have at least a master's degree.

Although the complex isn't new, it is constantly renovated and is extremely well maintained. There is a $1,000 fee to have your name placed on the waiting list. The entrance fee ranges from $37,000 to $1.5 million, depending on the apartment and whether you must have an ocean view. Monthly fees vary from $1,200 to $2,500 for a spacious apartment.

events. Shops, boutiques, and cafes are within blocks. About ½ mile north of Chateau La Jolla Inn are all the temptations of La Jolla. Monthly rents begin at about $2,000.

Fredericka Manor
183 3rd Ave., Chula Vista
(619) 422-9271, ext. 22

There's no entrance fee or deposit for this senior complex that really is one of the nicest you'll find. To say that the individual cottages are cozy doesn't do them justice—they are downright darling and inviting. The grounds are pristine and the people who choose to live at Fredericka Manor are typically active folks. In addition to the

Senior Organizations

You'll find a weekly listing of clubs, hobby groups, volunteer needs, and special activities in the *North County Times* and the *San Diego Union-Tribune*. Most organizations that help seniors always need dependable volunteers to deliver meals, visit shut-ins, and provide helping hands at activities. Volunteering is a great way to make new friends and learn new skills.

Alzheimer's Association
8514 Commerce Ave., San Diego
(858) 537–5040
www.sanalz.org

This organization provides and coordinates a countywide effort to give information and referrals. They also offer respite programs, support groups, and education programs. The organization coordinates the "Safe Return" system, a wanderers alert program.

City of San Diego Senior Citizen Services
202 C St., Downtown, Central San Diego
(619) 236–6905

The brochures, free newspapers, and general camaraderie of those working or visiting at this busy desk are all good reasons to visit. The office (actually a few cubicles and a counter) is located on the first floor in the city administration building along with several other agencies. Services include referrals for medical and psychological services and housing. This office also issues senior identification cards. Seniors who don't drive can use these cards to get discounts on bus fares, at restaurants, for accommodations, and for other services. Information is available on discounts for special events and tours

that help seniors get out to enjoy a play, for example, or a performance of the opera. The city of San Diego offers a variety of senior services that you can access through this office. There are liaisons with the city attorney's office, environmental services, the libraries, and the mayor's office. It's a good idea to become familiar with their programs no matter where you live. Stop by to pick up a copy of their free handbook.

Jewish Family Service Senior Services
3715 6th Ave., San Diego
(619) 291–0473
www.jewishfamilyservicesd.org

This office is open to all seniors and services are available on a sliding scale. Licensed clinical social workers give free consultations and provide information and recommendations on physical and mental-health issues. You'll find people willing to help with issues of housing, managed care, adult day care, and counseling. There is even a hot meal delivery service available.

Meals-On-Wheels
Administration
(619) 260–6110, (800) 573–6467
www.meals-on-wheels.org
Central San Diego
(619) 225–9510
North County
(760) 736–9900
East County
(619) 447–8782
South Bay
(619) 420–2782

This agency provides two home-delivered meals per day to seniors who are ill or disabled, for a suggested fee based on a sliding scale. The association accommodates special and restricted diet choices, too. Dependable volunteers are always needed.

National Association of Hispanic Elderly
22 W. 35th St., Ste. 127, National City
(619) 425–3734

This organization helps Hispanic seniors with social and economic concerns and provides programs to help with temporary employment and training.

Coronado is home to several retired Navy admirals and their families. PHOTO: JAMES BLANK, COURTESY OF THE SAN DIEGO CONVENTION & VISITORS BUREAU

Senior Centers

Most communities throughout the county have senior centers. The easiest way to find them is by calling each city's main phone number or its parks and recreation office. Senior centers and activities geared to the senior community are also available at religious centers. Many churches provide meal service, counseling, support groups, and housing referrals. Hospitals take an active part in helping seniors with a variety of programs, from those addressing substance and elder abuse to those offering respite and hospice assistance. Be sure to look at the Health and Wellness chapter for some tips to finding medical and wellness programs.

It's always best to call and find out what your neighborhood's center has available, as things do change. Most serve a well-balanced hot lunch one or more days a week for a suggested donation of about $2.00. A number of the centers can arrange for delivery of hot mid-day meals to the homebound. Many of the centers have bilingual staff members who serve as trans-lators for elderly Spanish-speakers needing assistance with medical care or housing .

The programs at the centers may include exercise and stretch classes, painting and craft activities, language arts and writing, bridge and poker, dance classes and performances, and discussions of current events. Most of the centers offer tax and financial information, senior advocacy programs, and medical checkups. Some centers have social workers on staff and weekly support groups that deal with many issues, from grief management to dealing with stress. Most of the services are free; however, it's always wise to ask.

A growing number of centers have classes coordinated with the YMCA program and local colleges. For instance, Palomar Family YMCA, 1050 North Broadway Street, Escondido, (760) 745–7490, holds senior fitness classes including low-impact aerobics, senior water aerobics, strength training. Fallbrook Senior Citizen Centers, 399 Heald Lane, Fallbrook, (760) 723–9282, offers art classes through Palomar College.

Senior Resources

AARP
(800) 523–5800

Adult Protective Services, Inc
9335 Hazard Way, San Diego 92123
(800) 510–2020

A.G.E.—Jewish Family Services Senior
Services
2930 Copley Ave., San Diego 92116
(619) 563–5232

Alpine Community Center
1830 Alpine Blvd., Alpine 91901
(619) 445–7330

Alpine View Lodge
973 Arnold Way, Alpine 91901
(619) 445–5291

Beech Street Community Center
1551 Fourth Ave., San Diego 92101
(619) 232–1181

Borrego Springs Senior Center
580 Circle J Dr., Borrego 92004
(760) 767–3116

Broadway Sr. Community Center
928 Broadway, San Diego 92101
(619) 232–2919

Casa De Servicios
1188 Beyer Way, San Diego 92154
(619) 423–1902

Casa Palmera Care Center
14750 El Camino Real, Del Mar 92014
(858) 481–4411

Centro Hispano Senior Center
4186 42nd St., San Diego 92105
(619) 283–2111

Clairemont Friendship Senior Center
4425 Bannock St., San Diego 92117
(858) 483–5100

College Avenue Senior Center
4855 College, San Diego 92115
(619) 583–3300

Community Care For Adults
602 Civic Center Dr., Oceanside 92054
(760) 433–9942

Coronado Senior Center
1019 Seventh St., Coronado 92118
(619) 435–2616

Escondido Joslyn Senior Center
210 E. Park Ave., Escondido 92025
(760) 839–4688

Flames, The
4538 35th St., San Diego 92116
(619) 281–1384

Florence Riford Senior Center
6811 La Jolla Blvd., La Jolla 92037
(858) 459–0831

George G. Glenner Alzheimer's Family
Centers, Inc.
3702 Fourth Ave., San Diego 92103
(619) 543–4704

Golden Hill Senior Center
2600 Golf Course Dr., San Diego 92102
(619) 235–1138

Grossmont Hospital Senior Resource Center
9000 Wakarusa St., La Mesa 91942
(619) 644–4214

Harmony Grove Elderly Care
2364 Avenida Del Diablo, Escondido 92029
(760) 741–3140

Hope Adult Day Health Care Center
11239 Camino Ruiz, San Diego 92126
(858) 653–5916

Imperial Beach Senior Center
1075 Eighth St., Imperial Beach 91932
(619) 424–7077

Jewish Family Service
3715 Sixth Ave., San Diego 92103
(619) 291–0473

La Jolla Recreation Center
615 Prospect, La Jolla 92037
(858) 552–1658

Lakeside Senior Center
9841 Vine St., Lakeside 92040
(619) 443–9176

La Mesa Senior Adult Center
8450 La Mesa Blvd., La Mesa 91941
(619) 464–0505

Lemon Grove Senior Center
8235 Mt. Vernon St., Lemon Grove 91945
(619) 460–0430

Linda Vista Sr. Community Center
2202 Comstock St., San Diego 92111
(858) 278–0771

Memorial Senior Center
610 S. 30th St., San Diego 92113
(619) 235–1141

Mesa Valley Grove Senior Day Program
8235 Mt. Vernon St., Lemon Grove 91945
(619) 460–0430

Mid-City Adult Day Healthcare Center
4077 Fairmount Ave., San Diego 92105
(619) 584–0250

Mira Mesa Senior Center
8460 Mira Mesa Blvd., San Diego 92126
(858) 578–7325

Mount Soledad Care Facility
2189 Crownhill Rd., San Diego 92109
(858) 274–2461

Neighborhood House Senior Center
841 S. 41st St., Central San Diego 92113
(619) 263–2108

Norman Park Senior Center
270 F St., Chula Vista 91910
(619) 691–5086

North County Adult Day Health Center
651 Eucalyptus Ave., Vista 92084
(760) 758–2210

North Park Recreation Center
2719 Howard Ave., San Diego 92104
(619) 235–1161

Ocean Beach Recreation Center
4726 Santa Monica Ave., San Diego 92107
(619) 531–1527

Pacific Beach Recreation Center
1405 Diamond St., San Diego 92109
(858) 581–9927

Paradise Hills Seniors Home
5907 Bataan Cr., San Diego 92139
(619) 470–8519

Paradise Senior Center
1880 Logan Ave., San Diego 92113
(619) 235–1148

Parkside Special Care Center
444 W. Lexington, El Cajon 92020
(619) 442–7744

Pleasant Care Nursing and Rehabilitation
Center of San Diego
2828 Meadowlark Dr., San Diego 92123
(858) 277–6460

Ramona Adult Day Care Center
2138-A San Vincente Rd., Ramona 92065
(760) 789–1553

Ramona Senior Center
434 Aqua Ln., Ramona 92065
(760) 789–0440

Rancho Bernardo Jewish Senior Center
16934 Chabad Way, Poway 92064
(858) 674–1123

Rancho Bernardo Joslyn Senior Center
18402 W. Bernardo Dr., San Diego 92127
(858) 487–9324

Rivera's Care Home
1611 Parkland Way, San Diego 92114
(619) 267–0983

Senior citizens can stay physically fit and young at heart playing tennis. PHOTO: THORN VOLLENWEIDER

Samahan Senior Center
2926 Market St., San Diego 92102
(619) 234-1360

Sandiesen Senior Center
2221 Morley Field Dr., San Diego 92104
(619) 692-4919

San Marcos Joslyn Senior Center
111 W. Richmar Ave., San Marcos 92069
(760) 744-5535

San Ysidro Senior Center
125 E. Park, San Ysidro 92073
(619) 428-9214

Senior Community Centers of San Diego
1535 Third Ave., San Diego 92101
(619) 235-4522

Senior Community Centers of San Diego
928 Broadway, San Diego 92101
(619) 235-6538

Sharp Cabrillo Senior Resource Center
3475 Kenyon St., San Diego 92110
(619) 221-3779

Sharp Chula Vista Senior Resource Center
751 Medical Center Ct., Chula Vista 91911
(619) 482-5802

Solana Beach Senior Center
120 Stevens Ave., Solana Beach 92075
(858) 755-9735

South Crest Senior Center
4149 Newton Ave., San Diego 92113
(619) 527-3413

Spring Valley Community Center
8735 Jamacha Blvd., Spring Valley 91977
(619) 460-0430

St. Jude's Senior Center
3751 Boston Ave., San Diego 92113
(619) 264-4771

Suncrest Residential Senior Care
1484 Gibson Highlands, El Cajon 92021
(619) 441-9961

Wells Park Community Center
1153 E. Madison Ave., El Cajon 92020
(619) 441-1680

Wesley Palms Retirement Community
2404 Loring St., San Diego 92109
(858) 274-4110

Senior citizens enjoy a day in Balboa Park playing a rousing game of lawn bowling. PHOTO: COURTESY OF SAN DIEGO CONVENTION AND VISITORS BUREAU

There's no need to limit your activities to senior centers, however. Most community recreation centers offer exercise and arts and crafts classes that are open to students of all ages. San Diego's community colleges and universities have significant numbers of students over age 50. Sign up for the class schedules and ponder all those things you always wanted to learn. Enjoy your endless opportunities.

Senior Publications

San Diego Eldercare Directory
2375 Northside Dr., #300, San Diego
(619) 718–5245

An annual publication listing senior services from healthcare to legal advice along with living options such as assisted care and skilled nursing services. It's available at San Diego Gas and Electric offices throughout the county, Sharp Health-Care System, and various other locations. Cost is $10.

New Lifestyles
414 North Central Expressway, Ste. 100,
Dallas, TX 75204
(800) 869–9549
www.newlifestyles.com

This national publisher puts out an excellent small magazine with information on retirement communities, assisted living facilities, home care agencies, and nearly every type of facility you might require. The comprehensive listings will give you a great overview of what's available throughout the county.

Media

Newspapers
Magazines
Special-Interest Publications
Television
Radio

Once San Diego was established as a full-fledged city, it wasn't long before journalists began surfacing, eager to report the daily news. Even though the city has only one major newspaper that covers the entire county, there's plenty of competition from community newspapers. More than 50 community and neighborhood newspapers are published, and although some come and go, many have become old-timers in their respective neighborhoods.

Radio runs the gamut from adult contemporary to news/talk, and, of course, all three established television networks are represented, as well as Fox and WB. The city has a thriving film industry and the San Diego Film Commission coordinates the various production companies wanting to take advantage of San Diego as a filming site. Among the feature-length movies shot in San Diego are *Top Gun*, *The Lost World*, *Mr. Wrong*, *Traffic*, and *Almost Famous*. A couple of television series have been filmed here too, including the popular series *Silk Stalkings*.

The following listings should give you a good idea of what's available to read, watch, and listen to locally.

Newspapers

Newspapers listed here are the major dailies and weeklies, and those that cover a broad area of the county. For news and information specific to a neighborhood or community, look for weekly or bi-weekly publications that are easily found in neighborhood newsstands, coffeehouses, convenience stores, and restaurants.

Daily

North County Times
207 E. Pennsylvania Ave., Escondido
(760) 745–6611
www.nctimes.com

North County's only full-sized daily newspaper has nine zoned editions covering Escondido, San Marcos, Valley Center, Ramona, Fallbrook, Bonsall, Poway, Rancho Bernardo, Oceanside, Carlsbad, Vista, Encinitas, Cardiff, and Solana Beach. It features international, national, and local news and sports. Comparable to the *San Diego Union-Tribune*, the paper focuses on local news and editorials that pertain to North County. Its expanded Sunday edition features special sections on lifestyle, entertainment, and real estate. The paper has a circulation of 82,000.

The *San Diego Union-Tribune*
350 Camino de la Reina, San Diego
(619) 291–3131, (800) 244–6397
www.uniontribune.com

Founded in 1868 by William Jeff Gatewood, the *San Diego Union-Tribune* is the oldest business in San Diego County and the second-oldest newspaper in Southern

Insiders' Tip

Looking for a job? How about an apartment, or even a used surfboard? Your best bet is the Sunday edition of the *San Diego Union-Tribune* in its expanded classifieds section.

A film crew sets up for a street scene in the Gaslamp Quarter. PHOTO: CECE CANTON

California. It began as a weekly and has been a daily since 1871. The *San Diego Union-Tribune* is the end product of a 1992 merger of *The San Diego Union* and *The Evening Tribune,* which was founded as an afternoon newspaper in 1895.

John D. Spreckels, a San Diego founding father, took over as publisher of *The San Diego Union* in 1890 and subsequently founded *The Evening Tribune.* He remained publisher until 1926, and after his death the two newspapers were purchased by Colonel Ira C. Copley. The Copley family has remained at the helm since 1947, with David C. Copley as the newspaper's current publisher.

The original building occupied by the newspaper still stands in Old Town State Historic Park. Today the *Union-Tribune* is published from an editorial and administrative building and printing plant in Mission Valley, not far from its original location in Old Town.

Five separate editions are published daily: San Diego City, North County Coastal, North County Inland, East County, and South County. The *Union-Tribune* also publishes *Enlace,* a free weekly newspaper in Spanish.

Thursday editions have the tabloid "Night and Day" section, which has a wealth of information about night life, concerts, special events, performing arts, movies, restaurants, and leisure activities throughout San Diego County.

Sunday's edition features special sections on travel, the arts, and homes, and has many feature-length articles to help pass the time on a lazy Sunday morning. Circulation on weekdays is 380,500; Sunday's is 455,660. Circulation for *Enlace* is 45,000.

Almost Daily

San Diego Daily Transcript
2131 3rd Ave., San Diego
(619) 232-4381
www.sddt.com

A broadsheet newspaper, the *Transcript* is published Monday through Friday and covers business, financial, legal, construction, real estate, and government news

A scene from a movie is being filmed on location in downtown San Diego. PHOTO: CECE CANTON

and includes legal notices, as well. The *Transcript* is the only publication to provide listings of every publicly traded corporation based in San Diego. Its circulation is 15,000. The *Transcript* became the first online newspaper in San Diego in 1994.

Weekly and Semiweekly

Beach and Bay Press
4645 Cass St., San Diego
(858) 270-3103
www.sdnews.com

This community news group publishes four weekly newspapers that cover issues of interest to residents of coastal San Diego from Ocean Beach north to La Jolla. The *Beach and Bay Press,* the *Peninsula Beacon,* the *La Jolla Village News* and the *Golden Triangle News* together reach some 75,000 readers. Each paper has occasional features on local personalities and brings readers up to date on political issues affecting their neighborhood. Opinion polls are a common feature, too, giving readers the chance to have their voices heard.

East County Californian
2144 Alpine Blvd, Alpine
(619) 445-3288

Published twice weekly, the *East County Californian* reports news affecting the East County cities of El Cajon, La Mesa, Spring Valley, Lemon Grove, Santee, Lakeside, Rancho San Diego, Jamul, Alpine, and the surrounding communities. It also covers issues dealt with by the various East County city councils and has a comprehensive editorial and commentary section.

La Jolla Light
565 Pearl St., La Jolla
(858) 459-4201

The *La Jolla Light* and its sister newspapers, the *University City Light,* and the *Clairemont Light,* are published weekly. Together these community newspapers cover the areas of La Jolla, Torrey Pines, the Golden Triangle, and Clairemont, and reach 54,000 readers. The *La Jolla Light* and the *University City Light* focus on "town and gown" news about the interaction between UCSD and the residents of La Jolla. With less of an educational slant and more of a community focus, the *Clairemont Light* has stories about residents and neighborhood activities in Clairemont.

Pomerado Newspapers
13247 Poway Rd., Poway
(858) 748–2311
Published weekly on Thursday, the Pomerado Newspapers include the *Poway News Chieftan,* the *Corridor News,* and the *Rancho Bernardo News Journal.* In addition to the communities of Poway and Rancho Bernardo, coverage includes Rancho Peñasquitos, Carmel Mountain Ranch, Sabre Springs, and Scripps Ranch. Besides neighborhood news, the papers feature profiles of community leaders and in-depth features on issues affecting these North County cities, such as local politics and real estate development. Each week 42,000 readers are reached.

San Diego Business Journal
4909 Murphy Canyon Rd.,
Ste. 200, San Diego
(858) 277–6359
cbjonline.com
The *Business Journal* provides weekly news and commentary on San Diego County businesses and industries to 18,500 readers. Each issue has news, features, and columns about San Diego's business environment. Its national award-winning weekly lists of businesses, agencies, and services and its annual *Book of Lists* keep readers in touch with San Diego's growing industries. It is part of a national chain of business journals in major cities. The *Business Journal* can be purchased at newsstands throughout the city of San Diego and is also available by subscription.

Magazines

San Diego Home/Garden Lifestyles
4577 Viewridge Ave., San Diego
(858) 571–1818
Local architecture, interior design, and gardening are the features of this monthly magazine. It also includes articles on remodeling, art, local personalities, and San Diego issues. The monthly

guide to arts, culture, and entertainment is an excellent source for information about what's happening in San Diego. The magazine's circulation is 45,000.

San Diego Magazine
1450 Front St., San Diego
(619) 230–9292
www.sandiego-online.com
The first city magazine in the country, *San Diego Magazine* celebrated its 50th anniversary in 1998. This glossy monthly contains a selection of articles about San Diego, past and present, and its notable political, social, and business leaders. The magazine also has an extensive thumbnail-review section on arts, entertainment, and restaurants. It has a circulation of over 53,000 and can be purchased at newsstands, supermarkets, and bookstores or by subscription.

San Diego Metropolitan Magazine
1250 6th Ave., Ste. 1200, San Diego
(619) 233–4060
www.sandiegometro.com
San Diego Metropolitan is a monthly newsprint magazine that focuses on the downtown community. Its emphasis is on downtown businesses, arts, retail, and

Insiders' Tip
Most San Diego publications and other media now have Web sites that include the contents of the latest issue, along with expanded sections on entertainment, dining, and local events. In addition to the sites in each listing, check out the *Union-Tribune's,* www.signonsandiego.com, and Cox Cable's, www.sdinsider.com.

human-interest items. Downtown redevelopment, urban real estate, and political happenings are subjects that are frequently covered, and at least one local business leader is profiled in depth each month. Monthly columns cover legal issues, money matters, and the business of sports. It's distributed free to 50,000 readers.

Special-Interest Publications

ComputorEdge
3655 Ruffin Rd., San Diego
(858) 573–0315

San Diego's free computer magazine is published weekly, and 85,000 copies are distributed to newsstands, computer stores, and libraries. It contains feature articles and columns with information on software and hardware for the computer buff. For true aficionados, *ComputorEdge* has a calendar of events to keep computer-heads entertained and up to date, as well as a listing of local Web sites and user group lists. The magazine also has a classifieds section advertising computers and accessories for sale.

Gay & Lesbian Times
3911 Normal St., San Diego
(619) 299–6397

With a circulation of 15,750, the *Gay & Lesbian Times* is San Diego's largest publication specifically for the gay community. Heavy on guest commentaries, the newspaper also has news and articles of interest to gays and lesbians. *The Gay & Lesbian Times* extensive arts and entertainment section covers nightlife that often is neglected in mainstream publications. It's most easily found in libraries, bookstores, and coffeehouses in the Hillcrest and Downtown areas.

La Prensa San Diego
1950 5th Ave., San Diego
(619) 231–2873

Bilingual *La Prensa* is published weekly and distributed throughout San Diego County, from San Ysidro in the South Bay to Oceanside in North County and east to El Cajon. It's available free of charge at libraries, government buildings, coffeehouses, and convenience stores throughout San Diego County. In publication since 1976, *La Prensa* views the news and events through a Hispanic/Chicano perspective. A continuing feature is its "Noticias de Mexico" column, which is a collection of wire-service news items from Mexico. The newspaper reaches 30,000 readers.

San Diego Family Magazine
1475 6th Ave., San Diego
(619) 685–6970

Published monthly, this free magazine is full of articles, columns, advice, and helpful hints to benefit families. Pick up a copy at libraries, drug stores, and convenience stores all over the county. Monthly features include columns titled "Family Science," "Health Tips," "Classes," and "Resources," as well as in-depth articles on parenting, camps, teen issues, and safety. It includes a comprehensive directory of private schools as well as a listing of classes for youngsters. The magazine is distributed to 120,000 readers.

San Diego Parent
3160 Camino del Rio S., Ste. 313,
San Diego
(619) 624–2770

San Diego Parent is a monthly magazine distributed free to 80,000 readers. It features monthly columns on parenting classes, health notes, and family fun, as well as feature-length articles on topics such as vacation options, summer camps, and exercising. Each issue also includes a calendar of events for parents and kids. It's usually located right next to *San Diego Family Magazine* in libraries, drug stores, and convenience stores.

The San Diego Reader
1703 India St., San Diego
(619) 235–3000

This free weekly tabloid is noted for its comprehensive entertainment section. The section gives detailed information and reviews on the arts, dining, sports, and things to do around San Diego. Each issue also contains feature articles and columns about San Diego life and politics. *The Reader* is distributed to locations throughout San Diego County and reaches 156,000 readers.

San Diego Voice and Viewpoint
1729 N. Euclid Ave., San Diego
(619) 266–2233

Distributed weekly throughout San Diego County, the *Voice and Viewpoint* is a publication geared toward the local African-American community. The newspaper prints local and national news, editorial, and commentary, and it recognizes African-Americans of distinction in special features. It includes a weekly calendar of events, and its circulation is 18,900. The newspaper can be purchased at newsstands throughout the county.

SLAMM (San Diego's Music Magazine)
3530 Camino Del Rio South, Ste. 105, San Diego
(619) 281–7526 x109

A free bi-weekly tabloid, *SLAMM* features articles and reviews on arts, film, theater, entertainment, and, specifically, the local music scene. Repeating columns are "Sordid Tales," "Ms. Beak," and irreverent music and movie reviews. Each issue also has a local club directory and calendar of events for theaters and museums. It has a circulation of 36,000. Pick up a copy at over 700 locations throughout the county, including libraries, coffeehouses, music stores, and restaurants.

Television

Like most other cities, local television stations have beloved anchor people and quirky personalities whose goal is to inform and entertain. With a good antenna the major network stations as well as Fox and the WB can be pulled in without cable. But reception is iffy, and most San Diegans subscribe to cable. The three network affiliates, Channels 8, 10, and 39, and local Channels 6 and 51 all have news broadcasts throughout the day.

Insiders' Tip

Check out *San Diego Magazine*'s January issue for its annual "50 San Diegans to Watch" article. It features profiles of the city's movers and shakers and up-and-coming leaders.

Local TV Stations and their Network Affiliates

KFMB Channel 8 (CBS)
News at 5:30 A.M., 4:00, 5:00, 6:30, and 11:00 P.M.

KGTV Channel 10 (ABC)
News at 5:30 A.M., noon, 4:00, 5:00, 6:00, and 11:00 P.M.

KNSD Channels 7 and 39 (NBC)
News at 5:30 A.M., 4:00, 5:00, 6:00, and 11:00 P.M.

KPBS Channel 15 (Public TV)

KSWB Channel 69 (WB)

KUSI Channel 51 (Independent)
News at 5:30 A.M., 7:00, and 10:00 P.M.

XETV Channel 6 (Fox)
News at 10:00 P.M.

XEWT Channel 12 (TVA-Tijuana)

Cable Providers

Three main cable companies cover the majority of San Diego County. For the most part, each has exclusive rights to its area, and the area is divided roughly as follows: south of Interstate 8 and part of North County is Cox Communication's

Reporters frequently cover news of construction and development as new architectural landmarks change the San Diego skyline. PHOTO: JAMES BLANK, COURTESY OF THE SAN DIEGO CONVENTION & VISITORS BUREAU

territory, north of I-8 and Coronado belong to Time Warner Cable TV. Confused? Obviously there's quite a bit of overlap, so if you have any doubt about which cable company controls your area, call any one of them. They'll be able to help you figure it out. Basic cable service can be purchased for around $15 per month, which will tune you in to the network stations as well as a few local independents. But if you wish to take advantage of the more than 200 premium and special-interest channels available in San Diego, expanded packages can be added, including digital cable.

Cox Communications (San Diego)
1535 Euclid Ave., San Diego
(619) 262–1122

Area Covered: Alpine, Santee, Lemon Grove, Jamul, Rancho San Diego, National City, Imperial Beach, Chula Vista, Poway, and portions of San Diego, La Mesa, Del Cerro, El Cajon, and Pine Valley.

Cox Communications (North County)
520 W. Valley Pky., Escondido
(760) 599–6060

Area Covered: Escondido, San Marcos, Ramona, Leucadia, some of Cardiff, Vista, Oceanside, Camp Pendleton, Solana Beach, Encinitas, Olivenhain, Fairbanks Ranch, and Rancho Santa Fe.

Time Warner Cable
8949 Ware Ct., San Diego
(858) 695–3220

Area Covered: Del Mar, La Jolla, Poway, Rancho Santa Fe, Mission Valley, Mission Beach, Pacific Beach, Bay Park, Linda Vista, Clairemont, University City, Serra Mesa, Tierrasanta, Mira Mesa, Rancho Bernardo, Rancho Peñasquitos, Carmel Valley, Lake San Marcos, Carlsbad, Fallbrook, Del Mar, parts of San Marcos, Vista, Encinitas, Solana Beach, and Scripps Ranch.

Radio

Whatever your favorite format, you're likely to find it somewhere on the dial. Some stations come in clear in some parts of the county and not so clear in others. If a station's signal originates in North County, for example, it'll be clear and strong in the northern regions, somewhat weaker in San Diego and probably nonexistent in the South Bay. Don't give up, though. The old boom box has plenty of entertainment to please every taste.

Adult Contemporary

92.5 FM XHRM
93.3 FM KHTS
96.5 FM KYXY
100.7 FM KFMB
102.1 FM KXST
102.9 FM KLQV

Insiders' Tip

The best lowdown on the club scene is found in *The San Diego Reader.* This weekly will help you decide which of San Diego's numerous clubs is the most happening.

Alternative

550 AM KCR
1320 AM KKSM
91.1 FM XTRA
92.1 FM KFSD

Children

1240 AM KSON (Radio Disney)

Christian

910 AM KECR
1210 AM KPRZ
100.1 FM KBNN
107.9 FM KWVE

Classic Rock

101.5 FM KGB

Classical

540 AM XBACH
92.1 FM KFSD

Country

97.3 FM KSON
99.3 FM XHCR

Jazz

88.3 FM KSDS
98.1 FM KIFM

Oldies

1360 AM KPOP
94.1 FM KJQY
94.9 FM KBZT
95.7 FM KJQY
103.7 FM KPLN

Rock & Roll

105.3 FM KIOZ
107.1 FM KLYY

Spanish

800 AM XEMM (Spanish Variety)
860 AM XEMO (Banda Music)
1040 AM KURS (Regional Music)

1420 AM XEXX (Spanish News/Sports)
1470 AM XERCN (Spanish News/Talk/Sports)
1550 AM XEBG (News/Talk/Sports in Spanish)
88.7 FM XHITT (Tijuana Public Radio)
91.7 FM XGLX (English/Spanish Contemporary)
97.7 FM XTIM (Radio Amor)
98.9 FM XMOR (Rock Hits in Spanish)
102.5 FM XHUAN (Ranchera)
104.5 FM XLTN (Spanish Contemporary)
106.5 FM KLNV (Ranchera/Banda)
107.3 FM XHFG (Spanish Contemporary)

Talk

600 AM KOGO (Talk/News/Rush Limbaugh/Padres Baseball)
690 AM XTRA (All Sports)
760 AM KFMB (Talk/News)
1000 AM KCEO (Talk/News)
1130 AM KSDO (Talk/News/Sports)
1170 AM KCBQ (Talk/Entertainment)
89.5 FM KPBS (National Public Radio)

Worship

While driving around our easygoing communities from Pacific Beach and Alpine to Bonita and Fallbrook it might seem that Insiders are too laid back to care about spiritual beliefs and values. If you've already read the Attractions, Shopping, and Balboa Park chapters you might be asking yourself: "How do they have time when there's so much to do?"

The answers are simple: Yes, we care and yes, we make time.

San Diegans are diverse, and run the gamut from conservative and orthodox to outrageous and unconventional. So you won't be surprised to learn that our places of worship also reflect a variety of spiritual preferences.

Whether we attend a nontraditional service or one that's steeped in ancient customs, religious beliefs are alive and active throughout the county.

But while our beliefs are both strong and diverse, we all still live the San Diego lifestyle, and so we hope you won't be shocked to learn that even at the most conservative services, the faithful may walk in with bare knees and toes. People in San Diego are comfortable in their breezy wardrobes as they mix with congregation members who might prefer to be dressed to the nines.

Services

The choices of religious services available throughout the county are extensive. If you're here on a vacation, finding a worship center that's right for you might be as easy as looking in the Yellow Pages of your hotel's phone book. Someone on the staff at the front desk should be able to tell you which of the listings are closest. Many visitors, regardless of their faith, attend mass at one of our missions. The services are a way to touch San Diego's rich history and feel the past of our diverse community. (Be sure to read over our History chapter for more about religion's role in our past.)

San Diego County's churches are far flung; most will require a drive to get there. The good news is that if you're attending a Sunday morning service, the freeway traffic will usually be light. But as always, allow extra time for unplanned gridlock.

The Friday edition of the *San Diego Union-Tribune* has a directory of religious services which includes church addresses, phone numbers, and times of services. However, not every San Diego house of worship is included. So think of this resource as a starting point. For instance if you're visiting Bonsall and you want to find a Roman Catholic service close to this North County Inland city, you could call one of the Roman Catholic churches listed in the telephone directory and ask for the name of the Catholic church nearest you.

If you're moving to San Diego, you may decide on specific neighborhoods or parts of our county that will be close to

Insiders' Tip
Most religious services welcome visitors dressed in California casual; i.e., it's not necessary to wear suits or dresses and high heels. If you're in doubt, call first. On any first visit, slacks and a blazer are always appropriate.

the house of worship of your choice. Some congregations have cultural events and groups for teens, singles, or seniors; others are focused around the young family unit, with everything from preschool programs and after-school programs to family campouts and church camps. As throughout the country, a number of churches in our region specifically support the gay and lesbian community.

Those courting a new church might check out the San Diego Reader's "Sheep and Goats" column, a weekly review of area churches. The column lists data such as congregation size and type of dress parishioners prefer, rates the sermon (content and delivery) and the after-service refreshments, and gives a lengthy commentary. Opinionated? Yes. But also informative, with plenty of direct quotes from the minister and congregation.

As you visit and consider where you'll put down your spiritual roots, remember it's okay to call and ask about the philosophies being shared or the programs in which the religious group is involved. If singles groups or senior day care are important, see if your needs are met as you connect with the congregation.

When you do decide on your new spiritual "home," you'll probably feel like you belong right away. People are friendly here in our county and you won't feel like a stranger for long.

History of Worship in San Diego

The Misión Basílica San Diego de Alcalá, the first in the chain of 21 missions established in California, still holds services and celebrates christenings and weddings. It's been doing so since 1777, when the church was blessed by Father Junipero Serra. (The first was built at the site of today's Presidio Park; the second, at the present location, was burned by the Indians in 1774 and subsequently rebuilt.) Like the San Diego de Alcalá mission church, Oceanside's Misión San Luis Rey continues to hold services in Spanish as well as English. Tours of both missions are available, and the gardens and museums alone make them popular tourist attractions. (Be sure to read about the missions in our Attractions chapter.)

While criollos (people of Spanish descent born in Mexico), Spaniards, and other Europeans who settled San Diego were Catholic, many other religions came to San Diego with the farmers, cattle owners, and tradespeople that began to call our county home. (See our History chapter for more information on early settlers.)

As they cleared the land, established homesteads and tried to figure out how to get water to make everything grow, these independent folks were determined to feed their souls, too. Just as it happens today, not everyone could decide on that spiritual "meal" or how it should be served, so diverse churches and houses of worship sprang up around the county.

If you stepped back in history, 50 or 100 years, you'd find a spiritual scene much like today's. On any Sunday you could choose to attend a spiritualist church or a Baptist church or a Catholic one. The only difference between then and now is that today you'd have even more choices.

Humanitarian Activities

Our scores of religious institutions also happen to be a vital part of humanitarian activity in San Diego. At any one of them you may find a way to express your own faith by helping with these efforts. At **Saint Vincent De Paul's Village** in San Diego (see the Close-up in this chapter) volunteers and paid staff members assist those who need a helping hand emotionally, physically, and spiritually. If you volunteer here you might be asked to read a book at the day-care center, help with distribution at the food bank, serve lunch, or work at a fundraiser. The main center is located at 3350 E Street, San Diego, (619) 233-8500.

The **Salvation Army**'s community center at 4170 Balboa Avenue, San Diego (858-483-1831), offers a homework assistance program, before-and-after-school and vacation programs for students, Bible study classes, youth chorus and band, and women's league in addition to Sunday worship. The downtown location (730 F Street, San Diego, 619-231-6020), provides shelter, clothing, and food for some of our less fortunate citizens. The Salvation Army always needs volunteers too.

Talk with the pastor, rabbi, or head of your spiritual center to find out about volunteer opportunities sponsored by your group. While many religious groups cry out for financial support, it's often the priceless gift of willing hands that is the greatest contribution you can make.

Cultural Activities

Our religious centers are more than sites where we join one another to worship.

They're often places to enjoy the arts and cultural activities, or centers where people can help themselves to a better life here on earth.

For instance, the **First United Methodist Church of San Diego** (2111 Camino Del Rio South, San Diego; 619-297-4366, www.fumcsd.org) often hosts a performance of spirituals and gospel music in January in honor of the Dr. Martin Luther King Jr. The church is known for its monthly concerts ranging from piano or organ music to renaissance, baroque, classical, and romantic compositions played on brass instruments. Almost all feature well-known performers. This outgoing church also hosts a good number of singles and family events.

Praise Chapel Christian Fellowship (6460 El Cajon Boulevard, San Diego; 619-582-0526, www.praisechapelsd.com) has appointed a "drama ministry" of artisans committed to spreading the Word through theatrical presentations, using both their own and professional scripts.

This form of worship draws people from all walks of life to celebrate God's blessings through song, music, and sermon—it's definitely a family affair.

The **Taoist Sanctuary of San Diego** (4229 Park Boulevard, San Diego; 619-

Father Joe: God's Hustler

He's been called a "genius," a "saint," and a "hustler." He's been referred to as a "con artist," and "that guy you wanta' watch." Perhaps what best describes Father Joe Carroll is "anomaly." Here's a Bronx-born priest who has instituted one of the nation's most effective programs for helping the homeless get back on their feet. And although Father Joe started out in South Bronx, the miracle happened here in San Diego.

Born in New York City in 1941, Joe Carroll was raised in a closeknit neighborhood where people valued roots. One of eight Carroll kids, he was part of a family that never forgot to pray for "the less fortunate," although living at the time in a two-room apartment. Father Joe says, "Given those circumstances, we'd be homeless today."

When he relocated to Southern California at age 22 with $50 in his pocket, Joe Carroll had one desire: to be a millionaire. What he got was something entirely different.

Joe's easy and gregarious personality, coupled with the compassion for the poor he'd learned as a child, eventually led him to the priesthood. Following his ordination in 1974, Father Joe immersed himself in parish work, where he also found outlets for his businessman's instincts. Parish life enabled Father Joe to apply fund-raising skills, which he used among his growing cadre of friends and supporters. Those skills would become for Father Joe a magnetic extension of his vision. This vision, which originally had a more personal nature, turned into one of universal proportions.

Visions like Father Joe's are contagious, and this one eventually caught the interest of Bishop Leo T. Maher. The bishop was appalled by the number of San Diegans sleeping nightly in cars, in the parks, and on the public beaches. He dreamed of a comprehensive center to address their immediate needs. He assigned Father Joe the task.

The priest accepted Bishop Maher's task with his usual gusto. Daunted but determined, he and his colleagues leased a hotel and set about understanding the causes of homelessness. He also devised a plan for an urban oasis that would provide not only emergency care but a free clinic, a public school, a children's library and play area, rooms for 350 residents, and a kitchen serving 2,000 meals daily. The center would also offer resources where "street people" could search for work, brush up on professional skills, and prepare for job interviews. The cost of this plan? Try $11 million and change.

We know him as Father Joe. Formally he's called Rev. Msgr. Joseph Carroll, president of Saint Vincent de Paul Village. PHOTO: COURTESY OF SAINT VINCENT DE PAUL VILLAGE

Like dynamos of less lofty persuasions, Father Joe scrounged for money. It came. The big break happened when a local television station aired his public-service spot. Viewers were captivated. "I'm a hustler," said the man in the clerical garb. Then he grinned and added, "And I want your money." Then as images of San Diego's homeless families were shown in the same commercial, Father Joe explained the need for a residence where people could galvanize themselves and work toward another try.

Father Joe's plan worked, and worked well. Offers of help poured in from every corner of the county. One Insider likes to tell about the times Father Joe was honored at various social functions: "He even made appeals for the center during grace." With God's help and through the hands of compassionate Insiders, the millions were raised. The dream turned into reality.

Opened in September 1987, the Joan Kroc Center is situated in what was once one of San Diego's seediest neighborhoods. Rising from its modest surroundings, the structure is a beacon of hope to the thousands of residents and nonresident homeless who partake of its services every day. It's been called the "Taj Mahal of homeless shelters," and building it took five years of selling, begging, wheeling, dealing, arm-twisting, hand-shaking, and Father Joe's brand of friendly persuasion.

An outspoken conservative, the good father doesn't believe in handouts. "Handouts are not the answer to today's volatile economy. People have to learn how to take care of themselves; that means learning how to spend, how to save, and how to maintain security for themselves and their families. We don't want to see our residents come back. If they do, then its time to re-evaluate our methods. Part of our job is to instill personal responsibility, tenacity, and the will to succeed. Of course the onus of this process lies squarely on the shoulders of our residents. But we have to help them to recognize that they can do it."

Since its opening day, the "Miracle of 15th Street," as the Joan Kroc Center is lovingly called, has become just one in half a dozen structures making up the Village and bursting out of that original dream. Actually located at 3350 E Street, San Diego, the center and its satellite sites provide a plethora of services, including medical programs, counseling and chemical dependency help, computer training programs, the meal plans, and the Village's Harbor Summit School. The school provides more than 100 resident children with education, techniques to bolster self-worth, social skills, and a sense of security. Additional programs coordinated with the school include tutoring, family literacy, children's therapy, medical services, a foster grandparent program, parenting classes, and teen and preteen clubs.

Many services are directed at families or children. The Toussant Teen Center is a residential center to protect, educate, and improve the self-esteem of runaway, abused, or abandoned teens. The average age of these children is 16; the center boasts a 70 percent success rate in returning them to their homes or helping them establish themselves successfully in the community. At press time, architects are designing a new center in rural Campo. PromiseLand Ranch is meant to shelter 250 young people in a beautiful country setting, while reuniting siblings and teaching strategies for success.

"Yet, there's still work to be done," says Father Joe, and smiles with pride when discussing another village. Because there are other villages now. The one in Las Vegas helps that city's growing homeless population and has become the largest facility of its kind in the state of Nevada.

Today, St. Vincent de Paul Villages continue to lead the country in nongovernment solutions to homelessness. Each case manager, counselor, administrator, volunteer, and donor seeks greater opportunities for people who come to the center. And Father Joe Carroll remains at the center of the activity. He is a clear-headed, determined businessman meeting the demands of severe federal cutbacks. After getting to know Father Joe, or about him, you won't be surprised that he's always looking for good volunteers—to serve meals, conduct medical exams, or teach someone how to read. To volunteer and be part of this successful mission, call (619) 233–8500, ext. 1575.

692–1155, www.taoistsanctuary.org), offers eight-week seminars in fall, winter, and spring to help students incorporate balance, harmony, and self-transformation into their daily lives. The center's philosophy mingles Chinese medicine, martial arts, and spiritual discipline, and often introduces newcomers to these practices during evening open houses in the summer months.

San Diego has two **Self-Realization Fellowships**, at 939 Second Street in Encinitas, (760) 436–7220, and in central San Diego at 3072 First Avenue, (619) 295–0170, www.yogananda-srf.org. The church, brought to the United States in 1920 by Parmahansa Yogananda, teaches self-realization through meditation and prayer. The church offers study lessons and group meditations in addition to weekly services. The larger temple in Encinitis has a particularly lovely meditation garden overlooking the beach, and both offer retreats for men and women.

Lawrence Family Jewish Community Centers (Mandell Weirs Eastgate City Park, 4126 Executive Drive, La Jolla; 858–457–3030, www.lfjcc.org) provides the community with a Jewish Film Festival and Jewish Book Fair. Affectionately know as "the J," this center also has a performance venue, an excellent physical fitness center, and an Olympic-size swimming pool that can be used by people of all faiths. There are a variety of activities for young Jewish couples, and for those looking for lifelong companionship, a dating service meant to help Jewish singles meet potential mates in a fun, safe setting.

The **First Spiritualist Church** (3777 42nd Street, San Diego; 619–284–4646, www.1st-spiritualistchurch.org) has been active in San Diego since the late 19th century. Very active in the community, it hosts a yearly psychic fair and regular programs such as Sufi dancing and full moon celebrations, and classes on how to communicate more effectively with angels and spirit guides, herbology, and Tarot card reading. Healing sessions and church services are held Sunday mornings and evenings.

So if you're looking for a place to worship, to put your faith to work in social service, and to enjoy the companionship of others, our community has much to offer. As with all of San Diego, just ask some Insiders and you'll receive a cornucopia of choices.

Insiders' Tip

On Good Friday and the Sunday before Easter, the *San Diego Union-Tribune* prints a list of Easter services. Many of these, including those at Las Flores Church of the Nazarene, 1400 Las Flores Drive in Carlsbad, (760) 729-0231, are held outdoors. If you're determined to wear a new spring outfit, bring a jacket.

Index

About the Authors

Jacquelyn Landis

A native San Diegan, Jacquelyn Landis has never seriously considered settling anywhere else. Her San Diego roots run deep: Jackie's ancestors arrived in San Diego in the early 1900s and quickly established themselves in the business community. Landis Street, which stretches east from North Park all the way through City Heights, was christened in honor of her great-grandfather, a physician, and her grandfather and great-uncle, who owned a drug store and soda fountain in Mission Hills.

An alumna of the University of San Diego, Jackie credits her demanding philosophy professors for pounding home the fundamentals of writing, while at the same time encouraging her love for the craft. Formerly the managing editor for Emery-Dalton Books, Jackie is now a freelance writer who ghostwrites health and psychology self-help books and celebrity autobiographies. But when the opportunity arises to write about her hometown, she has yet to be able to resist. Her work has appeared in *San Diego Magazine,* San Diego pictorial books, and a variety of San Diego business and community newspapers. She also is an editorial consultant, offering advice and guidance to other writers.

Jackie currently lives in Linda Vista, overlooking bustling Mission Valley. Wanderlust strikes occassionally, and it has taken her to the four corners of the world. But San Diego always beckons. Jackie knows she's spoiled. When you can go to the beach in January, drive a short hour to play in the snow in the Laguna Mountains, and keep going over the mountains to the warmth of the Borrego Desert, why live anywhere else?

Eva Shaw

As far as Eva Shaw is concerned, there's no other area on the planet that compares to San Diego. It has been her hometown for almost 30 years, chosen for the climate, diversity, and spectacular array of outdoor activities.

Eva teaches creative writing with Education to Go, the University of California Extension Programs, and at conferences throughout the United States. She holds a doctorate in eschatology from Westbrook University. She is the award-winning author of more than 40 books, including the best-selling *Writing the Non-Fiction Book, The Successful Writer's Guide to Publishing Magazine Articles,* and *For the Love of Children,* as well as *What to Do When a Loved One Dies.* She's currently working on books about safety for women and gardening as therapy, and she "dabbles" in writing fiction.

Her writing has appeared in the *San Diego Union-Tribune, San Diego Business Journal,* and scores of national publications. Eva is a ghostwriter, lecturer, public speaker, and advocate for family and women's issues. She was recently honored with North San Diego County's Woman of Merit Award. A nationally recognized television guest on Leeza, A&E Network, MSNBC, and Maury Povich, Eva has enlightened audiences with her expert knowledge on topics ranging from grief management to wellness.

Eva lives in Carlsbad, a pearl on the string of coastal communities in San Diego County. When not writing, teaching, speaking, and volunteering at the Florence Crittenton Center and other charities, Eva tends her flower garden (at last count there were nearly 100 rose bushes); plays fetch with Zippy, a Welsh terrier; and hikes San Diego County and the world with her husband, Joe, and their son, Matt.

About the Revisers

Maribeth Mellin

Maribeth Mellin is an award-winning journalist who has been covering San Diego for over two decades. Like many San Diegans, she is a transplant from the East Coast, but after nearly 30 years living by the Pacific Ocean, she's most definitely content to be called a Southern Californian. Maribeth developed her knowledge of the inner workings and far-flung regions of the county as senior editor at *San Diego Magazine*. In the role of travel editor, she covered vacation destinations around the globe and was always delighted to return to her home in San Diego. Her articles on social, legal, and medical issues have garnered over two dozen awards from journalism organizations. Her travel books on California, Mexico, and other Latin American countries have also received commendations, and she is the recipient of the prestigious Pluma de Plata award for her coverage of Mexico.

Jane Onstott

Jane Onstott is a professional editor, travel writer, and translator. She moved to San Diego in 1976 to attend San Diego State University, where she received a B.A. in Spanish language and literature. She tempers her adulation for America's Finest City with frequent forays to Spanish-speaking countries, and has lived and worked in Oaxaca, Mexico and the Galapagos Islands, in Ecuador. She's written for many years about Mexico and South America for Fodor's Travel Publications. She has contributed her knowledge of San Diego to several different guide books, including *Best Places San Diego*, edited by colleague Maribeth Mellin. In November 2001 Jane's *National Geographic Traveler Mexico* was published by the National Geographic Society.